Jewish Solidarity

The Ideal and the Reality in the Turmoil of the Shoah

This volume is based on the lectures presented at the international
conference "All of Israel are Responsible for One Another?"

The conference was supported by
The Gertner Center for International Holocaust Conferences
and **The Gutwirth Family Fund.**

Jewish Solidarity

The Ideal and the Reality in the Turmoil of the Shoah

Edited by

Dan Michman and Robert Rozett

YAD VASHEM
THE WORLD HOLOCAUST
REMEMBRANCE CENTER

THE INTERNATIONAL INSTITUTE
FOR HOLOCAUST RESEARCH

Jewish Solidarity

On the Challenges to Jewish Solidarity during the Holocaust

Language Editor: Evelyn Grossberg
Production Editor: Dania Valdez

ISBN 978-965-308-648-7

Typesetting: Hava Salzman

Printed in Israel by Ayalon Amit and Raffi Ltd.

Contents

Introduction 7
    Dan Michman and Robert Rozett

Perspectives on and Interpretations of the Meaning of Jewish Solidarity

On Solidarity among Jews during the Holocaust Period 21
    David Engel

Exploring the Concept of "*Kol Yisrael Arevim Zeh Lazeh*" 41
    Steven T. Katz

Challenges to Solidarity in Ghettos and Urban Concentrations

Children's Voices: Solidarity and Survival of Families in the
Warsaw Ghetto 65
    Dalia Ofer

Medical Activity in the Warsaw Ghetto as a Test of Jewish
Solidarity in the Face of Persecution 97
    Miriam Offer

Testing Solidarity: Collaborators Attempt to Seize Key Positions
in the Kovno Ghetto 129
    Rami Neudorfer

Unexpected Alliances and Limits of Solidarity: Non-Jewish Aid
Organizations and the Jewish Community—Assisting Jews and
"Non-Aryans" in Vienna, 1938–1945 151
    Michaela Raggam-Blesch

**Challenges to Solidarity in Concentration, Labor, and Extermination
Camps**

Cohesion and Conflict among Jewish Prisoners in Dachau
and Lichtenburg: A Social Study of the Extreme Situation 179
    Kim Wünschmann

Family, Local, and Class Solidarity in the Vaihingen and
Hessental Concentration Camps 199
    Idit Gil

Jewish Concentration Camp Inmate Functionaries: Karl Demerer in
Blechhammer—A Case Study 223
  Verena Buser

Communes in Auschwitz: The Communal Idea in the Holocaust 245
  Avihu Ronen

Solidarity and Rivalry in Rescue Attempts and Operations

Information, Knowledge, and Desperation: Jewish
Communications during the Holocaust 269
  David Silberklang

Poale Zion Left in Belgium and Rescue by the Comité de Défense
des Juifs 291
  Jeannine (Levana) Frenk

DELASEM: A Jewish Relief Organization in Italy under the Fascist
Regime and Nazi Occupation 315
  Liliana Picciotto

The American Jewish Joint Distribution Committee and the Va'ad
Hahatzala: Fundraising Competition and Begrudged Rescue
Cooperation, 1939–1943 335
  Efraim Zuroff

Religious Perspectives: Interpretations and Acts

Jewish Unity, Disunity, and Assigning Blame for the Holocaust 367
  Gershon Greenberg

Requests for Atonement in Responsa Literature: Complex Dilemmas
Regarding Jewish Solidarity during the Shoah 387
  Moshe Tarshansky

Renée Reichmann and Her Rescue Enterprise in Tangier 417
  Esther Farbstein

List of Contributors 439

Index 447

Introduction

What is the meaning of "solidarity," and what should one expect regarding Jewish solidarity in modern times? Dictionaries define solidarity as "unity (of a group or class) that produces or is based on a community of interests, objectives, and standards";[1] "unity or agreement of feeling or action, especially among individuals with a common interest; mutual support within a group";[2] and "the support that people in a group give each other because they have the same opinions or aims."[3] These definitions raise the following questions: To what extent is there "unity"—"unity or agreement of feeling," "a common interest," "the same opinions or aims," and/or "mutual support"—among Jews in modern times? Are they still a collective bound by a "community of interests, objectives, and standards"?

Jews considered themselves and were perceived by others as a group defined by religion until the modern period, and this religion had national characteristics. However, from the seventeenth through the twentieth centuries, especially from the beginning of the nineteenth century, Jewish history was characterized by historical developments that transformed Jewry in nearly every aspect. These developments include emancipation; secularization (skepticism, agnosticism, atheism); democratization and deep involvement in (Jewish and non-Jewish) politics; economic modernization and the emergence of new classes; migration; and modern, national awareness. The interaction of these developments radically changed the modes of Jewish self-organization, self-understanding, and cohesion. Consequently, we can observe unending religious and ideological clashes among Jews around various issues, such as social and linguistic integration into national societies versus the creation of supranational organizations; and the assimilation

1   https://www.merriam-webster.com/dictionary/solidarity.
2   https://www.lexico.com/definition/solidarity.
3   https://www.macmillandictionary.com/dictionary/british/solidarity.

and the abandonment of ties with other Jews versus demonstrating an accentuated "Jewish" presence (way of dressing, impressive synagogues, openly Jewish organizations), among others. As David Engel writes so persuasively in this volume, "Jewish society on the eve of the Holocaust was far from a paragon of harmonious cooperation and mutual support, and [was] actually fragmented." Furthermore, he argues that one cannot write about a general breakdown of solidarity in the Jewish community as a result of the Holocaust, because that presupposes widespread solidarity to begin with.[4]

Therefore, what would constitute reasonable expectations of "Jewish solidarity" during the period of the Holocaust (1933–1945)? High expectations in retrospect undoubtedly result from the post-factum knowledge that Nazi Germany and its allies waged a war against **all** Jews without distinction. Moreover, the often emphasized, national characteristic of the post-World War II Jewish world that emerged with the establishment of the State of Israel shortly after the Holocaust reflects an attitude that did not exist before 1933. Consequently, the concept and practice of "Jewish solidarity" during the Holocaust is not easy to define or analyze.

The essays in this volume were first presented at the biannual scholarly conference convened at Yad Vashem in December 2014. The theme of the conference was chosen by the Yad Vashem International Institute for Holocaust Research in the wake of a statement by the historian Saul Friedländer during a lecture that he had delivered at Yad Vashem on September 2, 2010. Friedländer, who had published his widely acclaimed, two-volume magnum opus *Nazi Germany and the Jews*

---

4   See also Dan Michman, "The Jewish Dimension of the Holocaust: The Context of Modern Jewish History," in Dan Michman, *Holocaust Historiography: A Jewish Perspective: Conceptualizations, Terminology, Approaches and Fundamental Issues* (London and Portland: Vallentine Mitchell, 2003), pp. 61–66; Bernard Wasserstein, *On the Eve: The Jews of Europe before the Second World War* (London: Profile Books, 2012). For the paths of emancipation, integration, acculturation, and assimilation in countries throughout Europe, all of which affected the sense of overall Jewish solidarity, see Pierre Birnbaum and Ira Katznelson, eds., *Paths of Emancipation: Jews, States and Citizenship* (Princeton: Princeton University Press, 1995). For examples of local, national, and international Jewish solidarity that have emerged since 1840 as a counterweight to the processes of decomposition, see Benjamin Pinkus and Ilan Troen, eds., *Solidariyut Yehudit Le'umit Ba'et Hahadasha* (Hebrew) (Sde Boker: Ben-Gurion University of the Negev Press, 1988); and Hasia R. Diner and Gennady Estraikh, eds., *1929: Mapping the Jewish World* (New York: New York University Press, 2013).

three years before,[5] claimed that solidarity among Jews had collapsed and that people had cared only for their own and their closest relatives' survival, and, in the best case, for "their own Jews," that is, German Jews for German Jews but not for Polish ones, longtime French Jews for similar Jews but not for foreign ones, etc. His statement engendered a fierce debate among the audience in the lecture hall, and several people responded on the spot. Yet a broader and more documented discussion seemed to be a desideratum. As the chapters in this compendium demonstrate, Jewish solidarity during the Holocaust is a multifaceted, multilayered issue, replete with complexities and shadings that make the attempt to encapsulate it a challenge. Yet it is clear that the extreme thesis that Jewish and, for that matter, human, solidarity disappeared entirely is not substantiated.

As Steven T. Katz writes so eruditely, the concept of solidarity is built into Judaism, Jewish civilization, and Jewish culture: *"Kol Yisrael Arevim Zeh Lazeh"* (All Israel [all Jews] are responsible for one another). According to the medieval exegete Rashi, the original Midrashic expression is slightly different—*"Kol Yisrael Arevim Zeh Bazeh"* (All Israel are interwoven with each other, i.e., are guarantors for each other)—and relates to the idea of Jews being responsible for preventing other Jews from sinning. Owing to this injunction, Jews often have displayed solidarity on many levels throughout Jewish history, especially regarding communal welfare. The question then is: What elements of this tradition remained intact during the Holocaust?

If the ideal of Jewish solidarity for all Jews everywhere was not prevalent on the eve of the Nazi era, that does not mean that there was no solidarity at all during the Holocaust. This can only be ascertained by studying solidarity during the Holocaust from all angles and examining every level. There were many, diverse concentric circles of solidarity and usually, although not always, the farther away they were from the ideal that all Jews are interwoven together, the weaker the sense of solidarity. Indeed, there were also many cases of individuals who focused solely on their own survival, and this too must be addressed openly. Perhaps somewhat counterintuitively, even the cases that Friedländer cited as

---

5   Saul Friedländer, *Nazi Germany and the Jews, 1933–1939: The Years of Persecution* (London: Weidenfeld and Nicolson, 1997); Friedländer, *Nazi Germany and the Jews, 1939–1945: The Years of Extermination* (New York: HarperCollins, 2007). This study was published in several languages and received a great deal of attention, which gave special weight to Friedländer's apparently authoritative statement on Jewish solidarity.

proof of the lack of comprehensive Jewish solidarity actually point to its presence—but within smaller circles. These circles of solidarity were indeed a reflection of the state of Jewry in modern times.

Of course, the broadest angle and perhaps the top level of this phenomenon is what may be termed international Jewish solidarity among Jews who sought to support, help, and sustain Jews who were far removed from their more immediate circles of responsibility—their family, friends, community, and country—and who did what they could to help distant Jews simply because they were fellow Jews. The negotiations carried out by the Slovak Working Group under the de facto leadership of Rabbi Michael Ber Dov Weissmandel and Gizi Fleischmann is a prime example of international Jewish solidarity. After the Working Group paid the SS a sum of money to halt the first wave of deportations from Slovakia in the autumn of 1942, they sought to stop the deportation of Jews from all parts of Europe to Poland. The members of the group learned about these additional deportations from the couriers they had sent out to learn what had happened to the Slovak Jews who had been transported eastward. Although the money that they had paid the SS to stop the deportations from Slovakia apparently was not the reason they had ended, from their vantage point, the Working Group believed that the payment had been the key. They began new negotiations, known as the Europa Plan, in an attempt this time to protect Jews from all over Nazi-dominated Europe and not only Slovak Jews. For many reasons, this chapter in the negotiations with the SS ultimately did not come to fruition, but it certainly was an expression of Jewish solidarity.[6]

This was not the only instance of attempts by Jews to protect Jews who were far away from them. For example, soon after the Nazis seized power in 1933, Jews in the United States organized a boycott of German goods in hopes of restraining Nazi Germany's anti-Jewish activities. They too did not actually succeed, but their efforts were a clear expression of wider Jewish solidarity.[7] Another demonstration of solidarity in the 1930s was the assistance provided by various Jewish communities, including newly established refugee committees, to Jews fleeing from Germany, and the establishment of the World Jewish Congress in 1936, headed by Nahum

---

6   Yehuda Bauer, *Jews for Sale? Nazi-Jewish Negotiations, 1933–1945* (New Haven: Yale University Press, 1994), pp. 60–101.

7   David Cesarani, *Final Solution: The Fate of the Jews 1933–1949* (London: Macmillan, 2016), pp. 39–49.

Goldmann, which intervened on behalf of "World Jewry" with Mussolini to counter persecutions and extended help to Jews under Nazi rule in the 1940s, for instance.[8] It is worth noting that from the point of view of the Working Group, their negotiations did indeed reflect international Jewish solidarity. However, after the war, Rabbi Weissmandel accused the Zionists in the free world of not supporting his group's efforts, because they did not provide the funds that he had asked for—in other words, he thought that they had limited their solidarity solely to Zionists.[9]

As this volume demonstrates, there were other instances, perhaps more limited in scope than those noted above, where Jews reached out over space and time to help fellow Jews. Esther Farbstein, for example, writes about Renée Reichman in Tangier, who sent packages to Jews in Auschwitz, Lublin, Theresienstadt, and other places, and also worked to obtain foreign papers to help protect Jews from the Nazis in Europe. In New York, the Va'ad Hatzala (Rescue Committee), an Orthodox rabbinical group sought to help yeshiva students, primarily from Lithuania, from where many of the Va'ad members had come, find refuge in the United States, Canada, and Shanghai. Their solidarity had a long geographic reach but, as Efraim Zuroff writes, was essentially limited to assisting only one sector. The extent of this partisanship was such that it sometimes led to merely reluctant cooperation within the broader framework of aid established by the American Jewish community and to not a little open discord. Obviously, this form of solidarity, which differs from that of the Working Group, should be understood in the context of the fragmented, modern Jewish world.

Of course, owing to the state of the Jewish world on the eve of the Holocaust, the Rescue Committee of United States Orthodox Rabbis was not the only rescue effort that was essentially sectorial. For instance, in early 1943, when Zionist leaders and youth movement members in Hungary and Slovakia began sending emissaries to Poland to try to assist Jews to reach Hungary by way of Slovakia, they initially had lists of fellow Zionists whom they hoped to assist. However, the reality of the

---

8   For more on this topic, see Gregory Wallance, "The World Jewish Congress during World War II," in Menachem Z. Rosensaft, ed., *The World Jewish Congress, 1936–2016* (New York: World Jewish Congress, 2017), pp. 25–39; David Silberklang, "Jewish Politics and Rescue: The Founding of the Council for German Jewry," *Holocaust and Genocide Studies*, 7:3 (1993), pp. 333–371.

9   For more about Rabbi Weissmandel's activities and thoughts, see Michael Dov Weissmandl, *Min Hametzar* (Hebrew) (New York: Emunah, 1960).

disastrous situation led them rather quickly to put aside their lists and rescue whomever they could. Eventually they helped up to 2,000 Jews from Poland arrive relatively safely in Hungary.[10]

Within countrywide frameworks, Jewish solidarity that was more narrow than international Jewish solidarity but that was not focused only on one sector often found expression in aid to Jews, both native and refugee, within a country's borders. Sometimes, as Jeanine Frenk writes regarding Belgium, succor began as a more restricted phenomenon but then became broader as the situation unfolded. In Belgium, the Linke Poale Tzion (Left Workers of Zion) activists first acted within their limited political sphere, but then expanded beyond it. Operating more broadly, they rescued approximately 3,000 children and about 5,000 adults, and their leading underground publication *Unzer Wort* (Our Word) offered many Belgian Jews support in a virtual community. In Italy, as Lilianna Picciotto writes, the rescue committee DELASEM— Delegazione Assistenza Emigrante Ebrei (Delegation for Assistance to Jewish Emigrants)—engaged in rescue activities throughout Italy from the start, focusing at first on Jewish refugees who were under threat and then, as the situation deteriorated, helping native Jews as well. In her closing remarks at the conference, Yad Vashem's chief historian Dina Porat also noted other local efforts by Jews to rescue and aid Jews, such as the activities of L'Armée juive in France that included, among others, the smuggling of Jews across the border into Spain. As Michaela Raggam-Blesch writes, some expressions of solidarity may even be somewhat surprising within a countrywide framework.

Raggam-Blesch demonstrates that in Austria, following the *Anschluß*—the political union of Austria with Germany through annexation in 1938—there was significant cooperation between the Jews and the Christians. The latter included those who found themselves classified as Jews owing to the racial definition that had been adopted by the Nazis at Nuremberg in 1935. As Porat also pointed out, Jewish solidarity was sometimes evident within activities carried out together with Christians who did not have Jewish origins, such as those of the Westerweel Group in Holland, whose membership included both Jews and Christians. Concomitantly, this rescue initiative also demonstrates

---

10 Robert Rozett, "From Poland to Hungary: Rescue Attempts, 1943–1944," *Yad Vashem Studies*, 24 (1994), pp. 177–193.

solidarity between Christians and Jews.[11] Among its other actions, this group smuggled Jews from the Netherlands to Spain by way of France. In Budapest during 1944, Jewish activists from the Budapest Relief and Rescue Committee, the Zionist youth movements, and other local Jews worked with non-Jewish diplomats from neutral counties to create an atmosphere of rescue that helped keep about 100,000 Jews alive to see the city fall to the Soviets early in 1945. This too is an instance of solidarity between Jews, and between Christians and Jews.[12]

The extremely harsh conditions in many of the ghettos in Eastern Europe, however, did little to nurture solidarity among Jews. Undoubtedly, there was often a breakdown of communal and even familial solidarity. Nevertheless, as a number of the articles in this compendium demonstrate, there were certainly significant instances of solidarity even under the most adverse conditions. For example, the Yidisher Sotsyale Alaynhilf (Jewish Self-Help) organization in Warsaw and other ghettos was instrumental, on a grassroots level, in trying to deal with the food and health crisis before the deportations. It could not actually succeed in stemming the tide of suffering and death, but it did what it could. As Miriam Offer writes, many doctors, nurses, educators, and others dedicated themselves completely to helping fellow Jews in many of the ghettos.

Within families in the ghettos, the increasingly deteriorating situation could, and often did, lead to a breakdown of solidarity. Dawid Sierakowiak wrote poignantly about this in his diary, noting that even a father could succumb to the endless, gnawing hunger and, in a moment of weakness, eat the bread that was meant for his children.[13] In other cases, however, as Dalia Ofer demonstrates, some family members acted selflessly to the point of doing irreparable damage to themselves. She also shows how, as death began to take an ever-increasing toll, family solidarity became more and more difficult to maintain, even among

---

11 Hans Schippers, *Westerweel Group: Non-Conformist Resistance against Nazi Germany: A Joint Rescue Effort of Dutch Idealists and Dutch-German Zionists* (Oldenbourg: De Gruyter, 2019), pp. 119–159.

12 Robert Rozett, "International Intervention: The Role of Diplomats in Attempts to Rescue Jews in Hungary," in Randolph Braham and Scott Miller, eds., *The Nazis' Last Victims: The Holocaust in Hungary* (Detroit: Wayne State University Press, 2002), pp. 137–152.

13 Alan Adelson, ed., *The Diary of Dawid Sierakowiak: Five Notebooks from the Lodz Ghetto* (New York: Oxford University Press, 1996), p. 177.

the last surviving members of the family. Yet elements of solidarity sometimes prevailed, even in the direst of situations, in the face of the massive deaths and mass deportations to the unknown. David Silberklang discusses another aspect of solidarity: efforts to warn fellow Jews about the destruction as it unfolded. He presents examples of people who did their best to send out warnings of the impending mass murders to their family members and friends, as well as to local, and even international Jewish institutions, sometimes using coded language that the authorities would not understand, but that those who received the messages probably would.

Avihu Ronen describes yet another form of solidarity in some of the ghettos that predated the Holocaust and generally continued throughout the war years: the cohesive spirit of youth movement groups. He writes about the role of these movements in supporting their members in various ways, including by establishing Zionist training farms, which benefitted not only the young farmers, but also the wider community. He also discusses the issue of social responsibility, which they grappled with regarding the organization of armed resistance, or escape to join the partisans. The youth movement members were keenly aware that even if they themselves succeeded in carrying out such operations, their family, friends, and communities who did not take part in these activities themselves would probably have to pay a steep price. This was a serious dilemma for all of them, which perhaps is one of the reasons that, in general, they engaged in armed uprising only when liquidation appeared to be imminent.

Even in the camps, there were acts of solidarity among Jewish prisoners, but they were generally circumscribed in some way. Idit Gil discusses how origins also affected solidarity in two work camps, Vaihingen and Hessental. Inmates from the same city or region felt more cohesiveness with one another than with prisoners from other places. As Kim Wünschmann writes, political affiliations, more than geographical origins, tended to lead like-minded political prisoners to display more solidarity among themselves than with other prisoners in the early prewar camps. In a similar vein, Ronen demonstrates how later as events progressed, members of Zionist youth movements continued to pursue their ideal of mutual responsibility and support for one another in the camps, despite the brutal conditions. Finally, as is well documented in the literature, solidarity among relatives, prewar acquaintances, or people who befriended each other in the camps crucially affected their chances to survive the deadly brutality of so many of the camps. Once again, this much more limited solidarity is very different from both the ideal in traditional Jewish sources and the international solidarity of the Working Group.

As has already been noted inter alia, any serious discussion of Jewish solidarity must include an examination of cases of its breakdown. It may be said that, especially in the public mind, the prevailing image of Jews who became ghetto and camp functionaries is that they embodied murderous treachery rather than solidarity. Rami Neudorfer demonstrates in his analysis of two individuals who sought to and, to a certain degree, succeeded in undermining the efforts of the police in the Kovno ghetto and in maintaining solidarity with and responsibility toward the ghetto's inhabitants, that this sometimes was indeed the reality. There were Kapos and other functionaries in the camps who gradually identified with the system that gave them their power and status and, thus, they treated the Jewish prisoners with extreme brutality and ruthlessness. This phenomenon has been described in the literature, but as Verena Buser shows regarding the Jewish camp functionary Karl Demerer in Blechhammer, it appears that he acted in this manner when he felt compelled to do so. It seems that he hoped that his brutality would prevent the German camp personnel from perpetrating even worse violence on a given prisoner. It appears that he also used violence and force as a sort of ruse to persuade the camp personnel that he was acting as they expected, so as to maintain his status and remain in a position to avert even worse violence and suffering. This was certainly not a situation that can be easily understood and analyzed in terms of solidarity or treachery. It is clear, however, that the behavior of Demerer, apparently like that of some other Jewish functionaries, was complex and indicated both solidarity and its antithesis.

Similar behavior is poignantly described in an oral testimony by the late Rabbi Yehoshua Eibeshitz of blessed memory, which he gave publicly at Yad Vashem in 2018. He recounted how a Kapo in Auschwitz brutally forced him to go to work one morning and not linger behind with the ill. When they returned from their day's forced labor, he discovered that everyone who had been left behind had been taken to be gassed. The Kapo, who had seemed to be so cruel to him earlier that day, had actually cared for him and had acted to save his life, having known beforehand that those in the barracks that day would be murdered. He could not warn Eibeshitz, or any other person, because it would have meant his own death. In this case, it may be said that cruelty was a tool that served to disguise solidarity.[14]

The cataclysm of the Holocaust upended most aspects of normative Jewish life in every sphere, including Judaism. Regarding responsa—rabbinic responses to questions of Jewish law—Moshe Tarshansky shows that here too the catastrophe engendered many queries and dilemmas that revolved around solidarity while it was underway, such as: Should one prisoner voluntarily give up his life to save another? Could a crying child be put in a potentially lethal situation to preserve quiet during a search for Jews in hiding? Is it moral to endanger innocent people in order to rescue others? The Holocaust, in this sphere as in many others, often tested the limits of morality and solidarity. As Gershon Greenberg writes, the issue of Jewish unity during and after the war was central to attempts by some important Orthodox Jewish thinkers to fathom the *hurban* (destruction; the term for the Holocaust used by most Orthodox thinkers). Some saw the suffering of the Jewish collective as just that, a test, based on the concept of "*Kol Yisrael Arevim Zeh Bazeh*"; whereas others tried to explain the catastrophe as punishment for the divisions that modernity had engendered and that had broken Jewish unity asunder.

Unquestionably, the Holocaust shattered most, if not almost all, prevailing frameworks and cast the struggle for survival in its starkest form. As we search for and examine the details to understand what it obliterated and how, we must be careful not to study history beginning with a false premise: that widespread solidarity was the norm and that the Holocaust had destroyed it completely. We must also be careful not to idealize the solidarity that somehow managed to prevail. Especially in its more limited forms and in not a few situations, acts of solidarity by some Jews could and often did mean that other Jews would pay the price for it—sometimes overtly, sometimes indirectly, and, all too often, probably with their very lives. Yet despite these caveats, it is important to recognize that the Holocaust did not necessarily lead Jews to act as lone wolves, caring only about their own survival. The ideal of "*Kol Yisrael Arevim Zeh Lazeh*" may not have predominated during the Holocaust, but

---

14 A special case in this text are the relations between members of the Sonderkommando in Auschwitz-Birkenau. The paper on this topic in the conference was not included in this volume as it was published elsewhere; see Gideon Greif, "Solidarity and Animosity among Sonderkommando Prisoners in Auschwitz-Birkenau," *Journal of Holocaust Research*, 33:4 (2019), pp. 239–253.

neither did it wholly cease to exist. Solidarity was expressed in different forms in different situations during the Holocaust, and that solidarity deserves to be ascertained, studied, made known, and discussed. This book aims to do just that.

Dan Michman and Robert Rozett

Perspectives on and Interpretations of the Meaning of Jewish Solidarity

On Solidarity among Jews during the Holocaust Period

DAVID ENGEL

I
t appears difficult to speak about solidarity or its absence[1] in the Jewish world during the Holocaust period without looking backward from that era to earlier intervals in the Jewish past. Some scholars, noticing what has seemed to them an ongoing process of social disintegration among Jews under the German yoke, have wondered if Jewish society ever displayed a significant measure of internal cohesion at any time in its history.[2] Others, in contrast, have been impressed by what they have regarded as the extraordinary ability of Jews under Nazi rule to maintain social institutions, to construct self-help mechanisms, and to support the needy under conditions more oppressive than any their predecessors in former generations

---

1 The word "solidarity" has been used to signify many things. In this essay, it is employed as an approximate synonym for "group cohesiveness" or "a feeling of mutual responsibility." In other words, it functions as a routine lexical item, without reference to any of the various social theories in which it figures. Those seeking the theoretical implications of the present discussion may think of "solidarity" as an emotion that generates the social formation that sociologist Helen Fein has termed the "universe of obligation": "that circle of persons toward whom obligations are owed, to whom the rules apply, and whose injuries call for expiation by the community"; see Helen Fein, *Accounting for Genocide: National Responses and Jewish Victimization during the Holocaust* (Chicago: University of Chicago Press, 1979), p. 4. On the connection between the universe of obligation and solidarity, as Fein understands the terms, see Fein, "Explanations of the Origin and Evolution of Antisemitism," in Fein, ed., *The Persisting Question: Sociological Perspectives and Social Contexts of Modern Antisemitism* (Berlin: Walter de Gruyter, 1987), pp. 8–9. The present discussion is not committed either to this specific understanding or to any other theory.

2 For example, Saul Friedländer, *The Years of Extermination: Nazi Germany and the Jews, 1939–1945*: (New York: HarperCollins, 2007), p. 192: "One of the striking aspects of the dramatically changing Jewish condition [under Nazi rule] appears to be the ongoing disintegration of overall Jewish solidarity—**insofar as it ever existed.**" (emphasis added).

21

had known. Many of those scholars have attributed this ability to a longstanding Jewish tradition firmly anchored in the Jews' collective character as a people.[3] Yet another group of scholars has portrayed the Holocaust period as one in which long-lasting practices of solidarity were temporarily suspended due to conditions that effectively prevented Jews from giving practical expression to their traditional sense of mutual obligation.[4]

Similar inferences from one historical era to another occurred during the Nazi period itself. *SS-Obergruppenführer* Erich von dem Bach-Zelewski offered a prominent example in a testimony he gave to an Austrian–American, Jewish psychiatrist, Leo Alexander, in 1946.[5] The testimony was part of a plea bargain that allowed the Nazi general to avoid prosecution as a war criminal, even though he had commanded the SS and police forces in occupied Belarus during the German invasion of the USSR and had supervised the murder of

3   For example, Ilan Troen, "Irgun Hatzalatam Shel Hayehudim Batekufah Hamodernit," in Benjamin Pinkus and Ilan Troen, eds., *Solidariyut Yehudit Le'umit Ba'et Hahadasha* (Hebrew) (Sde Boker: Ben-Gurion University of the Negev Press, 1988), pp. 3–4: "The Jews have maintained their solidarity as a people despite having lived in exile for nearly two thousand years....The bonds uniting modern Jewry have been sorely tested, and they have shown themselves vital with respect to the commitment of a people in exile to be "*Arev Zeh Lazeh*" (responsible to one another)....Such was the case in tsarist and in Bolshevik Russia, in Hitler's Germany, and in many Middle Eastern states....The tradition of solidarity has been a part of Jewish history ever since the *mitzvat pidyon shevuyim* (commandment to redeem captives) was imposed upon the Diaspora communities.... Over time, [the Jewish community] has rendered ever increasing aid to the educational, cultural, and spiritual activities necessary for guaranteeing the continuity and perpetuity of Jewish life wherever [such continuity and perpetuity] have been endangered."

4   For example, Binyamin Pinkus, "Petah Davar," in Pinkus., ed., *Yahadut Mizrach Eropa Bein Shoah Litkuma, 1944–1948* (Hebrew) (Sde Boker: Ben-Gurion University of the Negev Press, 1987), p. ix: "Jewish national solidarity and aid to persecuted Jews have been the foundation stone of individual and communal Jewish thought and practice throughout the generations; they reached the peak of their extent and variety during the modern era. Because of its unprecedentedly horrifying dimensions, the Holocaust brought about an almost total paralysis of rescue efforts at the most fateful moment in the Jewish people's existence, precisely when rescue was most needed. This was the source of the powerful determination among the leaders of Jewish organizations around the world and in [Mandatory] Palestine to undertake energetic, sustained action to aid the surviving remnant."

5   Leo Alexander, "War Crimes and their Motivation: The Socio-Psychological Structure of the SS and the Criminalization of a Society," *Journal of Criminal Law and Criminology* 39 (1948), pp. 298–326; Bach-Zelewski's remarks appear on pp. 309–318.

about 45,000 Jews between July and November 1941.[6] During those months, Bach-Zelewski told Alexander that he had warned the Jews of Białystok, Moghilev, and Baranowicze of the fate that awaited them and encouraged them to prepare appropriately. He explained that his sister, who was married to a Białystok Jew, had felt compelled to flee to Brazil following the Nazi takeover in Germany. Consequently, Bach-Zelewski stated, he retained a measure of sympathy for his brother-in-law's people. Yet he claimed that his warning had fallen upon deaf ears—a response that aroused in him a form of cognitive dissonance, since it did not chime with what Nazi doctrine had led him to believe.

> Contrary to the opinion of the National Socialists that the Jews were a highly organized group, the appalling fact was that they had no organization whatsoever. The mass of the Jewish people was completely taken by surprise. They did not know at all what to do; they had no directives or slogan as to how they should act. This is the greatest proof of the lie of anti-Semitism because it gives the lie to the old slogan that the Jews are conspiring to dominate the world and that they are so highly organized. In reality, they had no organization of their own at all, not even an information service. If they had some sort of organization, these people could have been saved by the millions; but instead they were taken completely by surprise.[7]

Raul Hilberg offered this story as proof that "the Jews were not oriented toward resistance."[8] This interpretation constitutes an unwarranted inference concerning the responses of Jews to the Nazi murder campaign, a matter about which Bach-Zelewski's observations cannot

6   Bach-Zelewski was tried in 1951, in 1958, and in 1961 for participating in the liquidation of Communist activists during the early years of the Nazi regime and in the murder of SA members during the Night of the Long Knives, the purge of the Nazi leadership and other political opponents (June 30–July 2, 1934). He was convicted and sentenced to prison terms of varying lengths of which he served only a portion. For biographical details, see Tomasz Żuroch-Piechowski, "Eryk z Bogdańska, niewinny z Norymbergi," *Tygodnik Powszechny*, September 22, 2006. For the text of the testimony that he gave at the request of the prosecution at Nuremberg, see *Trial of the Major War Criminals before the International Military Tribunal, Nuremberg, 14 November 1945–1 October 1946*, vol. 4 (Nuremberg: International Military Tribunal, 1947), pp. 474–496.

7   Alexander, "War Crimes and their Motivation," pp. 314–315.

8   Raul Hilberg, *The Destruction of the European Jews* (Chicago: Quadrangle Books, 1961), pp. 662–663.

testify at all, certainly not as a general description and perhaps not even with regard to the specific incidents that he described. Even more, they deflect attention from a significant component of Bach-Zelewski's own words. Those words actually incorporate two postulates that cut to the heart of the understanding of Jewish solidarity before and during the Holocaust. Those words actually incorporate two postulates that cut to the heart of the understanding of Jewish solidarity before and during the Holocaust. Those postulates were a product of his Nazi education and, as such, merit further consideration.

Bach-Zelewski belonged to the prestigious Nazi echelon of the *alte Kämpfer* (old fighters)—party veterans from the years of the struggle for power before 1933. He joined the SS in 1930. As a result, he underwent many years of Nazi indoctrination. His education presented an image of the Jewish people as a tightly knit, highly organized, social formation, alert and aware, ready to confront any danger, whenever and wherever danger appeared. The Nazi regime gave that image currency, representing the Jewish people as a great and powerful enemy, whose forces were deployed across the globe, bound together with a most impressive internal cohesiveness. That cohesiveness, Nazi leaders taught, gave the Jews their power. However, during World War II, Bach-Zelewski saw that power vanish; the horrific enemy he had been taught to fear turned out to be, in his eyes, as docile as a lamb being led to slaughter. That impression, in turn, led him to two conclusions. One was a proposition about history: in fact, he suggested, the Jews had actually never been as united or as cohesive as his instruction as an SS officer had led him to believe. The other was speculative and counterfactual: if the Jews had actually been as united and as cohesive as he had been taught to believe, the outcome of their encounter with the Third Reich would surely have been different from what it was.

Remarkably, both of Bach-Zelewski's conclusions parallel a discussion among Jews about that encounter. The discussion began during the Nazi era's very first days and has continued long after its awful conclusion. Nazis, it appears, were not the only ones who pondered the foundations of Jewish existence. It turns out that from the beginning of the Third Reich, Jewish leaders from around the globe regularly represented internal cohesiveness—the same force that Bach-Zelewski eventually found illusory—not only as a real but as a vital weapon in the struggle against the new Nazi threat, one that they believed would ultimately decide the struggle in the Jews' favor. A prominent physician and Zionist activist from Vilna (Vilnius), Jakub Wygodzki, gave early expression to that belief in a comment on the outbreak of violence that beset Jews in Germany following Adolf Hitler's appointment as chancellor on January 30, 1933.

> The pogrom that the Hitlerite bands are visiting upon the Jews of Germany...has made clear to all the danger facing Jews the world over [at this moment]. Jews who only yesterday thought themselves full citizens with equal rights have today been humiliated and degraded to the level of homeless dogs. Jews [in every country] who today consider themselves full and equal citizens, are liable tomorrow... to fall into the same abyss of suffering and despair as the German Jews. The fate of our unfortunate brothers in Germany is accordingly not their problem alone; it is of concern to all of us. Only our united Jewish power can extricate us from our tragic condition and rescue us from the abyss into which we are sinking. If we Jews come together.... and confront our enemies...with firm, steadfast resistance, ready not only to defend but to assume the offensive, we will overcome the danger that is standing in our way. That is certain.[9]

Ozjasz Thon, a Kraków rabbi and Zionist leader, expressed a similar conviction in an article that he wrote for the Polish-language Jewish newspaper *Nowy Dziennik* (Current Daily) in advance of the Jewish New Year in 1933.

> For [world] Jewry, Hitlerism means...a struggle for our very existence.... We know...that a teaching so *zacny* [noble-minded] as Hitlerism can spread rapidly throughout the world, infecting the public in other countries....Hence it is up to us...to defend ourselves with all our might, with every particle of energy at our disposal....We [Jews] number 16 million and we are not without resources, material as well as spiritual.... We are not without weapons...we are an ancient people [who are] *dobrze zszyte* [well sewn together], and the threads that bind us are not easily pulled apart....There may be losses, and the losses may be many and painful, but our solid core is able to withstand all blows.[10]

9   "Kol Koyre Tzu Ale Yidn" (Yiddish), YIVO, RG 29/2.16.
10 Ozjasz Thon, "De mortuis...," *Nowy Dziennik*, September 22, 1933. It is possible, of course, that the pronouncements of Thon and Wygodzki, along with similar proclamations by Jewish spokesmen in various countries during the early years of Nazi rule in Germany,

Thon was mistaken, of course. He did not imagine the force of the blow that the enemy would soon bring down upon the Jews of Europe from one end of the continent to the other. That force would no doubt have shattered even the most solid of cores. However, after the anti-Nazi struggle had failed, and the Jews stood powerless before the German murder machine, the belief that the failure had begun when the core disintegrated from within began to permeate Jewish circles. In fact, seeds of this notion can be found even during the Nazi era, when the struggle was still going on. In the 1930s, various Jewish leaders expressed concern over internal disintegration and over the dire consequences that it was liable to bring. At the inaugural session of the World Jewish Congress in August 1936, for example, Rabbi Stephen S. Wise of New York, one of the pillars of this newly formed, international Jewish organization, railed bitterly against the opposition that he had encountered from Jewish organizations to the congress' effort to unite Jews throughout the world under a single political roof. He also derided what he saw as the Jewish people's unwillingness to mobilize the copious resources at its disposal for the anti-Nazi fight. In fact, he declared the lack of solidarity to be the greatest danger facing the Jewish people, because this more than anything else encouraged the Jews' enemies to give their enmity practical expression.

> When one considers how little the Jews of the world, who enjoy some degree of possessions and power, are prepared to do on behalf of Jewish self-defence and survival, one wonders that our enemies do not press us even harder than they do....Unconsciously it may be, but none the less truly, we hold out every inducement and encouragement to our enemies by reason of our failure to stand together except when we do so momentarily in order to relieve calamity. Our unreadiness to act organisedly in defence of and for the safeguarding of the rights of Jews—these are invitation, temptation, provocation to the enemies of Israel to do their cruelest and foulest....One wonders whether men and nations would have dared to deal as brutally with Jews had it not been felt that these were almost wholly unorganized and were unready or unwilling to defend themselves, save for unorganized, uncoordinated, unrelated protests, on back of which

were nothing more than a rhetorical gesture with nothing behind them, an effort to raise the spirits of Jews who feared their future by describing their situation in terms that those doing the describing did not believe themselves.

lay the ever-present dread that the peoples or groups who made such protests might be imagined to be related to one another. A further encouragement to our foes is the failure of Jews of leadership to come together from many lands earnestly to consider Jewish problems and to bend their united strength toward an effort of solution....Not one-tenth of one percent of Jewish possessions has been given for the relief of Jews of Germany....What will history say of them, good Jews, who in the presence of the cruelest, widest-spread persecution, economic insecurity, political uncertainty, cultural sterility, refuse to meet openly with their fellow-Jews, whether because of fear or any other expediency[?][11]

As years passed, the view that the absence of internal cohesion among world Jewry had mortally wounded the ability of Europe's Jews to withstand and to overcome the Nazi threat became a staple feature of attempts to explain how the Nazis and their fellow travelers had managed to smite Israel hip and thigh without interference. If only the Jewish people had had the sense to set their internal quarrels aside and to confront the enemy in battle with ranks truly united—as even today many scholars and non-scholars alike maintain, in a manner strikingly similar to the evaluation of Bach-Zelewski—the results of the deadly encounter with the Third Reich would have been different from what they were. The charges are familiar: organizational rivalries among the Jews of Germany prevented them from laying the groundwork for timely emigration;[12] the leadership of Polish Jewry on the eve of the war proved incapable of coordinating positions among organizations and parties, or of bringing the Jewish public together for the struggle that awaited them;[13] conflicts and disagreements among underground Jewish political movements delayed the development of armed resistance in the Warsaw ghetto and elsewhere;[14] the leaders of Palestinian Jewry sabotaged plans

---

11 *Protocole du premier Congrès Juif Mondial, Genève, 8–15 août 1936* (Geneva: World Jewish Congress, 1936), pp. 14–16. Wise's speech was transcribed in English.

12 Avraham Margaliot, "Hapulmus Bishe'elat Hanhagatam Shel Yehudei Germaniya Bishenotav Harishonot Shel Hareich Hashelishi (1933–1938)," in Margaliot, *Bein Hatzala Le'avadon: Iyunim Betoledot Yehudei Germaniya, 1932–1938* (Hebrew) (Jerusalem: Yad Vashem, 1990), pp. 1–15.

13 Emanuel Melzer, *No Way Out: The Politics of Polish Jewry, 1935–1939* (Cincinnati: Hebrew Union College Press, 1997), pp. 97–112.

14 Israel Gutman, *The Jews of Warsaw, 1939–1943: Ghetto, Underground, Revolt*

for an anti-German economic boycott that could have choked the Reich in its infancy, and they undercut rescue efforts that did not involve immigration to [Mandatory] Palestine, because in their minds the battle for the future of that country took precedence over the saving of Jewish lives in the Diaspora;[15] the Jews of the United States stood by silently upon learning that European Jewry was being systematically slaughtered, because ever since arriving in their new homeland from a continent that they regarded as accursed, an emotional gulf separated them from the families whom they had left in the old country;[16] and many additional similar arguments, all implying that the Jewish people's internal fissures contributed in some measure to their bitter fate when calamity struck.[17]

This Jewish narrative about the role of solidarity or its absence in determining the dimensions of the Holocaust thus affirms Bach-Zelewski's speculative, counterfactual conclusion. However, it does not necessarily confirm his historical findings. From his observations of Jewish behavior in 1941, Bach-Zelewski made an inference about Jewish history in general: the Jews had always been as they were at the moment that he observed them. His statement entails the proposition that the Jews had never been a well-organized or cohesive people, had never coordinated their activities together, and had never developed true mechanisms for exercising power. The Jewish narrative does not appear to incorporate such an all-encompassing historical inference. On the contrary, the narrative that emerges from the statements of Wygodzki, Thon, and Wise is one of deterioration and atrophy: those statements, taken together, suggest that on the eve of the Nazi era, and even at that era's outset, world Jewry gave all indications of being a highly cohesive entity, and its internal cohesiveness constituted the chief assurance

(Bloomington: Indiana University Press, 1982), pp.169–171, 445n35; Sara Bender, *The Jews of Bialystok during World War II and the Holocaust* (Hanover: University Press of New England, 2008), pp. 166–169; Yehuda Bauer, "Jewish Baranowicze in the Holocaust," *Yad Vashem Studies*, 31 (2003), pp. 95–151.

15 Shabtai B. Beit-Zvi, *Hatziyonut Hapost-Ugandit Bemashber Hashoah: Mehkar Al Goremei Mishgeiha Shel Hatenu'a Hatziyonit Bashanim 1938–1945* (Hebrew) (Tel Aviv: Bronfman, 1977); Edwin Black, *The Transfer Agreement: The Untold Story of the Secret Pact between the Third Reich and Jewish Palestine* (New York: Macmillan, 1984).

16 Gulie Ne'eman Arad, *America, Its Jews, and the Rise of Nazism* (Bloomington: Indiana University Press, 2000).

17 Expressions of this explanation appear in the works cited above in notes 12–16. The authors of the works are not themselves of one mind concerning the validity of the explanation.

of the Jews' physical security and material well-being everywhere. According to this understanding of history, only after the Nazis took power did the internal threads that tied them together—the threads that purportedly connected all parts of the Jewish world to one another and enabled them to mobilize resources on a global scale on behalf of their weakest, most threatened parts—begin to unravel. This version thus suggests that nothing at all can be learned from the behavior of different Jewish communities during the Nazi era about Jewish history before the Holocaust. By implication, the Holocaust constitutes an absolute rupture in the ongoing flow of Jewish history. Accordingly, the actions of Jews during the Holocaust must be understood only against the background of that period itself—of the extreme, immediate situation in which the Jewish people found themselves during those years.

Clearly, both views—one of the Holocaust as a period that reveals certain unchanging, essential Jewish characteristics, and the other that treats the era's darkness as a barrier to seeing anything beyond it—miss the mark when formulated in such decisive, all-or-nothing terms. They also distort thinking about Jewish solidarity. After all, solidarity is not a digital quality, as it were, one that either exists or does not exist. It is instead better represented analogically, as a quality that manifests itself to varying degrees at different moments. Developing a well-considered, reliable understanding of Jewish solidarity thus requires examining its history and the possible connections between it and the outcome of the Nazi murder campaign empirically. Such an examination requires tools for assessing its variability over time. Those tools, in turn, ought to enable measured, cautious answers to a series of questions of paramount importance for both historians of the Holocaust and for historians of the Jews: In what ways and to what degree did different parts of the Jewish Diaspora, during the Holocaust and earlier, display characteristics of belonging to a cohesive people whose bonds transcend geopolitical boundaries? How did such cohesiveness find practical expression at different times? Has a feeling of global Jewish solidarity shown itself to be a permanent feature of Jewish history, or have this feeling and its practical expressions changed over time in accordance with varying local conditions? Did Jewish cohesiveness really serve as a source of power before the Holocaust? If so, how was that power manifested, and what were its limits? Did the Nazi regime succeed in injuring the Jewish sense of solidarity or in impairing the manner in which it could be expressed? If this was the Nazi regime's effect, what was the extent of the injury, and which expressions were impaired? How did that injury, if indeed there was one, influence the development of Nazi policies toward the Jews or the results of the murder campaign? A firm empirical basis for consideration of these questions does not yet exist. Nevertheless, enough has been learned to date to discern at least one long-term trend that bears upon the discussion of the link between Jewish solidarity and Jewish power that unfolded during the Holocaust period.

This link is reflected in the rabbinic maxim that many have taken as proof of the existence of an ancient Jewish tradition of solidarity: "*Kol Yisrael Arevim Zeh Bazeh*" (All Israel is responsible for one another). Some will undoubtedly object, claiming that this saying cannot be taken as a description of a permanent social reality but only as an expression of a social ideal. It appears clear, however, that the saying's original intent was indeed descriptive, although the description pertained to a theological rather than a social situation. The maxim comes from Sifra, an early rabbinic midrash on the Book of Leviticus. The text interprets Leviticus 26:37—"With no one pursuing, they shall stumble over one another as before the sword; you shall not be able to stand your ground before your enemies"—as if "over one another" should be read "one for the offenses of another," which teaches that every person of Israel is responsible for every other one. According to this reading of the biblical verse, every individual Jew is liable to be punished for the transgressions of another Jew, and the entire Jewish people may be punished for the sins of a single Jewish individual. That every Jew is supposed to be held responsible for every other Jew is thus considered a legal guarantee stemming from the special relation between the Jewish people and God; it exists independently of the actual conditions of Jewish life on earth. In modern times, however, a secular interpretation was added to the rabbinic text. That interpretation, too, is purported to be descriptive.

A newly founded Jewish organization, the Alliance Israélite Universelle, adopted it in 1860 to represent its fundamental working assumption that all Jews throughout the world are linked to one another not only by virtue of their obligations to God but also by a set of tangible worldly interests. For the founders of the Alliance Israélite Universelle, the existence of these worldly connections meant that what happened to Jews in one part of the world directly influenced the situation and the fate of Jews everywhere else. It appears that the new organization's members understood that they were employing an ancient text in a novel way. One of the Alliance Israélite Universelle's first publications declared,

"We must create a new sort of bond [among the Jews of the world], to establish solidarity among [the Jews in] every country. This solidarity must embrace within one vast network all that is of Jewish concern." The same text also explained why such a "vast network" was needed: its purpose was to create "a cohesion powerful enough to triumph over all obstacles and to resist persecution."[18] This document appears to contain one of the earliest expressions of the idea that solidarity is directly connected to power. That idea would later become the foundation for the view that the extent of Jewish losses at Nazi hands was, among other things, a function of their purported lack of internal cohesion.

Notice that the "vast network" of which the founders of the Alliance Israélite Universelle spoke was supposed to inculcate a secular sense of solidarity. The founders did not posit that this sense of solidarity existed from time immemorial. Quite the contrary, the organization adapted the rabbinic saying about mutual responsibility in order to use it as a mobilizing slogan, thereby adding to it the character of a moral imperative.[19] Nevertheless, it appears that during the organization's initial stage, its founders operated less with that presumed imperative in mind than in response to strategic considerations. Bringing together all the Jews of the world under a single organizational roof was supposed to assist Jews in the West, who enjoyed a relatively high level of physical security at the time, to wage an effective struggle on behalf of the Jews in other countries, whose security was precarious in comparison to their own. The test of the new organizational structure promoted by the Alliance Israélite Universelle—one predicated upon the foundation of "solidarity"—was thus to be found in the outcome of an ongoing battle in the international political arena.[20]

The first such test was encountered at the Congress of Berlin in 1878, when an international Jewish coalition, led by the Alliance Israélite Universelle, demanded placing the matter of the rights of Balkan Jewry on the congress' agenda. After the congress not only took up the matter

18 Alliance Israélite Universelle, *Alliance Israélite Universelle* (Paris: A. Wittersheim, 1860), p. 15.
19 The words *"Kol Yisrael Arevim Zeh Bazeh"* were cited (in Hebrew typeface) on the cover page of the organization's publication, *Bulletin de l'Alliance Israélite Universelle*, beginning in July 1865.
20 For further discussion, see Lisa Moses Leff, *Sacred Bonds of Solidarity: The Rise of Jewish Internationalism in Nineteenth-Century France* (Stanford: Stanford University Press, 2006), pp. 157–199.

but enshrined civic equality for the Jews of Romania, Bulgaria, Serbia, and Montenegro in an international covenant, most Jewish observers were persuaded that the new structure and its underlying assumptions had proven themselves. The results of the congress reinforced the belief that solidarity among Jews was a source of significant power for them.[21]

Recent historical research has shown that this belief was distorted. It turns out that the results of the Congress of Berlin stemmed from the complex, multilateral relations between the European powers at the time. The results were influenced as well by the behind-the-scenes activity of a single Jew, the banker Gerson Bleichröder, whose interventions proved more effective than the organized, collective, Jewish diplomatic efforts.[22] Indeed, although during the four decades that followed the Congress of Berlin, Jews in the West sometimes managed to develop sufficient power to induce political action on behalf of their fellow Jews in Eastern Europe and elsewhere—as, for example, in 1911, when the United States Senate, responding to a demand from Jewish leaders, refused to renew a commercial treaty with Russia over the objection of U.S. President William Howard Taft.[23] Their success stemmed not so much from their organizational capacity as from the dependence of many governments upon the monetary resources, commercial acumen, and political support of a small coterie of wealthy Jewish financiers like Bleichröder, Jacob Schiff, the Warburg family, and the House of Rothschild. During the late nineteenth and early twentieth centuries, these and other Jewish private bankers served as a principal source of funding for government activity. This situation gave these financiers considerable leverage in international politics. For reasons beyond the scope of the present discussion, some members of the Jewish financial elite displayed from time to time an interest in using their leverage on behalf of the Jews in the Russian Empire and in other countries where the Jews suffered from exclusion, discrimination, and persecution.[24] However, their ability

21 N. M. Gelber, "She'elat Hayehudim Lifnei Hacongres HaBerlinai Bishenat 1878" (Hebrew), *Zion*, 8 (1943), pp. 35–50; Narcisse Leven, *Cinquante ans d'histoire: L'Alliance israélite universelle (1860–1910)* (Paris: Felix Alcan, 1911), pp. 213–232.

22 Fritz Stern, *Gold and Iron: Bismarck, Bleichröder, and the Building of the German Empire* (New York: Alfred A. Knopf, 1977), pp. 351–393.

23 Naomi W. Cohen, *Jacob H. Schiff: A Study in American Jewish Leadership* (Hanover: Brandeis University Press, 1999), pp. 144–152.

24 Derek J. Penslar, *Shylock's Children: Economics and Jewish Identity in Modern Europe* (Berkeley: University of California Press, 2001), pp. 152–158.

to employ that leverage effectively did not depend upon the support of any worldwide Jewish community, no matter how cohesive and united that community might have been. In fact, it is far from certain that a cohesive, united, worldwide Jewish community can be said to have existed at all during the decades when the financial elite's power was at its height. Indeed, the Alliance Israélite Universelle ultimately proved unable to bring the vast network of which it dreamed into being on a permanent basis. Rather, as early as the 1870s, it took on the character of an emphatically French national organization, while parallel Jewish organizations, similarly reflecting a particular national orientation, were formed in Great Britain, Germany, Austria, and the United States before World War I. Sometimes these organizations worked in concert with the Alliance Israélite Universelle, sometimes in opposition to it, and sometimes with no reference to it at all.[25]

The leaders of these organizations, including of the Alliance Israélite Universelle, understood quite well that the Jewish people had not suddenly banded together as one in accordance with their wishes. They knew that their ability to intervene on behalf of their fellow Jews whose physical security was threatened depended almost entirely upon the essential role of the Jewish economic elite in international finance and upon that elite's willingness to employ its power to promote overall Jewish interests. This dependence was brought home to the Jewish organizations in 1919 at the Paris Peace Conference, where Jewish financial magnates did not play an active role. Some of the Jewish organizations that assembled in Paris took part in an effort to resurrect the "vast network" of the Alliance Israélite Universelle in a different form, this time as a worldwide, representative, Jewish political body tasked with fighting for the recognition of the Jews of Eastern Europe as a minority nation in the new national states carved from the ruins of the Russian and Habsburg Empires. This effort led to the founding of a new organization, the Comité des Délegations Juives. About ten years later, that body initiated the process that culminated in the establishment of the World Jewish Congress in 1936.[26] At the Peace Conference, the Comité des Délegations Juives supported the

25 These organizations included the Anglo–Jewish Association (founded 1871), the Israelitische Allianz zu Wien (1872), the Hilfsverein der deutschen Juden (1901), and the American Jewish Committee (1906).

26 For an extended discussion, see David Engel, "Manhigim Yehudim, Tihnun Astrategi Vehazira Habeinle'umit Le'ahar Milhemet Ha'olam Harishona" (Hebrew), *Michael*, 16 (2004), pp. 165–178.

idea of anchoring the rights of Jews in the new states in international treaties. Other Jewish organizations that sent delegates to the Peace Conference, including the Alliance Israélite Universelle, also supported the idea, although they objected to certain features of the Comité des Délégations Juives' plan of action and did not join the new body. In the end, the Peace Conference adopted the general concept of international guarantees, forcing a series of Minorities Treaties upon fourteen states, in most cases, over those states' objections.[27] However, recent studies have established that the efforts of the Comité des Délégations Juives and of other Jewish organizations had only marginal influence on the Peace Conference's actions.[28] The Comité des Délégations Juives was well aware that the conference's convening governments had actually given the Jewish body only scant attention, and its leaders complained bitterly about this seeming neglect. Nevertheless, in the wake of the conference not only did the Comité des Délégations Juives claim exclusive credit for the creation of the international mechanism for the protection of minorities, it attributed its self-proclaimed success to its ability to speak for all of world Jewry with a single, unified voice. Its behavior actually constituted a conscious attempt by a Jewish leadership group to cultivate an illusion—the illusion of significant Jewish political power based upon a foundation of national unity.[29]

An episode from the beginning of the Nazi era sheds further light upon this move. In the second week of April 1933, Stephen Wise received a letter in New York from a Nicholas (Nicolas) Sorin.[30] Information about this person is lacking.[31] Possibly the name was an alias, since it is known

---

27 Carole Fink, *Defending the Rights of Others: The Great Powers, the Jews, and International Minority Protection, 1878–1938* (Cambridge: Cambridge University Press, 2004), pp. 132–264.
28 David Engel, "Metsav Hayehudim BePolin Vehadiyunim Al Amanat Hami'utim Beve'idat Hashalom BeParis, 1919—Ha'araha Hadasha" (Hebrew), *Divrei Hakongres Habeinle'umi Lemada'ei Hayahadut*, 12 (1997), pp. 183–190.
29 David Engel, "Perceptions of Power: Poland and World Jewry," *Simon Dubnow Institute Yearbook*, 1 (2002), pp. 17–28.
30 Letter from Nicholas (Nicolas) Sorin to Stephen Wise, April 5, 1933, Central Zionist Archives (CZA), A405/84a. The document in the archival file is a typewritten copy; the writer's first name appears in two different forms, one in the heading, the other in place of the signature. It is not possible to tell from the typescript which form is correct, nor to know whether the writer pronounced his name in English or in French. The letter was sent from Vanves, a suburb of Paris.
31 He described himself as "a Russian aristocrat who has political friends also in Jewish

that during the first months following the Nazi accession to power in Germany, Wise received reports on the situation in that country from a secret informer whose identity he was keen to conceal.[32] To preserve secrecy, Wise made it a practice to destroy the reports. However, he made a limited number of typewritten copies for distribution to close associates.[33] In any event, the person who wrote the letter in question, the mysterious Mr. Sorin, reported that a short time earlier he had received a visit from a man who presented himself as a delegate from "Hitler's 'Quartier General' in Paris and London, seeking contact with political high quarters in order to get information—whether the 'Jewish conspiration' [sic] against Germany is a serious danger or only a bluff." The author of the letter informed Wise that he had told his interlocutor, "Starting a war with the Jews, Hitler made the greatest stupidity which will do him the greatest harm and perhaps destroy him. Remember the fate of the tsar and of the Old Russia." By contrast, Sorin warned Wise confidentially, in his own opinion, that "the Jews will be the victims" of the political upheaval in Germany. "Only God knows how to save them."[34]

The letter prompted Wise and his colleagues from the American Jewish Congress—yet another of the many bodies preaching the vital importance of Jewish solidarity, while simultaneously insisting upon their organizational independence—to conduct a survey of the resources available to the Jewish people that might be used to counter the threat articulated by Sorin. Sorin had reported warning the German delegate

circles." His letters mention personal connections with influential people in Germany and in France, including a Baron Ungern-Sternberg, probably a member of the Baltic German noble family, one of whose other members, Roman von Ungern-Sternberg (1885–1921), was an officer in the Russian army during World War I who fought against the Bolsheviks during the Russian Civil War and later in Outer Mongolia against the Bolsheviks and the Chinese.

32 Stephen Wise, *Challenging Years: The Autobiography of Stephen Wise* (London: East and West Library, 1951), pp. 161–163; letter from Stephen Wise to Ruth Mack Brunswick, April 6, 1933, CZA, A405/84a.

33 In the corner of the copy of the letter from Nicholas (Nicolas) Sorin to Stephen Wise, April 5, 1933, that is preserved in CZA, A405/84a, Wise instructed the recipient (Judge Julian Mack of Chicago), "Please destroy this item at once." Mack did not carry out the instruction. The document was preserved thanks to his failure (or unwillingness) to do so.

34 A week later, he sent a different assessment: "Hitler and Co. are totally terrorized by the Jewish world resistance....We are not weak, we are powerful and we can bite Germany on its many acheable spots"; letter from Nicholas (Nicolas) Sorin to Stephen Wise, April 12/14, 1933, CZA, A405/84a. The typewritten copy of the letter in the archival file bears two different dates: April 14 in the heading and April 12 at the end.

that "[As long as] Hitler remains in office and continues his antisemitic policy, Germany will never get any political concessions," including with regard to the Saar region, loan forgiveness, or revision of the Treaty of Versailles.[35] He had also intimated that world Jewry had the power to place the suffering of German Jews at the center of press coverage worldwide in a way that could force Germany to change direction. However, only a short while later, Wise and his colleagues, including David Sarnoff, who as chairman of the NBC radio network and a founder of RKO Motion Picture Studios understood well the media of mass communication, noted that the Nazis paid little attention to world public opinion and were not influenced by it. They concluded that if Hitler could not achieve his territorial aims with the agreement of the world's great powers, he would achieve those aims by force, surmounting the powers' opposition.[36]

Wise's first thought in response was to "fight it out in Germany by making the Germans see and believe that we have the power to hurt her economically and commercially."[37] However, over the following weeks, as he and his associates examined the German economy in depth with the aim of identifying its weaknesses, they found no easy point of attack. An economic boycott was unlikely to be effective, they noted, because most of the commerce that the Jews in Western countries conducted with Germany involved firms owned by German Jews, and the role of those firms in Nazi economic plans was nearly nil.[38] Moreover, they despaired of the possibility of interfering with German credit in the international bond market, since the influence of the great Jewish financiers had virtually vanished after World War I, and the United States government was determined to thwart any step that might induce the Germans to suspend loan repayments.[39] Consequently, they determined that their

35 Letter from Nicholas (Nicolas) Sorin to Stephen Wise, April 5, 1933, CZA, A405/84a.
36 Letter from Stephen Wise to Felix Frankfurter, April 26, 1933, CZA, A405/84a; letter from Stephen Wise to Ruth Mack Brunswick, April 28, 1933, CZA, A405/84b; letter from Ruth Mack Brunswick to James McDonald, May 4, 1933, CZA, A405/83a.
37 Letter from Stephen Wise to Ruth Mack Brunswick, April 15, 1933, CZA, A405/84a.
38 See, for example, the undated, handwritten, Russian-language analysis bearing the section headings *Poseshchaemost' Germanii inostrannymi turistami* (Visits to Germany by Foreign Tourists); *Otrazhenie boikota na vneshnei torgovle Germanii* (The Reflection of the Boycott in Germany's Foreign Trade); *Proverka nemetskikh dannykh ob eksporte* (Monitoring German Export Data); and *Prichiny slabogo otrazheniia boikota v statistike* (The Reasons for the Weak Reflection of the Boycott in the Statistics), CZA, A126/603. The document incorporates data from early 1932 until mid-1933.
39 Memorandum from Stephen Wise and Bernard Deutsch, April 28, 1933, CZA,

ability to convince Germany of the harm Jews might do to it was more important strategically than the harm itself. In other words, the strategy for confronting the threat to German Jewry developed by one of the central institutions of Jewish foreign policy during the early months of the Nazi era rested upon creating an illusion of power that could effectively mask actual powerlessness. Over time, other organizations and individuals who took part in formulating the initial responses of Jews around the world to Nazi anti-Jewish policies adopted a similar strategic principle: where power is absent, make it appear present. However, all faced the same problem: how to conjure up the requisite deception.[40]

This context appears to provide the key to understanding the Jewish solidarity narrative that found expression before and at the outset of the Nazi period. The Comité des Délégations Juives and the groups in the Jewish world that supported it were concerned with strengthening to the greatest extent possible the image of the Jews as a people whose internal cohesion gave them serious clout in great power politics, in international financial markets, and in world public opinion. Such an image, they believed, might dissuade unfriendly governments from adopting measures that adversely affected their well-being. For this reason, evidently, Jewish spokesmen in Poland were not quick to rebut the charges that circulated in that country following the Peace Conference about a hidden, international Jewish hand that had undermined Polish independence by forcing the new state to accept the strictures of a Minorities Treaty. On the contrary, they operated with the insight that the appearance of power can move people who believe in it as effectively as can power itself.[41] It appears, moreover, that the intended audience for the bold declarations made by Jewish leaders like Wygodzki and Thon in 1933 about the power of Jewish solidarity to defeat the Nazi regime was not so much the Jews as the Germans, especially the German policymakers in Berlin. To be sure, Jewish strategists did not expect the

A405/84a; letter from Stephen Wise to Ruth Mack Brunswick, April 28, 1933, CZA, A405/84b; letter from Louis Brandeis to Stephen Wise, May 16, 1933, CZA, A405/83a; letter from Mark Brunswick to Ruth Mack Brunswick, May 16, 1933, CZA, A405/83a. See also Walter Lippmann et al, eds., *The United States in World Affairs, 1933* (New York: Council on Foreign Relations, 1934), pp. 113–115; Adam Tooze, *The Wages of Destruction: The Making and Breaking of the Nazi Economy* (New York: Viking, 2007), pp. 52–53, 86–89.

40 See Arad, *America*, pp. 157–180.

41 Letter from Nicholas Sorin to Stephen Wise, April 5, 1933, CZA, A405/84a.

leaders of the Third Reich to read a Polish-language Jewish newspaper—although German bureaus did survey such newspapers and reported their contents—let alone a Yiddish-language leaflet that circulated locally in Vilna in a small number of copies. Yet just as in earlier decades, such declarations served primarily a tactical function in the service of a broader strategy. The idea behind them was evidently that if Jews everywhere saw themselves as connected by powerful bonds to a large, unified people who controlled considerable resources across the globe, Germans too would see them as such and, if they were not dissuaded from tangling with them altogether, they would at least seek to reach accommodation with them.[42] The architects of the strategy were quite familiar with the feature of Nazi doctrine that attributed mysterious power to "international financial Jewry," which they considered a weakness that could be exploited to the benefit of global Jewish interests.

Jewish efforts to cultivate the illusion of cohesion and power were evident later during the Holocaust period as well, for instance in the attempts by the Working Group in Bratislava and the Aid and Rescue Committee in Budapest to save Jewish lives by negotiating with Nazi officials. These stories are well known and need not be retold here.[43] Suffice it to point out that during its twelve-year existence, the Nazi regime displayed periodic interest in bargaining with Jewish agents and in suggesting possibilities that might allow some Jews to escape death. Such occasional interest suggests that the Jewish strategy of cultivating an illusion of power did not rest entirely upon illusory premises. However, instead of being deterred by their assessment of Jewish power and abandoning their hostile designs, as Jewish strategists had anticipated they might, the Nazis looked instead for ways to make that

42 See, for example, the *vertraulich* (confidential) memorandum sent from Baden to the Comité des Délégations Juives, September 1, 1933, CZA, A126/603. The author of the memorandum, whose name is not known, spoke of the "*unzulänglichkeit*" (inadequacy) of the steps that have been taken to date for the rescue of German Jewry. He attributed the ineffectiveness to the inability of the major international Jewish organizations to form "*eine einheitliche Abwehrfront*" (a unified front for defense). "Until all of the defense forces are in constant contact with one another, and until there is a responsible authority for [maintaining] this contact and the united action that stems from it," he wrote, "Jewish defense [efforts] will look like...a series of individual initiatives of limited influence." Only the "united front," which he called for, could, to his mind, "preserve operational capability vis-à-vis—the German authorities."

43 For an extended discussion, see Yehuda Bauer, *Jews for Sale: Nazi-Jewish Negotiations, 1933–1945* (New Haven: Yale University Press, 2004).

power serve their own global strategic aims. As a result, if Jews wished to make use of their illusory power, they were compelled to employ it not against Germany but against a third party—the Western Allies. It was their misfortune that at that moment the governments of Great Britain and the United States were no longer influenced by the stereotype that had nourished the Nazi image of "international financial Jewry." Policymakers of those governments understood that since World War I, the power of the Jewish financial elite had waned to insignificance. With that power gone, the Jews lost all international political leverage. They could raise their voices against British and American inaction on their behalf but, in the end, they would surely take the British and American side in the war against their greater enemy. Even absolute solidarity among Jews the world over could not change their most unfavorable strategic position.[44]

Thus, it appears that the narrative that attributes decisive weight to the absence of solidarity, or to its loss, in determining the fate of European Jewry at Nazi hands rests upon the weakest of foundations. Perhaps, in theory, solidarity may enhance collective resilience, but the theory does not apply equally in all historical situations. Its applicability in any particular situation requires empirical demonstration. In the case of the encounter between the Third Reich and European Jewry, such a demonstration has yet to be provided. To be sure, solidarity may be expressed in other domains beyond politics; it may also manifest itself in the social sphere, as when a group transfers resources from some of its sectors to others in order to strengthen its weakest members and to improve their living conditions when they are in distress. Such expressions of solidarity were evident among European Jews during the Holocaust, but their extent and their results require further investigation.[45] Still, it seems doubtful that such investigation will reveal more extensive activities of the type that could have altered the magnitude of Jewish losses from the Nazi mass murder campaign to any statistically significant extent. In short, the connection between solidarity and power in Jewish history seems illusory in its own right.

---

44 For further discussion, see Shlomo Aronson, *Hitler, the Allies, and the Jews* (New York: Cambridge University Press, 2004).

45 An initial attempt at a comparative examination of the countries of Western Europe has been made in Bob Moore, *Survivors: Jewish Self-Help and Rescue in Nazi-Occupied Western Europe* (Oxford: Oxford University Press, 2010).

Why then might the subject of Jewish solidarity be significant for the study of the Holocaust? Its significance lies in no small measure in its connection to long-term processes in modern Jewish history. It turns out that the Holocaust occurred at a particular moment in Jewish history, a moment in which the ability of Jews to influence their surroundings had reached its lowest ebb. Accordingly, the study of the variations in that ability during the decades that preceded the Nazi rise to power and of the factors that influenced them will show that the Holocaust was the result of historical developments vastly more complex than a failure of Jewish solidarity, on the one hand, or a sudden explosion into Jewish history of an overwhelming external, destructive force, on the other.

One final observation: it is true that the presence or absence of solidarity among the Jews cannot explain the dimensions of the Holocaust, but understanding the Holocaust as the product of a particular moment in modern Jewish history can enhance explanatory efforts. Raul Hilberg missed the mark, to be sure, when he employed Bach-Zelewski's words as evidence of the absence of Jewish resistance, but he was correct when he observed in the same connection that "it is the interaction of perpetrators and victims that is 'fate.'"[46] Indeed, it was not Nazi enmity alone that brought about the murder of two-thirds of European Jewry: such a lethal outcome became possible only after the social, economic, and political mechanisms that had served in the past to moderate or to neutralize enmity had collapsed. It seems that Jewish solidarity was not one of those essential mechanisms. Nevertheless, the question remains: Would the collapse have borne such catastrophic results had a regime no less hostile to Jews than that of the Nazis taken power in Germany, or in another country, at an earlier point in Jewish history? In other words, were the Jewish people at all times equally vulnerable to mass annihilation, or could the Holocaust have happened only at one particular juncture in the Jewish past?

The implications of that question extend far beyond the scholarly realm, but it is scholars of the Holocaust and of Jewish history who are best positioned to answer it in a manner that will withstand critical scrutiny. The search for answers demands solidarity among scholars of both subjects.

---

46 Hilberg, *Destruction*, p. 662.

Exploring the Concept of "Kol Yisrael Arevim Zeh Lazeh"[1]

STEVEN T. KATZ

K ol Yisrael Arevim Zeh Lazeh (All Israel are responsible for one another), the complex and multifaceted ideal that Jews are responsible for one another, is a pillar of traditional Jewish thought. It is a concept that entails a range of obligations, which over the centuries has been subject to diverse interpretations. Furthermore, it has come to be appreciated as a broad category that involves moral, psychological, ontological, and metaphysical implications.

The exact phrase "Kol Yisrael Arevim Zeh Bazeh" originated with Rashi, the great French medieval exegete. In his commentary on the Torah, Rashi employs a nonliteral, midrashic, hermeneutical style of interpretation to explain the biblical verse Leviticus 26:37: "They will stumble, each man over his brother as if from a sword." That is, all Israel is bound together as a community, and the sin and corruption of any member of the community affects the status of the entire collective.

When framing this interpretation, Rashi certainly knew the explanation provided in the Mekhilta of the Sinai covenant by Rabbi Yehuda Hanasi: "'I am the Lord, your God.'[2] This speaks of the merit of Israel. When they stood at Sinai to receive the Torah…they pledged themselves each for the other."[3] Rashi was undoubtedly also familiar with the explanation in the Babylonian Talmud of verse Leviticus 26:37: "And they will stumble one upon another. It is not written 'one man because of his brother,' but 'one man by his brother,' the sin of his brother—whereby we are taught that all of Israel are responsible, one for the other."[4] This

---

1 This article is the final version of the paper that Steven Katz presented in the keynote address at the conference. An earlier version of this article was published in Steven T. Katz, *Holocaust Studies: Critical Reflections* (New York: Routledge, 2019).

2 Exod. 20:2.

3 Mekhilta de Rabbi Ishmael, Yitro 5.

4 See also B. Sifra, Behukotai 26:37.

teaches that all must act as sureties for one another and, as such, they have the power to restrain their fellowman from evil but do not.

Accordingly, as summarized by Rabbi Bachya ben Asher in his *Commentary on the Torah*, the *p'shat* (simple explanation) of the text in Leviticus is that the Israelites "disregarded their reciprocal responsibility and this was their undoing." However, this interpretation immediately raises a host of fundamental theological, philosophical, and ethical questions. Like all things biblical and rabbinic, it implicates us in a web of interpretations in which each individual element supports, and requires support from, all the other elements in the architectonic design of the whole. That is, to deconstruct both the literal and midrashic exegesis of the original biblical phrase, we must ask and answer four questions: (1) What is the meaning of the notion of *ahariyut hadadit* (mutual responsibility)? (2) What is the source from which the notion of *ahariyut hadadit* is derived? (3) What is the basis of authority of the notion of *ahariyut hadadit* in Jewish tradition; that is, from where does it receive its authority? (4) To what extent does the notion of *ahariyut hadadit* regulate Jewish ethical behavior?

Before proceeding, I must note that answering these and the related questions that the primary text provided by Rashi raises is not a straightforward exegetical or philosophical matter because, in spite of the popularity of the observance of *Kol Yisrael Arevim Zeh Lazeh*, there is relatively very little specific discussion about it in the long history of Jewish thought. Other than a few glosses by later biblical commentators who were aware of Rashi's reading, it rarely appears as a distinctive idea that is analyzed separately, on its own, in the writings of later philosophical, kabbalistic, and ethical commentators. Therefore, it is necessary to construct that web of reinforcing parts from which the notion derives its full meaning and significance.

In the Torah, the source of ethical obligation within the community of Israel, *Kol Yisrael Arevim Zeh Lazeh*, lies in three interconnected concepts. The first concept is the collective nature of the covenant between God and Israel; the second emerges from the obligation, that is, the commandment, to love one another; and the third is the "election of Israel." The covenant was first established between God and the patriarchs and then between God and Israel after the Exodus from Egypt. It forges a shared reality that by its very nature establishes a sense of kinship, of "family," and fosters a feeling of solidarity among all Jews. By its nature, it is all-embracing and without temporal limits. The relationship that it established between God and Israel is "eternal." As Moses reminds the People of Israel regarding God's words at Sinai, "It is not with you alone that I make this covenant and this oath [of obedience], but with those who are standing with us this day before God, our God, and with those who are not with us today…the secret things belong to the Lord, our God, but that which has been revealed is for us and our children forever to carry out all the words of the Torah."[5] At a minimum, it engenders what Rabbi Joseph Soloveitchik labeled a "Covenant of Fate," and, at a maximum, it creates a shared "Covenant of Destiny."

It is against this foundational context that Maimonides (Rambam) quite remarkably defined a heretic as someone who is indifferent to the well-being of the People of Israel.[6] The experience at Sinai ties all Israel together who then bind themselves as a collectivity in a compact with the Almighty. The covenant relates primarily to the Jewish people as a whole, not to individual Israelites, and the responsibility of maintaining it with fidelity is a shared one. The entire Jewish people benefits from appropriate societal behavior, and all Israel suffers from individual transgressions that disturb or violate the common obligation. The covenant entails at its core mutual responsibility. Israel is elected as "a kingdom of priests and a holy nation," that is, the community of Israel is not a group of individuals, some of whom do the right things and some of whom do the wrong things, with each person being judged accordingly.

The actions of Moses in two different incidents makes this clear. In the first, he intercedes for a slave and the text speaks of his intercession on behalf of "his beaten brethren."[7] Moses understands that he has an a priori moral obligation to his fellow Jew even though he is a prince and the other individual is a slave. He knows that he is responsible for his "brethren" and that he must choose to act.[8] In the second episode, Moses encounters God after the sin of the Golden Calf. An angry God tells Moses that He will destroy Israel and initiate a new nation through his (Moses') offspring. However, Moses, who is fully aware of the people's colossal wrongdoing and the legitimacy of Divine intention, nevertheless replies to God's offer in the following manner:

5   Deut. 29:13–14, 28.
6   Moses Maimonides, *Mishne Torah*, Hilchot Teshuva 3:11. For an English translation by Rabbi Eliyahu Touger, see Maimonides (Rambam), *Mishneh Torah: Hilchot Teshuvah* (New York: Moznaim, 1990).
7   Exod. 2:11–17.
8   The midrashic mode of analysis of the content of the biblical tale is employed here.

> Now it came to pass on the next day that Moses said to the people, "You have committed a great sin. So now I will go up to the Lord; perhaps I can obtain atonement for your sin." Then Moses returned to the Lord and said, "Oh, these people have committed a great sin, and have made for themselves a god of gold! Yet now, if You will forgive their sin—but if not, I pray, blot me out of Your book which You have written.[9]

For Moses, God's plan was unacceptable and he would not be party to it. Being a member of *Am Yisrael*, the People of Israel, means showing ultimate concern for the others in the community, even when they have fallen short of their obligations. For the leader of the nation, the values governing in this context go beyond strict justice and demand recognition of the interdependence of all Israelites. In the course of making this choice, Moses reminds God of His moral obligations to the patriarchs and, at the same time, lives up to his responsibility to ensure the future of the Jewish people.

The foregoing episode prompted the midrash that compares Noah, Abraham, and Moses as ethical models. Noah did not plead for his fellow human beings and was therefore inferior to Abraham, who pleaded for the righteous at Sodom. However, although Abraham did challenge God's severe judgment against Sodom, he pleaded **only** for the righteous, whereas Moses appealed for the sinners who danced around the Golden Calf and linked his future to theirs, and thus Moses surpassed Abraham.

The notion of covenantal responsibility appears throughout the Torah. For example, regarding false teachers, Israel is told, "All Israel will hear and fear."[10] The threat that such people pose is not primarily to individuals but rather to the well-being of the national community. Again, in response to those who violate the covenant, the Torah demands that the witnesses against them be the first to raise a hand to kill them, and then "the hand of the entire people afterward, and you will destroy evil from your midst."[11] Every Israelite is responsible for the maintenance of the "contract" between God and Israel. These are highly challenging obligations; God makes great demands. Later this principle of interdependence became the normative assumption that justified the

9 Exod. 32:30–32.
10 Deut. 13:12, 21:21.
11 Deut. 17:7.

critique of Israel's behavior by the prophets. The prophet was both a member of the nation and a severe critic within it who was tasked with maintaining its integrity.

Likewise, in the case of the rebellious son, the Torah commands, "All the men of his city will pelt him with stones and he will die; and you will remove evil from your midst; and all Israel will hear, and they will fear."[12] Israel is a collective enterprise. As such there must be a concern on the part of all its members for the way in which the behavior of individual members affects the community. Hence, the obligation that the nation "sweep out evil from your midst,"[13] lest evil consume the nation. Though this rule was not enforced, it nevertheless reflects the high bar that God ideally sets for the behavior of His covenantal partner.

The themes of mutual accountability and Israel's inescapable connectedness again find expression in and through the event recounted in Joshua 7.

> The children of Israel were unfaithful in regard to the consecrated property: Ahan, the son of Karmi, the son of Zimri, the son of Zerah, of the tribe of Judah, took some of it. So, the Lord's anger burned against the children of Israel.[14]

And as a result:

> The Lord said to Joshua, "Stand up! Why do you fall on your face?" Israel has sinned; they have violated My Covenant that I commanded them [to keep]. They have also taken from the consecrated property; they have also stolen, they have also lied, they have put it with their own possessions. That is why the children of Israel will not be able to stand against their enemies; they will turn their backs and run because they have become worthy of destruction. I will not be with you anymore unless you destroy the transgressor from your midst.[15]

God declared not that Ahan had sinned but that "Israel had sinned." Israel, defined by its collective integrity, was held liable for not preventing

---

12 Deut. 21:21.
13 Deut. 13:6, 17:7, 19:19, 21:21.
14 Josh. 7:1.
15 Josh. 7:10–12.

Ahan's crime and, after the fact, for not punishing it, thereby becoming an accomplice.

A self without concern for others, a social order that does not respond to evil in its midst, even if it otherwise dedicates itself to its own religious virtuosity, is, in actuality, a transgressor who betrays the fundamental imperative of the Torah and Jewish life. In the real social and political drama of communal existence, Jews are not allowed to be "bystanders." The bystander is not neutral, as is often mistakenly believed, but an ally of those who do evil. Moses is Moses because he came down from Sinai to join in the national experience and to share in the fate of Israel. So too the later prophets did not abandon their social environments but remained firmly within them and made severe demands upon them.

The second foundational principle that mandates our mutual ethical concern is the biblical command *"v'ahavta l're'eha kamoha* (love your neighbor as yourself): I am the Lord."[16] This verse, found almost exactly in the middle of the Torah, as if to emphasize its centrality, demands that we be other-directed. Egotism is the source of sin and selfishness— what the sages identified as *middot S'dom* (the ethics of Sodom). Ezekiel recalled this when he exhorted Israel: "Behold, this was the inequity of your sister Sodom…it did not strengthen the hand of the poor and needy."[17] Further drawing on this tradition, the Talmud teaches, "He who closes his eyes against charity is like an idolater."[18] In contrast, love is always directed toward another person: one unique being encountering another unique being and responding to his/her need. As Martin Buber noted, love means responsibility for the other.

This ethical norm, which should define our relationships with one another, is expressed in such biblical laws as those of the Jubilee Year and the rules governing the Israelite slave.[19] The Israelite whose impoverishment leads to voluntary enslavement is to be shown respect and granted freedom after six years. According to the ruling in Exodus 21, "If you buy a Jewish bondsman, he will work for six years; and in the seventh he will go free, for no charge."[20] Even if the Israelite slave refuses,[21] he is to be liberated. According to the rabbinic interpretation,

16 Lev. 19:18.
17 Ezek. 16.49.
18 B. Ketubot 68a.
19 Deut. 15:13; Lev. 25:42.
20 Exod. 21:2.
21 Exod. 21:2–6.

the phrase "he will serve [him] forever"[22] should be understood as: until the Jubilee Year. There must be an end to degradation and subjugation for the Israelite slave for he too belongs rightfully **within** the national community. The Torah, likewise, instructs us:

At the end of every three years, bring all the tithes of that year's produce and store it in your towns, so that the Levites who have no allotment or inheritance of their own, and the stranger, and the fatherless, and the widow who lives in your towns may come and eat and be satisfied, that the Lord your God may bless you in all the work of your hands.[23]

"Loving one's neighbor" means ensuring that everyone in the community is fed. Looking after the welfare of all the members of society, of every social class, reflects our primordial interconnectedness and is a non-negotiable obligation. As Maimonides observed, "We have never seen nor heard of an Israelite community that does not have a charity fund."[24] This involvement rather than the indifference of the modern autonomous self is obligatory for every Jew. Drawing on the ruling in the Talmud, Maimonides even concludes that the *Beth Din* (the rabbinic court) "may take from a person what it is proper for that person to give. It may [also] pawn possessions for purposes of charity, even on the eve of the Sabbath."[25] Moreover, according to Halacha (Jewish law), *tzedaka* (charity) must be provided in a way that preserves the dignity of the recipient. This, as much as the giving itself, is what defines a just and decent society.

Similarly, as taught in Leviticus and Deuteronomy, all debts must be canceled and all sales of land over the previous forty-nine years must be annulled in the Jubilee Year: "And you will hallow the fiftieth year and proclaim liberty throughout the land unto all the inhabitants thereof... you will return every man to his possessions, and you will return every man to his family."[26] The purpose of this practice was to eliminate economic inequity by recreating the fair, original division of the land. If enacted, there would be no rich and no poor.

22 Exod. 21:6.
23 Deut. 14:28–29.
24 Maimonides, *Mishne Torah*, Matnot Aniyim 9.3.
25 B. Baba Batra 8b.
26 Lev. 25:10; see also Lev. 25:8–24 and Deut. 15:1–11.

These and all similar rules are predicated on the duty that one must "love your fellow as yourself." We must take on the obligation to protect others, even to protect them against themselves, against their weaknesses, mistakes, and inadequacies. There are elements of prudence and pragmatism in these various ethical prescriptions but, ultimately, as is the case of our love of self, these initiatives are not grounded in utilitarian concerns. Moreover, we can never legitimately say, "This is not my affair," or "I have no stake in this and, hence, no responsibility for what occurs." One must **always** respond to the needs of others. Especially, in the repeated language of the Torah, to the widow, the stranger, and the orphan. Moreover, one must work toward creating a society in which the political, economic, and social institutions promote this inclusive goal.

The third concept that is essential for an understanding of *Kol Yisrael Arevim Zeh Lazeh* is the "election" of the Jewish people. There has been much debate over the centuries regarding the interpretation of election, and the very claim has had many critics, both inside and outside the Jewish community. Mordecai Kaplan, for example, argued for its elimination from Jewish theological discussion, and Richard Rubenstein has done so more recently. Both thinkers reject the idea as too narrow and self-centered. However, the main interpretation that has been given to this central biblical doctrine in rabbinic tradition is that election means responsibility **not** privilege—duty not pride. "You will do the good and the right."[27] With regard to this command, I am reminded that it is repeated in the description of God's covenant with Abraham: "I have chosen [Abraham] so that he will direct his children and his household after him to keep the way of the Lord by doing what is right and just." [28]

The election of Israel, independent of our individual autonomous choices, imposes a unique and inescapable ethical and theological charge on those who belong to the Nation of Israel. Exodus describes the special character of Israel: "You will be a kingdom of priests and a holy nation."[29] Leviticus explains, "You [the entire community of the People of Israel] are to sanctify yourselves and you will be holy for I the Lord your God am Holy."[30] Further elucidation is provided in Deuteronomy: "God supreme...shows no favor and takes no bribes, but upholds the cause of

---

27 Deut. 6:18.
28 Gen. 18:19.
29 Exod. 19:6.
30 Lev. 11:44.

the fatherless and the widow, and loves the stranger, providing him with food and clothing."[31]

Being "chosen" entails high ethical standards and imposes demanding moral goals that have dramatic consequences. In the words of the prophet Amos, "You only have I known of all the families of the earth; therefore, I will punish you for your iniquities."[32] Jeremiah exhorts:

> Thus says the Lord: Do justice and righteousness, and deliver from the hand of the oppressor him who has been robbed. And do no wrong or violence to the resident alien, the fatherless, and the widow, nor shed innocent blood in this place. For if you will indeed obey this word, then there will enter the gates of this house kings who [will] sit on the throne of David, riding in chariots and on horses, they and their servants and their people. But if you will not obey these words, I swear by myself, declares the Lord, that this house will become a desolation.[33]

Being Israel requires that the Jews and the Jewish people, individually and collectively, pursue social justice and the well-being of others. This demand, this obligation, is inescapable. This inescapability is the core of the essential meaning of being the *Am Segula* (Chosen People), of "being elected." This is not a voluntary undertaking. In answer to Cain's question, "Am I my brother's keeper?"[34] the answer is emphatically "yes." A Roman once asked Rabbi Akiva, "Why does your God, who is the God of the poor, not feed the poor?" and Akiva aptly replied, "So that we can escape damnation."

It is important to remember that this notion of *Kol Yisrael Arevim Zeh Lazeh* has strong halachic, that is, legal, implications. Consider, for example, apart from the more usual, daily legal principles governing social and economic justice, the ruling that was so important in premodern times addressed the absolute responsibility of all Jewish communities to redeem Jews taken as captives and slaves. In his authoritative *Shulchan Aruch*, Joseph Karo declares, "*pidyon shvuyim* (redeeming captives) takes precedence over sustaining the poor and clothing them, and there

---

31 Deut. 10:17–18.
32 Amos 3:2.
33 Jer. 22:3–5.
34 Gen. 4:9.

is no commandment more important than *pidyon shvuyim*...every moment that one delays *pidyon shvuyim* where it is possible to do so quickly, one is like a person who sheds blood."[35] If funds are limited, this requirement has priority over almost all other obligations. A Jewish community is required to help other Jews in distress, even if this means assisting someone unknown to them or an individual from a distant land. Moreover, they must do so even when it will come at the expense of other pressing local needs.[36]

The relationship that must exist between moral obligations and the halachic process may be summarized by citing two great authorities on the requirements that must govern the process of legal decision-making. First, there are the instructions of Rabbi Moses ben Nachman (Ramban), the thirteenth-century Spanish sage, in his commentary on and explanation of the verse in Deuteronomy: "Do what is right and good in the sight of the Lord."[37] This "refers," he wrote, "to compromise and conduct *lifnim mishurat hadin* (beyond the requirements of the law)...now God says that with respect to what He has not [explicitly] commanded, you should take heed to do the right and the good."[38] This should be understood to mean that the *posek* (halachic judge) is enjoined not to decide the cases that come before him according to the standard of the religious elite and the most pious in the community. Rather, he is to rule so that his decision does not impose unnecessarily strict burdens on the community as a whole. Second, which is a point of decisive importance, when Rabbi Haim Brisk (1853–1918) was asked by his students about the primary responsibility of a rabbi, he replied, "To redress the grievances of those who are abandoned and alone, to protect the dignity of the poor, and to save the oppressed from the hands of the oppressor."[39]

According to Halacha, our responsibility for others can be seen in the legal requirement that even the high priest, who, as a general rule, is

---

35 Joseph Karo, *Shulchan Aruch*, Yoreh De'ah 252:1–3.
36 I would note that, for example, when destitute Jews in the Ottoman Empire were unable to pay the taxes imposed by the state, wealthy Jews paid these taxes so that their poor brethren would not be pulled into debt slavery.
37 Deut. 6:18.
38 Moses ben Nahman, *Commentary on the Torah*, Deut. 6:18. For the English translation, see Rabbi Charles Chavel, *Moses ben Nahman, Ramban: Commentary on the Torah*, 5 vols. (Zurich: Books'n Bagels, 2000).
39 Joseph Soloveitchik, *Halakhic Man* (Philadelphia: Jewish Publication Society, 1983), p. 91.

commanded to avoid the dead, must attend to the burial of a corpse on Yom Kippur, if there is no one else to undertake this task.[40] This is known as an act of *hesed shel emet* (true kindness).[41] The usual, elevated, ritual rules that apply to maintaining the purity of the high priest are here set aside. The fact that the high priest is the central actor in the Temple service on Yom Kippur is of secondary significance. All that matters is our unshakeable commitment to our fellowman. "Come and hear," the ancient sages taught, "great is human dignity, since it overrides a negative percept of the Torah."[42] Furthermore, this norm is a corollary of the still more encompassing halachic category of *kevod ha'beriot* (respect for creation), the imperative that we be concerned with the intrinsic value of all human beings. Applying this understanding, the sages instructed that in order to show our common humanity in a final act of concern for others, everyone should be buried in a shroud of the sort that is available to all men and women so as to not embarrass the poor.[43]

To grasp the full meaning of *Kol Yisrael Arevim Zeh Lazeh*, it is also of interest to note that not only halachists but also medieval Jewish philosophers emphasized the priority of moral action as the primary Jewish obligation, while highly valuing contemplation. Thus, after reflecting on the speculations of philosophers, notably Aristotle's *Nicomachean Ethics*, Abraham ibn Daud observed that "the reason of all philosophy is proper conduct [vis-à-vis others]."[44] His fellow medieval rationalist, Joseph ibn Tzaddik argued, in a very Jewish reading of the proper role of philosophy, that philosophy is meant "to lead one to know the Creator, but the fruit and effect of its teachings is to cause one to emulate according to one's ability the Creator's moral qualities."[45] As the Almighty is selflessly concerned with us, we must be selflessly concerned with others.

Maimonides, the greatest of the medieval Jewish thinkers, generally adopted Aristotle's view that ethics is to be understood as a precondition

---

40 B. Berakhot.

41 Kindness that is done for the deceased is true kindness, since there is no possibility for the recipient to reciprocate.

42 B. Menachot 37b.

43 B. Moed Katan 27.

44 Abraham ibn Daud, *The Exalted Faith* (Rutherford and London: Fairleigh Dickinson University Press and Associated University Presses, 1986), p. 4.

45 Joseph ibn Tzaddik, *Olam Katan: Sefer Ha'olam Hakatan* (Hebrew) (Jerusalem: H.m.l., 1967), p. 64.

for the ultimate human end, the life of contemplation,[46] but demurred from endorsing this hierarchical order when discussing the biblical term *hesed*, which means, depending on the context, "love," "kindness," or "loving kindness."[47] In this context, he reiterates the "responsibility that Jews have for one another." Consider as paradigmatic his instructions regarding the proper behavior relative to festive meals on holidays.

> [W]hile one eats and drinks himself, it is his duty to feed the stranger, the orphan, the widow, and other poor and unfortunate people, for he who locks the doors to his courtyard and eats and drinks with his wife and family, without giving anything to eat and drink to the poor and the bitter in soul, his meal is not a rejoicing in a Divine commandment but rejoicing in his own stomach. Rejoicing of this kind is a disgrace to those who indulge in it, as Scripture says, "And I will spread dung upon your faces, even the dung of your sacrifices."[48]

Again, Maimonides tells us that when instructing a convert to Judaism, the convert's teachers must inform the proselyte of the transgressions involved in the law of *leket* (gleanings), *omer she nishkah* (forgotten sheaves), *pe'ah* (the corner of a field, vineyard, or orchard left unharvested for the poor), and *ma'aser oni* (the tithe for the poor).[49] These are essential rules that bind Jews to each other.

In the *Guide for the Perplexed*, Maimonides insists that acts of *hesed* are not to be done to repay an obligation, or in order to acquire indebtedness, and in anticipation of future gain. Instead, they are to be done only out of a sense of responsibility, that is, they should be the outcome of love. Imitating God, we must love other human beings with whom we share the *Tzelem Elohim* (Divine image). As God created the world and takes on a self-imposed duty for it without self-interest, we must do likewise.

Complementarily, there is the challenging ethical idea that the kabbalists drew from the act of creation. Just as God, through the act of *tzimtzum* (Divine contraction) made space for creation, so we, too, following His example—*v'halachta be'drachav* (and walk in his ways)—

---

46 Aristotle, *Nicomachean Ethics*, Book 10, 7–8, *The Internet Classics Archive*, http://classics.mit.edu/Aristotle/nicomachaen.10.x.html (accessed March 27, 2022).

47 See Maimonides' Commentary on Pe'ah 1:1.

48 Ibid.; Mal. 2:3.

49 Maimonides, *Mishne Torah*, Issurei Biáh 14:2.

have to make room for and recognize the needs of others. Moreover, this obligation, which demands that we be answerable for the other, is asymmetrical, that is, it does not depend on the reciprocal actions of the other or his/her correct or incorrect behavior.[50]

It is significant that the Torah commands us to both love God—"love the Lord your God with all your heart and with all your soul, and with all your might"[51]—and to love our fellow human beings.[52] Both require taking responsibility. Love of Heaven is, as the rabbis put it, "manifest through adhering to the rules regarding the rejection of idolatry and acting for the sake of Heaven." It is instantiated through the many, most usually ritualistic, acts *bein Adam leMakom* (between man and his Creator). The command to love God assuredly entails heavy and continuous demands. However, the command to "love our fellowmen" is even more demanding. Loving God, who is perfect, is relatively easy. Alternatively, loving our fellowmen, who are often mean-spirited and miserable, is far more difficult. But this is the law. The fulfillment of this commandment requires us to engage with the world and attempt to make a positive difference in it. This, of course, is the great challenge: to take responsibility for the other who is not oneself, whose self is decidedly independent and different, yet whose existence as a human being makes an absolute demand on us to which we are obligated to respond. *Kol Yisrael Arevim Zeh Lazeh* means that I am responsible for the other.

The concept of "*arevim*" entails many things. It denotes that we are required to acknowledge the pain of others, to be concerned with their suffering, and to seek to assist those in need. Furthermore, it requires that we help them to establish and maintain their self-esteem. To refuse to hear the pained cry of the other is immoral. As Isaiah demanded, "When you see the naked, that you cover him; and that you hide not yourself from your own flesh."[53] The suffering of others irrevocably obligates us.

---

50 The notion of *Kol Yisrael Arevim Zeh Lazeh* is central not only to halachists, philosophers, and kabbalists. At a still more basic level of Jewish spirituality and religious obligation, it needs to be recognized that Jewish prayer is usually framed in the plural, i.e., we pray not, or even primarily, for ourselves, but rather, for the entire *Knesset Yisrael*. Moreover, the **normative** organization of prayer involves a **minyan**, a group of ten men, representative of the entire community.

51 Deut. 6:5.

52 Lev. 19:18.

53 Is. 58:7.

In the words of the prophet, we are instructed in God's name: "Learn to do good. Seek justice. Vindicate the victim. Uphold the rights of the orphan. Defend the cause of the widow."[54] In T. B. Ta'anit, we learn that Moses was known to say, "Seeing that the People of Israel suffer, I suffer with them." It is relevant to note that the sages likewise attributed to God the saying, "I am with them in their suffering."[55]

The foregoing is not intended to introduce some comforting theodicy that "explains" suffering. Neither appeals to the *yissurin shel ahava* (tribulations of love) nor to the doctrine of vicarious suffering as described in Isaiah 53, not theological "explanations" that invoke Job nor the *Akedah* (binding of Isaac) can provide adequate explanations. In fact, to introduce theodicy is to hide, to seek to avoid the reality of the all too real suffering that we encounter and see everywhere around us. The demand of *Kol Yisrael Arevim Zeh Lazeh* is to be compassionate, not to provide false explanations of why others are in pain. The reality of pain and suffering transcends the false promises of theodicy.

Since this lecture was originally written to be delivered at the closing event of a conference on Jewish behavior during the Holocaust, it is not inappropriate to add that these ethical and existential considerations, the morality of other-directness and the concern with the welfare of the community, were fully in evidence in the halachic decisions made by the sages in the ghettos of World War II. In this unprecedented context, the *poskim* knew that their responsa had to meet the needs of the inquirer. Their obligation was not only, or even primarily, to get the decision right halachically—though they always tried very diligently and honorably to do this—but rather to meet the living, pressing needs of those posing the questions. Their answers clearly indicate that they gave priority to lightening the burden of their fellow Jews.

Though the *teshuvot* (rabbinic responsa) from the war years that we have are relatively few in number, those that have survived indicate a profound awareness of the unprecedented situation that the Jewish people and the individual Jew were in. Therefore, in their replies, the rabbinic sages of the period took it upon themselves, as best as they could, to alleviate the religious burdens of the faithful by suggesting the most practical and "lenient" course of action possible. Consider the following four responsa: The first of these responsa, provided by Rabbi

54 Is. 1:17.
55 B. Ta'anit 11a.

Ephraim Oshry in the Kovno ghetto,[56] deals with the issue of the use of contraception by Jewish women.

> On 20 Iyar 5702—May 7, 1942—the evildoers issued an edict that if a Jewish woman was found pregnant, they would kill her. I was asked whether Jewish women in the ghetto might utilize contraceptives to avoid pregnancy and the concomitant risk of death.

> **Responsa**: I ruled that because there was an absolute danger to their lives if the defiling evildoers should discover them pregnant, women might use contraceptive devices before intercourse.[57]

The second halachic decision, also given by Rabbi Ephraim Oshry, involves the possibility of a Jew serving as a cook on the Sabbath.

> **Responsa**: I ruled that he [a Jew] was allowed to cook on Shabboss, because the alternative of slave labor in the airfield on Shabboss was no less a desecration of the Sabbath than the cooking. In neither case would he be desecrating the Sabbath willfully, but solely out of compulsion. It was therefore preferable that he work in the kitchen [on the Sabbath] because there he would get enough food to eat. I allowed him to eat the black soup that he himself would cook on Shabboss because it is not forbidden to eat the product of Shabboss labor where one eats it to preserve life.[58]

The third, again the reply of Rabbi Oshry, provided the following ruling about eating on Yom Kippur:

> But after they grew weak from hunger and from the pressures of hard labor, a number of them [Jewish laborers] came to me in the pre-Yom Kippur days of 5702—late September 1941—and asked if they

---

56 Rabbi Oshry survived the Holocaust. After the war his responsa were translated and published. See Rabbi Ephraim Oshry, *Responsa From the Holocaust* (New York: Judaica Press, 1989). For an explanation about how Rabbi Oshry came to publish his responsa see, Moshe Tarshansky, "The Writings of Rabbi Ephraim Oshry of the Kovno Ghetto, Orthodox Historiography?" *Yad Vashem Studies*, 47:1 (2019), pp. 59–104.

57 Ibid., p. 71.

58 Ibid., p. 13.

might be permitted to eat the soup since their lives would ultimately be endangered if they did not eat it.

Responsa: Medical experts maintained that it was impossible for the person to survive with the nutrition then available to the Jews. The laborers' lives were certainly in danger; famine is an extremely agonizing, drawn-out way to die. I ruled that they might eat the soup now because of the eventual danger to their lives. The rabbi of Kovno, the *gaon* Rav Avrohom Dov Ber Kahana-Shapira, concurred with me.[59]

Finally, we have the following, interesting reply by Rabbi Katriel Tchorsh, written in Tel Aviv after the end of the war, that deals with our responsibility to the dead in the "world above":

Question: Is one who did not have relatives who perished in the Holocaust obligated to say Kaddish for the martyrs, or should one only say Kaddish if he had relatives who perished?

Responsa: Obviously, it is understood that just as each individual is obligated to join with the community and share the grief, so also is each individual obligated to do something for the spirits and souls of the departed. We find that the Kaddish has great importance, and we are obligated to [say] it for parents and relatives (Sh. AR. YD 376:4, according to Rema).[60] So, also, is every person obligated to add to the purity of the many souls of the entire house of Israel.[61]

In this last ruling, which is linked to the essential concept of caring for the dead, one finds that the charge to say Kaddish is based on the general obligation to perform acts of kindness. Although Rabbi Tchorsh cited as his authority Rabbi Moses Isserles, the Rema, who lived in sixteenth century Kraków, it is clear that he was also aware of the ruling of Maimonides who wrote the following:

---

59 Ibid., p. 22.
60 R. Moses Isserles (Rema), *Shulchan Aruch*, Yoreh De'ah, 376:4.
61 Katriel Fishel Tchorsh (Kazryel Fiszel Tchorz), "Hiyuv Ha'Kadish Haclali' Lezeher Hanispim Bashoah" (Hebrew), *Shana Beshana* (1969), https://daat.ac.il/he-il/shoa/maamarim/thoresh-kadish-klali.htm, pp. 131–140 (accessed March 28, 2022).

It is a positive rabbinical precept to visit the sick, to console mourners, to accompany the corpse, etc. It is true kindness that we practice with the dead, for there is not selfish calculation of accepting anything from the dead in exchange, and we do it only for the sake of the obligation to practice kindness. This is sufficient to establish the significance and precious value of saying the Kaddish even for the deceased person who is not a family relative. Therefore, it is clear to us that no Jew anywhere should refrain from practicing kindness to the dead, and it is each Jew's duty to join in saying Kaddish in memory of the dead and for the elevation of their soul.[62]

This is a maximal representation of *Kol Yisrael Arevim Zeh Lazeh*. One's obligation extends even to Jews who have died no less than to Jews with whom one lives.

Beyond the ethical demands of caring and the responsibility that we bear for those who suffer and are in need, the principle of *Kol Yisrael Arevim Zeh Lazeh* also raises the crucial issue of justice. *Kol Yisrael*, all Israel, carries the communal implication that we must create a just society in which the rights of all are guaranteed and protected. That obligation mandates that the laws, practices, and institutions of Jewish society be equitable and "blind." "You will not show partiality in justice."[63] Accordingly, Moses instructed the children of Israel as they were about to enter the Land of Israel: "Judges and officials you will appoint for yourselves in your cities. They will rule the people with just justice; justice will you pursue."[64] Indeed, this is a required precondition for Israelite society in *Eretz Israel*. It is only on the basis of creating a just society that, as the Torah teaches, "you may live, and inherit the land that the Lord your God is giving you."[65] The concept of the *kedusha* (holiness) of *Eretz Israel* is inseparable from justice. Hence, Isaiah insists, "The Holy God is sanctified through justice."[66]

This imperative entails creating state institutions to protect the rights of everyone in the society and, as such, must embody the values of responsibility and respect for the dignity of all those who appeal to them. They must limit violence and coercion, refrain from giving

---

62 Maimonides, *Mishne Torah*, Evel 14:1.
63 Deut. 16:19.
64 Deut. 16:18.
65 Deut. 16:20.
66 Mikdash be' Bedakah 5:16.

preferential treatment to the powerful and the wealthy, and ensure that Jewish society protects and treats every member of the community fairly. Injustice represents the manifest failure to honor the principle of *Kol Yisrael Arevim Zeh Lazeh*. With respect to Solomon, it is written: "All Israel heard the judgment that the king rendered. They saw that the wisdom of God was in him, to do justice."[67] Furthermore, to guarantee this outcome the king, like all state institutions, must be subordinate to the law and is to be judged by its statutes and ordinances.

To conclude this section, I must call attention to a few of the many consequential examples of *Kol Yisrael Arevim* during the Holocaust. I begin by recalling the existence of "self-help efforts": the creation of orphanages, hospitals, and schools; the special collections for children; and the communal support of the elderly. Almost everyone was starving in the ghettos, yet the Jews organized themselves to share the little that they had.

Second, it is important to note that during the intense debates between the heads of the Judenräte and the leaders of the underground and resistance movements in various locations, the former warned the primarily young resistance fighters that their activities, including their attempts to escape, could bring reprisals against those who remained behind. This argument was intended to dissuade those who wanted to escape. This is related in the *Pinkas Shavli*, the records of the Shavli ghetto.[68] On February 5, 1943, a meeting was held between the Jewish underground and the ghetto leaders to discuss the possibility of armed resistance. During this meeting, it became clear that the plan to escape, which involved fleeing to the Soviet partisans operating in the not-too-distant marshlands of northern Lithuania, meant leaving the women, children, and elderly, who would remain behind exposed and vulnerable. The majority of the young Jews present, moved by this appeal to *Kol Yisrael Arevim Zeh Lazeh*, decided that they could not so endanger the other ghetto residents and the plan was abandoned.[69]

Similar debates went on in other ghettos as well. In Vilna, Zelig Kalmanovich, one of the intellectual leaders of the community, wrote, "The attempt to arm is the result of irresponsibility."[70] The head of the

67 I Kings, 3:28.
68 Eliezer Yerushalmi, ed., *Pinkas Shavli* (Hebrew) (Jerusalem: Bialik Institute and Yad Vashem, 1958).
69 Ibid., p. 315.
70 Zelig Kalmanovich, "A Diary of the Nazi Ghetto in Vilna," *YIVO Annual*, 8 (1953),

ghetto, Jacob Gens, supported him. Consequently, although there was organized resistance, no revolt broke out inside the ghetto until the ghetto was about to be liquidated. This same moral confrontation took place in the Silesian ghettos of Będzin and Sosnowiec, headed by Moshe Merin, as well as in Lwów and in Bielorussia. Regarding the outcome of these tense life and death discussions, Shalom Cholawsky wrote, "Collective responsibility was the chief constraint to Jewish resistance in the ghettos."[71]

Third, we must remember the heroic actions of the Kovno ghetto Jewish police. The Nazis arrested the entire Jewish police force on March 27, 1944, and tortured its members to force them to reveal the hiding places of Jews in the ghetto, but none of the policemen betrayed their fellow Jews. Here the responsibility of *Kol Yisrael Arevim Zeh Lazeh* was taken with utmost seriousness and, as a result, all of these policemen— including the head of the police, Moshe Levin, and his lieutenants, Yehuda Supovitz and Ika Grinberg—were killed in the Ninth Fort.

Of course, such moral courage and faithful solidarity on behalf of their fellow Jews was not always the rule among the Jewish ghetto police. In Warsaw, for example, relations between the ghetto police and the resistance movement were not good. In the Łódź ghetto, most of the inhabitants also came to loathe and fear the police. In these, and comparable contexts, the profound desire to live sometimes led to immoral acts, such as those perpetrated by the ghetto police in Warsaw and in Łódź. Honoring the principle of selfless ethical action in the midst of the Holocaust called for exceptional moral integrity. Yet, remarkably, there were numerous instances of selflessness unto death. The principle of *Kol Yisrael Arevim Zeh Lazeh* was neither altogether absent nor devoid of influence during the Holocaust, and we must not allow that fact to go unnoticed.

Fourth, it is incumbent on us not to forget the acts of the Jewish leaders, such as Itzhak Wittenberg, head of the Communist underground forces in Vilna, who committed suicide when the Nazis required that he hand himself over, threatening the destruction of the entire ghetto if he did not meet their demands. Wittenberg could have tried to find shelter, or to attempt to escape, but he understood how perilous

---

pp. 9–81.

71 Shalom Cholawsky, *The Jews of Bielorussia during World War II* (Amsterdam: Harwood Academic Publishers, 1998), p. 136.

that would be for the ghetto community. His personal interests were sacrificed out of a profound sense of responsibility for the protection of the remaining Jews of Vilna.[72] This concern to protect the Vilna ghetto community was witnessed a second time on September 14, 1943, when Jacob Gens, the head of the Jewish Council, was ordered to report to Gestapo headquarters. Although he was warned of what awaited him if he appeared as ordered, he understood that the Nazis might carry out reprisals against the ghetto if he did not comply and he delivered himself to the police. He was shot at 6:00 P.M. the same day.

Fifth, I cannot fail to mention the extraordinary behavior of Janusz Korczak and the unbreakable bond that he had with the children in his charge at the orphanage that he headed in the Warsaw ghetto. Concerned solely with the children's welfare, he refused to abandon them and chose to accompany them to their death. He would not compromise his obligation to them in order to save his own life, although he was encouraged to do so by the Polish underground. He submitted to the merciless Nazi demands without attempting any evasion, because of his fidelity to his wards.

Then there was the exceptional heroism of the doctors and the nurses in many of the ghettos located throughout Nazi-occupied Europe. Dr. Adina Szwajger-Blady provided the following testimony about the final phase of the liquidation of the Warsaw ghetto. She reported that in early 1943, the hospitals were being cleared and their patients, including sick children, were being rounded up and sent to Treblinka. In response to this circumstance, she assumed ultimate responsibility for those in her care.

I asked Mira what we should do, and she said, "Help them, surely." So we helped them too. And by the window there was this woman, swollen from starvation and suffering from circulatory insufficiency, and she kept on looking at us, pleading with her eyes. She was the last one we gave an injection to...

72 Discussed in N. N. Shneidman, *Jerusalem of Lithuania: The Rise and Fall of Jewish Vilnius: A Personal Perspective* (Oakville: Mosaic Press, 199), pp. 440–441; see also Eric Sterling, "The Ultimate Sacrifice: The Death of Resistance Hero Yitzhak Wittenberg and the Decline of the United Partisan Organization," in Ruby Rohrlich, ed., *Resisting the Holocaust* (Oxford and New York: Berg Publishers, 1998), pp. 59–76; and Zila Rosenberg-Amit, *Lishmor Al* (Hebrew) (Tel-Aviv: Bet Lohame Hageta'ot and Hakibbutz Hame'uhad, 1990), pp. 46–49.

...So when I left the room, I...got two large containers of morphine. We didn't say a word to each other, just squeezed each other's hand, I think. I took the morphine upstairs. Dr. Margolis was there, and I told her what I wanted to do. So, we took a spoon and went to the infants' room. And just as, during those two years of real work in the hospital, I bent over the little beds, now I poured this last medicine in those tiny mouths. Only Dr. Margolis was with me. And downstairs there was screaming, because the Szaulis and the Germans were already there, taking the sick from the wards to the cattle trucks. After that we went to the older children and told them that this medicine was going to make their pain disappear. They believed us and drank the required amount from the glass. And then I told them to undress, get into bed, and sleep. So they lay down and after a few minutes—I do not know how many—but the next time I went into the room, they were asleep. And then I don't know what happened after that.[73]

Conclusion

The Holocaust tested the obligation of *Kol Yisrael Arevim Zeh Lazeh* more profoundly than any prior event or experience in Jewish history. In the ghettos, forced labor camps, and death camps, Jews were called upon to live up to the requirements of covenantal responsibility, the ideal of "love of neighbor," and the implications of "election." Not surprisingly, these ethical mandates were not always met. In spite of the normative precepts that everyone was aware of, there were uncountable acts of selfishness, repeated manifestations of cruel indifference, and both minor and serious instances of rampant corruption. The Jewish Councils were imperfect and at certain times and places even less than imperfect. The Jewish police in the many ghettos often took advantage of their positions to protect themselves and their own. There were Jewish informers and Kapos who discharged their duties with brutality. Moreover, all too many Jews and Jewish communities were passive while all sorts of Jewish individuals who possessed some degree of power took unfair advantage of their neighbors. Despite these

---

73 Adina Szwajger Blady, *I Remember Nothing More: The Warsaw Children's Hospital and the Jewish Resistance* (New York: Simon & Schuster, 1992), pp. 52–57.

severe and significant failures, and in no way diminishing them, I am still inclined to judge that in the midst of the Holocaust, the majority of Jewish communities generally acted with courage, dignity, and an abiding sense of obligation that flowed from their instinctive sense of *Kol Yisrael Arevim Zeh Lazeh.*

CHALLENGES TO SOLIDARITY
IN GHETTOS
AND URBAN CONCENTRATIONS

Children's Voices

Solidarity and Survival of Families in the Warsaw Ghetto

DALIA OFER

This chapter is part of a broad study on the family in the East European ghettos during the Holocaust. In previous work, I related to the tension between disintegration and solidarity among families in these ghettos.[1] The topic brackets various issues associated with the conduct of family life, including conjugal relations, questions of livelihood, professional aspirations, sibling relationships, and links among members of the extended family. Children represent one of the most, if not the most, important focal point of family life, and aspirations concerning their education and the shaping of their futures were and are central among Jewish families of whatever class.

The characteristic dynamism of Jewish life in interwar Eastern Europe, and the political and social changes that swept through the countries of that region placed the family and their way of life under enormous pressure. For major segments of the Jewish population, economic stress often accompanied these changes. In the aftermath of World War I, families who had lost a breadwinner faced even more dire economic hardships. Bourgeois and haut bourgeois households were overwhelmed by the changes in culture and religious faith that would shape their family life and their children's futures. Given the diversity and pluralism of Jewish society, one cannot generalize about the Jewish milieu at large because differences in class, attitudes toward faith and tradition, and ideologies created substantial differentiations within the Jewish collectivity. All of these found expression in Jewish family life, but this is not the place to elaborate.[2]

---

1   Dalia Ofer, "Cohesion and Rupture: The Jewish Family in East European Ghettos During the Holocaust," *Studies in Contemporary Jewry*, 14 (1998), pp. 143–165.

2   For elaboration, see Ido Bassok, *Teḥiyat Hane'urim: Mishpaḥa Veḥinuh Beyahadut Polin Bein Milḥamot Ha'olam* (Hebrew) (Jerusalem: Zalman Shazar Center, 2015), pp. 39–99.

The families that we encountered in the East European ghettos constituted a mosaic that represented the diverse complexions of the Jewish population. However, the pauperization of the Jews pursuant to Nazi occupation and ghettoization, particularly in large and medium-size cities, obliterated class differences and created a level of equality, which the writer Anatole France referred to as "*La majestueuse égalité des lois, qui interdit au riche comme au pauvre de coucher sous les ponts, de mendier dans les rues et de voler du pain.*" (In its majestic equality, the law forbids rich and poor alike to sleep under bridges, beg in the streets, and steal loaves of bread.)[3]

Reality in the Jewish ghetto was dynamic and was subject to many changes. Immense suffering was the portion of all the Jews who had been torn from their homes, whether they had been relocated to a ghetto in their own city or had been banished from villages in the subdistrict where the ghetto was set up. Nevertheless, significant economic differences were accompanied by cultural and ideological divergences among the ghettoized population. The place of the family in the new class constellation and the new relationships that evolved in the ghetto were major factors in the family's likelihood of survival. The prewar wealth and social status of a family were also very important factors.

In this chapter, I discuss the tension between solidarity and disintegration in parent–child relationships, which I learned about by listening to the voices of children that were recorded in the extant sources. I relate to the questions of what constitutes solidarity and how solidarity is examined, and to adolescents' remarks about the family from sources written before the war. Then I describe the documentation from the Ringelblum Archive on which I base my remarks, present the methodology, and categorize the life stories that the children narrated or wrote. Finally, I analyze comments by children who were refugees and deportees in Warsaw and those who were adolescents when ghettoized.

Family Solidarity: How Should One Define It?

It seems that the explicit assumption is that, in general, there is solidarity within the framework of the family. The question is how to deconstruct

3 Quoted in Frederick Wilmot-Smith, *Equal Justice: Fair Legal Systems in an Unfair World* (Cambridge: Harvard University Press), p. 29.

the concept into a set of obligations between parents and children, and vice versa. What elements should we examine when we take up the question of solidarity in a family context? Solidarity should find expression in actions, not mere rhetorical commiseration. To my mind, family solidarity should be defined in reference to actions by parents for their children and vice versa. A cardinal manifestation of this solidarity is parental responsibility for their children's physical well-being, that is, nutrition, clothing, and safety in and near the home. On a higher level, parents are responsible for children's psychological welfare and a framework that ensures warmth, love, and concern for their emotional needs. Another facet, largely related to or even emanating from the two aspects mentioned above, concerns socialization processes in the broadest sense of the term: equipping children with the capabilities that they will need in their lives as adolescents and adults, including the ability to communicate with peers and figures of authority, to cope with social norms, and to recognize the virtue of mutual responsibility. All of these ultimately enable children in their various growth phases to function responsibly vis-à-vis those close to them, to others, and to the society in which they live and act.[4]

In contrast, the manifestations of solidarity among children relative to the family are divided into various stages of child development. Relatively large families, although not as large as those in the nineteenth century, were common among the Jews. Children were deemed responsible for appreciating their parents' efforts to provide them with security and education and were expected to function within the various systems in accordance with requisite norms. Older girls, especially firstborn daughters, had the responsibility of helping to run the household, particularly watching over younger siblings, and often their responsibilities overwhelmed them. Children were expected to respect their parents' values even when they clashed and differed from those of the general society.

Some inequalities and tensions in parent–child relationships originated in economic and social changes that followed in the wake of World War I. Two precipitants of major change in the attitudes of

---

4 For an edifying source about parents' obligations to children, set in the early modern era in Eastern Europe but of concrete significance in the twentieth century as well, see Gershon David Hundert, "Jewish Children and Childhood in Early East Central Europe," in David Charles Kraemer, *The Jewish Family Metaphor and Memory* (New York: Oxford University Press, 1989), pp. 81–94.

children and youth were schools and youth movements. After Poland introduced compulsory education, most Jewish youngsters moved from traditional educational settings to public schools. Even if many of them attended schools that had a Jewish majority, owing to their place of residence, the curriculum became increasingly diverse and various subjects were taught by non-Jews. Moreover, Jewish children developed more contacts with their non-Jewish peers, and they read more Jewish and non-Jewish literature.[5]

Many young Jews attended school for only four to six years due to their parents' penury; afterward, they were apprenticed to artisans. These young people, too, were increasingly exposed to a reality that challenged their parents' traditional world of values. Parallel to these changes, these years saw the expansion of youth movement activity that placed adolescence, creativity, and national or class responsibility at the center of consciousness and education.[6] Grown children rarely had to look out for their parents, but the assumption was that they were responsible for them when they reached old age. The phenomenon of old age homes in Poland—a development of the interwar years—signaled a change in the pattern, but there was still an economic obligation.[7]

Owing to the severe economic plight of many Jewish households in the eastern reaches of Europe, particularly Poland and much of Romania, there was greater emphasis on the aforementioned parental responsibility for children's physical security. Fathers and mothers who put in long hours of work away from home had to enroll their children in preschools or schools at a very early age. Homes were crowded, food was basic, and attention to other elements of life was much scantier— although it should be remembered that these remarks pertain primarily to the lower classes, which accounted for the majority of the Jewish collectivity.

---

5   See the interesting article concerning the era preceding the present discussion, which is
     instructive about the patterns of change in Jewish family life as a result of modernization
     processes and the Haskalah movement in Eastern Europe: David Biale, "Childhood,
     Marriage, and the Family in the Eastern Jewish Enlightenment," in Steven M. Cohen
     and Paula E. Hyman, eds., The Jewish Family: Myths and Reality (New York: Holmes &
     Meier, 1986), pp. 45–61.
6   Bassok, Tehiyat Hane'urim, pp. 207–231.
7   Shaul Stampfer, "What Happened to the Extended Jewish Family? Jewish Homes for the
     Aged in Eastern Europe," Studies in Contemporary Jewry, 14 (1998), pp. 128–142.

Adolescent and Young-Adult Perspectives on the Prewar Period

In the 1930s, middle-class educators and parents took a growing interest in the inner world of adolescents. This concern is reflected in autobiographical contests that YIVO conducted in 1932, 1934, and 1939. These autobiographies, along with documentation relating to youth movements, educational systems, orphanages, and other institutions are indicative of the trends that evolved among youth.[8]

The generation that reached adulthood in the 1920s and 1930s developed an awareness of psychological issues, emotional needs, and affective deficiencies that had been theirs at the time of their childhood and adolescence. Sima Petliuk, born into a lower-class family in 1913, was twenty-one when she submitted her autobiography for the second YIVO contest in 1934. Her submission reflects psychological and class insights about herself and her parents.[9]

My father was a strict and difficult man who never received tender emotions from his parents and never heard a good word from anyone. He didn't know his mother at all; she died while giving birth to him. In his early childhood, he was thrown out of his home and when he was ten, he had *esn tog* [meals with a different family each day] in a strange city. Consequently, the man hadn't been trained for family life. He never developed paternal emotions. This aside, he was religious and very stingy; he always hated to work.[10]

However, in reference to her mother, she wrote,

My mother was the absolute opposite of my father. She was the youngest daughter in her family. She was always surrounded with tenderness and love; she came from a family of fishermen who were

---

8 Abraham Nowerszstern and Ido Bassok, eds., *Alilot Ne'urim: Oṭobiyografiyot Shel Bene'i No'ar Yehudim MiPolin Bein Shtay Milḥamot Ha'olam* (Hebrew) (Jerusalem and Tel Aviv: Beit Shalom Aleichem, Tel Aviv University, and Zalman Shazar Center, 2011); Jeffrey Shandler, ed., *Awakening Lives: Autobiographies of Jewish Youth in Poland before the Holocaust* (New Haven and London: Yale University Press, 2002), particularly the introduction, pp. xvii–xxvi.

9 Shandler, *Awakening Lives*, pp. 227–256.

10 Ibid., p. 235.

once considered "householders." She got married by happenstance. Her father, who loved her dearly, died. Her mother was afraid that she would remain an old maid and also understood very little about her daughter's psychology.[11]

Petliuk dealt with psychological approaches that relate to parent–child relationships in early childhood, growing processes, and class distinctions—matters that contribute to psychological understanding or the lack thereof. In parallel, she reflected on traditional attitudes toward a girl's need to get married lest she "remain an old maid," heaven forbid.

If I relate to these remarks through my chosen binary of solidarity versus disintegration, the disintegration of the family is evident in Petliuk's life story. "From the time I remember myself, the house was always in an uproar; father and mother were clashing and quarreling incessantly."[12] She centered her hard feelings toward her father on his personality and his inability to give his children warmth and love. However, she understood the reasons for his shortcomings and associated them with his motherless childhood and his removal from his home at a young age.

The middle and upper-middle classes were aware of questions surrounding children's psychological strength and their need for more warmth and love. Calel Perechodnik expressed this by stressing the difference between himself and his parents. In regard to the latter, he wrote,

> These [the parents] were honest people, possessed of a strong family instinct, characterized on the part of the children by affection and attachment to their parents, and on the part of the parents by a sacrificial devotion to the material well-being of the children. I emphasize "material" because there were no spiritual bonds that tied me or my siblings to our parents. They did not try or were unable to understand us.[13]

He described his marriage to Anna Nusfeld "as a loving one." They had fallen in love years before they married, during his studies, and their feelings for one another continued throughout their years together

---

11 Ibid.
12 Ibid.
13 Nowersztern and Bassok, *Alilot Ne'urim*, p. xxii.

and upon the birth of their daughter. As he saw it, his marriage and his partnership with his wife reflected the difference between his generation and that of his parents. Just the same, when he was an adult, Perechodnik affirmed his responsibility for his parents and their responsibility for his family.[14]

Under the Nazi Heel: The Ghetto

In view of the foregoing discussion, the limits of our research on families in the ghettos have to be acknowledged. We cannot trace family histories on the basis of extant relevant documentation, because that documentation has little to say about relationships within the family and, above all, about the intergenerational tensions that preceded the Nazi occupation and ghettoization. Sometimes diaries yield a more or less complete picture of one family. One such example is the diary of Fela Szeps.[15] Another is the work of Noemi Szac-Wajnkranc from the Warsaw ghetto.[16] Although letters or reports about one family or another in the ghetto reveal something about the life of that family and the relationships among its members in the prewar years, can we assume that the strength or weakness of this particular family in those years had some effect on its members under Nazi rule and in the ghetto?

Yet the crux of our inquiry is the Nazi occupation period and life in the ghettos. It should be borne in mind that the difficult situations that families had faced before the war in respect to livelihood, nutrition, and vision of the future, which often seemed to defy any solution, took on new dimensions in the realities of the ghetto. They were ten times more extreme. Quotidian life in the ghetto presented inhabitants with new hardships in every domain that had formerly seemed familiar and well known. Work, breadwinning, relations with the surroundings and with neighbors, questions of compliance and authority, and basic assumptions about routine life had to be redefined. The struggle for existence itself took on massive magnitudes of insecurity and uncertainty.

14 Ibid., p. xxiii.
15 Fela Szeps, *Balev Ba'ara Hashalhevet: Yomana Shel Fela Szeps, Ma'ane Ha'avoda Grinberg* (Hebrew) (Jerusalem: Yad Vashem, 2002).
16 Noemi Szac-Wajnkranc, *Halaf im Ha'esh: Reshimot al Geto Varsha Shenihtevu Bemahvo* (Hebrew) (Jerusalem: Yad Vashem, 2003).

In her book, Sarah Rosen reports on research on Jewish families in the ghettos in Transnistria during the Holocaust. Rosen contends that survival was easier in cases where solidarity was sustained. However, the ability to maintain family solidarity was often associated with the family's economic situation and class in the ghetto. In her far-reaching study on refugees in the Warsaw ghetto, Leah Prais devotes a chapter to the refugees' families. She demonstrates how the collapse of the home habitus and the economic anchor, along with the deprivation of roots and the cruelty of the surroundings, shattered family integrity. Thus, many families reached Warsaw without a spouse and, in not a few cases, without some of the children. In Warsaw, many set up residence in public buildings, where there was no privacy. Often hunger and the death of a family member claimed family solidarity as an additional victim, although many ghetto inhabitants attempted to sustain mutual responsibility among family members with the last of their strength. In various monographs about East European ghettos, the fate of Jewish families is mentioned as part of the description of ghetto life, and the space given to the family in the account varies from one researcher to the next.[17]

From here on, I focus on two kinds of documentation from the Ringelblum Archive. The first collection comprises seven responses by children to interviewers' questions about "what they experienced during the war." The youngsters' remarks were evidently written down by the interviewers, who played an active role in a study on children in the ghetto. Although most of the texts in this collection are in the third person, several are in the first person, possibly as quotations of the children's remarks.[18] The second collection contains thirty-four texts written by children in a day residence at 25 Nowolipki St. in Warsaw. In their compositions, the youngsters answered the question, "What changes did you undergo during the war?" The interviewer's hand is not evident (or less evident) in these texts, which were written in the form of brief first-person essays.[19]

---

17 Sarah Rozen, *Behevel Eretz Nidah: Hayehudim Begeta'ot Tzefon Transnistria, 1941–1944* (Hebrew) (Jerusalem: Yad Vashem, 2020); Lea Prais, *Displaced Persons at Home, Refugees in the Fabric of Jewish Life in Warsaw, September 1939–July 1942* (Jerusalem: Yad Vashem, 2015).

18 United States Holocaust Memorial Museum (USHMM), RING-A I/678, no.1002, Mf. ŻIH – 816. Elisheva Shaul translated the original documents into Hebrew, and then Dalia Ofer translated the Hebrew into English.

19 USHMM, RING-I/676, no.1002, Mf. ŻIH – 816.

Also preserved in the archives are five compositions by children who attended school in the ghetto. In three of them, there are references to "the school on Nowolipki St.," possibly the Tarbut school at 68 Nowolipki St. The topics that they wrote about were "What We See in the Streets"; "Our School"; "Memories of the Beginning of the War"; and "Deportation."[20] I examined a total number of forty-six texts for the present study.

I resorted to these collections to "listen" to the children and to ask how their unique voices further our understanding of their families' lives and self-organization during the war and how their fate was sealed. I separated the discussion into stories told by children and adolescents who had been deported with their families to Warsaw and had reached that destination before the establishment of the ghetto, and those of youngsters who had lived in Warsaw and were evicted from their homes and sent to the ghetto. I make this differentiation because the first group is composed of refugees and deportees—the city was strange to them and their families, and its physical and social space was more threatening. Some of the Varsovian youngsters also experienced uprooting during the bombardments and the immense destruction that Warsaw had sustained in the three weeks of war in September and afterward, when they were relocated to the ghetto.

My question is whether the children's unmediated voices around the time of or actually during the events is particularly important and significant for historical research.[21] It should be remembered that we have copious information about the situation of families and children from diverse sources, including Jewish self-help institutions in the ghettos, the Judenräte, and other ghetto institutions, and from the testimonies of adults. All of these have been preserved in ghetto archives and in declarations taken immediately after the war, or later. Memoirs written by adult survivors, or by adults who were children during the

---

20 USHMM, RING-I/407, no. 305, Mf. ŻIH – 783.

21 Several scholars have carried out important studies concerning children's lives during and after the war based primarily on children's testimonies at those two junctures in time. The testimonies were taken by the historical committees in Poland and the displaced persons camps and by counselors and caregivers in orphanages in Poland and elsewhere. The writings emphasize the need to understand the setting and the event during which the testimony was given and the importance of the children's voices; they note several collections. See Boaz Cohen, "The Children's Voice: Postwar Collection of Testimonies from Child Survivors of the Holocaust," *Holocaust and Genocide Studies*, 21:1 (2007), pp. 73–95; Joanna B. Michlic, "Who Am I? Jewish Children's Search for Identity in Post-War Poland 1945-1949," *Polin*, 20 (2007), pp. 98–121.

war, also have much to say about their lives under occupation and their survival.

The methodological approach presented above argues that the history of a family, even if murky, is important for understanding the family's situation in the ghetto, which is manifested in the writings of the authors who investigated the children's situations and, to be more precise, the behavior of specific groups of children in the ghetto. The goals of this research are set forth in a text written for the Ringelblum Archive research project, "Guidelines for Research about Street Children": "To learn how to define the phenomenon [of street children] and the reasons for its formation: lone children; street children who have families; beggars; life in the street; criminality among street children; and methods of countering and preventing the phenomenon."[22]

The authors of the study wanted to see whether street children, who busied themselves panhandling, roving, pilfering, and so on, came from families who had been mendicants before the war, or whether "Due to the tumult of the war, many problems in today's daily life that also predated the war to one extent or another now received a definitive place or came about as a result of the war." The designers of the study focused the inquiries regarding the past and at the time of the study, the current circumstances of the parents, and their responsibilities toward their children. They took parental responsibility for the children's safety as a given, and presented several possibilities including the following:

> Some children collect alms because they have no home, no one to look out for them, and nothing to eat (i.e., compelled by realities). Other children are sent into the street by their parents, because it is easier to evoke pity together with a child, or the child alone (children sent out by parents or who beg on their own)....[What is] the family's attitude toward a mendicant child (forcing the child, passive approval, condemnation), [and] the attitude of "street children" toward their families and siblings (to raise money for the family and look out for their siblings). Is the beggar child as a phenomenon distinct from the family typical of certain families?[23]

22 USHMM, RING-I/558.
23 Ibid.

Even though the research questions concern street children, they are instructive in connection with the attitude of the Oyneg Shabbes researchers. Thoroughly cognizant of the prewar realities of the lives of the Jews in Warsaw and in Poland at large, they found it necessary to establish a link between the family's past and the behavior of the children and adolescents in the ghetto.

Voices of Children of Refugee and Evicted Families in Warsaw

The narrator is Bajla Brinberg, born on March 27, 1927, in Warsaw. Her family lived at 25 Radziminska St. in the city.[24] She attended primary school and advanced to the fifth grade. Her mother passed away four weeks before the war began, and as Warsaw was being bombarded, their home was struck and most of its contents were destroyed. The surviving members of the family moved in with an aunt, who "treated us like beggars, harassed us, even though I did my best to help her, because I knew she was feeding us out of kindness." Her father, a cobbler, sought a solution to the family's distress, because "the harassment was unbearable." Thus, he moved with his children and the aunt to the town of Węgrów. Their situation improved; Bajla's father worked, and "We ate well," she recalled. Sometime later, however, they were evicted and, after wandering, returned to Warsaw, where the Germans captured them and took them to the ghetto, and settled in a refugee center. Bajla continued, "We reached this gathering place and that's where the disasters began. In the summer of 1941, my little sister died. Father worked as a tanner until the winter of 1941. He earned a pittance, went hungry, had diarrhea, and was sent to the hospital, where he died."

Death continued to erode the family; Bajla's second sister also died. Bajla continued describing the distress that reduced her to begging. Her account shows her acute reluctance to beg and how badly the situation affected her.

---

24 All quotations in this section are sourced to USHMM, RING-I/678, Mf. ŻIH – 816. The remarks were committed to writing after April 1942, as noted at the top of the document. Individual records are undated.

I also suffered a great deal from hunger at the gathering places. I spent whole days not eating a thing. When you're hungry, it's hard to stand; you haven't got the strength. I had nothing to live on. I began to beg. The best center was on Leszno St. Sometimes I was ashamed, but hunger plagued me. There were various situations. Sometimes I gorged myself on bread that I'd received until I burst, but when it rained, not many people were around and then I went hungry. A woman stranger took an interest in me and sent me to the "holding room" at 40 Chlodna St., where there were street children. It was good there.[25]

Bajla exhibited strong self-awareness. She had the strength to review her actions and to explain why she did what she did. She was also able to appreciate assistance and distinguish among different situations: good, less good, and bad. At the center where she stayed with the street children, things were good. "It was sad at first," she explained, "but now I've made friends with the children and I love the teachers....I'd like to work in order to move my body around. I'm not a little girl anymore." [She was fourteen or fifteen at the time].

Bajla showed social sensitivity and the ability to form social relationships. In reference to the issues that I raised above, her remarks may be decoded as evidence of having internalized the values that her family represented: respect for labor in the sense that labor dignifies those who perform it. A sensitive reading of her remarks, including expressions describing the state of her family during their stay with her aunt—the aunt's disdain for them as beggars, because they lacked a source of livelihood, and Bajla's awareness of the concept of "feeding us out of kindness," even though they were in the home of a relative—suggests criticism of the aunt and her family. The way that she expressed herself, however, reflects values associated with independence and appreciation of labor and breadwinning that allow some degree of independence. The same is true regarding the contrast between her shame over begging and her melancholy awareness that there was no other way. I contend that Bajla's wish to go to work, even when her situation improved and she was not allowed to work in her new setting, also expresses the sense of responsibility of someone who is no longer a little girl and, accordingly, feels duty bound to take part in the breadwinning effort. However, it is

25 Ibid.

also worth considering the possibility that Bajla knew of the stigma that her interviewer associated with begging and that her remarks reflected her wish to appease him. Her desire to work also suggests a utilitarian approach: She hoped to improve her nutrition and perhaps that of her younger sister.

Bajla was mindful of her own distress as well as that of her sister. After "getting along" through the services of the woman whom she had encountered, she displayed responsibility and related, "I found out about CENTOS and I placed my sister [there]." Her emotional bond and solidarity with her little sister had not vanished. This too can be seen as the internalization of the family values that her father had modeled. Her response about the future reinforced this feeling. When asked about her future plans and the things that she deemed important, Bajla replied, "If God lets me survive, that will already be good....And most important, I have a sister on Cegielna St."

Bajla's comments may be summed up by noting that her family projects the image of a working household, both parents toiling for their livelihood. After the occupation began, her father displayed responsibility for and devotion to his children and to Bajla's aunt, even though the latter, in Bajla's opinion, mistreated them. Her father was a dynamic and creative individual, who spared no effort to support his children and the aunt until the difficulties of the situation overwhelmed him and took his life, evidently owing to dysentery.

The records of talks with other children in the same home allow one to probe more deeply and to detect additional points of view about the youngsters' existential situation: their state of being refugees—due to dislocation, displacement, escape, or eviction from home—and peregrination among villages and towns until they reached Warsaw. There, too, there was no balm for their vicissitudes. On the contrary, they encountered disconnection, subhuman living conditions, extreme hunger, and, consequently, a race to death as parents, siblings, and other relatives and friends succumbed. The children described their parents' helplessness with understanding, appreciating their inability to give them the most basic form of security, that is, keeping them fed. With profound sadness, they reported their parents' physical and mental decline into total dysfunction.

The absence of family was accompanied by a sense of orphanhood and loneliness. Even though the children were not asked about these emotions, they stand out in the subtext of the youngsters' narratives.

When asked about something pleasant or joyful, the children often noted the presence of a family member, such as a younger or older sibling, whether they assisted these relatives or were assisted by them. The case of twelve-year-old Zanwel Krigsman, expelled with his family from Piaseczno in February 1941, is telling. His father, a barber, died of tuberculosis in 1939. His mother was deported to Warsaw along with her four children. "Mother was helpless; she died of starvation in March 1942. My little brother died in April 1941; my sister in February 1941; my second brother in March 1941."

Zanwel began by describing his mother's situation and her death from starvation. Then he mentioned the dates of the deaths of family members and siblings before his mother's death and around the time of the family's deportation and arrival in Warsaw. Did he see a connection between the events? Did his mother's helplessness trace back to the loss of her three children? He did say that she held on for another full year. Finally, he tallied the death toll. "Now I have no one, they've all died of hunger."

I contend that the structure of his narrative explains the continuation of his mother's life after the death of the children. Zanwel supported his mother and himself by smuggling. As 1942 approached, bringing cold days and with no warm clothing available, smuggling became more difficult than it had been before. When the Germans began to shoot smugglers, Zanwel stopped smuggling, leaving the family with no food. He described his smuggling days with a touch of pride.

> Until mid-1941, it wasn't so bad. I did some smuggling. I took the tram to Piaszeczna. I came [back] with potatoes, beets. All the 'goyim' knew me there; they all treated me well, even the police. Once a gendarme caught me and wanted to take away all the goods. He asked what I'd rather have, thirty lashes or everything that I'd smuggled. I told him thirty lashes. Then he let me go.[26]

After Zanwel stopped smuggling, however, hunger increased to an unbearable degree. Still, he was active. "I took care of my mother. If it weren't for me, she would've died sooner." I ask again, is it coincidental that he noted the time when the smuggling stopped along with the date of his mother's death?

26 Ibid.

Zanwel's story reflects the internalization of family solidarity. He expressed a mordant sense of reality. He accurately assessed the dangers that he faced and displayed resourcefulness. Even the policeman gave in to the kid who was willing to take thirty lashes for the sake of his contraband. We can picture this twelve-year-old boy, who lost his father at the beginning of the occupation, the firstborn son, who assumed responsibility for his family and ultimately strove to watch over his mother, the last remnant of his family. Although no emotion is expressed directly, Zanwel's narrative is fraught with emotion and a sense of responsibility. When the interviewer prodded him to open up about his emotions, he spoke about the fear that he had experienced in his smuggling endeavors and the blows that he had received on the "Aryan" side. When asked about a pleasant experience, in contrast, he replied, "[It was] when I managed to bring 'goods' from the other side," and "Before the war, it was pleasant to go into the forest with our landlords. I would go to Warsaw with father and that was also very pleasant." The recent and distant experiences in the past blended into pleasant recollections that were as far from one another as east is from west.

Other children who were interviewed in spring 1942 also revealed the internalization of the values that they had acquired from their families. Chil Brajtman, born in 1927, described the suffering that his family endured after they had been deported to Warsaw in November 1940. His father died in March 1941 and his mother passed away in June of that year; then things got even worse. His older brother worked for some wealthy people, but did not earn enough and did not help them. He ate his first meal, he reported, at the CENTOS kitchen at 2 P.M.—he did not say that this was his only meal, but one can infer as much from the text—and tried to decide about what to do. He saw two possibilities: panhandling and smuggling. He recounted the following:

> Hunger plagued me and I felt that I would die from it. I didn't want to panhandle [so] I began to engage in smuggling. It was a hard way to make a living. I got hit with a crowbar once. It couldn't be helped: it was better to get beaten than to starve to death. Several times beggars put handguns to my head....After these incidents, I'd come home hungry and depressed. I survived, but my seventeen-year-old brother died of hunger in February 1941. Afterward, my sister died of

German measles in March 1942. Another sister, who is twenty-one, is still in the refugee center and is suffering from hunger.[27]

Chil described the violent reality among the beggars who vied for the kindness of passersby and fought each other for each favor given. Danger and violence were the youthful smugglers' regular fare. Just the same, Chil preferred smuggling over panhandling. Why? Was panhandling a more difficult way to obtain food? Or was it because at home he had internalized the message that panhandling is unworthy? His father, he related, worked "from 4 A.M. to 3 P.M. at odd jobs and fixed shoes in the afternoon." His mother was a housekeeper and they—four children and their parents—lived in one room. He went to school and did not work to support the family. Did the home and his father's hard work, which provided basic sustenance, guide his thinking and actions?

Chil expressed the internalization of family solidarity regarding another matter. At the time of the interview, he was housed and fed in a residence. He promised the manager of the facility that he would stop smuggling, possibly as a condition for his admission to the home. This promise, however, came at a price that saddened him and made him doubt that he had done the right thing. "I'm sorry I promised [the manager] at the home that I would stop smuggling because I could have continued helping my sister." Chil kept his word, but felt guilty about it and pitied his hungry sister.

Izrael Lederman, born in 1927 in Góra Kalwaria, the son of a heder teacher, went through much tribulation with his family until, totally destitute, they reached a gathering place in Warsaw. The situation there was grim and he lost his parents:

It was bad at the gathering place. Father didn't work. Father died of paralysis in April 1941. Mother died of hunger in July. My grandmother also starved to death. I remained alone. I slept at the gathering place and ate with one of my aunts. As long as my aunt was working, there was something to eat. Afterward, they sent me here. It's not bad here but my father was a pious Hasid from Góra Kalwaria, and for me it's...[an inappropriate place].[28]

27 Ibid.
28 Ibid.

Lederman missed the devoutly religious atmosphere that he had enjoyed at home and at his father's heder. Among the children whose remarks are in our possession, only he criticized the goings-on at the day center. He did not describe his activities and did not explain what he did to help his family or the aunt with whom he had taken his meals since his parents' death. Unlike Zanwel and Chil, he was pessimistic. He did not even know what he wanted to do. One can infer the depth of his loneliness and sadness from the answer he gave when asked about a pleasant experience that he remembered: "The most pleasant experience? The heder and being with that saintly man on the Sabbath. The rabbi got sick not long ago, and there weren't more experiences like those." It suggests the extent to which the absence of a religiously observant framework weighed on him and exacerbated his loneliness.

Another manifestation of the persistence of a deep family relationship even after the family perished has to do with the youngsters' perception of the future. Some of the respondents could not even imagine a future. Chil expressed this when asked about his future plans. "What plans? Nothing. It seems to me that it'll be like it is now as long as I live." He could not imagine life outside the given moment. One can hear bitterness verging on ridicule in his answer about future plans, as though wondering how a person can even think about the future when he is filled to the brim with the ghastly present.

Some of the respondents, however, did hesitantly disclose a more animated plan. Luba Glicensztejn, born in 1929, for example, who lost her mother in early childhood and was raised by a stepmother, was deported from Kalisz, and reached Warsaw with her family after a great deal of wandering and suffering. Her father, a photographer, found work in Warsaw but did not earn enough to spare his family from hunger. He contracted typhus and died in February 1942. Luba's stepmother had died a day earlier. Asked about her future plans, Luba replied, "I don't have many, but I'm thinking about America. I have relatives there."

Some of the children hoped to follow in their parents' footsteps in the future. Ten-year-old Hejnoch Jarzebski wanted to be a cobbler like his father and older brother. His father had died. His brother evidently was still alive and looked out for him. When asked about a pleasant experience, he noted, "[It happened] when I was with my married brother, and he took very good care of me."

Sara Widawska, deported from Konstantynów to Łomża and thence to Warsaw, where she lost her parents in December 1941 and in early

1942, reacted differently. After pondering the question at length, she replied, "In the future, I'll do some sewing."

The children did not view their pasts and the prewar lives of their families through rose-colored lenses. Their approach was matter-of-fact and very realistic: Their parents worked hard and put in long hours. The family lived in crowded conditions. Food was doled out, but no one went hungry. Daily life was fraught with hardships. Zanwel Krigsman described his father as a barber, who worked hard and lived with his mother and their four children in one room. Luba Glicensztejn reported that her mother died while Luba was a baby and her father, a photographer, remarried. They too lived in one room. Izrael Lederman, the son of a heder teacher and a mother who took in seamstress work, related, "They didn't have it too good, but bread wasn't lacking at home." Quotidian life that met basic needs with respect to housing, clothing, and nutrition was typical. Just as the young interviewees did not complain, they did not express any enthusiasm, although they definitely felt nostalgic about some of what they described. They expressed themselves in terse sentences or, at least, that was what the interviewer noted.

The children reported on the period following the onset of the occupation in relatively abundant detail and expressed their family's gradual decline. First, their home and most of their possessions were lost. The sense of shock was great at that stage. It was not yet clear how things would develop. The family then wandered, dependent on villagers and strangers. The children did not say exactly how long this period lasted, but they had already experienced dislocation and displacement, acute deprivation, and, sometimes, hunger. The story of decline that devolved into tragedy reached a critical turning point when they were forced into the ghetto. From there it was a short way to the refugee "point" or to blatantly unreasonable living conditions. The children were aware of their parents' helplessness and often described their parents as being traumatized, unable to find a way to resume their mundane lives and to find a job that would ensure the family their barest needs. Nevertheless, they neither criticized nor expressed disappointment in their parents, most of whom were already gone. They often noted that their father worked but did not earn enough to fend off starvation. Hunger was the dominant theme of their remarks.

Although the children's families disintegrated and essentially no longer existed, a painstaking reading of these forlorn texts shows that the youngsters regarded them as "present absentees." Their presence is expressed in the internalization of values that the children had learned from their parents, as noted above. The existence of a family member, a remnant of the crumbling family, was a source of joy and perhaps also of comfort and hope for the future. Thus, when the interviewer asked Luba Glicensztejn to recall a happy memory, the latter noted, "After she gave it much thought, she answered, 'Just four weeks ago, I found out that my sister is alive. It made me really, really happy.'"

When asked about the meaning of the war, all of the children mentioned hunger as its absolute embodiment. "There are two wars," said Izrael Lederman, "a war of hunger and a war of bullets. The war of hunger is worse because then you suffer, but you die straight away from bullets."

Families that Lived in Warsaw from the Onset of Occupation to Ghettoization

The ghetto documentation includes compositions by children bearing the title "How Have Things Changed among Us during the War?" This collection, as noted, contains thirty-four narratives by children at a day center on 25 Nowolipki St. who described their lives and those of their families until they reached that facility. Quite a few of the young composition writers were offspring of families from Warsaw or Praga that had been evicted from their homes and found it difficult to reorganize in the city. Most of the youngsters began their ghetto lives in an apartment; some, one presumes, did so in one room in an apartment. Their accounts yield a picture of a stable economic situation before the war, although some of the families barely made ends meet. Parents put in lengthy hours of work and older siblings helped to support the family. According to not a few youngsters, mothers worked and helped to support the family. A smaller number were housekeepers. The writers of most of the compositions indicate that there were three or four children in their family.

With the onset of the occupation, if the home was destroyed and belongings were lost, most of the narratives describe their parents' efforts to find an alternative, such as moving in with relatives, or renting. Parents usually managed to find work, even when they could not continue to practice their original occupations. The alternative livelihoods usually had to do with commerce, working for the Germans, and holding jobs in sundry workplaces. Older siblings who fled to the East sent parcels to their families and helped to sustain them.

The young narrators described their families' gradual disintegration. A monumental crisis occurred after the Jewish quarter—the expression that the children commonly used to refer to the ghetto rather than the more rarely used term "ghetto"—was sealed, mainly due to the loss of the alternative livelihood and the inability to find a substitute. This triggered the slow sale of the family's possessions until they were gone. Thus, the family's economic situation and state of physical and mental health were gravely impaired. Fathers and mothers were unable to cope with the daily routine, because of the prevailing hunger and their inability to find solutions to the growing distress. Parents died slowly or quickly, propelling their children down a steep, slippery slope. Even when they continued to inhabit a room at home or moved in with relatives, whose situation was also worsening, their distress was immeasurable, centering on acute hunger and an inability to function. The children were sent to a residence, a "center," because they had no chance of surviving at home, where hunger had already claimed its victims, and the family had in effect ceased to exist, even if some members of the family still survived.

The reality described here is well known from the research literature. I wish, however, to express it in the children's voices in an effort to appreciate their view of these matters. I divide my remarks into the way the children described their prewar situation, and how they wrote about the transition to a situation of war and to the ghetto. I also ask whether their descriptions offer a vision of the future and how the destruction of their families affected the way they perceived their situations.

The Children's Voices

From Prewar to Ghettoization

The children's descriptions of their families' prewar situations fall into three categories:[29]

- Complex but not negative
- As neutral as possible—no reference to good or bad
- Highly positive

29 All the quotations in this section are from USHMM, RING-I/676. Mf. ŻIH – 816.

Complex but Not Negative

For example, H. Wlodawer (first name unknown) wrote,

> Before the war, I lived with my parents and brothers in Praga. My
> father was a cobbler. He worked all day long to support us. I was
> in fifth grade at a primary school. I was supposed to go on to high
> school, but the war ruled that out. Each year, I went to a summer
> camp or a village where I spent my vacations very happily. And then
> the war broke out.[30]

So far, this is a matter-of-fact account. The expression "all day long"
in describing his father's work is indicative of a difficult economic
situation. Still, H.'s family enrolled him in school and intended, he said,
to send him on to high school—an unusual course of action for children
from poor homes. The positive part of H.'s composition has to do with
vacations, which he spent "very happily" at a summer camp. However,
the next sentence, "**And then the war broke out**"[31] marks a dramatic
change. At first, H. mentioned the war as if en passant to explain why
he did not go to high school, but then the drama began. Here he wrote
about the grim reality: escaping from his home in Praga to join his aunt
in Warsaw, the destruction, the anxiety, fleeing from homes to shelters,
and the many who were killed or injured. His account then took a very
vivid turn.

> Once, as we were being shelled, we found refuge in one of the shelters.
> Bombs and shells flew from all directions. Suddenly I heard a terrible
> noise and my eyes went dark. When I recovered, I saw people pushing
> toward the window to climb out through it. I followed them and
> jumped out of the window to the street. Here I saw lots of injured
> people; panes flew out of the windows. People didn't know where to
> run. When the gunfire finally died down a little, I went home and lay
> down to sleep, hungry and worn out.[32]

---

30 Ibid.
31 I boldfaced this text because as I read it, I felt that had I heard the delivery of the
  description aloud, as often happens in oral documentation, I would have heard his voice
  and tenor rising.
32 Ibid.

These were the last atrocities that occurred before the ceasefire. H. skipped over the period that preceded relocation to the ghetto, summarizing it laconically, "We returned to Praga, to our home, but there was nowhere to get money to survive. Then my older brother signed up for work with the Germans. He received a wage of 3.20 złotys." The transition to the ghetto and its hardships in H.'s story is highly dramatic: "One day all of a sudden, all the Jews in Praga were ordered to leave. They forced us to move to Warsaw, to a little apartment, where we had no way of getting by, because the place where my brother was working was liquidated." Interestingly, H. mentioned not the establishment of the ghetto but the eviction from his home in Praga to a small apartment in Warsaw.

In his book about Warsaw, Israel Gutman described the difficult move made by most of the Jews of Praga, who belonged to the impoverished strata of Warsaw Jewry, in the last week before the ghetto was sealed. Buoyed by sundry rumors, many hoped that a ghetto would be established in Praga as well.[33] This may explain why H. wrote, "One day, all of a sudden..." As we have seen, however, H.'s words have an element of expressing suddenness that creates a dramatic turning point. Beniek Frylegsztejn also described a complex reality.

> Until two years ago, before the war, I lived with my parents and brothers in Warsaw, where I was also born and raised. My father made briefcases and even though he didn't make much money, we didn't go hungry and things were very good for us. When I got a little older, my parents sent me to school, where I was a really good pupil and got good marks. Right before the war began, in September, I went to summer camp in Jarosław and was there until September 1.[34]

In his factual description, Beniek assessed his family's economic situation. His father "didn't make much money." School was immensely important to him and the family, and Beniek proudly mentioned his scholastic success. "I was a really good pupil and got good marks." In contrast to H.'s account of the war and the family's plight in Warsaw, Beniek's transition to these topics was dispassionate. "When I came back [from the summer camp], the first battles began. They ended quickly

---

33 Israel Gutman, *The Jews of Warsaw 1939–1943: Ghetto, Underground, Revolt* (Bloomington: Indiana University Press, 1989), p. 60.
34 USHMM, RING-I/676. Mf. ŻIH – 816.

with the siege of Warsaw and the arrival of the German army in the capital." Continuing, Beniek reported the destruction of his family's home and noted that his father took his mother and sister away from the house shortly before this event. He considered this a miracle. "My mother and little sister were saved from death miraculously, because an hour earlier my father and brother went to the apartment to wake them up and take them downstairs; bombs were falling all the time and it was at night." Beniek was sensitive to the numerous losses and the devastation that he saw around him, noting that many had been killed or injured.

Other accounts of the prewar situation are laconic and anodyne. Bela Dymlecht, for example, related the following: "Before the war it wasn't bad. I lived at 23 Krochmalna St. Papa was a porter; he had a pushcart. He made a good living and we had enough to eat. Mama was a housewife. My brother finished school and began to learn house painting. The kids went to school; only my little sister was in kindergarten." Abram Brajtman also reported tersely, "Before the war, my father worked, my big sister worked in a fruit shop, and I went to school. Thank God, we lived, made a living, and didn't have to ask anyone to help us." Hela Gestel provided undetailed but clear information.

In 1939, war broke out. We were living in Warsaw, at 26 Lubecki St. My father died in 1930 **and after his death mother began a soap business and made a really good living. We didn't have it bad** [emphasis added]. In 1938, mother enrolled me in school. I finished fifth grade and got a job with a seamstress. I apprenticed for eight months and afterward earned 5 złotys per week and I was happy.[35]

Gitla Szulcman took a more emotional approach. "Before the war, when I still had my dear mother, I had it good, because mother was working and I went to school and studied. Father died before the war."

Cyla Rozenblum encapsulated a complex situation.

Two years before the war, father died. Mother tried to fill his shoes, but I was already big enough to understand that I was missing the most important person who had looked out for me. We lived at 71 Stawki St., apt. 9. In 1939, the war broke out. During the bombardments, we

35 Ibid.

moved in with my aunt. Mother bartered cucumbers. It was bad for us. But since they established the Jewish quarter, it's been worse.[36]

As Neutral as Possible: No Reference to Good or Bad

The following quotations describe prewar life very concisely and factually. The contents themselves are highly diverse and are typified by an absence of judgmentalism. Fajga Lazewnik stated,

Before the war, I lived at 68 Miła St. I went to school. I finished third grade. In the summer of 1939, I went with mother to Otwock. We came back to Warsaw, and mother started working in commerce, and father worked. Afterward, they locked us up in the Jewish quarter.[37]

Jozef Kantorowicz recounted the following:

Until I was 7, I lived in eastern Poland, where my father worked as a secretary for a nobleman named Olenski. In 1937, we were living in Warsaw, at 64 Targowa St., where my father worked as an official at the Ministry of Finance and mother was a housekeeper. My brother and I went to school. During vacations, we went to Grodno.

Kantorowicz described the vacations in Grodno in detail. He mentioned sailing, fishing, and Russian friends, and compared the smaller houses in the city of Grodno with those in the great city of Warsaw.

L. Bakauer related,

Before the war, I lived with my mother and brothers on Furmanska St. in Warsaw. I didn't have a father, because he had left us four years earlier. Mother was a seamstress and she supported three children. My brothers and I went to a Polish school and we were good students.[38]

Szlama Zalewas recalled,

Father worked in the textile industry. He earned enough to keep us fed. Mother was a housewife. My brothers did the work that father

36 Ibid.
37 Ibid.
38 Ibid.

did. I went to school. I liked my studies a lot. When I got promoted to third grade, mother died. She left me in deep grief. But I forgot soon afterward, because a big danger came to all the populations in Europe. War, I mean.[39]

Highly Positive

M. Rubinsztein reported,

I, like my brothers and sisters, was born in Warsaw. My father was a carpenter of antique furniture. We had a workshop of our own on Bagno St. There they made furniture for various places. There were seven people in my family. My father's brother had a sewing workshop. His profits went to us, because he was also a member of our family. Apart from that, I had my mother and three little sisters. As the only son, I was very much loved by my parents. Whatever I wanted, I got. I went to school, as my sisters did. My father and uncle worked to support us, and mother kept up the home. That's how our lives were, quiet and peaceful.[40]

Fela Brzezinska recounted, "Before the war, I lived at 57 Nowolipki St. Life was very good. My father and older brother worked and my younger brother and I went to school."
Hela Goldzand recalled,

On September 1, 1939, war broke out. Before the war, we lived at 65 Pawia St. in Warsaw. Father was a porter. We weren't rich but we had enough to get by. Mother made sure that I went to school. I went to School No. 84 and was in fifth grade. I had a great life. I didn't know how the day went by. In the winter, things were really happy for us. We had a phonograph and various games.

Beniek Fredler related the following:

Before the war, our situation was very good. My father was a housepainter, who had lots of work and was well paid. Mother had

39 Ibid.
40 Ibid.

a shop, and my brothers had a barbershop and earned nicely. Every year we went away on vacation, and I had a great time there. In September 1939, when we returned from the vacation to Warsaw, war broke out.[41]

Chana Szuzman asserted, "Before the war, we were well. We were all together. We had a nice room. Before the war, we all worked, and we had a lot of food."

After Ghettoization

In many compositions, the sealing of the Jewish quarter, or the move to it, is described as a very significant watershed in the deterioration of the children's circumstances. In other narratives, however, hardships are depicted in a steady sequence with no specific reference to the ghetto. The accounts that follow reveal that some of the children experienced the difficult loss of a father or mother before ghettoization—months, or in one case of the death of a father, two years before the war began.

Tadek Fruchtgarten began his composition with a positive description of life prior to the war before narrating an unbroken string of dire events.

Before the war, we were very well off. Father worked at the Tourchette plant as its manager. My sisters and I went to school, and we led comfortable lives until the war. On September 1, 1939, the war between Poland and Germany broke out and, after a month of fighting, the German armies occupied Warsaw. Then my father lost his job and decided to move to the Soviet Union, and that's what he did. A week later, we received a letter saying that father was in Białystok and, a few months later, we got word that he was returning to Warsaw. Then we had no news for fifteen months. At this time, mother became seriously ill and was sent to a hospital. Eight weeks ago, my father returned from Grodno, from prison. Right after he came back, he changed apartments, arranged a home for me and a job for my sister, and now he's looking for employment for himself. On April 1, 1941, at 6 A.M., mother died and I sank into sadness and

41 Ibid.

pain. A few weeks later, however, I forgot about it. In the meantime, I'm at the home, where I get meals four times a day and also study.[42]

After writing about the good life before the war, Fela Brzezinska described how their situation deteriorated.

In 1939, on September 1, the war broke out. The schools were shut down. We sold everything that we had at home. Father came down with a liver disease and was out of work. Sometime later, mother fell ill with diabetes and went to the hospital. She died there. Afterward, father fell down the stairs and broke a hand and some ribs. I came down with typhoid fever just then and was put in a hospital, and father and my sister were placed in quarantine. When I came back from the hospital, and father and my sister returned from quarantine, we slept in the stairwell over the window for three days, because the apartment was locked. Two days after we got into the apartment, my seventeen-year-old sister died. The next day, they buried her in a common grave with lots of other people. I don't know exactly where. We lost everything we had. All that was left were the clothes that we were wearing. We were really hungry. For lack of choice, I had to go around to the neighbors and collect leftovers. Then this woman pitied us and signed me and my brother up for half residence [staying during the day in a children's shelter and sleeping at home]. It's very good for us there, because we get four meals a day.

Most of the compositions, however, show a gradual decline toward the final crisis. Everything else notwithstanding, being forced into the ghetto, or the sealing of the ghetto led to a precipitous deterioration of the situation. Chana Rozenblum provided the following account:

Two years before the war, my father died. I didn't immediately realize that I'd lost my most loving protector. Mother tried to compensate for father's love and concern....I went to school and didn't [demonstrably] feel the loss of my father, but the pain in my heart didn't go away. We lived three people in one room. Mother worked and we were at school. The war came. During the shelling, mother abandoned the apartment, and the three of us went to [live

42 Ibid.

with] our aunt. Mother had no source of income. I stopped going to school, and the two of us, my sister and I, decided to think about making money. Until they sealed the Jewish quarter, we were able to live on what my sister and I earned. We lived modestly. Afterward, the cost of living became horrible, and hunger began to trouble us. Critical times came, and my mother decided to sell everything she had so that we could survive. Everything was sold, and mother looked for help for us and found it.[43]

In contrast, Szlama Zalewas wrote,

The Germans created a Jewish quarter, and hunger and poverty spread throughout the population. Young and old began to die from starvation. **My brothers stopped sending parcels** [emphasis added]. My uncle stopped helping us. We had nothing to live on. For whole days, I wondered how I could save myself from starving to death.[44]

Aron Zajdner noted,

Things went very well for us until they sealed the Jewish quarter. From then on, mother stopped making money to support us. We began to sell everything in our flat. Father died sometime later. That caused me a lot of pain, and mother, too. Six weeks after father died, **mother managed to place me and my younger brother in a half-residence** [emphasis added]. It's very nice for us here. We get meals four times a day and hope to survive the war.[45]

Andzia Baranek described the situation differently.

When they locked up the Jewish quarter, mother stopped doing business. Then hunger began to bedevil us. Mother sold everything in the apartment, even an armoire, a table, and chairs. But that didn't suffice for long. Then winter came and it was even worse. Mother would bring only two food rations and we lived on [them] for a whole

43 Ibid.
44 Ibid.
45 Ibid.

day. Mother's legs swelled up and she spent the whole winter lying in bed. **A neighbor suggested that we sell the ration cards. Mother sold [hers], and I brought home something to eat** [emphasis added].[46]

Toward a Conclusion

The title of this chapter refers to solidarity and survival among families in the extreme situations of war and confinement in the ghetto as represented in children's narratives. This juxtaposition seems to leave room for two possible poles of relationships: fracturing or solidarity, as well as something in between. In the documentation that underlies this essay, the children do not attest to fracturing. On the contrary, they speak of solidarity. These children and adolescents strained to help support their families by smuggling, or in other ways, however dangerous they might have been. Even after remaining on their own, or living on and off with a sibling, they did not shirk their responsibilities and tried to help. Recollections of their destroyed families also lent meaning to their survival efforts, as manifested in the wish to follow the family's path in the future, be it in the choice of an occupation or in joining relatives who had emigrated.

I should stress again that these testimonies relate to children who were old enough to have memories of the period before the war and were aware of the different stages in the changes that their families had experienced. This is important to remember, since younger children who were unable to write or relate memories of their lives before the outbreak of the war, or of their confinement to the ghetto, are mute for us. Without making a comprehensive comparison of diaries of children, or adolescents, which merits a separate discussion, I dare say that even when the youngsters were critical of their parents, they demonstrated understanding of their hardships and were able to express empathy.

Most of the parents whom we encountered belonged to the middle and lower-middle classes; none had higher educations or practiced liberal professions. Heads of households managed to support themselves by working but could not afford to be out of work for long. Many had limited possessions that they could sell or barter. They did not have connections among the central authorities of the ghetto: Judenrat

46 Ibid.

officials, Jewish self-help organizations, or other individuals of authority and influence. Some were not totally strange to their surroundings.

After reading the youngsters' stories, both those written in first person and those written by counselors and rendered in third person, I find them convincingly credible. They appear to present a rather balanced picture, with few positive superlatives about their families' past but also no complaints or protests against their nuclear or extended family. Despite their grim life experiences, the children came across as artless storytellers.

The dispassionate and matter-of-fact descriptions of the family past are also credible. It is my feeling as a reader that the young narrators were enveloped in their vanished pasts. In most cases, they described normal working and breadwinning parents, although they sometimes stressed the poverty and overcrowding that pervaded their homes. Hunger was mentioned only in the context of the realities of ghetto life, where it was dominant. One may cite several main crossroads in family life after the onset of the war and occupation: loss of home, due to the bombardments, and loss of livelihood, as a result of the occupation. However, ghettoization produced the most extreme change, whether prompted by deportation and displacement, or the sealing of the Jewish quarter, as described by those who lived in or near the ghetto, or in Praga.

Each time a family moved, their situation worsened. Parents became unable to overcome the extreme circumstances, although their children noted their initiative and creativity in striving to meet their families' most elementary needs. Children reported having worked together with their parents as long as work was available, being active in smuggling until the winter, and so on. They could not, however, stop the process that ultimately led to the disintegration of their families. At that point, the youngsters' stories took on a salient tenor of tragedy and responsibility, as they examined whether they truly had spared no effort to help. Some of the youngsters stated that for some time they had managed to avert the disaster that was ultimately inevitable. This probing attitude reflects a reality that led inexorably to an abyss and, at the same time, to pro-activism as they sought to stop the unstoppable.

Until the final, sad denouement, family members remained in contact with one another and, to some extent, shared mutual responsibilities. A brother who had fled to the East sent parcels. A father, mother, or other relative placed children in a home on the assumption that they would be better off there. A mother who was no longer able to endure the distress, hoping to better her situation by leaving the city, consigned her two daughters to an institution and stayed in touch with them by sending a letter. An older son, an uncle, or an aunt in the ghetto tried to offer assistance, however scanty, and there were children who spent their days in a children's shelter, while living with family members. The youngsters themselves, including those who remained almost totally on their own, even after being placed in shelters, still worried about any remaining members of their families and siblings in institutions such as theirs. In this sense, the family remained part of the world of their youth, even when it no longer existed.

When emotions are expressed in the children's compositions, they are usually restrained—sorrow, sadness, horror over what had happened to them: a mother's death, a father's death, distancing from or absence of relatives, and also appreciation for and satisfaction with having had someone to take care of them, who wished to do well by them by placing them in a day residence, or watching over them in their own homes.

Some of the children evidenced prospective thinking. They assumed that the war would end and that another way of life would become possible, for example, to be a cobbler like one's father, or to emigrate to America. In most of the compositions and questionnaires, however, the focus is on the present, and the question "Who knows if I will survive?" thunders relentlessly.

Medical Activity in the Warsaw Ghetto as a Test of Jewish Solidarity in the Face of Persecution

MIRIAM OFFER

First World Congress of Jewish Physicians: Emergency Assembly to Raise Awareness in the Enlightened World

On the first day of the month of Iyar 5696 (April 23, 1936), three years after Hitler's rise to power in Germany, a formative event occurred in the history of Jewish medicine: the initiation of the First World Congress of Jewish Physicians. The congress was held in the Ohel Shem Hall in Tel Aviv, founded in 1929 as a cultural center for residents of the Jewish *Yishuv* (pre-independence Israel) in *Eretz Israel*. No less than 1,200 people attended the opening ceremony. Among the dignitaries were Meir Dizengoff (1861–1936), the first mayor of Tel Aviv, and Prof. Chaim Weizmann (1874–1952), a chemist of international renown and one of the first Zionist leaders, who later became the first president of the State of Israel.[1]

At that time, the Jewish *Yishuv* in *Eretz Israel* had a population of approximately 380,000, including about 1,960 Jewish physicians.[2] Most of them had immigrated after dismissal from their posts when Hitler rose to power and as a reaction to the Nuremberg Laws passed on September 15, 1935. More than 200 physicians from overseas attended the congress, representing approximately fourteen Jewish communities worldwide.[3]

The congress was dedicated to discussing the difficult situation facing the Jewish physicians and Jewish communities throughout Europe—the increasing waves of antisemitism and the barring of Jewish

---

1   David Arie Friedman, ed., *Sefer Hakongres Haolami Harishon Shel Rofim Yehudim* (Hebrew) (Tel Aviv: Harefu'ah, 1936).
2   Nissim Levy and Yael Levy, *Rofeyha Shel Eretz Yisrael, 1799–1948* (Hebrew) (Zikhron Ya'akov: Itai Bahur, 2012), pp. 34–35. This updated and expanded edition was published for the centenary of the Israel Medical Association, 1912–2012.
3   Ibid., pp. 54–57.

physicians from their workplaces and universities.[4] The manifesto of the First World Congress of Jewish Physicians reflects the organizers' sense of identification, concern, responsibility, and proactiveness in arousing global awareness of the plight of the Jewish physicians in Europe.

> The recent calamities and severe decrees that are revisited daily on our people in various countries have damaged the status of physicians, in particular, who were admired and respected even in more trying times for our people than the present. The massive increase in the number of physicians in all countries has led to tough competition with the Jewish physicians. With the added racial hatred and political struggle, this has deprived thousands of families of physicians of their source of livelihood....This wave of fierce animosity on the part of our enemies is endangering not only the economic status of a large segment of the Jewish people, and not only the professions and the disciplines held by many complete generations of the cultured among us, but it is also endangering the health of the multitude of the Jewish people as a result of the various persecutions.[5]

Thus, this congress had a clear nature of solidarity. It called for the formation of a system of international collaboration among the Jewish medical organizations as a defense against the "recent calamities and severe decrees that are revisited daily on our people," especially the damaged status of physicians. The aim of this gathering was to discuss the future of Jewish medicine and physicians, as well as the health of the Jews and the Jewish nation. It was hoped that this joint, international, Jewish activity would prompt "the whole of the enlightened, culturally humane world to stand by us and assist us."[6]

The World Congress of Jewish Physicians was not the only international organization for the protection of the rights of Jews during this period. In August 1936, only a few months after the physicians' congress, the World Jewish Congress (WJC) in Geneva was founded by a plenary assembly of 230 young Jewish adults from thirty-two countries. The WJC opened a liaison office in Geneva, which initiated diplomatic

---

4   On the state of Jewish medicine in Poland during the interwar period, see Miriam Offer, *White Coats in the Ghetto: Jewish Medicine in Poland During the Holocaust* (Jerusalem: Yad Vashem, 2020), pp. 51–96.

5   Friedman, *Sefer Hakongres Ha'olami Harishon*, pp. 10–11.

6   Ibid., p. 11.

activity with the League of Nations. Its aims were to urge the Jewish people and the democratic powers to act against the Nazi offensive, to fight for equal political and economic rights in all locations, to assist in the establishment of a Jewish national home in Mandatory Palestine, and to found a worldwide, representative Jewish organization based on the idea of a united Jewish people, with a democratic structure and the ability to work on common issues.[7] In 1936, the atmosphere among the Jewish communities was ridden with anxiety regarding the plight of the German Jews under the Nazi regime and the rising antisemitism in the other countries in Europe. This is what led influential Jews to form an international Jewish front to do whatever was possible in response to the difficulties and dangers facing the Jewish people.

The First World Congress of Jewish Physicians may be seen in the broader historical context of national Jewish solidarity initiatives, which increased in scope and diversity in the new era and operated in different arenas—locally, nationally, and internationally—and were sometimes set in motion by individuals and sometimes by organized public initiatives. Jewish history is full of events that bear the stamp of commitment to Jewish solidarity. Helping Jews in times of distress and persecution is central to individual and public Jewish thought and behavior.[8] National solidarity developed among the Jewish people, on one hand, through the multitude of hardships in the Jewish Diaspora throughout Jewish history, which created the constant need to help and to rescue Jews persecuted because of their faith and national belonging, and, on the other hand, in view of Jewish culture and Halacha, which ascribe supreme value to saving a life and exalt helping others, ransoming prisoners, and the Jewish principle that "all of Israel are responsible for one another."[9]

7   See the World Jewish Congress website, http://www.worldjewishcongress.org/he/about/communities.

8   Prominent Jewish organizations that engaged in solidarity activity in the new era included the Alliance Israélite Universelle in Paris, founded in 1860; the Hebrew Immigrants Aid Society (HIAS) in New York, founded in 1884; Hilfsverein der Deutschen Juden in Berlin, founded in 1901; and the American Jewish Joint Distribution Committee (AJJDC), commonly known as the JDC, founded in 1914. See Benjamin Pinkus, ed., introduction to *Yahadut Mizrah Eropa Bein Shoah Litkuma, 1944–1948* (Kiryat Sde Boker: Ben-Gurion University of the Negev, 1987).

9   Ilan Troen, "Irgun Hatzalatam Shel Hayehudim Batkufa Hamodernit," in Benjamin Pinkus and Ilan Troen, eds., *Solidariyut Yehudit Le'umit Ba'et Hahadasha* (Sde Boker: Ben-Gurion University of the Negev Press, 1988), (Hebrew), pp. 3–18; Ya'akov Blidstein, "Pidyon Shvuyim Bamasoret Hahilkhatit: Metahim Umediniyut," in Pinkus and Troen, *Solidariyut Yehudit Le'umit Ba'et Hahadasha*, pp. 19–27.

Dr. Israel Milejkowski, Head of the Judenrat Health Department in the Warsaw Ghetto

Among the participants in the aforementioned World Congress of Jewish Physicians was Dr. Israel Milejkowski, a physician from Poland.[10] At that time, he was serving as the deputy chair of the Organization of Jewish Physicians in Poland and was a prominently active member of the Jewish medical organization Towarzystwo Ochrony Zdrowia Ludności Żydowskiej (Society for Safeguarding the Health of the Jewish Population, TOZ), which was founded in 1921 and operated in the Jewish communities throughout Poland.[11] Dr. Milejkowski was also an active member of the international committee of physicians who organized this important congress. He did not imagine that three years later he would be shouldering the burden of managing the Health Department in the largest ghetto, the Warsaw ghetto. His personality and experience as a Jewish, Zionist physician, oriented toward social involvement,

10 Dr. Israel Milejkowski (1887–January 18, 1943) completed dermatology studies in 1914 and practiced in Warsaw. Before World War II, he was the highly esteemed chair of the Jewish Medical Association. On September 18, 1939, in the midst of the siege of Warsaw, he was appointed chair of the Medical Aid Desk of the Jewish Civilian Committee that public representatives had set up in the Jewish community building. During the occupation, he headed the Judenrat Health Department in the Warsaw ghetto. He strove prodigiously to set up the underground medical school in the ghetto and also headed the team that performed scientific research on hunger. He is described as a man of noble bearing and courage. As the liaison between the Judenrat and the German health authorities, he dared to criticize the occupation authorities' cruel edicts and stayed in his post to the end. In an *Aktion* that began on January 18, 1943, members of the Ordnungsdienst (Jewish ghetto police) entered courtyards and ordered the residents to come down from their apartments. Jews who held "life numbers," particularly Judenrat officials, placed their trust in these documents and did as told. Many physicians who held important posts in the Judenrat institutions, including Milejkowski, were snared in the trap that the Nazis had set. See Adam Czerniaków, *The Warsaw Diary of Adam Czerniaków: Prelude to Doom* (New York: Stein and Day, 1979), p. 75; Louis Falstein, ed., *The Martyrdom of Jewish Physicians in Poland* (New York: Exposition Press, 1963), p. 419; Naomi Menuhin, "Ha'intelektual Hayehudi BePolin Bein Shtei Milhamot Ha'olam: Doktor Izrael Milikovski Kemikre Mivhan" (Hebrew) (PhD diss., Ben-Gurion University of the Negev, Kiryat Sde Boker, 2016).

11 TOZ was founded in 1921 against the background of Poland's establishment as an independent state in which Jews were recognized as a national minority. On TOZ and its widespread, professional activity during the interwar period and the Holocaust, see Offer, *White Coats in the Ghetto*, pp. 75–81, 177–199.

apparently left its mark on the development and character of the medical system in the Warsaw ghetto, as we will see further on.

Solidarity and Mutual Responsibility

In this article, I will attempt to examine whether significant components of mutual responsibility and solidarity can be identified in the health and medical activities, which were run by the Judenrat and the health and welfare organizations in the ghetto. First, however, I will briefly address the terms "solidarity" and "mutual responsibility." A brief look at the definitions shows that two different principles and values are prominent in these concepts. Solidarity, from the subroot "solid"— uniform and compacted—emphasizes the feeling of identity, unity, and even full agreement with the stance of the other,[12] whereas "mutual responsibility," *arevut hadadit* in Hebrew, from the root *arev*, meaning "guarantor," emphasizes the value of responsibility and obligation.[13]

In his article, "Solidariyut" (Solidarity), Israel Sorek defined the term as a person or a group's identification with a person, a group, or a specific community, based on empathy or on ideological or ethical partnership. He asserts that solidarity may be more sharply defined as a type of voluntary commitment to the other, expressed either through emotions or behavior.[14] Sorek differentiates among three manifestations of solidarity:

1. Demonstration of solidarity—expressing solidarity in itself is perceived as a good deed, even if one is unable to help the person or the group with whom one identifies.
2. Cooperation—even in the presence of asymmetry between organizations or between the material gain from a particular

---

12 On the etymology of the word solidarity, see, for example, https://etymologeek.com/eng/solidarity (accessed September 6, 2020).

13 *Arev* is defined as: 1. A person who undertakes to repay a debt for someone else who does not pay on time, or a person who takes responsibility for something. 2. Responsible: "All of Israel are responsible for one another." See Avraham Even Shoshan, *Hamilon* (Hebrew), vol. 3 (Jerusalem: Kiryat Sefer Ltd., 1986), p. 1015.

14 Israel Sorek, "Solidariyut" (Hebrew), *Lexi-Kaye*, 3 (January 2015), pp. 24–25, https://www.kaye.ac.il/lkey/%D7%A1%D7%95%D7%9C%D7%99%D7%93%D7%A8%D7%99%D7%95%D7%AA/ (accessed September 6, 2020).

agreement between them, cooperation is still possible because of shared values, ideological identification, or similarity of identity.

3. Altruism—the highest level of active solidarity, when at least one of the sides is willing to suffer, to risk the loss of possessions or life in order to realize the sense of brotherhood and solidarity.

Arevut hadadit is a concept originating with the Jewish sages of the Mishnaic, Tosefta, and Talmudic eras, which emphasizes that every individual Jew is responsible for other Jews' adherence to the commandments: "All Jews are guarantors for one another."[15] Unlike the concept of solidarity, which constitutes a voluntary, internal, moral development in relation to the other, *arevut hadadit* is, in fact, a commandment and is not merely subject to freedom of choice—it is a religious, social commandment based on interaction between individuals and society, and founded on mutual obligation and responsibility. According to the sages, this responsibility is so great that one individual may even be punished for a sin committed by another.[16] This idea, a cornerstone of Jewish thought, draws on various Jewish sources that position the individual's concern for another as a centrally important value, as well as a moral, religious commandment. This idea of "Will one man sin, and will You be wroth with all the congregation?"[17] is referenced also in the following midrashic parable from the teachings of Rabbi Shimon Bar Yochai:

> A group of people were traveling in a boat. One of them took a drill and began to drill a hole beneath himself. His companions said to him, "Why are you doing this?" The man replied, "What concern is it of yours? Am I not drilling under my own place?" They said to him, "But you will flood the boat for us all!"[18]

---

15 B. Shevuot 39a:22.

16 This concept appears in various Jewish sources in the Bible and in the writings by the Sages. See, for example, Lev. 26:37, "And they will stumble one upon another, as it were before the sword, when none pursues; and you will have no power to stand before your enemies"; see also the Midrashic source, M. Sifra, Behukotai 7:5; B. Sanhedrin 27b.

17 Num. 16:22.

18 Midrash Vayikra Rabbah 4:6, Yalkut Shimoni, Yirmiyahu, sec. 334. For the English translation, see, for example, https://www.chabad.org/library/article_cdo/aid/386812/ jewish/The-Boat.htm (accessed September 6, 2020).

Nevertheless, an examination of these noble traits of solidarity and *arevut hadadit* in Jewish society in the ghettos, in general, and in the Warsaw ghetto, in particular, puts the manifestations of these traits to a special test under the extreme circumstances of all the Jews in the ghetto. Therefore, when evaluating health and medical activity in the ghetto, we will examine whether these components of mutual responsibility, partnership, identification, and altruism were expressed through the activities of those who provided medical services in the ghetto. Did the extreme circumstances in the Warsaw ghetto, where there was a shortage of all the required infrastructures for human life and thousands of Jews starved to death every month throughout 1941, suppress the traits of compassion and solidarity within the society that was fighting for its life? Did other traits, such as individualism and egoism, become dominant components that drove the activities of the medical and health staff in the ghetto?

The Jewish Medical System in the Warsaw Ghetto: Mutual Responsibility and Solidarity

Health and medicine play a central role in daily life in "normal" times, and how much more so under the living conditions in the ghettos. Almost all the families in the ghetto, especially in the Warsaw ghetto, which was the largest of the ghettos, had to cope with morbidity and the untimely death of close family members. A review of the characteristics of the medical system established by the Jews in the Warsaw ghetto leaves much food for thought regarding the values and motivation that drove the medical workers in the ghetto. This includes an evaluation of the place of the values of mutual responsibility and solidarity among the range of motives that led to the formation of patterns of Jewish activity, in general, and in particular, patterns of Jewish medical activities in the Warsaw ghetto.

The medical system in the Warsaw ghetto was professional and well organized. It included services for preventing disease and fighting epidemics, aiding and treating patients in the ghetto clinics and through hospitalization, and conducting medical research, especially on the diseases and epidemics that broke out in the ghetto, alongside medical instruction and training frameworks. The activity was steered by the head of the Judenrat, Adam Czerniaków who, in this capacity, established departments for the practical care of health and the treatment of disease, primarily the Health Department, which ran six health centers in the ghetto, two hospitals, regional clinics, professional committees, such as the Health Council, an organization to fight tuberculosis, medical services for refugees, and more.[19]

The workers of the Judenrat and the TOZ Jewish health organization, which was active in the interwar period, shouldered the main burden of operating this system. The main institutions that functioned as part of the medical services in the ghetto included Czyste Jewish Hospital, which had served the Jewish population of Poland in the interwar period and was not included within the ghetto boundary. The director at this time was Dr. Josef Stein.[20] Jews reestablished the hospital in dilapidated buildings scattered throughout the ghetto.[21] Another main

19 Offer, *White Coats in the Ghetto*, pp. 161–396; Isaiah Trunk, *Judenrat: The Jewish Councils in Eastern Europe under Nazi Occupation* (New York: Macmillan, 1972), pp. 159–160, 102–103; Jonas Turkow, *Hayo Hayta Varsha Yehudit* (Hebrew) (Tel Aviv: Mifaley Tarbut Vehinuh, 1969), pp. 18–19.

20 Dr. Josef Stein (1904–1943) completed his studies in 1927. He was a teaching aide and lecturer at the University of Warsaw. His research work on the micropathology of typhus was very well known among German pathologists, who visited the ghetto to study the disease. In the ghetto, Stein researched the pathological anatomy of hunger and helped to set up the ghetto medical school. In a display of immense courage, he refused an opportunity to be rescued from the ghetto and participated in the April 1943 uprising. See Falstein, The *Martyrdom of Jewish Physicians*, p. 461.

21 On the fate of Czyste Hospital in the ghetto, see, for example, Isaiah Trunk, "Epidemics and Mortality in the Warsaw Ghetto, 1939–1942," *YIVO Annual of Jewish Social Sciences*, vol. 8 (1953), pp. 82–122; Dr. Henry Fenigstein testimony, "Varshever Yid: Shpital Betn Nazi-Rezhim," Aroysgegebn Durkh Farlag Ibergang Bey der Federatsiye fun Poylishe Yidn in Deytshland, Amerikaner Zane, 1948 (Yiddish), YVA, O.33/1074, https:// digitalarchive.mcmaster.ca/islandora/object/macrepo%3A81178#page/1/mode/2up (accessed July 10, 2022). See also, Yad Vashem Archives (YVA) O.33/1074; Dr. Chaim Einhorn testimony, YVA, O.3/1836; Sabina Gürfinkel-Glocer, "Goralo Shel Beit Haholim Tzhista," in Itzhak Gruenbaum, ed., *Entziklopedia Shel Galuyot: Varsha* (Hebrew), vol. 6, part 2 (Jerusalem: Encyclopedia of the Jewish Diaspora Co., 1959), pp. 587–590; Dr. Emil Apfelbaum testimony, History of Czyste Hospital, YVA, 4510; Charles Gordon Roland, *Courage Under Siege: Starvation, Disease and Death in the Warsaw Ghetto* (New York: Oxford University Press, 1992), pp.77–94; Falstein, *The Martyrdom of Jewish Physicians*, pp. 227–230; Mordechai Lensky, *A Physician Inside the Warsaw Ghetto* (New York and Jerusalem: Yad Vashem and The Holocaust Survivors Memoirs Project, 2009), pp. 22–24, 99–100, 200–201; Reuven Ben-Shem, "Batei Holim Yehudiyim BeVarsha," in Gruenbaum, *Entziklopedia Shel Galuyot: Varsha*, vol. 1, pp. 579–585.

institution was Bersohn and Bauman Children's Hospital, directed by the dedicated physician Dr. Anna Braude-Heller during the interwar period and throughout the entire ghetto period.[22] The Jews in the ghetto established a professional network of clinics that served the patients,[23] a chemical and bacteriological laboratory set up by scientists in the ghetto,[24] a first-aid station,[25] and approximately nineteen pharmacies.[26]

22 On the Berson and Bauman Children's Hospital in the ghetto and Dr. Anna Braude-Heller, see, for example, Yehudit Braude testimony, YVA, O.3/2360; Sabine Sanderman testimony, YVA, M.49.E/5883; Adina Blady Szwajger, *I Remember Nothing More: The Warsaw Children's Hospital and the Jewish Resistance* (New York: Pantheon, 1990); Israel Rom (Rotbalsam), "Mahalot Hayeladim Begeto Varsha," in Mark Meir Dworzecki, ed., *Hama'avak Lakiyum Velabriyut Biymei Hashoah* (Hebrew) (Jerusalem: Israel Directorate of the World Jewish Congress and the Association of Holocaust Survivor Physicians— Ghettos, Camps, Forests, 1958); Dr. M. Tursz testimony, YVA, O.3/438; Shmuel Stanisław Waller testimony, YVA, O.3/2358; Roland, *Courage Under Siege*, pp. 94–97; Dr. Israel Rotbalsam (Rom) testimony, YVA, O.3/2357; Joseph Kermish, ed., *To Live with Honor and Die with Honor! Selected Documents from the Warsaw Ghetto Underground Archives "O.S." (Oneg Shabbath)* (Jerusalem: Yad Vashem, 1986), pp. 403–404. For photos of Bersohn and Bauman Children's Hospital, see AŻIH, ARI.989.

23 Jewish Social Self-Help, Statistics Department Report, no. 6, November 1941, ŻIH, ARI.32; Turkow, *Hayo Hayta Varsha Yehudit*, pp. 20–21, 23; Yehudit Braude testimony, YVA, O.3/2360; Lensky, *A Physician Inside the Warsaw Ghetto*, pp. 87–89; Judenrat Statistics Department Report, no. 29, March 13, 1942, Ghetto Fighters' House Archive (GFH), no. 11250, p. 10; Chaim Einhorn, "Harofe Begeto Varsha," in Dworzecki, *Hama'avak Lakiyum Velabriyut Biymei Hashoah*, p. 12; Rom (Rotbalsam), "Mahalot Hayeladim," p. 15; Roland, *Courage Under Siege*, pp. 54, 70; Dr. M. Tursz testimony, YVA, O.3/438.

24 Report from a chemo-bacteriological institute, YVA, AR.1/191; see also Roland, *Courage Under Siege*, p. 70; Ludwik Hirszfeld, *The Story of One Life* (New York: University of Rochester Press, 2010), p. 208.

25 Jerzy Ross (Rosenberg), "Tahanat Ezra Rishona Begeto Varsha" (Hebrew), *Yalqut Moreshet*, vol. 14 (1972), pp. 67–76; Emmanuel Ringelblum, *Notes from the Warsaw Ghetto* (New York, Toronto, and London: McGraw-Hill, 1958), pp.114, 179, 185, 332; Roland, *Courage Under Siege*, pp. 67–68.

26 On pharmacies in the Warsaw Ghetto, see Roland, *Courage Under Siege*, pp. 71–77; Emmanuel Ringelblum, *Yoman Vereshimot Mitkufat Hamilhama: Geto Varsha, September 1939 Detzember 1942* (Hebrew) (Jerusalem: Yad Vashem, 1993), pp. 94, 190; Ringelblum, *Notes from the Warsaw Ghetto*, p. 166; Czerniaków, *The Warsaw Diary*, p. 98; Chaim A. Kaplan, *Scroll of Agony: The Warsaw Diary of Chaim A. Kaplan*, ed. and tr. by A. I. Katsh (Bloomington: Indiana University Press, 1999), pp. 223–224; Trunk, *Judenrat*, pp. 157, 159, 160, 605; Lensky, *A Physician Inside the Warsaw Ghetto*, pp. 47, 104; Judenrat Statistics Department Report, no. 29, March 17, 1942, GFH, no. 11250; Warsaw Municipal Caregiving Committee Report, internal publication, Jewish Social Self-Help, Statistics Department Report, no. 6, November 1941, ŻIH ARI.32, p. 24.

The medical system dealt not only with emergency medicine and the treatment of patients, but continued during this difficult period with activities characteristic of medical systems, such as medical studies, in-service training, and research. Thus, the Jewish school of nursing, under the direction of nurse Luba Bielicka-Blum, continued to function, training approximately eighty students during the ghetto period.[27]

Surprisingly, the Jewish physicians and scientists in the ghetto risked their lives to establish a clandestine faculty of medicine that maintained high academic standards, which had 500 students. This was made possible under the camouflage of courses in epidemiology to prevent epidemics in the ghetto, which the Germans authorized, because they feared outbreaks caused by Jews who "carried bacteria," according to the antisemitic stereotype of Jews, and by the subhuman conditions that they imposed on the Jews in the ghetto.[28]

About thirty physicians conducted an underground study of hunger disease in the ghetto.[29] The doctors who took part in the research, themselves suffering from hunger and the other ravages of ghetto life, investigated and documented the tragic reality using scientific tools. Despite the wretched working conditions—limited medical equipment, deficient physical facilities, insufficient laboratory resources—after five months of research, they managed to present a professional, high-quality, and unique study that would normally have taken an entire year

27 Aleksander Blum, "The Nursing School in the Warsaw Ghetto," in Michael A. Grodin, ed., *Jewish Medical Resistance in the Holocaust* (New York and Oxford: Berghahn, 2014), pp. 173–177; see also Luba Blum-Bielicka, "Szkoła Pielęgniarstwa przy Szpitalu Starozakonnych w Warszawie (1923–1943)," BŻIH, 40 (1961), pp. 66–67; Czerniaków, *The Warsaw Diary,* p. 178; Blady Szwajger, *I Remember Nothing More,* p. 62; Roland, *Courage Under Siege,* pp. 73–74; Helena Szereszewska, *Memoirs from Occupied Warsaw, 1940–1945* (London: Vallentine Mitchell, 1997), p. 28; Nachman Blumental, "Batei Hasefer Bageto," in Gruenbaum, *Entziklopedia Shel Galuyot: Varsha,* vol. 6, part 2, p. 546.

28 Czerniaków, *The Warsaw Diary,* pp. 225, 233; Ringelblum, *Notes from the Warsaw Ghetto,* p. 225; Roland, *Courage Under Siege,* pp. 187–192; Ludwig Stabholz, "Hora'at Anatomiya Bamahteret" (Hebrew) (paper presented at the conference on "The Medical Faculty in the Warsaw Ghetto and Polish–Jewish Medical Collaboration in the Holocaust, Sackler Faculty of Medicine, Tel Aviv University, May 5, 2005); Hirszfeld, *The Story of One Life,* pp. 201, 204–205; Prof. Adam Drozdowicza testimony, YVA, O.3/3647.

29 Moshe Shechter, "Simfonia Bilti Gmura Shel Rofim Yehudim Mishnat 1942" (Hebrew), *Harefuah,* 44:9 (1953), pp. 202–205; Rachel Auerbach, *Behutzot Varsha: 1939–1943* (Hebrew) (Tel Aviv: Am Oved, 1954), p. 329n4; Ringelblum, *Notes from the Warsaw Ghetto,* p. 294.

to produce.[30] In addition, approximately twenty physicians conducted an extensive study of typhus, led by Dr. Jakub Penson, who directed the Department of Infectious Diseases at Czyste Hospital in the ghetto.[31]

Thus, it can be seen that under the difficult conditions in the ghetto, a hierarchical and highly disciplined medical system was created, which set objectives for itself to meet the public health challenges according to modern standards: improved sanitation, immunizations, disease quarantine, quality control of food, medical training, and medical research.[32] This system was established by the Jews themselves, the persecuted society, and not by the Germans or any external authority. This is an apparently unprecedented phenomenon in any case of genocide or mass atrocities.[33]

This alternative medical system established by the Jews had, of course, a very limited ability to provide adequate medical assistance to cope with the morbidity that prevailed as a result of the conditions created in the ghetto by the Germans. There were severe shortages of food, medical equipment, medication, hospital beds, mattresses and bed linens, heating fuel for wards in the freezing winter, etc. In addition, the terrible hunger

30 Myron Winick, *Hunger Disease: Studies by the Jewish Physicians in the Warsaw Ghetto* (New York: Wiley, 1979), p. 4.

31 Dr. Jakub Penson was born on April 23, 1899, in Poland and completed his primary and secondary studies in Plock. After taking part in the Polish–Soviet War as a volunteer soldier (1918–1921), he studied medicine at the University of Warsaw. After surviving the war, Penson was named head of the Internal Medicine Department at the Medical University of Gdańsk and became a pioneer in clinical nephrology in Poland. See Joanna Muszkowska-Penson, "Prof. Jakub Penson (1899–1971) Część I: Okres Przedwojenny I Okupacji," *Annales Academiae Medicae Gedanensis*, 32 (2002), pp. 321–330; Boleslaw Rutkowski, "Jakub Penson and His Studies on Acute Renal Failure during Typhus Epidemics in Warsaw Ghetto," *Journal of Nephrology*, 17 (2004), pp. 175–179; Jakub Penson, "Cechy kliniczne epidemii duru plamistego w latach 1940 I 1940/1941 w Warszawie: Badania nad przemiana azotowa ze szczegolnym uwzgl´dnieniem nerek. Metoda wczesnego rozpoznawania," *Polski Tygodnik Lekarski*, 46–52 (1946), pp. 1399–1404, 1478–1487, 1538–1542, 1553–1569. Dr. Milejkowski notes that research on typhus took place; see Kermish, *To Live with Honor*, p. 743.

32 For elaboration on these tasks, see Walter Holland, Roger Detels, and George Knox, eds., *Oxford Textbook of Public Health*, vol. 1 (Oxford: Oxford University Press, 1984), p. 20. For a broader look at the role of public and social medicine in the interwar years and its manifestations in European countries, see Iris Borowy and Anne Hardly, eds., *Of Medicine and Men: Biographies and Ideas in European Social Medicine between the World Wars* (Frankfurt am Main: Peter Lang, 2008).

33 For a comparison of the study of medicince during the Holocaust and the study of medicine in other cases of genocide, see Offer, *White Coats in the Ghetto*, pp. 635–639.

imposed by the Germans on about half a million ghetto inhabitants led to diseases with serious complications and to death, and the physicians lacked the equipment to save all the patients. Before the first deportations were carried out, more than 80,000 Jews in the ghetto had already died, mainly of hunger disease and its complications. The medical staff documented for posterity the terrible state of health and the helplessness that accompanied their work in the ghetto, alongside the gradually increasing tragic dilemmas that climaxed during the deportations.[34]

Nonetheless, from the first days of the Nazi regime until the Final Solution was decreed in mid-1941, and up to the deportations from the Warsaw ghetto in July 1942, the ghetto inhabitants, including the physicians and nurses, believed that a large proportion of the Jews would remain alive and would survive the war, despite the gradual destruction. The Nazis' anti-Jewish policy and the Final Solution did not follow a direct, linear development. When the ghettos were first set up, the Final Solution had not yet been decided. The ghettos were a temporary mechanism to contain the Jews until a solution could be found for them "elsewhere." Therefore, at first, the Germans also recognized the need for some form of medical service for the Jews, even if they provided no concrete assistance in establishing and sustaining it. They cast the responsibility for preventing epidemics on the Jewish physicians in the ghetto, allowing Jewish medical organizations solely for epidemic prevention and even largely relying on them until the Final Solution was underway. Thus, despite the impossible challenges that faced the medical staff and ghetto leadership under genocide conditions, they found a reason to continue fighting against epidemics and to cure patients to the best of their ability.[35] In addition, the preservation of life as a supreme Jewish value motivated the staff to continue their work notwithstanding the appalling conditions.[36]

The speed at which the medical system in the ghetto was organized was not generated out of a void but drew on the infrastructure of Jewish medicine that had been developed during the interwar period. Following the accelerated modernization and secularization processes in Jewish society at the turn of the century, an increasing number of Jews flocked

---

34 On the work of the doctors and nurses, and on the tragic dilemmas, see, for example, Ibid., particularly chap. 4, pp. 319–345, and chap 10, pp. 577–626, respectively.
35 Ibid., pp. 645–648.
36 Ibid., p. 651.

to the universities and completed their medical studies. At the same time, however, antisemitism was on the rise in independent Poland. Many of the 4,000 Jewish physicians, approximately 40 percent of all physicians in interwar Poland, were dismissed from medical organizations and positions of public employment. As a result, the Jewish society in Poland, which was characterized by a largely independent Jewish group culture and self-awareness in the interwar period, rapidly developed a separate system of Jewish medical institutions with a kind of state infrastructure. Many Jewish physicians worked for the TOZ health organization, which was founded in 1921 and served all of the large Jewish population throughout Poland.

The abundance of certificates and documents that were left in the JDC Archive indicate that the goals of the Jewish health organization TOZ were based on clear social objectives, which were directed at working with weak populations and laypersons, and focused on preventive medicine, with an emphasis on disseminating knowledge and health services among all the strata of the people.[37] Thus, for example, various activities were developed to protect the health of mothers and children, to teach medicine and hygiene in schools, to offer lectures for the general public, and more. It seems that the principles of mutual responsibility and social responsibility for all the strata of the population were an inseparable part of this organization during the interwar period and in the ghetto. This was due to the influence, on one hand, of a particularly Jewish slant on socialist ideas, which present a social challenge and encourage benevolent activities to help the weak, the sick, the traveler, the orphan, and the widow. On the other hand, the Jewish medical services followed the general trend of modernization in public health, the development of pediatrics, obstetrics and gynecology, and preventive medicine.[38]

---

37 Leon Wulman, "Hevrat TOZ," in Gruenbaum, *Entziklopedia Shel Galuyot: Varsha*, vol. 1, pp. 581–586.

38 Jewish Self-Help (ŻSS) report concerning TOZ, March 1942, ŻIH, ARII.92; Dr. M. Tursz testimony, YVA, O.3/438, pp. 3–7. To get an impression of the extent and content of the activity, see, for example, TOZ Budget Report, April 1, 1936–March 31, 1937, JDC, AR.3-44, files 821, 840; Friedman, *Sefer Hakongres Haolami*, pp. 63–65; Leon Wulman, "OZE–Hesegeha Beavar Vetohniyoteha Latkufa Sheleahar Hamilhama" (Hebrew), *Harofe Ha'ivri*, 2 (1944), pp. 85–94; Leon Wulman, ed., *In Fight for the Health of the Jewish People: 50 Years of OSE* (New York: World Union, OSE, and the American Committee of OSE, 1968); Falstein, *The Martyrdom of Jewish Physicians*, pp. 118–121. Much important information about TOZ's activities in Poland and Warsaw is preserved in the JDC archives. See, for example, Miriam Offer, "Ma'arach Harefu'a Begeto Varsha Bitkufat Hashoah: Irguno

In the ghetto, under the leadership of Dr. Jakob Rozenblum,[39] TOZ continued its activities and provided medical services for all the ghetto inhabitants, especially the thousands of refugees, schoolchildren, and the poor. In other words, the concept of social medicine for weak populations persisted during the ghetto period.[40] Throughout the entire period of the Nazi occupation, the organization did not only operate in the largest ghetto, the Warsaw ghetto, but it continued to operate branches in many ghettos around the Generalgouvernement, at certain times, assisting 195 cities and small towns.[41]

Identifying the Foundations of Mutual Responsibility and Social Solidarity of Medical Activity in the Ghetto

An examination of the historical picture of the medical activity in the ghetto indicates that the social principles that guided the organization in the interwar period continued to guide it during the war. A large number of those who had been active in the organization before the war continued to work for TOZ in the ghetto. Therefore, it is no wonder that

Ve'etgarav Hamiktzo'iyim Bithumei Harefu'a Veha'etika Beheksher Histori" (Hebrew) (PhD diss., Bar-Ilan University, Ramat Gan, 2010), vol. 2, Appendix A.12, pp. 48–51.

39 Dr. Jakob Rozenblum (1895–1943) completed his studies at the University of Warsaw in 1930. He continued his medical activity at the university's laboratories and at the Jewish-owned Czyste Hospital, even after losing a leg in a tram accident in 1937. Until the war, he was active in TOZ in Warsaw. In September 1939, with the war underway, he was appointed to a senior post in the TOZ administration. On January 18, 1943, he was sent to Treblinka. See Dr. M. Tursz testimony, YVA, O.3/438, pp. 18–20; Falstein, The *Martyrdom of Jewish Physicians*, p. 443.

40 Wulman, "Hevrat TOZ," pp. 584–586; Roland, *Courage Under Siege*, pp. 55–57; Dr. M. Tursz testimony, YVA, O.3/438. From the beginning of the war until the deportations from the ghetto, TOZ in Warsaw sent out detailed monthly reports to the JDC in the United States and other free countries with comprehensive documentation of its preventive and therapeutic actions. See, for example, JDC, AR.33–44, file 841; Report Jewish Self-Help (ŻSS) concerning TOZ, March 1942, ŻIH, ARII.92; report by Dr. Emanuel Patt on the social service work among Polish Jews, March 1941, JDC, AR.33–44, file 814; Report on ŻSS activities in Warsaw, July–August 1940, ŻIH, ARII.17; Report of the Warsaw Municipal Caregiving Committee, internal publication, Jewish Social Self-Help, Statistics Department Report, no. 6, November 1941, ŻIH, ARI.32; Judenrat Statistics Department Report, no. 29, March 17, 1942 GFH, no. 11250.

41 TOZ, activity report, May 1940, JDC, AR.33–44, file 840; Wulman, "Hevrat TOZ" pp. 584–585; Dr. M. Tursz testimony, YVA, O.3/438, pp. 18–19.

they carried out their activities according to the principles and values that had previously motivated them. In fact, under the Nazi occupation they continued to constitute a Jewish medical network. The distribution of medical services to other small towns and ghettos underscores the commitment to solidarity that characterized TOZ, which had branches in Jewish communities throughout Poland, even before the Holocaust, and served the entire Jewish population in Poland.

Research on some of the prominent figures who set the medical system in the Warsaw ghetto in motion reveals that the men and women who headed this system held diverse and contradictory worldviews. The human mosaic of this staff expresses a large part of the dissension and differences that characterized Jewish society in Poland in the interwar period and that prevailed in the ghetto as well. For example, Dr. Anna Braude-Heller, who devotedly directed Bersohn and Bauman Children's Hospital, was a member of the Bund;[42] Dr. Israel Milejkowski, the head of the Judenrat Health Department in the ghetto and one of the initiators and leaders of the hunger study, was an enthusiastic Zionist activist, well known and well respected among the Jewish physicians in Poland; Prof. Ludwik Hirszfeld, an internationally acclaimed scientist in the fields of bacteriology and serology, who had converted to Christianity and continued to go to church while in the ghetto, was very active in the medical field in the ghetto;[43] Adam Czerniaków, head of the Judenrat,

---

42 Dr. Anna Braude-Heller (1888–1943) studied in Switzerland and Germany, and graduated in 1911. In 1914, she returned to Poland as a pediatrician and was appointed chief physician at Bersohn and Bauman Children's Hospital. In 1916, the hospital was deactivated and shut down due to a shortage of funds. Dr. Braude did much to have it reopened. On her activity, professionalism, and devotion during the Holocaust, see Offer, *White Coats Inside the Ghetto*, p. 196. On Dr. Braude-Heller and her lifework, see Falstein, *The Martyrdom of Jewish Physicians*, p. 322; Rom (Rotbalsom), "Mahalot Hayeladim," p. 14; Roland, *Courage Under Siege*, pp. 94–95; Blady Szwajger, *I Remember Nothing More*, pp. 19, 37–38; Yehudit Braude testimony, YVA, O.3/2360; Shmuel Stanisław Waller testimony, YVA, O.3/2358; see also the testimony of Dr. Polisiuk in Nachman Blumental and Joseph Kermish, eds., *Hameri Vehamered Begeto Varsha* (Hebrew) (Jerusalem: Yad Vashem, 1965), pp. 310–317. Polisiuk witnessed Dr. Braude's doings in the last hours of her life. See Dr. Adolf Polisiuk diary, GFH, no. 3182; Polisiuk's diary is cited in Offer, *White Coats in the Ghetto*, pp. 266–267.

43 Ludwik Hirszfeld (1884–1954) was born in Warsaw. He studied medicine in Berlin and worked at the cancer research institute in Heidelberg and subsequently at the Institute of Hygiene in Zurich. A world-renowned researcher on blood groups, he also discovered the Paratyphoid C bacterium. In 1915, he went to Serbia to help fight the spread of typhus in the ranks of the Serbian army. Continuing his research on blood

who was considered an "assimilated Jew" in terms of that period, was party to all the medical initiatives and measures taken in the ghetto; Prof. Juliusz Zweibaum, a renowned histologist in the medical faculty in Warsaw, who established the underground medical faculty in the ghetto, was among the founders of the Friends of the Hebrew University in Jerusalem in 1933 and was a member of its directorate; nurse Luba Bielicka-Blum managed the nursing school in the ghetto and was also a member of the Bund. However, from the description of these people's activities and thoughts, as expressed in different sources, we learn that despite the differences and friction that existed between the Zionist, the Bundist, the assimilated Jew, and the apostate, this group cooperated at all the central junctures of the fight for survival, and displayed social and historical responsibility alike. Hence, can anything be learned about the values and ideals that motivated those who played a part in this impressive system? This is almost a rhetorical question.

It is my belief that it is difficult to explain the impressive system, with all its aforementioned limitations, which was established under the conditions that prevailed in the Warsaw ghetto, without observing the continuity of the ethical and professional principles that were the basis for establishing these systems in the interwar period. The 800 Jewish physicians who operated in the Warsaw ghetto brought with them the experience that they had acquired in the interwar period and the ethical perceptions that propelled this system, including the value of mutual responsibility and helping others.

---

types in Salonika, he was able to determine that Type A blood is common mainly among European peoples, whereas Type B is the preponderant among soldiers from Asian countries. In 1919, the Institute of Hygiene in Warsaw named him director of the departments of bacteriology and serology. In 1920 he converted to Catholicism. In 1924, he was appointed lecturer at the Free University and, in 1926, he received the degree of docent. He also served as lecturer on bacteriology. After Warsaw surrendered to the Nazis, Hirszfeld was dismissed from his position at the Institute of Hygiene and, as an apostate Jew, he had to leave his apartment on the "Aryan" side of Warsaw and move to the ghetto in February 1941. There, he was active in many medical fields. After Poland was liberated, he received a professorship at the University of Lublin. Settling in Wrocław, he served as dean of the medical school and established Poland's first institute of immunology, which still bears his name. See Hirszfeld, *The Story of One Life*, introduction, pp. xix-xxxv; Stefan Lutkiewicz, "Hirszfeld Ludwik," in *Encyclopaedia Judaica*, vol. 9 (Jerusalem: Keter, 1971), p. 530; Mordechai Lensky, "Rof'im Yehudim Mefursamim," in Gruenbaum, *Entziklopedia Shel Galuyot: Varsha*, vol. 6, part 2, p. 318.

Solidarity Projects for Medical Aid by Jewish Organizations outside of the Areas Under Nazi Occupation

It is noteworthy that the initial findings regarding the issue of delivering medicines to the ghetto from outside authorities sheds a small amount of light on the external help from Jews who were fortunate to be in countries not under Nazi occupation. The quantity of medicines sent through these channels was very limited, and, of course, was inadequate for the amount required. This subject warrants further study, and there is much to learn about the trend toward solidarity from the range of authorities that dealt with this issue, as well as about the tensions and complexities of the authorities that were active in this area. However, we can point to several channels for dispatching medicines.

The following people appear to have been the main agents of this activity: Dr. Boris Tschlenoff, head of Obshchestvo Zdravookhraneniia Evreev (Society for the Safeguarding of Jews' Health, OZE),[44] who subsequently described the OZE medication project for the Jewish population in Poland and other occupied countries in a report he wrote;[45] Saly Mayer,[46] the president of the Association of Jewish Communities in

44 OZE was established by Russian Jews in 1912 in Saint Petersburg. Additional societies of a similar nature came into being in other countries. In 1921, the Soviet authorities forced OZE to desist from its activity. In 1923, OZE relocated to Berlin and established an international association. The OZE board in Berlin was chaired by Albert Einstein. Ten years, later, when the Nazis rose to power, OZE moved its activity to Paris. In late June 1940, the board relocated to the unoccupied portion of France. In early 1943, the Central Committee transferred the seat of its activity to Geneva. See Michel Ilan, "OZE," in Israel Gutman, ed., *Encyclopedia of the Holocaust* (New York: Macmillan, 1990), pp. 1081–1082; see also Mania Ostrovsky, "Zihronoteha Shel Ahot Be'irgun Oze, 1916–1917" (Hebrew), *Korot*, 11 (1995), pp. 65–72.

45 Tschlenoff report, November 1940–January 1943, GFH, no. 1194; see also the correspondence between Dr. Tschlenoff and Tropper and the letter from Dr. Tschlenoff to Lisbon regarding medicines for TOZ Poland, JDC, AR.33–44, file 940.

46 Saly Mayer (1882–1950) was a Swiss Jewish leader, who served as president of the Schweizer Israelitischer Gemeindbund (Association of Jewish Communities in Switzerland, SIG) from 1936–1942. In 1940, he was appointed representative of the Swiss branch of the JDC, which involved passing information between all parts of occupied Europe and the JDC office in Lisbon. In addition, he was responsible for the Jewish refugees who arrived in Switzerland. He was involved in rescue attempts with the resistance movement in Slovakia and in Kastner's activities in Hungary. After the war, Mayer was accused of not doing enough to save Jews. Yehuda Bauer claims that this was an injustice. Even though he was apparently no saint, he succeeded in providing aid under

Switzerland who assisted OZE to dispatch the medicines; Dr. Michael Weichert, the controversial figure whom the Germans appointed to head the Jewish welfare institution in the Generalgouvernement;[47] and the most interesting of them all, Elias Sternbuch, president of the Bikur Cholim Association in St. Gallen in Switzerland, who privately initiated and orchestrated a large operation to dispatch medicines and medical equipment to the Warsaw ghetto and to other ghettos, and who enlisted members of Agudath Yisrael in the United States to participate in this project.[48] All this notwithstanding, did the medical system reflect only solidarity, or is it possible to claim that egoistic motives were behind this system?

The Medical System in the Ghetto: Individualism and Egoism

We will now examine criticism voiced against the medical services in the ghetto that focused on the egoistic motives of the workers in the medical system. The sources throw light on the deep-seated tensions among the different organizations, alongside the impressive medical and welfare systems. They have also left an uncomfortable impression on readers and influenced historians who have attempted to assess the dynamics of

impossible conditions and faithfully served the last remnants of the Jews of Europe. See Yehuda Bauer, "The Negotiations Between Saly Mayer and the Representatives of the SS in 1944–1945," in Israel Gutman and Efraim Zuroff, eds., *Rescue Attempts During the Holocaust: Proceeding of the Second Yad Vashem International Historical Conference* (Jerusalem: Yad Vashem, 1974), pp. 5–46.

47 Weichert and his activities stirred controversy during and after the war. In the context of heading the Jüdische Soziale Selbsthilfe (Jewish Social Self-Help, JSS) during the war, the main criticism concerned his continuing to run the organization under Nazi supervision after the Germans had begun the systematic murder of Polish Jewry, at which time the organization was renamed Jüdische Unterstützungsstelle (Jewish Relief Office, JUS). After the war, Weichert was placed on trial before a Polish court on the charge of collaborating with the Germans and was acquitted. He was tried then before a public tribunal of the Central Committee of Polish Jews. Regarding these trials, see David Engel, "Remove the Evil from the Midst of Thee: On the Concept of Collaboration in the Trials of Michael Weichert," in Shmuel Almog, David Bankier, Daniel Blatman, and Dalia Ofer, *The Holocaust: History and Memory—Essays Presented in Honor of Israel Gutman* (Jerusalem: Yad Vashem, Avraham Harman Institute of Contemporary Jewry, Hebrew University, 2001), pp. 1–24.

48 Offer, *White Coats in the Ghetto*, pp. 292–302; see also GFH, files: 21351, 21356, 1933, 21352, 21368, 21342, 21344, 21339, 21338.

the Jewish society in the ghetto, which, for example, Dr. Joseph Kermish described as an "excellent school of evil and corruption in interpersonal relations and between individuals and society."[49]

Criticism of the health system was directed at the Judenrat's activities, as well as at the corrupt behavior of physicians. The criticism of the Judenrat's activity, usually from the dozens of underground newspapers in the ghetto, systematically pointed an accusatory finger at the Judenrat in general as an authority imposed by the Germans. The criticism is very important, but should be considered with great caution. Organizations working alongside the Judenrat voiced criticism as well, such as workers in the Jewish self-help organizations,[50] physicians in the Jewish health organization TOZ, and in the CENTOS organization, which continued its activities initiated before the war, focusing on the care and nourishment of children.

TOZ and the self-help organizations operated, for the most part, legally and independently, in parallel with the Judenrat and were supported by the JDC, mainly until the end of 1941, when the United States joined the war. TOZ continued its prewar activities and was recognized and appreciated as a respected, professional organization. The Jewish self-help organizations were initiated and created by public leaders in the Jewish community. Thus, the population had far greater trust in these organizations than in the Judenrat, which was perceived as a tool enforced by the Germans.

49 Joseph Kermish, "Nigudim Ma'amadiyim Begeto Varsha," in Gruenbaum, *Entziklopedia Shel Galuyot: Varsha*, vol. 6, part 2, pp. 577–579.

50 Jewish self-help institutions in the German-occupied Generalgouvernement, operating legally or quasi-legally, went by different names as the German authorities dictated and they are designated differently in the primary sources in Polish, German, Yiddish, and Hebrew. JHK (Jüdisches Hilfskomitee), ŻSS (Żydowska Samopomoc Społeczna, JSS (Jüdische Soziale Selbsthilfe), ŻTOS (Żydowskie Towarzystwo Opieki Społecznej), and JUS (Jewish Relief Office). These institutions operated in connection with the Polish Komitet Opiekuńczy Miejski (Municipal Relief Committee, KOM), which functioned as a branch of the national Polish relief organization Rada Głowma Opiekuńcza (Central Relief Council, RGO). On relief activity in the Generalgouvernement in general and in Warsaw in particular, see, for example, Israel Gutman, *The Jews of Warsaw, 1939–1943: Ghetto, Underground, Revolt* (Bloomington: Indiana University Press, 1989), pp. 40–47, 102–106; Turkow, *Hayo Hayta Varsha Yehudit*, pp. 20–21; Czerniaków, *The Warsaw Diary*, pp. 107, 126–127, 154, 157, 168, 180–181, 185, 198, 293, 314, 329, 333–335, 375; Ringelblum, *Yoman Vereshimot*, p. 93; David Ben-Shalom, "Ha'ezra Ha'atzmit Hayehudit Kemisgeret Lepe'ilut Va'adei Habatim Begeto Varsha" (Hebrew) (master's thesis, the Hebrew University of Jerusalem, 1995), pp. 29, 35.

The criticism of the Judenrat included inter alia accusations of lax and corrupt management of the health institutions, criticism of the policy of the health tax imposed by the Judenrat, and inadequate treatment of epidemics and sanitation. Not infrequently, the criticism of the unethical behavior of individual physicians was systematically projected onto the Judenrat. In a letter from TOZ and the self-help organizations to Adam Czerniaków, head of the Judenrat, in June 1941, they lodged an array of complaints, severely and unrestrainedly criticizing the management of the Judenrat:

To the Chairman of the Judenrat:

1. Public outcry against the frightening mortality rate among the Jewish population of Warsaw.

2. The tragic state of the hospital....

...The mortality is a consequence of the tragic state of the hospitals under the management of the Judenrat....The feeding of patients at the hospital is a pipe dream...A second pipe dream is the state of cleanliness at the hospital. Patients often lie [in bed] without underwear...the employees of the hospital are also bloated from hunger and are struggling along at the hospital....

...First, it is worth emphasizing that the tragic reality is characterized by the nonfunctioning of the Judenrat, the entity responsible for the hospital. The hospital's budget is in catastrophic condition....

...Moreover, the hospital staff's starvation wages have not been paid for months....The management of the maintenance of the hospital is inefficient, making the disorder at the hospital all the worse....

...After describing the features of the tragedy, our consciences cannot remain silent and order us to take remedial measures. While we do not overestimate our capacity, we do not lack confidence....

...Our groups of activists in the community, from ŻTOS and TOZ, have not lost faith in the Jewish population. We are building on this faith. We are aware that the entire Judenrat is—and it is no secret—corrupt. We do not wish to lose our faith in the community. Therefore we activists in the TOZ and CENTOS organizations have decided to act on our own, and only then is there a chance for success.[51]

A review of the suggestions for improvement proposed by the members of TOZ and the self-help organizations further in the letter show a large gap between the writers' perception of the difficulties and their understanding of the limitations under the Nazi regime. The letter reflects hope for changes that were virtually impossible in the tragic reality of the ghetto.

Undoubtedly, the Judenrat was not immune from errors and lapses in managing the medical institutions, especially in light of the difficult conditions under which it had to work. However, I wish to point out that the research indicates that the apparent dichotomy between the Judenrat's activities and the activities of TOZ and the self-help organizations, as presented in this document and in other sources, is exaggerated and does not reflect the reality. The impression received from the sources that TOZ was the only organization to help the weak and the refugees, whereas the Judenrat dealt only with institutional issues, violates the perception of a full, balanced picture of the overall medical system in the ghetto. Many of those active in this organization cooperated with the head of the Health Department, Dr. Israel Milejkowski, who represented the health policy of the Judenrat and was himself a central actor in the TOZ organization. Many of the TOZ workers were members of the medical committees initiated by the Judenrat. Some of them worked for both the Judenrat and TOZ institutions. The cooperation was expressed also in all the clandestine medical activities, such as the establishment of the underground medical faculty and the performance of medical research. These were set in motion with the support of the Judenrat and of Adam Czerniaków himself. I contend that both in spite of and because of its clear professional advantages and social emphasis, TOZ contributed its part to the joint effort, and despite the disagreements and criticisms voiced, continued to act to unite the fronts, and was, consciously and by choice, an important part of what may be defined as the medical system in the Warsaw ghetto.

Even though Czerniaków was not immune from errors in the policies that he led, the establishment of an alternative, all-inclusive

---

51 Anonymous public appeal from doctors and public figures concerning the state of the hospital, June 1941, YVA, AR.10.M.1/315.

health system, in which he played an important role—in collaboration with all the medical and sanitary authorities in the ghetto—overshadows the points of criticism. In other words, this discussion calls for a deeper examination of the texts that describe the tensions between the Judenrat and the TOZ and the social self-help organizations. It is through the essential differences among the authorities in particular that their collaboration may be viewed as an indication of the strong foundation of mutual responsibility for advancing the goals of their shared interest.

Regarding the criticism voiced in the ghetto against the physicians' unethical behavior, there was no shortage of corrupt behavior by physicians as a result of the tragic ghetto conditions. This was manifested in different ways, and especially in relation to the disinfection enforced by the Germans in the struggle against epidemics. The decree imposed by the German physicians responsible for the Warsaw ghetto regarding the disinfection of apartments and buildings in which typhus cases were discovered was one of the harshest decrees recorded in diaries and protocols written in the ghetto. The measures included a two-week quarantine of the inhabitants which, under the ghetto conditions, was tantamount to a death sentence for many who were unable to obtain meager food supplies for this period. In addition, the disinfection methods were destructive and suitable disinfection substances were in short supply. In many cases, the sparse contents that remained in these dwellings were ruined during the disinfection procedure. All the inhabitants of the building and of adjacent buildings, sick and healthy alike, were sent in groups to the few bathhouses in the ghetto. As well as losing their last set of clothes, they were forced to wait their turn outside in freezing conditions to wash in cold water with no soap, and a large number became infected with typhus, even if they had not been ill beforehand. Entire streets were closed off for two to three weeks and the process was frequently repeated. To evade these devastating measures, a system of corruption developed whereby ghetto inhabitants who could afford to pay bribed doctors and disinfection teams not to report the typhus patients in their dwellings. Those who lacked financial means, however, had to suffer this procedure again and again, which cost many of them their lives. [52]

---

52 Ludwik Hirszfeld, *Die Geschichte eines Lebens* (n.p.: n.p., 1950), p. 141; Hirszfeld, *The Story of One Life*, p. 214. For a detailed account, see Offer, *White Coats in the Ghetto*, pp. 533–565.

In an anonymous document in the Ringelblum Archive, the corruption that spread among the physicians is described as follows:

> I may be accused of antipathy and excessive criticism, but I must denounce the doctors for the quality of care and their attitude toward the sick. Their role in the horrific ghetto is highly important—a matter of life and death. It's as important as the problem of bread... Many Jews studied medicine before the war and many were jobless. Now everyone's working, even people who just finished courses, feldshers, and nurses. It wasn't enough and the situation became abnormal...while the doctors are off enriching themselves.... Almost all of them are exploiting the difficult situation for their own benefit. The doctors want money and they're getting it. They offer the unwitting ill all sorts of expensive tests....The doctors also pass patients from one to another and advise [them] to go to another doctor; he'll help....There's no cure whatsoever without injections, no matter what the illness is....Jewish patients believe in doctors. A doctor is God. Every injection costs the patient 10 złotys. (That's a lot of money in the ghetto.) Sometimes the patient has to pay for injections every day and is selling his last shirt to buy a piece of bread....The fact is that in the ghetto it's better to live the way the doctors, the bakers, the high bureaucrats, and the smugglers do.... These doctors aren't to be envied, but [nonetheless], they should spend more time at the hospital, where they're so badly needed. A doctor's decency should be evident even in the hard times of the ghetto. I have nothing against bakers, butchers, merchants. But for God's sake, who can one turn to in such dire distress as this....There are doctors who are kindhearted and sincerely willing to help those in need. They are few but there are some in the ghetto[53]

"In times of war, physicians were no different from any other human being who knows that he has a stomach that must be filled," asserts Opochinsky.[54] There is no doubt that both heroic and courageous deeds and low unethical behavior was evident among the physicians in the ghetto. Some physicians failed the moral tests with which they were faced.

---

53 Report on various aspects of life in the ghetto, ŻIH, ARI.428.
54 Peretz Opochinsky, *Reshimot Migeto Varsha* (Hebrew) (Tel Aviv: Hakibbutz Hame'uhad, 1970), p. 60.

Egoism and Solidarity: Between the Individual and the Collective

Nonetheless, according to different sources, most of the physicians actually did withstand the tests during that difficult period. Dr. Mordechai Lensky, for instance, asserts the following:

> It is noteworthy that among the 830 physicians were isolated individuals who did not live up to ethical standards. Individual physicians embezzled rather than honored their mission and abused the population's trust in them out of greed....But these were only a few cases, and the number of villains among the physicians—and no society can take responsibility for their misdeeds—was marginal.[55]

An ethical evaluation of the physicians is complex, just as that of other leading officials, and certainly of the ordinary person. It seems that, as individuals, the physicians' behavior was not markedly different from the behavior of many others in official positions in the ghetto: they were all forced to face impossible ethical tests. Some failed and some withstood them admirably. Nonetheless, the collective picture, which is completely different, is most interesting. It would have been impossible to establish a system of treatment, training, and research without collaboration and devoted professional commitment, and without mutual responsibility on the part of the staff who formed the medical system in the ghetto.

Altruism

It must be noted that there is not a small number of examples of medical workers, both women and men, who not only behaved honestly and fulfilled their roles responsibly but who behaved with unquestionable altruism. For instance, it is noteworthy that in the course of their work in the ghetto, physicians were exposed to infectious diseases, such as typhus and tuberculosis, which were widespread there. Physicians and nurses died after being infected by patients, whom they refused to abandon. This was the case even in the refugee centers inhabited by

---

55 Lensky, *A Physician Inside the Warsaw Ghetto*, p. 104.

tens of thousands of destitute, Jewish refugees, who had been cruelly deported to the ghetto by the Germans. Epidemics raged throughout these centers. In addition, while some of the physicians took advantage of their prewar connections with Polish colleagues and patients, and successfully escaped to hideouts on the Aryan side of Warsaw during the *Grossaktion* in the Warsaw ghetto throughout the summer of 1942 and in subsequent *Aktionen*, according to testimonies from that time and from post-Holocaust memoirs, some physicians and nurses chose to remain with their patients until the end, despite the possibility of leaving for the Aryan side. Some of them died in the bunkers under the hospital during the Jewish uprising that broke out on April 19, 1943, and others escorted patients who had difficulty fulfilling the German command to walk to the *Umschlagplatz*, boarded the trains with them, and shared their bitter fate at the Treblinka extermination camp. Historian Emmanuel Ringelblum provided the following account:

> We previously mentioned the passive and quiet heroism of the educators, beginning with Dr. Korczak. We recounted how they walked to their deaths willingly, accompanying the children whom they had been nurturing for years. The conduct of the doctors and nurses at the Jewish hospital on Stawki St. was similar...Everyone knew that the hospital would not be spared from deportation.... Therefore, some doctors and nurses left. However, a group of a few dozen doctors and nurses remained and did not abandon the patients until the very last moment. When this tragic moment came and more than 1,000 patients were loaded into the [railroad] cars, a handful of doctors and nurses went with them. Such was the comportment of the people whom the Nazis deemed subhuman.[56]

The Worldview of Dr. Israel Milejkowski, Head of the Judenrat Health Department

Dr. Israel Milejkowski, who was deported to Treblinka during the *Aktion* of January 1943, left valuable writings, including those from which we can learn about the values that motivated him as head of the Judenrat

---

56 Emmanuel Ringelblum, *Ktavim Aharonim: Yahasei Polanim–Yehudim, Yanuar 1943– April 1944* (Hebrew) (Jerusalem: Yad Vashem and Ghetto Fighters' House, 1994), p. 37.

Health Department and those around him to act constructively in the Warsaw ghetto. One of the documents is his answer to a questionnaire written by members of the ghetto's underground archive, the Oyneg Shabbes Archive. His answer discloses his perceptions and his evaluation of the complex reality in relation to the social dynamics in the ghetto. His identification with Zionist ideology is clearly discernible, as are the stratification and ideological and social contradictions in the ghetto, which he describes. He viewed the responsibility to the public as a whole, with all its diversity, as a Jewish value and as a duty in this unique period in the ghetto.

I discern two layers in the Ghetto which can perhaps be illustrated in the following manner: the entire Jewish community in the Ghetto can be said to have been cast into a large cauldron of boiling water atop a high flame—the flame of our tribulations. In the boiling water two layers can be discerned—an upper and a lower. The upper layer seethes, but more quietly, with less fuss...to appreciate the true face of the Ghetto, we must plunge below the surface...in its layer of the Jewish Ghetto population we find modest but highly important phenomena, full of light and vigor...which find expression in the house-committees...organized Jewish life where the true Jewish qualities of mercy and charity find realization....

In addition, quiet, unassuming work also is going on in other fields...public kitchens, medical courses, as well as other studies in order to equip the younger generation to grow up with skills. Intensive medical research being carried out on death through starvation and typhus. The entire clinical—and unfortunately plentiful—material is being studied and conclusive medical results of the research are being prepared....We simply want later—after the cataclysm—to be able to show the world that even these terrible trials could not break us....

...And now a few words on my attitude towards converts in the Ghetto. My attitude is a direct result of my two positions regarding the problem: firstly, the medical and, secondly, the Jewish-ethical. I understand the soul and disposition of the convert who was brutally cast into the Ghetto with us. I can feel how difficult it must be to be a *"Zwangs Jude"* (a Jew by force), to live and suffer with the masses of Jewry from whom he's always tried to flee, and to make a final break forever.

The convert was led to conversion because of the woeful manner in which he was raised by parents who tried to free their child of the Jewish burden. For the most part he did it himself for material reasons. And suddenly there came to the world the mammoth Hitlerian cataclysm...which unfurled the flag of zoological anti-Semitism not only with respect to first-generation converts from Judaism, but also with respect to half and quarter Jews up to the fourth generation.

How should we receive these dissident brethren of our origin? The Gemara says that even if a Jew sins, he is still a Jew. And here my conscience dictates to adhere firmly to the Jewish ethical prescription: "Though shalt neither avenge nor bear grudge"—In our ethical development we stand high above petty account settling with brother sinners, and particularly in times of trouble. As a doctor I see the converts who live with us in the Ghetto as people with a severe spiritual complex. Therefore from this viewpoint—no, not viewpoint, but feeling—I relate to them without hatred whatsoever, but also without fondness.[57]

According to the text, there is no doubt that Milejkowski's worldview drew from the Jewish systems of compassion and ethics, expressions that he himself chose to use. He identified these values of mutual responsibility among some strata of the population, if not among everyone. This document reflects the personality and policy of the man who headed the health system. A connecting thread can be identified between Dr. Israel Milejkowski, deputy head of the TOZ Health Organization, who represented the large Jewish physicians' organization in Poland at the First World Congress of Jewish Physicians, and Dr. Israel Milejkowski, who spearheaded the establishment of the medical system in the ghetto and his impressive activities. In both cases, the sense of a mission and of taking responsibility to act for the sake of the public is dominant. A study of the backgrounds and the attempts brought by other men and women physicians indicates a similar outlook in many of them.

---

57 Kermish, *To Live with Honor*, pp. 741–746.

Solidarity and Altruism: Motives for Significant Action of the Individual and Society from a Historical, Sociological, Philosophical, and Psychological Viewpoint

It may be possible to say that the case study of the medical activity in the Warsaw ghetto and the collective achievement of the ability of the Jews to establish a medical system that was an expression of modern professional perceptions, and of social responsibility and mutual responsibility, reinforces the philosophical perception that views the principle of solidarity and group cohesion as an integral part of the individual and group foundation. Identification with such principles, even in extreme situations, is of great importance. These values prompted the Jews of the ghetto to establish a professional medical service, despite the negligible possibility of overcoming the epidemics. These values by no means canceled out the displays of individualistic and egoistic desires, but were unquestionably present in the public medical activity.

The sociologist Emile Durkheim contended in his research that social cohesion is what motivates all societies and constitutes a framework according to which humans may belong to one society or another. A lack of cohesion or excessive cohesion delineates the development or the stagnation of the society. In Durkheim's view, society is composed of collective awareness and its power to influence the individual. In his famous study of suicide, he showed that the strength of social attachment and the strength of protection that the society is capable of offering to the individual can help the individual to overcome crises. Thus, for example, a link was found between the degree of cohesion of the social group to which people belong and the chance that they will commit suicide. The greater the social cohesion of the society and the greater the consensus, the more protection it will provide to the individual against anxiety, and against internal and existential conflicts.[58] On this issue, it is interesting to note that different studies have proved that the suicide rates in the Warsaw ghetto were lower than expected. For instance, Lucy Dawidowicz claimed that the suicide rate was 65 percent of that prior to the war. Dr. Lensky, a physician in the Warsaw ghetto, wrote that social and family

---

58 Émile Durkheim, "Suicide: A Study in Sociology," in Ian McIntosh, ed., *Classical Sociological Theory: A Reader* (New York: New York University Press, 1997), p. 217.

cooperation prevented the outbreak of the pathological symptoms of the individual's psychological makeup.[59]

In March 1942, about three months before the *Grossaktion*, Chaim Kaplan wrote about the collective strength of the Jews of Poland.

> This secret power works wonders in us; as evidence, we don't have cases of suicide....Proud, filled with self-esteem, thousands of German and Austrian Jews put an end to their lives. Not so the...Jews of Poland...this will of ours to live in the midst of terrible calamity is the outward manifestation of a certain hidden power whose quality has not yet been examined. It is a wondrous, superlative power with which only the most established communities among our people have been blessed.[60]

Ringelblum also drew attention to the low suicide rate as a unique and astonishing phenomenon in light of the difficult conditions with which the Jews had to cope. These studies and testimonies reinforce the assumption that the values of solidarity and cohesion, even if influenced by egoistic values, were not a marginal phenomenon in the Warsaw ghetto, and support the picture presented here regarding expressions of mutual responsibility as manifested in the collective reaction of the medical activity in the Warsaw ghetto.

It is interesting to refer to several early twentieth century philosophers, who draw attention to the centrality of the social values of solidarity. For example, the philosopher and zoologist, Peter Kropotkin (1842–1921),[61] an advocate of anarcho-Communism, contradicted Darwin's thesis of natural selection. He claimed that animals in the wild develop not only through natural selection but also, with emphasis on "also," through solidarity. This is an interesting claim, which only eighty years later, sociobiological studies proved to be correct.

Another nonmainstream philosopher, who therefore was pushed to the sidelines, was George Herbert Mead (1863–1931),[62] a contemporary who was oppositional to Freud. He claimed that from a psychological

---

59 Mordechai Lensky, "Problems of Disease in the Warsaw Ghetto," *Yad Vashem Studies*, 3 (1959), p. 87.
60 Kaplan, *Scroll of Agony*, p. 131.
61 Peter Kropotkin, *Mutual Aid: A Factor of Evolution* (Mineola: Dover, 2006).
62 George Cronk, "George Herbert Mead (1863–1931)," The Internet Encyclopedia of Philosophy, http://www.iep.utm.edu/mead (accessed August 29, 2021).

point of view, our personality construct is social and not individualistic, and that we need each other to develop the sense of "I." The source of this claim is the Jewish philosopher, Edmund Gustav Albrecht Husserl (1859–1938), who was known as the father of phenomenology, which asserts that the significant factor in understanding human behavior is people's personal, subjective interpretation of how they perceive the world. Following the Nazis' anti-Jewish legislation in 1933, he was barred access to the library in Freiburg and was dismissed from his post. His ideas were later expanded in existentialist philosophy,[63] especially by the religious Jewish philosopher, Emmanuel Lévinas (1906–1995), who emphasized the value of "sociality" and "otherness" as a highly important part of the life of the individual and the group.[64]

Additional inspiration in this direction may be drawn from the work of the American Jewish psychologist Marshall B. Rosenberg, who established an important center in California for education to promote nonviolence and solidarity—The Center for Nonviolent Communication (NVC). His approach, which he developed in the 1960s, is also referred to as compassionate communication. It seems that Rosenberg's work originated in thinking about the concentration camps. Whereas all the sociological and psychological literature dealt with the question of the loss of humanity, Marshall Rosenberg was interested specifically in the opposite question: How did people who were living under impossible conditions still succeed in preserving their humanity and displayed astonishing aspects of humaneness, compassion, solidarity, and closeness? He claims that these phenomena were far more significant than the "usual," expected phenomena of the loss of humanity.[65]

---

63 See, for example, Edmund Gustav Albrecht Husserl, *Al Hafenomenologiya Shel Habein-subyektiviyut* (Hebrew) (Tel Aviv: Resling, 2016); Husserl, *Mivhar Ma'amarim* (Hebrew) (Jerusalem: Magnes, 1993); Shamay Zinger, *Kinun Ha'ani Ha'aher Bafenominologiya Shel Husserl Vehabikoret Shel Sartre* (Hebrew) (Jerusalem: The Hebrew University of Jerusalem, 2000).

64 See, for example, Zeev Levy, *Ha'aher Veha'ahrayut: Iyunim Bafilosofia Shel Emmanuel Levinas* (Hebrew) (Jerusalem: Magnes, 1997); Emmanuel Lévinas, *Humanism of the Other* (Champaign: University of Illinois, 2003); Lévinas, *Difficult Freedom: Essays on Judaism* (Baltimore: Johns Hopkins University, 1997); Chilik Weizman, *Solidariyut Yehudit Lifnei Ve'aharei Hashoah—Leshe'elat Musag Hayahid Vehayahad Bayahadut* (Hebrew), http://www.yadvashem.org/he/articles/general/solidarity.html (accessed August 29, 2021).

65 Marshall Rosenberg, *Nonviolent Communication: A Language of Life* (Encinitas: Puddle Dancer Press, 2003), pp. 1–14.

The research of Kristen Renwick Monroe,[66] a professor at the University of California and the recipient of an abundance of academic prizes, poses an interesting challenge for those seeking the motivating factors for human behavior in situations of genocide. Kristen, an expert in political psychology, has written a trilogy on altruism. Among the people whom she researched are Holocaust survivors and their rescuers, who saved Jews at great personal risk. She interviewed Holocaust survivors and their rescuers, including the Righteous Among the Nations, and presents an emotional, cognitive, and sociopolitical "model" of altruism. It seems that the examples mentioned earlier in relation to the medical system and the physicians' activities in the ghetto may strengthen these theories to a large extent and may illustrate more intensely how human beings are naturally altruistic, or at least, are capable of performing altruistic deeds, even in extreme situations.

Conclusion

I have described the characteristic components of the establishment of the Jewish medical system in the ghetto and have pointed out the inhuman difficulties that confronted the medical staff, without disregarding the darker side of those who did not behave according to medical and humane standards. Nevertheless, when observing the medical and nursing activities of the Jews in the ghetto in the broader context of sealed locations in wartime, and especially when comparing these events to other cases of genocide, this was doubtlessly an extraordinary phenomenon.

In the eyes of a considerable number of researchers and witnesses, the majority of physicians, nurses, and other medical staff were moral saints who were altruistically motivated to risk their lives and to work relentlessly for the sake of their sick and needy brethren. Based on the examples presented in this article, this appears to be a one-sided and rose-colored picture, since the reality was far more complex. Alongside the medical staff's extraordinary heroic and altruistic acts were cases in

---

66 Kristen Renwick Monroe, *The Heart of Altruism: Perceptions of A Common Humanity* (Princeton: Princeton University Press, 1996); Monroe, *The Hand of Compassion: Portraits of Moral Choice during the Holocaust* (Princeton: Princeton University Press, 2004); Monroe, *Ethics in an Age of Terror and Genocide: Identity, Political Psychology, and Moral Choice* (Princeton: Princeton University Press, 2011).

which basic egoism overcame solidarity and concern for others, and led to immoral behavior. The behavior of the medical staff, as individuals, did not differ significantly from the behavior of other officials in the ghetto. All of them were faced with unparalleled ethical and moral tests. Collectively, however, the Jewish medical system that was established in the Warsaw ghetto drew out the best of the physicians and scientists. Despite the immense diversity among them, they were motivated by a sense of mutual responsibility and solidarity, which has been manifested in times of distress throughout Jewish history, and even during the Holocaust, they set up a professional, humane medical system, which was much greater than the sum of its individual parts.

Testing Solidarity

Collaborators Attempt to Seize Key Positions in the Kovno Ghetto

RAMI NEUDORFER

This study investigates tensions in the Kovno (Kaunas) ghetto between the Ältestenrat (Council of Elders, Jewish Council) and two collaborators who attempted to take over the council and the Jüdische Ghetto-Polizei (ghetto Jewish police) in Slobodka (Vilijampolė), Josef Caspi-Serebrovitz and Benjamin (Benno) Lipzer.

Many ghettos saw a great deal of tension between the population and the Ältestenrat and, a fortiori, between the population and the Jewish police, which was largely perceived as a collaborationist force.[1] Against this background, alternative leaderships such as self-help organizations, political movements, and underground groups, surfaced in many ghettos, and the acute stress between them and the German-imposed official leadership sometimes escalated into outright confrontations.

In the Kovno ghetto, matters were totally different. The Ältestenrat there was headed by people whom the ghetto population usually found acceptable. Under the grim conditions of the ghetto, the population mostly perceived them as doing their best for the masses under the dire conditions of the occupation. The Jewish police, too, who in other ghettos helped to carry out the murder and transport of the Jews to their death, were highly regarded, relatively speaking, largely due to their widely known assistance to underground activity in the ghetto. However, it is necessary to note there were also severe allegations of corruption and

---

1 The Warsaw and Łódź ghettos come to mind. For a detailed analysis of the relationship between the Jewish ghetto community and the Jewish police, see Aharon Weiss "Hamishtara HaYehudit BaGeneral Gouvernemant UviShlezia Ilit Bitkufat Hashoah" (Hebrew) (PhD diss., the Hebrew University of Jerusalem, 1973). Very few police forces were viewed as acting with the interests of the ghetto residents in mind.

favoritism, even among the council and police employees. In this essay, I review the factors that, in my opinion, explain the sense of relative solidarity in the Kovno ghetto; identify the people who attempted to take control of the council and the elements that supported them; and determine how far their efforts succeeded and in what ways they failed, and why.

When the Germans occupied Kovno, on June 24, 1941, they found about 35,000 Jews there, including refugees from occupied Poland, who together accounted for about one-fourth of the total population. By July 8, 6,000–7,000 of them had been murdered, most of them by Lithuanian "partisans," and many without the involvement of the Germans.[2]

On July 8, 1941, the Jews of Kovno were given until August 15 to move to a ghetto that would be established in a suburb called Slobodka, in the Jews' parlance. On August 4, at an assembly replete with emotion, community activists elected Dr. Elchanan Elkes, a well-known and respected physician, as the chairman of the Ältestenrat, which became operative on August 8.[3] The council's initial members were Leib Garfunkel; Michael (Moisei) Kopelman, commander of the Jewish police; Grigory Wolf; the noted literary researcher Dr. Chaim Nachman Shapira; and Hirsch Levin of the Betar movement. The Ältestenrat immediately recruited the core members of the Jewish police force, placing Zionist-minded, young people who were active in the ghetto resistance in command. Therefore, at least relative to other ghettos, there was a measure of solidarity between the population and the Ältestenrat in Kovno. Even the police were generally thought of favorably. Let us try to understand why.

The Composition of the Ältestenrat and the Police

The Jews themselves appointed the Ältestenrat members. Dr. Elchanan Elke, a revered and familiar figure was named chairman. His deputy, Leib Garfunkel, was a long-time Zionist operative, a former member of the Lithuanian Seimas (parliament), and a well-known newspaper

---

2   For sources on the numerical estimates, see Christoph Dieckmann, *Deutsche Besatzungspolitik in Litauen 1941–1944*, vol. 1 (Göttingen: Wallstein, 2011), p. 331n140.

3   This term is German; in Yiddish, it was rendered in transliteration: Eltestenrat. It was known in Hebrew as Va'ad Ziknei Ha'eda (Committee of Elders of the Community).

editor in Kovno. The police force was headed largely by representatives of the Zionist youth movements, who combined ongoing underground movement activity with their service in the police.

Relations with the Ghetto Resistance

An underground Zionist entity—a secret umbrella organization set up shortly after ghettoization—operated in the ghetto in parallel with the Ältestenrat. Its name, Matzok, was an acronym of the Hebrew Merkaz Tsiyonei Slobodka–Kovno—the Slobodka–Kovno Zionist Center. Most of its leaders were high-level officials in the Ältestenrat and the police.[4] Elkes, Garfunkel, and the Ältestenrat secretary, Avraham Golub (later Tory), were members. The police commanders obeyed Matzok's instructions and assisted in clandestine cultural activities in the ghetto. Furthermore, most of the commanders of the police were also leading or prominent figures in the ghetto Zionist underground movements. As time passed, the Ältestenrat and the police cooperated closely and, together with the Communist resistance, smuggled more than 150 equipped and armed fighters to partisan bases in the Rudniki forests, approximately 150 kilometers from Kovno—a heroic operation that was basically unmatched in any other ghetto.[5]

Economic, Social, and Cultural Factors in the Kovno Ghetto

The economic conditions in the Kovno ghetto were better in comparison to most other ghettos. No one starved to death and the Ältestenrat managed to set up and maintain a rather large area of farmland that greatly improved the inhabitants' nutrition. The council also attempted to promote the population's welfare through mutual aid, education, culture, health, and social services with the assistance of the police. There were no overt conflicts between the Ältestenrat and the police; the latter obeyed the former unstintingly.

---

4   Dov Levin and Zvie A. Brown, *The Story of an Underground: Resistance of the Jews of Kovno in the Second World War* (Jerusalem: Gefen, 2014), p. 63.
5   Ibid.

Selection of the Jews for Transport

From the establishment of the ghetto to the March 1944 Children's *Aktion*, when the Jewish police was liquidated, the Ältestenrat was not forced to select Jews for transport to murder. The reason for this may have been the Germans' fear that the Ältestenrat would refuse to comply.

The Demise of the Jewish Police

In retrospect, the bitter end of the Jewish police abets the relatively positive assessment of the force. On March 27, 1944, all the members of the police force were transported to the Ninth Fort, where they were interrogated under torture in order to extract information about the resistance organizations.[6] Forty policemen were murdered, including most of the commanders, who had been members of the Jewish resistance.[7] The force was obliterated at this time and was replaced by the Ordnungsdienst (Order Service) under the command of a collaborator who obeyed the Germans in every matter. All sources perceive the Ordnungsdienst as the antithesis to the prevailing assessment of its precursor.[8]

Two of the many testimonies that are presented below capture the inhabitants' feelings about the comportment of the Ältestenrat and the police. One of the survivors of the ghetto, Prof. Kalman Perk, wrote the following in his memoirs:

> The Jewish police in greater part were accepted among the residents of the ghetto, and some of the policemen, especially the commanders,

---

6   For a fascinating testimony about the ex post reassessment of the police, see Eliezer Yerushalmi, *Pinkas Shavli: Yoman Migeto Lita'i (1941–1944)* (Hebrew) (Jerusalem: Bialik Institute and Yad Vashem, 1958), p. 64. In his entry for February 21, 1941, Yerushalmi presents an especially derogatory description of the police: "Its people are irresponsible, vile, and morally corrupt....They gorge themselves on food and drink and lead lives of debauchery at the expense of their oppressed, deprived brethren." On March 30, 1944, he added a footnote on the same page: "All the information about the Jewish police was not reported objectively and does not square with the truth."

7   For a quantitative analysis, see Rami Neudorfer, "Hamishtara Hayehudit Begeto Kovna: Hronika Shel Nigudim" (Hebrew) (master's thesis, Tel Aviv University, May 2015), p. 85.

8   The Ordnungsdienst was commanded by the collaborator Benjamin (Benno) Lipzer.

were members or associates of the resistance. Thus, their murder left the Jews of the ghetto defenseless.[9]

Irena Adamowicz, a young Pole born in Warsaw and a pious Catholic who had been active in the Armia Krajowa (Home Army), provided a gripping testimony that compares the situation in the Kovno ghetto with that in other ghettos in Poland and Lithuania. In the summer of 1942, she had carried out dangerous missions for Jewish resistance groups in the Warsaw, Białystok, Vilna, and Kovno ghettos, in which she visited and met with the ghetto leaderships and Zionist youth movements. She relates,

> I saw the Jewish police while I was in the Kovno ghetto and saw how they went about their work. They looked to me like what you might call an internal *hagana* [the Hebrew word for defense] and not like a tool in German hands. The internal organization in the ghetto and cooperation among [political] parties, Matzok in particular, seemed altogether amazing to me. I compared it with everything I knew about other ghettos. There, everything was so different. The fragmentation and the contrasts there were so deep....To me, the way of your leadership, combining organic work and resistance, was smarter.[10]

Due to this state of affairs in which there were no severe conflicts between the ghetto leadership and the police, and between both of them and the public, alternative leaderships of the kinds described above were not formed in the Kovno ghetto. However, other individuals and entities did attempt to seize positions of power in the ghetto. At issue are collaborators who operated overtly in the ghetto throughout its existence, along with established groups of supporters who aided them and tried to exploit their strength, their influence on the German authorities, and the distress of the ghetto inhabitants in order to seize key positions in the ghetto Jews' "self-rule" mechanisms. They sought material emoluments, "respect," and to incite fear among the Ältestenrat heads and the police. They also wished to please their German masters

---

9 Kalman Perk, *Shetihiye Ben Adam: Darki Mehashoah Leolam Hamada* (Hebrew) (self-pub., 2013), p. 25.
10 Irena Adamowicz testimony, May 8, 1958, Oral History Division, Avraham Harman Institute of Contemporary Jewry, the Hebrew University of Jerusalem, E/415.

and show them how helpful they could be to carry out their schemes. The two main characters who acted in this manner were Josef Caspi-Serebrovitz and Benjamin (Benno) Lipzer. Their actions spanned the German occupation era, from June 24, 1941, through the establishment of the ghetto on August 14, 1941, and up to the liquidation of the ghetto on July 8, 1944.

The massive Ghetto Police Archive (hereinafter Police Archive), has not yet been researched adequately. The narrative, entitled "Geshikhte fun der Viliampoler Geto Politsei" (History of the Vilijampolė Jewish Ghetto Police), in particular, sheds new and fascinating light on these people and their incessant attempts to dominate the Ältestenrat, the police, and the Labor Office.[11] This new information makes many references to Caspi-Serebrovitz and Lipzer in the research literature and in important memoirs about the Kovno ghetto.[12] Both of them and the terror that they inflicted on the ghetto and its inhabitants are mentioned in many of the testimonies and memoirs of the ghetto residents. Reports about Caspi-Serebrovitz and Lipzer reached beyond the ghetto boundaries as well.

11 Anonymous, *The Clandestine History of the Kovno Jewish Ghetto Police: By Anonymous Members of the Kovno Jewish Ghetto Police*, trans. and ed. by Samuel Schalkowsky (Bloomington: Indiana University Press and the United States Holocaust Memorial Museum, 2014). The archives were buried in the ground during the infamous Children's *Aktion* on March 27, 1944, and were found twenty years later as foundations for a building were being dug. On the interment of the archives, see Azriel Levi testimony, September 1991, Massuah Archive, AR-T-022-5, pp. 11–12. On the discovery of the archives in 1966 and what happened to them, see Dov Levin and Ester Meirovitsh-Shvarts, "Geshikhte fun der Yidishe Politsei in Kovner Geto" (Yiddish), *YIVO Bleter,* (*New Series*, vol. 3) (1997), pp. 206–294. The archive contains about 30,000 documents and 40,000 pages. The collection is kept in the Lithuanian Central State Archives (LCVA), R-973-1, R-973-2, R-973-3.

12 A study of major importance in describing the duo's misdeeds is Avraham Tory, *Surviving the Holocaust: The Kovno Ghetto Diary* (Cambridge: Harvard University Press, 1990). The book and the documents have also been published in Hebrew and Lithuanian. The book also contains many of the archive documents that Tory buried; almost all of them are in German and Lithuanian and about half are of Jewish provenance. Important details are also revealed in Yosef Gar, *Umkum fun Yidisher Kovne* (Yiddish) (Munich: Farband Fun Litvishe Yidn in der Amerikaner Zone in Deitshland, 1948). Both collaborators are also mentioned in Leib Garfunkel, *Kovna Hayehudit Behurbana* (Hebrew) (Jerusalem: Yad Vashem, 1959). Additional important sources are the books by Moshe Segalson, who was in charge of the large ghetto workshops, and his nephew, Arie Segalson; see Moshe Segalson, *Mayne Zikhroynes, 1941–1948* (Yiddish) (self-pub., 1961); Arie Segalson, *Belev Ha'ofel, Kilyona Shel Kovna Hayehudit: Mabat Mibifnim* (Hebrew) (Jerusalem: Yad Vashem, 2003).

The first to attain a position of influence in the ghetto was the Gestapo agent Josef Caspi-Serebrovitz. A native of Rokiškis (known as Rakishok by the Jews), he was a school principal, a teacher of Hebrew literature, a journalist, and a member of the Betar Movement. Before the war, he had evidently been a Lithuanian police detective.[13] After spending the 1940–1941 period of Soviet occupation in prison, Caspi-Serebrovitz was released when the Nazis moved in and he became a Gestapo informant. He was allowed to continue living in Kovno with his family, to carry a firearm that he had received from the Germans, and to move about without donning the yellow star. Yosef Gar remarks,

> Caspi-Serebrovitz, who had belonged to the Revisionist Movement in Lithuania before the war, tried to persuade his Gestapo masters that Ahimeir's Revisionist faction, of which he was a member before the war and which was called Kegn Strom [against the current], was pronouncedly anti-British and that the Kegn Strom movement identified with Hitler and with the *Aks Melukhes* [Axis powers].[14]

Caspi-Serebrovitz launched his career of betrayal immediately after the Germans occupied the area. He attempted to arrange the liquidation of the heads of the town's Jewish community and have himself appointed as chair of the Komitet, the committee in charge of transferring the Jews of Kovno to the ghetto in Slobodka, which was established when the Germans issued the ghettoization order on July 8, 1941. In the Kovno SD archives, I found unmediated and clear proof of Caspi-Serebrovitz's denunciations of the leading Jewish activists in Kovno, including the head of the Komitet, Garfunkel; Grigory Wolf; the scholar Dr. Chaim Nachman Shapira; journalists; and numerous "Communists."

The main target of Caspi-Serebrovitz's denunciation was the attorney Leib Garfunkel, deputy chair of the Ältestenrat, a Zionist leader, a public activist in Lithuania, a cofounder and first editor of the Yiddish-language Zionist daily newspaper *Di Idishe Shtime*, secretary of the executive committee of the Nazionalrat (national council) of Lithuanian Jewry and subsequently its vice president, and a member of the Lithuanian

---

13 Gar, *Umkum*, p. 114; Anonymous, *The Clandestine History*, pp. 23, 24, 302–318. Yosef Gar was a functionary in the Jewish Labor Office in the Kovno ghetto. After the war he wrote several books and articles about his life and about the ghetto.
14 Ibid.

Seimas (parliament). In the Kovno ghetto, he headed the Komitet and then served as the de facto chairman of the Ältestenrat in the absence of the frequently bedridden Elchanan Elkes.

The Kovno SD archives, preserved in the Lithuanian Central State Archives (LCVA), contain numerous documents from the early days of the German occupation. They yield detailed incriminating information against many Jews who lived in Kovno, including serious, trumped-up charges against Ältestenrat heads whom the Germans themselves had appointed.[15] The documents are clearly signed by SS *Hauptscharführer* Helmut Rauca.[16]

In an intelligence report dated July 29, 1941, titled "Deutschfeindliche Jüdische Politiker" (Anti-German Jewish politicians), Rauca notes Leib Garfunkel's age, occupation, and address, and then devotes a full page to dire accusations against Garfunkel in regard to German affairs. For example, he describes Garfunkel as a *"Persönlicher Freund des Pro-Englisch jüdischer Politikers Prof. Weizmanns"* (a personal friend of the pro-English Jewish politician Prof. Weizmanns [sic]) and a personal friend of the Socialist leader Chaim Arlosoroff.[17] Rauca continues, depicting Garfunkel as an important member of the boycott Germany committee in 1934–1936 and a man of Marxist and pro-British worldviews. He adds that Garfunkel had raised funds for the Spanish Red Army during the Spanish Civil War. Rauca concedes that Garfunkel had been imprisoned by the Bolsheviks, but specifies that this was only until the end of October 1940. Garfunkel was then released, says Rauca, with the help of a fellow Communist Party member named Grinberg, who had denounced many right-wing *"prominenti"* in Lithuania and helped to have Garfunkel set free by so doing.[18] As for what really happened, Grinberg had headed

---

15 For numerous denunciation documents against the heads of the Komitet, senior Ältestenrat officials, journalists, and public figures who had socialist or communist leanings, and who are all presented as dangerous enemies of the Reich, see LCVA, R-1399-1-15.

16 Rauca was a member of Einsatzkommando 3 and a prime culprit in the murder of the Jews of Kovno. After the war, he fled to Canada. In 1983, he was extradited to West Germany, following protracted legal proceedings. He died there before his trial could begin. See *Federal Republic of Germany and Rauca*: Canada, Ontario Court of Appeal, April 12, 1983, International Law Reports 88 (1992), S. 278–301.

17 Arlosoroff, of course, had been assassinated eight years before.

18 Grinberg is almost certainly Ika Grinberg, a leading personality in the Irgun Brit Zion (ABZ), a Zionist underground movement, which had initially operated against the Soviet authorities. Grinberg, a Zionist and an anti-Communist, had no entrée to

an anti-Soviet, Zionist, resistance movement called Irgun Brit Zion (ABZ), which had been established when the Soviet occupation began, but continued to operate against the Germans after the Nazis moved in. Even while in prison, Rauca relates, Garfunkel did not conceal his antipathy to the Germans and was released only due to the exertions of highly influential friends in Mandatory Palestine, Britain, and America.

The intelligence paper on Garfunkel combines copious information on its subject's personal and political life with false and tendentious allegations designed to besmirch him in German eyes. It is almost certainly the product of betrayal; the more closely it is studied, the stronger this conjecture becomes.[19] A painstaking study of the denunciation documents shows that some of them bear the expression "*abgegeben durch V-Mann S*" in Rauca's tiny penmanship. *V-Mann* is a common abbreviation of *Vertrauens-Mann*, meaning that the information had been submitted by "undercover agent S." It is my conjecture that "S" denotes Serebrovitz, Rauca being his handler. After presenting this torrent of incriminating details about the Ältestenrat leaders, Rauca notes that the latter will have to be done away with one day but adds, "For practical reasons, we found it undesirable for a member of the Kegn Strom group to be represented on the Komitet—the precursor of the Ältestenrat."[20]

In view of Gar's aforementioned quotation, the betrayer who attempted to oust the heads of the Ältestenrat must have been Caspi-Serebrovitz. This is almost certainly the same man who tried to denounce and succeed the chair of the Ältestenrat in an act that recalls the Prophet Elijah's outrage: "Would you murder and also inherit?"[21] Garfunkel did not know who had falsely denounced him. In his important book, *Kovna Hayehudit Behurbana* (Jewish Kovno in Ruins) published in 1959, he

the Soviet officialdom in Lithuania. Eventually he became a high-ranking officer in the Kovno ghetto Jewish police. He was murdered during the Children's *Aktion* on March 27–28, 1944, because of his connections with the resistance.

19 Another document by Rauca assails the "plutocrat" Grigory Wolf, who was also an "enemy of Germany. According to Rauca, Garfunkel and Wolf were the de facto leaders of the Ältestenrat who should not be left in office in view of their psychological influence on the Jewish masses. The SD archives contain much additional information about Jews and also non-Jews, who had to be dealt with, under the headings "Dangerous Bolshevik Agents" and "German-Hating Jewish Journalists." On each man, there is terse biographical information and rationales for labeling him an "enemy of Germany" who deserves to be liquidated.

20 LCVA, R-1399-1-15.

21 I Kings 21:19.

bluntly decried Caspi-Serebrovitz's adverse influence on the ghetto but added, "In fact, he caused neither the entire ghetto nor individual Jews the troubles that someone so close to the authorities could have caused."[22] Today, however, we know from many testimonies that Caspi-Serebrovitz betrayed hundreds of Jewish "enemies of the Reich" to the Germans. This, however, was not the end of Caspi-Serebrovitz's attempts to take over the ghetto institutions. Before I document them, I will describe his complex and contentious persona and try to follow the traces of the organization that he ostensibly headed, Kegn Strom.

While Caspi-Serebrovitz, as mentioned, was allowed to live outside the ghetto, he visited the ghetto often, not wearing the yellow star and armed with a handgun, inciting fear among the heads of the police and of the Ältestenrat. He dominated the Jewish police in practical terms for several months in the course of various power struggles in the ghetto. Caspi-Serebrovitz was not only an informer for the Gestapo but he also established close friendships with the Gestapo hacks in Kovno. On June 22 or 23, 1942, for example, he threw a party in his home—evidently an orgy of sorts—in which he hosted Rauca and other senior Gestapo officials.[23]

According to "Geshikhte fun der Viliampoler Geto Politsei," the police maneuvered Caspi-Serebrovitz into being their representative, if not their patron, vis-à-vis the Ältestenrat. It is hard to understand from the document who did this maneuvering and how. Further on, however, the authors of "Geshikhte Fun der Viliampoler Geto Politsei," willingly or not, report that they depended on Caspi-Serebrovitz and leaned on his broad shoulders. Thus, for a short time he became the de facto boss of the police. He spent whole days sitting at headquarters and wielding his control from there....Ten times a day he proclaimed himself the chief of police and the others [the members of the force] heeded him and gave him their respect—first, because they were afraid, and second, because they needed him.[24]

Caspi-Serebrovitz set up an organization within the force called "A getreie grupe politsisn" (A Loyal Group of Policemen), made up of Revisionist policemen, cronies, and personal friends—a force within the force, as it were. The group, the author of "Geshikhte fun der Viliampoler

---

22 Garfunkel, *Kovna Hayehudit Behurbana*, p. 244.
23 Tory, *Surviving the Holocaust*, p. 99.
24 Anonymous, *The Clandestine History*, pp. 303–304.

Geto Politsei," alleges, pledged allegiance to Caspi-Serebrovitz and took part in his orgy.[25] "Geshikhte fun der Viliampoler Geto Politsei," paints an excoriating, complex, and highly contradictory portrait of Caspi-Serebrovitz. It describes him as a pathological honor seeker, a drunkard, a hedonist, a skirt chaser, an indefatigable babbler, and also a healthy and very handsome man who was, however, "sick" in body and soul. He is depicted as follows:

> He was an amiable Jew, a fervent nationalist, constantly proclaiming to be a Revisionist Zionist....
> ...On the other hand, it did not bother him, as a Jew and a Zionist, to sell out to the Gestapo...to be the one at whom fingers were quietly pointed, "here goes the Jew who serves the Gestapo."[26]

In his diary, Avraham Tory (Golub), also mentions in disgust a long and vainglorious speech that an armed Caspi-Serebrovitz delivered to the Ältestenrat. In his speech, Caspi-Serebrovitz described himself as a savior of the ghetto, and the handgun he was given by the Germans, as a symbol of real power.

> "The moment will come," Caspi-Serebrovitz prophesied, "when there will be a need to take out twenty-five innocent men....Delegations come to me and to Lipzer, Caspi-Serebrovitz continued...This may cost us in blood. The situation, must be brought to an end. The dreamers and fighters have discovered a new phenomenon: a Jew with a gun. Namely me, Caspi-Serebrovitz, a living legend who will go down in Jewish history. I will be with you at every stage, but you have to accept me the way I am."[27]

Many witnesses testify that Caspi-Serebrovitz snitched on ghetto inhabitants in many other cases. Zvi Levin, a prominent member of the Ältestenrat, states that Caspi-Serebrovitz denounced Communists to the Gestapo.[28] According to another witness, it was Caspi-Serebrovitz who provided the Germans with the list of individuals who would be

---

25 Ibid., p. 310–311.
26 Ibid., p. 311.
27 Tory, *Surviving the Holocaust*, p. 358.
28 Zvi Levin interview by Dov Levin, June 3, 1973, Oral History Division, Institute of Contemporary Jewry, the Hebrew University of Jerusalem, film 100/339.

murdered in the "Intellectuals *Aktion*."[29] Tory (Golub) recorded two additional cases in his diary: a hunt for three escapees from the ghetto in November 1941 and the arrest of Erich Kohn, whom Caspi-Serebrovitz had denounced to the Gestapo.[30]

Did Caspi-Serebrovitz truly head a pro-Nazi Jewish students' organization called Kegn Strom? Had such a Jewish organization existed anywhere in Lithuania, let alone in Kovno? Apart from Garfunkel's testimony, which accurately reports Caspi-Serebrovitz's remarks, and apart from the German intelligence documents, I found no evidence of the existence of such an entity in prewar Lithuania. However, an extreme, right-wing, Jewish periodical under that name appeared in Kovno between the wars, and perhaps Caspi-Serebrovitz was involved in it. A police investigation file from May 1942, however, contains documents on the investigation of Jews who were suspected of the forbidden smuggling of letters into the Vilna ghetto; one of those interrogated mentioned his membership in the organization.[31] The suspect—Leibas Ippas (in Lithuanian; Leib Arie Ipp in Yiddish), a twenty-seven-year-old student whose letter to the Vilna ghetto was intercepted by the Germans, was interrogated:

- To whom in Vilna were the letters that you sent addressed?
- To a friend and colleague of mine in Josef Glazman's movement.[32]
- What kind of colleague in the movement?
- Both of us belonged to a right-wing students' organization called Kegn Strom, [composed] of Fascist Jews.[33]

---

29 Wolfram Wette, *Karl Jäger: Mörder der litauischen Juden* (Frankfurt am Main: Fischer Taschenbuch, 2011), p. 99.

30 Tory, *Surviving the Holocaust*, p. 191. Kohn had served in the German army in World War I and had been awarded the Iron Cross. Caspi-Serebrovitz denounced him for not wearing the yellow star while purchasing food in Kovno.

31 LCVA, R-973-2-69, documents 54–84.

32 Ibid. Yosef Glazman was a partisan leader, an associate of the Betar movement, and a leading personality in the Vilna ghetto resistance during the Holocaust. After a stint as head of the ghetto police, he was ousted by Jacob Gens, due to his underground activity. Together with Abba Kovner and others he established the Fareynikte Partizaner Organizatsye (United Partisan Organization, FPO). In 1943, he fell as a partisan in combat against the Germans.

33 Ibid.

The suspect goes on to mention another man of like mind in the Kovno ghetto, Hirsch Levin. Hirsch (Zvi) Levin, however, was a senior member of the Kovno ghetto Ältestenrat. Not only was Levin, like Glazman, not pro-Nazi, but he was in charge of the relations between the Ältestenrat and the Communist underground and acted indefatigably to smuggle armed partisans to the forests. Ippas stated that the Bolsheviks had exiled most members of Kegn Strom to Siberia and that only ten of them remained by the time of the investigation.

Ostensibly, we have found a document that confirms the existence of a pro-German organization headed by Caspi-Serebrovitz. Ippas even insinuates that Josef Glazman, a leader of the anti-German resistance in the Vilna ghetto, as previously stated, belonged to it. Various witnesses, including Zvi Levin himself, who survived the war and gave his testimony to Prof. Dov Levin in the 1960s, state that Caspi-Serebrovitz himself had orchestrated the interrogations, and that the organization had never existed. Caspi-Serebrovitz had apparently put the remarks about the pro-Nazi organization in the suspect's mouth in order to play down the gravity of the offense or, perhaps, to burnish his status in the Germans' eyes.[34] Another possibility is that Caspi-Serebrovitz had belonged to a pro-fascist, Lithuanian organization before the war. Zelik Kalmanovitz of Vilna mentions this rumor in his diary.[35] Somehow, Caspi-Serebrovitz managed to smooth over the forbidden smuggling of letters, which in fact did take place between the Betar members in Kovno and in Vilna, and no one was punished.

To secure status among the Jews in the ghetto that would overstep German support, Caspi-Serebrovitz exploited his influence with the Germans to release from detention Jews who had been interned in the ghetto. Generally, however, he terrorized the ghetto population. He frequently visited the Vilna ghetto, where he also terrified the population and probably tried to establish a dominant position there too. Herman Kruk of Vilna mentions him five times in his important diary.[36] On September 17, 1941, for example, he writes:

34 Zvi Levin interview by Dov Levin, June 3, 1973, Oral History Division, Avraham Harman Institute of Contemporary Jewry, the Hebrew University of Jerusalem, film 100/339.
35 Zelik Kalmanovitz, "Yoman Geto Vilna" (Hebrew), *Yalkut Moreshet*, (1977), p. 74.
36 Herman Kruk, *The Last Days of the Jerusalem of Lithuania: Chronicles from the Vilna Ghetto and the Camps, 1939–1944*. (New Haven: YIVO Institute for Jewish Research, 2002), pp. 114, 121, 151, 208, 339.

A guest came from Kovno. The visitor, one Kasper Serebrovich, was in the apartment of the Police Chief Gens. A witness told about it: a young, handsome, lively fellow came into the room, and insolently tore open the coffers, and took out chocolate. Leather gloves, leather, cloth...[37]

On September 29, Kruk describes the terror that Caspi-Serebrovitz had inflicted on the Vilna ghetto several weeks after it was established.

Kasper Serebrovich, a man with a disgusting past, a Kovno Revisionist, by the way, is one of them. Here, in this sad situation, he has emerged as a patron of Kovno Jewry. He shouts, he orders, and everybody trembles...often comes from Kovno to Vilna and tries to extend his rule here too.[38]

One of Caspi-Serebrovitz's most harmful practices was his incessant attempt to scale back the number of Ältestenrat and police personnel, and increase the number of forced laborers in the ghetto.

Caspi-Serebrovitz's senior status in the ghetto as the superintendent of police affairs is evidenced in two documents from the Police Archive that were sent to him as chief of police on July 1 and July 2, 1942.[39] In the first, signed by police commander Kopelman and written in a somewhat obsequious tenor ("Humbly..."), the commander gives a brief account of changes in the structure of the police headquarters that were made due to pressure by Caspi-Serebrovitz. In the second, Kopelman elaborates on the reasons that, in his opinion, the police contingent should be left untouched. Kopelman lists new tasks assigned to the police, such as inspecting the paving of the ghetto's two streets, beefing up of the police presence at the workshops, and the need for more police to guard the gardens. Kopelman concludes by expressing his hopes that Caspi-Serebrovitz, too, will realize that downsizing the force will impair its duties and asks him to "convey this position to the competent authorities." Several days later, nevertheless, the police force was reduced by twenty posts.[40]

---

37 Ibid., p. 114. Kruk mistook Caspi-Serebrovitz's name, referring to him as "Kasper-Serebrovich."
38 Ibid., p. 121.
39 LCVA, R-973-2-69-25-26, R973-2-94-1.
40 Anonymous, *The Clandestine History*, p. 312.

Another person, who was also boastful of his close relations with the Germans, helped Caspi-Serebrovitz at this time: Benjamin (Benno) Lipzer. Lipzer was something like a mirror image of Caspi-Serebrovitz. Born in Gardinas (Grodno) on March 22, 1908, he had been an agent for a radio company before the war. Arrested by the Lithuanians early in the war, he assembled a group of skilled workers in prison—tailors, cobblers, mechanics, and carpenters—and offered their services to the Gestapo even before the ghetto was established. He headed this collectivity while serving as a "brigadier"—a foreman of a group of forced laborers—of the Jews who worked at the offices of the German security services. Lipzer envied Caspi-Serebrovitz for his "senior" status and aspired to succeed him as the Germans' leading collaborator. He initially presented himself as the head of the labor group at the SD headquarters. He later signed documents as the "Authorized Representative of the SIPO and the SD," with the Germans' knowledge and approval.[41]

In the early months of 1942, Caspi-Serebrovitz and Lipzer served concurrently as an alternative establishment, as it were, to the Ältestenrat, to which Jews turned to obtain various emoluments from the Germans. In June–July 1942, however, the two men entered into a power struggle, both approaching the German authorities with "efficiency" proposals—fewer police and Ältestenrat personnel, and referral of more Jews to grueling forced labor. On June 29, for example, Judel Zupovich was dismissed from his post as deputy police commander at Caspi-Serebrovitz's initiative.[42] The next day, June 30, two important meetings took place. During the first, which was held in Caspi-Serebrovitz's residence outside the ghetto, he issued threats against the Ältestenrat and particularly against Hirsch Levin. During the second, in the Ältestenrat offices with both Caspi-Serebrovitz and Lipzer in attendance, it was agreed that by order of the Gestapo and in return for their pro-German efforts, Lipzer would be given overarching responsibility for the Labor Office and Caspi-Serebrovitz for the Jewish police.[43] The next day, July 1, 1942, Lipzer sent a document to Rauca, advising him that he had "decided" to slash the Ältestenrat headcount by 75 percent and allow only those

41 For example, Lipzer letter, December 29, 1942, LCVA, R-973-2-19-224.
42 Judel Zupovich, a senior police commander and a leading figure in the resistance, was murdered at the Ninth Fort on March 28, 1944.
43 Tory, *Surviving the Holocaust*, p. 101.

incapable of physical labor to continue working there.[44] Lipzer also recommended broader enforcement of the forced labor requirement in the ghetto. The Germans accepted his "decisions" partway, demanding "only" a 50 percent cutback and ultimately compromising on 25 percent. Within three days, the Ältestenrat's external advisory committee, audit committee, and courts were dissolved and the schools were closed. It was Lipzer who announced this decision to the Ältestenrat. It is very likely that these grave decrees were also adopted at his recommendation.[45] On July 4, 1942, Caspi-Serebrovitz and Lipzer clashed sharply over their "rule" in the ghetto.[46]

The two collaborators struggled for power in the course of 1942, mainly over the question of who could harm the Ältestenrat more. They worked out a "division of labor" of sorts—Caspi-Serebrovitz took charge of the police while Lipzer did the same for the Labor Office, one of the Ältestenrat's most important functions. The Caspi-Serebrovitz–Lipzer feud ended in late July 1942, when Caspi-Serebrovitz and his family were murdered en route to Vilna. The Germans may have discovered Caspi-Serebrovitz's involvement in stifling the investigation of the letters to Vilna. Lipzer may have been involved in Caspi-Serebrovitz's demise. Either way, it is unlikely that he regretted it.[47]

From the elimination of Caspi-Serebrovitz until the destruction of the ghetto, Lipzer was central in ghetto life and institutions. No longer having a rival of Caspi-Serebrovitz's ilk, he enjoyed some success in extending his control to the ghetto police. After Caspi-Serebrovitz's death, Lipzer, the ghetto's "superintendent for labor affairs," attempted to take over additional domains of ghetto institutional life, foremost the police. The heads of the Ältestenrat were so frustrated by his incessant meddling that on September 5, 1942, Garfunkel proposed that the Ältestenrat resign so that Lipzer could replace it with people

---

44 Tory knew only about Lipzer's recommendation to downsize the force by "only" 50 percent; Ibid., p. 102.

45 Ibid., pp. 101–102.

46 Ibid., p. 104–105. The Ältestenrat refused to accept permits to move about freely to the city for its senior members without escorts that Caspi-Serebrovitz provided, because they did not want to be seen as collaborators.

47 One of the documents from the investigation that Caspi-Serebrovitz presided over, as stated, attempts to incriminate Lipzer in knowing about the prohibited exchange of letters. Kruk, worried, noted in his diary on July 29, 1942, that Caspi- Serebrovitz had been posted in Vilna. See Kruk, *The Last Days of the Jerusalem of Lithuania*, p. 339.

loyal to him. The proposal was voted down after a tumultuous debate on the grounds that abandoning the ghetto to Lipzer would be an act of "national irresponsibility."[48] Lipzer demanded the types of powers with which he could manage the police.

On January 1, 1943, Lipzer received a document signed by Elkes giving him responsibility for the police.[49] After demanding this of Elkes, Lipzer was named "Honorary Commander of the Jewish Police" on January 11, 1943.[50] The letter of appointment, dated January 12, 1943, kept in the Police Archive, attests to the ghetto leaders' apprehensions about Lipzer.[51] In this fawning document, the commanders of the police who signed it thank Lipzer for his devotion to the ghetto community in general and particularly to the Jewish police, and name him an honorary member of the police high command. To demonstrate his power, Lipzer also signed the letter of appointment and added the word *einverstanden* (agreed). Lipzer was now authorized to wear a police uniform and to participate in meetings of the police leadership. The next day, the appointment was conferred upon Lipzer in a festive ceremony in which he delivered remarks in Yiddish, written for him by Tory (Golub), as the commanders of the force looked on. In his speech, Lipzer elaborated on everything he had done for the ghetto and said that he had sought neither gratitude nor honor during his term of service, without sensing the irony of the words that Tory (Golub) had placed in his mouth.[52]

On January 4, 1943, Lipzer visited the Ältestenrat offices only to find the heads of the council away at a Matzok meeting.[53] Enraged, he threatened to dismiss the members of the Ältestenrat for having been absent upon his arrival. He was not empowered to take any such step, of course, and the heads of the Ältestenrat forced him to apologize for having offended them. The tension persisted anyway.

48 Tory, *Surviving the Holocaust*, p. 132.
49 For a copy of the document, see Avraham Tory, *Geto Yom-Yom: Yoman Umismahim Migeto Kovna* (Hebrew) (Jerusalem and Tel Aviv: Mossad Bialik and Tel Aviv University, 1988), photo section following p. 302.
50 Ibid., p. 178. Tory despised Lipzer, calling him "unrefined, brazen, and ignorant." Nevertheless, he had to pander to him and posture as his friend because he feared Lipzer's connections with the Gestapo. Tory describes the appointment contemptuously. Evidently, however, Lipzer's involvement in police affairs was meaningful if not central.
51 LCVA, R-973-2-112-1.
52 Tory mentions the speech in his diary but does not reproduce it there. For a copy of the speech, see the LCVA, R-973-2-112-2.
53 Tory, *Geto Yom-Yom: Yoman Umismahim Migeto Kovna*, p. 136.

On January 22, 1943, Lipzer interfered in police affairs in a harsh and crude manner. The head of a labor company that returned to the ghetto with large quantities of food in its rucksacks refused to share the loot with the police gate squad, which had allowed him to smuggle the food in, as was the standard practice in the ghetto. He was arrested and delivered to the ghetto tribunal, where Lipzer sentenced him to ten lashes—the first time that such a thing had happened in the ghetto.[54] Lipzer continued to incite fear among the police. This inanity, Tory (Golub) relates, reached its apex at a performance of the police orchestra that Lipzer arranged on June 5, 1943. At this event, one of Lipzer's cronies wrote a supremely obsequious poem titled *A brief tsu dier* (a letter to you). Lipzer ordered the orchestra director Michel Hofmekeker to set the lyrics to music and play the resulting work at a concert in his honor.[55] The program lists this sycophantic song as "dedicated to Herr B. Lipzer, from the coworkers of his brigade."

The Police Archive also contains thousands of documents in which Lipzer, by now calling himself the "Authorized Representative of the SIPO and the SD," interfered in police affairs to have people arrested at the Germans' behest, sometimes on his own authority, and to release from detention people who applied to him.[56] In a document dated December 29, 1942, for example, Lipzer complained that only a day earlier the police had felt it correct to advise him of the arrest of a woman, whose name is not mentioned, and when he concluded that her detention was unjustified, he ordered her to be released after obtaining his German masters' permission to make this decision.[57]

On January 17, 1943, the police command began to conduct its meetings in Yiddish.[58] That very day, Lipzer started taking part in these meetings and led the discussion. He was also the first to sign the summary of the discussions, in huge handwriting, above the signatures of the police

---

54 Ibid., p. 149. The Germans often invoked the punishment of lashings; this, however, was the first and almost the only time that it was administered at the initiative of Jews.

55 Tory, *Surviving the Holocaust*, p. 369. The concert program was found in the ghetto archives; see LCVA, R-973-2-232-40.

56 Lipzer initially defined himself as the head of the group of Jewish workers at the SD and the SIPO headquarters.

57 LCVA, R-973-2-19-224.

58 Until then, they had been held in Lithuanian. The switch may have taken place, because Lipzer did not know Lithuanian. Summaries of the police command discussions in 1941–1943 appear in LCVA, R-973-2-11.

commander, Kopelman, his deputy, Abramovich, and the person who was considered the de facto commander, Zupovich.[59] Lipzer intervened intensively in all the discussions between the police commanders and submitted proposals on various matters, all of which were accepted. On July 11, 1943, he ordered affixing a sign at the entrance to his apartment: "B. Lipzer, Representative of the Gestapo in the Ghetto and Chief of the Jewish Police."[60]

On August 17, 1943, after months of service as the de facto chief of police, Lipzer surprisingly announced his resignation,[61] offering no reasons for this move and merely noting that it was irrevocable. Attached to his letter were his policeman's certificate, armband, and cap. Despite the resignation, he chaired three subsequent meetings of the police command, doing so until September 15, 1943, the last meeting for which a summary is found in the archives. My conjecture is that Lipzer quit, because he knew about the Germans' intentions of liquidating the police force due to its connections with the resistance.[62] If so, Lipzer and Caspi-Serebrovitz may be understood as tragicomic mirror images of each other. Both boasted about their connections with the Germans. Both appropriated vacuous honors. Both gathered a group of sycophants within the police. Both asked for and received appreciation and respect from the Ältestenrat. Both gave pompous lectures before the council. Both spread fear and terror among the ghetto population.

59 About ten days later, on January 28, 1943, the management of all police affairs began quickly to shift from Lithuanian to Yiddish. On February 1, as noted in *The Clandestine History*, pp. 312–318, "Everything was changed to Yiddish." Lithuanian almost totally disappeared from the archive documents. However, it remained in use in intermittent criminal investigations. In "Geshikhte fun der Viliampoler Geto Politsei," no explanation for the switching of languages is given. The reason may have been that Lipzer did not know Lithuanian and, therefore, demanded, first, that the discussion proceedings take place in Yiddish and, after two additional meetings, that all police affairs be conducted in Yiddish. Another possibility is that Lipzer, who emphasized his "folksy" nature and his closeness to the oppressed population, demanded that Yiddish be adopted so that he could commune with "the people."

60 Tory, *Surviving the Holocaust*, p. 419.

61 Benjamin (Benno) Lipzer's letter of resignation, LCVA, R-973-2-110-7.

62 The process of *Kasernierung* (barracking) in the ghetto began about a month later, in the autumn of 1943. The management of the ghetto was turned over to the SS, the ghetto was officially declared a concentration camp, and its inhabitants were scattered among labor camps near Kovno, or even far from the city. The powers of the police were greatly diminished and the Ältestenrat lost its influence.

Was Lipzer an informer, too? He almost certainly played a key role in liquidating the police force and having its commanders executed in the Children's *Aktion*. According to one testimony, the final selection of the policemen who survived the *Aktion*—one that determined whether they would live or die—was made on the basis of hints that a Gestapo man named Keitel had received from Lipzer.[63] After the police force was liquidated, Lipzer was placed at the helm of its successor, the Ordnungsdienst. The service was subordinate not to the Ältestenrat, which was dissolved on April 8, 1944, but directly to the SD. Lipzer collaborated with the Germans, helped them to flush out bunkers and hiding places, and earned infamy among the ghetto inhabitants.

Lipzer's demise also resembled Caspi-Serebrovitz's. As the ghetto was being liquidated in July 1944, he attempted to go into hiding and, when his place of refuge was discovered, he tried to slip into the ranks of those being deported from the ghetto. However, Wilhelm Göcke, the commandant of the Kovno camp who had searched for him several days later, had him shot because he "knew too much." Still showing signs of life, Lipzer was tossed into the flames of a burning hospital.[64]

Despite all the foregoing, it is important to note that the power and influence of Caspi-Serebrovitz and Lipzer in the ghetto were far from absolute. Despite the honors and the obsequious treatment that they received, they did not exert de facto control over the ghetto police. The Ältestenrat and the police continued to do their jobs; the police commanders continued to aid residents in digging underground hideouts and to help the resistance smuggle partisans to the forests, concealing these feats from both collaborators until their bitter end. Each of these collaborators, however, "succeeded" in harming the ghetto and its population immensely. Dozens, and probably hundreds, of people were murdered because of their denunciations. It is very likely that the liquidation of the Jewish police should also be "credited" to Lipzer. He was certainly the main beneficiary of that act because he was placed at the head of the Ordnungsdienst that did his German masters' bidding. As in many other cases, their betrayals and collaboration did not help to protect them. The Germans murdered both as soon as they were no longer of any use to them.

---

63 Segalson, *Belev Ha'ofel*, p. 28. Gar also mentions Lipzer's "highly suspect" role in the affair. See Gar, *Umkum*, p. 116.

64 Gar writes this with more than a touch of schadenfreude; see Ibid.

To a large extent, solidarity in the Kovno ghetto meant support of the efforts of the Ältestenrat and the Jewish ghetto police, and the lack of an alternative leadership, such as youth movements, self-help organizations, and emerging resistance groups. This situation resulted from two factors:

1. The heads of the council and the senior members of the Jewish ghetto police were themselves also the heads of the youth movements and the secret resistance groups. The members of these groups received privileged and preferential treatment from the departments of the Ältestenrat in the ghetto.
2. Opposition to the official ghetto leadership came from pro-Nazi collaborators, who were suspect and often loathed by the populace.

Unexpected Alliances and Limits of Solidarity

Non-Jewish Aid Organizations and the Jewish Community Assisting Jews and "Non-Aryans" in Vienna, 1938–1945

MICHAELA RAGGAM-BLESCH

fter the "*Anschluss*" (Nazi takeover) in Austria, thousands of people belonging to different religious communities or without denomination were declared Jewish by Nazi racial laws. Since the Jewish community was responsible only for their members, those who were newly defined as Jews—or "non-Aryans"—were left without support, often experiencing exclusion from their Christian congregations. While the Catholic Church officially remained indifferent, the Protestant Churches immediately distanced themselves from their members who were former Jews and excluded them from attending church services. Therefore, the assistance of non-Jewish aid organizations for so-called "non-Aryans" proved to be crucial. In Vienna, there were four main organizations: the Aktion Gildemeester (later, AHO) founded by the Dutch philanthropist Frank van Gheel-Gildemeester; the Society of Friends (Quakers); the Catholic Hilfsstelle (Archiepiscopal Aid Agency for "Non-Aryan" Catholics); and the Protestant Schwedische Mission (Swedish Mission), which was run by Swedish pastors independently from the Austrian Protestant Churches. While initially, the Catholic Hilfsstelle mainly provided help to Catholics who had been declared "non-Aryans," the Schwedische Mission cared for Protestants who had been expelled as Jews from their local communities. The Quaker and the Aktion Gildemeester functioned as non-denominational aid organizations. Only the Catholic Hilfsstelle was able to continue its activities until the end of the war. All the other associations were closed down with the onset of the deportations between the fall of 1941 and 1942.

This paper will focus on the situation of those who were declared "non-Aryan" by Nazi regulations,[1] as well as their helpers, some of whom were also of Jewish descent. After an overview of all the non-Jewish aid organizations in Vienna, I will examine whether there were instances of cooperation between these different aid groups and will investigate the role the Jewish community played during this time. This paper will explore the relations and the limits of solidarity between Jews and those who were declared "non-Aryan" by Nazi regulations, and will also assess whether the Vienna Israelitische Kultusgemeinde (Jewish Community, IKG)—the representative body of Viennese Jewry—extended their solidarity toward them. Finally, it will focus on the heterogeneous community of the Ältestenrat (Council of Elders), the successor organization of the IKG, during the last years of the war. It will thereby disclose unexpected alliances between the Ältestenrat and the Catholic aid agency for "non-Aryans" at a time when the majority among the remaining Jewish population were members of intermarried families.

Aktion Gildemeester/AHO (Emigration Aid Organization for Non-Mosaic Jews in the Ostmark)

The Aktion Gildemeester was initiated by a group of industrialists of Jewish descent, who founded this aid organization for "non-Aryans" with the help of the Dutch philanthropist Frank van Gheel-Gildemeester in March of 1938. Gildemeester was instrumental in its formation, since he was known for his aid to political opponents of the Austro-fascist regime, mainly Social Democrats and National Socialists. Therefore, he could count on the support of the Nazi authorities. The well-connected industrialist Arthur Kuffler (1869–1940), who was of Jewish descent, served as his deputy. While Gildemeester appeared as the head of the organization, it was the businessman Hermann Fürnberg (1897–1976), who led the organization behind the scenes.

---

1   In the summer of 2015, Yad Vashem hosted a workshop on "non-Jewish Jews"—people who were declared "non-Aryan" by Nazi laws regardless of their denomination— advocating for a new awareness of this victim group and thereby attempting to coin a new term outside of Nazi terminology. While commending this important attempt, I nevertheless decided against using this term, since it does not succeed in honoring the self-identity of those defined as "non-Aryan."

During the first two months of its existence, Aktion Gildemeester was the only institution that offered help to the persecuted Jewish population. Following a raid on March 18, the Jewish community had been closed down by the authorities shortly after the *"Anschluss"* and was only reinstated six weeks later. During the anti-Jewish riots that immediately followed the Nazi takeover in Vienna, the Jewish population was without protection. Therefore, the work of the Aktion Gildemeester was crucial for those who tried to escape. When the Jewish community opened again early in May of 1938, there was a great deal of distrust of Gildemeester, because of his "murky connections" with Nazi functionaries, regardless of his aid activities.[2]

The Aktion Gildemeester was the first organization to implement a system in Austria whereby the wealthy financed the escape of impoverished Jews by paying 10 percent of their assets to a fund in exchange for their own expedited escape.[3] The organization used these funds to organize the emigration of their clients, and provided information, assistance, and financial support for their less privileged members. In addition, the Aktion Gildemeester tirelessly advocated for the release of their "non-Aryan" participants, who had been arrested in the course of the November pogrom—an activism that was severely criticized by the Nazi authorities.

In order to participate in the emigration scheme of the Aktion Gildemeester, affluent members had to entrust their assets to the Gildemeester Fund, which was supposed to be sold on their behalf. This fund was managed by Nazi Party members with close ties to Adolf Eichmann's Zentralstelle für jüdische Auswanderung (Central Office

---

2   Charles J. Kapralik, "Wien 1938/39," Leo Baeck Institute (LBI), ME 352, p. 5; Theodor Venus and Alexandra-Eileen Wenck, *Die Entziehung jüdischen Vermögens im Rahmen der Aktion Gildemeester: Eine empirische Studie über Organisation, Form und Wandel von "Arisierung" und jüdischer Auswanderung in Österreich 1938–1941, Österreichische Historikerkommission*, vol. 20/2 (Vienna and Munich: Oldenbourg, 2004), pp. 125–131; Doron Rabinovici, *Eichmann's Jews: the Jewish Administration of Holocaust Vienna, 1938–1945* (Cambridge: Polity, 2011), p. 82.

3   This system was inspired by the Altreu Fund of the Allgemeine Treuhandstelle für die jüdische Auswanderung GmbH (General Trusteeship for Jewish Emigration, Ltd.) in Berlin, which established a similar model. Later on, Eichmann's Zentralstelle für jüdische Auswanderung also adopted this system, forcing the Jewish community to do the same. See Dieter J. Hecht, Eleonore Lappin-Eppel, and Michaela Raggam-Blesch, *Topographie der Shoah: Gedächtnisorte des zerstörten jüdischen Wien* (Vienna: Mandelbaum, 2018), pp. 131–132, 327–328.

for Jewish Emigration)—a cynical name, considering the organization's crucial role not only in reinforcing expulsion and expropriation but particularly in implementing deportation procedures later on.[4] In many cases, these Nazi Party members intimidated the participants of the Aktion Gildemeester, who had to agree to sell their property at prices that were far below the actual value. Therefore, the role of the Aktion Gildemeester remains ambivalent: while it was instrumental in helping "non-Aryans" to escape, it also supported the appropriation policy of the Nazi authorities.[5]

The most ambitious project of the Aktion Gildemeester was a colonialization plan for Austrian Jews in Abyssinia (today Ethiopia), which was an Italian colony. Frank van Gheel-Gildemeester and Hermann Fürnberg frequently traveled to Rome to conduct negotiations with the Italian government. In order to further support their arguments, they presented a leaflet about the fate of the persecuted Jewish population in Austria. This initiative, however, backfired and resulted in an accusation of "atrocity propaganda." Fürnberg, who was defined as a "non-Aryan" himself, immediately had to flee and managed to escape to the U.S. via Lisbon; Gildemeester was denied entry into the German Reich.[6] Shortly thereafter, in January of 1940, the Aktion Gildemeester was dissolved by the Nazi authorities and reorganized as Auswanderungs-Hilfsorganisation für nichtmosaische Juden in der Ostmark (Emigration Aid Organization for Non-Mosaic Jews in the Ostmark, AHO). While most of the staff and its agenda remained the same, the organization lost its independence and was placed under the official supervision of the Zentralstelle für jüdische Auswanderung. The AHO functioned as a centralized platform for all "non-Aryans" of different religious denominations. On October 31, 1942, after the conclusion of the mass deportation of the Austrian Jewish population, the organization was

4   Gabriele Anderl and Dirk Rupnow, *Die Zentralstelle für Jüdische Auswanderung als Beraubungsinstitution, Österreichische Historikerkommission,* vol. 20/1 (Vienna and Munich: Oldenbourg, 2004); Hans Safrian, *Die Eichmann-Männer* (Vienna: Europaverlag, 1993).
5   Anderl and Rupnow, *Die Zentralstelle,* pp. 184–188; Hecht, Lappin-Eppel, and Raggam-Blesch, *Topographie der Shoah,* pp. 323–329; Venus and Wenck, *Die Entziehung jüdischen Vermögens,* p. 159.
6   Herbert Rosenkranz, *Verfolgung und Selbstbehauptung: Die Juden in Österreich 1938–1945* (Vienna: Herold, 1978), pp. 238–240; Doron Rabinovici, *Eichmann's Jews,* pp. 182–183; see also Hermann Fuernberg Collection, 1936–1946, LBI, AR 7194.

dissolved. Most of its staff, including its last executive director, Erich Fasal (1909–1943), were deported and killed.[7]

The Quakers (Society of Friends)

The Quakers' activities in Austria date back to 1919, when they opened a branch in the center of the city in order to aid the starving postwar population of Vienna. Their relief effort was nondenominational. During the years of Austro-Fascism (1934–1938), they mainly aided Social Democrats, as they had fallen victim to political persecution. The International Center of the Society of Friends, directed by a team of British and American Quakers, coordinated the aid work in Austria. The branch of Austrian Quakers, who mainly focused on the religious aspects of Quakerism, quickly subordinated themselves to the new authorities after the Nazi takeover, and distanced themselves from their fellow "non-Aryan" believers. This prompted outrage within the international leadership team of the Society of Friends who, on the contrary, were committed to aiding those who were defined as Jewish by the Nazi regime.[8] Their international networks enabled them to assist thousands in their effort to escape and also to provide welfare to those in need. The Quakers were particularly instrumental in organizing the famous Kindertransporte (children's transports) to rescue children by taking them abroad, mainly to Great Britain. According to the historian Sheila Spielhofer, about 1,200 children and teenagers from Vienna were rescued through the efforts of the Society of Friends.[9] Since those who were desperate to leave often contacted more than one of the local relief organizations, these aid groups also had to cooperate with each other. Therefore, it is sometimes difficult to determine which organization was pivotal in organizing the escape of a particular individual. Consequently, the numbers of those who were saved by the Quakers cannot be established with certainty. Historians

---

7 Hecht, Lappin-Eppel, Raggam-Blesch, *Topographie der Shoah*, pp. 331–334.

8 Sheila Spielhofer, *Stemming the Dark Tide: Quakers in Vienna 1919–1942* (York: William Sessions Ltd., 2001), pp. 106–117; Hans A. Schmitt, *Quakers and Nazis: Inner Light in Outer Darkness* (Columbia: University of Missouri Press, 1997), pp. 107–108, 136–138, 183.

9 Spielhofer, *Stemming the Dark Tide*, pp. 116–118; Spielhofer, "Response to Kindertransport," *Among Friends*, 112 (Autumn 2008), p. 4.

have estimated between 2,408 and 4,500 persons were helped in Austria.[10] Following the outbreak of the war and the expulsion of the British Quakers, the American members of the International Center of the Society of Friends, including the director Emma Cadbury, returned to the U.S. They left the organization in the hands of the two Austrian group members, the former secretary Käthe Neumayer and Franz Lipovsky. The group was supported by the German Quaker Grete Sumpf, who joined Neumayer and Lipovsky in aiding persecuted "non-Aryans." During the onset of the mass deportations in February 1941, they desperately tried to arrange the exemption of people from the transports by attempting to obtain last-minute exit permits and supplied deportees with basic necessities. In the fall of 1941, the interim director Käthe Neumayer was removed from her position by the German branch of Quakers due to criticism of her lack of involvement in religious activities. The aid work of the Center of the Society of Friends came to a halt shortly thereafter.[11]

The Catholic Hilfsstelle (Archiepiscopal Aid Agency for "Non-Aryan" Catholics)

"Non-Aryan" Catholics were initially supported by Aktion K,[12] an unofficial aid organization initiated by the Jesuit Georg Bichlmair, an opponent to the Nazi regime who was, however, also known for his antisemitic writings within the Catholic Church prior to the Nazi takeover.[13] After his imprisonment and expulsion in November of 1939,

10 Spielhofer, *Stemming the Dark Tide*, p. 115; J. Ormerod Greenwood, *Quaker Encounters: Vol. 1, Friends and Relief* (York: William Sessions Ltd., 1975), p. 267; Schmitt, *Quakers and Nazis*, p. 163.

11 Spielhofer, *Stemming the Dark Tide*, pp. 136–158; Claus Bernet, "'Ja-sagen zum Judentum': Die Quäker und ihr Verhalten gegenüber Juden in Deutschland von 1933–1945," in Daniel Heinz, ed., *Freikirchen und Juden im "Dritten Reich": Instrumentalisierte Heilsgeschichte, antisemitische Vorurteile und verdrängte Schuld* (Göttingen: V&R Unipress, 2011), pp. 35–64; Sarah A. Glaser, "State and Religion: Austrian Quaker Nazi Identity in World War II" (master's thesis, Haverford College, 2012), pp. 29–36; Hecht, Lappin-Eppel, and Raggam-Blesch, *Topographie der Shoah*, pp. 334–339.

12 Aktion K was named after the co-initiator, Countess Emanuela von Kielmansegg, who was a leading social worker for the city of Vienna.

13 Georg Bichlmair, "Der Christ und der Jude," *Reichspost*, March 19, 1936; see also Bruce F. Pauley, *From Prejudice to Persecution: A History of Austrian Anti-Semitism* (Chapel Hill: University of North Carolina Press, 1992), pp. 161–163; Gershon Greenberg, "Irene

the organization was closed down. The Viennese cardinal Theodor Innitzer (1875–1955), who in March of 1938 had publicly welcomed the Nazi takeover to appease the new authorities,[14] took over in June of 1940 and together with the Catholic Caritas Institute founded a Catholic help organization for "non-Aryan" Catholics, the Diözesanstelle (Diocesan Office).

After renewed difficulties with the authorities, Innitzer finally established an official aid organization for "non-Aryan" Catholics, the Hilfsstelle, in the archdiocese of Vienna in December of 1940, which remained active until the end of the war. Most of the staff members from the Aktion K. and the Diözesanstelle became activists of the Hilfsstelle. More than half of the staff members and volunteers of the Catholic Hilfsstelle also were of Jewish descent. In fact, eight of them became victims of the Shoah, whereas others managed to escape.[15] The employees who remained until the end of the war were Verena Buben, a nun with the Caritas Socialis; the journalist Gertrud Steinitz-Metzler; Luise Ungar-Perner; and the Jesuit priest Ludger Born, who was in charge of the organization.[16] They supplied "non-Aryan" Catholics with financial assistance, clothes, food, and medicine, and visited them in their homes, as well as in the Jewish hospital and old age homes. In addition, the Catholic Hilfsstelle provided medical and dental care free of charge. While all helpers worked with great empathy for the persecuted, the missionary aspect was not completely dismissed.[17] Father Born also cared for a group of girls, most of them "half-Jewish" children of

---

Harand's Campaign Against Nazi Anti-Semitism in Vienna, 1933–1938: The Catholic Context," in Donald J. Dietrich, ed., *Christian Responses to the Holocaust. Moral and Ethical Issues* (Syracuse: Syracuse University Press, 2003), pp. 132–150.

14 Innitzer, worried about the situation of the Catholic Church in Germany, thought that he could safeguard the position of Catholics in Austria with a public welcoming of the annexation to Nazi Germany; see Maximilian Liebmann, *Theodor Innitzer und der Anschluß: Österreichs Kirche 1938* (Graz and Vienna: Styria, 1988).

15 Notes in the holdings of Father Born, Archive of the Diocese of Vienna (DAW), box 3, folders 1, 4; see also Hecht, Lappin-Eppel, and Raggam-Blesch, *Topographie der Shoah*, pp. 341–343.

16 Ludger Born, *Die Erzbischöfliche Hilfsstelle für nichtarische Katholiken in Wien* (Vienna: Wiener Katholische Akademie, 1979), pp. 99–100.

17 This becomes particularly clear in the autobiographical novel written by a former employee of the Hilfsstelle after the war, who described the activities of the organization; see Gertrud Steinitz-Metzler, *Dass ihr uns nicht vergessen habt…Tagebuch-Aufzeichungen aus dem "Stall"* (Vienna: Dom Verlag, 2008).

intermarried families, who gathered each Thursday in a room above the chapel of the Jesuit church. Among them was Ilse Aichinger (1921–2016), a renowned writer after the war, who later paid tribute to the Hilfsstelle's aid work in her publications.[18] Together with the AHO, the Hilfsstelle initiated a school for "non-Aryan" children and hosted a day care. Funding for the Hilfsstelle came from Cardinal Innitzer, as well as from private donations of a few Austrian bishops and a number of parishes.[19] During the mass deportations, they also tried to obtain the release of people from transports, even if most of these attempts were bound to be futile. They stayed in touch with deportees whenever it was possible and sent monthly food parcels to community members deported to Theresienstadt. The Hilfsstelle was the only remaining, non-Jewish aid organization until the end of the war.[20]

The Schwedische Mission

The Schwedische Mission at Seegasse 16, across from the old age home of the Jewish community, was founded in 1920 by Swedish Protestant missionaries. After the Nazi takeover, the German pastor Friedrich Forell, who had been director of the Schwedische Mission since 1933, immediately had to flee together with his wife, because of their Jewish descent. They fled to Paris and managed to escape to the U.S. The deaconess Martha Hellmann also escaped for the same reason and found refuge in Sweden. The Swedish pastor Göte Hedenquist took over and was courageous in his assistance to "non-Aryans." In close cooperation with the Aktion Gildemeester and later the AHO, the Schwedische Mission managed to support the escape of more than 1,500

---

18 Ilse Aichinger, *Kleist, Moos, Fasane* (Frankfurt am Main: S. Fischer, 1987), pp. 24–27.

19 Two priests in the second district, where the Jewish population was being concentrated, were particularly active in the aid activities. The support of Alexander Poch of the parish of St. Leopold and the vicar Arnold Dolezal of St. Nepomuk went beyond just financial and material help, as both of them also opened the doors of their communities to the persecuted. See Therese Lindenberg, "Die Leopoldstadt unter Hitler, " in Ruth Steiner, *Was ich dich noch fragen wollte...: Eine Christin auf der Suche nach ihrer jüdischen Identität* (Vienna: Dom Verlag, 2006), pp. 34–70; Gerhard Baader interview by Michaela Raggam-Blesch, July 2, 2012, Vienna.

20 Born, *Erzbischöfliche Hilfsstelle*, pp. 7–13, 21–35, 40–46, 67–72, 138; Hecht, Lappin-Eppel, and Raggam-Blesch, *Topographie der Shoah*, pp. 344–348.

persons.[21] It also established a soup kitchen and an old age home to care for the persecuted "non-Aryan" population. "Non-Aryan" Protestants, who were barred from their local parishes, found a new home with the group of Swedish deaconesses and pastors at Seegasse. In March 1940, Hedenquist was expelled by the Nazi authorities because of his commitment to the persecuted. The Schwedische Mission was able to continue for another year, under the direction of his successor Johannes Ivarsson and the deaconesses Anna-Lena Peterson and Greta Andrén. It was closed down by the authorities in June of 1941.[22] Thereupon, the Austrian Protestant Churches expressed their concern in a letter to the Gestapo that Protestant "non-Aryans" would return to their parishes and thereby "cause unrest"—a reaction that may be considered characteristic of the Protestant Churches in Austria.[23]

Cooperation and Distrust

After the Nazi takeover, a number of aid organizations supported individuals who were classified as Jews only by Nazi racial laws. As shown above, some of those who were now defined as "non-Aryans" contacted more than one organization in their despair to find possibilities to escape. Cooperation between aid organizations was therefore essential. This also included the Jewish community that was officially prohibited from

---

21 As in the case of the Quakers, it is difficult to estimate the exact number, since all non-Jewish aid organizations worked together. While Göte Hedenquist gives the number of 3,000 persons, the historian Thomas Pammer considers this number exaggerated. It is, however, safe to assume that the Schwedische Mission was involved in the support of more than 1,500 people. See Göte Hedenquist, "50 Jahre Schwedische Mission in Wien," *Christusbote: Vierteljahresbrief der Schwedischen Mission für Israel*, 11:32 (1972), pp. 9–10; Thomas Pammer, *"Die Arche Noah ist auf dem Kanal vorbeigefahren"*: *Geschichte der Schwedischen Israelmission in Wien* (Vienna: Mandelbaum Verlag, 2017), pp. 104–105.

22 Anna Lena Peterson, "Unser Altenwohnheim in Weidling," *Christusbote: Vierteljahresbrief der Schwedischen Mission für Israel*, 11:32 (1972), p. 13; Evangelische Akademie Wien, ed., *Hoffnungsort Seegasse 16: Hilfsaktionen der Schwedischen Israelmission im Nationalsozialismus* (Vienna: Mandelbaum, 2015); Hecht, Lappin-Eppel, and Raggam-Blesch, *Topographie der Shoah*, p. 350.

23 Letter from the Protestant Oberkirchenrat [Superior Church Council] to the Gestapo, Vienna, July 11, 1941, Holdings of the Schwedische Mission, Protestant Church Archive, Vienna (EKA).

assisting "non-Aryans" by order of the Nazi authorities.[24] This cooperation became most evident in the organization of the children transports that were arranged not least because of the political influence of the Quakers in London. Since the Quakers assisted all denominations, they also aided Jewish children, such as Otto Tausig (1922–2011), who arrived with a Kindertransport in England at the beginning of 1939 and became a popular actor after the war.[25] At the same time, relationships between staff members of different aid associations were not devoid of competition and occasional distrust.[26] While these differences are not surprising, it is noteworthy to point out the various forms of cooperation over time.

Most non-Jewish aid organizations cooperated closely with the Aktion Gildemeester and later the AHO in their efforts to supply their "non-Aryan" members with exit permits and visas. Given the role of the AHO, which was responsible for the "non-Aryan" population, this does not appear to be unusual. Nevertheless, this cooperation went beyond the official framework, since the AHO even helped to fund urgent cases of other organizations and often appealed to the authorities on their behalf. The same was true for the IKG, which enabled the last-minute escape of ten "non-Aryan" Catholics by lending the Hilfsstelle $3,500 in October of 1941, shortly before the onset of the deportations and the ban on all emigration.[27] In fact, a closer examination reveals the multifaceted interconnections between all these organizations. The Catholic Hilfsstelle had a particularly close relationship with the AHO. The Diözesanstelle, the short-lived predecessor of the Hilfsstelle, even had its office in the same building as the AHO. In December of 1940, the Hilfsstelle and the AHO jointly initiated a school for "non-Aryan" children, which also received funding by the Quakers and the

---

24 "Aktennotizen," December 19, 1938, and December 20, 1938, Joseph Löwenherz Collection, IKG Wien Memos 1941–1945, LBI, AR 25055; Spielhofer, *Stemming the Dark Tide*, pp. 112–113.

25 Spielhofer, *Stemming the Dark Tide*, pp. 116–118; Otto Tausig, *Kasperl, Kummerl, Jud: Eine Lebensgeschichte* (Vienna: Mandelbaum, 2010), pp. 28–30; Hecht, Lappin-Eppel, Raggam-Blesch, *Topographie der Shoah*, p. 353.

26 Ben Barkow, Raphael Gross, and Michael Lenarz, eds., *Novemberpogrom 1938: Augenzeugenberichte der Wiener Library London* (Frankfurt: Jüdischer Verlag im Suhrkamp Verlag, 2008), pp. 858–864.

27 The fact that it was a U.S. dollar amount was not insignificant. The Hilfsstelle had very limited access to foreign currency, which was necessary to organize ship passages and exit permits, while the IKG had access through the help of international Jewish aid organizations; Born, *Erzbischöfliche Hilfsstelle*, pp. 126–127.

Schwedische Mission. The Hilfsstelle established a nursery and day care center, as well as a sewing shop in the "Gildemeester House" in the city center. While the AHO provided the Hilfsstelle with office space, it remains unclear how much it was involved beyond that. The fact that staff members of the Hilfsstelle—such as the founding member Lotte Fuchs (1906–1944) and the director of the nursery, Gertrude Brunner (1902–1942)—appeared on membership lists of the AHO indicates their close-knit cooperation.[28]

The Schwedische Mission also worked closely with the AHO, which often advocated their cases before the authorities. After the Schwedische Mission was closed down in June 1941, the AHO took over the building at Seegasse 16, where it opened an old age home for "non-Aryans." When the AHO was dissolved after the conclusion of mass deportations in October 1942, the successor organization of the Jewish community—the Ältestenrat—took over the old age home, although most of the remaining residents were Catholic or Protestant. The Schwedische Mission and the Quakers were also bound by multiple cooperations in their efforts to assist the escape of those defined as "non-Aryans." Before his expulsion, pastor Johannes Ivarsson entrusted Käthe Neumayer of the Quakers with a list of those who relied on the support of the Schwedische Mission in order to ensure their care.[29] The Swedish Quaker Malla Granat-Horn continued to assist "non-Aryan" Protestants and also cooperated with the Catholic Hilfsstelle until her expulsion in 1944.[30]

The Ältestenrat (Council of Elders)

At the end of October of 1942, after the deportation of the majority of the Austrian Jewish population, the Jewish community in Vienna was

---

28 "Liste der Mitarbeiter der Auswanderungs-Hilfsorganisation, Fürsorgeaktion und des Altenheimes, die unbedingt bis 30: September 1942 benötigt werden," Central Archive of the History of the Jewish People (CAHJP), A/W 2716. This list, titled "Urgently Needed Staff Members," was thereby an attempt to plead for exemption from deportation for the people on the list.

29 Letter from Pastor Ivarson to Käthe Neumayer, Society of Friends, June 14, 1941, Holdings of the Schwedische Mission, EKA.

30 Thomas Pammer, "Barnen som var räddning värda? Die Schwedische Israelmission in Wien 1938–1941, ihre Kindertransporte und der literarische und wissenschaftliche Diskurs" (PhD diss., Vienna University, 2012), pp. 35, 39; Born, *Erzbischöfliche Hilfsstelle*, pp. 10–11, 183.

officially dissolved and reorganized as the Ältestenrat by the authorities. After the dissolution of the AHO—the central organization for "non-Aryans"— the Ältestenrat was put in charge of all people who were defined as Jewish by Nazi racial laws, regardless of their denomination. The composition of the former Jewish community, therefore, changed significantly. The majority of the people left behind were protected from deportation, because they had an "Aryan" spouse or parent. Of the 7,989 people defined as Jewish in January of 1943, a total of 5,564 were married to non-Jews. The rest had a non-Jewish parent, or were employees of the Ältestenrat, while a small, additional group was protected by foreign citizenship.[31] Consequently, the newly established community also included many "non-Aryans" in "mixed marriages," who until now had often kept a distance from the Jewish community in order not to endanger their precarious position and their attempts to blend in with the general society. In fact, more than half of the people who were obliged to become members of the Ältestenrat in 1942 were not Jewish by religious denomination.[32] It is therefore not surprising that this new, heterogeneous community was faced with many challenges from the start.

This also becomes apparent in the community newspaper, *Jüdisches Nachrichtenblatt*. Front-page headlines, such as "Return" and "No Conversion," were intended to appease new members, emphasizing the mutual respect among people of different religious backgrounds and the importance of unity. Other articles focused on the achievements and services of the Ältestenrat and its institutions, arguing their vital importance to the new members as well.[33] The fact that topics like these were recurrent themes in the community paper indicates that the process of building cohesiveness and solidarity within the new community was not without difficulties. In January of 1944, Josef Löwenherz (1884–1960), the head of the Ältestenrat, hinted at some of the problems that he had encountered in his annual report to the Nazi authorities.

In 1943, the Ältestenrat was put to the test, since for the first time the attempt was made to unite the Jewish community in one

31 "Bericht über die Tätigkeit des Ältestenrates der Juden in Wien im Jahre 1942," January 1943, CAHJP, A/W 116, pp. 18, I-III.
32 Hecht, Lappin-Eppel, Raggam-Blesch, *Topographie der Shoah*, pp. 484–492.
33 *Jüdisches Nachrichtenblatt*, November 27, 1942, December 11, 1942, January 15, 1943, January 22, 1943, Yad Vashem Archives (YVA), O.30/167.

organization—without consideration of religious denomination. It cannot be denied that there are the most heterogeneous elements among the obligatory members of the community, and that there are many differences regarding religious denomination....Members [who are spouses] in privileged mixed marriages[34] have ever since refused to deal with any Jewish organization and consider contact with such an organization, the acceptance of directives, mailing, and summons an interference with their rights. It required the utmost care and discretion in regard to existing differences to actually include all members in one organization, to lead them, and to make them understand that the Ältestenrat in Vienna represents their rights in its dealings with the authorities.[35]

One point of contention between the Ältestenrat and its new members was the latter's reluctance to pay the compulsory membership fees, since many of them did not want to be part of the organization. However, the Ältestenrat relied on these payments to be able to finance its activities, such as social welfare and soup kitchens, as well as its institutions, including the hospital, the children's home, and the old age home with residents of different religious backgrounds. This was not always easy to achieve. In October of 1943, Franz Berger, an employee of the Ältestenrat, was sent to the home of Franziska Criba, who was married to a non-Jew, to collect her membership fees. Upon arriving, he was harshly rebuffed by her "Aryan" husband, who refused to help support the "Polish Jewish scum" of the Ältestenrat[36] in order "to secure their remaining in Vienna." When Berger reminded him that he was married to one of them, he threatened to slap him, whereupon Berger left the apartment immediately. Franziska Criba ended up paying her fees, not

---

34 The Nazis differentiated between privileged and non-privileged "mixed marriages." Privileged couples were families with an Aryan head of the household (male partner), or those with children who were not members of the Jewish community, thus *Mischlinge*. See Joseph Walk, ed., *Das Sonderrecht für die Juden im NS-Staat: Eine Sammlung der gesetzlichen Maßnahmen und Richtlinien—Inhalt und Bedeutung* (Heidelberg: Müller, 1981), p. 348.

35 Translation from the original German by the author; "Bericht über die Tätigkeit des Ältestenrates der Juden in Wien im Jahre 1943," January 1944, CAHJP, A/W 117, pp. 31–32.

36 The head of the Ältestenrat, Josef Löwenherz, was born in 1884 in Piwowszczyzna, Galicia (formerly Poland, today Ukraine) and therefore had Eastern Jewish roots.

without complaining about Berger's supposedly threatening conduct.[37]

The distant attitude toward the Ältestenrat was not always due to a lack of understanding. Jewish spouses in intermarried families who had previously left the IKG often feared that close association with Jewish organizations would compromise their safety. This was a valid concern, since their fate had not been decided definitively. At the same time, many of them had adopted other religions and did not identify with this new Jewish identity that had been forced upon them. The Ältestenrat was well aware of these reservations and tried to gain their trust, since it relied on their support. This trust was put to an initial test regarding subscriptions to the monthly *Jüdisches Nachrichtenblatt*, to which every member of the Ältestenrat was required to subscribe, since one of its purposes was to publish every new edict pertaining to Jewish life. At the same time, subscription fees were part of the contributions that financed the Ältestenrat. Many of the new members had misgivings about this, since receiving official mail from the Ältestenrat undermined their attempts to blend in. Therefore, a solution was found, and the paper was sent in an envelope, without disclosing the sender. Josef Löwenherz even succeeded in convincing Johann Rixinger, the Gestapo officer in charge of Jewish affairs, to allow postal mailings to members in privileged "mixed marriages"[38] without the compulsory addition of the name "Sara" (for women) or "Israel" (for men), which immediately identified the recipient as Jewish.[39] Not only does this demonstrate that the local Nazi authorities had a way of handling official edicts liberally, it moreover illustrates that intermarried couples who had ties to the non-Jewish population were at times treated with caution by Nazi officials.

37 "Bericht über die Tätigkeit des Ältestenrates der Juden in Wien im Jahre 1943," October 10, 1943, "Abgelegte Akten" (cast off documents), CAHJP, A/W 275; see also Michaela Raggam-Blesch, "Survival of a Peculiar Remnant: The Jewish Population of Vienna During the Last Years of the War," *Dapim: Studies on the Holocaust*, 29:3 (2015), p. 201.

38 Hecht, Lappin-Eppel, Raggam-Blesch, *Topographie der Shoah*, pp. 484–492.

39 "Aktennotizen," February 12, 1943, Joseph Löwenherz Collection, IKG, Wien Memos 1941–1945, LBI, AR 25055; "Bericht über die Tätigkeit des Ältestenrates der Juden in Wien im Jahre 1943," January 1944, CAHJP, A/W 117, pp. 31–32; see also Raggam-Blesch, "Survival of a Peculiar Remnant," pp. 200–201.

Privileged and Non-Privileged "Mixed Marriages" and Their Families

The majority of the remaining Jewish population, who became members of the Ältestenrat at the end of 1942, were people in "mixed marriages." This group complicated the proclaimed racial homogeneity of the Nazi regime and was considered an "unsolved problem" in the Wannsee Conference and its follow-up meetings in March and October of 1942. Internal conceptual differences within the Nazi Party leadership, as well as concerns that "Aryan" family members would incite public unrest, ultimately spared them from the full force of the radical measures applied to the general Jewish population. Plans for the inclusion of "half-Jews" and intermarried "Jewish" spouses in the "Final Solution," however, were never abandoned.[40]

Nazi authorities decided to provide privileged status to certain "mixed-marriages" and their families in order not to evoke objections from non-Jewish relatives.[41] Families with a male non-Jewish partner (head of the household) were given privileged treatment. Intermarried families with children who were baptized or without denomination—so-called *Mischlinge*—were also declared "privileged," regardless of whether the mother or father was "Aryan." At the same time, all intermarried families with *Geltungsjuden* (children raised in the Jewish faith) were designated "non-privileged."[42] While most of the non-privileged families had already been members of the IKG, privileged "mixed marriages" and their families now comprised the majority of the new members of the Ältestenrat. The latter received the same food ration cards as the general non-Jewish population and, for the most

---

40 Raul Hilberg, *The Destruction of the European Jews*, vol. 2 (New Haven: Yale University Press, 2003); Jeremy Noakes, "The Development of Nazi Policy towards the German–Jewish 'Mischlinge,' 1933–1945," *Leo Baeck Institute Yearbook*, 34 (Oxford: Oxford University Press, 1989), pp. 291–354.

41 The distinction between privileged and unprivileged "mixed marriages" was introduced shortly after the November pogrom and the surge of anti-Jewish legislation. The privileged group was thereby exempt from some of the anti-Jewish laws and taxes. See Noakes, "Development of Nazi Policy," p. 337.

42 The first supplementary decree of the Nuremberg Laws, issued on November 14, 1935, defined people with a Jewish and an Aryan parent either as "*Mischlinge* of first degree" or as "*Geltungsjuden*"—depending on their denomination at the time of the introduction of the Nuremberg Laws in 1935. See Walk, *Das Sonderrecht*, pp. 127, 139–140, 233, 379.

part, were permitted to remain in their apartments. Non-privileged "mixed families" who were, or had been in the past, members of the Jewish community were subject to treatment similar to that of the general Jewish population, including gradual exclusion from certain food rations and eviction from their homes, often with very little notice. The edict of September 1941 required Jewish spouses in non-privileged "mixed marriages," along with their children, to wear the degrading yellow star on their clothing, thus publicly identifying them as Jews and making them vulnerable to assaults by the public.[43] As long as the "mixed marriage" remained intact, the Jewish spouse and the children were usually protected from deportation.[44]

Generally, privileged families were able to remain in their apartments. There were, however, exceptions. Oskar Baader—despite being an "Aryan" himself—was already expelled from his municipal apartment together with his Jewish wife and son in December 1938, prior to the official revocation of Jewish tenancy rights in April 1939.[45] In fact, The Nazi-led Viennese municipality was eager to appropriate apartments in the popular municipality buildings and expelled all Jewish tenants by the end of 1938.[46] The Baaders thereafter found an apartment in the second district, known as Leopoldstadt, in a building that later became a *Judenhaus*.[47] Unlike other privileged families, they

---

43 Ibid., p. 347. The edict of September 1, 1941, required Jews to wear a yellow star that identified them as Jews.

44 For the deportation guidelines of October 11, 1941, and January 31, 1942, see Alfred Gottwaldt and Diana Schulle, *Die "Judendeportationen" aus dem Deutschen Reich 1941–1945: Eine kommentierte Chronologie* (Wiesbaden: Marix Verlag, 2005), pp. 56–58, 140–144; Wolf Gruner, *Widerstand in der Rosenstraße: Die Fabrik-Aktion und die Verfolgung der "Mischehen" 1943* (Frankfurt am Main: Fischer TB Verlag, 2005), pp. 50–52.

45 Law on Tenancies with Jews, April 30, 1939, RGBI I., p. 864.

46 In Austria, the law protecting tenants was only valid for buildings built before 1917, which excluded tenants in the municipality buildings built by the Social Democrats in the 1920s. See Hecht, Lappin-Eppel, and Raggam-Blesch, *Topographie der Shoah*, pp. 49–52.

47 The term *Judenhaus* refers to a building that mainly hosted crowded apartments with Jewish inhabitants, who had been moved there not by their own choice. See Saul Friedländer, *Das Dritte Reich und die Juden: Gesamtausgabe* (Munich: DTV, 2008), pp. 313–314. Due to the fact that *Judenhaus* was a contemporary term, usually carrying a derogative meaning, recent German Holocaust research often favors the term *Ghettohaus*. In this paper, the original term is used, since the concept of *Ghettohaus* could be misleading in the context of international Holocaust studies.

witnessed the crammed living conditions and the terror of deportation of their Jewish neighbors. During this time, the family received regular visits from the Hilfsstelle, since Oskar Baader and his son Gerhard were nominally Catholic. At the same time, Oskar's wife, Cecilia, continued attending synagogue service during the High Holidays, even if the family kept a distance from the Jewish community otherwise. At the invitation of the local parish, their son Gerhard became a member of the church youth group, where he found acceptance among his non-Jewish peers for the first time, in spite of his Jewish descent. He recalls his first awakening to his Jewish identity already at the funeral of his maternal grandmother in 1942. Gerhard was counted in the minyan during Kaddish recital, given the absence of Jewish men due to the ongoing mass deportations.[48]

Non-privileged families, such as the family of Lotte Freiberger,[49] often kept their distance from the Jewish community as well. This distance was intensified by her grandmother, who never accepted her Catholic daughter-in-law, even though Lotte Freiberger's mother Mimi had converted to Judaism prior to her wedding. As a result, the family hardly participated in Jewish festivities.[50] Intermarried families, such as the family of Walter Eckstein, who were deeply involved in Jewish life and attended the synagogue regularly, were more of an exception. After Walter's father was murdered in Buchenwald in 1939, his mother's sole objective was to save her son. She therefore canceled her son's membership with the Jewish community and even considered baptism in order to have him recognized as a *Mischling*, which never succeeded.[51] Walter survived as a *Geltungsjude* in Vienna. After the war, he immediately registered with the Jewish community, not least because

---

48 After a career as a medical historian, Gerhard Baader became an active board member of the Oranienburg synagogue in Berlin; Gerhard Baader interview by Michaela Raggam-Blesch, July 2, 2012, Vienna; see also Michaela Raggam-Blesch, "'Privileged' under Nazi Rule: The Fate of Three Intermarried Families in Vienna," *Journal of Genocide Research*, 21:3 (2019), pp. 385, 387, 394.

49 Lotte Freiberger was the daughter of Moritz and Mimi Freiberger.

50 Lotte Freiberger interview by Michaela Raggam-Blesch, April 30, 2009, Vienna; see also Raggam-Blesch, "'Privileged' under Nazi Rule," p. 383.

51 Conversion or termination of membership in the Jewish community after the cut-off date of the introduction of the Nuremberg Laws in 1935 did not have any bearing on the racial categorization; see Walk, *Sonderrecht*, pp. 127, 139–140; Österreich, *Gesetzblatt für das Land Österreich*, 51/150 (May 27, 1938) p. 421.

he wanted to become a member of the popular Hakoah sport club, where he became a well-regarded member of the water polo team.[52]

Interactions between Members of this Heterogeneous Community

After the Nazi takeover, the Jewish population of Vienna was evicted from their apartments and gradually concentrated in Leopoldstadt, the city's second district, where they were forced to live in crowded *Sammelwohnungen* (communal apartments).[53] Three or more families were typically made to share one apartment, depending on its size. Conflicts and tensions within the crowded apartments were common, particularly in light of the uncertain fate of the inhabitants. Lotte Freiberger's non-privileged family lost their apartment in 1939. She lived in several crowded dwellings until 1944, when she and her Jewish father and "Aryan" mother were moved into a room of an apartment for mixed-marriage families, which they shared with six other people. "Cooking took place in a small kitchen. There were daily arguments and bickering. Everyone's nerves were on edge; living together became an ordeal," she recalled.[54] Tensions were also caused by religion, particularly when secular people and Orthodox Jews lived together. Stefanie Metschl was divorced by her Catholic husband, Johann, immediately after the Nazi takeover. Together with her seven-year-old daughter, Susanne, she had to leave their home and was forced to live in an apartment of an Orthodox family in the second district, where they shared a room with her mother and aunt. Since none of the women kept kosher, the owner of the apartment, Rubin Wolf Kramer, refused to allow the new subtenants

---

52 Walter Eckstein interview by Michaela Raggam-Blesch, November 17, 2014, Vienna; see also Michaela Raggam-Blesch, "Alltag unter prekärem Schutz: 'Mischlinge' und 'Geltungsjuden' im NS-Regime in Wien," *Zeitgeschichte*, 43:5 (2016), pp. 292–307.

53 Gerhard Botz, *Wohnungspolitik und Judendeportation in Wien 1938 bis 1945: Zur Funktion des Antisemitismus als Ersatz nationalsozialistischer Sozialpolitik* (Vienna: Geyer, 1975); Hecht, Lappin-Eppel, and Raggam-Blesch, *Topographie der Shoah*, pp. 395–409.

54 Translation from the original German by the author; Lotte Freiberger interview, Dokumentationsarchiv des Österreichischen Widerstandes (DÖW), ed., *Jüdische Schicksale: Berichte von Verfolgten: Erzählte Geschichte*, vol. 3 (Vienna: ÖBV, 1993), p. 204.

to use the kitchen. Therefore, the women had to prepare their meals on a hot plate in their room. One time, eight-year-old Susanne Metschl unsuspectingly entered the kitchen eating a *Wurstsemmel* (roll with sliced sausage) that even had a layer of butter in it. Kramer was exasperated by this transgression. Susanne understood the reason for the commotion she had caused only years later. It was in this apartment that she was introduced to Jewish traditions of which she had been oblivious. She was particularly fascinated by the wedding of Kramer's older daughter, which took place in the apartment.[55] Due to the many complaints in shared apartments, the Ältestenrat established a conciliation committee to resolve conflicts. Normal juridical procedures were no longer available to Jews. By December of 1941, the committee had already handled 3,000 cases—an indication of its high demand.[56]

In some cases, the Ältestenrat was responsible for organizing the move of one evicted, intermarried couple into the apartment of another by order of the authorities. This was not always met with understanding and cooperation. In June of 1943, Franz Berger, the aforementioned unfortunate employee of the Ältestenrat, was sent to the apartment of Alexander Pompan, who lived with his Catholic wife in an apartment in the first district. When Berger informed him about the need to accommodate another intermarried couple in his place, Pompan reacted angrily. He refused to house any "rabble" in his apartment, dismissing the fact that his own marriage was considered a "mixed marriage" by Nazi ideology.[57] Encounters of this nature highlight the limits of solidarity between members of this heterogeneous community.

---

55 The name and fate of Kramer's daughter and her husband could not be determined. Rubin Wolf Kramer and his wife, Dwora, were deported to Litzmannstadt (Łódź ghetto) on November 2, 1941, and subsequently murdered. After the deportation of Kramer and his family, Susanne, her mother, grandmother, and aunt were moved to another communal apartment in the second district; Susanne Metschl interview by Eleonore Lappin-Eppel and Michaela Raggam-Blesch, February 20, 2013, Vienna, Database of Austrian Shoah Victims, https://www.doew.at/erinnern/personendatenbanken/shoah-opfer (accessed May 16, 2020).

56 The conciliation committee existed until the end of the war, however, most of its files did not remain; "Bericht des Leiters der Schlichtungsstelle, December 29, 1941," CAHJP, A/W 2972; "Bericht über die Tätigkeit des Ältestenrates der Juden in Wien im Jahre 1942," January 1943, CAHJP, A/W 116, p. 5; see also Raggam-Blesch, "Survival of a Peculiar Remnant," pp. 202–204.

57 Diverse Wohnungsangelegenheiten, CAHJP, A/W 441; see also Raggam-Blesch, "Survival of a Peculiar Remnant," p. 204.

The Ältestenrat and Its Cooperation with the Catholic Hilfsstelle

After the conclusion of the mass deportations, most institutions of the former Jewish community—the old age home, the hospital, the children's home, the soup kitchen, and the mikveh (ritual bath), as well as the offices of the Ältestenrat and the synagogue—were moved to Leopoldstadt, where the majority of the remaining Jewish population was being concentrated. Until the end of the war, these institutions were the last venues of Jewish communal life. They not only served the needs of the community, but also provided a number of people with employment, which protected them at least temporarily from deportation until the end of the war. Given the fact that most members of the community were living in crowded dwellings without bathrooms, the function of the mikveh also changed, since it served as a washroom facility for many non-religious members.[58]

During this time, the majority of the inhabitants of the old age home and many of the patients in the Jewish hospital were Christians. Therefore, the Ältestenrat allowed priests and members of the Catholic Hilfsstelle to care for their members and to celebrate church services on the major Catholic holidays in these Jewish institutions.[59] The cooperation with the Ältestenrat also led to joint Hanukka and Christmas celebrations at institutions such as the Jewish children's hospital. Sophie Löwenherz, the wife of the head of the Ältestenrat, Josef Löwenherz, was in attendance, presumably in order to reach out to the new members of the Ältestenrat. Mignon Langnas, who survived in Vienna as a nurse in the Jewish children's hospital, wrote about one of these early celebrations in a letter on December 10, 1942, to her cousin Hala Dornstrauch, who had escaped to Zurich:

My dearest Halinka!
Yesterday we had a little celebration here in the hospital—a joint Hanukka and St. Nicholas party,[60] because we have all together three Jewish children; the other children are all *Mischlinge*. It was very, very nice. I spent the weeks before [the party] sewing during my night

58 Hecht, Lappin-Eppel, and Raggam-Blesch, *Topographie der Shoah*, pp. 484–490.
59 Born, *Erzbischöfliche Hilfsstelle*, pp. 33, 37–38.
60 St. Nicholas is a Catholic saint; St. Nicholas Day is usually celebrated with sweets and small gifts for children on December 6.

shifts—mittens, washcloths, shawls—everything made only out of old socks, but these little gifts turned out to be pretty and delighted all the children. The wife of Dr. Löwenherz, with whom I get along very well, was also among the guests. I had to promise to visit her tomorrow. Do you know her? She is a very good-looking woman with a very good heart. Unfortunately, I have made acquaintance with all these people too late—a year earlier, this relationship would have made it possible to go to my children.[61] But I shouldn't complain, I really shouldn't! I have my work, which I love. I am with father, thank God; we have a light and warm place and, thank God, everything we need. Am I allowed to complain? Of course, I am desperately longing for you, my loved ones, but God will help us. Won't He?[62]

Celebrations of this kind also took place in the nearby Jewish children's orphanage and the day care center in Tempelgasse, located next to the ruins of the destroyed Leopoldstadt synagogue. The majority of children who remained in Vienna after the conclusion of the mass deportations were children of intermarried families. Some of the children in the orphanage had been transferred there from the nursery of the Hilfsstelle and, therefore, had been raised Catholic. Others were formal members of the IKG, often with limited familiarity with religious practice. Since the majority of the Jewish population and those who were defined as such were engaged in forced labor, child care was important. The Church-based aid agency for "non-Aryan" Catholics provided the Jewish children's home with food, medical supplies, and regular financial support. They also organized Christmas and Easter celebrations at the orphanage, which was a highlight for all the children, since they received special treats that were a rarity to them.[63] During the last years of the war, the Jewish population was already excluded from receiving milk products, meat, and regular bread rations, and had to live off very meager provisions. Therefore, the supplies that the Catholic aid organization

---

61 Mignon Langnas remained with her elderly parents in Vienna, while her husband and children escaped to the U.S. At the time of the writing of this letter, her mother had already passed away.

62 Translation from the original German by the author; Elisabeth Fraller and Georg Langnas, eds., *Mignon: Tagebücher und Briefe einer jüdischen Krankenschwester in Wien 1938–1949* (Vienna: Studienverlag, 2010), pp. 231–232.

63 Born, *Erzbischöfliche Hilfsstelle*, p. 92; activity report of the "Erzbischöfliche Hilfsstelle, 1944/45," DAW, box 3, folder 2.

provided were greatly welcomed. One of the former caregivers, Edith Taussig, recalled in an interview by the Shoah Foundation:

There were all kinds of inventions that we could eat....I know, we made dumplings out of black flour, which tasted just terrible, you know....And I got jaundice because the food sometimes was just awful, what we ate, and what we got. And...I have to say that Father Born, he was Catholic, and he really sent us a lot of food. And there was a nun also, but she went in...you know, in regular clothing...and she came and she helped, and they brought us medicine. And they were very, very helpful.[64]

The children in the orphanage were regularly visited by a priest, who always had little treats for the children. As a result, some of the Jewish children decided to undergo baptism.[65] Their parents often agreed in the hope of improving their children's precarious position, which, however, was in vain. The IKG allowed these visits of clerics, since Catholic members of their community demanded religious education for their children in the day care.[66] This pastoral care was made possible in spite of the prohibition of education for all children defined as Jewish as of June 1942.[67] At the same time, Hugo Bondy, the director of the day care in Tempelgasse and former principal of the AHO school for "non-Aryan" children, secretly taught the children in the orphanage and day care. He also staged nativity plays with both Catholic and Jewish children during the Christmas season. Rosa Ringler, whose "Aryan" father had divorced her Jewish mother after the Nazi takeover, was one of the Jewish children in the day care. Bondy, who became her mentor, cast her regularly for the part of Mary, the mother of Jesus. The former children at the orphanage

64 Edith Taussig (née Löw) interview, November 13, 1996, New York, USC Shoah Foundation Visual History Archive (VHA), 22837, tape 2.
65 Rosa Kostenwein and Susanne Metschl were among the children from the day care who were baptized in 1944; Rosa Kostenwein interview by Michaela Raggam-Blesch, June 15, 2015, Weidling; Susanne Metschl interview by Eleonore Lappin-Eppel and Michaela Raggam-Blesch, February 20, 2013, Vienna.
66 Letter with an indecipherable signature, requesting to show consideration for the religious needs of the Catholic children in the children's home, January 13, 1943, "Abgelegte Akten" (cast off documents), CAHJP, A/W 275; Letter of the Archdiocese of Vienna to Joseph Löwenherz, requesting to facilitate religious education for Catholic children, February 2, 1943, "Abgelegte Akten" (cast off documents), CAHJP, A/W 275.
67 Walk, Das Sonderrecht, p. 379.

and day care remembered the Christmas performances and recalled that they were attended by members of the clergy and the Hilfsstelle, as well as by members of the Ältestenrat.[68]

By the fall of 1941, all "non-Aryans" of different religious denominations had to be buried in the Jewish section of the central cemetery by decree of the authorities. While documentation of the Hilfsstelle, as well as official reports of the Ältestenrat, suggest smooth cooperation, internal reports of the Jewish community's Cemeteries Department show its initial indignation when confronted with the new law. Initially, the IKG explicitly prohibited funeral ceremonies of other religions. Later, the Ältestenrat took into consideration its heterogeneous composition and permitted Christian funerals for their "non-Aryans" members at the Jewish cemetery.[69]

During the last years of the war, the remaining Jewish population came under the increased scrutiny of the authorities and even minor offenses could lead to imprisonment and deportation.[70] Survival strategies, such as obtaining extra rations of food, which were forbidden to Jews, became infractions against Nazi laws. Those who were defined as Jewish were restricted in their daily lives in a tightening network of edicts and regulations. Even things like going to restaurants and cinemas could be fatal. In order to enter them, it was necessary to remove the stigmatizing yellow star, which itself was a major offense.[71] Therefore, deportations of smaller groups still continued until the end of the war. These transports also included members of intermarried families who had lost their protection due to divorce or the death of an "Aryan" spouse. The Ältestenrat also was forced to continually reduce its staff, and those who lost their position were deported on one of the next transports.

---

68 Rosa Kostenwein (née Ringler) interview by Michaela Raggam-Blesch, June 30, 2015, Weidling; panel discussion with former children of the Jewish children's home on the occasion of the opening of the photo exhibit "Die Kinder der Tempelgasse," ESRA Psychosocial Center for Holocaust Survivors, April 28, 2015, Vienna.

69 Born, *Erzbischöfliche Hilfsstelle*, p. 39; "Bericht über die Tätigkeit des Ältestenrates der Juden in Wien im Jahre 1944," January 1945, CAHJP, A/W 118, p. 27; memo of the Cemetery Department of the Jewish Community, September 24, 1941, Jewish Community Archive Vienna (IKG/A), A/VIE/IKG/II/FH/3/2. I would like to thank Tim Corbett for this information; see his book on Jewish cemeteries in Vienna, Tim Corbett, *Die Grabstätten meiner Väter: Die jüdischen Friedhöfe* (Vienna: Böhlau Verlag, 2020).

70 Raggam-Blesch, "Survival of a Peculiar Remnant," pp. 212–213.

71 Walk, *Das Sonderrecht*, p. 347.

Consequently, many of the Ältestenrat's employees had a packed suitcase ready, in case their name appeared on the list of the next transport.[72]

These transports also included children from the orphanage and day care. The social worker of the IKG, Franziska (Franzi) Löw, fervently tried to prevent the deportation of children in her care and did not hesitate to provide false papers for children in order to save them. This was possible in cases of children born out of wedlock, provided that the name of the father did not appear on the birth certificate. With the help of Father Ludger Born from the Catholic Hilfsstelle, who gave her access to baptism records, Franzi Löw researched names of potential "Aryan" fathers in order to provide evidence of the alleged "half-Jewish" descent of these children.[73] Some of them were thus able to remain in Vienna until the end of the war. One of these children was Adolf Silberstein, who had been raised by Jewish foster parents. His Jewish mother had to give him up at birth in 1936, since she had contracted tuberculosis. When his birth family was to be deported in April of 1942, Adolf was picked up at the home of his foster parents as well. In the transit camp before deportation, he became severely ill, which ended up saving his life. He was transferred to the Jewish children's hospital that was situated next to the Jewish children's home. There, the medical staff most likely found out that he had been born out of wedlock and notified Franzi Löw. The social worker was able to come up with an "Aryan" father for Adolf, who survived the war in the Jewish orphanage.[74]

Conclusion

After the Nazi takeover in Austria, a number of non-Jewish aid organizations were instrumental in the care of those who were suddenly

---

72 Maria König interview, DÖW, *Jüdische Schicksale*, pp. 245; Rosa Müller interview, DÖW, *Jüdische Schicksale*, pp. 251; Hecht, Lappin-Eppel, and Raggam-Blesch, *Topographie der Shoah*, p. 489.

73 Franzi Löw interview, DÖW, *Jüdische Schicksale*, pp. 189–192.

74 Adolf Silberstein interview by Michaela Raggam-Blesch, October 19, 2016, Vienna; see also the website on an exhibit on transit camps in Vienna, which includes interview excerpt, https://www.oeaw.ac.at/ausstellung-letzte-orte/ (accessed May 5, 2020). Adolf Silberstein's birth mother and grandparents were murdered in Maly Trostinec; Database of Austrian Shoah Victims, https://www.doew.at/erinnern/personendatenbanken/ shoah-opfer (accessed May 16, 2020).

declared "non-Aryan" by Nazi racial laws. Some of these organizations had staff members and volunteers who were considered "non-Aryans" themselves. While some were able to escape, others stayed on and eventually became victims of the Holocaust. In spite of moments of mistrust and competition between these organizations, they eventually cooperated closely with each other. This cooperation also included the Jewish community, even though the IKG was officially prohibited from taking care of "non-Aryans." When the Ältestenrat was put in charge of all people defined as Jewish by Nazi racial laws in late 1942, the newly-created, heterogeneous community faced a number of challenges, since many of the new members had kept a distance from the Jewish community until that time. Solidarity, therefore, was not a given.

At the same time, the remaining institutions of the community also provided a limited number of employees with protection from deportation in their functions as doctors, nurses, cooks, cleaning staff, caregivers, or clerical workers. Jewish institutions, such as the hospital and old age home, were able to persevere until the end of the war in order to take care of Jewish members of "mixed families." They were an "unsolved problem" for the Nazi authorities and therefore ultimately spared from deportations. During the last years of the war, unexpected alliances came into being. While the Catholic aid agency initially had mainly cared for "non-Aryans" after the Nazi takeover, it began to extend its assistance to all those who were defined as Jews, including members of the IKG. It provided financial support, food, and medical supplies to the institutions of the Ältestenrat, and supported the Jewish social worker Franzi Löw in her efforts to save Jewish children from deportation. The fact that Father Ludger Born also went as far as forging baptism records in order to save children should not be left unmentioned.[75] While documentation on the Hilfsstelle therefore demonstrates its genuine commitment to help those defined as Jewish, it nevertheless was not devoid of missionary motives.

The Ältestenrat, on the other hand, depended on the support of its new members, many of whom were Catholic by religious denomination. It therefore strove to gain their trust and participated in joint holiday celebrations in institutions such as the Jewish orphanage and the children's hospital. Members of the Ältestenrat attended nativity plays in the Jewish children's home, where Jewish and Catholic children performed

75 Franzi Löw interview, DÖW, *Jüdische Schicksale*, pp. 190, 196.

together. The Ältestenrat also facilitated visits of Catholic clergy and members of the Hilfsstelle to its own institutions, since its new members requested this. Due to the precarious situation of the remaining Jewish population during the last years of the war, the differences between members of this heterogeneous community were incrementally set aside in order to secure mutual survival. It was also the close cooperation between the Catholic Hilfsstelle and the Ältestenrat that contributed to the continued existence of Jewish institutions. After the war, this unusual alliance slowly fell into oblivion. One of the reminders of this period is the section of Christian gravestones in the Jewish cemetery that not only points to the discriminatory Nazi edicts but also to the heterogeneous community that was forced to stand together.

CHALLENGES TO SOLIDARITY IN CONCENTRATION, LABOR, AND EXTERMINATION CAMPS

Cohesion and Conflict among Jewish Prisoners in Dachau and Lichtenburg

A Social Study of the Extreme Situation

KIM WÜNSCHMANN

O n March 25, 1933, the *Landrat* (district administrator) of Schmalkalden, a town in the center of Germany, ordered the arrest of Ludwig Pappenheim, a Jewish journalist and Socialist politician who served as a deputy in the parliament of the Prussian province of Hesse-Nassau. Pappenheim, a pacifist by conviction, was taken into *Schutzhaft* ("protective custody") on the spurious grounds that he had hidden vast stores of weapons. An emergency decree issued by President Paul von Hindenburg less than a month earlier, on February 28, 1933, served as the pseudo-legal basis for the detention of Pappenheim, as well as for that of many others who were declared enemies of the state. The decree, which was issued only hours after the Reichstag in Berlin had gone up in flames, suspended central constitutional rights and gave the executive branch the power to impose *Schutzhaft*.

Vague and ambiguous in its definition, *Schutzhaft* became "the embodiment of the political fight against the opposition," and the "foundation stone of the new extra-constitutional order" in Germany.[1] Those who fell victim to it were detained without trial and without access to legal defense. *Schutzhaft* prisoners suffered disenfranchisement and arbitrary, violent treatment. Clearly, they were held against their will and

---

1 "Order of the Reich President for the Protection of People and State, 28 February 1933," *Reichsgesetzblatt* (Reich Law Gazette), 1 (1933), p. 83; Martin Broszat, "The Concentration Camps 1933–45," in Helmut Krausnick, Hans Buchheim, Martin Broszat, and Hans-Adolf Jacobsen, eds., *Anatomy of the SS State* (London: Collins, 1968), p. 400; Jane Caplan, "Political Detention and the Origin of the Concentration Camps in Nazi Germany, 1933–1935/36," in Neil Gregor, ed., *Nazism, War and Genocide: Essays in Honour of Jeremy Noakes* (Exeter: University of Exeter Press, 2005), p. 26.

not for their "protection." Imprisoned in the Breitenau concentration camp near Kassel, Pappenheim protested against this unlawful treatment. In a letter to state officials, he laid bare the twisted nature of *Schutzhaft* and demonstrated that he saw through its pretenses. "The arrest warrant against me is maintained on the grounds that I would need protection....I forego the protection, no decent people are threatening me....I do not wish to be kept here as the object of primitive feelings of revenge."[2]

The Reichstag Fire Decree served as the basis for the establishment of hundreds of concentration camps. After Hitler's assumption of power on January 30, 1933, the National Socialists radically intensified their forceful campaign to transform what had remained of the crisis-ridden Weimar Republic into a one-party dictatorship. Before long, a massive wave of terror swept through the country. The long-expected moment of reckoning with all those regarded as the Nazi movement's enemies had come. Within months, tens of thousands were arrested and sent to improvised detention sites. Established on the initiative of local state authorities, self-empowered Nazi potentates, and paramilitary activists practiced in the use of political violence, these "camps of revenge" emerged as extrajudicial prisons.[3]

Concentration camp imprisonment confronted the individual with the most extreme experience of terror. In contrast to regular prison sentences, *Schutzhaft* lasted for an indefinite period of time, and camp inmates often did not know the reasons for their arrest. They did, however, feel the criminalizing effect of concentration camp detention. They knew that they had fallen victim to arbitrary terror and were held unjustly, and many felt humiliated. The popular perception was that there was little difference between imprisonment in a jail and detention in a concentration camp. Both were widely considered "penal institutions for those who had committed crimes and therefore deserved punishment."[4]

2 Letter from Ludwig Pappenheim to Governmental President Kassel, March 31, 1933, quoted in Dietfrid Krause-Vilmar, *Das Konzentrationslager Breitenau: Ein staatliches Schutzhaftlager 1933/34* (Marburg: Schüren, 1998), p. 73.

3 Günter Morsch, "Oranienburg – Sachsenhausen, Sachsenhausen – Oranienburg," in Ulrich Herbert, Karin Orth, and Christoph Dieckmann, eds., *Die nationalsozialistischen Konzentrationslager: Entwicklung und Struktur*, vol. 1 (Frankfurt am Main: Fischer Taschenbuch Verlag, 2002), p. 122.

4 Michael Berkowitz, *The Crime of My Very Existence: Nazism and the Myth of Jewish Criminality* (Berkeley: University of California Press, 2007), p. xix; see also Reinhard Bendix, *From Berlin to Berkeley: German–Jewish Identities* (New Brunswick: Transaction Books, 1986), pp. 122, 147.

In his memoir, a former concentration camp prisoner admitted feelings of deep humiliation, shame, and self-pity stemming from the profoundly upsetting experience of "an outrageous injustice that was done to me."[5] These experiences of injustice and humiliation, as well as the uncertain prospects regarding the future, weighed heavily on the prisoners, who were isolated from each other, which made their living together in the camps' adverse conditions of unbounded violence extremely difficult. How did prisoners deal with the quarrels and fights that arose among them? How did they try to resolve arguments that resulted from differences of opinion? Moreover, how could they get along with each other in the climate of violence of the camps, where scrambling for the limited resources was the order of the day and where survival often came at the expense of filching from fellow prisoners?

Whereas research on the inmates' attempts to resolve conflicts in the concentration camps is still in its infancy, studies on the ghettos in German-controlled Eastern Europe have fruitfully explored the social dynamics at work within these Jewish "communities of coercion."[6] Self-administered institutions of policing, jurisdiction, and incarceration existed in many ghettos. To be sure, the structures and modus operandi of these institutions differed from place to place, just as the patterns of Jewish leadership could vary significantly. In Warsaw, Łódź, Vilna, and Kovno, for example, the Judenräte (Jewish Councils) set up ghetto courts that tried incidents that the German authorities did not want to pursue themselves. They dealt with a wide range of cases, including litigation between tenants, smuggling, and quarrels resulting from forced labor assignments.[7] Ghetto jurisdiction was often improvised since

---

5   Ludwig Bendix, "Konzentrationslager Deutschland und andere Schutzhafterfahrungen 1933–1937," (unpublished manuscript, 1937–1938), vol. 1, pp. 34, 57, and vol. 5, p. 108, Leo Baeck Institute Archives, ME 40.

6   The term *"Zwangsgemeinschaft"* (community of coercion) was used by H. G. Adler to analyze the social dynamics in the Theresienstadt ghetto; see H. G. Adler, *Theresienstadt, 1941–1945: Das Antlitz einer Zwangsgemeinschaft. Geschichte, Soziologie, Psychologie* (Tübingen: Mohr, 1955), pp. 237–238, 449–88.

7   Isaiah Trunk, *Judenrat: The Jewish Councils in Eastern Europe under Nazi Occupation* (New York: Macmillan, 1972), p. 181; Dina Porat, "The Justice System and Courts of Law in the Ghettos of Lithuania," *Holocaust and Genocide Studies*, 12:1 (1998), pp. 49–65; Andrea Löw, *Juden im Getto Litzmannstadt: Lebensbedingungen, Selbstwahrnehmung, Verhalten* (Göttingen: Wallstein, 2006), pp. 112–116; Barbara Engelking and Jacek Leociak, *The Warsaw Ghetto: A Guide to the Perished City* (New Haven and London: Yale University Press, 2009), pp. 190–215; Svenja Bethke, *Tanz auf Messers Schneide:*

prewar legal standards and rules of procedure had to be adapted to a new reality of life and death in an extreme situation. Sometimes, these courts resorted to rabbinic traditions regarding the settlement of disputes. Research has demonstrated that, all in all, a remarkable effort was put into maintaining legal forms of conflict resolution to "ensure a minimum of social stability and a certain sense of 'normalcy'" in the ghettos.[8]

In the search for conceptual tools with which to analyze the dynamics of conflict and cohesion among concentration camp inmates, we may turn to studies in the social sciences. Curiously, former prisoners, such as Bruno Bettelheim, Curt Bondy, Viktor Frankl, and Paul Martin Neurath, pioneered theories of terror that rationalized the effects of camp detention on the inmates and their social conduct under extreme conditions. The present study draws in particular on Neurath's work, which offers valuable insights into the power structures, behavioral codes, and concepts of justice that governed the daily life of the inmates living together in the camps, which he observed.[9]

Studies in the fields of behavioral science and correctional education explore conflicts arising in institutions of confinement by focusing primarily on the relationship between staff and inmates. Since these studies mostly take "the perspective of inmate control, the psychological reasons for conflict and riots, and the bureaucracy's strategy to deter violence," there is a tendency to neglect the prisoners' perceptions of cohesion and conflict, as well as their initiatives in dealing with these dynamics.[10] We do, however, learn from this research that to a significant degree collective violence is generated by tensions and strain prevailing in institutions of confinement in general and among their

Kriminalität und Recht in den Ghettos Warschau, Litzmannstadt und Wilna (Hamburg: Hamburger Edition, 2015), p. 169.

8 Bethke, *Tanz auf Messers Schneide*, p. 298. On the application of religious law, see Ibid., p. 177.

9 Bruno Bettelheim, "Individual and Mass Behavior in Extreme Situations," *The Journal of Abnormal and Social Psychology*, 38:4 (1943), pp. 417–452; Bettelheim, *The Informed Heart: Autonomy in a Mass Age* (New York: Avon, 1960); Curt Bondy, "Problems of Internment Camps," *The Journal of Abnormal and Social Psychology*, 38:4 (1943), pp. 453–475; Viktor E. Frankl, *Ein Psycholog erlebt das Konzentrationslager* (Vienna: Verlag für Jugend und Volk, 1947); Christian Fleck, Albert Müller, and Nico Stehr, afterword to Paul Martin Neurath, *The Society of Terror: Inside the Dachau and Buchenwald Concentration Camp* (Boulder: Paradigm, 2005).

10 Gregory Gathright, "Conflict Management in Prisons: An Educator's Perspective," *Journal of Correctional Education*, 50:4 (1999), p. 144.

inmate populations in particular. The observation that "batch living, regimentation, mass movement, depersonalization, lack of autonomy and freedom, monotony, sexual deprivation, fear, frustration, alienation, and high levels of anxiety" generate conflict accords with Erving Goffman's by now classic social theory of confinement.[11]

That inmates suffered from syndromes of "barbed wire disease" was established as early as World War I, when the mass internment of soldiers and civilians was invoked on an unprecedented scale.[12] What we can also take away from sociological studies is an awareness of the heterogeneity of inmate populations. Instead of perceiving them as one coherent group of (in this case) men, we have to pay attention to their subjective understanding of camp detention, as well as their individual problem-solving skills or patterns of acting-out behavior.[13]

The present chapter ventures into the social dynamics at work among Jewish prisoners. Through a critical evaluation of memoirs and other ego documents, I explore the way conflicts were acted out in the "Jewish blocks." In doing so, I focus on the prewar concentration camps, the sites of terror for all those who were forcibly excluded from the Nazi *Volksgemeinschaft* (national community) in the making. Owing to Nazi racist dogma, Jews were separated from non-Jewish prisoners in special housing units that evolved in Dachau and Oranienburg as early as in 1933. To be sure, the conditions that Jewish prisoners confronted in the prewar camps were different from those that prevailed in the camps during World War II, where Jews were subjected to systematic, biological annihilation on an industrial scale. Moreover, whereas the prisoner population of the wartime camps was international, Jews in the prewar camps were overwhelmingly German or from German-speaking countries. This means that there were also different issues at stake in their attempts to cope with the extreme situation, to survive physically and mentally, and to get along with others.

Whereas antisemitic violence challenged German Jews not only as Jews but also as Germans, Jewish prisoners from other countries did not

---

11 Edith Elisabeth Flynn, "From Conflict Theory to Conflict Resolution: Controlling Collective Violence in Prisons," *American Behavioral Scientist*, 23:5 (1980), p. 758; see also Erving Goffman, *Asylums: Essays on the Social Situation of Mental Patients and Other Inmates* (Garden City: Doubleday & Co., 1961).

12 For a pioneering study on this phenomenon, see Adolf Lucas Vischer, *Die Stacheldraht-Krankheit: Beiträge zur Psychologie des Kriegsgefangenen* (Zurich: Rascher, 1918).

13 Gathright, "Conflict Management in Prisons," pp. 143–144.

have to defend their—however troubled—national identities with the same urgency. In their condemnation of SS terror, they could thus more easily interpret the camp as a "German hell," as Polish Jewish prisoner Yehoshua Friedmann did in his memoir.[14] Arguably, such methods of "othering" were not naturally available to Jews from German-speaking countries, some of whom were fighting fiercely against their demotion from "citizens of Jewish faith" to outlawed "Jews," who were violently executed in the concentration camps. Recent research has investigated the unique ability of German-speaking Jews "to 'capture' their captors in a way non-German Jews could not" and has discovered in the victims' perceptions of their compatriot tormenters an urgent need to make sense of their predicament and to defend their self-worth. In their testimonies, a shared cultural background; a common language; and a set of social norms, ideals, and stereotypes served as the basis for strong arguments to devaluate the adversary and to assert oneself against violent humiliation. German Jewish men, in particular, had to affirm their gender identities as Great War veterans, bourgeois family patriarchs, cultivated citizens, or steely revolutionaries of the antifascist class struggle vis-à-vis the camp guards' claims of embodying the new men of fascist Germany.[15]

The fact that the inhabitants of the "Jewish blocks" in the prewar camps were mostly Germans should not, however, mislead us into assuming that they had a common background and thus shared a distinct group consciousness. In reality, Jews imprisoned in the prewar concentration camps came from many different milieus. Members of the workers' movement, left-wing parties, and trade unions were to be found in significant numbers among the Jewish prisoners in the early concentration camps of 1933–1934. However, there were also liberals and conservatives; bourgeois civil servants; entrepreneurs; and the unemployed, "assimilates"; Zionists, liberal, or Orthodox religious

14 Yehoshuah Friedmann, "Sachsenhausen: Die deutsche Hölle" (unpublished manuscript, c. 1944–1945), Yad Vashem Archives (YVA), O.33/1098; see also Calel Perechodnik, *Am I a Murderer? Testament of a Jewish Ghetto Policeman*, ed. and tr. by Frank Fox (Boulder: Westview Press, 1996), p. 19.

15 Mark Roseman, *Barbarians from Our "Kulturkreis": German Jewish Perceptions of Nazi Perpetrators* (Jerusalem: Yad Vashem, 2016), p. 8; Kim Wünschmann, "Männlichkeitskonstruktionen jüdischer Häftlinge in NS-Konzentrationslagern," in Anette Dietrich and Ljiljana Heise, ed., *Männlichkeitskonstruktionen im National-sozialismus: Formen, Funktionen und Wirkungsmacht von Geschlechterkonstruktionen im Nationalsozialismus und ihre Reflexion in der pädagogischen Praxis* (Frankfurt am Main: Peter Lang, 2013), pp. 201–219.

believers; atheists; and baptized Christians. A considerable number of Jewish prisoners arrested in the latter 1930s lived on the margins of society. They were social outcasts, some of whom had previously come into conflict with the police and had been convicted for legal offenses. Others were imprisoned for socially deviant and nonconformist behaviors; among them were a small number of homosexuals. Finally, they belonged to different generations and age groups, and there was even a significant number of female Jewish prisoners interned in special women's camps.[16] This social heterogeneity conditioned particularly diverse manifestations of companionable and conflicting behaviors. As this study shows, underlying political and social tensions were aggravated in the camps' climate of violence, just as a common heritage, however remote, could sometimes generate feelings of cohesion and help relieve distress.[17]

Social Life in the Concentration Camps

The sociologist Wolfgang Sofsky coined the term "absolute power" to describe the brutal setting of the concentration camp in which prisoners were exposed to near-omnipotent guards who violently dictated their every move.[18] A constant fear of punishment undermined the inmates' efforts to get along and manage the uncertainties of imprisonment collectively. The threat of terror weakened their ability to withstand the camps' cruel regimentation, monotony, and day-to-day humiliations. Whereas "absolute power" dominated the camps, and prisoners ultimately found themselves at the mercy of brutal overseers, there were, however, still situations in which they could escape total

16 Kim Wünschmann, *Before Auschwitz: Jewish Prisoners in the Prewar Concentration Camps* (Cambridge: Harvard University Press, 2015).

17 Falk Pingel observed that Jewish prisoners did not constitute a homogeneous group and that there was a great variation in social backgrounds and political affiliations among them in his groundbreaking study on "prisoners under SS rule." Upon examining controversies and conflicts among political prisoners, Pingel also stated that these were fueled by inmates' "pre-concentrationary" characteristics, that is, by behaviors, tactics, and beliefs adopted prior to imprisonment; see Falk Pingel, *Häftlinge unter SS-Herrschaft: Widerstand, Selbstbehauptung und Vernichtung im Konzentrationslager* (Hamburg: Hoffmann und Campe, 1978), pp. 51–60, 91–96.

18 Wolfgang Sofsky, *The Order of Terror: The Concentration Camp* (Princeton: Princeton University Press, 1993), pp. 16–27.

control and maintain a little influence over their daily routine. Spaces for inmates' interactions opened up in their rare free time in which they could occupy themselves with reading, writing letters, playing games, or attending lectures and discussions. These activities took place in the evenings before the "lights out" command on work-free Sundays and especially during the infamous isolation periods in the Dachau concentration camp, when Jewish prisoners were locked into their barrack for weeks, sometimes months. These were periods of total seclusion from the rest of the camp, and Jews were deprived of even the basic privileges of early concentration camp inmates: buying additional food in the canteen, smoking, reading books or newspapers, and, most crucially, postal correspondence. Apart from short periods of excruciating "camp sport" outdoors, prisoners were continually confined to the barracks and left to themselves. Especially during the isolations in the summer, the air inside became nauseating. The atmosphere was tense, and because the prisoners were nervous and irritable, "quarrels were constantly occurring at the slightest pretext."[19]

In an understanding that differs from Sofsky's concept of "absolute power," the sociologist Paul Martin Neurath, who had himself been imprisoned in Dachau and Buchenwald in 1938–1939, had a different understanding of the inner workings of the concentration camp, which he described as a "prisoner society," as opposed to Sofsky's concept of "absolute power." In Neurath's view, this prisoner society functioned as a self-devised "system of routine and cooperation." It was comparable, he noted, to the cohabitation of any other group of people while, at the same time, distinct by virtue of the camp's adverse living conditions. The prisoner society had vital functions in providing a meaningful frame of reference to govern the inmates' behavior. It gave them a feeling of belonging and could thereby counter the camp's destructive power. As in every other society, there were behavioral codes and standards according to which a prisoner was evaluated and treated. The prisoner society also developed its own concepts of justice, which found their expression in social pressure, ostracism, and punishment.[20]

It is important to note that what Neurath described as the social life of concentration camp inmates was in fact the clandestine network

---

19 Anonymous report by a former Dachau prisoner, 1930s, reprinted in Irmgard Litten, *A Mother Fights Hitler* (London: Allen and Unwin, 1940), p. 272.

20 Neurath, *Society of Terror*, pp. 131–137, 187.

set up by political prisoners, a dominant group in the prewar camps to which he himself belonged. As other Jewish political prisoners, Neurath identified with the majority of the non-Jewish "political" inmates. He joined their close-knit community, whose members consciously distanced themselves from other prisoners. Like Neurath, many Jewish "political" prisoners shared the group's ideals and principles but also their prejudices toward other categories of inmates, most obviously toward the "asocials" and "criminals," some of whom also wore the yellow triangle of the Jews and shared the same barracks with the "political" prisoners.[21]

Conflicts between "political" and "criminal" inmates—between the bearers of the red and the green triangles—outlived the period of imprisonment and also led to a discrepancy in remembrance. Whereas historians long neglected the concentration camps, it was the former political prisoners who wrote the dominant narratives in the first decades after the war. In their writings, some "political" prisoners of Jewish descent made no effort to conceal their hatred of Jews who were classified as "criminal" or "asocial" prisoners. They also expressed disdain for those "Jewish petit-bourgeois" who, in their view, had lived with the illusion that they "could adapt to life under fascism."[22] Others went so far as to insist that the memory of fellow Jews who had "always stood outside of our community" should be blotted out of the history books.[23] On the other hand, there are few sources that tell us about the fate of "asocial" and "criminal" prisoners in the concentration camps. We have little information about their personal backgrounds, their life stories, and their strategies for coping with victimization. In contrast to the political prisoners, social outcasts rarely wrote memoirs, not

21 The SS standardized the use of color-coded markings for concentration camps inmates in the late 1930s. Categories of imprisonment were matched with colored triangles in the following combinations: "political," red; "professional criminal," green; "emigrant," blue; "Jehovah's Witness," purple; "homosexual," pink; "asocial," black. Badges for Jewish prisoners were composed of two triangles—the underlying triangle was yellow, marking the prisoner as a Jews and the color of the top triangle varied, depending on the additional classification—"political," "asocial," etc. See Wünschmann, *Before Auschwitz*, p. 209–210.

22 Emil Carlebach, *Tote auf Urlaub: Kommunist in Deutschland: Dachau und Buchenwald, 1937–1945* (Bonn: Pahl-Rugenstein, 1995), pp. 19, 22, 24, 65.

23 Letter from Werner Neukircher to Oskar Winter, July 13, 1946, Dachau Concentration Camp Memorial Site Archives (DaA), 2237.

187

least because their stigmatization and discrimination continued after 1945.[24] It is due to this biased memoir literature that we know much less about the underground networks of nonpolitical prisoners, who also had their rules and codes. In light of this social fragmentation of the inmate population, it might be more appropriate to conceive of the camp population as being composed of different prisoner societies that existed—and often conflicted—in the concentration camp.

Generally speaking, scholars have been hesitant to explore the dynamics of conflict among concentration camp inmates. Studies on survival strategies, solidarity, mutual support, and collective acts of resistance dominate the historiographical picture of the prisoners' existence in the camps.[25] Could this bias in scholarly analysis possibly be influenced by the ways in which the prisoners' social life is depicted in witness testimonies? Indeed, some accounts glorify acts of organized resistance and perpetuate the myth of the one, united prisoner society that heroically "braved the terror, aided the ill and the weak...and saved those sentenced to death on the gallows."[26] However, usually such biased representations are clearly understood as promoting the ideological agenda of former political prisoners and, in particular, that of the Communists among them. Their status as martyrs and resistance fighters was thus affirmed retrospectively.

It may come as a surprise that, on the whole, primary sources describe many incidents of disagreement and clashes between concentration camp prisoners, sometimes even in great detail. The fact that these conflicts were neither forgotten nor left out of testimonies tells us to what extent

---

24 Wolfgang Benz, "Homosexuelle und 'Gemeinschaftsfremde': Zur Diskriminierung von Opfergruppen nach der nationalsozialistischen Verfolgung," *Dachauer Hefte*, 14 (1998), pp. 3–16.

25 See, for example, Nechama Tec, *Resilience and Courage: Women, Men, and the Holocaust* (New Haven: Yale University Press, 2003), pp. 161–204; Johannes Tuchel, "Selbstbehauptung und Widerstand in nationalsozialistischen Konzentrationslagern," in Jürgen Schmädeke and Peter Steinbach, eds., *Der Widerstand gegen den Nationalsozialismus: Die deutsche Gesellschaft und der Widerstand gegen Hitler* (Munich and Zurich: Piper, 1985), pp. 938–953. Svenja Bethke observes a similar phenomenon for scholarly investigations of "criminality" in the ghettos. Offenses such as smuggling are often interpreted as acts of resistance, which somewhat simplifies and obscures the diverse spectrum of motives for breaking rules and regulations of the ghetto inhabitants; see Bethke, *Tanz auf Messers Schneide*, pp. 283–291.

26 Walter Bartel, *Buchenwald: Mahnung und Verpflichtung* (East Berlin: Kongress-Verlag, 1960), p. 9.

they constituted a dramatic and decisive experience for the prisoners. The classic text, which most eloquently expresses the complexities and ambiguities of prisoners' lives in the concentration camp is Primo Levi's "The Gray Zone."[27] Warning us against the tendency to "simplify history" and divide the camp universe into "the good guys and the bad guys," Levi unsparingly disclosed that "the network of human relationships in the *Lager* (camps) was not simple: it could not be reduced to the two blocks of victims and perpetrators...here the righteous, over there the reprobates."[28] His writings make it very clear that conflicts and exploitation were everyday phenomena that troubled the inmates and hindered their subsisting together under the brutal living conditions in the camps.

Revenge

Primo Levi saw "the gray zone" of the concentration camps most strikingly represented in the workings of the Kapo system. Conflicts became inevitable when a privileged caste of prisoner functionaries ruled as a minority with great powers over the majority of the inmate population. For Levi, the "gray zone of '*protekcja*' and collaboration" constituted a "poorly defined" space, "where the two camps of masters and servants both diverge and converge." Here, the seemingly clear-cut division between perpetrators and victims becomes blurred.[29] Installed as a "perfidious measure" to co-opt prisoners in the implementation of terror and violence, the Kapo system developed into a parallel organizational structure of "divide and rule" that ensured the running of the camp on a day-to-day basis. Prisoners who held posts of influence and exerted power over fellow inmates may be divided into those who performed disciplinary tasks and those whose duties were administrative. The prisoner functionaries who enforced order and discipline in the inmates' living quarters belonged to the former. Each housing unit had a *Blockältester* (barrack elder) aided by a *Stubenältester* (room elder) and a *Tischältester* (table elder). Together they distributed food and other

27 Primo Levi, "The Gray Zone," in Primo Levi, *The Drowned and the Saved* (New York: Summit Books, 1988), pp. 36–39.
28 Ibid.
29 Ibid., p. 42.

goods, and ensured that the inhabitants of their block adhered to the strict routine of the day and kept their quarters spotlessly clean.[30]

Appointments of Jewish prisoners to functionary positions were very rare. Jews ranked too low in the camp hierarchy to assume tasks of influence in the Kapo system. Positions that would have made them superior to non-Jews were entirely outside their reach and, at least in Sachsenhausen, forbidden as a matter of course.[31] The highest ranking and most influential Jewish prisoner functionary of the prewar concentration camps was Heinz Eschen, the *Blockältester* of Dachau's "Jewish block." Arrested in February 1933 in Munich, the 23-year-old Communist and student of medicine had played a leading role in the resistance against the Nazi movement and its growing influence at German universities. At protest rallies and with numerous flyers, Eschen and his comrades urgently warned of the dangers of "academic fascism" and often clashed with SA paramilitaries and other Nazi radicals. When Eschen led a demonstration through Munich's university quarter on February 2, 1933, he collided with the police. Wounded in a gunfight with a policeman, he was arrested, tried, and sentenced to prison. After six months, in November 1933, he was taken to Dachau. Apparently, Eschen was appointed *Blockältester* of the "Jewish block" sometime in 1936, after having temporarily served as the Kapo of a work commando.[32]

30 Karin Orth, "Gab es eine Lagergesellschaft? 'Kriminelle' und politische Häftlinge im Konzentrationslager," in Norbert Frei, Sybille Steinbacher, and Bernd C. Wagner, eds., *Ausbeutung, Vernichtung, Öffentlichkeit: Neue Studien zur nationalsozialistischen Lagerpolitik* (Munich: Saur, 2000), p. 100; Nikolaus Wachsmann, *KL: A History of the Nazi Concentration Camps* (New York: Farrar, Straus and Giroux, 2015), pp. 122–124, 512–527. The origins of the term Kapo, which entered camp language in the prewar years, are uncertain. Eugen Kogon stated that it derived from the Italian *capo* (head) and the French *caporal* (corporal). According to Lutz Niethammer, it was the abbreviation of *Kameradschaftspolizei* (police of comrades). See Eugen Kogon, *Der SS-Staat: Das System der deutschen Konzentrationslager* (Munich: Heyne, 1996), p. 89; Lutz Niethammer, ed., *Der "gesäuberte" Antifaschismus: Die SED und die roten Kapos von Buchenwald: Dokumente* (Berlin: Akademie-Verlag, 1994), p. 15.

31 Günter Morsch, "Formation and Construction of Sachsenhausen Concentration Camp," in Günter Morsch, ed., *From Sachsenburg to Sachsenhausen: Pictures from the Photograph Album of a Camp Commandant* (Berlin: Metropol, 2007), pp. 149, 182–186.

32 Marion Ebner, "Heinz Eschen: "Jüdischer Widerstand im KZ Dachau," in *Deckname "Betti": Jugendlicher Widerstand gegen die Nationalsozialisten in München oder: Ein Plädoyer für "Junge Demokratie." Ein Projekt des Kreisjugendring München-Stadt und der DGB-Jugend München. In Zusammenarbeit mit dem Kulturreferat der Landeshauptstadt München* (Munich: Kreisjugendring München-Stadt, 1997), pp. 50–51; Karl Heinz

In the memoirs of the survivors of Dachau's "Jewish block," Eschen is portrayed as an ambiguous figure. Whereas some prisoners remembered him with great respect and defended his conduct, others, among them the almost 60-year-old Berlin lawyer Ludwig Bendix, were disgusted by the violent behavior of "the juvenile potentate of our company."[33] Those who respected him understood that the Jewish prisoner functionary was caught up in an impossible dual responsibility toward both prisoners and the SS. As *Blockältester*, he virtually "had the duty of mistreating fellow prisoners." Only by relentlessly executing the brutal "Dachau spirit" could he have secured the trust of the SS, which, in turn, was crucial if he was to gain the influence necessary to protect Jewish inmates from worse abuse. Ultimately, Eschen's ambiguous behavior should be assigned to that Levian "gray zone" in which prisoner functionaries had to maneuver. In exchange for the risks they ran, they enjoyed privileges, such as working inside the camp, mostly indoors, instead of in dangerous outside commandos. They were also allocated more food, as well as the occasional free hour to rest. During the isolation periods, a form of punishment for Dachau's Jews in August 1937, Eschen was the only one permitted to leave the "Jewish block" for a few hours each day.[34]

Whereas Eschen's brutal conduct was somewhat explicable when it was displayed in the presence of the SS, it is harder to make sense of his outbursts of violence in situations in which there was no direct guard surveillance. A prisoner who witnessed the way Eschen lashed out at the small group of religious Jews who regularly gathered to pray together rationalized his behavior as a necessary disciplinary punishment. He explained that after Eschen had found some of them guilty of having stolen the bread of their fellow inmates, he had their prayer books burned. He also made a point of ridiculing their religiosity in front of all the other prisoners. Acknowledging that this was a harsh measure, the witness nevertheless thought it necessary to act against those who displayed a

Jahnke, "Heinz Eschen—Kapo des Judenblocks im Konzentrationslager Dachau bis 1938," *Dachauer Hefte*, 7 (1991), pp. 24–26.
33 Bendix, "Konzentrationslager Deutschland," vol. 5, p. 69.
34 Anonymous report about Dachau sent to Oskar Winter (formerly Oskar Winterberger) (undated manuscript, p. 5), DaA, 1180; Alfred E. Laurence, "Dachau Overcome: The Story of a Concentration Camp Survivor" (unpublished manuscript, c.1970, p. 13), DaA; Hugo Burkhard, *Tanz mal Jude! Von Dachau bis Shanghai: Meine Erlebnisse in den Konzentrationslagern Dachau—Buchenwald—Ghetto Shanghai* (Nuremberg: Reichenbach, 1967), p. 94; Jahnke, "Heinz Eschen," p. 28.

"complete lack of solidarity" and thereby endangered the whole group.[35] In another such incident of brutal, self-administered justice, Eschen beat up a fellow Jewish prisoner, Max Schier, a man who was twenty to thirty years his senior. Schier had arrived in Dachau in February 1937 with a transport of Jews from the Lichtenburg concentration camp in Prussia. These men had brought their grudges and conflicts along with them. Upon their arrival in the Bavarian camp, two Jewish Communists from Lichtenburg denounced prisoner Schier for his alleged "antisocial behavior," and asked Eschen to "make an example and punish him for this." Without trying to find out what Schier had to say to these accusations, Eschen began hitting and kicking the defenseless man.[36]

Bendix, the lawyer from Berlin mentioned above, was among those who were appalled by Eschen's violent behavior. Defining himself as a liberal, Bendix viewed Communist Jews as dangerous fanatics who would have implemented their utopian vision of "the dictatorship of the proletariat" with a brutality similar to that of the Nazi movement's campaign of terror. Bendix testified that Eschen and his comrades envisioned Communist tribunals taking place after liberation in which they would not only punish their Nazi oppressors, but also the so-called traitors among the prisoners.[37] It is noteworthy that the Jewish "political" inmates, who dominated life in the "Jewish blocks" through their functionary positions, made up only a small minority of the prisoner group. In Dachau, no more than twenty to thirty political activists were grouped around Eschen.[38] As we have seen, the imbalance caused by the power of a highly politicized minority over the majority of "nonpolitical" Jewish inmates provoked conflicts and exacerbated the lack of unity within the heterogeneous prisoner group. Often, these conflicts fueled acts of revenge. A prisoner who had threatened to report Eschen to the SS fell victim to a rigid act of self-administered justice described as follows by former prisoner Alfred Laurence: He was

---

35 Alfred E. Laurence, "Leben für morgen: Autobiographischer Bericht" (unpublished manuscript, c.1938) DaA, 30.357, pp. 1170–1171; Alfred E. Laurence, "Heinz Eschen zum Gedenken," July 3, 1939, DaA, 9394, p. 3.
36 Bendix, "Konzentrationslager Deutschland," vol. 5, p. 69.
37 Ibid., vol. 4, pp. 59, 62–63.
38 Knut Bergbauer, Sabine Fröhlich, and Stefanie Schüler-Springorum, *Denkmalsfigur: Biographische Annäherungen an Hans Litten* (Göttingen: Wallstein, 2008), pp. 279–281; Carlebach, *Tote auf Urlaub*, p. 18; Laurence, "Leben für morgen," p. 167; Laurence, "Dachau Overcome," pp. 91–93; Litten, *A Mother Fights Hitler*, p. 268.

"most savagely beaten, he had a whole container of boot-black applied to his genitals and buttocks, which he could not remove for many days or even weeks."[39]

As a result of his exposed and ambivalent position as a Jewish prisoner functionary, Eschen made enemies among both prisoners and guards. Ultimately, these enmities brought about his downfall in late January 1938. It seems that a denunciation by a fellow inmate triggered an investigation that ultimately led to Eschen's death—whether by murder or suicide is unknown. According to one survivor's explanation of the incident, Eschen was denounced to the SS by his adversaries within the "Jewish block." An older inmate who had clashed with Eschen during the isolation period in August 1937 and had sought revenge ever since is said to have accused the prisoner functionary of having set up a Communist resistance cell in the "Jewish block." Around the same time, Eschen lost favor with the SS after he had complained about some of the noncommissioned officers (NCOs).[40] For the SS, a Kapo was just a cog in the machine of terror, replaceable at will at any time. The prisoners, on the other hand, feared their superiors. Some sought revenge after they had been put at a disadvantage by a Kapo who favored and protected first and foremost his own group of comrades.[41]

Justice

As the case of Heinz Eschen demonstrates, the violent setting of the concentration camp left prisoners little possibility of negotiating conflicts peacefully. Thus, all the more surprising is the attempt of Jewish prisoners in the Lichtenburg camp to settle arguments in court-like scenarios that were designed to resolve discords fairly. A number of such court scenarios are documented in Ludwig Bendix's lengthy memoir. Driven by the intention to seek justice through dispute and quasi-judicial negotiation of antisocial behavior, the conflicting parties

---

39 Laurence, "Dachau Overcome," p. 55.
40 Anonymous report of a former Jewish prisoner, undated, DaA, 28.309; Bergbauer, Fröhlich, Schüler-Springorum, *Denkmalsfigur*, pp. 284–290; Carlebach, *Tote auf Urlaub*, pp. 27–31; Benjamin Carter Hett, *Crossing Hitler: The Man Who Put the Nazis on the Witness Stand* (Oxford: Oxford University Press, 2008), pp. 238–239; Jahnke, "Heinz Eschen," p. 32; Laurence, "Heinz Eschen zum Gedenken," pp. 5–6.
41 Sofsky, *The Order of Terror*, pp. 138–140.

discussed the pros and cons of problematic issues. This way, the "defendant" was given a realistic chance to explain, justify, and represent himself and his conduct. Court scenarios were mostly held during the night. Both parties to the conflict argued in a quiet, whispering tone to support their claim, and a third prisoner, appointed "judge" or "referee," then decided the case.

Let us take as an example a conflict concerning property that, as it happened, could only have occurred in the concentration camp's adverse conditions. The object of the conflict was a tin can that Bendix kept under his bed to store food supplies. His opponent in this argument was fellow prisoner Werner Scholem, the older brother of philosopher Gershom Scholem and a lawyer like Bendix. As a professional politician, Scholem had belonged to the Reichstag until 1928. Being a founding member of the German Communist Party (KPD), Scholem figured as one of its most influential leaders in the early years of the Weimar Republic. A dramatic break with the KPD came in 1926, after his ultra-left-wing position had become incompatible with the Moscow-loyal party line. On the night of the Reichstag fire of February 27, 1933, Scholem was among the Nazis' very first captives. After two years in captivity in a state prison, he was deported to the Lichtenburg concentration camp in 1935, then to Dachau, and later to Buchenwald, where he lost his life in July 1940.[42]

Sharing a "Jews' cell" in Lichtenburg with Bendix and others, Scholem had kept a wary eye on Bendix's tin can for some time. Anxiously bearing in mind the SS order that prisoners should not keep any unnecessary items, Scholem feared that during the next inspection of the inmates' living quarters, the tin can could prompt the guards' anger. He knew all too well that a seemingly trivial issue could quickly turn into enough of a reason to spark antisemitic violence. However, Bendix, the owner of the tin can, refused to get rid of it. Bendix considered Scholem a fanatic of orderliness, a rigid and pedantic man who had no right to order him around. The conflict escalated when one day Bendix found that his tin can was gone. Scholem initially denied having removed it, but eventually admitted that he had taken it. With the antagonists being edgy and short-

42 Michael Buckmiller and Pascal Nafe, "Die Naherwartung des Kommunismus—Werner Scholem," in Michael Buckmiller, Dietrich Heimann, and Joachim Perels, eds., *Judentum und politische Existenz: Siebzehn Porträts deutsch-jüdischer Intellektueller* (Hanover: Offizin, 2000), pp. 61–81; Mirjam Zadoff, *Werner Scholem: A German Life* (Philadelphia: University of Pennsylvania Press, 2017).

tempered, it did not take long until a verbal confrontation developed into a scuffle, and blows were exchanged, but then something remarkable happened. Both Bendix and Scholem agreed to a hearing of each other's arguments in a court-like situation. They appointed an impartial third prisoner as judge, and each pleaded his case before him, using judicial language. Bendix argued that the unauthorized removal of the tin can was a breach of the peace in the "Jews' cell." He considered it a violation of the only value that remained among concentration camp prisoners: mutual respect and fair treatment by fellow inmates. Scholem, on the other hand, delivered strong arguments for the necessity of keeping order in the cramped accommodation that they shared so as to not provoke SS violence for being untidy. The judge finally decided the case in favor of Bendix.[43]

As a mediating instance between quarreling parties, several prisoners also intervened in a conflict between two other Jewish inmates. Ignatz Manasse, a tailor from Berlin, had viewed with great envy the privileged position that his fellow inmate and colleague Rubinstein had obtained by putting his sewing skills in the services of the camp SS. In return, Rubinstein received benefits and was treated "as if he were not a Jew." Friction between the two inmates arose every day and after it had escalated into a brawl, Rubinstein used his connections to the camp SS and reported Manasse for violently attacking him. As a consequence, Manasse was punished with six days of arrest. The incident caused great unease among the prisoners, and Bendix described how they discussed the extent to which such denunciations to the SS undermined the morale of the prisoners and put Jewish inmates in particular at great risk. They decided that such a drastic measure should remain a last resort and that its implementation be reserved for those among the prisoners who were appointed "judges" in the negotiation of conflicts. Ultimately, the discussion enhanced cohesion among the inmates and even led the two adversaries to make peace with one another.[44]

The phenomenon of these quasi-courts as a means of conflict resolution among Lichtenburg's Jewish prisoners may be attributed to the influence of lawyers such as Bendix, Scholem, and Hans Litten, who

---

43 Bendix, "Konzentrationslager Deutschland," vol. 4, pp. 75–78.
44 Ibid., vol. 4, p. 31. Whereas Bendix used Ignatz Manasse's real name, he used "Rubinstein" as a pseudonym for his adversary. Most likely he used the pseudonym to refer to the Lichtenburg prisoner Felix Rubin.

were deeply committed to the ideal of justice and who fought fiercely against the travesty that the Nazis made of the German legal system. A man of vast professional experience, Bendix had practiced law since 1907 and later also functioned as the presiding judge of the Berlin Labor Court. He was devoted to his profession and described himself as a "legal fanatic," forever seeking true justice. As his son later recalled, "His commitment to the law was more than the choice of a career. It was a dedication to German culture and society, more specifically, to the development and reform of German law in place of his family's traditional commitment to Judaism. The practice of law became his way of life."[45] The Nazis' *Schutzhaft* measures and antisemitic legislation aimed at professional bans had destroyed Bendix's career, as well as those of many other Jewish jurists. Moreover, given the high degree to which many of them identified with the legal profession, it destroyed their personalities and social lives, as well as the lives of their families. Fighting against all the odds for justice in the concentration camp may be interpreted as a means of resistance to this discrimination and as an attempt to assert oneself in the face of terror and inhumanity.

The observation that it was jurists who initiated modes of bipartisan conflict resolution among concentration camp inmates may be linked to the running of ghetto courts, which in many cases also involved legal professionals. The court personnel of the Łódź ghetto, for example, included the wife of the Judenrat head Regina Rumkowska, who had worked as a lawyer before ghettoization.[46] These jurists' education and experience in practicing law was crucial for organizing legal proceedings, which, in turn, had a direct bearing on the way inmates lived together in these institutions of confinement. Research into prison violence has revealed that "[c]onflict resolution requires that an attempt to work with the other parties by collaborating include an attempt to resolve an issue satisfactorily for both parties. It is doubtful that, without training, offenders can accomplish this skill with a high degree of success."[47]

45 Ibid., vol, 1, p. 38; Bendix, *From Berlin to Berkeley*, p. 50.
46 Bethke, *Tanz auf Messers Schneide*, p. 174; see also Porat, "The Justice System."
47 Gathright, "Conflict Management in Prisons," p. 145.

Concluding Remarks

In the larger context of the social dynamics in the "Jewish blocks," Lichtenburg's "Jewish courts" remained an exception. As observed above, the violent setting of the concentration camps left prisoners little possibility of negotiating conflicts peacefully. Life inside the camps was life in an extreme situation. It overwhelmed the human ability to cope with crises and conflict. With his unsettling observations on the Kapo system, Primo Levi led us into "the gray zone" of the concentration camps, a sphere in which standard, moral categories no longer existed. Levi, a survivor of Auschwitz, also allowed us to approach the imprisonment reality of the prewar camps and to see that the conditions prevailing there equally defied the human tendency to think in binary terms of good and evil, right and wrong, courage and cowardice. Any attempt to understand the prisoners' lives in these terms would be a gross oversimplification of the extreme situation of the concentration camp.

As this essay has shown, it is important to study conflicts within the prisoner society without making moral judgments. Research on the various ways that these conflicts were acted out can lead to a better understanding of the imprisonment reality of the camps and possibly also add to our understanding of human behavior in extreme situations. What emerges from the study of the social dynamics within the "Jewish blocks" of the prewar camps is the notion of the prisoners as actors who could, albeit to a limited degree, take initiatives that influenced their predicament. Upon examining survivor memoirs for manifestations of conflict and cohesion, we encounter camp prisoners as individuals who could reason and make decisions, even when real choices were almost nonexistent. The different ways in which disputes were handled point to the complexity of social life in the concentration camp. These findings challenge a common temptation to reduce prisoners to passive victims, tortured by their superiors and merely awaiting death. Showing their ambiguous behaviors in situations of conflict ultimately restores their dignity as human beings, the dignity that the Nazi regime of terror tried to deny them.

Family, Local, and Class Solidarity in the Vaihingen and Hessental Concentration Camps

IDIT GIL

n August 1944, a total of 2,187 Jewish prisoners who had been sent from the Szkolna concentration camp in Radom, which had been shut down as the Red Army approached, reached the Vaihingen concentration camp in Reich territory. Vaihingen was a new satellite camp of Natzweiler, and the inmates there, who were all Jewish males, were tasked with building an underground factory for Messerschmitt AG. In late October, when Allied bombardments forced the work to a halt, most of the prisoners were transferred to four other concentration camps nearby. Vaihingen became an infirmary camp for the entire Natzweiler constellation; 387 Jewish prisoners remained there, chiefly in administrative and maintenance positions.

This essay explores the relationships in terms of manifestations of solidarity, or the lack thereof, among members of the population of 2,187 prisoners who were interned in Vaihingen and Hessental. Both camps, which were in the Reich, were unique in their demographic composition. Until November 1944, only Jewish prisoners who had been transported from Radom were sent to Vaihingen. From then on, as additional prisoners arrived, the management of the camp remained in Jewish hands. Hessental, which housed 800 prisoners, all from the Radom transport, was one of the few concentration camps in the Reich that were populated solely by Jewish prisoners during the entire period of its existence.[1]

---

1   Letter from Chief G. B. Fromageot, South Bavarian Branch, Bureau of Documents and Tracing, United States Relief and Rehabilitation Administration (UNRRA), U.S. Zone, Munich, to Captain J. P. C. Heybrock, RNA, Chief, Death March Section, Bureau of Documents and Tracing, UNRRA, U.S. Zone, Wiesbaden, October 25, 1946, Arolsen Archives (AroA; previously ITS), United States Holocaust Memorial Museum (USHMM), 1.1.29.0/82129990; letter from F. C. Kern, Allied and German Military Graves Service, Schwäbisch Hall, to Dr. John R. Schwäbisch Hall and Dr. John R. Roth, Chief of Documentation, Wiesbaden, July 27, 1946, AroA, USHMM, 1.29.1/3141128.

The 2,187 prisoners from Radom were a diverse group. Their ages ranged from fourteen to sixty. About 40 percent were from Radom, more than 20 percent had been born in towns in the district, and almost all the others had come from elsewhere in Poland. Thirty-two prisoners had been born in the Soviet Union, Germany, Austria, Hungary, or the Netherlands.[2] Before the war, the inmates had been artisans, merchants, teachers, manufacturers, doctors, lawyers, students, and rabbis. Some were Orthodox—Hasidim from various courts, as well as Mitnaggedim— but the traditional, the secular, and the assimilated were also represented. In Poland, many had belonged to youth movements and political parties that had represented and segmented Jewish society in the interwar years: Agudath Yisrael, Betar, Akiva, Dror, Hashomer Hatzair, the Bund, and the Communists.[3] However, two contemporary diaries and hundreds of postwar testimonies relating to the last year of the war make no mention of acts of solidarity grounded in religious, ideological, or political party affiliation or shared creed. Instead, primarily three circles of solidarity are referred to in these sources: family, geographic origin, and socioeconomic class. I discuss these three circles, which reflect the social infrastructure of the prisoners' society in the camps, by examining three kinds of acts of solidarity—assistance in obtaining food, psychological support, and help regarding employment—and investigate the modalities and circumstances under which these actions were taken, as well as their significance for the prisoners.

Nutrition

While still in Radom, the members of this group had been interned in the Szkolna concentration camp, where most of them had worked

---

2 Transport list, Natzweiler file, Yad Vashem Archives (YVA), O.51/9.
3 On the Jewish political culture and schisms in interwar Poland, see David Engel, "'Masoret Nega'im?' He'arot Al Hamegamot Hapoliti'ot Vehatarbut Hapolitit Shel Yahdut Polin Bein Shtay Milhamot Ha'olam," in Israel Bartal and Israel Gutman, eds., *Kiyum Vashever: Yehudei Polin Ledorotehem* (Hebrew), vol. 2 (Jerusalem: Zalman Shazar Center, 1997), pp. 649–665; Emanuel Melzer, "Goral Yehudei Radom Bemahanot Ricuz Shonim Al Adamat Germania," Avraham Shmuel Stein, ed., *Radom Book* (Hebrew) (Tel Aviv: Radom Landsmanschaft, 1962), pp. 427–450; Bernard Wasserstein, *On the Eve: The Jews of Europe before the Second World War* (New York: Simon & Schuster, 2012), pp. 409–427.

at the Steyr-Daimler-Puch plant, forced to perform grueling labor. Men worked two shifts in most departments and many tended several machines simultaneously. Nevertheless, the living conditions were tolerable. Many inmates obtained food from the Poles on the job, or by relying on still-extant connections with former Polish neighbors in town. Some prisoners gave their basic rations to others who could not count on Polish acquaintances to supplement their nutrition. The survivors agreed unreservedly that no one went hungry in Szkolna.

All of this changed when they were transferred to the concentration camps in the Reich. The quantities and quality of prisoner rations in the camps dwindled badly in the last year of the war.[4] The situation was especially dire in the new camps that were established as the collapse of the Third Reich loomed. A total of 588 such camps, which were loosely inspected and unprofessionally managed, were opened in 1944.[5] On paper, prisoner rations were similar to those of the German civilians— about 75 percent of the nutritional requirements of individuals engaged in hard physical labor. However, the prisoners did not receive the official quantities. In Vaihingen, according to several testimonies, SS men regularly pilfered the meat and margarine that the prisoners were supposed to get on Sundays. The ingredients for soup often did not arrive, and the inmates went without lunch.[6]

The issue of hunger is noted again and again in two diaries kept in Hessental and Vaihingen and, of course, figures importantly in postwar memoirs and testimonies. Acute hunger was not due solely to the severely restricted quantities of basic foods, but also to the limited possibilities of augmenting their nutritional intake. Nevertheless, the men in Vaihingen and Hessental had several potential ways of supplementing their diet. In both camps, some prisoners worked for civilians, near civilians, or alongside foreign forced laborers who were afforded reasonable rations. Aware of the Jewish inmates' physical state, these employers and workers gave them small quantities of extra food. Several expert artisans among the prisoners regularly did private jobs for SS men in the camps and were

---

4   Eugen Kogon, *The Theory and Practice of Hell: The German Concentration Camps and the System Behind Them* (New York: Farrar, Straus and Giroux, 2006), p. 27.
5   Nikolaus Wachsmann, "The Dynamics of Destruction: The Development of the Concentration Camps, 1933–1945," in Jane Caplan and Nikolaus Wachsmann, eds., *Concentration Camps in Nazi Germany: The New Histories* (New York: Routledge, 2010), pp. 32–33.
6   Shlomo Hurvitz testimony, AroA, USHMM, 1.1.29.0/82130010.

usually paid with food.[7] In some workplaces, small food supplements were provided quite regularly and many recipients shared them with others. Benjamin Adler often spent Sundays repairing SS men's watches and, according to his brother Amek (Abraham), Benjamin's recompense, which he shared with him, another brother, and his father, helped the family to survive Vaihingen.[8] Samuel (Szmul) Migdalek also testified that he and his cousin were reasonably well fed, because his brother Charles (Cudyk), who worked in the mess, provided him with supplements. However, this lifesaving support could not be taken for granted. Once Charles was caught pilfering food from the mess and was punished with twenty-five lashes; he could hardly sit for many days thereafter.[9]

Most of the extra food randomly found its way into the prisoners' hands. For example, the camp was situated amid orchards and, in the autumn of 1944, fruit ripened on the trees and some fell to the ground. Even after several prisoners were executed for picking or gathering fruit, others were undeterred from gleaning. Local inhabitants were additional sources of nutrition. In both camps, prisoners were occasionally taken to Stuttgart and Schwabisch Hall to clear away bombardment debris, and they received food from homes where they were billeted. In the devastation that accompanied the final days of the war, they sometimes found cabbage, pickles, jam, and chocolate in abandoned supply vehicles, or among the belongings of downed Allied pilots, which they had to gather up.[10] Some prisoners did not share regular or onetime food supplements with others but consumed their pickings alone. Some bartered them for better food or for something other than food. Others held a communal "feast" in which each contributed his booty. Yet others, in a display of solidarity with their peers, shared or surrendered their extra victuals without demanding anything immediate in return.

The most conspicuous and numerous examples of such acts of solidarity involved kin. There was, however, a difference between those who received regular supplements and recipients of random increments.

7   Manfred Scheck, *Zwangsarbeit und Massensterben: Politische Gefange, Fremdarbeiter und KZ-Häftlinge in Vaihingen an der Enz 1933 bis 1945* (Berlin: Metropol, 2014), pp. 126–127.

8   Amek A. Adler, *To Hell and Back in Six Years* (unpublished memoir, 2009), p. 39.

9   Samuel Migdalek testimony, USC Shoah Foundation Institute for Visual History Archive (VHA), O.93/18519; Charles Migdalek testimony, VHA, O.93/26769.

10 Amek Adler interview, May 9, 2010, Toronto, Canada; Morris Grynbaum testimony, VHA, O.93/12066.

The former tended to give their surpluses to members of their nuclear families above all others, but not a few passed them on to more distant relatives or to acquaintances. Zdzisław Przygoda, an engineer by training, practiced his profession in Vaihingen and received two portions of soup. He ate one portion and half of the other and regularly shared the remainder with a prisoner who worked with him or with his brother-in-law.[11] Tobias Weisbord looked out for his father before anyone else. He worked at the Von Neurath farm and was well fed. Baroness von Neurath also wanted to give him cigarettes and asked him whether he smoked. He did not, he replied, but his father did. Instead of giving his father the pack of cigarettes that he received each day, he bartered it in the camp for food, which he gave to his father. Whenever he procured larger quantities of food in return for odd jobs in town that he did at the baroness' bidding, he gave them to his cousin. When the latter came down with a serious leg infection, Weisbord gave some bread to a doctor in return for surgery.[12]

Some family members not only shared the extra food that they managed to obtain intermittently but also their regular, paltry rations whenever one of them was in mortal danger. The three Gutman brothers maintained a strict regimen of sharing any supplemental nourishment that came their way. Hyman Gutman wrote in his memoirs, "When I mended socks for one of the soldiers and received a piece of bread, or Elek shaved someone and got something to eat, or Jacob received an apple or a sandwich from his *Meister* (boss), we always shared with one another." His brother added in his own memoirs that they worked different shifts and marched at the edge of the rank on their way to and from work so that they could share whatever they had, if anything, while walking past one another. Their solidarity was put to a severe test when Hyman fell ill and his ankles became swollen. Jacob realized that Hyman would die unless he were given solid food to reduce the edema. Jacob and Elek decided to augment Hyman's nutrition at the expense of their own small, basic rations. Thus, for an entire week, Hyman was given two slices of bread and all the vegetables in the soup at each meal, while his two brothers shared one slice of bread and the broth. After a week passed in this manner, Hyman's edema subsided. Hyman explained his

---

11 Zdzisław Przygoda, *The Way to Freedom* (Toronto: Lugus, 1995).
12 Tobias Weisbord testimony, VHA, O.93/4792; Tobias Weisbord telephone interview by the author, June 17, 2011.

brothers' behavior: "Due to our upbringing, we took care of each other wherever possible."[13]

There were cases in the Reich camps in which family members not only failed to maintain solidarity but even pilfered the little food that one of them had managed to acquire. Family loyalty was so ingrained in the culture, however, that some survivors considered this a base form of human behavior among prisoners. Several witnesses expressed astonishment at cousins or uncles who failed to help one another. I did not find explicit references in the testimonies about the lack of solidarity between brothers, but incidents of this kind in which a parent and child were involved were indelibly inscribed in four survivors' memories. Meir Blevis was horrified by a father and son who quarreled over crumbs that remained when a loaf of bread was divided into eight portions. Jehezkel (Henry) Zagdanski was appalled when he saw a boy stealing a piece of bread from his father. Isak Wasserstein was astounded by a father who took his dying son's regular bread ration. Leon Weinryb emphasized attempts by family members to help each other. When I interviewed him, he explained that one of the reasons he did not give official testimony was a spectacle that would haunt him forever: A boy gave his father a slice of bread for safekeeping and, upon discovering that his father had eaten it, he cried, "Father, you're killing me."[14]

Family was such an important source of strength that in at least two instances prisoners eased their loneliness by sharing food with others who became surrogate families in lieu of those they had lost. Steve (Szmul) Ross (Rosental) was fourteen years old when a fellow inmate in his barracks named Berek, aged fifty, asked Ross' brother for permission to adopt Steve Ross as a son in place of the children he had lost. The man, a talented smith, made rings for the Germans out of gold teeth. Ross relates, "When they [the Germans] gave him a piece of bread, he

13 Hyman Gutman, "What I Remember as a Survivor," in *Witnesses Speak: An Anthology* (*Memoirs of Holocaust Survivors in Canada Series*, vol. 15b) (Montreal: Concordia University Chair in Canadian Jewish Studies, 2001); Jacob Gutman, *A Survivor's Memoir: Memoirs of Holocaust Survivors in Canada Series*, vol. 4 (Montreal: Concordia University Chair in Canadian Jewish Studies, 1999).

14 Isak Wasserstein, *Ich stand an der Rampe von Auschwitz* (Norderstedt: Books on Demand, 2011); Henry Zagdanski, *It Must Never Happen Again* (Toronto: Colombo & Company, 1998), p. 134; Meir Blevis interview by author, June 2, 2014, Rishon Lezion, Israel; Leon Weinryb telephone interview by the author, September 23, 2008; Leon Weinryb interview by the author, May 7, 2010, Toronto, Canada.

gave it to me so I could call him *Tatuś* (Daddy). He wanted me to be his son."[15] Jakob of Piotrków asked Moshe Kuperwajs (Kfir) for a similar favor. Kuperwajs related that Jakob, his bunkmate, had told him that he strongly resembled his son, whose fate was unknown, and promised to watch over him. Jakob regularly gave him some of his bread and told him to his face that he loved him. Kuperwajs' father was also named Jakob, and Kuperwajs bonded with him.[16]

Berek and Jacob were not from Łódź or Wolanów, where Ross and Kuperwajs had grown up, but many prisoners whose families had perished felt firmly committed to fellow townspeople, particularly if the localities were small shtetlach. In Vaihingen, Gedalia Shapira worked in a cobbler shop outside the camp. While there, he received a nourishing meal and was given extra bread to take to prisoners in the camp. He handed the bread to the barracks superintendent and donated his basic ration to people from Jedlińsk, his home shtetl.[17]

Others often formed friendships with another person or persons, resulting in mutual assistance. The psychological support occasioned by such friendships was evidently reciprocal, but the material aid was not always so. Some prisoners shared food that they had obtained and had no expectations of material reward. Occasionally, friendship was more important than another slice of bread. Shamai Davidson, who studied the importance of social relationships among prisoners in Nazi concentration camps, found that "Pairing friendships were the most common bonding relationship and often the most effective." There were various types of these friendships. "Choice and compatibility in these couples were related to the specific needs of the situation as well as to individual psychological needs."[18] In Vaihingen and Hessental, pairs were often made up of people from the same town or social class. Nathan Cooper had twenty dollars that he used to buy bread for himself and his best friend, Israel Zilberberg. Zilberberg came from Cooper's

15 Steve Ross testimony, VHA, O.93/28997.

16 Moshe (Kuperwajs) Kfir, interview by the author, Netanya, Israel, August 16, 2010, Netanya, Israel.

17 Gedalia Shapira testimony, YVA, O.3/10505.

18 Shamai Davidson, "Human Reciprocity among the Jewish Prisoners in the Nazi Concentration Camps," in Israel Gutman and Avital Saf, eds., *The Nazi Concentration Camps: Structure and Aims, the Image of the Prisoner, the Jews in the Camps: Proceedings of the Fourth Yad Vashem International Historical Conference, Jerusalem, January 1980* (Jerusalem: Yad Vashem, 1984), p. 567.

hometown but was several years older, and it was only in Vaihingen that they became good friends.[19]

Postwar testimonies yield a diverse picture: some prisoners regularly showed solidarity, a few harmed others, and many attempted to survive on their own. A diary written in Hessental reveals the complexities involved in displays of solidarity. Yosef Giser, Avraham Fishman, and David Zeitlin regularly shared an apple or some other extra food that one of them had managed to get. Alongside several such cases that Giser described in his diary, however, he noted a different occurrence. While Fishman and Zeitlin went out in an attempt to find extra food for the three of them, Giser pilfered the bread that Fishman had deposited with him. Giser had gone "crazy hungry" and wolfed down his portion in the manner of someone who rarely had anything to eat. In the diary, Giser reported that, as he ate the bread, he knew that Fishman was no less hungry than he was and would remain hungry that evening and all the next day. Although he assumed that Fishman would not behave in this way, he was unable to stop eating and share the portion with his friend. The tension between comradery, loyalty, and the demands of hunger persisted even when the incident was over. At the end of the day, Giser wrote, "I fell asleep with mild pangs of conscience but with greater pleasure, because I had eaten some delicious bread. I did not allow the thought that Avraham would have to go hungry to enter my mind. I wanted to compensate him in some way, but it was hard for me to give some of my bread to him."[20] Giser also behaved differently and showed that the ability to feel valued was an important reward under the harsh conditions of the concentration camps.

As time passed, winter arrived, there was no more fruit to gather, and the prisoners became increasingly frail. They found every movement difficult and even struggled to speak. Whenever they did not have to work, they merely sprawled on their bunks. On Christmas, they discovered that outside the camp was a wagon laden with turnips. Giser made a prodigious effort to exit the barracks and slip away. "Happily and with an extraordinary sense of triumph," he noted in his diary,

I poured out the bag of turnips in front of Avraham. I had managed to get past the gate, fill a sack with turnips, get back in time, and not

---

19 Nathan Cooper testimony, VHA, O.93/30136.
20 Joseph Giser's diary in Radom and in the camps in Germany, December 12, 1944, Ghetto Fighters' House (GFH), no. 1387.

be caught by the Kapo at the gate. Avraham gazed at me gratefully. Seeing the look on his face, I grabbed another sack as if someone had lit a fire under me and went out again. Again I managed to return to the barracks with the loot. Avraham's eyes opened wide to express his gratitude for my agility, and David, who also benefitted from this, said feebly, turning to Avraham, "I told you Yossele is our genius." I went to sleep with uncommon pride, with a sense that the effort had been worth it. We had a satisfying Christmas.[21]

Psychological Support

According to some testimonies, the conditions in the concentration camps in the Reich were so harsh that every man looked out for himself and waged his own struggle for survival. Many witnesses, however, noted psychological and moral support that was no less significant than physical assistance. It fueled "the motivation to continue the struggle to live on."[22] In Vaihingen and Hessental, psychological aid came first and foremost from family members. The essence of knowing that kin would look out for each other spurred prisoners to trust that psychological or material assistance would be forthcoming when needed. Many family members who had been separated in the transports from Vaihingen to other camps made efforts to reunite, sometimes by switching places with others and, on other occasions, by bribing manifest officers.[23] Murray (Moses) Mapen even paid with a broken nose and two broken teeth for his struggle to join his brother in Hessental.[24]

Prisoners who had lost most of their families tried to cling to surviving kin as a source of stability, such as Alexander Donat, who switched places with a young man whose family had been murdered. The only surviving member was a brother from whom he refused to part.[25] When several family members survived but could not remain together, they divided up so that at least two or three would be together and none would be alone.[26] Even in the absence of explicit testimony about switching places,

21 Ibid.
22 Davidson, "Human Reciprocity," p. 560.
23 Alexander Donat, *The Kingdom of Death* (Washington, DC: USHMM, 1999), p. 221.
24 Murray Mapen testimony, VHA, O.93/5278.
25 Donat, *The Kingdom of Death*, p. 221.
26 Melvin Katz testimony, VHA, O.93/11862.

one may adduce that this often happened from the differences between names on transport lists from Vaihingen and subsequent lists from the camps to which they were transferred, or from testimonies about the concentration camps where the inmates were interned.

Many inmates from the shtetlach went to great lengths to avoid being separated. The statement "Everyone from our town tried to stay together" recurs frequently in the testimonies of survivors from Opatów, Bialobrzegi, Staszów, and Zaklików.[27] Ten men from Zaklików reached Radom from Budzyn. Two of them testified that back in Budzyn, all the Zaklikówers had struggled to stay together and to be sent to Radom as a group. Indeed, it was in this manner that they moved from Vaihingen to Hessental.[28] Many prisoners from the shtetlach felt inferior to their better educated peers from Radom and Warsaw. Remaining together in close proximity gave them strength; it was a counterweight to the city dwellers' advantage in schooling.[29] Max (Melech) Boimal noted this in so many words. Although he had many friends in Vaihingen, he stayed with a father and the father's two sons from his hometown. "They [the other Jews] were smarter than us, bigger than us, so we [the Jews from my hometown] stayed together all the time."[30]

Three prisoners from the Netherlands, who also felt different from the others, bonded together for mutual support. Jules Schelvis wrote in his memoirs,

We suffered together, cried, and laughed....We had stayed together as a unit, known to all as "*die drei Holländer*," the three Dutchmen, a synonym for reliability and fraternity, for Western civilization different from their own....Under the most difficult circumstances, we had supported and encouraged each other. We knew each other better than our wives had known us.[31]

27 Ibid.; Abram Piasek testimony, VHA, O.93/1969; Joseph Kirshen testimony, VHA, O.93/10350; Samuel Heller testimony, VHA, O.93/9013; Morris Grynbaum testimony, VHA, O.93/12066.

28 Samuel Heller testimony, VHA, O.93/9013; Morris Grynbaum testimony, VHA, O.93/12066.

29 Abe (Abram) Piasek telephone interview by the author, February 22, 2014.

30 Max Boimal testimony, VHA, O.93/51413.

31 Jules Schelvis, *Inside the Gates: A Report of Two Years in German Extermination and Concentration Camps* (Amstelveen: Elzenhorst, 1990), p. 115.

When Schelvis fell ill and had to part from his friends and return to Vaihingen, he envied the two of them for the support they would be able to give each other while he remained alone.[32] The psychological support that intimate familiarity afforded was one of the assets shared largely by people who had known each other before, even if they had not been close friends. Many prisoners, distrustful of each other and suspecting that their neighbors were collaborating with the Germans, preferred the company of those on whom they could count.[33]

For Joseph Kirshen (Kirshenworcl), solidarity among his townspeople, those of Staszów, was an important factor in the survival of many. "All the people from my town tried to be together. All of us were friends. Age did not matter. They could not give much help but being together gave us strength."[34] Eliahu Bines cites mutual support among seven members of his extended family as one of the reasons for their survival. Asked to explain the importance of this support, he replied, "The work was very hard. We had no rights, like slaves, and it helped a lot that we talked with each other."[35] Speech had power. It attested to life. In his diary, Giser described how he stopped relating to his friend Staszek when the latter was overtaken by exhaustion. Staszek lay prostrate, unresponsive to the lice that swarmed on his body and even to the revulsion that the other inmates expressed concerning his condition. Giser was overwhelmed by the realization that Staszek was about to die. He stopped emptying his urinal.[36]

The prisoners sustained their morale and hope by talking with each other. Abe (Abram) Piasek recalled a friend from the shtetl who told stories in the evening, saying that this helped them to forget their hunger.[37] Yisrael Lerman took pride in being able to encourage his comrades by apprising them of the status of the war on the various fronts, which he gleaned from reports that he received from a Belgian with whom he worked. He was particularly pleased when he found leaflets in Polish, French, and German with pictures of German soldiers

32 Ibid., p. 116.
33 Joe Aceman testimony, VHA, O.93/37111; Zagdanski, *It Must Never Happen Again*, pp. 116–117.
34 Joseph Kirshen testimony, VHA, O.93/10350.
35 Eliahu Bines interview by the author, June 16, 2009, Givatayim, Israel.
36 Yosef Giser's Diary in Radom and in the camps in Germany, January 1, 1945, GFH, no. 1387.
37 Abram Piasek testimony, VHA, O.93/1969.

fleeing from France and urging the Germans to turn their weapons on the Führer and not on the Allied soldiers. It was clear to him that the war was winding down and that they should make every effort to endure until the liberation.[38]

By the time that the prisoners arrived in the concentration camps in the Reich their communities and families had disintegrated. According to psychological studies, the prisoners whose bonding relations were based on a mutual, cultural background were often able to cope with severe difficulties at critical moments. The group gave them a sense of belonging to a community, helped restore part of their destroyed cultural past and, thus, restored their human identity.[39] In that vein, for the prisoners in Vaihingen and Hessental who were there without family members, the locality of origin served as the core for their group affiliation. Unlike the Landsmanshaft (society of refugees from the same town) in the Warsaw ghetto, these affiliations were not officially organized. In Warsaw, the Landsmanshaften, which were established by refugees from various communities outside of the city, were integrated into the self-help framework under the auspices of the Judenrat, and each Landsmanshaft had official representatives. In the concentration camps, the prisoners' organizational structure was very different. Whereas prisoners served as functionaries, there was not an institutionalized leadership. In Warsaw, veteran refugees gave practical help to those who had recently arrived at the large ghetto, and many of the Landsmanshaften only functioned for a few months until the refugees were assimilated among the Varsovians. In the concentration camps, on the other hand, those from the same locality tried to cope with the harsh conditions together. There was no hierarchy or division between long-term and new prisoners in the groups that they formed.[40]

On the Job

In Radom, workplace solidarity was manifested by arranging placement in easy tasks and helping to fill quotas at the armaments factory and the

---

38 Yisrael Lerner testimony, YVA, M.49E/2951.

39 Davidson, "Human Reciprocity," pp. 569–570.

40 On the importance and uniqueness of the Landsmanshaften in the Warsaw Ghetto, see Lea Prais, *Displaced Persons at Home: Refugees in the Fabric of Jewish Life in Warsaw, September 1939–July 1942* (Jerusalem: Yad Vashem, 2015), pp. 207–214, 258–267.

peat mine. The Judenrat Labor Office generally assigned four elderly, religious Jews to maintain the furnaces in the courtroom offices—four hours a day of cleaning and stoking—because this was considered one of the easiest forced-labor posts and places where Jews were not harassed.[41] There were no quotas in the concentration camps, and most of the work was in arduous construction and labor in the quarries. Moreover, living conditions were grim: severe overcrowding, hunger, wet and dirty clothing, shortage of blankets, and inadequate sanitation. According to one witness, a prisoner paid to have easier work assigned to himself and to a fellow prisoner.[42]

In contrast to the concentration camp in Radom, the range of jobs in the concentration camps in the Reich was much narrower, there was less mobility between jobs, placement was more centralized, and prisoners had fewer resources with which to "buy" preferable jobs. Thus, unlike the myriad testimonies that exist about "buying" work assignments in Radom, hardly any witnesses from the camps in the Reich report the "purchase" of jobs in cash or in kind.

In a few cases, family members or a townsperson managed to enlist a relative or acquaintance to work with them in the workshops in Vaihingen. Such placements, however, were short-lived, since those so employed were soon transferred elsewhere.[43] Even those who described sharing food with others did not willingly surrender a relatively easy job to anyone else. Jules Schelvis reported having attempted to teach a friend not to overexert himself as the rest of the crew strained to load gravel and sand, but the friend was unable to do this as well as Schelvis could. Schelvis then received a record keeping job that required no physical effort while his friend continued to do the difficult, enervating work.[44] Kalman Malc testified that his eldest brother assumed the role of his father for him and his other brothers after their real father had left home a year after he was born. In Radom, the brother, a master cobbler, looked out for Kalman and his brothers by arranging to have them assigned to easy work. In the selection that took place when the ghetto was liquidated, he kept them together with him. In Vaihingen, he worked in the cobbler shop. In late November, Kalman and his middle

41 *Dos yidishe Radom in khurves (Ondenbukh)* (Stuttgart: Komitet fun di Radomer Idn in Stuttgart, 1948), p. 146.

42 Nathan Cooper testimony, VHA, O.93/30136.

43 Morris Grynbaum testimony, VHA, O.93/12066.

44 Schelvis, *Inside the Gates,* pp. 121–122.

211

brother were placed in the second transport to Hessental, and although the eldest brother could have joined them, he chose not to leave his comfortable job in Vaihingen.[45]

Did solidarity at the workplace exist in the Reich concentration camps? There is hardly any evidence of it within the family or within the shtetl. Nevertheless, the assignment of jobs, the placement of people in transports to other camps, and the treatment of officials are described in the survivors' testimonies in terms of solidarity. Several survivors testified that the youngest inmates in Vaihingen were assigned to cleaning jobs in the living quarters of Germans and to kitchen duties. Apart from being relatively easy, the most important thing about these jobs was that they afforded better nutrition than other prisoners could hope for.[46]

In his testimony at the postwar trial of one of the Kapos at Hessental, the camp physician, Henry Fenigstein, stated that the Kapo, a lawyer by profession, had been named to this post because it was the tendency to assign members of the intelligentsia, who were unaccustomed to physical labor, to leadership duties.[47] Review of the survivors' remarks on this issue indicates that they are accurate in terms of the contexts of geographic origin and socioeconomic class. As noted in the testimonies, in Vaihingen most of those working in the Jewish prisoners' mess and that of the Nazi guards were fourteen to seventeen years old, the youngest age cohort in the camp. Although the witnesses do not say explicitly that all of these young people came from Radom, the testimonies imply that this was the case. Dr. Fenigstein's testimony was also easily corroborated. At Hessental, the leadership was staffed by the intelligentsia. Fenigstein, however, did not note that almost all the members of this leadership were from the Warsaw intelligentsia, many of whom did not speak Yiddish and found it hard to communicate with some of the prisoners. Most were actually more Polish than Jewish by identity, and some prisoners and civilian workers thought that they were not Jewish as their names were typically Polish: Mstysław, Wdowinski, Dzielinski.

45 Kalman Malc testimony, VHA, O.93/6814.
46 Leon Weinryb interview by the author, May 7, 2010, Toronto, Canada; Yehuda Rosenberg interview by the author, February 10, 2009, Herzliya, Israel; Shlomo Frischmann interview by the author, May 18, 2009, Lod, Israel; Meir Shapira interview by the author, February 11, 2009, Bnei Brak, Israel; Charles Migdalek testimony, VHA, O.93/26769.
47 Dr. Henry Fenigstein testimony at the rehabilitation trial of Władysław Friedheim, August 18, 1947, Munich, YIVO, RG294.1/18/195/62. I thank Rivka Brot for having shared this file with me.

Approximately 250 Varsovians were in the group that reached Vaihingen. Most had arrived in Radom in two transports. About 80 of them had come with the transport of 100 printworkers in May 1943, and more than 100 came from the Budzyn concentration camp in May 1944 as part of a group of 500 prisoners. The first group included some individuals who were not printers by trade but had been added as such by virtue of connections and/or payoffs.[48] The group from Budzyn also included Varsovians in the liberal professions who had attained a certain public stature by dint of having received leadership posts while in Budzyn. Upon arriving in Radom, they found all the leadership positions filled by locals and had to work in the arms factory as unskilled laborers. They reached out to acquaintances from Warsaw who had been in Radom for a long while and who gave them some financial aid from the money that the Warsaw courier Wladka Miedzyrzecki-Peltel (Wladka Meed) had delivered to the printworkers.[49]

The new concentration camps in the Reich offered new jobs and, ostensibly, new leadership posts. Two elite groups stood out in these camps: one among the Jews of Radom and one made up of Jews from Warsaw. The former controlled Vaihingen; the latter was dominant in Hessental. The Radom elite comprised thirty to forty successful businessmen—manufacturers and merchants—and members of the liberal professions. Twenty to thirty members of the Warsaw elite were well-known Zionists and social activists. Among them were lawyers, engineers, doctors, a publisher, a businessman, and Jewish community functionaries. Ted Back called them "true Polish Jewish intelligentsia." Many had been acquainted before the war and had traveled in the same social circles. They had attended the same schools and were friends or had friends in common.

---

48 Ted Back alleged that three members of the group were a violinist, his wife, and a secretary; see Ted Back testimony, VHA, O.93/9086. Additional testimonies indicated that there were also several lawyers and an engineer in the group. Back worked for a German officer.

49 Wladka Miedzyrzecki-Peltel, a member of the Warsaw ghetto resistance, delivered money to the Warsaw Jews in Radom twice, in late 1943 and in the summer of 1944. On the first occasion, she brought 10,000 złotys to the print shop; the second time, she delivered 50,000 złotys. The money was meant for the workers in the print shop and in the arms factory, as well as those who had arrived from Budzyn. About 100 men received 500 złotys each; see Wladka Meed (Wladka Miedzyrzecki-Meed) and Feygl Peltel, *On Both Sides of the Wall: Memoirs from the Warsaw Ghetto* (New York: Holocaust Library, 1979), pp. 244–250; Donat, The *Kingdom of Death*, p. 201; Adam Melcer testimony, VHA, O.93/9415.

Members of these two elite groups held all the senior leadership positions: heads and deputy heads of the camps; administrative officers, such as registrars and secretaries; and labor foremen. They were in charge of placing people in positions of responsibility: middle-level leadership, such as Kapos; barracks superintendents and their aides; barracks clerks; heads of infirmaries; and heads of workshops. The leadership in Vaihingen dealt with five transport lists to four concentration camps. Unsurprisingly, the members of both of these elite groups looked out mainly for people with whom they felt close. In Vaihingen, most prisoners worked at the quarry: loading gravel onto wagons, dragging bags of cement on ladders, hauling bricks, drilling and crushing stones, and digging foundations. A few jobs were considered easy and did not always require special skills: mess duty, work on the Von Neurath family farm, and unskilled labor in tailor and cobbler workshops. As noted, most kitchen workers were young people from affluent Radom families. Thirty workers were sent to the Von Neurath farm, where the work was easier and, most importantly, where they were given sizable food supplements. The very young were not specifically looked after, but men from Radom who, according to testimonies, were close to the camp leadership, were given special care.[50]

Several workshops within the camp turned out various products for the guards and the SS commanders, and some prisoners were placed in workshops outside the camp, in Vaihingen proper. Many of these inmates were unskilled.[51] In contrast, Samuel Migdalek was an expert tailor who had made caps for SS commanders in Radom. When he arrived at Vaihingen, he approached *Hauptscharführer* Johannes Hacker, superintendent of prisoners and one of the SS men who had arrived with the inmates from Radom, and asked to be placed in the tailors' workshop. According to his testimony, the inmates already employed there agreed to accept him "because they had known me from Radom." Despite his

---

50 Alfred Lipson, "Meine Odyssee von Radom nach Vaihingen," in Scheck Manfred, ed., *Das KZ vor der Haustüre: Augenzeugen berichten über das Lager "Wiesengrund" bei Vaihingen an der Enz* (Vaihingen: Selbstverlag der Stadt Vaihingen an der Enz, 2005), p. 174.

51 The utterly unskilled Oskar Goldberg was in charge of either the tailor or the cobbler workshop. See the list of prisoners in Vaihingen, KZ Vaihingen/Enz Haeftlings Kartai, Stadtarchiv Vaihingen H1.2/1155. I thank Dr. Manfred Scheck for sharing this file with me. See also (Meir) Macher Macharowski interview by the author, November 7, 2010, North Miami Beach.

expertise, he was always afraid that he would be sent to perform grueling construction labor. After Vaihingen became an infirmary camp, 387 prisoners remained there with light duties. Most were from Radom and, according to Moshe Fischmann, the majority were merchants.[52]

The largest group of Warsaw residents was sent to Hessental. According to the Hessental camp records, about half of the inmates worked in construction and damage repair at the airport; the rest were divided up for other duties. Some posts were preferred, owing to the nature of the work and the extra food that came with it. In late October, several quotas were established: 13 prisoners for the mess, 16 for camp leadership positions, 4 for the clinic, and 11 as technical staff. Gradually, the quotas were enlarged and sought-after jobs were added. Fifteen inmates worked for farmers in the vicinity and additional groups labored at the cobbler shop, a brewery in town, the garden of the local hospital, and as maintenance workers at city hall and the mayor's home.[53] All the work crews were supervised by 20 Kapos. Most of the prisoners who were assigned to these jobs had come from Warsaw and Budzyn.

According to Ted Back, the camp administration was run by the Warsaw elite[54]—"teachers, professors, liberal professionals, and the rich," as Abe (Abram) Piasek defined them."[55] In late November, the clinic was staffed by two doctors and five medical orderlies. Only one of the latter had some experience in first aid. The other four had neither schooling nor experience in the medical field. All had arrived from the Budzyn camp. The journalist and publisher Alexander Donat, for example, was chosen for the post because he was a friend of one of the doctors. The other doctor did not oppose his appointment because when he had reached Radom from Budzyn, Donat had been a member of the committee that had given the doctor 500 złotys from the funds that Wladka Miedzyrzecki-Peltel had delivered.[56] The cobbler shop employed ten inmates. Only one was a cobbler by trade; the other nine had no such skills and were employed there because of their ties to the camp leadership. Gedalia Shapira, who had been one

---

52 Yosef Margalit testimony, YVA, O.3/10531; Moshe Fischmann telephone interview by the author, August 21, 2009.

53 The Hessental camp commander's weekly report, October 22 and October 28, 1944, Hessental Archive, courtesy of Siegfried Hubele.

54 Ted Back testimony, VHA, O.93/9086.

55 Abe Piasek telephone interview by the author, February 22, 2014.

56 Donat, *The Kingdom of Death*, p. 222.

of the finest cobblers in Jedliṅsk, specialized in making ski boots and handsewn shoes. When he reached Hessental in the second transport in November 1944, the Jewish deputy commander of the camp assigned him to the cobbler shop and installed him at its head. The previous superintendent attempted to oppose this but the other workers, while also unhappy with the new man, understood why the decision had been made. After all, somebody had to make high-quality ski boots for the camp commander and his lover.[57]

Five of the ten potato peelers in the mess were rabbis.[58] One of them, Rabbi Shapira, had been a member of the rabbinical court in Warsaw. In Budzyn, he had already been one of the Jewish leaders who had been given an easy job assignment—at the bathhouse—on the recommendation of Władysław Friedheim. At his rehabilitation trial, Friedheim, who had been a Kapo at the bathhouse in Budzyn, as well as in Hessental, explained these job placements as acts of solidarity in consideration of the candidate's inexperience in physical labor and as a reward for his activity on behalf of the Jewish community.[59] Given these acts of solidarity, however, one can only wonder at the failure to assist the prisoner David Zeitlin, a writer and the scion of one of the best-known, intellectual families in prewar Poland. David's grandfather, Rabbi Hillel Zeitlin, was "synonymous with Polish Jewry." He engaged in philosophy, literature, and the press. His uncle Aaron was a playwright and his father, Elhanan, was a writer, editor of the Yiddish-language newspaper *Unzer Express*, and a social activist.[60] Information about Zeitlin's last days comes from two contemporary sources: a letter that he wrote and left with a Belgian with whom he had worked and Yosef Giser's diary. In Hessental, Zeitlin was assigned to the forest detail. In his letter, dated December 8, 1944, he noted that he could hardly clutch a pencil to write. His Belgian coworker described him as the most emaciated of all the Jewish prisoners. According to Giser's diary,

57 Gedalia Shapira testimony, YVA, O.3/10505.
58 Ted Back testimony, VHA, O.93/9086; see the list of prisoners in Vaihingen, KZ Vaihingen/Enz Haeftlings Kartai, Stadtarchiv Vaihingen, H1.2/1154.
59 Władysław Friedheim's statement at his rehabilitation trial, August 18, 1947, Munich, YIVO, RG294.1/18/195/62.
60 Mikhail Krutikov and Shachar Pinsker, "The Zeitlin Family," *The YIVO Encyclopedia of Jews in Eastern Europe*, http://www.yivoencyclopedia.org/article.aspx/Zeitlin_Family# suggestedreading (accessed April 30, 2015).

he had been hospitalized in the infirmary several times.[61] Nevertheless, although he was an intellectual and unaccustomed to hard labor, he was given neither an easy job nor a leadership position of the sort that the other members of the intelligentsia, who were considered unfit for hard labor, had received. Zeitlin did not survive.

Relations between the Radom and the Warsaw Elite

What kind of relations existed between the Warsaw and the Radom elite? At first glance, they were rivals. Their relations were typified by condescension on the part of the Varsovians, who considered themselves intellectuals as opposed to the Radomites, who were perceived as rich and provincial. This attitude is evident in three memoirs and a diary produced by four members of the Warsaw elite. Alexander S., whose grandfather had headed the Warsaw Jewish community and had served in the Polish Senate, noted in his memoir that he did not speak Yiddish and preferred to fraternize only with the kind of people who could converse with him about mathematics or philosophy.[62] He described his encounter with the Radomites as follows:

> The Radom camp administration struck me as repulsive. The Jewish functionaries there were only concerned with their own interests and often, without any scruples, acted as flunkies to the Germans. I saw the remaining people in the camp as a foreign, provincial mass, and I wasn't attracted to them at all. Perhaps there were some members of the intelligentsia among them, but I had no energy left to look for them.[63]

His references to Vaihingen are no less vivid. The Jews of Radom, he explained, were privileged; some were well-fed and maintained a ghetto

---

61 Letter from Gustaaf Hendrick regarding David Zeitlin, December 8, 1944, Hessental, YVA, O.33/1456; Yosef Giser's Diary in Radom and in the camps in Germany, December 12, 1944, GFH, no. 1387.

62 In his memoir, Alexander noted only his first name and his family relations. By examining several sources, I was able to find his full name in the transport list to Vaihingen. I respect his wishes not to disclose his full name.

63 Joanna Wiczniewicz, *And Yet I Still Have Dreams: A Story of a Certain Loneliness* (Evanston: Northwestern University Press, 2004), p. 92.

mentality.[64] Although Alexander S. is the most caustic, others also took an unsympathetic view of the Radom elite. In the diary that he kept at Vaihingen, David Wdowinski called the camp elder "the Yid commander."[65] In his memoirs, Alexander Donat fumed at the camp leadership in Radom, who preferred to sell jobs at the print shop to the local, well-heeled Jews rather than bring over his wife, who had been left behind in Majdanek, and who instead dismissed the twelve printers who had arrived with the Warsaw group from their jobs at the print shop. According to Donat, only printers, police, and the affluent of Radom remained at the shop.[66]

In his chapter on Vaihingen, Donat totally disregarded the Radomite leadership in the camp. The omission also stands out in the case of Zdzisław Przygoda, who had been transferred to Szkolna after having been caught on the "Aryan" side posing as a Pole. Two Jewish artisans from Radom mentioned Przygoda approvingly in their testimonies as someone who had given them ongoing support in Vaihingen.[67] In his memoirs, however, Przygoda made no mention of this, but rather wrote at length about the non-Jewish prisoners in the camp and elaborated on how he had helped them to prepare a Christmas tree. He did refer once to disputes between the Warsaw people and the Radom group, explaining that Henry Fenigstein was unable to work as a doctor at the infirmary barracks in Vaihingen because he had come from Warsaw. Only Radomites, he alleged, were allowed to work as doctors. Fenigstein was condemned to physical labor.[68]

Were relations between the two elite groups marked only by tension, as one might expect? Did each group reserve various workplaces for its own people? Did workplace solidarity find expression only at the local class level?

---

64 Ibid., p. 100.
65 David Wdowinski, "David Wdowinski's Diary (April 18, 1944–October 18, 1946) from the Concentration Camps and the D.P. Camp," in David Wdowinski, *Anahnu Lo Noshano* (Hebrew) (Jerusalem: Yad Vashem, 1986), p. 151. For Wdowinski's memoir about the Warsaw ghetto in English, see David Wdowinski, *We Were Not Saved* (New York: Philosophical Library, 1963).
66 It is true that print workers were dismissed, but many of the Varsovians who remained were not printers.
67 Gedalia Shapira testimony, YVA, O.3/10505.
68 Zdzisław Przygoda, *The Way to Freedom*.

While it is true that Alexander S. loathed the Radom elite, he included in his memoirs an example of an act of solidarity that this group had displayed toward him. His father was a lawyer and a good friend of David Wdowinski, a leading member of the Revisionist Zionist movement in Poland and a well-known physician. Wdowinski had taken Alexander under his wing and had arranged easy work for him and had given him money in Budzyn. In Radom and Hessental, Wdowinski was unable to help him, and Alexander was assigned to grueling physical labor. He fell ill in Hessental, and Wdowinski, who by then had been sent to another camp, and a doctor from Warsaw whom he had known in Budzyn recommended that he be admitted to the hospital on the grounds that he was a protégé of Wdowinski's and the grandson of a senator. "It saved my life." After recovering, he was not sent back to his arduous duties; instead, he was transferred to a convalescent barracks, where he found privileged and wealthy people from Radom with whom he chatted and played cards.[69]

An in-depth review of the testimonies and the lists of the transports to and from Vaihingen shows that even as the two elite groups competed with one another, there is also evidence of cooperation and class solidarity between them. Three factors support this contention: an examination of the prisoners who held leadership positions in Vaihingen, the registration of prisoners in the Natzweiler system, and the placement of the Warsaw elite on the transport to Hessental.

Leadership Positions in Vaihingen

Is it true that members of the Radom elite held all the leadership and medical positions in Vaihingen and that the arrivals from Warsaw were crowded out? The Radom Yizkor book lists those in the camp who received official appointments. Of the 7 highest leadership positions, 5 were held by Radomites, and 2 were staffed by inmates from Budzyn.[70] Alexander Donat noted that the night-shift Kapo at the concrete-mixing facility, who received an extra bowl of soup, "was one of our printworkers." One of the medics had also arrived in the printworkers'

---

69 Wiczniewicz, *And Yet I Still Have Dreams,* p. 97.
70 Melzer, "Goral Yehudei Radom Bemahanot Ricuz Shonim," p. 260.

transport.[71] Another physician from Warsaw, Dr. Feinstein, did not practice his profession at the infirmary barracks, nor was he assigned to construction work like the rest of the inmates. Instead, he was posted at a first-aid tent at the quarry, where he treated civilian workers, who tipped him generously for his services with food and tobacco.[72]

Registration of Prisoners in the Natzweiler System

Here, too, there is evidence of cooperation between the two elite groups. The prisoners from Radom received concentration camp numbers several days after they arrived, and the Jewish camp clerk was in charge of recording the numbers.[73] The 2,187 forced laborers from Radom were given numbers 24203–26389. The digits were issued on three lists, according to the prisoners' last names in alphabetical order. The number of names in the lists was 900, 300, and 987, respectively. Registration was based on cards that had been brought from the concentration camp in Radom.[74] There is no explanation for the existence of the three lists; presumably, there was some administrative reason for it. However, an interesting class correlation emerged when the rosters were examined. On the third list, almost all those in leadership positions were from Radom, Warsaw, and Budzyn, while only one Kapo appears on the second list. The only two individuals from Warsaw who do not appear on the third list were also not included in the original transport to Hessental. Information about the fate of the members of the entire group shows that the survival rate among those on the third list was much higher than that of those on the other two lists. According to what is known about the fate of the prisoners in the lists, 63 percent of the inmates on the third list survived as opposed to 39 percent of those on the first list and 32 percent of those on the second one. The roster of deaths shows a similar trend. In the third group, 19 percent are known to have perished as opposed to 24 percent in the first group and 31 percent in the second group.

---

71 Donat, *The Kingdom of Death*, p. 221; Wdowinski, *Anahnu Lo Noshanu*, p. 145.
72 Donat, *The Kingdom of Death*, p. 218; Wdowinski, *Anahnu Lo Noshanu*, p. 151.
73 Reuven Adler testimony, YVA, O.3/13084; Schelvis, *Inside the Gates*, p. 114.
74 Personal labor cards from the Szkolna camp, Radom, January 17–May 26, 1944, AroA, USHMM, 1.1.23.2.

Placement of the Warsaw Elite on the Transport to Hessental

In the two other camps in the Radom District, there was tension between the local Jews and the Jews who had come from Majdanek, many of whom were originally from Warsaw. Felicja Karay described a harsh dispute that broke out between the Radom people and the Majdanek contingent, none of whose members was given a leadership appointment in Skarzysko-Kamienna.[75] Christopher Browning also presented testimonies to the effect that during the move from Starachowice to Birkenau, Jews who had come from Majdanek strangled the principal jobholders from Starachowice in a fit of vengeance.[76] The elite groups of Radom and Warsaw found a different solution. When they had to prepare a transport of 600 Jews from Vaihingen to Hessental, the leadership cadre from Budzyn and the printworkers from Warsaw selected their men knowing that they would get the leadership positions in the new camps and would be able to give plum jobs to their cronies.[77] Thus, 43 percent of all the prisoners in this transport were Varsovians and others who came from Budzyn, even though they constituted only one-fourth of the total prisoners in Vaihingen. The Radom people may have been glad to be rid of the Warsaw elite and therefore enabled them to switch camps.

Hanoch Tenenbaum, who was known to have been an official denouncer to the Gestapo in Radom, was among those transported to Hessental. In Hessental, he became a Kapo and was tried before a Polish tribunal after the war. Upon surveying the lists of the additional transports from Vaihingen, one finds that the Jewish leadership had precise knowledge of the nature of the destination camps and had drawn up the lists accordingly. If so, the Radom leadership ceded Hessental to the Warsaw elite. Hessental was a less harsh camp than the destinations of the transports that followed: Bisingen and Dautmergen, which were part of the Wüste operation. In these two camps, the mortality rate was very high. In contrast, notables from Radom joined the third transport

---

75 Felicja Karay, *Death Comes in Yellow: Skarzysko-Kamienna Slave Labor Camp* (Amsterdam: OPA, 1996), pp. 112–116.

76 Christopher R. Browning, *Remembering Survival: Inside a Nazi Slave-Labor Camp* (New York: Norton, 2010), pp. 228–233.

77 Donat, *The Kingdom of Death*, p. 221; Ted Back testimony, VHA, O.93/9086.

to the camp in Unterriexingen, where, as a new concentration camp, leadership positions were given to Jews.

Conclusion

There are myriad testimonies concerning acts of solidarity among the contingent of forced laborers who were sent from Radom to Vaihingen in the summer of 1944. Even in the last year of the war, under the grim conditions that typified the concentration camps, not a few cases of solidarity have come to light. Recalling his experiences in Vaihingen, Alfred Lipson noted, "The prisoners developed friendships among each other as had not been before. We helped each other like family and shared the little that could be shared."[78] Food assistance and psychological support were reflections of family, local, and class solidarity. Placement in lifesaving jobs and on transport lists mirrored a solidarity that was based on class and geography. Moreover, these acts of solidarity demonstrate the complexity of the relationships that evolved within the society of Jewish prisoners in Vaihingen and Hessental.

78 Lipson, "Meine Odyssee von Radom nach Vaihingen," p. 173.

Jewish Concentration Camp Inmate Functionaries

Karl Demerer in Blechhammer—A Case Study

VERENA BUSER

*T*he roles of Jewish men and women who held privileged positions[1] during the Nazi dictatorship are still ambiguously evaluated in scholarly and popular literature today, usually within the questionable category of "Jewish collaboration."[2] There has not yet been a comprehensive study in which Jewish functionaries

1   The author is aware that the term "privileged" is an external ascription, either used by "ordinary" fellow inmates or scholars who work on the broad issue of "Jewish collaboration." It describes a kind of intermediate position between the perpetrators and the Jewish victims. Primo Levi described it as the "gray zone" between the "masters" and the "slaves." See Primo Levi, *The Drowned and the Saved* (New York: Summit Books, 1988).

2   The field within Holocaust scholarship that deals with the question of "Jewish collaboration" has meanwhile grown. There are case studies of Jewish individuals that entail the challenge of explaining and describing their behavior in ghettos or non-ghetto situations and under camp captivity. Additionally, there are microstudies about specific Jewish communities and camps and their respective "Jewish elites." On Judenräte, there is by now a broad corpus of scholarly research, much of it in Hebrew. For some important studies, see Isaiah Trunk, *Judenrat: The Jewish Councils in Eastern Europe under Nazi Occupation* (Lincoln: Nebraska University Press, 1972). For a critical discussion of Trunk and also Hannah Arendt's work, see Dan Michman, "Reevaluating the Emergence, Function, and Form of the Jewish Councils Phenomenon," in *Ghettos 1939-1945: New Research and Perspectives on Definition, Daily Life, and Survival— Symposium Presentations* (Washington, DC: USHMM, 2005), pp. 67–84; Freia Anders, Katrin Stoll, and Karsten Wilke, eds., *Der Judenrat von Białystok. Dokumente aus dem Archiv des Białystoker Ghettos 1941-1943* (Paderborn: Ferdinand Schoeningh, 2010). On functionaries in camps, see Tuvia Friling, *A Jewish Kapo in Auschwitz: History, Memory, and the Politics of Survival* (Waltham: Brandeis University Press, 2014); Hans-Dieter Arntz, *Der letzte Judenälteste von Bergen-Belsen: Josef Weiss—würdig in einer unwürdigen Umgebung* (Aachen: Helios, 2012); Galia Glasner-Heled and Dan Bar-On, "Displaced: The Memoir of Eliezer Gruenbaum, Kapo at Birkenau–Translation and Commentary," *Shofar: An Interdisciplinary Journal of Jewish Studies*, 27:2 (2009), pp. 1–23; Rivka Brot, "Julius Siegel: A Kapo in Four Judicial Acts," *Dapim: Studies on the Holocaust*,

are looked at in an integrated manner. Scholarly works dealing with individual case studies are most often concerned with members of the Judenräte (Jewish Councils). The *Judenältestester* (Jewish elder)[3] of the Litzmannstadt ghetto, Chaim Rumkowski, is foremost among these subjects,[4] but there is also research literature on Benjamin Murmelstein, the *Judenältestester* in the Theresienstadt ghetto.[5] In retrospect, it seems

25:1 (2011), pp. 65–127; René Wolf, "The Undivided Sky: The Auschwitz Trial on East and West German Radio," in M. Davies and C. Szejnmann, eds., *How the Holocaust Looks Now: International Perspectives* (London: Palgrave Macmillan, 2006), pp. 75–84; Orna Ben-Naftali and Yogev Tuval, "Punishing International Crimes Committed by the Persecuted," *Journal of International Criminal Justice*, 4:1 (2006), p. 128–178; Christopher Browning, "'Alleviation' and 'Compliance': The Survival Strategies of the Jewish Leadership in the Wierzbnik Ghetto and Starachowice Factory Slave Labor Camps," in Jonathan Petropoulos and John K. Roth, eds., *Gray Zones: Ambiguity and Compromise in the Holocaust and Its Aftermath* (New York: Berghahn, 2005), pp. 26–36; Sari Siegel, "The Coercion-Resistance Spectrum: Analyzing Prisoner-Functionary Behavior in Nazi Camps," *Journal of Genocide Research*, 23:1 (2021), https://www.tandfonline.com/doi/full/10.1080/14623528.2020.1768331 (accessed August 1, 2021); Sari Siegel, "Treating an Auschwitz Prisoner–Physician: The Case of Dr. Maximilian Samuel," *Holocaust and Genocide Studies*, 28: 3 (Winter 2014), pp. 450–481; Jörg Wollenberg, "Die 'roten Kapos' – 'rotlackierte Nazis' und 'willige Vollstrecker' der SS? Zum Versuch, den Gebrauchswert des Antifaschismus am Beispiel der KZ-'Funktionshäftlinge' neu zu bemessen," in Matthias Brosch, Michael Elm, Norman Geißler, Brigitta Elisa Simbürger, and Oliver von Wrochem, eds., *Exklusive Solidarität: linker Antisemitismus in Deutschland: Vom Idealismus zur Antiglobalisierungsbewegung* (Berlin: Metropol-Verlag, 2007), pp. 115–139. Also see Israel Gutman and Cynthia J. Haft, eds., *Patterns of Jewish Leadership in Nazi Europe 1933–1945* (Jerusalem: Yad Vashem, 1977); Evgeny Finkel, *Ordinary Jews: Choice and Survival during the Holocaust* (Princeton and Oxford: Princeton University Press, 2017).

3   The title *Judenältester* was also used in the camps, denoting the highest-ranking Jewish prisoner in charge. The *Lagerältester* was the counterpart of the *Judenältester* in the case of non-Jewish prisoners. A Kapo was an "ordinary" prisoner, Jewish or non-Jewish, who was responsible for supervisory tasks, such as cleaning barracks and assisting Germans to conduct roll call, for example.

4   On Rumkowski, see Richard L. Rubinstein, "Gray into Black: The Case of Mordecai Chaim Rumkowski," in Petropoulos and Roth, eds., *Gray Zones: Ambiguity and Compromise in the Holocaust and its Aftermath*; Michal Unger, "Reassessment of the Image of Mordechai Chaim Rumkowski," *Search and Research: Lectures and Papers*, 6 (Jerusalem: Yad Vashem, 2004); Lucille Eichengreen, *Rumkowski and the Orphans of Lodz* (San Francisco: Mercury House, 2000).

5   On Murmelstein, see Hans Guenther Adler, *Theresienstadt, 1941–1945* (New York: Cambridge University Press, 2017); Lisa Hauff, *Zur politischen Rolle von Judenräten: Benjamin Murmelstein in Wien, 1938–1942* (Göttingen: Wallstein Verlag, 2014); Anna Hájková, "Der Judenälteste und seine SS-Männer: Benjamin Murmelstein und

that a privileged position was most often accounted for by two apparently mutually exclusive patterns of behavior on the part of the respective individual. Either the individual was a collaborator—here collaboration is defined as the coerced participation of Jews in the victimization of fellow Jews, often in return for a privileged position—or the individual is characterized as a resistance fighter.[6] Only recently has this historic perspective begun to shift, as evident, for example, in the more nuanced understanding and broader frame of reference in the work of Holocaust historian Christopher Browning and his research on the Starachowice forced labor camp complex.[7] Other scholars have also raised questions far beyond the dichotomy of "good" and "bad" behavior during the Holocaust, such as, "What kind of Kapo[8] had one been?" Questions that address broader underlying issues regarding the human mind include: "What is a human being? How many faces does he have? What abysses are in his heart?"[9]

During the last decade, a large body of scholarship on the history of the concentration camp system has been published that illuminates the topography of camps under the auspices of the SS-Wirtschafts- und Verwaltungshauptamt (SS Main Economic and Administrative Department, SS-WVHA) in Nazi-occupied Europe. Owing to this research and the inherent broader historical perspective, the often one-

seine Beziehung zu Adolf Eichmann und Karl Rahm," in Ronny Loewy and Katharina Rauschenberger, eds., *"Der Letzte der Ungerechten"*: *der "Judenälteste" Benjamin Murmelstein in Filmen 1942–1975* (Frankfurt am Main and New York: Campus Verlag, 2011).

6   Tanja Schönborn, "Widerstand im Konzentrationslager: Formen, Voraussetzungen, Möglichkeiten und Verarbeitung aus literaturwissenschaftlicher und sozial- psychologischer Perspektive," *Tagungsbericht: Widerstand im Konzentrationslager: Formen, Voraussetzungen, Moglichkeiten und Verarbeitung aus literaturwissenschaftlicher und sozialpsychologischer Perspektive, Regensburg, July7–August 7, 2015*, H-Soz-Kult, November 5, 2015, https://www.hsozkult.de/conferencereport/id/tagungsberichte-6231 (accessed August 1, 2021); Tamar Rotem, "Kapo—or Hero?" *Haaretz*, April 5, 2002, https://www.haaretz.com/life/books/2002-04-05/ty-article/kapo-or-hero/0000017f- f660-d47e-a37f-ff7ced9f0000 (accessed March 15, 2018).

7   Christopher R. Browning, *Remembering Survival: Inside a Nazi Slave-Labor Camp* (New York: W. W. Norton, 2010); Browning, *Collected Memories: Holocaust History and Post- War Testimony* (Madison: University of Wisconsin Press, 2003).

8   Glasner-Heled and Bar-On, "Displaced: The Memoir of Eliezer Gruenbaum," p. 3.

9   Philip G. Zimbardo, *The Lucifer Effect: How Good People Turn Evil* (New York: Random House, 2007). These broader questions are related to the question of how "ordinary guards" became torturers.

sided view associated with the concept "concentration camps"—"camps as the places of absolute terror where daily life was not possible"—the narrative that emerged in Germany after the publication in German in 1992 of *The Order of Terror: The Concentration Camp* by German sociologist Wolfgang Sofsky has gradually been modified.[10] Nevertheless, the complex social hierarchies—the interactions and interdependencies within the prisoner societies in general and particularly within the respective Jewish prisoner society is relatively unexplored. Scholarship in this field was initiated through the work of Gideon Greif,[11] Bella Gutterman,[12] Esther Farbstein, and, more recently, Andrea Rudorff[13] and Kim Wünschmann, among others.[14] Holocaust scholars like Nikolaus Wachsmann[15] do not even discuss this issue, nor is it addressed in the *Encyclopedia of Camps and Ghettos*, which was edited by the USHMM.[16]

The concentration camps may be understood today as complex social environments. However, there has not yet been a comprehensive study about "life in the concentration camps." While there have been studies on the ghettos in Warsaw, Łódź, or Kovno (Kaunas), the camps in Sachsenhausen or Buchenwald, for example, have not been studied. Consequently, little is known about the tensions, solidarity, collaboration, and assistant services to the SS, or about supportive mutual aid among the prisoners. Only a few articles have been published on Jewish inmate functionaries.[17] One reason may be that this is a very complex

---

10 Wolfgang Sofsky, *The Order of Terror: The Concentration Camp* (Princeton: Princeton University Press, 1997).

11 Gideon Greif, *We Wept Without Tears: Testimonies of the Jewish Sonderkommando from Auschwitz* (New Haven: Yale University Press, 2005). The original edition in German was first published in 1994, and the Hebrew translation was published in 1999.

12 Bella Gutterman, *Narrow Bridge to Life: The Gross-Rosen Network of Labor Camps for Jews* (New York and Oxford: Berghahn Books, 2008).

13 Andrea Rudorff, *Frauen in den Außenlagern des Konzentrationslagers Groß-Rosen* (Berlin: Metropol Verlag, 2014).

14 Kim Wünschmann, *Before Auschwitz: Jewish Prisoners in the Prewar Concentration Camps* (Cambridge: Cambridge University Press, 2015).

15 Nikolaus Wachsmann, *KL: A History of the Nazi Concentration Camps* (London: Farrar, Straus and Giroux, 2016).

16 *Encyclopedia of Camps and Ghettos*, https://www.ushmm.org/research/publications/ encyclopedia-camps-ghettos/download (accessed August 1, 2021).

17 See, e.g., Hermann F. Weiss, "From Reichsautobahnlager to Schmelt Camp: Brande: A Forgotten Holocaust Site in Western Upper Silesia, 1940–1943," *Yad Vashem Studies*, 39:2 (2011), pp. 83–95; Weiss, "Preiskretscham (Pyskowice): A Forced Labor Camp for Jews in Upper Silesia, 1942–1944," *Roczik Muzeum Górnośląskiego W Bytomiu*, 10 (2016). Weiss was able to analyze a postwar interview of one of the camp's *Judenältesten*, Josef Slaim.

issue. There were not simply "two forces" during the Holocaust—good (victims) and evil (perpetrators)—and neither category comprehends all the Jewish functionaries, men and women, as many fall somewhere "in between." I am convinced that the individual behavior patterns of the Jewish functionaries were often dependent on two related aspects:

1. The assumption that there had been no "freedom of choice" implies that the individual functionary had no autonomy. Moreover, in many studies it is subliminally assumed that even if there had been "free choice," the respective Jews would have chosen "good deeds," which could have meant acting without harming others,[18] and if they had made decisions against fellow Jews, they had acted under coercion.[19] I contend that this is a simplification that ignores the "broad swathe of human behavior...between these extremes" of collaboration and resistance, but also that they found themselves in life-threatening situations, where altruism and solidarity were the exception rather than the rule.[20]

2. The unsubtle assumption that there was a homogeneous mass of Jewish victims—"the servants," according to Primo Levi— ignores the vastly different living conditions of Jews in the camps, the different "types" of Jewish functionaries, and the very different ethnic backgrounds of the Jewish inmates. In her research on Jewish witnesses in trials and honor courts, Rivka Brot refers to the assumption that Jews were a "homogeneous group" (of survivors) who "all represented the absolute good."[21]

This essay demonstrates that there was rarely a clear distinction between collaboration and resistance; rather, behavior tended to be ambiguous, conflicting, and paradoxical—exhibiting both "collaboration" and

---

18 In his book *The Lucifer Effect*, Philip Zimbardo impressively shows that the specific space, which he calls the "system," contributes to the behavior of individuals—without exempting them from their responsibility; Zimbardo, *The Lucifer Effect*.

19 Rivka Brot, "There Wasn't a Righteous Person Among Them: The Gray Zone of Collaboration in the Israeli Courtroom," in Gabriel Finder and Laura Jockusch, eds., *Jewish Honor Courts: Revenge, Retribution, and Reconciliation in Europe and Israel after the Holocaust* (Detroit: Wayne State University Press, 2015), p. 349, https://www.academia.edu/12925684/_There_Wasn_t_a_Righteous_Person_among_Them_The_Gray_Zone_of_Collaboration_in_the_Israeli_Courtroom (accessed January 27, 2021).

20 Brot, "Julius Siegel," pp. 65–127, in particular, p. 69.

21 Brot, *There Wasn't A Righteous Person*, p. 351.

resistance, most often combined in one person. Individual behavior in complex social environments or extreme situations, such as in Nazi camps or ghettos, was ambivalent, conflicting, paradoxical, and not mutually exclusive. The following case study of Karl Demerer,[22] a *Judenältest* (camp elder) at the "Jewish camp" in Blechhammer, provides an impressive illustration of this perspective. Demerer's life in that camp combined both "collaborational" patterns and aspects of resistance, or as some prominent Holocaust historians defined it, alleviation.[23]

First, there have to be some conceptual considerations. The term and the subject of "Jewish collaboration" was and remains a highly complex area of Holocaust research. As one can see from the Kapo trials in Israel, it was a huge challenge to judge crimes committed by persecuted individuals;[24] the same difficulties also emerged in the Jewish honor courts after the war had ended.[25] Saul Friedländer, for one, did not even mention the "gray zone" of Jewish collaboration in his works.[26] However, the omission of this highly important aspect of Jewish life during the Holocaust somewhat distorts the picture. For example, a look at the concentration camps reveals that compared to the total number of functionaries, Jews—both men and women—were a minority. Yet, among the survivors, there were quite a few, and a careful look at their testimonies reveals that many of them held a "privileged position," for example, as a *Lagerläufer* (camp runner/ messenger), or as a prisoner in the Kanada Commando, who sorted the belongings of the murdered, or as a physician or camp nurse.

Moreover, it is important to keep in mind that if one speaks today of "Jews" as a group, one might forget that it was the Nuremberg Laws of 1935 that defined who was a Jew, and that many people of Jewish descent who did not self-identify as Jewish were also persecuted. Now, to come full circle, if Holocaust researchers talk about a Jewish elite,

22 In 2018, Karl Demerer posthumously was granted the Jewish Rescuer's Citation in Poland by the Committee to Recognize the Heroism of Jews Who Rescued Fellow Jews during the Holocaust of the B'nai B'rith World Center, Jerusalem. Israeli researcher Zahava Mualem is also currently studying Karl Demerer.

23 See Raul Hilberg, *The Destruction of the European Jews* (New York: Holmes & Meier, 1985). For Hilberg's evolving interpretation of functionaries, see Adam Brown, *Judging "Privileged" Jews: Holocaust Ethics, Representation and the "Grey Zone"* (New York and Oxford: Berghahn Books, 2013).

24 Ben-Naftali and Tuval, "Punishing International Crimes Committed by the Persecuted," pp. 128–178; Brot, "There Wasn't a Righteous Person Among Them," pp. 327–360.

25 Jockusch and Finder, *Jewish Honor Courts*.

26 Siegel, "Treating an Auschwitz Prisoner-Physician."

leaders, or Jews in presumably privileged positions, as in the camps, one must be aware of the caveats. In order to acquire a better and more nuanced understanding of the Holocaust, including the responses of the persecuted, especially the functionaries, circumstances as well as individual behaviors must be considered most carefully. As human behavior and perceptions of reality are highly complex, the following hypothetical question may be posed: Would a non-Jewish individual who was persecuted as a Jew and imprisoned in a ghetto or a camp, and who became a Kapo be considered a "Jewish collaborator"?

The following questions, without any claim of completeness, may be helpful in illuminating the complexity of human behavior during the Holocaust: If an individual "collaborated" or cooperated with Nazi functionaries, what was the motive behind that act? How did he or she execute the daily tasks in the respective privileged position? For or against the fellow prisoners, or both? Did the person's behavior change with time?

I am convinced that the subliminally assumed and highlighted "solidarity of the victims/the persecuted" in many scholarly works was an important factor for many of the survivors, however, it was for many of them also an exception and not the rule. Primo Levi and other less well-known survivors noted that fact in their accounts.[27] Researchers tend to focus on the positive aspects of human coexistence in the ghettos or camps, which is not at all wrong, but sometimes I wonder if the historical weighting is balanced. The best sources for discussion of all those questions and subjects are the testimonies of the survivors—specific memories based on their personal experiences—which tell us a great deal about everyday life and the perversion of values and norms during the Holocaust.

Introduction to Blechhammer

Blechhammer[28] was established in 1940 under the administration of Organization Schmelt, which established a camp system in East Upper

---

27 Adam Brown, *Judging "Privileged" Jews*; Lawrence L. Langer, *Versions of Survival: The Holocaust and the Human Spirit* (New York: State University of New York Press, 1982).

28 Andrea Rudorff, "Blechhammer (Blachownia)," in Wolfgang Benz and Barbara Distel, eds., *Der Ort des Terrors: Geschichte der nationalsozialistischen Konzentrationslager 1933–1945*, vol. 5 (Munich: C. H. Beck, 2007), pp. 186–191.

Silesia that was separate from the concentration camp system.[29] The Schmelt camps are well known because the first systematic selection of Jews was carried out there, apart from "*Aktion* 14f13."[30] Trains to Auschwitz stopped at Cosel, where inmates were selected for forced labor. Blechhammer was a large complex that consisted of several small camp units—forced labor camps, prisoner of war camps, and work/re-education camps for political prisoners—with about 50,000 prisoners. The living conditions in the *Judenlager* (Jewish camp) in Blechhammer were somewhat less intolerable than other camps with Jewish inmates—at least until the spring of 1944, when it was incorporated into Auschwitz III. At times, there were 6,000 Jewish prisoners incarcerated in Blechhammer, but only 3,000 men and 200 women were living there when it was liquidated in January 1945, most of them Polish Jews, but also some from the Netherlands, France, Germany, and Belgium.[31] In January 1945, the last prisoners were forced to leave Blechhammer and were sent on death marches, the last of whom ended up in Bavaria.[32] Although the Schmelt camps comprised a separate camp system, in many ways they were similar to the other concentration camps.

Lagerälteste (Camp Elders) in General

The original meaning of the term *Lagerälteste* was fundamentally different from its use under National Socialism. The use in the context of the camp system shows that *Lagerälteste* is a National Socialist neologism. It was a feature of the concentration camp wherein the SS delegated supervisory functions to inmates and established a differentiated system of prisoner functionaries.[33] All of us know the term "Kapo." Himmler

---

29 Andrea Rudorff, "Arbeit und Vernichtung Reconsidered: Die Lager der Organisation Schmelt für polnische Jüdinnen und Juden aus dem annektierten Teil Oberschlesiens," *Sozial.Geschichte Online*, 7 (2012), pp. 10–39, http://www.stiftung-sozialgeschichte. de (accessed August 1, 2021); Wolf Gruner, "Juden bauen die Straßen des Führers," *Zeitschrift für Geschichtswissenschaft*, 44 (1996), pp. 798–808.

30 Sybille Steinbacher, "*Musterstadt*" *Auschwitz: Germanisierungspolitik und Judenmord in Ostoberschlesien* (Munich: Saur, 2000), p. 277.

31 Rudorff, "Blechhammer."

32 Heinrich Demerer, *Olam Shalem Karas Betohi: Hitbagrut Bamahanot Uvatzaʾadot Hamavet* (Hebrew) (Jerusalem: Yad Vashem, 2020).

33 H. G. Adler, "Selbstverwaltung und Widerstand in den Konzentrationslagern," *Vierteljahrshefte für Zeitgeschichte*, 8 (1960), pp. 221–236; Falk Pingel, *Häftlinge unter*

explained this perfidious system in an address to Wehrmacht generals on June 21, 1944.

> There we made use of...Kapos...From the moment he becomes a Kapo, he won't sleep among the other prisoners anymore. He is responsible for seeing that the work is done, that the prisoners don't commit sabotage, that they are clean, and that the beds are made well....Thus, he has to push his men. At the moment we become dissatisfied with him, he's no longer a Kapo, and he will sleep with the others again. He knows very well that they will beat him to death on the first night.[34]

The *Lagerälteste* in contrast to the Kapos, ranked at the top of the camp hierarchy and in the camp society of prisoners.

In the men's camps, the SS most often appointed experienced prisoners as *Lagerälteste*, many of whom had been incarcerated elsewhere before they were transferred to the men's camps. In exchange for favorable treatment, these inmates promised to be reliable about adhering to the rules of the camp. For the most part, they were ethnic Germans, classified as *Berufsverbrecher* (professional criminals) or "antisocials;" political prisoners also held these positions.[35] The SS— more specifically the respective *Schutzhaftlagerführer* (protective custody camp leader)[36]—appointed those functionaries. A great number of them stayed in the camps until 1945, and there were many instances of fellow prisoners executing them just before or just after liberation.

It was characteristic of the National Socialist regime to delegate

---

SS-Herrschaft: Widerstand, Selbstbehauptung und Vernichtung im Konzentrationslager (Hamburg: Hoffmann and Campe, 1978), pp. 102–117; Hermann Langbein, *People in Auschwitz* (Chapel Hill: University of North Carolina Press, 2004), pp. 178–190; Herbert Diercks, *Abgeleitete Macht–Funktionshäftlinge zwischen Widerstand und Kollaboration* (Bremen: Edition Temmen, 1998); Revital Ludewig-Kedmi, *Opfer und Täter zugleich? Moraldilemmata jüdischer Funktionshäftlinge in der Shoah* (Giessen: Psychosozial Verlag, 2001).

34 Ulrich Fritz, in Ulrich Fritz, Silvija Kavcic, and Nicole Warmbold, eds., *Tatort KZ: Neue Beiträge zur Geschichte der Konzentrationslager* (Ulm: Klemm and Oelschläger, 2003), p. 120.

35 The administration in Sachsenhausen or Buchenwald consisted of three *Lageraeälteste*.

36 The *Schutzhaftlagerführer* was subordinate to the *Lagerführer*. He was responsible for protective custody, a typical Nazi term; such custody supposedly was for protecting German society from the prisoners, be they antisocials elements, Jews, or homosexuals.

supervisory functions to the persecuted, and the SS established a differentiated system of prisoner functionaries. The *Lagerälteste* were at the top of the camp hierarchy, functioning as liaisons between the SS and the inmates. A look at the men's concentration camps, for example, Buchenwald, illustrates the daily tasks of *Lagerälteste*, whose clothes were an indicator of their privileged position and their areas of competence.

- *Lagerälteste* I was responsible for the whole administration.
- *Lagerälteste* II and his deputy administrated the *Arbeitseinsatz* (labor division).
- *Lagerälteste* III implemented the camp rules and imposed the penalties.[37]

The crucial criterion was most often knowledge of the German language. In some cases, the respective *Lagerführer* (camp leader), an SS officer, took into consideration "voluntary applications" by inmates, or made decisions based on whether they liked a person or not. Two former female prisoners testified about the selection of prisoner functionaries in Schlesiersee I, Lower Silesia, in October 1944: "We had to stand for *appell* [roll call] until late in the evening, and the SS man picked out the women for different positions. If the woman prisoner put on a friendly face, she got a better position."[38] Moreover, in some testimonies it was noted that prisoners had relative autonomy in appointing "their" *Lagerälteste*.[39]

In the Schmelt camps it was different—the *Lagerälteste* took responsibility for all of the daily tasks. The prisoner society in the *Judenlager* in Blechhammer consisted solely of Jewish men and women, so Jewish prisoners served as Kapos and *Blockälteste* (block elders), performed *Stubendienst* (barrack duty), worked in the *Schreibstube* (registry/office), and also served as camp physicians or nurses. Especially in the Schmelt camps—and later on in the Baltic concentration camps such as Vaivara in Estonia—with a population of only Jewish women

---

37 Harry Stein, "Buchenwald—Stammlager," in Benz and Distel, *Der Ort des Terrors: Geschichte der nationalsozialistischen Konzentrationslager*, vol. 3 (Munich: C. H. Beck, 2006), pp. 301–356, particularly p. 331.

38 Rozsi and Helen F. testimony, July 16, 1945, Deportáltakat Gondozó Országos Bizottság (National Committee for Attending Deportees) (DEGOB), Protokoll Nr. 2820, https://www.degob.org (accessed August 1, 2021).

39 Rudorff, *Frauen in den Außenlagern des Konzentrationslagers Groß-Rosen*.

and men, Jews such as Demerer were able to assume privileged positions, even as *Lagerälteste*.[40] There they were called *Judenälteste*, as in many ghettos.

Brief Biography of Karl Demerer

Karl Demerer was born in Vienna in June 1901.[41] In an oral history interview conducted in Yad Vashem in 1973, he noted that he was born into a nonreligious family. His father died when he was six months old, and his mother then went to Biała near Bielitz (today Bielsko-Biała) in Upper Silesia. He attended a Polish school, although his mother tongue was German. At the age of fifteen or sixteen, he returned with his family to Vienna. Deprivation and starvation were part of everyday life for the Demerer family, and the boy contributed financially. His first love was a non-Jewish woman, but his mother objected to the relationship. He spent a holiday in Kattowitz (today Katowice), where he met the woman he would marry—Henia, from Sosnowiec. They had two children— Halina, who was born in 1930 and Heinrich (Heniek), born in 1931.

The family's hometown, Sosnowiec, was invaded by German troops two weeks after the invasion of Poland in 1939. Karl Demerer was forced to leave his family to work as a laborer in various work camps for Jews in Upper Silesia, such as in Annaberg or Ottmuth, in 1940. From 1942 onward, he was interned in Blechhammer, which was administrated by Organization Schmelt, where he was promoted because he "spoke a real good German."[42] and became the highest-ranking prisoner in the camp. Demerer served as the *Judenältester* of the *Judenlager* until the camp was liquidated in January 1945.

As the Germans began purging East Upper Silesia of Jews in May 1942,[43] the entire population, including Demerer's family—most of whom were elderly, women, and children—were assembled in a sports stadium, held there for five days, and finally subjected to a selection. All the elderly and the children, including Heinrich Demerer's grandmother

---

40 Ruth Bettina Birn, "Vaivara—Stammlager," in Benz and Distel, *Der Ort des Terrors: Geschichte der nationalsozialistischen Konzentrationslager 1933–1945*, vol. 8, pp. 131–147.
41 Karl Demerer testimony, Yad Vashem Archives (YVA), O.3/3635.
42 Ibid.
43 Rudorff, "Arbeit und Vernichtung Reconsidered," p. 22.

and his cousin, who was also named Heinrich, were sent to Auschwitz, although Heinrich Demerer managed to escape. He went to live with his mother and sister in the ghetto of Środula (Szrodula), which was established for the Jewish population of Sosnowiec and finally liquidated in August 1943.

Owing to Karl Demerer's connections to Alfred Ludwig, an employee of Organization Schmelt, whose headquarters was in Sosnowiec, his family was transferred to Blechhammer before the final liquidation of the ghetto in Środula. This "reunification" was a survival strategy of the imprisoned Jewish forced laborers in the Schmelt camps and proved to be a lifesaving measure during this time in this region.[44] Jews who were living in a camp in 1943 had a chance to survive when all the ghettos in the region were liquidated and the people were deported to Birkenau. From August 1943 on, approximately 30,000 Jews were transferred to Auschwitz-Birkenau, and most of them were murdered in the crematoria. Karl Demerer's family survived the Holocaust and was reunited in Bavaria in 1945.[45]

Functional Cooperation

This essay is based on oral history interviews with survivors regarding Karl Demerer, which are housed in the archive of the USC Shoah Foundation Visual History Archive (VHA) and also in other archives, as well as on other sources. When I began looking for interviewees among individuals who had testified about the Blechhammer camp and its *Judenältester* Karl Demerer, I found that the following terms in the index were used to describe his function: "Jewish Camp Police, SS/SD personal, Jewish Survivor." Of course, this categorization reflects the interpretation of the person who indexed the respective interview on the basis of the information provided by the interviewee, but may also be understood as reflecting the position in which the survivor found himself before Demerer: Was this person part of his designated subgroup or not? Since Demerer was not able to protect all his fellow prisoners, some saw

---

44 For Jews, living inside a camp in 1943 meant a chance to survive, since all the ghettos in the region were liquidated and the people were deported to Birkenau.

45 For the story of the family, see Verena Buser, introduction to the Hebrew edition of Heinrich Demerer's memoir, Demerer, *Olam Shalem Karas Betochi*, pp. 7–17.

him as their protector, while others reported negative experiences. Just as Christopher Browning noted regarding Jeremiah Wilczek, the head of the "camp council" in the Starachowice factory forced labor camp, it is striking that Demerer was also remembered "more for whom [he] saved than for whom [he] mistreated."[46] How can that fact be explained? Moreover, is it possible to identify specific "strategies" that Demerer used to increase the chances of survival for at least some of his fellow prisoners?

After the war, Demerer reported that he had developed a close contact and a good relationship[47] with *SS-Sturmbannführer* Alfred Ludwig, who worked for Organization Schmelt.[48] Moreover, court files of the Central Agency for the Investigation of National Socialist Crimes in Ludwigsburg, Germany, reveal that Ludwig and Demerer shared some parallels in their biographies: Ludwig was around the same age as Demerer, in his early forties at the time, and also came from Vienna. Others confirmed that special relationship. According to former prisoner Harry Fransman, for example, even the Germans respected Demerer.[49]

A leading position in the camp meant that the favored prisoner lived a dual life marked by ambivalence: having to "serve" the camp personnel and the prisoners while being well aware of the fact that there were not merely two sides—of "masters" and of "slaves"—in the camps but a whole, coerced "society" of prisoners. Many decisions were taken every day to the detriment of others. Presumably, Demerer and others who found themselves in privileged positions could act spontaneously in response to a given situation and were in a sense good "actors." Frederika Kohensius[50] described Demerer's personality and how it affected his actions:

> After being in camp Gogolin for three months, 100 women, including me and my sister, were sent to camp Blechhammer in May 1943....The *Judenältester* was a Jew from Vienna by the name of Karl Demerer, a

---

46 Browning, "'Alleviation' and 'Compliance,'" p. 32.
47 Karl Demerer testimony, YVA, O.3/3635.
48 Investigations of Alfred Ludwig (b. 1902), Verfügung der Zentralstelle im Lande Nordrhein-Westfalen für die Bearbeitung von nationalsozialistischen Massenverbrechen bei der Staatsanwaltschaft Dortmund, April, 3, 1978, *Bundesarchiv Berlin* (BA), 205AR 1496/67, vol. 20.
49 Harry Joseph Fransman interview, May 9, 1995, Sydney, Australia, USC Shoah Foundation Visual History Archive (VHA), 2548.
50 Frederika Kohensius testimony, YVA, O.93/46023.

man with a clear head, who knew how to behave in different situations. There was a case in which a prisoner named Eisenberg, a tall, thin man, revealed to Demerer's deputy, a Jew from the Netherlands named Nibeks, that he had dollars, diamonds, and valuables hidden in a cellar in Sosnowiec. He asked the deputy to speak to a German officer and to ask him to take him [Eisenberg] to the cellar, and he would give him half of the valuables. The deputy spoke with a German officer who passed the information on. Before long, a few German officers, including the *Lagerführer* [Erich] Hoffmann, seized Eisenberg and brought him to Karl Demerer's office. As they entered the office, Karl Demerer immediately rose up and began to beat and curse Eisenberg. Eisenberg fell to the floor and Demerer continued to kick him. The Germans who were standing there told Demerer [that he had done a] "good job." That's how Demerer was able to save Eisenberg.[51]

Demerer had "good" connections, because he deliberately took advantage of the corruptibility of the *Lagerkommandant* (camp commander)[52] and bribed him; thus, for example, he managed to save some female prisoners by ensuring that they were not transferred to Birkenau.[53] In another situation, he adopted a strategy that might be defined as "embrace your enemies." Asked by the *Lagerführer*, "Tell me, Demerer, I am not the *Lagerführer* and you are not the *Lagerältester*, tell me, what do you believe, who will win the war?" Demerer, who later described himself as a "German Jew" who had become an "Israeli," answered, "We will, of course." The *Lagerführer* looked at him, asking what he meant. Demerer replied, "We Germans, *Herr Lagerführer*." Then both smoked a cigarette and Demerer told him about some diamonds that he said he had found by chance and with that, he saved forty children from being transferred to Birkenau. I have as yet been unable to prove this story.

Protection of Others Became Possible

Although the interpretation and implementation of camp rules were always in the hands of SS personnel and the highest-ranking prisoner

---

51 I wish to thank Zahava Mualem for the translation of parts of the interview.
52 Rudolf Höss, for example, was the *Lagerkommandant* of Auschwitz.
53 Karl Demerer testimony, YVA, O.3/3635, p. 7.

functionary, the rules were often interpreted arbitrarily. Demerer had a large say in building up a cohort of functionaries when camp positions had to be filled. According to his testimony,

There was no whip used to bring order. Not one Kapo carried a whip, no one was beaten; you only did it here and there, if you had to, in front of the SS, to show them that you were tough. Aside from that, it was a camp where they let you live, where it was possible to arrange things so that you would get what you needed.[54]

Demerer insisted that he beat fellow prisoners to "pretend that [I] was a hard man in front of the SS."[55] For the most part, other survivor testimonies back up Demerer's version of camp life in Blechhammer. Arthur Gelbart recalled that "[he] saved many lives; he would lie and cheat...[he] punished Kapos who beat up prisoners, he really ran that thing [and] kept [the] camp in order, [the] Germans appreciated this..."[56] Sam Schnitzer reported that Demerer "concealed things [from the SS], [he] bribed the Germans."[57] Emanuel Wajnblum described Demerer as follows:

He was acting as being cruel in the camp [to] appease [the Nazi staff] in the camp; he intervened in the camp so that the Nazis did not touch [the prisoners] directly [i.e., whipping or hitting them with rifles]; [he] used his whip and pretended to whip his fellow prisoners; [he was] an excellent actor.[58]

However, one has to keep in mind that at the same time Demerer was responsible for carrying out executions by hanging. Moreover, he benefited from his position as the *Judenältest*. He was able to save his family and establish a social network, as well as relationships with other women. Furthermore, he may have sometimes used his power to do what he wanted for his own sake to the detriment of others.

---

54 Ibid., pp. 6–7.
55 Ibid., p. 7.
56 Arthur Gelbart interview, December 17, 1996, Pepper Pike, OH, VHA, 24368.
57 Sam Schnitzer interview November 7, 1996, Bronx, New York, VHA, 22536.
58 Emanuel Wajnblum interview, November 20, 1996, Bentleigh East, Australia, VHA, 23432.

However, I contend that his decisions were—in contrast to those of the Judenräte in the ghettos—"lonely ones." He was not only responsible for the entire administration, but he also ran the Arbeitseinsatz (labor division) and had to enforce the camp rules and impose the penalties. He was in charge of the community of prisoners, but we do not know of any individual among the camp elite who testified after the war. Demerer's testimony reveals that he took most of his crucial decisions at his own risk and not with a cohort of fellow prisoners, which would have allowed him to discuss the advantages and disadvantages of a decision. For example, when he had to send women prisoners to another camp, not a single woman wanted to leave, since the destination of this specific transport was uncertain. Demerer decided to add the names of his wife, Henia, and daughter, Halina, to the transport list. This gave the other women a sense of security and most of them wanted to join Henia and Halina Demerer. Moreover, there is another story—or perhaps a myth— mentioned both in Demerer's Yad Vashem testimony and that I heard from his family: During the death marches, an SS man allegedly had offered Demerer a gun so that he could flee with his son. He recalled more than twenty-five years later that he had rejected the offer, because he felt a responsibility to lead the Jews to their final destination, although his son was only thirteen years old at the time.[59]

The Dark Side of Being Part of the Camp Elite

Compelled by his privileged position and his awareness of the all-too- often unpredictable camp penalties, Karl Demerer once beat his son. Karl Demerer had to punish his son, knowing very well what could happen to him as a consequence of being charged with sabotage. Both Karl Demerer and his son Heinrich recalled this event, which Karl related in his testimony, including the recollections of his son, Heinrich,[60] who lived with his father even after his mother and sister were sent to another camp. The reason for the beating was that the boy played with a spool of yarn, unaware of the fact that high-ranking SS officials had come to Blechhammer to conduct an inspection on that day. When they found the yarn, they suspected the prisoners of sabotage and demanded to know

---

59 Karl Demerer testimony, YVA, O.3/3635, p. 18.
60 Demerer, *Olam Shalem Karas Betochi*, pp. 58–59.

the person responsible in order to punish him. When Demerer learned that his son was the "evil doer" he offered to punish the boy himself, and proceeded to slap him twice. However, later, when he was alone with his son, Demerer beat him with a belt. In his testimony, Heinrich recalled,

> He then beat me so hard with his belt in the laundry barracks that I won't forget it for my entire life. I had red welts everywhere. I screamed so loud that many prisoners came over. Father sent them all away. Then he said to me, you can think about why you got this beating. I stood for a long time in the laundry barracks and wept. At first I was terribly angry with father…At the evening meal in the barracks, the cook told me that I should never do anything like that again, explaining that, for the Germans, everything could be sabotage, and for sabotage there is only one punishment: death.[61]

Heinrich survived because he lived with his father, the *Judenältest* and highest prisoner functionary. The two were never separated, which granted Heinrich a measure of emotional stability. His father provided a sense of connection to his former home and especially to his mother. Karl Demerer took care of his son when his son was repeatedly beaten by Kapos or by SS men, and during the death marches in January 1945, following the evacuation of Blechhammer via Groß Rosen and Flossenbürg.[62] However, when Karl Demerer refused to flee with his son from the death march—most probably because he felt some sense of responsibility for the prisoners—the son then endured some traumatic events, which had a lifelong impact.

As I noted above, according to the testimonies that were studied for this essay, most of these survivors benefited from an improvement in their living conditions through Karl Demerer's help. They explained that they owed him their lives, or were part of his group of friends in the camp, for example, his camp secretary or one of the girlfriends he supposedly had in Blechhammer. While most of the witnesses saw him as a rescuer—a "real mensch"—one person reported the following:

> I lost my parents…to the politics of Jews in the camps.…My brother-in-law's wife [the witness' sister] was there. The Jew in the

---

61 Ibid.
62 One transport went to Regensburg and another to Bergen Belsen.

camp—Demerer...he had a couple of girlfriends. The girlfriends were jealous of my sister. I had a very good-looking sister. Pure jealousy....The *Judenältester* said something to Mengele and he took my father, my mother, my sister, my brother-in-law, and another doctor and they went.[63]

This testimony is paradigmatic in that the witness does not explicitly evaluate the consequences of Demerer's actions as "correct" or "wrong"— although the readers of these testimonies who were born after these events had occurred may categorize them as "good" or "bad." Moreover, this testimony may have been intended to serve as a corrective against the background of the discussion of Demerer's behavior as being merely that of a hero. Thus, it demonstrates that there are different narratives of the events and their interpretation depends on who testified and with what intention, be it Demerer himself, or his fellow prisoners who received his help, or who were sent to other destinations or to their deaths.

German officials investigated Demerer in 1963. Israeli officials also later conducted an investigation concerning charges of accessory to murder. A former fellow prisoner, Israel F. from Rozniatow, accused him in 1963[64] of having two camp physicians, Dr. Ritter and Dr. Simons, sent to Auschwitz-Birkenau because "certain tensions prevailed," between them owing to the fact that Dr. Ritter in particular did not want to follow Demerer's instructions. According to the witness, Demerer was fully aware of the use of Zyklon B in Birkenau to carry out mass murders.[65] We will never know if he was a rescuer, or simply an egoist who had the ability to manipulate others but, ultimately, is that important? If we know that a rescuer can also have his dark side, we gain a greater understanding of human behavior. Philip Zimbardo, the American social psychologist who created the famous Stanford Prisoner Experiment and who, after 2003, was the psychological evaluator of one of the guards who tortured prisoners in Abu Ghraib in Iraq noted, "Given violent behavior, one searches for sadistic personality traits. Given heroic deeds, the search is one for genes that predispose toward altruism."[66] However, most often, the line between evil and good deeds is naturally permeable and is surely

---

63 Ezriel Zigmunt Rabinowicz interview, August 27, 1997, Melbourne, VHA, 32755.
64 Israel F. testimony, June 18, 1963, Staatsanwaltschaft bei dem Landgericht Mannheim, Landesarchiv Baden-Württemberg.
65 Ibid.
66 Zimbardo, *The Lucifer Effect*, p. 7.

dependent on the context in which they were performed and the time. According to Zimbardo's theory, individual behavior in extreme situations can only be adequately explained by dispositional, situational, and systemic factors rather than by individual choices—the choices approach seems far too monolithic or simplistic. It is important to remember that the Nazi camp system was designed to prompt victims to consider collaboration from the beginning, which was an integral part of that system. The "gray zone," as coined by Primo Levi, was a natural feature of the camps and not an exception. Isabella Leitner, who was transferred from Auschwitz–Birkenau to Birnbaumel in October 1944, was well aware of the ambivalence of her "privileged" position. "The German genius had, of course, variations of evil. One of which was to appoint the torturers from among the inmates themselves. Brother against brother, sister against sister."[67] It would be promising to read either the small number of *Selbstzeugnisse* (self-accounts)[68] or ego-documents by former Jewish functionaries against the background of the dispositional, situational, and systemic factors that led to the behavioral outcome, applying Zimbardo's approach.[69] This is because Holocaust survivors who testified about the respective functionaries focused most often on a narrow outcome of the behavior of certain individuals, either the "hero" who acted altruistically, or the "sadistic" Kapo who acted for his own benefit.

During a conversation with an Auschwitz survivor who was liberated in Berlin, I asked the woman if she had had any experiences with Kapos or other functionaries. She told me about a female prisoner who had guarded the female teenagers in a Berlin subcamp and who was very brutal. At the end she noted, "And only today, I understand her behavior because her parents were shot in front of her eyes in the Łódź ghetto."[70] I found several other testimonies in which the survivors focused not on a single event that was triggered by an assumed perverted personality structure but rather on the circumstances that had led to the behavioral outcome.[71]

67 Isabella Leitner, *Fragments of Isabella: A Memoir of Auschwitz*, ed. by Irving A. Leitner (New York: Thomas Y. Crowell, 1978), pp. 55–56.

68 Accounts about oneself.

69 Zimbardo, *The Lucifer Effect*.

70 Conversation between the author and A. B., Haifa, March 10, 2019.

71 In some testimonies, the survivors themselves said that the behavior of an individual was triggered by the camp environment or by experiences to which the person had been subjected. For example, a person became cruel after having witnessed the murder of his

Conclusion

Most often, scholars conclude that the Jewish elites or Jewish leaders were either collaborators or rescuers. Remarkably, nearly every survivor account focuses on prisoner functionaries—they are "nowhere and yet everywhere."[72] Yet despite their omnipresence in survivors' testimonies, they are not an integral part of the official history or of the collective memory of the camps. As has been noted, Nikolaus Wachsmann published a comprehensive study on the history of the concentration camps in which the existing research on functionaries is hardly mentioned.[73] There is neither a comprehensive study on that group nor an approach to analyzing testimonies about them and from them regarding inherent complexities, inconsistencies, specific structures, and themes that are "silenced," that is, not mentioned at all. According to former prisoners and one of the most prominent survivors, Primo Levi, the "network of human relationships inside the *Lager* was not simple; it could not be reduced to the two blocs of victims and persecutors."[74] This, we can agree, was true in all of the more than 40,000 camps that were built by Nazi Germany.

Levi's view regarding the analysis of the Kapos is sometimes very narrow. However, since he focused primarily on Auschwitz, as he himself was a prisoner in Monowitz, on the Sonderkommando, and on the role of Rumkowski in the Litzmannstadt ghetto, it would be most interesting to add current research to his elaborated thoughts, which have become an integral part of the Holocaust canon. According to Levi, as described in his book, *The Drowned and the Saved*, there was a scaled system of individual responsibilities and behavioral patterns among Jewish prisoner functionaries in the camps. They had "privileged positions," for example, as *Lagerläufer*; as prisoners in the Kanada Commando, who sorted the belongings of the murdered and the prisoners; as Kapos or as *Blockälteste*, who supervised fellow prisoners; as physicians or camp nurses; and, of course, as prisoners in the Sonderkommandos. Generally

---

parents. In the case cited here, the survivor said that the person was a killer, but added why this may have occurred.

72 Allison Ann Rodriguez, "Beyond Dichotomies: Representing and Rewriting Prisoner Functionaries in Holocaust Historiography" (master's thesis, University of North Carolina, Chapel Hill, 2007), p. 2.

73 Wachsmann, *KL: A History of the Nazi Concentration Camps*.

74 Levi, *The Drowned and the Saved*, p. 23.

speaking, the common features of their heterogeneous experiences were privileges in connection with food, supplies, housing, and contact with other prisoners. Much greater responsibility and agency was granted or placed on the *Judenälteste*, the Jewish camp elders.

Agency

The complexity of the individual agency of Jewish functionaries reflects the extremely difficult and complex living conditions of Jews in the camps. Jewish prisoners were not a homogeneous group of victims. Rather there existed a broad spectrum of positions that Jewish prisoners could occupy and, in some cases, like that of Demerer, they stood at the top of the prisoner hierarchy. How they performed their camp tasks was up to them. "Each [functionary] chose to act in his own way."[75] The broad variety of responses and actions in the camps of Jewish functionaries mirror the whole scale of human behavior. Thus, coerced choices did not automatically include actions that were considered morally "good"—nor was there only one possible option for survival. I contend that rather than evaluating their actions, we must be aware of the fact that they were human beings who were, in many cases, as Primo Levi put it, "brutal, egoistic, and stupid." Therefore, it is more important to "evaluate the various factors—dispositional, situational, and systemic—that led to the behavioral outcome."[76]

Non-Jewish Jews

Regarding the victims, we may speak today of "Jews" as an entity, but it was the Nuremberg Laws of 1935 that defined who was a Jew in Nazi Germany, and many people of Jewish descent who were not Jews themselves were also persecuted. Quite a few non-Jews—as defined through their self-perception—were persecuted as "racial Jews" and imprisoned in ghettos or camps.

Even if historians today try not to pass judgement, they have to ask themselves what legacy they want to give to future generations who are exposed to the results of their research, for example, in exhibitions

---

75   Brot, "Julius Siegel," p. 72.
76   Zimbardo, *The Lucifer Effect*.

or public projects. They will definitely ask questions regarding the functionaries, such as, was he or she good or bad—what do you think? Perhaps the correct answer would be they were both good and bad, because they were human. Hermann Joseph, the former *Lagerältester* in the Fürstengrube satellite camp of Auschwitz wrote the following to a former fellow prisoner on October 18, 1968:

> I once told a judge that, since I was in Auschwitz, I had become accustomed to wondering about each person whom I encountered— what he had done in the camp, whether in Fürstengrube…or in the Natzweiler penal camp, where I had been. And then I would rank him based on my experiences with people in this utterly incomprehensible situation. The judge then asked me what I thought he would have been doing had he been in a concentration camp. I told him that he might have become a *Blockältester*, obsessed with absolute cleanliness. He seemed to be satisfied with that, until I asked, Do you know how you would have achieved the highest degree of cleanliness?"[77]

77 Wollenberg, "Die 'roten Kapos,'" pp. 115–139.

Communes in Auschwitz

The Communal Idea in the Holocaust

AVIHU RONEN

Jewish Socialist Solidarity in the Holocaust

Solidarity is the cornerstone of every socialist idea. Therefore, research on Jewish socialist movements during the Holocaust, particularly the Zionist *halutzic* (pioneering) youth movements, presumes ab initio that one is dealing with a modus operandi centering on solidarity. In the context of these movements, then, the question is not whether there was solidarity under the extreme conditions engendered by the Holocaust but whether it was strong enough and resilient enough to survive under those conditions.

Another relevant question when investigating the solidarity of the Jewish socialist movement concerns the extent to which one can consider it "Jewish." Even if one stipulates the existence of a pattern of solidarity among Jewish organizations, that is, a "Jewish solidarity," the origins of this fraternity are universal, flowing chiefly from the idea of class and social solidarity. Thus, Jewish solidarity of the Zionist pioneering youth movements may not originate in Jewish principles, such as the idea of all Jews being responsible for one another. In the tradition of the youth movements, the French Revolution idea of *fraternité,* which jelled and metamorphosed into the famous rallying cry for proletarian unity, "Workers of the world, unite,"[1] works in tandem with the principles of *adat ha'ahim* (fraternal community) or *adat re'im* (community of companions) in the educational group to form a whole in which the value of the collectivity sometimes transcends that of its constituent parts.[2]

---

1 Karl Marx and Friedrich Engels, "Manifesto of the Communist Party: February 1948," in Karl Marx and Friedrich Engels, *Karl Marx and Frederick Engels, Selected Works,* vol. 1 (Moscow: Progress Publishers, 1969–1970), https://www.marxists.org/archive/marx/works/download/pdf/Manifesto.pdf (accessed April 10, 2022), p. 67n5.

2 "The Ten Commandments of Hashomer Hatza'ir," 1928, states: "The Shomer [member

In this essay, I identify the principal patterns of solidarity among the *bogrim*[3] of the Zionist pioneering movements during the Holocaust, which were based on communal self-organization, or kibbutzim, as such initiatives were called in Hebrew. I argue that a broad range of communal configurations appeared during World War II, evolving in accordance with the conditions and the developments in the course of the war: training collectives that came together in the Rikuz Vilna (the Zionist pioneering center in Vilna [Vilnius], Lithuania) at the beginning of the war; training communes that reorganized in the ghettos of occupied Poland; farms under the patronage of the Judenräte; other communal configurations in Nazi-occupied countries; and, finally, communes that took shape in labor and concentration camps.

In this overview, I identify the shared foundations of these communal initiatives, test their resilience against the processes that Jewish society underwent during the Holocaust, and assess them in view of the cultural conventions that were based on the premise that individuals survive under extreme conditions only by waging a cruel struggle for existence.

Kibbutzim en Route: Training Collectives at the Beginning of the War

Communal ventures were typical of *bogrim* of the Socialist Zionist or pioneering youth movements that had been organized in collective training camps in pre-World War II Europe. These included Dror-Freiheit, Hashomer Hatza'ir, Gordonia, Akiva, Hashomer Hadati, and Bnei Akiva—most of which were under the umbrella of Hehalutz. Making some allowances, one can also add Zukunft, the youth movement of the Bund.[4] Young people prepared themselves for *aliya* (immigration to the Land of Israel) and lives of collective toil in these communal settings, known as *kibbutzei hachshara* (training kibbutzim), or simply kibbutzim.

---

of Hashomer Hatza'ir] is loyal to the Shomeric community and accepts the discipline of its directors." See Israel Rosenzweig and Levi Dror, eds., *Sefer Hashomer Hatza'ir* (Hebrew) (Merhavia: Sifriyat Poalim, 1956), p. 44.

3   *Bogrim* refers to the "older" age group of the youth movements, ages 18–24.

4   The Bund did not set up training communes because it did not train members for aliya.

When World War II broke out in September 1939, the Zionist youth movements in Poland alone had more than 100,000 members, including thousands of *halutzim* (pioneers) who were concentrated in, or at least affiliated with, dozens of training communes.[5] They formed a powerful vanguard that intended to fulfill this way of life in the still-embryonic collective movements in Mandatory Palestine.[6] From the standpoint of Jewish society, one may say that the attractiveness of the collective idea reached a pinnacle at this time. Even general Zionist movements that had no socialist roots, such as Hano'ar Hazioni and Maccabi Hatza'ir, followed the collectivist lead by linking, albeit noncommittally, the idea of *aliya* with living on a kibbutz.[7]

Socialization for collective life was to be found mostly on European soil. The youth movements' activities for their younger age groups, which largely consisted of endeavors in primary education, dealt with the subject of the collective in stories and songs, as well as with the idea of trying out cooperative life in winter and summer camps. Another important level comprised training activities in which the movement's *bogrim* prepared for collectivist lives of labor in *Eretz Israel*. The difficulties of trying to maintain working lives and coping with crowded housing and deprivation, while maintaining the *halutzic* structure and traditions, resulted in the creation of social, cultural, and communal settings that stressed strong cohesion and profound organizational commitment.[8] Over the years, several Hehalutz training sites, such as the quarry in Klesów, the training farm in Grochów, and the urban training camp in Będzin, became important stepping stones for hundreds if not thousands of *halutzim*.[9] A spirit of fraternity prevailed in these facilities

5   According to Perlis, the movements amalgamated in Hehalutz—Dror–Freiheit, Hashomer Hatza'ir, Gordonia, and Akiva—had about fifty communes that comprised around 2,700 *halutzim*. See Rivka Perlis, *Tnu'ot Hano'ar Hehalutzi'ot BePolin Hakevusha* (Hebrew) (Tel Aviv: Hakibbutz Hame'uhad, 1987), pp. 458–459.

6   At that time, the kibbutz movement in Mandatory Palestine had only about 20,000 members.

7   Hano'ar Hatzioni established Usha, Tel Yitzhak, and Kefar Glickson in the late 1930s. Young Maccabi, the youth movement of the Maccabi sports organization, founded Kefar HaMaccabi (Maccabi Village) in 1936.

8   On the Hehalutz training sites, see Israel Otiker, *Tnu'at Hehalutz BePolin: Gidula VeHitpathuta, 1932-1935* (Hebrew) (Tel Aviv: Hakibbutz Hame'uhad and Ghetto Fighters' House, 1972); Levi Arye Sarid, *Hehakutz VeTnu'ot Hano'ar BePolin 1917-1939* (Hebrew) (Tel Aviv: Am Oved—Culture and Education, 1979).

9   See Haim Dan, ed., *Sefer Klosova: Kibbutz Hotzvei Avanim Al Shem Yosef Trumpeldor*

as the destitute anarchists who had disengaged from their parents' homes planned for a new tomorrow. The anthem of Klesów is a clear reflection of that life.

Who have we got, what have we got, we've got nothing here,
We stormed out of our homes, from everything dear.
Our hair unkempt, our clothing disheveled,
An abandoned bunch that croons sadly.
Mocked in suffering, taunted in pain,
Our voice in stone will stir reverberations;
Today is in our hands, tomorrow we will fortify,
Red in our arteries is our tempestuous blood![10]

In their essence, the training collectives had elements of permanence, even though they were perceived as temporary. Young people spent years waiting for the coveted "certificate"—the Mandatory Palestine immigration visa—and knew that the social framework created in the camp was supposed to be duplicated in *Eretz Israel*. This strengthened social relations and internalized the collectivist idea as an obligatory one. Thus, when the war broke out, these training camps became kibbutzim in almost every sense other than, of course, the possession of land in *Eretz Israel*. Moreover, given the absence of commitments—to family, children, breadwinning, and occupation—these collectives were much more capable of concerted and disciplined action than were other social organizations.

In the first few weeks of the war, all of these entities disintegrated amid the general chaos occasioned by Poland's rapid collapse. At some training camps, it was decided that members would return to their homes and recollectivize only after reconnecting with their families. At other centers, the choice was to take to the roads in an organized fashion,

---

BeKlosova Veplugotav: Mea'sef (Hebrew) (Tel Aviv: Hakibbutz Hame'uhad and Ghetto Fighters' House, 1978).

10 Abraham Globerman, *The Klesów Anthem*; translated into Hebrew from the Yiddish by Moshe Basok and thence into English by the author; Ruth Braude, *Mimispahat Ya'ari Lo Nishar Ish: Seva Hashanim Shel Hashomer Hatza'ir BePolin 1939–1946* (Hebrew) (Haifa: Yad Vashem, Moreshet, and Yad Ya'ari, 2018), pp. 42–46. This book includes a broad chapter on the Zionist *halutzic* center in Vilna (Vilnius) and a detailed description of the organization of about twelve Hashomer Hatza'ir training kibbutzim, which included 610 members.

first to the Soviet occupation zone and then on to Vilna. In yet other cases, members moved to Vilna in small groups, not because of faulty organization but owing to instructions from the central institutions of their movements—Hashomer Hatza'ir, Hehalutz, Hano'ar Hatzioni— which had begun to steer their people toward Vilna. From there, so it seemed at the time, they would be able to make their way to *Eretz Israel*. In any case, by the spring of 1940, approximately 2,000 *halutzim* of various movements, who had organized in about twenty training collectives, had set themselves up in Vilna.[11]

These collectives were essentially no different from their prewar incarnations, and the element of continuity was prominent. Their social settings were built on prewar configurations, mutatis mutandis. Moreover, the basic patterns of activity changed but little. Much attention in Vilna was focused on solving the problem of earning a livelihood. Various committees were established to oversee social and cultural life—an effervescent area of endeavor. Newspapers were issued, seminars and conferences were held, and, of course, efforts to make *aliya* continued. The presence of national leaderships or at least of members of such leaderships in Vilna institutionalized the collectives' activities and molded them into homogeneous and coordinated systems within and among the movements. The principle of continuity even in wartime was tellingly reflected in remarks by Josef Shamir, who summarized the activities of the Hashomer Hatza'ir council in Vilna in March 1940.

We are young. Our generation must cash in the note that we signed when we were children. During those lengthy evenings of conversation and stormy debates, at night around the bonfire, during Youth Weeks, and when we dreamed about the future, the new tomorrow, we knew: the time of trial would come. We believed we would withstand it. Now the great hour has come. Can we bear the weight of the burden?[12]

11 Perlis, *Tnu'ot Hano'ar Hehalutzi'ot*, pp. 86–91.
12 Anonymous editors, *Al Hurvot Polin* (Hebrew) (Merhavia: Hakibbutz Ha'artzi and Hashomer Hatza'ir, 1940), p. 171. Interestingly, the movement leaders did not, broadly speaking, pass the tests that they presented for membership. Although Shamir, like most of the Hashomer Hatza'ir and the Hehalutz leaders, moved to *Eretz Israel* over the next few months, the organizational and social infrastructure that they had established survived in occupied Poland.

In fact, the main change at this time was that the training collectives became refugee communes or, to put it in a positive way, they were turned into training collectives en route to *Eretz Israel*.[13]

This period ended with the Soviet occupation of Lithuania in the summer of 1940. Several collectives fell apart and their members went underground, but after the German occupation in early 1942, small groups set up Dror and Hashomer Hatza'ir collectives in Białystok and Grodno.[14] Several hundred *halutzim* managed to slip out and "make *aliya*" in legal and less-legal ways, even after the Soviets took over, until March 1941. Others began organized migration via the East in order to reach *Eretz Israel* in one way or another.[15] About 400 Hashomer Hatza'ir members founded Hashomer centers in the Soviet Far East—Uzbekistan and Kazakhstan—where, despite persecution and hardships, they survived the war in an organized and supportive fashion.[16] According to researcher Ruth Braude,

> Members of the movement [Central Asia] have fostered a cooperative lifestyle based on a common coffer, mutual assistance, and fellowship. They used to meet, creating an *Eretz Israel* atmosphere, and mainly to draw spiritual strength from the comradery in the face of the regime's hostility. The comradery, more than ideology, was the glue that consolidated the Hashomer Hatza'ir during the war.[17]

Some of them, including Shlomo Kless and Mordechai Rozman, repatriated to Poland after the war, and became heads of the Bricha Movement.[18]

---

13 Ibid.; Anonymous editors, *Beyemei Shoah, Bemilotehem Shel Shlichi Hehalutz* ((Hebrew) (Ein Harod and Tel Aviv: HeFederatzia Ha'olomit Shel Tnu'at Ha'avoda BePelestine and Hakibbutz Hame'uhad, 1940); Ruth Zariz, *Michtave Vilna 1939–1940* (Hebrew) (Ramat Gan: Yad Tabenkin and Ghetto Fighters' House, 1992).

14 Mordecai Tenenbaum-Tamaroff, *Dapim Min Hadeleika* (Hebrew) (Jerusalem: Yad Vashem, 1985), pp. 101, 218; Chaika Grosman, *The Underground Army: Fighters of the Bialystok Ghetto* (New York: Holocaust Library, 1987), pp. 55–78; Perlis, *Tnu'ot Hano'ar Hehalutzi'ot*, pp. 341–343.

15 Moshe Gal, "Al Pnei Aratzot Veyamim" (Hebrew), *Yalkut Moreshet*, 32 (1981), pp. 71–100.

16 Braude, *Mimispahat Ya'ari*, pp. 289–323.

17 Ibid., p. 399.

18 Shlomo Kless, *Gvulot, Mahteret Vebricha: Pe'ilut Tzionit Halutzit, BeBrit HaMo'atzot Veksharim im Hayishuv Ba'Aretz, 1941–1945* (Hebrew) (Tel Aviv: Moreshet and Sifriyat Poalim, 1989).

The era discussed here, the beginning of the war, is perceived as a transitional stage. However, it has a singularity of its own: when the war broke out, the collective framework served as an organizational model that could cope with the terrors of the occupation, instigate an organized exodus from Poland, and promote solidarity as a social entity that could mitigate the misery of the refugees' daily lives in Vilna by wielding the well-honed tools of the training collective. In addition to all of the foregoing, one should add the existence of strong central leaderships that regulated and supervised the communal structures and created powerful social networks based on solidarity.

Kibbutzim under Occupation: Training Collectives in Occupied Poland

If a refugee kibbutz or a kibbutz en route to *Eretz Israel* was the first model, as discussed above, the second model centered on the kibbutz under conditions of occupation and discrimination, such as the training collectives in the ghettos of occupied Poland, the Generalgouvernement, and the Reich-annexed sector. These communes were made up of young people from the movements' training camps who had not managed to slip out of occupied Poland and were in effect stuck there. The members of the new kibbutzim began to organize, sometimes in parallel with the organizing efforts in Vilna, and attempted to come together. In accordance with Meir Ya'ari's instructions and resolutions of the council in Vilna, several important members of Hashomer Hatza'ir, if not of other movements as well, were instructed not to move to Vilna but rather to renew the activities of the training collectives or cells that they headed.[19] The return of several emissaries from Vilna and the Soviet-occupied territories, such as Frumka Plotnicka, Tosia Altman, Zivia Lubetkin, Mordechai Anielewicz, and others, obviously strengthened these renewed initiatives.

Most of these communes were organized locally, often with available personnel, and thus were sometimes less firmly established. Their formation and the nature of their membership were influenced by rapidly changing circumstances. One of the most important collectives

---

19 Avihu Ronen, *Nidona LeHayim: Yomaneiha Vehayea Shel Chajka Klinger* (Hebrew) (Tel Aviv: University of Haifa and Yediot Books, 2011), pp. 84–86.

at that time, Dror in Będzin, was consolidated after the Hehalutz leadership in Warsaw oversaw an unsuccessful attempt to cross into Slovakia in the winter of 1940. Kibbutz Będzin, which had essentially disintegrated at the beginning of the war, was reorganized in the spring of 1940 after the Hehalutz leadership attracted new members. The newcomers had arrived with the intention of crossing the border and moving on to Mandatory Palestine, but when the operation failed, they remained in Będzin and began to function as full-fledged members of the collective. At its peak, this kibbutz had nearly 100 members.[20] In another case, Kibbutz Baderech (Kibbutz en Route), established by Hano'ar Hatzioni, moved from Łódź to Warsaw in the early autumn of 1939. After becoming known as a place where refugees could receive assistance, it became the Hano'ar Hatzioni center in that city.[21] Another collective was formed by members of Akiva in Kraków, who set up a kind of training brigade in Warsaw in 1940.[22] Surpassing all of these was the Dror urban kibbutz at 34 Dzielna St. in Warsaw, which over the summer expanded to about 300 members and served as the national center of Dror–Hehalutz.[23]

In some cases, central institutions of several movements in Warsaw established collectives scattered among various training farms in occupied Poland. Noteworthy among them were those of Hashomer Hatza'ir in Żarki, Gordonia in Opoczno, and Dror in Białystok. The leading movement in this respect was Dror–Hehalutz, which in 1941 had about 700 *halutzim* at its different training centers.[24] These collective entities adhered to all the rules of the prewar training kibbutz, mutatis mutandis. Most were supported by Judenrat agencies or semiofficial community institutions such as Zydowskie Towarzystwo Opieki Spolecznej (Jewish Mutual Aid Society, ŻTOS) in Warsaw. This support found expression in assistance to find sources of livelihood and to refer members of the collectives to various social service jobs, such as in public kitchens, but

---

20 Ibid., pp. 92–94.
21 B. Auerbach, "Hano'ar Hatzioni Begeto Varsha," in Yohanan Cohen et al., eds., *Shalos Shurot Bahistoria: Hano'ar Hatzioni, Akiva Veahahalutz Haklal Tzioni Betkufat Hashoah BePolin* (Hebrew) (Jerusalem: Massuah, 1999), pp. 168–169.
22 Hela Schüpper Rufeisen, *Preda Mimila 18: Sipura Shel Kasharit* (Hebrew) (Tel Aviv: Hakibbutz Hame'uhad and Ghetto Fighters' House, 1990), pp. 25–34.
23 Havkah Folman-Raban, *Lo Nifradeti Mihem* (Hebrew) (Tel Aviv: Ghetto Fighters' House, 1997), pp. 39–49.
24 Perlis, *Tnu'ot Hano'ar Hehalutzi'ot*, p. 462.

the kibbutz members themselves bore the primary responsibility for earning a livelihood. As the organizational auspices were sustained and even reinforced, the existence of secretariats, committees, meetings, and cooperative and egalitarian norms, to name only a few, is mentioned in almost all the testimonies about the collectives.

The *halutzim* who populated the communes were the main reservoirs for local movement activities. They took active part in rehabilitating movement cells, counseling young members, creating cultural systems, and developing an underground press. In some places, they were able to base all their local activity on firm and responsible foundations. Hela Schüpper Rufeisen subsequently related,

> We'd get up early in the morning....We'd eat three or four thin slices of bread, drink some tea with saccharine, and head out to work. We'd return at 1:00 or 2:00, eat the paltry soup with a thin slice of bread and set out for training. Many training activities took place in our apartment....After the activities, just before curfew, we would have a supper that usually comprised soup with a slice of bread. Only then did something of our social life begin.[25]

One may say that collective life, a natural modus operandi for participants in training camps and members of youth movements, was preserved in its organizational structure as a power base for the survival of the movement as an entity. This way of life offered people the basics for survival under the conditions of starvation and death that prevailed in the ghettos in Poland. Referring individuals to jobs, allocating food, and providing a roof over their heads were solutions for thousands of *halutzim* who, as refugees, were exposed to the mortal dangers of the ghetto. As Israel Gutman wrote in his book *Resistance*, for example,

> Kitchens in the urban clubs and communes also served the public under the supervision of the Self-Help organization. They were actually run by women living in the movements' hostels. The hostels of Dror on Dzielna Street and Hashomer Hatza'ir on Nalewski Street "were open to any hungry person."[26]

---

25 Schüpper Rufeisen, *Preda Mimila 18*, p. 29.
26 Israel Gutman, *Resistance: The Warsaw Ghetto Uprising* (Boston: Houghton Mifflin, 1994), p. 124.

Similar and even more detailed descriptions of the activities of the "kibbutzniks" are found in the testimonies of Yitzhak Zuckerman from Warsaw,[27] Rozka Korczak from Vilna,[28] Chawka Lenczner from Będzin,[29] Chaika Grossman from Bialystok,[30] Uziel Lichtenberg from Łódź and Warsaw,[31] and many others. The collective framework also provided individuals with spiritual and social support in a disintegrating world. It gave people something to believe in, something to dream about, and someone to trust. The following excerpt from Gusta Davidson Draenger's diary *Justyna's Narrative*, characterizes these feelings of brotherhood: "As always acutely aware of their positions as leaders of a youth movement, they felt themselves spiritually bound to their followers. They had total faith in each other; each had no doubt that any would rather die than betray a friend."[32] It is not incidental that these "kibbutzniks" would become the core of the armed groups that took part in the uprisings and attempted uprisings in Warsaw, Kraków, Częstochowa, Białystok, Będzin, and Vilna.

Training Farms under Judenrat Patronage

An edifying chapter in the history of the Holocaust-era kibbutzim is the creation of training farms and collectives under the patronage of the Judenräte and community institutions. Practically speaking, there was no major difference between these initiatives and those discussed above. In both, *halutzim* engaged in collective self-organization and were provided with organizational patronage by the Judenräte, which considered them part of their configurations. There was, however, a twofold difference. First, in some cases, the initiative behind the establishment of the training communes or farms came from the

---

27 Yitzhak Zuckerman ("Antek"), *A Surplus of Memory: Chronicle of the Warsaw Ghetto Uprising*, ed. and tr.by Barbara Harshav (Berkeley: University of California Press, 1993).

28 Ruzka (Reizl) Korczak-Marla, *Lehavot Ba'efer* (Hebrew) (Merhavia: Moreshet Vesifriyat Poalim, 1965).

29 Chawka (Lenczne) Rabinowicz, *Tzivu Alei Et Hehayim* (Hebrew) (Rehovot: HaSipur Sheli, 2010).

30 Chaika Grossman, *The Underground Army: Fighters of the Bialystok Ghetto* (New York: Holocaust Library, 1987).

31 Uziel Lichtenberg, "Havei Hageto," *Massuah*, 2 (1974), pp. 62 – 69.

32 Gusta Davidson Draenger, *Justyna's Narrative* (Amherst: University of Massachusetts Press, 1996), p. 63.

Judenräte, which wanted to base them on existing communal structures. Second, the membership of these enterprises was based on the Zionist pioneering movements at large rather than on affiliation with any particular movement.

This pattern appeared largely in Zagłębie and Łódź, where the Judenräte were chaired by authoritarian Zionist personalities: Moshe Merin and Chaim Rumkowski, respectively. In Zagłębie, Merin ran a youth department that was, at least officially, subordinate to a youth council made up of the heads of all Zionist pioneering movements in Zagłębie. This department, in conjunction with the council, ran a farm in Będzin and unsuccessfully attempted to set up three similar facilities in Sosnowiec and in neighboring towns. Merging into the communal idea here were farm labor, orientation in the field, and a general experience of freedom that was so different from that of the sequestered Jews in the cities. When the deportations began and the Żydowska Organizacja Bojowa (Jewish Fighting Organization, ŻOB), was established, the farm in Będzin, along with the Dror collective in the same city, became the headquarters of the underground that was established there and that existed until the last days of the Zagłębie community in August 1943. The following excerpt demonstrates the prevailing atmosphere at the Będzin farm:

We held memorial evenings for Herzl and Bialik. We sat, all of us, in the distant field. The singing of *Tehezkena* [Be Strong] carried into the silence of the night. Words of defiance and rebellion against Fascism, against the massive injustice being inflicted on the Jewish people, were heard. We resurrected the memory of those who had fallen on the fronts. Inadvertently, eyes swiveled to see what was happening around: Was no one listening in? Not being afraid in the open field—there's something of dropping the guard about it and we'll be punished for it one day.

As the words are heard, the heart's yearnings for *Eretz* [*Israel*], for the kibbutz, for the brother well up. Two girls from *Eretz* [*Israel*], are with us;[33] they had come to visit their parents and the war caught

33 For more on Chaike Bukhbinder and Sara Rechnitz of Kibbutz Degania, the two girls referred to here, see Idan Sagi, *Chajka VeSara: Haderech Habayta*, documentary film, directed by Idan Sagi (Israel: Idan Productions, 2020), https://www.youtube.com/watch?v=By5uX2euhM4&t=2648s (accessed April 11, 2021).

them by surprise here. They sing songs of *Eretz* [*Israel*], Galilee, [Lake] Kinneret for us. Songs of struggle. Suddenly the sadness and the longing go away and are no more, and the joy of youth and instinctive hope come. We dance. A harmonica turns up too. We dance passionately, abandoning all thought, all respite. Ceaselessly the voice rises: "Who lives? The People of Israel! Who's winning?..." Everyone listening in thus far forgets everything and is drawn in. So it went until well into the night.[34]

Rumkowski in Łódź acted in a similar way and allowed youth movement activists to take over the farming parcels in Marysin, where the movements did manage to maintain their separate settings and organized in collectives along the classic movement lines. However, relations between the movements' leaders and Rumkowski quickly deteriorated. The Marysin farm was dismantled before its first anniversary and its members returned to the Łódź ghetto, where they continued to function within the framework of the youth movements for some time.[35] In the Warsaw ghetto, too, the Grochów farm, which long predated the war, remained operative by dint of the youth movements and Hehalutz and functioned as a full-fledged collective until 1942.[36]

Given that these phenomena were predicated on youth movement models, they can hardly be considered totally different from the earlier pattern. Their importance stems more from the attention that the leaders of the large Judenräte invested in the *halutzim* and the collective way of life and, at least in the first stage of the occupation, they appear to have had a clear interest in this manner of self-organization. With the help of the *halutzim* on the farms, they were able to provide the starving ghetto population with small quantities of fresh food and enjoyed some degree of cooperation with an organized body of young people to whom they turned in connection with other areas of Judenrat activity, such as welfare and education. The selfsame Judenrat leaders, however, feared the strong cohesion of the *halutzim* within the framework of these farms, as attested

---

34 Chajka Klinger, *MiYoman Bageto* (Merhavia: Sifriyat Poalim and Kibbutz Haogen, 1959), p. 28.
35 Michal Unger, "Tn'uot Hano'ar Begeto Łódź" (Hebrew), *Yalkut Moreshet*, 66 (1988), pp. 19–50.
36 Sarah Segal and Arie Fialkov, eds., *Besdot Grochów: Kibbutz Hacshara Grochów Vekvutzot Ha'avoda Shelo: Ma'asef* (Hebrew) (Tel Aviv: Ghetto Fighters' House and Hakibbutz Hame'uhad, 1976).

by the dismantling of the Marysin farm and the conflicts between Merin and the *halutzim* in Będzin. Their concern was not groundless as it was from the ranks of the *halutzim* that the fighters and resistance activists were drawn. Either way, by adding the communal populations of the farms to those of the earlier configurations of training collectives, we arrive, according to Perlis' tally, at more than 3,000 members of sixty communes in occupied Poland.[37]

Communal Configurations in Other Nazi-Occupied Countries

Turning now from Poland to the rest of the Nazi-controlled sphere, we encounter a broad range of collective or communal ways of life that came about owing to the necessities and varying circumstances in each country at different times. The objectives of these training camps and communes essentially matched those of their contemporaries in Poland, of which they knew basically nothing, at least until 1944. The goal was to maintain the movement's organizational setting and provide *halutzim* who were stranded en route to *Eretz Israel* with a framework that would enable them to survive the tempest.

Several of these settings are noteworthy. In Horthy's Hungary, where Zionist activity was banned and the training camps were dissolved in 1940, members of Hashomer Hatza'ir established urban communes that they called *haym* (home in Yiddish). Each *haym* had four or five members who pooled their resources and divided all their income and living expenses. This form of collective, which may be defined as semi-underground, existed until nearly 1944, but steadily disintegrated as most of its members were mobilized for labor brigades.[38]

In Slovakia, Hashomer Hatza'ir and Young Maccabi maintained training camps until 1942 under the patronage of the Ustredna Zidov (Jewish Center, UZ), a kind of Slovakian Judenrat. In addition to their own members, these camps took in groups of young Jews who had organized collectively for *aliya* in 1938–1939. Unfamiliar with the movement norms, these groups pushed their way into the Hashomer

---

37 Perlis, *Tnu'ot Hano'ar Hehalutzi'ot*, pp. 460–464.
38 Avihu Ronen, *Hakrav Al Hehayim: Hashomer Hatza'ir BeHungaria, 1994* (Hebrew) (Givat Haviva: Yad Ya'ari, 1994), pp. 40–45.

Hatza'ir orbit in search of refuge from Nazi-occupied Czechoslovakia.[39] The communal framework resembled that of the ghettos in Poland for young people who had loose connections with a movement or with Hehalutz—an umbrella under which they could find support and cope together with the horrors and torments of the occupation. The training camps were disbanded when the deportations to Poland began in March 1942, whereupon dozens of their members were smuggled into neighboring Hungary in the first, organized rescue operation.[40]

In the Netherlands, two types of camps—*Mittlehachshara* for groups and *Einzelhachshara* for individuals—were set up by Hehalutz members from Germany who had been smuggled into the country in the 1930s and had joined the Dutch Hehalutz training farms. These facilities, in which adolescents who had been formally approved for vocational training were scattered in safe locations, mainly farms or homes of peasants, would form the basis of Joachim Simon (Shushu)'s and Joop Westerweel's rescue operation, in which about 300 *halutzim* were smuggled into Belgium and France.[41]

Interesting patterns developed in Theresienstadt, where the Hehalutz leadership was integrated de facto into the senior administrative echelon of the camp. While Hehalutz did not maintain a communal way of life, its members, who were central to various education and social activities, often invoked principles and ideas from the field of communal thinking according to their understanding of it.[42] Another fascinating story is that of the "Villa Emma children," a Youth Aliya group from Austria and Germany that moved from Yugoslavia via Slovenia and Italy to Switzerland, guided by a staff of educators who belonged to youth movements and led by Josef Indig (Ithai). The group practiced communal principles in its school, which helped it to remain cohesive and gave it the strength to survive during the years that it moved from place to place.[43]

39 Yaakov Ronen, "Yamim Goralyim (1938–1943): MiKosice Ad Nove Mast Nad Vahom," in Yosef Rav, ed., *Shomrim Tamid: Hashomer Hatza'ir BeCzecoslovakia 1920–1950* (Hebrew) (Kibbutz Dalia: self-pub., 1994), pp. 150–152.

40 Gila Fatran, *Hayim Ma'avak Al Hisardut: Hanhagat Yehude Slovakia Bashoah 1939–1944* (Tel Aviv: Moreshet and the Institute for Contemporary Jewry, 1992), p. 153.

41 Dan Michman, "Zionist Youth Movements in Holland and Belgium and Their Activities during the Shoah," in Asher Cohen and Yehoyakim Cochavi, eds., *Zionist Youth Movements during the Holocaust* (New York: Peter Lang, 1995), pp. 145–171.

42 Yehuda Reznichenko, Lisa Worzl, and Henke Fishel, *Theresienstadt* (Hebrew) (Tel Aviv: Mapai, 1948).

43 Joseph Ithai, *Yaldei Villa Emma* (Hebrew) (Tel Aviv: Sifriyat Poalim, 1983).

This diversity of the communal configurations among the youth movement members would form the infrastructure for organized rescue operations, some meant solely for movement members and others, such as the Zionist pioneering movement's resistance in Hungary, expanding into a mass rescue operation for the Jews of Budapest during the Szálasi regime, October 1944–January 1945.[44]

The story of the Zionist pioneering movement's resistance in Hungary, which I do not discuss here, illuminates another unique aspect of solidarity among these groups. During hard times, this solidarity was not limited to members of the communal or movement structure but expanded into something greater, to solidarity among non-Jewish entities, such as the Communist resistance, which the Zionist pioneering underground assisted. In this context, it is important to note the participation of the survivors of the Warsaw Ghetto Uprising in the Polish Warsaw Uprising in the summer of 1944 and of the Hashomer Hatza'ir members' participation in the Slovak National Uprising.[45] This was not incidental; the roots of this solidarity were universal, transcending the more limited characteristics of national solidarity.

Communes and Collectives in Concentration and Extermination Camps

A highly dramatic aspect of the subject at hand is the existence of collectives and communes in labor and concentration camps that culminated in communes in Auschwitz. The studies of Felicja Karay, Judith Tydor-Baumel, and Bella Gutterman suggest that such camps also featured mutual support groups with cooperative characteristics.[46]

---

44 Asher Cohen, *The Hehalutz Resistance in Hungary, 1942–1944* (Boulder: Social Science Monographs, 1986).

45 Ronen, *Hakrav Al Hehayim*, pp. 263–274; Akiva Nir, *Shvilim Bema'agal Ha'esh* (Hebrew) (Tel Aviv: Moreshet and Sifriyat Poalim, 1967); Zuckerman, *A Surplus of Memory*.

46 Felicja Karay, *Death Comes in Yellow: Skarzysko-Kamienna Slave Labor Camp* (Amsterdam: Overseas Publishers Association, 1996); Judith Tydor-Baumel, "Ruha'ke VeShtei HaRivkot: Tnu'at 'Banot' BeKrakow," in Avihu Ronen and Yehoyakim Cochavi, eds., *Guf Shlishi Yahid: Biyografyot Shel Havrei Tnu'ot Hano'ar Bitekufat Hashoah* (Hebrew), vol. 2 (Tel Aviv: Yad Ya'ari, Moreshet, and Ghetto Fighters' House, 1995), pp. 133–159; Bella Gutterman, *A Narrow Bridge to Life: Jewish Forced Labor and Survival in the Gross-Rosen Camp System, 1940–1945* (New York: Berghahn, 2008), pp. 142–160.

Here I focus on entities that functioned consciously as "communes" in Auschwitz as a case study that leads the present discussion to its culmination. In my study of the Hehalutz resistance in Hungary, I trace the experiences of the few members who were captured and sent to Auschwitz. Although the story of their internment in Auschwitz was beyond the scope of my study, I did ask them what happened to them there. To my surprise, they responded by telling a story that began, more or less, with the words, "and in Auschwitz, we had a commune..." As I continued to question them, I identified at least four "Hashomer Hatza'ir" communes in Auschwitz—two of men and two of women.

The foundations of these communes had been established earlier, as the inmates had been captured together or aboard the train, but sometimes also in reencounters in the camp itself. There was, of course, a strong element of arbitrary fate in this. One had to have had the good fortune to meet or to be with someone one knew—a movement member or someone else who could be trusted. Furthermore, one had to be lucky enough to clear the selection, to be sent to the correct side. Nevertheless, along with fickle fate and chance, it was the people themselves who chose with whom to share what they immediately perceived as the ghastliest possible experience.

Basic factors in the coalescence of these communes were the members' shared background, their youth, and the general uncertainty of their situation. Youth movement members clung to each other in the detention facilities, on the train, in Auschwitz, and in the labor camps, because they knew each other and, thus, knew whom they could trust and turn to in need; they also knew who would undertake to help them if they encountered trouble. The result was a sort of reciprocity in a state of uncertainty. Many sources make it clear that in Auschwitz and, to a large extent, in the labor camps as well, an individual's survival depended not only on luck and personal prowess but also on the availability of at least one supportive other at her or his side. The same consideration emerges from the writings of Jean Améry and Primo Levi, who best described Auschwitz as a Hobbsean *bellum omnium contra omnes*—a war of all against all.[47] For example, if a person had to use the latrine while standing in the lengthy queue for food, the presence or absence of someone who

47 Jean Améry, *At the Mind's Limits: Contemplations by a Survivor on Auschwitz and Its Realities* (New York: Schocken Books, 1980); Primo Levi, *Survival in Auschwitz* (New York: Simon & Schuster, 1996).

would save his or her place, or receive his or her ration and actually hand it over upon return, was often a matter of life or death.

Similarly, a daily struggle was waged over the spaces that were allotted for sleeping. These were physical power struggles in which inmates whose strength failed them even slightly might lose their place, forfeit hours of sleep, and be unable the next morning to endure the grueling labor that drove many to exhaustion and death. Mutual aid in the ongoing struggle for opportunities to sleep helped to safeguard against this and was even more important when a camp inmate's health failed. The specter of becoming a *"Muselman"*[48] was in everyone's thoughts. In an allocation of calories that fell far short of a person's normal needs even at rest, an additional spoonful of soup or something else for someone whose strength was waning might have a direct effect on whether he or she lived or died.[49]

The Auschwitz communes were primarily social structures that were meant to help the incarcerated cope with these existential questions. Often, they took the form of "quartets"—four inmates who shared one eating utensil. They shared their food and, if a portion was more than or less than the ration, they determined how it was to be apportioned to this or that member and the order in which it would be consumed. In such a commune, members sometimes decided to increase the portion of a member who had become weak by one or two spoonsful at the expense and with the consent of her or his stronger comrades. The cooperative model was also invoked in connection with clothing and equipment. The commune members, singly or collectively, busied themselves in their few leisure hours after having spent most of their time either working or standing for roll call by "organizing" additional gear—a spoon, an item of clothing, and so on—for the needs of the commune or the collective, as the groups were called.[50] "Organizing" often meant pilfering, a totally accepted norm in the chaotic world of Auschwitz. Within the framework of the commune, however, this expression took on an additional meaning in the prisoners' jargon: to organize for the group and to safeguard the group's property against others who might scheme to "organize" it.

---

48 *Muselman* is a term that was widely used among concentration camp inmates to refer to prisoners who were near death due to exhaustion, starvation, or hopelessness in the death camps.

49 Anna Csech (Metuka Klein) testimony in Ronen, *Hakrav al Hehayim*, p. 181.

50 Moshe Shapira testimony in Ronen, *Hakrav al Hehayim*, p. 180.

Support of ill members was particularly conspicuous in the women's groups. Members helped each other with personal care, covering for each other during inspections and selections and, of course, worrying incessantly about somewhat improving nutrition—the basic essential for convalescence. This support was also a feature in the men's groups but there it was manifested in assistance at work and during the terrible "death march."[51]

In tandem with physical support was the nearly self-evident provision of spiritual support. Members of communes or collectives conversed at length, analyzed their current situation, summoned memories, and dreamed about the future. If they had belonged to youth movements, they were able to share movement memories, ideals, and guiding principles as they applied to daily life in the camp, and dreams about a future together in *Eretz Israel*. One of the most riveting stories in this context was told by a woman, who had spent her youth in Hungary, about the time that she arrived in Auschwitz in the summer of 1944 and was sent with her friends to shower together with the other women in the transport. Given that the girls of Hashomer Hatza'ir had already heard stories about Auschwitz by then, they were sure that after stepping into the shower room they would be gassed and die.

> There were lots of people there. Terribly packed together. On the one hand, we laughed. Hysterical laughter. We were all naked and shaven. On the other hand, we thought, well, that's that. And as we had read in books, this was the time to sing "Hatikva."[52] As we sang "Hatikva," we laughed hysterically and hugged each other, and each of us thought about whomever she thought....After that, water [came out of the shower heads]. Not gas. It's a fact.[53]

The story of the naked girls' singing "Hatikva" in the shower has other implications. In her testimony, the woman related to the connection between the spiritual reality created by the commune and the empirical reality of Auschwitz. She insisted that this link was built on a delicate equilibrium of main factors along the timeline. Anyone who was overly

---

51 Ibid.
52 "Hativka" (hope), which became the national anthem of the State of Israel, was drawn from a poem composed by Naftali Hertz Imber in 1887.
53 Anna Csech (Metuka Klein) testimony in Ronen, *Hakrav al Hehayim*, p. 181.

mired in the past—in the form of a personal reality that had become unreal—could not cope with the reality of the present. Conversely, those who could not dream about the future, for example, about living on a kibbutz in *Eretz Israel*, had nothing to hope for and, perforce, lost strength in the daily struggle for survival. Singing "Hatikva" while naked could not influence the answer to the most important question of all, the one that remained unanswerable at that moment: What would emerge from the shower head, water or gas? It did, however, give the members of the group the strength to cope in the event that it would be water, and hope for future groups to cope were it to be gas, finding solace in the idea that the strength of the future is in the present.

Moreover, the unclothed singing of "Hatikva" was also a product of the past—Hungarian girls, singing Hebrew words in a Slavic tune on Polish soil. After all, someone at some time had taught them the lyrics of the song, someone had sung the melody with them, or they had sung it in movement activities, and they sang it together, not as a solo performance but as a chorus, standing at attention. Thus, there must have been something in the past of these girls, something that had taught them to sing, that told them to sing now. In fact, the witness claimed exactly this. At all times, she said, I heard an inner voice of sorts, something like a command from the movement: We have expectations of you; this is how you should behave and in no other way, because this is what makes us who we are, different from others. By implication, the strength to cope with the present is rooted in the past. Further, as the woman noted, the power of the past must not be allowed to overwhelm the reality of the present, because one of the biggest problems in Auschwitz was to know how to adapt to the present reality. Those who remained stuck in the past could not endure the daily hardships that transformed them into dirty laborers, fighting over pieces of bread and contracting typhus. One had to remember the past without wallowing in it.[54]

This, of course, ties into the views of Viktor Frankl, which in large part have become a web of banalities among us. The Franklian "meaning" of Auschwitz is perceived not as a substitute for the empirical meaning of the camp but as how one relates to it and influences it with other input. It preserves personal autonomy not as an escape from reality but as just the opposite: a "meaning" by which to cope with reality but in no way the sole and omnipotent "meaning." Frankl wrote,

54 Ibid.

The prisoner who had lost faith in the future—his future—was doomed. With his loss of belief in the future, he also lost his spiritual hold; he let himself decline and became subject to mental and physical decay. Usually this happened quite suddenly, in the form of a crisis, the symptoms of which were familiar to the experienced camp inmate. We all feared this moment—not for ourselves, which would have been pointless, but for our friends. Usually it began with the prisoners refusing one morning to get dressed and wash or go out on the parade grounds….He simply gave up. There he remained, lying in his own excreta, and nothing bothered him anymore.[55]

One has to reread Primo Levi in a similar manner. His reality of Auschwitz—an anti-spiritual reality, an *anus mundus*, a war of all against all in which nothing exists but the individual's power to survive— ostensibly clashes with Frankl's, but he nonetheless acknowledged the importance of both mutual aid and spiritual support in the struggle for survival. In his book, Levi writes about his friend Alberto, who helped him make improvised cigarette lighters to sell in Auschwitz.

We worked for three nights; nothing happened, nobody noticed our activity, or did the blanket or pallet catch fire, and this is how we won the bread, which kept us alive until the arrival of the Russians, and how we comforted each other in the trust and friendship, which united us.[56]

In another book, Levi writes, "Culture was useful to me; not always, at times perhaps by subterranean and unforeseen paths, but it served me well and perhaps saved me."[57]

An interesting testimony on this subject is that of Jean Améry, perhaps the pessimist among the intellectuals who survived Auschwitz. The skeptical agnostic, who felt the cessation of the human spirit in Auschwitz, could not help but admire the people who clung to their beliefs even in this terrible place—the religious and the Marxists.

---

55 Viktor Frankl, *Man's Search for Meaning* (Boston: Beacon Press, 2006), p. 74.
56 Primo Levi, *The Periodic Table* (New York: Schocken Books, 1984), p.146.
57 Primo Levi, *The Drowned and the Saved* (London: Abacus, 1989), p. 112.

Yet I must confess that I felt, and still feel, great admiration for both my religiously and politically committed comrades. They may have been "intellectual" in the sense we have adopted here, or they may not have been, that was not important. One way or the other, in the decisive moments, their political or religious belief was an inestimable help to them...their belief or ideology gave them that firm foothold in the world from which they spiritually unhinged the SS state.[58]

One may say that these elements, fellowship and spirituality, featured in the struggle for survival in Auschwitz. Levi did not sing "Hatikva" in the shower, but the fact that he found someone with whom to discuss Dante was meaningful for him, as was the help he received in his time of distress from a simple Italian laborer, Lorenzo. But there is a difference: in the individual world of the delicate Italian intellectual, Lorenzo and Dante did not come together. In the world of the girls of Hashomer Hatza'ir, they converged in the singing of "Hatikva." To connect a past that has become a fiction with a present that is but a figment of one's imagination—to fashion them into tools with which to cope each day with the ghastliest present that ever was—the "together" was necessary—a "together" manifested in this case in the singing of "Hatikva" by naked girls in the shower, face-to-face with the closed shower heads of the future.

Conclusion

The story of the communes in Auschwitz, although attesting to only a small part of the phenomenon dealt with here, expresses the mordant crux of the characteristics of communal solidarity during the Holocaust. Several commonalities surface in all the phenomena reviewed above—from traditional training collectives to impromptu communes, training farms, and various communal configurations:

1. They were relatively young groups for people of similar ages.
2. Their members maintained ideological partnerships and beliefs in a common idea.
3. Their members had a profound sense of fraternity or fellowship.

58 Améry, *At the Mind's Limits*, pp. 12–13.

4. Their members offered each other, as well as members of similar groups, material and spiritual support.
5. Their members kept egalitarian relationships and shared their scanty belongings.
6. The individuals in these groups typically had a clear sense of who they were and the group to which they belonged.

It probably was not incidental that these characteristics of the various communal groups became central in Jewish society in the Holocaust era, both in organized resistance to Nazism and in individual members' ability to survive. This also explains the presence of members of communal entities at the forefront of resistance and rescue operations.

Furthermore, the answer to the question of the role of the group in the individual's fight for survival is unequivocal. Membership in any kind of group—a nuclear family or a support group and, a fortiori, a movement that is based on long-internalized patterns and norms—enhanced the individual's chances for survival. Hardly any Holocaust survivor's story fails to mention support from someone else or a group. This argument is valid in its broad context, as well as in the patterns of the kibbutzim described above. Membership in a training commune, a farm sponsored by a Judenrat, or a movement institution rendered the individual's survival much more likely. In this context, those who chose to fight and die as rebels under the banner of the ŻOB consciously forwent opportunities to survive as individuals. It was, however, a collective choice, the meaning of which was not much different from singing "Hatikva" while naked in the shower.

Be that as it may, this phenomenon in its broad context—the collective patterns in the Holocaust—and its more focused context—the communes in the camps—plainly indicates that today's Darwinian conventional sayings in regard to both society and culture—that "a war of all against all" is the only kind of behavior that holds in a "natural state"—fails the test of the communal idea during the Holocaust.

Solidarity and Rivalry in Rescue Attempts and Operations

Information, Knowledge, and Desperation
Jewish Communications during the Holocaust

DAVID SILBERKLANG

To what extent were Jews in Nazi-controlled Europe able to share information in real time with others regarding their experiences during the Shoah? What information were they able to share and with whom? What did they hope to achieve by sharing information? Could the information they received affect their actions communally and not only individually? Questions such as these are at the heart of the Jews' efforts to help each other and of our endeavors to understand Jewish perceptions of events during the Holocaust. We can see this reflected in two stories regarding communications during that period, one familial and the other communal.

The first is the story of Feliks (Efraim) Rzeczyński, a Polish Jewish lieutenant from Warsaw, who spent most of the war in an officers' POW camp in Germany—*Offizierslager* (officers POW camp) VIIa— in Murnau, Bavaria. His wife, son, brothers, father, and brother-in-law were all in the Warsaw ghetto. Quite a number of Polish Jewish officers lived out the war years alongside their non-Jewish Polish fellow officers in various *Oflag*, and as recognized officer prisoners of war, they were permitted to correspond with their families. Rzeczyński managed to preserve a collection of letters from his family written in 1942 and 1943, along with other kinds of correspondence.[1]

---

1 The story of Feliks (Efraim) Rzeczyński is based upon a remarkable collection of more than fifty letters—the correspondence between him and his family and others in August 1942–February 1945. The correspondence and a brief testimony are in the Yad Vashem Archives (YVA), O.48.B/19-1. He and his brother-in-law, Bernard (Dov) Luxemberg also completed Pages of Testimony for the same family members. For a similar story of wartime correspondence until the bitter end, see Nusia and Inia Szifman, *"Dos Lebn Nokh far Mir"*: *Briev fun Getto un Lager* (Yiddish) (Tel Aviv and Jerusalem: I. L. Peretz Verlag and Yad Vashem, 1962). Dr. Lejb Szifman, a physician and reserve officer in the Polish army, was a POW in Oflag VI-E in Dorsten after being handed over to the Germans by the

On August 16, 1942, Rzeczyński's wife, Ada (Adela), wrote to him about the deportations from Warsaw then underway, and she and her brother, Bernard Luxemberg, both wrote to him in October, describing the deportations in detail. Luxemberg named the deported family members, adding that all the deportees were dead. Ada wrote on February 26, 1943 (posted only on March 6) that the Germans had decided that "Warsaw must be cleansed of Jews." On March 27, 1943, Ada and Adam, their son, wrote asking Rzeczyński to write to Stefan (Stefka) Fay and to ask him to turn to Chaim Y. Eiss (and to other people), both of them in Zurich, to arrange foreign papers for them.[2] "The matter cannot be delayed," urged his son. On April 9 and 10, they wrote again (received April 13 and 15), pleading desperately with him to do all he could to get them out of the country on foreign papers by turning to Chaim Eiss via Stefan Fay. They included Eiss' address in Zurich. Ada despaired of ever seeing her husband again.[3]

What could he, a POW, do? One thing he succeeded in doing was to send them financial support. Between January 23 and October 21, 1943, he sent them a total of 590 Reichsmarks in several mailings. He also wrote to Stefan Fay and others in Switzerland, who succeeded in arranging papers for his family so that they could leave. But on June 16, 1943, Fay wrote to him, informing him that a special messenger had been sent to rescue his wife and son from the ghetto, but that they were gone and there was no forwarding address. Of course, there was none; they were already in Poniatowa.

Romanians in early 1941. After his wife was deported to Treblinka in early September 1942, he continued to correspond with his daughters, eleven-year-old Inia (Irena) and fourteen-year-old Nusia (Anna) via the Red Cross. The girls worked at the Többens workshops and were transferred to Poniatowa in March 1943. The girls' letters were optimistic, and the correspondence continued until they were murdered in *Aktion Erntefest*.

2   Rabbi Chaim Yisroel Eiss was among the founders of the Agudath Yisrael Party and a rescue activist in Switzerland. With the assistance of Polish diplomats in Switzerland, he began arranging foreign papers for Jews in occupied Poland in 1941, especially Paraguayan papers. He tried to send couriers from Switzerland to deliver these papers personally, but he found that by the spring of 1943 most of the papers could not be delivered and were perhaps falling into the wrong hands, so he decided to stop sending them to ghettos. See Chaim Shalem, "'Remember, There Are not Many Eisses Now in the Swiss Market': Assistance and Rescue Endeavors of Chaim Yisroel Eiss in Switzerland," *Yad Vashem Studies*, 33 (2005), pp. 347–377. It is not clear who Stefan Fay was, other than a friend of the Rzeczyńskis.

3   YVA, O.48.B/19–1.

Rzeczyński's first contact from his deported family was in brief letters dated August 5, 1943, from his father and his brother in Poniatowa, where the Többens factory workers from Warsaw had been sent, informing him that they had arrived safely in the camp on April 22 and were working in the laundry. They indicated that they wanted to try to get U.S. citizenship. He tried in vain to contact his wife and son. A letter from the Poniatowa camp administration on August 25 informed him that his wife and son were not there, while Schultz (Trawniki camp) and Többens each referred him to the other. The office of the *SS- und Polizeiführer* (SS and Police Commander, SSPF), which was responsible for these camps, offered no information. His father and brother wrote on September 12, in response to five letters from him (July 22–September 2), telling him, "Your son is healthy."

On September 22, his brother-in-law wrote that he had escaped from the camp and was hiding in Warsaw under an assumed name; his "life was hanging by a thread." In his efforts to obtain information about his wife and child, Rzeczyński wrote to Többens; Schultz; Gottlieb Hering, the former commandant of the Bełżec death camp and now commandant of Poniatowa; the *Stadthauptmann* in Lublin; Majdanek; *SS- und Polizeifuhrer* (SSPF) in Lublin; a Polish lawyer in Warsaw named Szymański; the Polish Red Cross; his own commander in the *Oflag*; and more. He encountered lies and obfuscation from all the Germans and ineptness from all the others. Only twice did he receive any real information from the Germans. Többens wrote on July 30, 1943, that Rzeczyński's father and brother were in Poniatowa and were well, and Hering wrote on September 10, 1943, saying that he had still not received the 50 Reichsmarks that Rzeczyński had sent for them—it was cleared ten days later.

When Rzeczyński could not find his wife and son, he wrote to the Population Registry in Warsaw on September 7, only to be told on October 2, nearly half a year after they had been deported from Warsaw, that they had no record of a change of address. Still, in the hope that perhaps they were indeed still in Warsaw, he wrote that day, October 2, to the Israelitische Flüchtlingshilfe (Jewish Refugee Board) in Basel asking for their assistance. However, they had no contact with the Generalgouvernement. As late as May 17, 1944, German officials were still writing to him that they did not know where his family was. The *SS Standortverwaltung* (garrison administration) in Lublin wrote that some family members had "left" Poniatowa, but Rzeczyński tried in vain to get a forwarding address. On May 20, 1944, he received a letter from his Polish friend Janina Komorowska—the false identity of his Jewish friend whose real name was Joselson—in Warsaw telling him of the fate of the Poniatowa Jews, who had all been shot on November 4, 1943, in *Aktion Erntefest* (Harvest Festival operation). Still, he tried desperately to get specific information in a last hope that perhaps they had indeed "moved." Of course, Hering, Többens, Schultz, and the other German officials all knew his family's fate.

The volume of correspondence in this story is striking. Dozens of letters and postcards were sent between the Warsaw ghetto and the Murnau POW camp in Bavaria, and between the camp and the Poniatowa, Trawniki, and Majdanek camps. Moreover, Rzeczyński corresponded with people in Switzerland, and his wife and son knew of the rescue activities of Chaim Yisrael Eiss and even provided his address in Zurich. Information traveled. Whereas the story of Feliks Efraim Rzeczyński relates to familial solidarity and rescue efforts through contacts within Nazi-controlled Europe and outside it, the following well-known story of the Bund Report highlights communal rescue efforts through external communication that was based on information gathered through contacts in Poland and the Soviet Union.

On May 21, 1942, two Swedish businessmen left Warsaw with a long, detailed report from the Bund in the underground in the Warsaw ghetto to deliver to the Polish Embassy in Stockholm for transfer from there to the Polish government-in-exile in London. The report opened, "From the day the Russo–German war broke out, the Germans embarked on the physical extermination of the Jewish population on Polish soil." The report detailed places, numbers, and methods of killing, estimating "that the Germans have already killed 700,000 Polish Jews." It called on the government to intervene with the Allies to take action: "We are aware of the fact that we are calling upon the Polish Government to apply unusual measures. This is the only possibility of saving millions of Jews from inevitable destruction."[4]

---

4 See the Bund Report, YVA, M.10/AR.I/937; YVA, JM.3489. On the dispatch and receipt of the report, see Yehuda Bauer, "When Did They Know?" *Midstream*, 24:4 (April 1968), pp. 51–58; Samuel Kassow, *Who Will Write Our History? Rediscovering a Hidden Archive from the Warsaw Ghetto* (New York: Vintage Books, 2009), pp. 298–299; David Engel, *In the Shadow of Auschwitz: The Polish Government-in-Exile and the Jews, 1939–1942* (Chapel Hill and London: University of North Carolina Press, 1987), pp. 185–186; Martin Gilbert, *Auschwitz and the Allies: A Devastating Account of How the Allies Responded*

The response to the receipt of this report in London on May 31, 1942, is well known—a few reports in British newspapers and limited coverage over the European Services of the BBC but no coverage over the Home Service in the UK. The Allies related to this report ambivalently, as did, it could be argued, many American and British Jewish leaders.[5] The Oyneg Shabbes underground group sent out several comprehensive reports to the Polish government-in-exile in the spring and summer of 1942, and, through that government, to the Allies in an effort "to describe and explain the Final Solution as it was unfolding."[6] One striking point in this story is the extent of the communications by Jews during the Holocaust reflected therein. The report was based on extensive information gathered from widespread and varied contacts—with Jews from communities that had experienced mass murder, the Polish undergrounds, neutral figures, the government-in-exile, Jews outside Poland, and the Allies.

The present essay examines the extensive exchange of information among Jews during the Shoah, even about mass murder, along with the widespread efforts to evade deportations to death camps, whether by hiding or by escape. Yet, for Jewish communities and for most Jews, the extent of rescue that resulted from sharing reports, information, and mutual concern seems to have been only very minimal.

Jewish Communications during the Holocaust

Communications among Jews continued via various channels throughout the war.[7] At least some Jews in occupied and Axis countries

to the News of Hitler's Mass Murder (New York: Henry Holt and Company, 1981), pp. 39–44; Walter Laqueur, The Terrible Secret: Suppression of the Truth about Hitler's "Final Solution" (Harmondsworth: Penguin, 1980), pp. 73–76; Dariusz Stola, "Early News of the Holocaust from Poland," Holocaust and Genocide Studies, 11:1 (1997), pp. 6–9.

5   In addition to the sources in note 3, see also David Silberklang, "The Allies and the Holocaust: A Reappraisal," Yad Vashem Studies, 24 (1994), pp. 162–163; Jeremy D. Harris, "Broadcasting the Massacres: An Analysis of the BBC's Contemporary Coverage of the Holocaust," Yad Vashem Studies, 25 (1996), pp. 66, 74.

6   Kassow, Who Will Write Our History? pp. 295–299.

7   Parts of the next two sections are based on parts of my book, David Silberklang, Gates of Tears: The Holocaust in the Lublin District (Jerusalem: Yad Vashem, 2013), pp. 149, 198–203, 281–290, 335–354.

were able to maintain limited contact with relatives and friends, both in Nazi-controlled Europe and outside it. The material, psychological, and informational importance of these contacts was significant. The contacts brought some Jews limited material relief from abroad—e.g., from the United States, until December 7, 1941; or from the Soviet Union, until June 1941; or from family within Europe in the form of packages and money. Communications also allowed Jews to maintain contact with the outside and with each other, which somewhat relieved their sense of isolation. Finally, they also provided information, albeit limited and often in code. The entry of the Soviet Union and the United States into the war cut legal contact with these countries and the hope that it brought. Moreover, this occurred in conjunction with the beginning of the systematic mass murders in the former Polish, Romanian, and Baltic states territories of the Soviet Union in the summer of 1941 and with the opening of the Chełmno death camp the day after the attack on Pearl Harbor in December 1941.

Jews might have tried to maintain contact with other Jews, or non-Jews, through various means: communication among Jewish officials, whether the Judenräte or others; personal, "legal" communication, as permitted by the Germans; telephones; and clandestine communication. The Judenräte maintained official communications with each other via correspondence, telephones, and, in parts of Poland, personal visits by Judenrat officials. In the Generalgouvernement, from January 1940, Jews were not permitted to use the regular post offices, and the Judenräte were forced to create a Jewish postal service. Private individuals maintained a measure of contacts via letters sent legally through these Jewish postal systems, letters sent secretly with couriers, and telephone calls through operators to the few official Jewish offices that had telephones. The Jewish postal systems in the Generalgouvernement operated under close German scrutiny. In general, Jews would bring their letters to the Judenrat or its Postal Department. The Judenrat's representative or the Jewish Postal Department would send and receive all the mail of the Jews at the regular Post Office, and the sorting would be done at the Jewish Postal Office. Generally, Jewish correspondence had to be written in Latin letters, in Cyrillic in countries where that was the alphabet, in German, or the local language; many wrote in Yiddish in Latin characters.

If assessed quantitatively, the total number of communications of all sorts would be in the hundreds of thousands. For example, in the autumn of 1940, the Postal Department of the Lublin Judenrat reported that it had processed 135,274 postal items in the first eight months of the year. Nearly 90 percent—120,350 items—was incoming, but the nearly 15,000 outgoing items reflect an active correspondence that continued until the deportations to Bełżec in March–April 1942.[8] The Lublin Judenrat's postal records indicate an increase in the volume of correspondence in 1941 and early 1942 to about 19,000 items monthly.[9] In Warsaw, approximately 10,000 to 13,000 postcards were sent each month from January to July 1942, as well as tens of thousands of packages monthly in 1941 and 1942, until the beginning of the Great Deportation.[10]

Yet, despite these impressive quantities of mailed items, there were many Jews whose contact with people outside their own community was severely limited, and others who had no such contact at all. Lublin's 15,000 outgoing postal items in eight months meant that approximately one person in three there sent one letter during that entire period on average, and this represented only a small fraction of the number of prewar communications. People often felt that they were not in touch with their loved ones. Small towns with poor infrastructures—of which there were many in Eastern and Southern Europe—were often the most isolated, especially in the winter.[11] Even those Jews who managed to maintain contact with the outside world, thereby deriving some relief and hope, lived under a brutal occupation regime, which by 1942 sought to kill them.

Private telephone calls could be made from telephones in the Judenrat offices, or in the Jewish Postal Department. With the permission of the German civilian administration, selected officials could have telephones in their offices. Many communities had at least one telephone, and some had several. All phone calls went through an operator, German or local, and could be tapped by the German authorities. Thus, the Germans could

8   Wojewódstwo Archiwum Państwowe w Lublinie (APL), Rada Żydowska (RZ) 21, 22, 52; Lublin Judenrat Annual Report, APL, RZ 8, pp. 69–70; YVA, O.6/9; Nachman Blumental, ed., Te'udot Migeto Lublin: Judenrat Lelo Derech (Hebrew) (Jerusalem: Yad Vashem, 1967), Protocol 2 (63), February 5, 1941, p. 213.

9   APL, particularly RZ 6, 52. The Jewish Postal Department's monthly reports for 1941 indicate an average of an additional 6,000 items per month for the Lipowa 7 POW camp, APL, RZ 6; United States Holocaust Memorial Museum Archive (USHMMA), RG-15.101M, reel 2.

10   Israel Gutman, Yehudei Varsha, 1939–1942: Geto, Mahteret, Mered (Hebrew) (Jerusalem: Yad Vashem, 2011), pp. 77–78, 214–217.

11   For example, on Krzeszów, see Moshe Becher testimony, YVA, O.3/8403; on Turobin, see Dov Freiberg, To Survive Sobibor (Jerusalem: Gefen, 2007), p. 151.

monitor Jewish contacts, while distancing the Jews from the general postal service and from direct dealings with their neighbors and the outside. Still, despite these restrictions, these limited communications offered a glimmer of normality and hope.

Communications during Murder and Deportations

News of the murder of the Jews in the Soviet Union spread fairly rapidly after it began. For example, in its September–October 1941 issue, the Warsaw ghetto underground newspaper *Neged Hazerem*, published by Hashomer Hatza'ir, reported on the murders in Vilna.

> At first everything was "normal"...However, later the [Lithuanian] authorities began kidnapping Jews and sending them to Lukiszki Prison, where they were sorted into those fit for work and those unfit. Those fit for work were apparently sent to work at the front (which meant death), while the unfit were simply killed. The killing was done at Ponary....The hangmen [were] all Lithuanians....
>
> In three months, the Jewish population of Vilna was reduced from 70,000 (under the Soviets) to 35,000.[12]

Numerous reports of the mass murder in the Soviet Union reached Warsaw and other places via refugees and messengers, and many reports appeared in the Warsaw ghetto underground press.

When the murders began in Poland, news traveled very quickly across the country. Murder by gas van began in Chełmno on December 8, 1941, and by January 19, 1942, the escapee Szlamek Winer had brought news of the murders to Jews on the outside. Following his escape, he made his way to Grabów and to the home of Rabbi Yaakov Sylman, where he told the rabbi, "Rebbe, I am a Jew from the world to come." After Winer had related the story of Chełmno in detail, the rabbi sent him to Warsaw under the pseudonym Jakub Grojnowski. Winer also wrote warnings to people in various localities, including Łódź and Warsaw, and he himself reported on Chełmno in the Jewish communities he passed through on his way to Warsaw.

---

12 Joseph Kermish and Israel Shaham, eds., *Itonut Hamahteret Hayehudit BeVarsha: July–Oktober 1941* (Hebrew), vol. 3 (Jerusalem: Yad Vashem, 1984), pp. 404–405.

In Warsaw, he was interviewed by Hersh and Bluma Wasser of the Oyneg Shabbes underground archive. His highly detailed story of Chełmno was widely discussed and reported in the Warsaw ghetto, as well as in the various places that he had passed through.[13] The Wassers helped Winer continue on to reunite with his family in Zamość, where he wrote to the Wassers in April about the newly opened death camp in Bełżec, a place known to Warsaw Jews who were sent to the murderous forced labor camps there in the summer and autumn of 1940: *"Der Bajs Olem is in Bełżyc,"* and Jews from Lublin, Rawa Ruska, and Biłgoraj have already been killed there.[14] What was the connection, if any, between the information on the murders and the Jewish responses, attempts to help others, and rescue? The Lublin District and Warsaw can serve as illustrations.

The deportations from Lublin to Bełżec began at dawn on March 17, 1942. Four companies of *Hiwis,* or *Hilfswillige* (Red Army renegades who had joined the Germans) who were trained at Trawniki—about 400–500 men—joined local SS and policemen for the operation. Only Jews who worked or those with useful skills were to be left behind.[15] The

13 Grojnowski testimony, YVA, M.10.AR.1/412; YVA, JM/1209-4; Lea Prais, "'Jews from the World to Come': The First Testimonies of Escapees from Chełmno and Treblinka in the Warsaw Ghetto, 1942–1943," *Yad Vashem Studies,* 42:1 (2014), pp. 52–60; Kassow, *Who Will Write Our History?* pp. 287–292; Shmuel Krakowski, *Chełmno, A Small Village in Europe: The First Nazi Mass Extermination Camp* (Jerusalem: Yad Vashem, 2009), pp. 69–80.

14 Postcards from Szlamek Winer, as well as from others working for the Zamość Judenrat, to Hersh Wasser, February–April 1942, YVA, M.10.AR.1/596. For a detailed discussion of Szlamek's identity, see Kassow, *Who Will Write Our History?* pp. 287–292; Ruta Sakowska, "Two Forms of Resistance in the Warsaw Ghetto—Two Functions of the Ringelblum Archives," *Yad Vashem Studies,* 21 (1991), p. 202. Sakowska identified Szlamek as the same person who had reported to Oyneg Shabbes on Chełmno in February. Kassow expands on this discussion significantly. Copies of the original letters can also be found in Ruta Sakowska, ed., *Archiwum Ringelbluma: Listy o Zagładzie* (Warsaw: Wydawnictwo Naukowe PWN, 1997), pp. 125–134.

15 YVA, TR.10/756 (Staatsanwaltschaft bei dem Landgericht Hamburg gegen Karl Richard Josef Streibel u.a., 147 Js 43/69), pp. 63–76; TR-10/869 (Landgericht Hamburg, Schwurgericht, Urteil in der Strafsache gegen Karl Richard Josef Streibel u.a., 147 Ks 1/72), vol. 3, pp. 325–327, and vol. 5, pp. 5–19 ; TR.10/859 (Landgericht Wiesbaden, Urteil gegen Josef Hermann Worthoff, 8 Ks 1/70), pp. 50–78; TR.10/736 (Anklageschrift die Staatsanwaltschaft Wien, gegen Ernst Lerch und Helmut Pohl, November 17, 1971, 15 St 2.696/62), pp. 26–30; See also Ida Rapoport-Glikstein testimony in Itzhak Gruenbaum, ed., *Entziklopedia Shel Galuyot: Lublin* (Hebrew), vol. 5 (Jerusalem and Tel Aviv: Encyclopedia of the Jewish Diaspora Co., 1957), p. 694–695; Ida Rapoport-

Germans and the *Hiwis* woke the sleeping Jews at 5:00 A.M. and drove them out of their homes. Whoever was slow to emerge or who tried to avoid joining the deportation was dragged out violently and beaten or shot. Following the intervention of the Judenrat, some of these Jews were then allowed to return to the ghetto as skilled laborers. The rest were marched under heavy guard to the freight rail station to be sent to Bełżec. The operation grew more brutal as it progressed, and "rivers of blood" flowed in the streets.

The opening moments of the roundup—the surprise, the shouting by the Germans and the Ukrainians, the victims' cries, the beatings, and the shootings—terrorized the Jews, as did the death threats and examples made should anyone try to escape.[16] The shooting of Jews accompanied every stage of the operation—from their homes to the trains. Once a section of the ghetto had been cleared, the Trawniki troops were sent back to search for all the Jews who were too ill to walk or were hiding. These people were shot on the spot. As the roundups progressed, increasing numbers of Jews tried to hide in impromptu hideouts, which created some difficulties for the Germans. At the end of each day, a special, Jewish burial unit collected all the dead and buried them in the Jewish cemetery. By March 29, 1942, approximately 18,000 Jews had been deported and at least 1,000 had been shot.

After suspending the operation in Lublin for two days for logistic reasons, the Germans resumed the deportations on March 31. Now, the Germans found it much more difficult to meet their daily quotas— the Jews had gone into hiding. This led to even more violence on the part of the angry and frustrated Germans and Ukrainians.[17] By April 14, 1942, when the deportation operation from Lublin to Bełżec ended, 2,000 or more Jews had been shot on the spot and about 30,000 had been deported to the camp and killed. The remaining Jews were sent to the remnant ghetto in the Majdan-Tatarski neighborhood. Although that ghetto was equipped to accommodate perhaps 2,000 people, 7,000–

Glikstein, *Dos Bukh fun Lublin* (Yiddish) (Paris: S.I.R.N., 1952), p. 395; Sarah Erlichman-Bank, *Biyedei Temai'im* (Hebrew) (Tel Aviv: Ghetto Fighters' House and Hakibbutz Hame'uhad, 1976), p. 36.

16 Klajnman-Fradkopf testimony, YVA, O.33/1134; Yehoshua Kaniel testimony, YVA, O.3/10622; Memo from Dr. Hasse to the Lublin-Land Kreishauptmann, March 17, 1942, regarding a March 4 court verdict, APL, Kreishauptmannschaft Lublin-Land 75; YVA, O.53/82.

17 YVA, TR.10/859, pp. 50–78. See also the pretrial interrogations, YVA, TR.10/1146Z.

8,000 were squeezed in, half of them without the necessary new identity cards. At 5:00 A.M., on April 20, 1942, the Majdan-Tatarski ghetto was surrounded by *Hiwis*, while SS men divided the Jews into those with the new IDs and those without. New identification papers were issued to 3,300 people, whereas the more than 4,000 "illegal" Jews who were caught were shot the next day in the mass graves that they themselves had been forced to dig in the Krępiec Woods.[18]

Parallel to the deportations from Lublin to Bełżec, about 90,000 Jews were deported from Mielec, Theresienstadt, Germany, Slovakia, and Austria to the Lublin District from mid-March to mid-June 1942, while the deportation and murder operation in the district spread to other localities. By mid-June, at least 140,000 Jews had been killed. The rest of the district's Jews, except for a small number of skilled laborers, were murdered between August and December of that year. Among this latter group were the last Jews of Lublin, who were killed in three operations in September, October, and November.

What did the Jews understand as the deportations got underway and what did they try to do? It is clear that the Jews of Lublin were taken by surprise. For example, only three days before the deportation operation began, the Judenrat was still looking ahead to communal matzah baking for the upcoming Passover holiday, which in that year began on April 1.[19] However, it seems that at least some of the Lublin Jews had quickly discovered the fate of the deportees.

On March 17, 1942, at 7:30 A.M., Josef Siegfried, a Judenrat deputy chairman and Marek Alten's Jüdische Soziale Selbshilfe (JSS) deputy in the Lublin district, telephoned the Kraków headquarters of JSS to inform them that mass deportations of the Lublin Jews had begun. He reported that the SD was deporting all nonessential people. Twenty thousand were to be deported at a rate of 1,400 daily. Two days later, Siegfried called Kraków again to report that all the deportees were being sent to Bełżec.[20] Although Siegfried did not refer to the fate of the deportees, at

---

18 Blumental, *Te'udot Migeto Lublin*, Protocols, 22 (146) and 23 (147), April 14 and 19, 1942, pp. 324–327; Zörner order, April 16, 1942, Moreshet Archive (MA), D.1.5868; YVA, TR.10/859, pp. 194–200; TR.10/736, pp. 33–35; TR.10/756, p. 68; TR.10/1146Z; Worthoff interrogation, September–November, 1960, p. 1357; Ida Rapoport-Glikstein's testimony in Gruenbaum *Entziklopedia Shel Galuyot: Lublin*, vol. 5, pp. 701–708; Rapoport-Glikstein, *Dos Bukh fun Lublin*, pp. 399–402.

19 Blumental, *Te'udot Migeto Lublin*, Protocol 13 (137), March 14, 1942, p. 309.

20 YVA, JM.1576, pp. 122, 123, 124. See also Blumental, *Te'udot Migeto Lublin*, pp. 65–67.

least part of the truth was revealed within two days. The mere fact that the destination was Bełżec was enough to strike terror in the hearts of all of the Jews, especially those who recalled the brutal conditions of those labor camps in the summer–autumn of 1940, which many thousands of them had experienced and whose notoriety was widely known in the district and across Poland.

Symcha Turkeltaub testified on numerous occasions after the war that by March 20, 1942, the Jews in Lublin had heard of the fate of the deportees from Poles.[21] The former head of the Zamość Judenrat and head of the JSS there, Mieczysław Garfinkel, reported that he had received a telephone call from the Lublin Judenrat in late March 1942, asking him to check on the deported Lublin Jews' whereabouts and fate. Since telephone calls by JSS officials were routine, it is likely that such a call could have been made by Siegfried or Alten to Garfinkel in that capacity without drawing the attention of the German authorities. Garfinkel called the Judenrat in Tomaszów-Lubelski, a few kilometers from Bełżec, asking them to look into the matter. They, in turn, learned from Polish railroad workers that all of the Jews who were sent to the camp were being killed and reported this to Garfinkel, who then informed the Lublin Judenrat.[22] According to Hava Goldminc, her family paid a Polish courier 20,000 złotys to follow the trains in order to find out where the Jews were being sent and discover their fate. By the eve of Passover, they knew what was happening to the deportees.[23]

These illustrations of Jews acquiring information on the fate of the deportees do not suggest that large numbers of Jews clearly understood the Nazis' plans for them. Yet the fact of the deportations and their extreme violence, coupled with the memories of earlier violent roundups for forced labor, drove many Jews into hiding. In fact, hiding was so widespread that it left its mark on the Germans' memory, as noted above. Still, most of the Jews were caught. Those who managed to survive the

21 Symcha Turkeltaub testimony, YVA, TR.10/756, p. 75; YVA, TR.10/1146Z, vol. 20, p. 4285.
22 Mieczysław Garfinkel testimony, YVA, JM/3536a; Mieczysław Garfinkel testimony, December 5, 1945, Polish War Crimes Commission, Lublin; Mieczysław Garwin (Mieczysław Garfinkel had moved to Rhodesia and changed his name to Garwin), YVA, TR.10/1146, vol. 17, pp. 3724–3274; YVA, O.33/322; YVA, TR.10/859, pp. 74–75; See also *Pinkas Zamość* (Yiddish) (Buenos Aires: Zamość Landsmanschaft, 1957), pp. 1117–1158.
23 Hava Goldminc (Kirszenblat) interview, January 16, 2000, YVA, O.3/11397.

initial deportations informed friends and relatives in other places about what was happening in Lublin. For example, Chaim Kaplan in Warsaw heard about the deportations within a few days and wrote about them in his diary as early as on March 22, 1942, and within less than four weeks, he was well informed by refugees from Lublin regarding the fate of those Jews.[24] Similarly, Avraham Lewin and Shimon Huberband recorded the growing tension in Warsaw in reaction to the horror stories reaching the ghetto from refugees as well as from letters.[25]

As the deportations progressed, Jews increasingly contacted relatives and friends, seeking help or conveying information and warnings in the hope that others might save themselves. Although the number of such letters sent cannot be known, those that have survived highlight the writers' creativity in evading the postal censors and getting their messages and warnings out. On March 29, 1942, Daniel Lewkowicz wrote to his sister in Warsaw from a cellar in Lublin, where he had been hiding with a cousin since the deportations began, reporting that 15,000 Jews had already been deported and 1,000 had been shot.[26] When such information was sent to loved ones through the legal post, it would be couched in cryptic messages, such as "*Malach Hamowes is in die gass*" (the Angel of Death is in the street).[27]

Some letters bore clear warnings to relatives or friends to hide, because otherwise they too would be caught in the deportations and murders. For example, a cryptic warning in Yiddish, dated June 1,

24 Chaim Aron Kaplan, *The Warsaw Diary of Chaim A. Kaplan*, ed. and tr. by Abraham I. Katsh (New York: Collier, 1973), pp. 304–305, 312–314. This is an incomplete translation of the original Hebrew; for the original Hebrew, see MA, D.2.470, pp. 236, 249–252.

25 Havi Ben-Sasson and Lea Preiss, "Twilight Days: Missing Pages from Avraham Lewin's Warsaw Ghetto Diary, May–July 1942," *Yad Vashem Studies*, 33 (2005), diary entries for May 15 and June 13, 14, 15, 1942, pp. 22–34; and Lea Prais, "An Unknown Chronicle: From the Literary Legacy of Rabbi Shimon Huberband, Warsaw Ghetto, May–June 1942," *Yad Vashem Studies*, 38:1 (2010), diary entries for May 10, 27, and 28, and June 21, 1942, pp. 75–76, 88–90, 97–99.

26 Letter from Daniel Lewkowicz to his sister, March 29, 1942, YVA, M.10/A.R.I/552; YVA, JM.3489.

27 See the postcard from Chelm to Warsaw, April 13, 1942, YVA, M.10/A.R.I/568; YVA, JM.3489; the postcard from Janina Szylska in Sosnowiec (Chelm County) to Ludwik Hirszberg in Warsaw, May 27, 1942, YVA, M.10/A.R.I/579; YVA, JM.3489; the cryptic letter from M. Altman in Międzyrzec-Podlaski to J. Berkal in Warsaw, May 5, 1942, M.10/A.R.I/558; YVA, JM.3489. Hela Ferstman reported that in Bełżyce she received information about the Lublin deportations almost immediately; see Hela Ferstman diary, YVA, M.49.P/2.

1942, was sent from Włodawa to Warsaw, probably by courier, after the deportation of about 1,300 Jews from Włodawa to Sobibór in a very violent operation on May 22–23, 1942, after many of the remaining Jews had fled from the town.[28] The letter warned the recipients that "Uncle wants, H[as] V[ehalila] [God forbid], to have his children's party by you, H[as] V[ehalila]....Perhaps you don't even know this. Therefore, I am writing to you now...specially, so you should know." The writer urged the addressees to "rent apartments out of town...because Uncle wants *vayigaresh et ha'adam* [and He expelled man], and then you will be together with Shlomo Velvel, A[lav] H[ashalom] [of blessed memory]." The warning to hide was repeated cryptically with references to biblical verses, pleading "Remember, be in your apartments [outside town] at all costs, so that you won't be with Shlomo Velvel A[lav] H[ashalom], and for sleeping the only *segula* [good fortune] is that of *yoshev beseter* [He who sits secretly]. Remember well that we are *kedoshim vehanotar mimenu ad boker, vekhu'* [holy and that which is left until morning, etc.]."[29] The biblical references and acronyms would have been clear to almost any Polish Jew at the time. The last reference that refers to the first Passover sacrifice by the Israelites in ancient Egypt was not completed—"shall be burned by fire"[30]—is the end of the verse. The writer was convinced that the murder operation would also reach Warsaw and, by implication, all of the Jews of Poland. It is not clear what the writer knew specifically, but the warning was clear: get out of town and hide, because the Germans are planning to kill all of you as well.

Information about the murders was also included in letters sent to the outside world. For instance, Shmuel Zitomirski, who had fled from Lublin to Hrubieszów, wrote on March 29, 1942, to Nathan Schwalb, director of the World Center of Hehalutz in Geneva, that "Uncle Gerush"

28 For details regarding the May 1942 deportations from Włodawa to Sobibór, see the testimonies in the Israel police investigations regarding Włodawa, YVA, TR.11/01238; the indictment and verdict in the case of Anton Müller et al., Hanover, 2 Js 165/61, and 2 Ks 4/63, YVA, TR.10/631. Ruta Sakowska believes the letter was copied by Eliahu Gutkowski, second secretary of Oyneg Shabbes; see Sakowska, "Two Forms of Resistance," p. 206.
29 Letter from Włodawa to Warsaw, June 1, 1942, YVA, "Oyneg Shabbes," AR-I/563; YVA, JM/3489. See also Sakowska, "Two Forms of Resistance," p. 206, where a partial and at times inexact translation appears. For a copy of the letter, see Sakowska, ed., *Archiwum Ringelbluma*, pp. 152–155.
30 Exod. 12:10.

(expulsion) had visited the Jews in Lublin.[31] Isser Roizman wrote to Schwalb from Zamość on April 20: "Mr. Kilayon (annihilation), whom you know from Mr. Haim Nahman of Nemirov, visited us. He looks bad and meeting him cost me half my health." The report referred to the April 11, 1942, deportations from Zamość, and the reference to Haim Nahman was to Bialik and his poem about the 1903 Kishinev pogroms, "In the City of Slaughter."[32]

The activists in youth movements and political parties were not the only ones who were able to maintain contact with others outside their country or outside Nazi-controlled Europe. For example, the family of Mordechai and Edzia Rotgold in Paris exchanged letters with their close family in Poland and sent them several packages.[33] On March 8, 1942, Edzia's father, Rafael Goldnadel, wrote to his grandchildren, Edzia and Mordechai's five children, thanking them for their letters. Ten weeks later, on May 18, the Jews of Łaskarzew were deported to Bełżec.[34] Fajga Rotgold wrote to her brother Mordechai and his family in Paris on May 4, 1942, informing him that they had left Lublin and were now in Łęczna, their hometown, whereas some members of the family had been "evacuated from Lublin to an unknown destination." She asked that they send her supplies, because, "imagine my dears that we have nothing left, because we left everything in Lublin."[35]

Letters reached Mandatory Palestine and even Australia. For example, Berta Böhm (Weisz), a deportee from Slovakia to Opole-Lubelski, wrote to Rene Kadlecik in Australia on April 2, 1942: "The weather here is not good. We're always waiting for a storm."[36] Josef Szalavec, another Slovakian Jewish deportee in Opole, wrote to Ferdinand Fels in Haifa

---

31 See the letter from Shmuel Zitomirski, Hrubieszów, to Nathan Schwalb, March 29, 1942, in Ruth Zariz, ed., *Michteve Halutzim MiPolin Hakevusha, 1940–1944* (Hebrew) (Tel Aviv: Yad Tabenkin and Ghetto Fighters' House, 1994), pp. 136–137. See also the letter from Moshe Wilnicki, Częstochowa, to Nathan Schwalb, March 28, 1942, Ibid., p. 135.

32 See the letters from Isser Roizman, Zamość, to Nathan Schwalb, April 20, 1942, p. 139.

33 See the letters from Rafael Goldnadel in Łaskarzew, Poland, to his daughter Edzia and his son, Jacques, in Paris, October 17, 1941, and March 3, 1942, thanking them for the packages and the news that they sent, in Serge Rodgold and Adina Drechsler, eds., *Edzia Yekirati, Yeladim Yekarim: Mishpahat Rodgold Mikhtavim 1940–1944* (Hebrew) (Jerusalem: Yad Vashem, 2008), pp. 52, 90.

34 Ibid., p. 90. On the deportation, see Silberklang, *Gates of Tears*, p. 318.

35 Rodgold and Drechsler, eds., *Edzia Yekirati*, p. 113.

36 YVA, O.75/162.

on August 11, 1942, asking for financial help.[37] Prior to his letter, in the period from March to May 1942, more than 5,000 Slovakian Jews had been deported to Opole-Lubelski, and about 6,000 local and other Jews had been sent from Opole to Bełżec and Sobibór.[38]

What did Jews outside the Lublin District understand about the deportations and how did this affect their own reactions to them? As the deportations began, many tried to discover the whereabouts and fate of their loved ones. For instance, on March 24, 1942, Markus Hirsch, in Rosulna, near Stanisławów (Galicia), wrote to the Lublin Judenrat to inquire about the whereabouts of his wife Ryfka Frieda, from whom he had not heard in a while. He included a stamped, self-addressed response postcard.[39] Hirsch's inquiry came one week into the mass deportations from Lublin to Bełżec—just as deportations from other localities, including the Galicia District, were beginning and, ironically, only six days before the deportations from Stanisławów County were to begin.[40]

It is difficult to know exactly what Markus Hirsch and other inquirers like him had understood about the deportations, but the numerous extant letters and records of telephone calls reflect ongoing communication among Jews even during the deportations, which was one of the most significant factors in spreading information about the Holocaust and warning the intended victims. This communication offers a glimpse of the Jews' anxiety, anguish, and fear, and the attempts of many to cry for help or to try to forewarn others.

The Oyneg Shabbes underground archive in the Warsaw ghetto collected a great deal of information from refugees and couriers, and

---

37 YVA, O.75/375. See also the letters from Moses Rubin, a Slovakian Jewish deportee in Chełm, to his children in Prešov, particularly his last letter, September 3, 1942, YVA, O.75/57.

38 Silberklang, *Gates of Tears*, pp. 294–309, 316–319.

39 Letter from Markus Hirsch to Judenrat in Lublin, March 24, 1942, APL, RZ 22; YVA, O.6/395. This file in APL contains dozens of inquiries of this sort. See, for example, Klara Herschthal in Lemberg to the Judenrat in Majdan Tatarski, May 1, 1942, inquiring about her brother Marek Alten; and a letter from Necha Ejbuszyc in Warsaw to Marek Alten, June 11, 1942, inquiring about her mother, who disappeared in Lublin on April 3 or 4, 1942.

40 For deportation dates from various places in the GG, see Yitzhak Arad, *The Operation Reinhard Death Camps: Belzec, Sobibor, Treblinka* (Bloomington: Indiana University Press, 2018), pp. 447–462. On Stanisławów, see Dieter Pohl, "Hans Krüger and the Murder of the Jews in the Stanislawów Region," *Yad Vashem Studies*, 26 (1998), pp. 239–264.

smuggled out detailed reports, hoping in this way to inform the Polish underground, the world, and the other endangered Jews. Some hoped their information would prompt solidarity among their Christian countrymen, as well as rescue activity on behalf of the Jews. Moreover, if Jews in other communities knew what was happening, perhaps they could save themselves. Letters from the Lublin District were among the important sources that the Oyneg Shabbes underground used to compile reports, such as the one in early April 1942 that reported that Jews in Lublin and towns in the area were being deported to Bełżec, where they were being killed "in the same way as in Chełmno; that is, they are poisoned by gas," clearly borrowing from Winer's message.[41] The abovementioned Bund Report of May 1942 is the best known. As news spread across Poland and elsewhere, we can say that by early summer 1942 the Jews in Poland had succeeded in sending out detailed information regarding deportations from dozens of communities.[42]

Yet, at the same time, many reports that circulated were inaccurate, such as those describing murders by electrocution in Bełżec, murders by drawing the air out of a room in Treblinka, or murders by quicklime

---

41 "Mitteilungen far der Untererdishe Presse, Mitteilung nr. 1, di Yiddishe Bafelkerung untern Zeichen fun Phizisher Oysrottung!" (Yiddish), YVA, M.10/AR.I/259.

42 See the reports, dated April 3 to July 18, 1942, in the "Oyneg Shabbes" Archive, YVA, M.10/AR.I/558; YVA, JM.3489; letter from M. Altman in Międzyrzec-Podlaski to J. Berkal in Warsaw, May 5, 1942; letter from Janina Szylska in Sosnowiec to Ludwik Hirszberg in Warsaw, May 27, 1942, A.R.I/579; YVA, JM.3489; undated report from Lublin (apparently early April), YVA, M.10/A.R.I/948; report on Lublin and Izbica, April 3, YVA, M.10/AR.I/262; YVA, JM.3489; report on Izbica, April 25, YVA, M.10/A.R.I/949; reports on Lublin, September 1939 to April 1942, YVA, M.10/A.R.II/305; YVA, JM.3488; report on Rejowiec, undated (apparently mid-May), YVA, M.10/AR.I/1215; YVA, JM.3489; report on Hrubieszów, June 1942, YVA, M.10/AR.I/998; YVA, JM.3489; report by Mr. Rotring on Tyszowiec, June 1942, YVA, M.10/AR.I/1061; YVA, JM.3489; a report on the Lublin District, May 5, 1942, YVA, M.10/AR.III/27; "Di Megilah fun Pein un Oystorung" (Yiddish), a report by Eliahu Gutkowski, May 29, YVA, M.10/AR.I/1062; YVA, JM.1209/1; reports on deportations, June 18, July 3, and July 18, YVA, M.10/AR.I/472; reports of May 5 and June 18, 1942, YVA, M.10/AR.I/317; YVA, JM.3489; June 25, 1942, report on GG, "z Kraju," and a July report, "Service prasowy," YVA, M.10/AR.I/471; YVA, JM.2719; a June 30, 1942, report, "z Kraju," YVA, M.10/AR.I/261; YVA, JM.3489; undated report on Poland, apparently the Bund Report that was compiled in mid-May and smuggled out to England, YVA, M.10/AR.I/937; YVA, JM.3489; undated report, probably July, "Gehenna Żydów Polskich pod Okupacja Hitlerowska," YVA, M.10/AR.I/144; YVA, JM.3489. Reports continued to arrive and to be circulated after July as well, of course.

in Izbica.[43] For example, Yehoshua Wohlfuss wrote in his diary on April 1, 1942, "Every day 18–20 train cars take Jews from Lemberg to Bełżec. People say that the barbarians exterminate the elderly, women, and children by electrocution."[44] Chaim Kaplan noted the same rumor in his diary on April 17, as did the Polish physician Zygmunt Klukowski in his diary on April 8, and as the underground newspaper of Po'alei Zion (ZS) *Unzer Weg* reported on May 1.[45] Yisrael Cymlich heard in Treblinka I that murder in Treblinka II was done by sucking air out of the murder chamber, while Jan Karski witnessed murder by quicklime when he was in a satellite camp of Bełżec at Izbica, and he reported this to the West.[46]

To what extent did information influence reactions? Did warnings help the endangered communities? It seems that whereas the actions of individuals may have been affected by the news, communities were less so, as might be expected. Moreover, even when information and warnings led to action, decisions were often fraught with insoluble dilemmas. For example, following a warning by a Polish Communist friend about the impending liquidation of the Ryki ghetto, Yehezkel Kesselbrener fled the ghetto on the eve of the deportation of May 6, 1942, leaving his wife and six children behind. He and his wife believed that women and children would not be harmed, but his family was deported the next day.[47] Assistance and action often resulted in more difficulties, such as in the case of Winer, who was assisted to get to Zamość only to be killed a few weeks later, or the case of Yitzhak Leibusz Perec, who fled with

43 "Oyneg Shabbes," YVA, AR.1/472; YVA, AR.1/317: YVA, JM.3489; YVA, AR.III/27; YVA, JM.1209.1; a July 1942 report, "Gehenna Żydów Polskich," YVA, M.10/AR.I/144.

44 Diary of Yehoshua Wohlfuss, ca. April 1, 1942, *Sefer Zikaron Lekehillat Rava Ruska Vehasviva* (Yiddish) (Tel Aviv: Rava Ruska Immigrants' Society, 1973), pp. 236–239, quotation from p. 238. Rawa Ruska was in the Galicia District of the Generalgouvernement, on the border of the Lublin District, very close to Bełżec. On March 20, 1942, about 1,500 Jews from Rawa Ruska were deported to Bełżec. Trains bearing Jews from Lwów and the Lwów District to Bełżec passed through Rawa Ruska during March and early April 1942.

45 *Diary*, entry of April 17, 1942, p. 313; Zygmunt Klukowski, *Diary from the Years of Occupation 1939–1944* (Urbana and Chicago: University of Illinois Press, 1993), entry of April 8, 1942, p. 191; Joseph Kermish and Israel Shaham, eds., *Itonut Hamahteret Hayehudit BeVarsha: Mars 1942–Yuli 1944* (Hebrew), vol. 6 (Jerusalem: Yad Vashem, 1997), p. 230.

46 Israel Cymlich and Oskar Strawczynski, *Escaping Hell in Treblinka* (Jerusalem: Yad Vashem and the Holocaust Survivors' Memoirs Project, 2007), p. 45; Jan Karski, *The Story of a Secret State* (Boston: Houghton Mifflin, 1944), pp. 379–381.

47 Yehezkel Kesselbrener testimony, YVA, O.3/2089.

his wife to Warsaw, after being warned by the head of the Hrubieszów Judenrat, Jokel Brand, of the impending deportation in June 1942, only to face deportation there a few weeks later.[48]

News of the deportations from the Warsaw ghetto reached the remaining Jews in Lublin almost immediately after they began in late July 1942. Jews in Majdan Tatarski lined up at the Judenrat office to telephone their loved ones in Warsaw, only to discover that the latter seemed unaware of the fate that awaited them. Some were confident that their work IDs would protect them.[49] As one Jewish man from Zamość in 1942 described the difficulty in believing the stories about the murders: "an expulsion is like a funeral procession—when a funeral procession passes by, heaven forbid, everyone thinks it is not for him. That's how it was with us."[50]

In general, even when warnings were received and heeded and communal action was taken, Jews found little possibility of saving significant parts of their communities. Thus, Jokel Brand in Hrubieszów succeeded in warning individuals but could not find a way to try to save the community. In Lublin, the Judenrat of the remnant community's last seven months of existence, debilitated by the deportations, locked behind a fence in Majdan Tatarski, and riddled with dubious personalities imposed on it by the SS, succeeded nonetheless in increasing the number of "legal" Jews in the remnant ghetto from 3,000 to more than 4,500 by June 1942, and legalized at least 130 more by giving them the ID cards of Jews who had died. Unfortunately, this had no impact on the remnant community's ultimate fate.[51]

As news and warnings spread, mass escapes and the efforts to hide increased. In Markuszów, when Judenrat head Shlomo Goldwasser, who

48 Yitzhak Leibusz Perec testimony, YVA, O.3/4238; Mischa Stahlhammer testimony, YVA, O.3/4312; Ahuva Shamai-Grossfeld testimony, YVA, O.3/3135.

49 Ida Rapoport-Glikstein, *Dos Bukh fun Lublin*, p. 404; Ida Rapoport-Glikstein's testimony in Gruenbaum, *Entziklopedia Shel Galuyot: Lublin*, vol. 5, p. 711.

50 Fiszelzon Report, June 6, 1942, YVA, M.10/AR.1/946. The extensive familiarity with detail in this testimony would suggest that this was written by either Baruch Fiszelzon, who had been a member of the Judenrat in Zamość, or Berek Fiszelzon, a Jewish policeman.

51 See requests from the Judenrat to the SS for additional *Ausweise* (ID cards), May 5–11, 1942, APL, RZ 159, pp. 17–110; handwritten list of 130 names of people who received the *Ausweise* of people who had died or been killed, dated June 12, 1942, APL, RZ 159, pp. 111–120; the September 1942 list of 4,641 Jews in Lublin who had received *Ausweise*, APL, RZ 164.

had heard about the Lublin deportations, received information about the impending deportation from his town, he warned the Jews. The result was mass flight to the nearby forest on the morning of May 9, 1942, as all the Jews were ordered to report to the town square. However, here as elsewhere nearly all of the Jews who escaped and went into hiding were eventually caught.[52]

In Łuków, rumors spread on Saturday evening, October 3, 1942, at the beginning of the Shemini Atzeret holiday that sixty freight cars were waiting for the 10,000 Jews there. The people knew about Treblinka and understood what this news meant. They prepared bunkers and guessed correctly that the deportation would not take place on Sunday. On Monday, October 5, the Jewish quarter was surrounded by German, Polish, and Ukrainian forces. The bulk of the German forces came from Reserve Police Battalion 101. The fact that the Jews had hidden themselves hampered the operation, but this proved to be only a minor nuisance for the Germans, and 7,000 Jews were eventually deported to Treblinka. On Thursday, October 8, the Germans announced that all the remaining Jews, including those in hiding, should report to the Judenrat to receive new work stamps. Two thousand reported and were deported to Treblinka.

A series of roundups took place during the following weeks. A young man named Finkelstein (first name unknown) was seized at 4:00 A.M. on November 8 and loaded onto the last train from Łuków to Treblinka. Some of the younger people on the train broke through the door of their freight car and hundreds escaped, including Finkelstein. Many of the escapees were caught by local villagers and returned to Łuków, where German policemen from Battalion 101 shot them in the Jewish cemetery between November 8–11, 1942. The first shot only singed Finkelstein's head. He was shot again, this time through the arm and neck but not killed. After the Germans left, Poles came to loot the bodies. Despite his injuries, Finkelstein was able to flee to the home of a Polish friend and from there he made his way to Warsaw in two weeks to join his brother and two sisters.[53] Whereas hiding and escape made a difference for

---

52 David Shtokfish, ed., *Hurbn un Gvurah fun Shtetl Markushov* (Yiddish) (Tel Aviv: Markuszów Immigrants' Association, 1955), pp. 159–194; Shmuel Krakowski, *The War of the Doomed* (New York: Holmes and Meier, 1984), pp. 61–62.

53 "Hurbn Lukov" (Yiddish), YVA, M.10.AR.2/306, late November 1942; Christopher R. Browning, *Ordinary Men: Reserve Police Battalion 101 and the Final Solution in Poland* (New York: Harper Perennial, 1992), pp. 110–112.

him temporarily, hiding and attempted escape were futile for the large majority of the Jews in Łuków. Indeed, for the Jews in general, regardless of the warnings received and the impact of information on their actions, the fate of the communities remained the same.

Amidst the despair and hopelessness, measures of solidarity continued at least for some people. In Lublin, for example, Rabbi Zvi Elimelech Talmud produced Jewish calendars for Rosh Hashana 5703 (Jewish New Year 1942/1943).[54] Rabbi Talmud was in deep turmoil and despair, as noted in his clandestine letters to Rabbi Haim Arieh Berglas on July 28 and in early October 1942. He knew about the murders all across Poland and the deportations from Warsaw to Treblinka as they happened. He despaired of the God who had unleashed His wrath on European Jewry: "It is difficult for me; I cannot accept under any circumstances the notion that we are all guilty, all sinners to such an extent that a deluge of blood and fire and belching smoke should wash us away in wrathful waters." Yet, he also reported that High Holiday services in Majdan Tatarski had been held without incident and were attended diligently, even by secular Jews.[55] On the one hand, "there is not even a spark of hope to survive," and God was inexplicably killing off His people, while, on the other hand, the remaining Jews of Lublin came together to attend High Holiday services and make Jewish calendars for the coming year. Less than two months into that new Jewish year, the remnants of this Jewish community were gone.

The pain and frustration that too often resulted despite the communications, information, warnings, and action undertaken by Jews are reflected in Feliks Rzeczyński's own summation in his brief account of his experiences during the war, which he attached to the letters that he gave to the Yad Vashem Archive in 1956. Regarding his efforts to save his family on April 5, 1943, he said:

---

54 See ten such calendars, most written by hand by Jews in the ghetto, apparently by or at the initiative of Rabbi Zvi Elimelech Talmud, APL, RZ 32; see also Symcha Turkeltaub's testimony in Gruenbaum, *Entziklopedia Shel Galuyot: Lublin*, vol. 5, p. 737.

55 Letter from Rabbi Zvi Elimelech Talmud to Rabbi Haim Arieh Berglas, ca. early October 1942, following the Shemini Azeret holiday, APL, RZ32. See also Talmud's letter to an unnamed correspondent (n.d.), and his letter of the third day of Parshat Ekev, 5742 (July 28, 1942) to Rabbi Haim Arieh Berglas, APL, RZ32 (copies of both letters in YVA, O.75/897); and Symcha Turkeltaub's testimony in Gruenbaum, *Entziklopedia Shel Galuyot: Lublin*, vol. 5, p. 737.

I received two alarming letters from my wife and son in Warsaw that I should get them foreign papers in Switzerland, otherwise there is no hope that we'll ever see each other alive again. It was Friday, 12 noon. At 2 P.M., I went to Lieutenant Freisinger (Abwehr) and in my despair asked him to allow me to send a telegram to Switzerland in order to get papers for my wife and son. He asked me to wait for Captain Oleschko, who returned to the office a few minutes later. After listening to my pleas and reading the desperate letters from Warsaw, he [Oleschko] answered in these words: "Herr Lieutenant, for us it does not matter what religion you are; for us you are an officer prisoner of war and we are obligated to help you. Telegrams are forbidden to prisoners of war by the OKW [Oberkommando der Wehrmacht (High Command of the Armed Forces]. I will however allow [you] to do this all by letter and you can send as many letters as you wish."

He [Oleschko] went into the censor's room and asked Captain Pohl to give orders to give me as many forms for letters as I wish. He asked him to censor the letters as soon as I wrote them, that same day, meaning Friday, and to send them the next day, on Saturday, so that they would not wait until Monday. The letters took eight days to reach Zurich. The papers were ready in May; a special Swiss courier went to Warsaw. The ghetto was still smoking. It was too late.[56]

From all the above, it appears that at least at some point by 1942 or 1943 quite a few Jews had surmised enough of what the Germans were doing to recognize that their lives were in danger. Many sought to warn others and to alert their government and the world in the hope of saving Jews. However, it is also clear that this collective concern and numerous reports and warnings yielded little by way of rescue. For most Jews, there was no hope for rescue, which came too late.

---

56 YVA, O.48.B/19-1. My thanks to Dr. Marta Marzańska-Mishani for her assistance in the translation of this excerpt.

Poale Zion Left in Belgium and
Rescue by the Comité de Défense des Juifs

JEANNINE (LEVANA) FRENK

t the outbreak of World War II, Belgium had a Jewish population of around 65,000. Approximately 55 percent survived to witness the liberation. Before the war, most of the Jewish collectivity resided in the country under provisional working permits, or as legal residents. About 90 percent were noncitizens, but even under the German occupation, they benefited from some kind of protection, unlike the noncitizen Jews in Bulgaria, Romania, and even France.[1] A more interesting feature of the Holocaust in Belgium, as pointed out by Maxime Steinberg, the principal authority on the subject, is that two-thirds of the victims, that is, 17,000 Jews, were arrested from August to September 1942, during the first two months after the first deportations began. The remaining third of the deportees, around 8,000, were arrested during the following two years under Nazi rule, from late September 1942 to the liberation in September 1944. The number of arrested victims declined drastically during the first two or three months after the massive manhunts of August–September 1942.[2] This specific phenomenon should be attributed to the response of the Jews themselves and to a turning point in local public opinion, particularly in the Francophone Walloon region, as well as to the fact that the municipal police forces ceased to participate in the hunt for Jews.

With respect to the response of the Jews, two important points

---

1 Bulgaria did not protect foreign Jews from the annexed provinces of Thrace and Macedonia who were deported to the death camps. Romania, which was not even occupied by Germany, deported the Jews from the reacquired provinces of Bessarabia and Bucovina to Transnistria.

2 Maxime Steinberg, *L'étoile et le fusil, 1942: Les cent jours de la déportation des Juifs de Belgique*, vol. 2 (Brussels: Vie Ouvrière, 1984).

should be emphasized: the gradual move of most Jews into hiding from August 1942 on and the formation of Le Comité de Défense des Juifs in September 1942. In accord with the "three protective screens" theory coined by the French sociologist Jacques Sémelin in the context of the conditions under which unarmed civilian resistance develops, the Comité was the first screen, a buffer between the victims and their pursuers, which created a protective cordon around them.[3] The Comité operated under the patronage of one of the country's strongest resistance movements, Le Front de l'Indépendance,[4] which constituted the second protective screen. These two shields were supported by the active mobilization of various sectors among the Belgian population and the state apparatus.

To this day, historiography considers Jewish Communists as central in establishing and running the Comité, although it represented a larger coalition until the liberation. This essay focuses on the role of the members of Poale Zion Left and their unique status, which allowed them to act as bridges between the Comité's diverse constituents. Dov Ber Borochov, the revered spiritual leader of Poale Zion Left, met with Lenin in Liège in 1907, at which time he explained his theory at length, placing special emphasis on his efforts to integrate Zionism and Socialism. Poale Zion Left, as we recall, was adamant about being fully Zionist and fully Socialist, and, consequently, it seceded from the Poale Zion World Union in 1920. During that encounter in Liège, Lenin remarked that the future party would, practically speaking, sit on two chairs, and what mattered was not what was on each chair but what was between them. By this, he was alluding to the risk of "falling between the chairs," that is, into the vacuum between them.[5] I contend that under the circumstances created by the German occupation, the Poale Zion Left membership in the Comité de Défense des Juifs transformed this "sitting on two chairs" into a pronounced advantage. It allowed them to merge and fuse contrasting

---

3   Jacques Sémelin, *Unarmed Against Hitler: Civilian Resistance in Europe, 1939–1945* (Westport and London: Praeger, 1993).

4   Le Front de l'Indépendance, established during 1941 under the patronage of the Belgian Communist Party, represented a broad amalgamation of political and trade organizations that shared the goal of liberating Belgium from the German occupation. Although the Communists strongly influenced its operations, they were not an absolute majority among its constituents.

5   See the memoir of the wife of Poale Zion Left's spiritual leader, Lyuba Borochov, *Prakim Miyoman Hayïe* (Hebrew) (Givat Haviva: Baderekh, 1971), pp. 24–25.

forces: the Communists and the Zionists, which included Poale Zion and Poale Zion/Tzeirei Zion, as well as the General Zionists. Poale Zion Left's contribution to the cohesion of the Comité created a dynamic that led to the mobilization of many others for the rescue of Belgian Jewry.

Consolidation of Poale Zion Left in the Interwar Era

The Poale Zion Left Party in Belgium was established in 1921, a year after the secession from the Poale Zion World Union at its congress in Vienna. In 1928, Brussels hosted the first convention of representatives of the branches of the Poale Zion Party that operated in Western Europe: France, Switzerland, Germany, Austria, and Belgium. These delegates were actually members of branches of the Poale Zion Party in Eastern Europe who had arrived in the West with the various waves of Jewish migration. The Jewish immigrants brought their customary way of life, institutions, political parties, and the socioeconomic structure in their communities of origin to those that they established in the West, in general, and in Belgium, in particular. These new frameworks served them as substitutes for what they had left behind and as vehicles that would ease their integration into their new countries of residence.[6]

David Trocki and Judah Tiberg were the representatives of Poale Zion Left in Belgium at the 1928 convention. Trocki, born in Vilna, was about to finish his studies in chemical engineering at the University of Ghent, where he ran a very vibrant party circle. During the 1930s, he also served as a *zamler* (local correspondent) for the YIVO Institute in Vilna, to which he submitted articles and studies about Belgian Jewry. Tiberg was the titular head of the party in the interwar years. He managed to complete his studies at the University of Warsaw before emigrating and made his living as a journalist. In Warsaw, he belonged to the circle of historians and political activists that gathered around Emanuel Ringelblum and Raphael Mahler. In 1930, Abusz Werber joined the party after having left his home in Radom, Poland. He was immediately integrated into the Belgian leadership. A year after reaching Belgium, he married Trocki's sister, the Yiddish poetess Sziffra (Sophie) Werber, making the party connection one of kinship as well. Although

6   Rudi van Doorslaer, *Enfants du Ghetto: Juifs révolutionnaires en Belgique, 1925–1940* (Brussels: Editions Labor, 1997), p. 28.

Werber made a living as a shoemaker, he was an autodidact who was knowledgeable in Jewish and universal culture. In this respect, he fit the profile of the members of the revolutionary Yiddishland, who were noted for their struggle against "fascism" throughout Europe.[7]

By the time World War II erupted, Poale Zion Left had established itself and had become particularly strong in Brussels. In 1939, it garnered 32 percent of the votes cast in the Belgian capital in the World Jewish Congress elections—that is, one-third of the Zionist voters in Brussels. However, it had somewhat less success in Antwerp.[8] This was an especially impressive achievement given that Poale Zion Left had joined the international Jewish/Zionist institutions only two years earlier. Together with the General Zionists, it garnered 56 percent of the votes. Owing to their activities in the leather/furrier workers and the garment trade unions, and in the cultural field, the Poale Zion Left members were accepted by the capital's "Jewish street" and the Yiddish-speaking immigrants. In the party ranks, there were radical intellectuals alongside workers and laborers, Yiddish lovers, litterateurs, and not a few autodidacts, such as Werber himself. The party directed its activities toward the Jewish working class, with whom and for whom they promoted the social and national revolution for which they yearned. Toward that end, they cultivated the Yiddish language as a medium of communication and education for the Jewish proletariat in particular.

The goal of Poale Zion Left was to integrate Zionism and Socialism. The party's members promoted the liberation of the Jews from the fetters of the "ghetto" and the flattening of the "upside-down pyramid" (i.e., eradicating the socioeconomic structural anomaly of European Jewry, as Borochov taught) and concurrently aspired to Jewish statehood in *Eretz Israel* at some future time. In practice, however, in the interwar years and at least up to 1943, Poale Zion Left in Belgium was more of a Socialist party than a Zionist one. It was the "leftmost" Zionist party and the closest in its social outlook to that of the Communists. Given that its members did not join the international Zionist institutions until 1937, they had not had the time to develop a pioneering movement that favored

7   For more about the life of Abusz Werber, his relatives, and the members of his party, see his son's publication, Michel Werber, *La Parole d'Abusz Werber* (Brussels: Institut d'Études du Judaïsme, 2015).

8   Rudi van Doorslaer, "Het Belgische Jiddischland: Een politieke geschiedenis van de joodse gemeemschappen in België tussen de twee wereldoorlogen," *Les Cahiers de la Mémoire contemporaine*, 11 (2014), p. 64.

the immediate emigration of youngsters who would pursue the goal of settling in *Eretz Israel*, nor did they embrace the Zionist "constructivism" of settling mainly in a kibbutz. Instead, they prioritized the Jews' struggle as something to pursue arm-in-arm with the international proletariat in their current countries of residence. Poale Zion Left saw the Jewish working class as the motive force of history, the carrier of the Socialist project. This clashed with the prevailing Zionist outlook of the time, which gave preference to the selective pioneering spearhead that would secure *Eretz Israel* and instill the value of "Hebrew labor." In addition to these differences, Poale Zion Left was zealously adamant about fostering the Yiddish language and culture, in contrast to the rest of the Zionist movement, which promoted the revitalization of Hebrew.

Poale Zion Left's Response to the Outbreak of War

The German invasion of Belgium on May 10, 1940, caused a panic among the local population including the Jews, who joined the great mass exodus to the south. Several Poale Zion Left stalwarts—Trocki, Werber, Tiberg, Hochberg, and their families, as well as the Tabakman clan—joined the wave of refugees and found temporary shelter in the Toulouse area in southern France. During their six months in that region, they wrestled with the dilemma of whether to return to Belgium, remain in France, or exploit the possibilities of immigrating to the United States. They had been offered the latter when the Jewish Labor Committee in New York sent Frank Bohn as a special emissary to the south of France. Bohn searched for left-wing political activists who would be in mortal danger if they fell into Nazi hands, and once he tracked them down, he offered them provisional immigration visas that exceeded the Americans' formal quotas.[9]

Several prominent leaders of Belgian Jewry decided to emigrate and did not return, including Aryeh Leon Kubowitzki, a Poale Zion leader who managed to reach *Eretz Israel* and then went to New York on a mission for the Jewish community there. Judah Tiberg and Shlomo

---

9 Catherine Clomp, "The Jewish Labor Committee, American Labor and the Rescue of European Socialists, 1934–1941," *International Labor and Working-Class History*, 68 (2005), pp. 112–133. After Bohn returned to the United States, Varian Fry, whom Yad Vashem recognized as Righteous Among the Nations in 1994, completed the mission of rescuing imperiled political activists and intellectuals.

Hochberg of Poale Zion Left accepted the visas that they were offered and reached the United States. Abusz Werber, David Trocki, and their families, as well as Israel and Meyer Tabakman—father and son—elected to "go home." Returning to Belgium, they mobilized to rehabilitate the party's institutions. In fact, with the exception of the youth movements that operated, although without emissaries, until mid-1942, Poale Zion Left in Belgium was the only Zionist party anywhere on the spectrum that resumed full operation under Nazi occupation. Werber replaced Tiberg at the helm of Poale Zion Left, which was joined by the surviving Poale Zion activists.

Going Home

In a letter to a party member in Switzerland, dated April 4, 1944, Werber hinted at several factors that prompted him to return to Belgium.

> We are not sorry that we are here. On the contrary, it pleases us immensely. We could not, we could not conceive of it, abandon our weak and ill elderly parents to improve our personal situation. It is a moral dilemma! Furthermore, it is our duty to family, to all humanity! The service that we have provided and will continue to provide to Uncle **Yishuv**, Aunt **Kibutzeinu**, and the **Merem** family gratifies us so much that we are very satisfied, despite the deprivation....Above all, I have such good and brave children. They are so devoted that nothing stops them.[10]

This letter, written during the German occupation, was meant to serve as a report to the Jewish institutions in Switzerland about the party's activities in Belgium from the beginning of the war. Werber used a code to outwit the censor, inserting Hebrew words (boldfaced in the translation) in the French text. The letter reflects the moral obligation of Werber and his comrades to the fate of "our...elderly parents," that is, the weaker Jews, the reference being to concern for the entire Jewish population in the form of "Uncle Yishuv," then concern for "Aunt Kibutzeinu," meaning the Zionist camp in the community, and, finally, concern for the "Merem family," party members, whose name is the

10 Yad Tabenkin Archive (YTA), 15–1/1–3.

contraction of Moshe Erem, a Poale Zion Left leader in the *Yishuv* in Mandatory Palestine. Werber, alluding to his status as the head of the party's underground organization, stressed the dedication of its activists—"such good and brave children"—to the rescue of Jews. As noted in a 1945 report about the activities of Poale Zion Left during the war, "Throughout the entire cruel occupation, the party did not abandon the Jewish masses; it gave them material and moral assistance and defended Jewish honor."[11]

In other words, Poale Zion Left mobilized to assist and relieve the Jewish population on the basis of solidarity with the impoverished proletariat and the wish to sustain their morale and their dignity. Thus, as Samuel Kassow describes it in his book on Emanuel Ringelblum's activities in Warsaw, Poale Zion Left always compensated for its penury, weakness, and marginality in the Zionist and Communist camps by the especially strong devotion of its members—a quality manifested in times of crisis in general and specifically during the Nazi occupation.[12]

These pronouncements were not made solely on paper. Immediately after they returned to Belgium, Werber, Trocki, and their associates sought to rehabilitate the party institutions, particularly in Brussels. From the fall of 1940 until December 1941, they took the following steps to sustain regular activity and restore preoccupation normality:

* Reestablish the Yiddish library.
* Reactivate the party's supplemental education school, Shul un dertsiyung (Study and Education).
* Reorganize the party's youth movement, Yung Bor (Borochov Youth).
* Reopen the party's sports club, Der Stern (the Star), through the efforts of Meyer Tabakman.
* Reactivate the two trade unions of the needleworkers and the leather/furrier workers through the efforts of Abraham Domb.
* Establish Le Secours mutuel (mutual aid; in Yiddish, Kegnzaytike Hilf), the party's mutual aid institution, which operated in parallel with its Communist counterpart, Solidarité juive (Jewish solidarity).
* Publish *Unzer Vort* (Our Say), the party's underground journal,

---

11 Abusz Werber report to the World Jewish Congress, Switzerland, about party activity under German occupation, Yad Vashem Archives (YVA), O.29.2/4, p. 55.
12 Samuel D. Kassow, *Who Will Write Our History?* (London: Penguin, 2010).

whose twenty-eight editions were published from December 1941 until the liberation in September 1944. In contrast, the Communist Party's *Unzer Kamf* (Our Struggle), published only five issues, and the Bund's *Der Morgen* (The Morning) issued only four.

Trade Union Activity

Abraham Domb reestablished the leather/furrier workers trade union in conjunction with Jacob Gutfreund of the Communist Party. Together they protected Jewish workers' terms of employment, fought against wage cuts and layoffs without severance pay, and protested the employment of Jews in enterprises that worked for and produced goods for the German army. They urged those conscripted for forced labor in northern France in May–June 1942 and then later in the "East" to refuse to comply with the summons.

Le Secours mutuel

Le Secours mutuel was established in September 1940. It created a fund that dispersed loans and grants to poverty-stricken Jews. Under its auspices, Israel Tabakman established a warehouse for the distribution of clothing and food to the needy.[13] From May–June 1942 on, his son Meyer devoted his efforts to searching for safe dwellings and jobs with non-Jewish Belgians, primarily in the countryside, reasoning that a labor contract in Belgium would spare a Jew from conscription for forced labor. Jobs as child caregivers, domestics, and servants were found for women. Meyer Tabakman also set up an agricultural training facility to provide young Jewish men with farming jobs—but that was an initiative that proved to be short-lived.[14]

---

13 Israel Tabakman, *Mayne Ierlebungen unter Natsistisher Okupatsye in Belgye* (Yiddish) (Tel Aviv: I. L. Peretz, 1957).

14 Dan Michman, "Les mouvements de jeunesse sionistes en Belgique durant l'occupation allemande: Etude d'un point de vue comparatif," in Rudi van Doorslaer, ed., *Les Juifs de Belgique: De l'immigration au génocide, 1925–1945* (Brussels: Centre de recherches et d'études historiques de la Seconde Guerre mondiale, 1994), pp. 173–192; English version: "The Belgian Zionist Youth Movements During the Nazi Occupation," in Dan Michman, ed., *Belgium and the Holocaust: Jews, Belgians, Germans* (Jerusalem: Yad Vashem, 1998), pp. 373–395; particularly p. 390.

The Secours mutuel and Solidarité juive, the social service organization that the Jewish members of the Communist Party had set up, worked together under the umbrella of Esra, the community's social service organization. As time passed, they became pillars of the underground social services that operated under the Comité de Défense des Juifs. Much like Alaynhilf, which was established on the initiative of Emanuel Ringelblum in Warsaw, and the Colonie scolaire, which was formed in Paris through the efforts of David Rapoport—both founders of Poale Zion Left—the Secours mutuel was based on the mutual aid tradition that had evolved over the years in the context of the struggle for the working class.

Unzer Vort and L'Association des Juifs en Belgique (AJB)

The publication of the Yiddish underground newspaper *Unzer Vort* was one of Poale Zion Left's most important projects. The newspaper started out as an initiative of Abusz Werber, his brother-in-law, David Trocki, and Abraham Ryba, who together made up the editorial board. The monthly gazette was published for two-and-a-half years for the benefit of the Jewish population of Brussels and the vicinity. During this period, the persecution and the deportations were at their worst. There was a brief moratorium in the summer of 1942 during the major deportation *Aktionen*, when the Poale Zion Left leadership was occupied laying the foundations for the activities of the Comité.

The production and distribution of *Unzer Vort* were accomplished through the collective efforts of the party members. Each edition comprised four to six pages of stencil-printed, single-spaced text in cramped print on both sides of the pages. The production staff included the poetess Sziffra Werber, Abusz's wife; Charles Grabiner, founder of the Dror movement in Belgium; and Baruch Mayzel, a doctor who had been dismissed from his post. A separate four-member team proofread the newspaper before printing 700–1,000 copies. Initially, *Unzer Vort* was distributed by party members and sold to the Jewish community institutions for one Belgian franc. When most of the Jews went underground, the Comité liaisons, who delivered money for sustenance, forged ID cards, and food parcels to fugitives, also brought them the newspaper.

The editors, Werber, Trocki, and Ryba, contributed articles, as did many others. Israel Tabakman, the party's liaison to the community welfare institutions—orphanages, hospitals, and soup kitchens for adults—reported on conditions in those facilities. Sziffra Werber wrote about the children's plight. Chaïm (Charles) Perelman and Leopold Flam, two philosophers who were active members of the Comité, also contributed articles, as did the future sociologist Georges Goriely. The viability of the publishing enterprise should be credited to the many intellectuals among the party members and to "fellow travelers"[15] who gathered around it, and *Unzer Vort* became an extensive collective project of the underground Poale Zion Left.

The importance of *Unzer Vort* traces to the alternative voice that it created—the grassroots voice of those deprived of the right to speak up and speak out could be heard. The paper's premiere edition appeared in December 1941, just as the Germans decreed the establishment of the AJB and barred Jewish children from attending Belgian schools. The AJB, Belgian Jewry's sole representative institution, was tasked with passing on the Germans' directives, which made it akin to a local Judenrat.[16] The paper did not spare criticism of officials who agreed to serve this institution. *Unzer Vort* and Poale Zion Left's various manifestos conveyed the party's daily instructions and urged disobedience of the AJB's orders.

- If the union demands that you pay dues, refuse.[17]
- If you encounter AJB members, show your disdain and contempt for them, as traitors deserve.[18]
- The AJB is setting up separate schools. Do not withdraw your children from the Belgian education system.[19]
- Refuse to send your children to the ghetto schools.[20]

---

15 "Fellow travelers" is a concept used for those who support the party from outside but refuse to be considered rank-and-file members.

16 About the AJB, see Jean-Philippe Schreiber and Rudi van Doorslaer, eds., *Les Curateurs du Ghetto: L'Association des Juifs en Belgique* (Brussels: Editions Labor, 2004).

17 Jewish resistance poster, "Public Appeal to the Jewish Masses in Belgium," presumed date, May 1942, YTA, 15-3/1-9; see also, *Unzer Vort*, no. 2, March 1942, YVA, O.29/3727420.

18 "Public Appeal to the Jewish Masses in Belgium," presumed date, May 1942, YTA, 15-3/1-9.

19 *Unzer Vort*, no. 1, December 1941, YVA, O.29/3727420. Adjurations of this kind appeared in the paper until June 1942. On the adaptation of the Jewish community to the dismissal of Jewish children from the Belgium school system, see B. Dickschen, "L'AJB et l'enseignement," in *Les Curateurs du Ghetto*, pp. 233–260.

20 *Unzer Vort*, no. 1, December 1941, YVA, O.29/3727420.

- Without you, the Nazis will not be able to open special schools for our children.[21]
- Do not assist the enemy. The Jewish working class should turn its back on this dirty and repulsive work....It amounts to a knife in the back of our Soviet brethren who are fighting for their liberation and ours.[22]
- If the AJB sends you a summons, refuse to report.[23]
- The call to go into hiding appeared as early as June 1942.

Poale Zion Left acquired a mass communication medium in *Unzer Vort* by which it could circulate its members' protest among the public outside its own circle of intimates. The newspaper, the only one to appear in Belgium in Yiddish until March 1943, helped to shape public opinion. One cannot understand the noncompliance movement and the move into hiding of most of Belgian Jewry, which occurred when the deportations began, without considering the contribution of the *Unzer Vort* to their psychological preparation and gradual adjustment to the idea of illegal life. Some Jews had had to adjust to a semi-legal lifestyle as early as the 1930s; others were forced to do so during the occupation years when they were ousted first from the labor market and then from all economic life in Belgium. It stands to reason that the newspaper's urgings to go into hiding were discussed and heeded by other Jewish circles, abetting practical measures in advance of their going underground. This phenomenon and the fact that the AJB was partly neutralized by the Jewish Resistance also count among the arguments that explain the survival of more than half of the Jews in Belgium.

Poale Zion Left Accommodates Outside Activists

Given that Poale Zion Left was the only Zionist political setting that continued to exist and to operate on "the Jewish street," it attracted activists from different circles. Former members of Poale Zion, such as Baruch Mayzel, Fela Perelman, and Charles Grabiner, found a new home there. Before the war, Perelman and Grabiner had been aides to the

---

21 Ibid.
22 Ibid.
23 Ibid.

chair of the Jewish community administration, Aryeh Leon Kubowitzki, who had since emigrated. From the onset of the mass arrests, Fela Perelman had coordinated activity as head of the Secours mutuel. Georges Goriely, a philosopher with close ties to Trotskyist circles, participated in underground activities as well. Poale Zion Left also welcomed secessionists from the Communist Party. The philosopher Leopold Flam, who left the Communists in protest over the signing of the Ribbentrop–Molotov pact in August 1939, is a case in point. Flam established one of the three Antwerp branches of the Comité and edited the Comité's Flemish-language organ, *De Vrije Gedachte*, until he was arrested.[24] The philosopher Chaïm (Charles) Perelman, Fela's husband, was a member of the AJB who joined the Comité and became active in the unified group that gathered around Poale Zion Left.

Recruitment of Former Members of the Hashomer Hatza'ir and Dror Youth Movements

Werber, nicknamed "the diplomat" owing to his prowess as a mediator,[25] worked strenuously to recruit alumni of the pioneering movements for the Comité's rescue activities. He made a special trip to Antwerp in the spring of 1942 to enlist Hashomer Hatza'ir members for the struggle, but they professed no interest in what was happening in the Diaspora. When the first summonses for forced labor in northern France under Organisation Todt were received, the *bogrim*, the eldest members of Hashomer Hatza'ir, decided to move to Switzerland and to use that country as a springboard for immigration to *Eretz Israel*. Approximately thirty of them and a similar number of Tzofim *bogrim* (the Scouts' younger group), altogether about sixty members of the Belgian Hashomer Hatza'ir youth movement, managed to slip into Switzerland illegally and found shelter there for the last two years of the war.[26]

---

24 According to Lieven Saerens, there were actually three different Comités de Défense des Juifs in Antwerp, which were dismantled one after the other following the arrest of their leaders. One of them was run by Orthodox Jews; see Lieven Saerens, *Étrangers dans la cité: Anvers et ses Juifs, 1880–1944* (Brussels: Editions Labor, 2005).
25 Werber, *La Parole*, p. 125.
26 Janiv Stamberger, "Zionist Pioneers at the Shores of the Scheldt, the Hashomer Hatza'ir Youth Movement in Antwerp, 1924–1946," *Les Cahiers de la Mémoire contemporaine*, 11 (2014), pp. 95–99.

Werber had greater success among alumni of Dror, some of whom were arrested, others who had moved to Switzerland, and still others who were scattered across Belgium itself. By the end of 1943, Werber had successfully integrated a few of them into the Secours mutuel. Icek Szatan, who also reestablished the Poale Zion Left/Tzeirei Zion partisan alignment, commended Werber for his enterprise in a letter sent to Switzerland in April 1944.

> Zerubavel [Werber], who had stayed in touch with many members, began doing this work long before we did. He proposed to us that we join the Secours mutuel, which he had established.…After five months of work, we are taking care of 200 of the 500 families whom Secours mutuel is supporting.[27]

Thus, clearly, Secours mutuel had already been supporting and aiding Jews in hiding for some time. It maintained its independence and operated autonomously under the Comité de Défense des Juifs alongside the Communist Solidarité juive.

List of Poale Zion Left Members

Seventy to eighty members of Poale Zion Left, including those sympathizers who joined the party under Nazi rule, were active in the Jewish Resistance throughout the war years. According to his testimony, given in the 1960s, Werber maintained regular communication with all of them during the entire existence of the Comité.[28] A list of party members that came into the hands of Dr. Chaim Pozner, deputy head of the Jewish Agency Immigration Department in Geneva, in November 1943, confirms this.[29] Upon receiving the list, Pozner

---

27 YVA, P.7/38, p. 83.
28 Abusz Werber testimony, February–March 1964, Oral History Division, Institute of Contemporary Jewry, The Hebrew University of Jerusalem.
29 List of Poale Zion Left members who were candidates for protective documents from the Jewish Agency in Switzerland: Labor Movement Archive, Pinchas Lavon Institute, III-37A-2-25. On Dr. Pozner's contribution to the issuance of protective papers and the rescue of Jews by the Jewish Agency, see Menahem Michaelson with contributions by Sir Martin Gilbert, *Chaim Pazner—Ha'ish Sheyada: Hayedi'a Al Hapitron Hasofi Uma'amatzei Hahatzala* (Hebrew) (Jerusalem: Yad Vashem, 2007), pp. 165–185.

acted to equip those registered with protection papers as Palestinian/ British citizens so that they could be included in an exchange for Germans in British detention, including several hundred Templers from Mandatory Palestine. The list sent to Pozner includes twenty-six names of families who were affiliated with Poale Zion Left. The names of wives, many of whom were involved in concealing children, are not included. Together with the wives, the list of party members comprises more than fifty people, but many more names of important party activists are absent from the roster, such as Israel Tabakman, who together with his deputy, Israel Broder, and with the assistance of one of his daughters and another woman courier, took care of roughly 120 families in hiding. Menachem Konkowski, founder of the Ninth Brigade—a combat unit that party members joined—is also missing, as is his aide, Israel Schlesinger, as well as many others. The register does, however, confirm Werber's count of party activists in the underground who participated in the Comité's rescue operations.

Relations with the Communists

Werber also maintained contact with associates who were active in the Communist Party. The rapprochement with the Communists intensified after the Wehrmacht invaded the USSR in June 1941. Until then, the Communist Party had remained on hold, in expectation of changes to come. The invasion brought an end to the waiting period that the Ribbentrop–Molotov pact had created and marked a watershed in mobilization against the German occupation. *Unzer Vort* reflected Poale Zion Left's unreserved support of the Soviet struggle and its total confidence in a Soviet victory over Nazi Germany. The editors viewed the war as an opportunity to set in motion a revolutionary process that would transform European society from the ground up. Those who wrote for the newspaper were unstintingly confident that the Red Army's triumph would eventually lead to a radical change in the existing social order: the obliteration of a society dominated by "exploitation of man by man,"[30] that is, the elimination of the capitalist regime. To bring this about, they said, the ranks must be unified and all forces marshaled for progress toward the exalted goal. *Unzer Vort*

---

30 *Unzer Vort,* no. 2, March 1942, and no. 24, late April 1944, YVA, O.29/3727420.

urged all Jews to unite and join the Belgian population in this struggle and to stamp out the German occupation. It also called for support of the Communist-sponsored Le Front de l'Indépendance, which had extended its patronage to the Comité from the beginning of the latter's activities in mid-September 1942.

Historiography to date has emphasized the initiative of Hertz Jospa, a Jewish engineer and a member of the Communist Party to establish the Comité. By the spring of 1942, however, Werber had already contacted another Communist Party member, Loszek Merinfeld, to promote the idea of cooperation between the Communists and Poale Zion Left. However, the national leadership of the Communist Party was in no hurry to assent to such cooperation and the date for the establishment of the Comité was postponed. The Communist Party went out of its way to cultivate a pan-national image in which no specific regional or religious characteristic would be highlighted. It was only in June–July 1942 that Jospa got the go-ahead to set up the Comité as a Jewish subsection of the Communist Party. At that point, Jospa again approached Werber to expedite the initiative of activating a united Jewish front. Werber undertook to persuade the Zionist members to join the project. Werber and Jospa approached Chaïm Perelman, who, after initially frowning on partnering with the Communists, changed his mind because of the gravity of the situation and the bridging role that the Poale Zion Left members played.

Initiation of Mass Arrests of the Jews, July 1942

The exacerbation of the Jews' situation as mass arrests and deportations to the "East" had begun prompted Perelman to join the Comité. The first transport set out from the Mechelen-Malines detention camp bound for Auschwitz on August 4, 1942. In the panic triggered by the initial *Aktionen*, the women in Poale Zion Left who were active in the Secours mutuel mobilized to hide children and arranged hiding places for hundreds of them even before the Comité came into being. The exigencies on the ground led to the activation of a special service within the Secours mutuel to hide children, which was coordinated by Sziffra Werber. Yvonne Jospa, Hertz's wife, and Ida Sterno, who were active in Solidarité juive, established a parallel service that carried out similar operations.

Children's Department of the Comité

When the Comité went into action on September 15, 1942, its Children's Department engineered a merger between the service that had already been set up by the Secours mutuel and the parallel agency of Solidarité juive. Yvonne Jospa, named to head the joint department, centralized the handling of appeals that were sent to her by both constituent entities. The agreement between them was established on the basis of an equal division of labor. The duties of the joint Children's Department included placing youngsters in hiding with foster families or in schools; escorting children to their hideouts; covering their monthly living expenses; providing them with forged papers, clothing, food parcels, and medical care; and forwarding letters. The department also required access to alternative hiding places if a child was in jeopardy. These actions entailed regular contact with the Belgian rescuers through the Comité's couriers or social workers. In 1943, Sziffra Werber opened an office that raised funds from parents or relatives of hidden children to help pay for their care and feeding, when such kin could be found and if they could still afford to meet these expenses.

Department for Adults

Parallel to the Children's Department was an office that provided relief and assistance to adults. Its duties included finding safe apartments or other hideouts; forwarding a basic monthly allowance to those in hiding; and equipping them with forged papers, ration cards, and parcels. Chaïm Perelman headed this department in addition to his duties at the AJB. His assistants were Werber, who specialized in obtaining forged papers of various kinds, and "Robert" Mandelbaum, who was replaced after his arrest by Icek (Richard) Wolmann. Mandelbaum and Wolmann were members of the Communist Party. As in the case of the Children's Department, Poale Zion Left and the Communists were the forces behind this entity, on a parity basis. Although others took part in various capacities, Perelman and Werber, who managed to avoid arrest from the beginning of the occupation to the end, provided the Comité's Department for Adults with stability and continuity throughout the war.

A national representation of the Comité de Défense des Juifs was established in the fall of 1943, which functioned within a framework that struck a balance between the Communists and Poale Zion Left, and without any others on the national level. The members of its national committee were Werber, its representative in Brussels, and Flam, his counterpart in Antwerp, both on behalf of Poale Zion Left. They were joined by two Communist members—Pinkas ("Pierre") Broder of Charleroi and Albert Wolf of Liège.

The Comité's Two Underground Journals

In addition to his position in the Department for Adults, Werber was in charge of the Comité's information and propaganda section. In March 1943, he and Flam began to publish two underground journals under the Comité's auspices—seven issues of the French *Le Flambeau* (The Torch) and six issues of the Flemish *De Vrije Gedachte* (Free Thought) were printed. Both had an explicit agenda: to inspire Belgians to make greater efforts to rescue Jews. Their declared goal was to save lives by conveying information about the unique fate of the Jews, who were being deported to Poland, shattering antisemitic stereotypes, and encouraging bystanders to assist those being persecuted. The journals were distributed together with the publications of Le Front de l'Indépendance. Practically speaking, *Le Flambeau* was an abridged version of *Unzer Vort*. Ryba translated into French articles that had previously appeared in Yiddish in the Poale Zion Left journal—apart from issues 5 and 6 of *Le Flambeau*, which were undoubtedly the work of Leopold Flam.

In June 1943, Benjamin (Beno) Nykerk, a Protestant manufacturer of Dutch origin who was fond of Jewish culture and who sympathized with the plight of the Jews, served as treasurer of the Comité. He set out from Brussels for Switzerland on a mission for the Comité to request assistance from the international Jewish institutions that maintained a presence there. He also met with representatives of the World Jewish Congress, Jewish Agency officials, Nathan Schwalb (the Hehalutz emissary in Geneva), and, foremost, Saly Mayer, an agent of the American Jewish Joint Distribution Committee (JDC). None of them had any idea who Nykerk was. To introduce himself and establish his bona fides as the emissary of a committee acting for the rescue of Belgian Jewry, Nykerk showed them several editions of the Jewish underground press that he had put onto microfilm and concealed in a fountain pen. On the basis of this evidence, Nykerk was able to raise money in Switzerland and acquired a letter of commitment from the JDC to repay loans after the war. This also allowed him and his successor David Ferdman to raise funds in Belgium itself to finance the Comité's rescue operations. The sum raised, about 48 million Belgian francs, was used to finance monthly maintenance payments for children in hiding and basic allowances for adults who had gone underground, among other things. Thus, the underground press played an indirect but important role in saving lives. Nykerk made three trips to Switzerland, also returning with copies of the free press, again on microfilm. Thus, issue 15 of *Unzer Vort* (August 1943) announced that from then on it could publish reports on Jewish life in the free world and on Mandatory Palestine, based on "authoritative sources in neutral or Allied countries." Nykerk persisted in his activities until he was arrested and deported to a concentration camp, where he died.

Reporting Forbidden and Alternative Information

In contrast to the Comité's two other journals, *Unzer Vort* was Poale Zion Left's sole organ. In response to the German policy of isolating the Jews from the surrounding society by means of a total information embargo, *Unzer Vort* continued to provide Yiddish readers with alternative, uncensored information about the course of the war and the armies' progress. Each edition began with a background analysis of international political developments, and of the progress of the Red Army and the other Allied forces on the various fronts. These background articles were written on the basis of "reverse" analysis and cross-referencing of sources garnered from the official Belgian and German presses, the BBC and Radio Moscow broadcasts, and, later, press organs in the free world that had begun to arrive from Switzerland. Thus, readers of *Unzer Vort* were exposed to information that served to bolster their morale and their confidence in the supremacy of the Allied and Soviet armies, and their ultimate victory over the maleficent Axis.

Similarly, *Unzer Vort* conveyed information about the Jews of Belgium: arrests, the Mechelen-Malines detention camp in the Dossin barracks, deportations,[31] and the phenomenon of denunciation by traitors. From June 1943, the journal transmitted the testimonies that came from the vicinity of the Auschwitz camp, alternately known as

---

31 On the Dossin barracks, see the study by Laurence Schram, *L'antichambre d'Auschwitz—Dossin* (Brussels: Racine, 2017).

"the Hell" or "the Slaughterhouse" of Upper Silesia. The information was based on the experiences of two Jews who had escaped from a labor camp in Upper Silesia and a report from Victor Martin, a sociologist whom the Comité had sent on a fact-finding mission to Poland in order to corroborate the rumors about systematic extermination. The June 1943 issue of *Unzer Vort* also reported on the Warsaw Ghetto Uprising and the widespread devastation of Jewish communities in Eastern Europe, particularly in Poland. The circulation of reports about deportations from Belgium and the bitter fate of those deported to the East was crucial in prodding the Jewish population to take the necessary precautions to avoid arrest as the Comité provided fugitives with means for survival. By spreading information about the extermination campaign, *Unzer Vort* made an important contribution to rescue efforts.

Dedication of Each Edition to a Formative Event in the History of the Proletarian Struggle

Alongside the background articles on progress on the battlefield and international political developments, each edition of *Unzer Vort* singled out a symbolic formative event or milestone in the party membership's collective memory. The first edition in December 1941, for example, was dedicated to the anniversary of Ber Borochov's death and to his teachings. The February 1942 edition centered on the history of Poale Zion, but also marked the establishment of the Red Army—"the spearhead of freedom" that would bring deliverance to the oppressed of the world. The March 1942 issue focused on the founding conference of the Poale Zion Party in Poltava in 1906 and the Paris Commune in 1871.[32] An edition in late April 1942, as May Day approached, was devoted to the festival of the international proletariat and the solidarity of peoples. It also noted the anniversary of the death of I. L. Peretz, the voice of oppressed Jews. The November 1942 edition dealt with the surrender of Germany at the end of World War I as a portent of the impending conclusion of the current war.

---

32 The Paris Commune refers to the insurrection of the population of the French capital in the wake of France's defeat in the Franco–German War and the collapse of Napoleon III's Second Empire that led to the emergence of the Third Republic. The event is considered to be a milestone in the collective memory of the international workers' movement.

These references combined events in Jewish history with historical episodes of a universal nature as manifestations of the Socialist Jewish identity of the newspaper's contributing editors. By marking past events, the editors evoked glorious struggles that could inspire the beleaguered Jews in their daily struggle for survival. The memories of the past were brought as examples from which one could derive the strength to cope with the vicissitudes of the present. Apart from reminding readers of the annual cycle of ordinary times, they created a bridge and established continuity between past and present.

For individuals who were isolated from each other, the pages of *Unzer Vort* resurrected shared symbols and images that created a bond and a sense of belonging to an imagined community. As the sociologist Benedict Anderson shows in the context of the formation of nations,[33] there is nothing like a newspaper and a novel to unite individuals who are strangers to each other, who do not even know each other's names, around shared symbols and a common agenda. It was certainly true for Jews who had been cut off from any form of community and, in some cases, were also confined to an isolated hideout.

An Imagined Community

Unzer Vort offered its readers a sense of imagined community. On its pages and with its mediation, the AJB officials and the members of the Resistance could engage in an indirect dialogue and an exchange of ideas. Those in the Resistance lost no opportunity to criticize the behavior of the members of the AJB. They did so, first, "because we protest the very existence of this institution and it is high time for these overlords to realize it,"[34] and, second, because those in the Resistance were still outraged by the contemptuous treatment of the needy by the bureaucrats of the AJB and its welfare agency, Esra. The representatives of the AJB were notables and members of the establishment who, according to contributors to *Unzer Vort*, were guided in their actions by the principle of "sending as many *shnorrers* [beggars] to Malines as possible so that there will be fewer and fewer supplicants."[35]

33 Benedict Anderson, *Imagined Communities: Reflections on the Origin and Spread of Nationalism* (London: Verso, 1991).
34 *Unzer Vort,* no. 24, April 1944, YVA, O.29/3727420.
35 *Unzer Vort,* no. 9, March 1943, YVA, O.29/3727420.

Unzer Vort also published the responses of the AJB and Esra to these accusations. In March 1943, it reported, "The comment we published last month about Esra's draconian methods...stirred much interest among the circles involved." In February 1944, it further elaborated, "The AJB responded gravely to the accusations that we lodged against them." Then in May 1944, the paper informed its readers, "Every article we publish about the AJB's behavior touches off a riot among those hooligans." The AJB members read and followed what was being written about them in *Unzer Vort*, and its editors kept abreast of the responses to its contents in the AJB circles, thanks to officers who operated on both sides of the divide. The indirect dialogue that went on between the parties brought results. *Unzer Vort* reported in May 1944, "The behavior of the Esra and social service people...toward applicants for relief...has become more humane....They have stopped treating the starving Jews like beggars." Furthermore, the paper noted, food distribution in Esra's soup kitchen had become more egalitarian and the atmosphere there had improved. If so, the criticism seems to have paid off, and if it was not the criticism, it was the newspaper's threat to pursue a reckoning over the AJB's conduct on liberation day that had this effect. *Unzer Vort* also opened its pages to debates between the Communists who favored assimilation, and the national-minded Zionists over the nature of the community after its reconstruction—a subject that triggered a caustic confrontation between them after the liberation. Despite the disagreements, however, the unified front held together until the end of the occupation.

Building a New Future

A common past assures a common future. The creation of a partnership of fate in an imagined community was expressed chiefly in co-opting readers into drafting plans for the construction of the future society and shaping the features of the community that would arise after the liberation. The contributing editors of *Unzer Vort* were confident that a more egalitarian and just society—without class differences and social disparities—would arise atop the ruins of the war. Alongside their dream of social justice, they dreamed of establishing a Jewish state in *Eretz Israel*. If the possibility of sustaining Jewry in exile as a national minority was still plausible until mid-1943, it totally vanished from the discourse as reports about the magnitude of the devastation escalated.

Hence, pursuant to the "lesson of blood"[36] that history had taught the Jews, the demand for the establishment of a national home for the Jewish people in their historical homeland gathered strength.

From mid-1943 to the liberation, the topic of *Eretz Israel* assumed ever greater importance and accounted for more and more space in the press. Now that news items from the free world and the *Yishuv* were arriving, *Unzer Vort* presented its readers with many reports about the development of the *Yishuv*, the establishment of communal and cooperative settlements, agricultural and industrial achievements, and the enlistment of Jews in the Palmach and the Jewish Brigade, and their participation in combat on the side of the Allies. The paper also reported the Allied powers' positions on the idea of establishing a Jewish state.

Unzer Vort informed at length on American Jewry and its congress in New York in February 1944. It spelled out the conferees' demands: rescind the White Paper policy, open the gates of *Eretz Israel* to Jewish immigration, restore the Jews' basic rights, and make property restitution. It emphasized the need to prosecute writers, intellectuals, and pseudoscientists who had spread the toxin of antisemitism and incited the murder of the Jews—anyone who had spread words that kill. Its proposal in this regard recommended the establishment of an international tribunal composed of reputed intellectuals who would hand down a ruling against antisemitic manifestations that would outlaw them. Alongside this demand, *Unzer Vort* continued to spread "lifesaving words," that is, instructions to remain in hiding and be doubly cautious in order to avoid capture. It also urged its readers to demonstrate solidarity with the Belgian people and to enlist in the struggle of the various Resistance movements and those of the country to bring liberation day closer.

The *Unzer Vort* enterprise owed its viability to the many intellectuals who gathered around its editors, drawn by their messianic faith in being able to change the world order after the liberation and their stubborn solidarity with the working class, without which the future society would not be built. *Unzer Vort* and the two underground journals supported the Comité's rescue operations in which the Poale Zion Left people acted in tandem with members of the Communist Party and, in so doing, Poale Zion Left played a mediating and bridge-building role between the Communists and the Zionists. The Secours mutuel,

36 Ibid.

together with its Communist counterpart, Solidarité juive, was the supportive pillar of the infrastructure of the Comité's rescue operations. The Comité constructed the first protective screen around the harried Jewish population. The Communist Party's resistance movement put up the second screen by giving the Comité its patronage. The cohesion of its active cadre, in solidarity with the Jews at large, attracted additional members so that the Comité de Défense des Juifs succeeded in rescuing approximately 3,000 Jewish children and 5,000 adults, with the support of segments of the Belgian population.

DELASEM

A Jewish Relief Organization in Italy
under the Fascist Regime and Nazi Occupation

LILIANA PICCIOTTO

The Italian Fascist regime officially ushered in anti-Jewish persecution by introducing legislation that would turn Jews into second-class citizens. The first of these anti-Jewish decrees, which the government called "Measures for the Defense of the Italian Race," were issued on September 5, 1938, and others followed well into 1944.

Fascist Italy embarked on the path of state antisemitism long before its alliance with Nazi Germany, which was initially a pact between equals, and it continued this policy as its relationship with Germany evolved. After the announcement on September 8, 1943, that Italy had signed an armistice with the Allied governments, the Germans reacted by invading the country and restoring Mussolini's control over part of its territory under their own strict oversight. Italy's status thus changed from a German ally to a hybrid state of alliance and occupation.

From 1938 to 1943, a series of laws were issued with the specific goal of forcing Jews into a hopeless "pariah" situation that included curtailing their rights in the fields of schooling, higher education, employment, and military service; expelling Jewish refugees or, later, denying them freedom of movement; prohibiting mixed marriages; and innumerable other restrictions. Just like Nazi Germany, the Italian government originally envisioned ridding itself of Jews by encouraging them to emigrate through the enactment of laws that made life difficult for them in Italy.

However, starting in November 1943, two months after the onset of the Nazi occupation, Italian edicts began to focus on hunting and arresting Jews, imprisoning them, and confiscating their property. The threat was no longer just to their dignity and rights, but their very lives were now in danger. In short, these were two separate phases marked by anti-Jewish laws that had different objectives. During this second stage,

315

the only ways that Jews could save themselves were to (a) go into hiding; (b) sneak across the Swiss border; (c) cross the front lines to the south; or (d) join the partisan resistance.

In this essay I look at the work that the Jewish relief organization Delegazione Assistenza Emigranti (Delegation for the Assistance of Emigrants, DELASEM) carried out during both of these periods. The group first became active when the Fascist regime was still an independent ally of Nazi Germany (1939–1943), and continued to operate underground when Italy, which was still allied with Germany, was occupied by it (1943–1945).

"Official" Activity, 1939–1943

In the second half of the 1930s, large groups of foreign Jews who had fled Nazified or antisemitic countries found themselves temporarily in Italy while waiting for visas for other countries. The Germans and Austrians among them were traveling without any belongings, as they had been forced to abandon their possessions and property when they left. These refugees knew little Italian, had no information as to how to find housing, passage on ships, or the documents necessary to leave Italy, and were often in need of clothing and medical care,[1] so several astute leaders from the Italian Jewish community rallied to help them.

On November 20, 1938, at the initiative of Raffaele Cantoni,[2] the Comitato Assistenza Ebrei in Italia (Committee for the Assistance of Jews in Italy, COMASEBIT) was founded in Milan at 3 Via degli Amedei, on the model of an earlier committee.[3] Renzo Luisada was its director, assisted by Umberto Nahon, and Federico Jarach, who was also president of the Unione delle Comunità Israelitiche Italiane (Union of Italian Jewish Communities, UCII)—the organization officially tasked with representing Italian Jews, which had been established by law in

---

1 Klaus Voigt, *Il rifugio precario: Gli esuli in Italia dal 1933 al 1945*, 2 vols. (Florence: La Nuova Italia, 1993, 1996).

2 This Florentine Jew was a Jewish community leader, an anti-fascist in the Giustizia e Libertà Movement, and a rebellious, resolute spirit, who was later sentenced to internal exile. He was the first president of the Union of Italian Jewish Communities (UCII) after the war.

3 Massimo Leone, *Le organizzazioni di soccorso ebraiche in età fascista (1918–1945)* (Rome: Carucci, 1983), pp. 150–167.

1931, following negotiations between the government and the Jewish communities.

COMASEBIT was not subject to government oversight and was outside the scope and purview of the UCII, even though it was chaired by Federico Jarach, who had also chaired the UCII since 1937. Its founding followed in the wake of the September 7, 1938, decree, which barred foreign Jews from taking up permanent residence in Italy and mandated their expulsion. That edict was followed by another on November 17, 1938, which included Article 24 that called for foreign Jews to leave the country by March 12, 1939.[4] These measures cast the refugees into utter despair, forcing them to leave Italy, which up to then had seemed like a refuge, however temporary and precarious. At that point, their first concerns were to find countries willing to take them in and to secure visas.

The Fascist government, which aimed for total control over all public and private manifestations of thought, belief, education, and social interaction, could not allow an agency to operate without being subject to the oversight of the UCII, which was considered the sole representative of Italian Jewry. On July 24, 1939, Police Chief Arturo Bocchini[5] ordered the prefect of Milan to shut down COMASEBIT.[5]

The relief organization had done everything possible to help the many refugees who had entered Italy over the mountain passes to the north to either leave by sea or to cross the French border to safety.[6] One of COMASEBIT's achievements in its ten short months of existence was its aid to the groups of refugees in the border town of Ventimiglia, who were looking for a way to slip into the French Côte d'Azur without being turned back by the French authorities. According to studies by Paolo Veziano, the source of the following information,[7] they would cross the border either by sea or by land along rocky, dangerous paths that led over the foothills of the Maritime Alps. Small rowboats clandestinely crossed the sea, coming ashore along a stretch of coast between the Italian border and Monaco.

---

4   Royal Decree Law No. 1381 of November 17, 1938, *Provvedimenti nei confronti degli ebrei stranieri*; Royal Decree Law no. 1728 of November 17, 1938, *Provvedimenti per la difesa della razza italiana*, reprinted in Michele Sarfatti, ed., "1938: Le leggi contro gli ebrei," *La Rassegna Mensile di Israel*, Special Issue, 54:1–2 (1988).

5   Leone, *Le organizzazioni*, pp. 162–167.

6   Voigt, *Il rifugio precario*, vol. 1, pp. 381–382.

7   Paolo Veziano, *Ombre di confine: L'espatrio clandestino degli ebrei stranieri dalla Riviera dei Fiori alla Costa Azzurra 1938–1940* (Saluzzo: Fusta, 2014), pp. 129–148.

Given the growing demand, this traffic was eventually organized and became a profitable business managed by a speculator named Mario Toselli, who created an underground ferryboat company. For a hefty fee, Toselli would provide larger motorized vessels. These secret voyages were arranged by the local COMASEBIT representative, Ettore Bassi, and local authorities actually encouraged rather than hindered them, in the spirit of the laws calling for refugees to leave Italy. Thus, the government's policies were contradictory: officially, attempts to leave the country in secret were to be penalized, yet clandestine expatriation by Jews was actually helped along in every way. Many of these sea voyages took place from March 19, 1939, until at least May 2, 1940. According to Paolo Veziano's research, at least 2,000 people managed to enter France illegally from the western Italian Riviera.[8]

Another way of helping foreigners out of Italy was devised by Raffaele Cantoni, who managed—at least until September 1939, when war broke out between Germany and France—to obtain temporary visas from the French consul in Milan, allowing the bearers to visit France for the official purpose of joining the Foreign Legion. This meant that they could cross the border in the open, and their entry was guaranteed.[9] There were also secret crossings by Jews into Switzerland during this period, facilitated by Italian border guards. After the forced closure of COMASEBIT in July 1939, all aid was suspended for several months and refugees seemed to have been left high and dry. One of them, Bernardo Grosser, formed a private committee in the apartment of a Mr. Fabiszkiewicz in Milan. Along with his collaborators, Enrik Schlaph and Gino Friedmann, Grosser sought out refugees to find out what they needed and to offer them assistance.[10]

The UCII with its new president, Dante Almansi, elected on November 13, 1939, conscious of its own responsibilities toward the many Jews in need of help, decided to tackle the refugee problem directly. On December 1, 1939, it set up the Delegazione Assistenza Emigranti, better known by its acronym, DELASEM.[11] Bernardo Grosser joined

---

8   Veziano, *Ombre di confine*, p. 112
9   Opera di soccorso, Organizzazioni di assistenza, DELASEM, Archivio della Fondazione Centro di documentazione ebraica contemporanea (ACDEC), file 15, folder 3.
10 *Due anni Delasem: Emigrazione, informazioni, distribuzione sussidi, distribuzione alimenti [ecc.]* (Genova: DELASEM, 1942) , pp. 9–10.
11 Settimio Sorani, *L'assistenza ai profughi ebrei in Italia (1933–1947): Contributo alla storia della DELASEM* (Rome: Carucci, 1983); Rosa Paini, *I sentieri della speranza:*

this new organization, as detailed below, but the other members of the private committee that he had formed probably managed to leave Italy. One should note that the antisemitic campaign was in full swing at that point, with new restrictions on Jewish activity coming hard and fast. Indeed, the name DELASEM did not contain the word *ebrei* (Jewish), perhaps out of caution or perhaps because the government discouraged the group from including it.

The new organization's mission was twofold: (a) to facilitate the emigration of the many foreign Jews then in the country and (b) to provide them with any and all assistance that they might need while they were in Italy waiting for the opportunity to emigrate. These goals continued to be consistent with the government's desire to rid Italy of all foreign Jews, so as to prevent them, among other things, from becoming a financial burden on the country. Thus, despite the anti-Jewish laws already in force, DELASEM had government backing, which allowed it basic autonomy, freedom of movement, and international contact with similar institutions abroad, all of which was unusual at the time. Like the earlier committees, DELASEM requested funding from international Jewish aid organizations: the Hebrew Immigrant Aid Society (HIAS), the European merger group HICEM—HIAS, the Jewish Colonization Association (JCA), the United Jewish Emigration Committee, and the American Jewish Joint Distribution Committee (JDC; the Joint).[12]

The first contingent of migrants in Italy aided by DELASEM was made up of 3,000 Polish, Romanian, German, and Austrian Jews, whose number grew as the international situation deteriorated. DELASEM, like COMASEBIT before it, helped arrange and fund the smuggling of foreign Jews into France in an ongoing operation that continued to

---

Profughi ebrei, Italia fascista e la DELASEM (Milan: Xenia, 1988); Voigt, *Il rifugio*, vol. 2, pp. 335–364; Sandro Antonini, *DELASEM: Storia della più grande organizzazione ebraica italiana di soccorso durante la seconda guerra mondiale* (Genoa: De Ferrari, 2000); Susan Zuccotti, *Under His Very Windows* (New Haven: Yale University Press, 2000), p. 75; Klaus Voigt, "La ricostruzione virtuale degli archivi della DELASEM," in Liliana Picciotto, ed., *La Rassegna Mensile di Israel: Saggi sull'ebraismo italiano del Novecento in onore di Luisella Mortara Ottolenghi*, 69:2 (2003), pp. 395–414; Liliana Picciotto, *Salvarsi: Gli ebrei d'Italia sfuggiti alla Shoah, 1943-1945* (Turin: Einaudi, 2017), pp. 86–119.

12 *Due Anni Delasem*, pp. 9–10; on the JDC, see Yehuda Bauer, *American Jewry and the Holocaust: The American Jewish Joint Distribution Committee 1938-1945* (Detroit: Wayne State Univeristy Press, 1981).

function even after December 1, 1939.[13] DELASEM's mission was solely to provide aid: underwriting the refugees' stay in Italy; finding cheap room and board; helping get baggage through customs; identifying countries that would accept immigrants; helping with emigration paperwork; and providing clothes, books, meal tickets, and advice on visas for other countries. The work was frenzied and kept its agents busy to the point of exhaustion.[14]

As there were already many refugees in the port city of Genoa hoping to find passage to North or South America, it was chosen as DELASEM's center of operations. The lawyer Lelio Vittorio Valobra, then vice-president of the Unione delle Comunita Israelitiche Italiane (UCII), was named to head the organization. He was assisted by Enrico Luzzatto Pardo, the secretary general; Berl Grosser, the vice-secretary; Federico Baquis, the treasurer; and Raffaele Noah, Elio Piazza, and Harry Klein. A local representative and secretary were appointed in each Jewish community: representative Mario Falco and secretary Alberto Nizza in Milan; representative Emanuele Montalcini and secretary Giulio Bemporad in Turin; representative Gino Friedmann and secretaries Salvatore Donati and Aldo Conegliani in Modena; representative Giuseppe Fano and secretary Carlo Morpurgo in Trieste; and representative and secretary Mario Finzi in Bologna, among others. The most important office was the one in Rome, where contacts with ministries and high-level officials could be arranged; the representative there was Gustavo Volterra, and Settimio Sorani was the secretary.[15]

Many different kinds of actions were taken on behalf of refugees in addition to those already described: financial support, donation of garments, medical care, childcare, and spiritual support through the distribution of prayer books and matzah for Passover.[16] Moreover, it was necessary to maintain contacts with the Italian authorities, who constantly had to be asked for favors and authorizations. There was almost daily personal interaction and correspondence between UCII

13 Veziano, *Ombre di confine*, p. 33.
14 *Due anni Delasem*, p. 20; Donato Grosser, *Refugees and Rescuers in Fascist and Post War Italy (1933–1946): Composed from Recollections and Documents of My Father Bernardo (Berl) Grosser* (self-pub., 2016).
15 *Due Anni Delasem,* List of Offices.
16 See the telegrams from DELASEM cited in Sandro Antonini, *DELASEM: Storia della più grande organizzazione ebraica italiana di soccorso durante la seconda guerra mondiale* (Genova: De Ferrari, 2000).

President Dante Almansi and the Ministry of Interior.[17] Fundraising campaigns also had to be carried out, targeting generous individuals who still had the means. One noteworthy figure among these DELASEM supporters was Carlo Shapira of Milan, who also funded another Jewish relief organization in Milan led by Lithuanian engineer Israel Kalk, known as the Mensa dei Bambini (Children's Refectory).[18]

From a financial standpoint, the total sums collected and distributed by DELASEM over the course of 1940 reached the remarkable total of about 4.5 million lire, 2 million of which was raised from Italian donors and 2.5 million from foreign aid organizations.[19] The sums from abroad were acquired primarily in the first half of 1940, as fundraising was curtailed when Italy entered the war alongside Nazi Germany in June of 1940, which resulted in a very serious reduction in the available monies.[20] In December of 1941, the American government outlawed the transfer of dollars to German-allied countries, such as Italy. Thus, DELASEM had to make renewed appeals to the generosity of Italian Jews, although the latter were increasingly impoverished themselves, owing to the antisemitic laws in effect since 1938.

The situation became untenable until DELASEM, and the JDC began implementing a financial agreement on indirect compensation with the American relief organization, reimbursing people outside of Italy after the fact for the costs of certain services that DELASEM was paid for in advance in one way or another. For example, the JDC sometimes funded the studies abroad of young Jews who had emigrated because of the anti-Jewish laws, and their families would make donations to DELASEM in Italy, or Italian Jews would turn their money over to DELASEM before emigrating, with the understanding that once abroad, they would receive an equivalent sum in dollars. This financial exchange took place in Switzerland. Valobra, on the Italian side, and, initially, Richard Lichtheim, a representative of the Jewish Agency, and then Saly Mayer, president of the Federation of Swiss Jewish Communities, on the Swiss side, negotiated the agreement that

---

17 Sorani, *L'assistenza*, p. 58.
18 On the work of Israel Kalk, see Fondo Israel Kalk, CDEC-Digital-Library, ACDEC; Klaus Voigt, "Israel Kalk e i figli dei profughi ebrei in Italia," *Storia in Lombardia*, 1:2 (1990), pp. 201–250; Lucia Realini, "La mensa dei bambini a Milano 1939–1943," *Italia Contemporanea*, 232 (2003), pp. 365–400.
19 The exchange rate at the start of World War II was about 20 liras to the U.S. dollar.
20 *Due Anni Delasem*, p. 20.

enabled DELASEM to rely on \$3,000–\$5,000 a month from the JDC.[21]

DELASEM's objectives changed and expanded considerably as the months went by. The situation had become more difficult for foreign Jews owing to three pivotal events:

1. The government order in June of 1940 that called for their internment.
2. The territorial expansion of Italy, which annexed portions of Yugoslavia in April of 1941.
3. The impossibility of crossing the Atlantic after the United States entered the war in December of 1941.

In late June of 1940, foreign Jews who had not managed to leave Italy by March 12, 1939, as the decree required,[22] became subject to grave measures, which resulted from Italy's entry into the war alongside Nazi Germany on June 10, 1940, as well as from the antisemitic perspective of the Ministry of Interior. The pretext was that many Jews were citizens of enemy countries and might act against the national interest, so they should be locked away in camps or other places of confinement. There was an inherent contradiction in the imprisonment of these Jews, however, since most were not from **enemy** countries, but from Axis allies. As Spartaco Capogreco points out, "the fact that most strikingly reveals the racist motivations for this decision was above all the arrest of Jews with German citizenship."[23] Polish, Romanian, German, and Austrian Jews were imprisoned in concentration camps—Ferramonti di Tarsia and Campagna, near Salerno—or ended up in remote villages in the hinterland in a kind of forced residence called "free internment."

Rather than being discouraged by this disastrous new situation for foreign Jewish families, DELASEM increased its activities: it set up branches in these far-flung locations, where the internees themselves

---

21 Voigt, *Il rifugio*, vol. 2, pp. 343–344.
22 Royal Decree Law no. 1728 of November 17, 1938, *Provvedimenti per la difesa della razza italiana*, Gazzetta Ufficiale del Regno d'Italia, 264 (November 19, 1938), https:// www.gazzettaufficiale.it/eli/gu/1938/11/19/264/sg/pdf (Accessed May 2, 2021), pp. 2–4; also reprinted in Sarfatti, "1938: Le leggi contro gli ebrei."
23 Carlo Spartaco Capogreco, "L'entrata in guerra dell'Italia e l'internamento degli ebrei stranieri: il campo di Ferramonti," in Costantino Di Sante, ed., *I campi di concentramento in Italia: Dall'internamento alla deportazione (1940-1945)* (Milan: Franco Angeli, 2001), p. 85.

would appoint a local representative to maintain contact with the head office in Genoa and with DELASEM leader, Valobra. The Fascist government continued to hope that the Jews would leave Italy as soon as possible, even if they were shut away in camps or other places of confinement. For about a year, foreigners who obtained the necessary papers were still able to leave the country. In November of 1940, there were 3,500 refugees in Italy who needed assistance.[24]

On April 6, 1941, another international event affected DELASEM operations. Italy and Germany launched a surprise attack on the Kingdom of Yugoslavia from every border country—Austria, Hungary, Bulgaria, and Albania—as well as from Italy. On April 17, 1941, Yugoslavia signed an unconditional surrender in Belgrade, and the country was split up among Germany, Italy, Hungary, and Bulgaria. The northern Dalmatian coast and the islands of the Adriatic were officially annexed by Italy, as was Slovenia, which became the ninety-fifth Italian province, known as the Province of Ljubljana. These territories were forced to adopt the Italian language and Italy's laws and bureaucracy, including the anti-Jewish legislation then in force. DELASEM extended its activity to those regions, not for native Jews, but for the refugees who were caught there. UCII president, Dante Almansi, who was now also responsible for aiding the foreign Jews in the newly acquired territories, wrote to Police Chief Carmine Senise on September 12, 1941, asking permission for Valobra and Secretary Luzzatto to inspect the situation in the cities of Ljubljana, Sušak, and Split, and at the 2nd Army Corps headquarters.[25]

Eugenio Bolaffio was the DELASEM agent in Ljubljana, and Vittorio Morpurgo was named to that post in Spalato (Split), the capital of Italian-annexed Dalmatia. Working in conjunction with the main office, the two agents provided relief to refugees from Bosnia, Bohemia, and Poland and attempted to streamline the process of their confinement in Italy, or their emigration.[26] In contrast, the organization was barred from operating in the area of Italian military and civil occupation called the Second Zone, a strip of land directly behind Dalmatia.

---

24 *Due Anni Delasem*, p. 27. There were far more than 3,500 refugees in Italy, but not all asked DELASEM for help.

25 Letter from Dante Almansi to Police Chief Carmine Senise, September 12, 1941, reprinted in Sorani, *L'assistenza*, pp. 87–88.

26 Leone, *Le organizzazioni*, pp. 197ff.

In the wake of the dismemberment of Yugoslavia, Italy backed the rise of Ante Pavelić, head of the Ustaša movement, who founded the so-called New Independent State of Croatia, which also included Bosnia-Herzegovina and Vojvodina, and established a cruel dictatorship that dealt violently with the Jews, Roma, and Greek Orthodox Serbs. Zagreb became the capital of this new state. The Jews soon began to flee westward, toward Italian Dalmatia or the militarized Second Zone, or more rarely—because there was more risk of being turned back—toward the Italian border town of Fiume. The Italian authorities, swamped by this exodus, sent those who crossed the eastern border to concentration camps or places of confinement in Italy, or sent them back. As a result, the foreign Jews with whom DELASEM worked were soon mostly from the former Yugoslavia who were confined to villages in Veneto, Emilia, and Val d'Aosta. At that point, while not all the refugees in Italy required aid, 6,700 of them did—of which at least 2,500 were from Slovenia and Dalmatia.[27]

The foreign Jews who were imprisoned after June 1940 were particularly unfortunate, because at this point, owing to the spread of the war, there was no way to flee to a democratic country. However, they were at an advantage from a social standpoint, because they were educated people, sometimes professionals who had held important positions in their hometowns. Though socializing was prohibited, those in small villages were able to arrange contacts with prominent local figures. Moreover, in dozens of cases, the local parish priest would regularly engage in an intellectual dialogue with the internees about religion, literature, and philosophy.

As time went on, DELASEM's Genoa location became less important, because it was far away from the small towns where Jews were confined, and passenger ships were no longer leaving its port as the war had spread to the seas. Some of the offices and the stockpiles of clothing and other basic supplies were moved to Nonantola, near Modena, where the organization had rented Villa Emma. Little by little, the prospects for leaving Italy vanished: on June 30, 1941, the American consulates closed; emigration to Brazil ceased in July; and on December 15, 1941, the Cuban Legation in Rome stopped issuing visas. Eventually, the only way to get out of Italy was to take a plane from Rome to Barcelona or Lisbon.[28]

27 *Due Anni Delasem*, pp. 24–25.
28 Sorani, *L'assistenza*, p. 67.

Assisting Refugee Groups in Italy

The Jews best prepared to face the worsening situation were the foreign refugees who had already experienced Nazi brutality and had no illusions about what Italy's future would be under German occupation. When the time came, they reacted without delay, and many were involved in extraordinary episodes of group flight that brought them to safety. The best-known and most adventurous of these all had two features in common: they were undertaken by foreign rather than Italian Jews, and they took place between September 9 and 13, 1943, just after the September 8, 1943, announcement of the armistice signed by the Badoglio government and the Allied forces, which demonstrates the quick thinking, determination, and organizational skills of the designated or self-designated leaders. There were four main episodes of this kind:

1. The flight into Italy of Jews who had been forcibly relocated to Saint-Martin-Vésubie in the territory under military occupation by Italian troops in France, at the foot of the Maritime Alps. [29]
2. The flight into Italy and then into Switzerland of young people from occupied Yugoslavia, who were staying at Villa Emma in Nonantola, near Modena.[30]
3. The flight into Switzerland of Jews who had been forcibly relocated to Aprica.[31]

---

29 Bronka Halpern, *Keren or bachoschechà* (Jerusalem: Rubin Mass, 1967); Alberto Cavaglion, *Nella notte straniera: Gli ebrei di St.-Martin-Vésuvie* (Turin: Nino Aragno, 2012); Harry Burger, *Biancastella: A Jewish Partisan in World War Two* (Niwot: University Press of Colorado, 1997); Alfred Feldman, *One Step Ahead: A Jewish Fugitive in Hilter's Europe* (Carbondale: Southern Illinois University Press, 2001); Danielle Baudot Laksine, *Les grands visiteurs* (Châteauneuf: Ed. du Bergier, 2005); Susan Zuccotti, *Holocaust Odysseys: The Jews of Saint Martin-Vésubie and Their Flight through France and Italy* (New Haven and London: Yale University Press, 2007); Adriana Muncinelli and Elena Fallo, *Oltre il nome: Storia degli ebrei stranieri deportati dal campo di Borgo San Dalmazzo* (Aosta: Le Château, 2016).

30 Klaus Voigt, *Villa Emma: Ragazzi ebrei in fuga 1940–1945* (Florence: La Nuova Italia, 2001); Josef Indig Ithai, *Anni in fuga: I ragazzi di Villa Emma a Nonantola* (Florence: Giunti, 2004).

31 Alan Poletti, *Una seconda vita: Aprica-Svizzera 1943, la salvezza* (Madonna di Tirano: Museo Etnografico Tiranese, 2012).

4. The flight to the Adriatic coast of Jews who had been forcibly relocated to Asolo, near Treviso.[32]

These flights all took place under grim conditions, with little chance of success, and involved dozens of people traveling together as families with children and grandparents, except in the case of Nonantola, where they were all young people and children. The friendly response of the civilian population, which proved willing to offer sympathy and solidarity, played a fundamental role in saving these groups. The flight of Jews from Saint-Martin-Vésubie and that of Jewish youth from Croatia, as described below, relate directly to DELASEM and its work.

The Flight of Jews from Saint-Martin-Vésubie to Italy

Just after the armistice, on September 9–10, 1943, a group of Jews traveled on foot from Saint-Martin-Vésubie—the French village in the Italian-occupied Maritime Alps, where they had been confined—along the steep paths of the Colle della Finestra and the Colle di Ciriegia, at about 2,500 meters above sea level, to reach the Val di Gesso near Cuneo.

The 4th Italian Army, stationed in southern France, was beating a chaotic retreat toward the Alpine passes, because it was known that German forces would soon be there. The latter were sweeping along the Côte d'Azur and would be in the foothills of the Maritime Alps before long. The only real way out was up the mountain—a frightening, uncertain prospect but one that was marginally possible. After a few dramatic meetings, the fleeing Jews decided to set out. The idea was to follow the soldiers up the Alps and come back down on the Italian side, which they assumed the Germans had not yet invaded. Crossing the border high up in the mountains, the soldiers shed their uniforms and scattered through the Val di Gesso. Lacking supplies, and with children and old people in tow, and unaware that German divisions were beginning to patrol the border, the Jews reached Entracque and Valdieri, tiny villages near Borgo San Dalmazzo, by noon on September 13, 1943.

On September 18, 1943, the day before the massacre of the local civilians in nearby Boves, an SS commander—identified only as Captain

---

32 Emilio Drudi, *Un cammino lungo un anno: Gli ebrei salvati dal primo italiano Giusto fra le Nazioni* (Florence: Giuntina, 2012).

Müller—had a notice posted ordering the Jews to present themselves at the German headquarters, or face execution, if caught.[33] He sent a soldier to Piazza di Valdieri and another to Piazza di Entracque, where many fugitives, weary of the endless flight, stressed and exhausted from dragging old people and children from place to place, turned themselves in. A total of 328 people surrendered; the rest—about 700, although the exact figure is uncertain—scattered throughout the area and hid with the aid of locals who showed extraordinary courage, since anyone caught abetting them would be shot, as the notice on the village walls clearly stated. The arrested Jews were locked up in the empty Alpini barracks in Borgo San Dalmazzo, where they remained for a month, until an SS group was summoned from Nice on November 21, 1943. The SS loaded the prisoners onto trains, sending them first to Nice and then to Drancy, on the outskirts of Paris, where a police and transit camp had been set up. The group of fugitives from France, arrested in Italy, was deported in three separate convoys, on December 7 and 17, 1943, and January 20, 1944, to the Auschwitz-Birkenau death camp in Upper Silesia.[34]

Most of the remaining fugitives hid in the surrounding forests. During those first few days after September 8, 1943, anti-Jewish persecution in Italy was not yet in full force and DELASEM, which had not yet gone underground, immediately swung into action to aid the foreign Jews scattered in the mountains. The fugitives who had escaped were foreigners of various nationalities. If caught by the Italian authorities, they would have been arrested and imprisoned, as were all the foreigners who managed to cross other borders into Italy. The heads of DELASEM tried to channel this flood of refugees toward various cities, with the idea of sending them south, as close as possible to the advancing Allied lines.[35] The cities involved in the operation were Genoa, Florence, Rome,

33 The notice, printed in block letters, read: German Command in Borgo San Dalmazzo. By 1800 hours today, all foreigners in Borgo San Dalmazzo and neighboring municipalities are required to report to the German command station in Borgo S. Dalmazzo, ALPINI BARRACKS. After this time, any and all foreigners who have not complied will be shot. Anyone harboring said foreigners in their homes will incur the same punishment. Borgo S. Dalmazzo, September 18, 1943; see Cavaglion, *Nella notte*, p. 66.

34 Serge Klarsfeld, *Le Mémorial de la déportation des Juifs de France: Listes alphabétiques par convois* (Paris: FFDJF, 1978, 2012); Liliana Picciotto, *Il libro della memoria: Gli ebrei deportati dall'Italia (1943–1945)* (Milan: Mursia, 2002), p. 60.

35 Michele Sarfatti, "Agli ebrei italiani: la Salvezza è al sud!" *Diario del mese* (January 24, 2003), pp. 18–23.

and, to some degree, Turin, which was the nearest metropolis. This was the episode in which DELASEM was most closely involved and which bolstered to its reputation for courage and heroism.

Those who escaped the roundup hid in Alpine huts and natural caves in the mountains overlooking Cuneo. Some joined the Resistance.[36] DELASEM entrusted the partisan priest Don Raimondo Viale[37] with bringing the refugees comfort and sustenance.[38] Other priests also did their part. Don Francesco Brondello,[39] the curate of Valdieri, aided many "French" Jewish families and directed them to more viable places, helping them reach Florence and then Rome. In early October 1943, Don Brondello received an envelope of money from DELASEM envoy Guido De Angeli to meet the needs of these fugitives.[40]

A succession of DELASEM emissaries arrived to lead the "French" Jews to Genoa, Florence, and Rome, where they could find less precarious shelter. Cardinal Maurilio Fossati, the archbishop of Turin who had jurisdiction over the Cuneo area, was part of a chain of bishops involved in this task, and, through his assistant, Don Giovanni Barale,[41] more than once had a hand in finding temporary places of refuge through priests scattered across various parts of Piedmont.[42]

Out of the thousand migrants who set out from Saint-Martin-Vésubie, almost half ended up in Auschwitz—328 were deported from the Alpini barracks in Borgo San Dalmazzo; approximately 100 were rounded up on November 6, 1943, in an empty movie theater rented by DELASEM and deported; and about ten others were arrested in Rome. The rest survived in safe hiding places that DELASEM had found for them with the help of clergy in Florence, Lucca, and Rome.

---

36 Burger, *Biancastella*.

37 Don Raimondo Viale was named Righteous Among the Nations by Yad Vashem in Jerusalem in 2000; see Israel Gutman, Sara Bender, Bracha Rivlin, and Liliana Picciotto, eds., *I giusti d'Italia: I non ebrei che salvarono gli ebrei 1943–1945* (Milan: Mondadori, 2006), pp. 235–236.

38 On Don Viale's work, see Elena Giuliano and Gino Borgna, *Cella n. zero* (Cuneo: Aga Editrice, 1994); Nuto Revelli, *Il prete giusto* (Turin: Einaudi, 1998); Cavaglion, *Nella notte*.

39 Don Francesco Brondello was named Righteous Among the Nations in 2004; see Gutman et al., *I giusti d'Italia*, pp. 66–67.

40 Andrea Villa, *Ebrei in fuga: Chiesa e leggi razziali nel Basso Piemonte, 1938–1945* (Brescia: Morcelliana, 2004), p. 224.

41 In 1955, Monsignor Vincenzo Barale received a gold medal from the UCII.

42 Villa, *Ebrei in fuga*, pp. 220–230.

The Flight of Jewish Youth from Croatia to Nonantola and then Switzerland

Another extraordinary episode of group flight involved German and Yugoslavian young people who were staying at Villa Emma in Nonantola, near Modena. The German scholar Klaus Voigt reconstructed their amazing story.[43] Recha Freier, a committed Zionist from Berlin, had founded the Youth Aliya organization in Berlin in 1933 and in Vienna in 1938, which offered young people a Zionist education to prepare them for *aliya* (immigration to *Eretz Israel*). From October 1940 to December 1941, she was in Zagreb, then still a free Yugoslavian city, where she secretly smuggled young people in from Germany and Austria with the idea of finding them visas to go to Mandatory Palestine.

The young people were welcomed by the Jewish community, and Josef Indig, Zehava Weiner, and the young Armand Moreno from Vienna attended to their needs. Ninety of them managed to obtain the necessary papers and left for *Eretz Israel* shortly after Freier, while the rest of the group was left in the care of Indig and Moreno. However, the invasion of Yugoslavia in April of 1941 put an end to all hope of leaving, and the young people were trapped in Zagreb.

In early June, Indig went to Ljubljana, which had been annexed by Italy. There he met with Eugenio Bolaffio, the local DELASEM agent, who put him in contact with the delegation's central office in Rome. It took considerable effort on DELASEM's part to convince the Italian authorities to let the young people cross over into Slovenia. Finally, on July 4, 1941, forty-three young Jews led by Indig and four guides crossed the border between Croatia and Slovenia and were put up in an abandoned castle in Lesno Brdo, which DELASEM had rented for this purpose, using funds from the JDC. However, soon after they arrived, clashes erupted nearby between the Italian army and Yugoslavian partisans, so DELASEM sought and obtained permission from the Italian government to temporarily transfer the young people to Villa Emma; they arrived there in the summer of 1942.

In December of that year, DELASEM asked that another group of several dozen Bosnian and Croatian Jewish young people, who had taken refuge in the coastal town of Spalato (Split) in Italian Dalmatia, be allowed to join them in Nonantola. They made the voyage by sea and soon

43 All of the details related here are from Voigt, *Villa Emma*.

settled into Villa Emma along with the first group of young German Jews. DELASEM organized all this and continued to look after the children and teens, funding their stay in Italy for as long as possible.[44] By this point, there were 102 people, counting the emissaries, staying in the large house that had been rented by the local DELASEM agent, Gino Friedmann.[45]

During their time at Villa Emma, the young people won the hearts of the local population through their interactions with neighbors, craftsmen, grocers, the local doctor, and the parish priest, all of whom played key roles when they were in mortal danger. After the armistice was announced, on September 8, 1943, the first priority was for them to scatter before German soldiers could arrive there. Indig was able to rely on the Russian musician Georg Bories (Boris Jochvedson),[46] the Polish Marco Schoky (Marek Silberschatz), and Armand Moreno for assistance, as well as on the caretaker at Villa Emma, Goffredo Pacifici, a good-hearted man whom everyone adored—the young people jokingly referred to him as Cicibù. At 7 P.M., half an hour after hearing the announcement of the armistice on the radio, the group leaders visited the local doctor Giuseppe Moreali[47] to ask him for advice. The latter immediately went to see Don Arrigo Beccari,[48] the bursar at the seminary next to the abbey, which was empty in the summer, to see if the young people could stay there temporarily.

The exodus from Villa Emma began at nightfall, with forty younger members of the group moving from Villa Emma to the seminary. The nuns took charge of the girls and the cooking. The older youths, meanwhile, were taken in by farm families, sleeping on ricks of straw, in barns, or in makeshift beds all over town.[49] In addition to the priests from the seminary and the nuns, about thirty families took the young people

---

44 Ibid.

45 Voigt, *Villa Emma*, pp. 333–336.

46 Klaus Voigt, *Chi era Boris Jochvedson?* (Nonantola: Municipality of Nonantola, 2001).

47 Dr. Giuseppe Moreali was named Righteous Among the Nations in 1964; see Gutman et al., *I giusti d'Italia*, pp. 171–173.

48 Don Arrigo Beccari was named Righteous Among the Nations in 1964; see ibid., pp. 40–43.

49 About ten of them were put up by Ernesto Leonardi, the tenant farmer at Villa Emma; ten more by Romolo Casari, an acquaintance of Dr. Giuseppe Moreali; others, with the aid of the priest Don Ennio Tardini, found hospitality with the families of the villa's repair man Barani; the carpenter Erio Tosatti; his father-in-law Mauro Pignatti; the basket-weaver Emilia Sitti Piccinini; the tobacconist Marcellina Nascimbeni Guerzoni; the Bruzzi, Raimondi, Borsari, Serafini, and Zoboli families; and others in Nonantola.

in for a few days. Some youths stayed behind to burn what remained of the DELASEM records, most of which had been transferred to the former headquarters in Genoa. At this point, these files had become pointless and risky. Many of the forged papers that DELASEM had given to foreign refugees had been fabricated right there in Nonantola.[50] After the first few days, most of the young people were transferred to houses further away from Villa Emma. Still, a full-fledged flight had to be organized to take the young people out of a place where everyone knew who they were. But where could they go? Who could they count on? That was the dilemma that faced Indig, who was now dressed up in a priest's cassock as a cautionary measure.

Goffredo Pacifici said he knew how to get to Switzerland by crossing the border near Varese. Indig decided to go with him to inspect the area, and above all to see whether, in the autumn, the River Tresa, which served as a natural border between the province of Varese and the canton of Ticino, was indeed low enough in some places to wade across and whether it would be possible to strike a deal with local smugglers. Pacifici was familiar with the area around Ponte Chiasso, as he had once worked there, and his brother, Aldo, lived nearby. After ascertaining that it would indeed be possible to wade cross the river, the pair returned to Nonantola to organize the escape. Out of caution, and to avoid being turned back en masse by the Swiss authorities, the young people were split into small groups that would travel separately. The first group left Nonantola with Goffredo Pacifici on September 27, 1943, but most of them were turned away at the border.

The second group set out from Nonantola on September 29, 1943, and were picked up at the station in Milan by Pacifici, who had come straight from the border and was unaware of what had happened to the first group. Once again, they were turned away, except for two children and a pregnant girl. The third group apparently set out on September 30, but could not cross the river, because the water level had risen too much in the meantime. The fourth group, which seems to have set out from Nonantola on October 1 managed to slip under the border fence unobserved and to move deep into Swiss territory. All of the young people who had been turned away made their way to Nonantola, dismayed and disheartened, and crept back under their guardians' wings. Anguished,

50 Eugenio Mortara referred to Marco Schoky's skill as a forger; see Eugenio Mortari interview by Michele Sarfatti, March and April 1996, ACDEC.

Indig and Pacifici decided to return to Ponte Tresa and to try to make contact with a Swiss courier who they knew crossed the border in both directions. On the morning of October 4, 1943, the pair managed to give him the telephone number of Nathan Schwalb, the Swiss representative of the Zionist youth movement Hehalutz, whom Indig had met in the past.

Meanwhile, time was running out. The young people who had not yet left Nonantola or who had been forced to return were in mortal danger, since the Germans could start roundups at any time. On October 5, 1943, word finally came: Schwalb had been reached and had arranged for the young people to cross at Ponte Tresa, where the Swiss Federal Council would order the police to let them through. After entering the Swiss Confederation, they were to seek help from the Yugoslav diplomat in exile there. Indig rushed back to Nonantola to prepare for the journey all over again, while Goffredo Pacifici saw to locating the smugglers and paying them whatever they asked. Just a few hours later, the young people bid an emotional farewell—a definitive one this time—to the good priests, monks, and nuns of Nonantola, who showered them with blessings and encouragement.

After all these unbelievable ups and downs, the young Jews of Villa Emma once again set out for Switzerland on October 6, 1943. The journey was a dangerous one, since the Italian police carried out constant inspections on trains. The railway line operated by fits and starts, and the journey from Modena to Milan seemed like it would never end. There were forty-three people in the group this time. At the Milan station, they had to wait several hours for a connecting train. After another journey and more anxiety, they got off at Ponte Tresa and embarked on an exhausting, three-hour march to the point where they were supposed to cross the river. Indig was worried, and the fact that it was the evening of Yom Kippur 1943 added to the pathos of an almost impossible undertaking: getting a group of forty-three people across the river unobserved.

When they reached the designated crossing point, they formed a human chain, because the current was very strong in places; some of the young people wailed, and some fell and were pulled out of the water with great effort. The tension was indescribable. On the other side of the border, the Swiss guards did not allow them to make any phone calls, so Indig had no way of contacting Schwalb directly. They were left in limbo all day and all night, not knowing whether they would be allowed into

Switzerland. At the end of the second day, when the good news arrived, Indig fainted from the strain.

The second group, made up of twenty-one young people, crossed over at the same crossing point, reaching Swiss soil on October 10, 1943, at about 10 P.M. Others had separated from the group and had headed southward, hoping to reach the Allied lines, but in vain; they crossed the Swiss border at Poschiavo a few days later.[51] Only Goffredo Pacifici did not cross, choosing to stay behind, because he now knew how to guide those in danger to Switzerland. This heroic figure, who has never received sufficient recognition, was arrested in Ponte Tresa on December 12, 1943, along with his brother, Aldo. They were both imprisoned together at the Fossoli camp and deported on August 2, 1944, to the death camp in Auschwitz, never to return.[52]

---

51 Beniamino Stern interview by Liliana Picciotto, October 5, 2010, Modena, Fondo Memoria della Salvezza, ACDEC.
52 Liliana Picciotto, *Il libro*, listings by name.

The American Jewish Joint Distribution Committee and the Va'ad Hahatzala

Fundraising Competition and Begrudged Rescue Cooperation, 1939–1943

EFRAIM ZUROFF

This article presents and attempts to analyze an unbridgeable ideological gap between the American Orthodox rabbis and the leaders of the American Jewish Joint Distribution Committee (JDC; the Joint), which significantly affected Jewish relief and rescue efforts from the United States during World War II. The main issues under debate were communal unity, rescue priorities, rescue tactics, fundraising strategies, and organizational credibility, all of which influenced the efforts to assist Jews in distress in four different cases during the years 1939–1943.[1]

---

1 Much of this article is based on Efraim Zuroff, *The Response of Orthodox Jewry in the United States to the Holocaust: The Activities of the Va'ad-Ha-Hatzala Rescue Committee, 1939–1945* (New York and Hoboken: Yeshiva University Press and KTAV Publishing House, 2000). In more recent research on the American Jewish response and rescue activities, this topic is unfortunately neglected and disregarded, in spite of its importance for the question of Jewish solidarity during the Holocaust. The only one who relates to this topic is Hurwitz, who confuses Agudath Yisrael with the Agudath Harabonim, which is the Hebrew name of the Union of Orthodox Rabbis of the United States and Canada (UOR), and who attributes activities undertaken by the former to the latter organization. See Ariel Hurwitz, *Jews without Power: American Jewry During the Holocaust* (New Rochelle: Multieducator, 2011), pp. 65–67, 82, 162; Richard Breitman and Allan Lichtman, *FDR and the Jews* (Cambridge, MA, and London: Belknap Press, 2013); Yehuda Bauer, *Could the US Government Have Rescued European Jewry?* (Jerusalem: The International Institute for Holocaust Research, Yad Vashem, 2017); David S. Wyman and Rafael Medoff, *A Race against Death: Peter Bergson, America, and the Holocaust* (New York: New Press, 2002); Rafael Medoff, *FDR and the Holocaust: A Breach of Faith* (Washington: The David Wyman Institute for Holocaust Studies, 2013); Samuel Merlin, *Millions of Jews to Rescue: A Bergson Group Leader's Account of the Campaign to Save Jews from the Holocaust* (Washington: The David Wyman Institute

On the eve of World War II, the primary American Jewish relief and rescue organization for Jews in distress overseas was the JDC. It had been established in the autumn of 1914, several months after the outbreak of World War I, initially by members of the mostly Reform, German Jewish elite, who were politically affiliated with the American Jewish Committee and who were joined shortly thereafter by the Orthodox Central Relief Committee. Slightly more than a year later, the People's Relief Committee, which represented the American Jewish socialist and labor organizations, also joined them, thereby unifying the overseas relief efforts of the American Jewish community. In terms of fundraising, the JDC conducted its own campaign until January 1939, at which point, in the wake of the *"Kristallnacht"* pogrom, a unified fundraising mechanism known as the United Jewish Appeal (UJA) was created.[2] The beneficiaries were the JDC, the United Palestine Appeal (later known as the United Israel Appeal), and the National Coordinating Committee for Aid to Refugees and Emigrants Coming from Germany. This was the situation at the outbreak of World War II.[3]

However, this ostensibly optimal situation did not last very long; within less than ten months, a new American Jewish overseas relief and rescue organization was created, which challenged the communal fundraising unity. The event that sparked the decision to establish the new relief and rescue organization, which would become the Va'ad Hahatzala (Va'ad Hatzala; the Va'ad), was the escape of hundreds of rabbis and yeshiva students from Eastern Poland to the city of Vilna that began in mid-October 1939 in the wake of the Soviet invasion of Eastern Poland on September 17, 1939, and the subsequent decision of the Soviets, announced in early October, to turn over the city, known as "Jerusalem of Lithuania," and its environs to the independent Republic of Lithuania.

---

for Holocaust Studies, 2011); Rafael Medoff, *The Jews Should Keep Quiet: Franklin D. Roosevelt, Rabbi Stephen S. Wise, and the Holocaust* (Philadelphia: The Jewish Publication Society, 2019); Rafael Medoff, "'The Holocaust, America and American Jewry' Revisited," *The Israel Journal of Foreign Affairs*, 6:2 (2012).

2 In January 1939, the American Jewish Joint Distribution Committee, the United Israel Appeal, and the National Coordinating Committee Fund banded together to establish the United Jewish Appeal (UJA).

3 Marc Lee Raphael, "From Separation to Community: The Origins of the United Jewish Appeal," *Forum*, 37 (Spring 1980), pp. 61–65; Raphael, *A History of the United Jewish Appeal 1939–1982* (Brown Judaic Studies, no. 34) (Chico: Scholars Press, 1982), pp. 1–11.

The motivation for this mass flight was clearly religious, but it was also based on politics. The inimical attitude of the Soviet authorities to Jewish religious life and educational institutions was well known to the Polish *roshei yeshiva* (yeshiva heads) and their students, many of whom had previously experienced severe hardships under Communist rule after World War I, and had opted to flee to Poland from the Soviet Union. In that respect, it was clear both to the students and to their rabbinic leaders that their institutions could not survive for long under the new Soviet regime.[4]

The Soviets and Lithuanians announced the transfer of Vilna on October 11, 1939,[5] and by the time that the Lithuanians took over the city on October 28,[6] about 1,500–1,600 rabbis and yeshiva students, as well as the families of the *roshei yeshiva* and the administrators, had arrived there as refugees. Practically the entire student bodies of some of the most prestigious yeshivot in the world—such as Mir (approximately 300 students); Kamenetz (200 students); Kletzk, Radin, Grodno, Bialystok, and Slonim—were among the refugees. Prominent *roshei yeshiva*, such as Rabbi Aaron Kotler of Kletzk, Rabbi Eliezer Yehuda Finkel of Mir, Rabbi Boruch Ber Leibowitz of Kamenetz, and Rabbi Elchanan Wasserman of Ohel Torah of Baranowicze, were also among the arrivals. Others who arrived in Lithuania at that time included Polish community rabbis, including Rabbi Yitzchak Ze'ev Soloveitchik of Brisk.[7]

---

4   For the background of the mass flight of the Polish yeshivot to Vilna, see Efraim Zuroff, "Rescue via the Far East: The Attempt to Save Polish Rabbis and Yeshivah Students, 1939–1941," *Simon Wiesenthal Center Annual*, 1 (1984), pp. 153–158.

5   Leonas Sabaliunas, *Lithuanian Crisis: Nationalism to Communism, 1939–1940* (Bloomington and London: Indiana University Press, 1972), p. 153. According to other sources, the announcement was made two days earlier. See Elchanan Herzman, *Mofa'it Hador* (Hebrew) (Jerusalem: n.p., 1976), p. 39; Rabbi Yaakov Nayman interview by Efraim Zuroff, July 26, 1977.

6   Yitzhak Arad, "Concentration of Refugees in Vilna on the Eve of the Holocaust," *Yad Vashem Studies*, 9 (1973), pp. 201–206.

7   Telegrams by Rabbi Chaim Ozer Grodzinski, November 5, 1939, and by Rabbi Yoseph Shub, November 6, 1939, to the Central Relief Committee, Archives of the Central Relief Committee (ACRC), Yeshiva University Archives (YUA); letter from Rabbi Eliyahu Bloch to Rabbi Moshe Blau, November 16, 1939, Archives of Merkaz Agudath Yisrael Be'Eretz Yisrael (AAYEY), file 62; letter from Y. Zacks to Rabbi Moshe Blau, November 17, 1939, AAYEY, file 62.

Practically all the refugee rabbis and yeshiva students were penniless when they arrived in Vilna,[8] so they naturally sought material assistance from the local Jewish institutions, in this case, from the Va'ad Hayeshivot, headed by Rabbi Chaim Ozer Grodzinski, the world-renowned leader of Orthodox Jewry.[9] Famous for his energetic efforts to support Torah education during the interwar period, Rabbi Grodzinski had become one of the major financial patrons of the Polish and Lithuanian yeshivot.[10] In that respect, his presence in Vilna was undoubtedly one of the factors in the decision of the rabbis and yeshiva students to flee to that city.[11]

Indeed, Rabbi Grodzinski and his assistants tried their best to feed, house, and clothe the refugee rabbis and yeshiva students, and to enable them to resume their Torah studies. However, the scope of the crisis was only growing as more and more refugees poured into Vilna, including more rabbis and yeshiva students. Under the circumstances,[12] it was only natural to appeal to the leaders of the Orthodox organizations in the United States, which during the interwar period had become the primary sources of support for the Polish and Lithuanian yeshivot: the Union of Orthodox Rabbis of the United States and Canada (UOR),[13] the largest Orthodox rabbinical association in North America; the Central Relief Committee, the Orthodox component of the JDC; and Ezrat Torah.[14]

---

8   Letter from Rabbi Elchanan Wasserman to Moshe Blau, November 1, 1939, quoted in Netanel Katzburg, ed., *Pedut: Hatzala Beyemei Hashoah: Mokorot Umehkarim* (Hebrew) (Ramat Gan: Bar-Ilan University Press, 1984), p. 16.

9   Abundant evidence regarding the prominent role played by Rabbi Grodzinski (1863–1940) in Orthodox life and his efforts on behalf of the yeshivot can be found in the collection of his letters regarding halachic and especially communal affairs. See Aharon Sursky, *Achiezer: Kovetz Igrot, Pirkei Chaim* (Hebrew) (Bnai Brak: Netzach, 1970), pp. 111–232, 645–736.

10 See, for example, the proposed budget of the Va'ad Hayeshivot for the years 1937–1938 and 1938–1939, ACRC, file 380-4; Sursky, *Achiezer*, pp. 672–676.

11 Zuroff, "Rescue via the Far East," p. 173; Zerach Warhaftig, *Palit Vesarid Beyemei Hashoah* (Hebrew) (Jerusalem: Yad Vashem and Ot Ve'eid, 1984), p. 31.

12 "Report about the Conditions of the Refugee Yeshivoth in Vilna," Papers of the Council of Jewish Federations and Welfare Funds (CJFWF), Brandeis University, Archives of the American Jewish Historical Society (AJHS), I-69, box 149.

13 The Union of Orthodox Rabbis of the United States and Canada (UOR), is also called by its Hebrew name, Agudath Harabonim or Agudas Harabonim.

14 For background on each of these organizations and their roles in supporting higher yeshiva education in Poland and Lithuania during the interwar period, see Efraim Zuroff, *The Response of Orthodox Jewry*, pp. 1–22.

Rabbi Grodzinski's pleas did not fall on deaf ears. The rabbinic leadership of American Orthodoxy had been closely following the developments in Eastern Europe after the outbreak of World War II and had already issued appeals for financial help for the yeshivot.[15] As the situation became worse and the appeals, especially from Rabbi Grodzinski, became more urgent, an emergency meeting of the Executive Committee of the UOR was convened. It decided to establish a special organization for the rescue of the rabbis and yeshiva students, and to launch a national fundraising campaign for that purpose.[16]

Hundreds of rabbis attended the November 13–14, 1939, emergency conference at which time the Executive Committee's decision to establish an exclusive rescue organization for rabbis and yeshiva students, known as the Emergency Committee for War-Torn Yeshivot, was announced by Rabbi Eliezer Silver of Cincinnati, who was chosen to head the operation. A leading spokesperson for American Orthodoxy and a respected Talmudic scholar, Silver had played a dominant role in the UOR for decades and was known for his energetic leadership.[17] In order to fully understand the rationale behind this step and the ensuing conflicts between the new rabbinic relief and rescue organization and the JDC, we have to take a closer look at the explanations offered by Silver and the leadership of the Emergency Committee for War-Torn Yeshivot. The conference concluded with the adoption of nine resolutions that stressed the rationale for establishing a national campaign "for the salvation of the great Yeshivoth which this war has uprooted from their sites, whose faculties and student bodies (approximately 4,000 bearers of the Light of Learning) are today refugees in Vilna, inadequately clad against the rigors of winter, starving and exhausted." To support their argument regarding the unique importance of Torah learning, the rabbis referred to Rabbi Yochanan Ben Zakai.

In the olden days of the Destruction of the [Second] Temple...[Rabbi Yochanan Ben Zakai] pleaded for the great Academy of Yavneh and

15 *Churbn un Rettung* (New York: Va'ad Hahatzala Book Committee, 1957), p. 153.

16 Eliezer Silver, "Jewish Rescue Work in Our Time," in *Churbn un Rettung*, pp. 21–22.

17 For details on the prominent role played by Rabbi Eliezer Silver (1881–1968) in Orthodox life in America, see Aaron Rakeffet-Rothkoff, *The Silver Era in American Jewish Orthodoxy: Rabbi Eliezer Silver and His Generation* (New York and Jerusalem: Yeshiva University Press and Feldheim, 1981); Aaron Shurin, *Keshet Giborim* (Hebrew) (Jerusalem: Mossad Harav Kook, 1964), p. 207.

her scholars, because he believed that the Torah was the Jewish citadel. In the tragedy that has befallen our people in the present day when complete destruction threatens the very life of the Jewish people, it should be our sacred duty to save our Yavnehs of today—the Holy Yeshivoth—in which the only salvation of Judaism and Jewish life lies.

Having made this point, the rabbis were obviously fully aware of the probable fallout from such a decision as it related to the UJA, and particularly vis-a-vis the JDC. Thus, the first of the nine resolutions passed by the convention specifically praised the JDC's efforts during World War I to which "millions of our brethren…owe their very lives and existence," noting the current plight of "millions of troubled, tormented and persecuted Jews," and calling upon American Jewry to "fulfill its duty toward its greatest and noblest world philanthropic organization."

In his keynote address, Silver also acknowledged that it was important for Orthodox rabbis to help the JDC expand its overseas relief, but explained that despite the situation, the rabbis had a special obligation to establish an exclusive rescue fund to save the yeshivot, which he referred to as Judaism's "columns of support."[18] However, despite the implications in terms of communal unity and unified fundraising, on the very next day, November 15, 1939, Rabbi Silver opened an office of the Emergency Committee for War-Torn Yeshivot, which began its operations at 673 Broadway, New York City—the same address as the offices of the UOR.[19]

One cannot understand this step without being aware of several additional factors that strengthened the rabbis' motivation to launch their own independent relief and rescue operation. One was the preeminent status of the yeshivot that had relocated to Vilna, which constituted the elite of the Torah world and the major sources of the rabbis and Torah scholars of the future.[20] A second factor was the rabbis' reluctance to

---

18 "Vi'eeda Chatzi-Shnatit Shel Agudat Harabanim" (Hebrew), *Hapardes*, 13:9 (Kislev 5700/ December 1939), pp. 4–9. To the best of our knowledge, there is no official protocol of the convention at which the Va'ad Hahatzala was established and, thus, we must rely on the convention resolutions, reports in the press, and the testimony of the participants for details of the events. See "The Resolutions of the Agudath Harabonim Convention," ACJFWF, I-69, box 149.

19 "Vi'eeda Chatzi-Shnatit," p. 9; letter from Rabbi Simcha Wasserman to Abraham Horowitz, December 19, 1939, ACJFWF, I-69, box 149.

20 "Vi'eeda Chatzi-Shnatit," p. 6; "Va'ad Hahatzala Layeshivot Be'Eropa" (Hebrew), *Hapardes*, 13:10 (Tevet 5700/January 1940), p. 4.

allow decisions of such import from their perspective to be made by an organization whose leaders were for the most part Reform Jews, and whose values and level of Jewish observance were in their opinion lacking in comparison to Orthodoxy. Moreover, although the Central Relief Committee was one of the founders of the JDC and had members on the JDC's Cultural Committee, which allocated support to Orthodox institutions, the fact remained that the dominant influence was that of the wealthy Jews of German origin, whose attitude toward traditional Torah education was quite different from that of the Eastern European born and bred leadership of the UOR.[21]

The fact that there were personal ties between the leadership of the UOR and the heads of the yeshivot stranded in Lithuania was another factor that influenced the decision to establish the Va'ad Hahatzala. All the members of the rabbinic association had been ordained in Eastern Europe after studying, in most cases, in the very institutions that had relocated to Vilna. Moreover, many of the American rabbis knew at least some of the refugee *roshei yeshiva* personally, having studied under or with them in their youth, or having met them when they had visited the United States to raise funds for their institutions and, thus, their sense of obligation to try and save them was particularly strong.[22] The fact that the appeals for help for this group came from Rabbi Chaim Ozer Grodzinski, who was considered a mentor to many, was also a factor,[23] which set a historical precedent. During World War I, after supporting the establishment of the JDC, the UOR founded Ezrat Torah as a separate relief framework for rabbis and yeshiva students on the premise that such persons should not be forced to turn to soup kitchens for help, lest they lose their standing in their community.[24] In this crisis, however, it was clear that Ezrat Torah could not handle

21 For biographical data on the leaders of the JDC, see Yehuda Bauer, *My Brother's Keeper: A History of the American Jewish Joint Distribution Committee, 1929–1939* (Philadelphia: Jewish Publication Society, 1974), pp. 19–22.

22 Zuroff, *Response of Orthodox Jewry*, pp. 1–22; William Helmreich, *The World of the Yeshiva: An Intimate Portrait of Orthodox Jewry* (New York and London: The Free Press, 1982), p. 41; Irving Bunim, who played an extremely active role in the Va'ad Hahatzala, acknowledged that the fact that he had met Rabbi Aaron Kotler when the latter visited the United States in 1935 and encouraged him to try to save himself.

23 Silver, "Jewish Rescue Work," pp. 21–22. Jacob Hellerstein was the recording secretary of the UOR from 1928 to 1972; see Jacob Hellerstein interview by Efraim Zuroff, November 29, 1973.

24 Zuroff, *Response of Orthodox Jewry*, pp. 1–22.

an emergency of such a scope; hence, the decision to opt for a new framework.[25]

In concluding this attempt to analyze the decision to establish the Emergency Committee for War-Torn Yeshivot, which would become the Va'ad Hahatzala, two additional elements should be taken into account. One was the personality of its founder Rabbi Eliezer Silver, who was known not only for his impressive Torah scholarship and active involvement in Jewish communal affairs, but also for his fiery personality, abundant charisma, and success as a fundraiser. His zeal in pressing to establish the Va'ad Hahatzala stemmed from his assessment of the severity of the crisis and most probably from his own desire to head the response to such a critical historical challenge, one that he considered well beyond the capabilities of Ezrat Torah and its leader Rabbi Eliyahu Henkin.[26]

The final factor that must be considered regarding the establishment of the Va'ad Hahatzala, is that its founders had no idea that it would develop into a full-fledged relief and rescue agency that would actively compete with the JDC for the charity dollars of American Jewry. That development was primarily the result of circumstances, rather than any long-range planning, as the rabbis did not initially harbor any grandiose plans. In fact, that was one of three explanations that the Va'ad used to try and counter the reservations expressed by JDC officials about the confusion that the Va'ad's fundraising activities had created in many Jewish communities. According to the rabbis, theirs was a "one-time campaign to be carried out this winter" that was solely undertaken for the relocation of the yeshivot, a task that was clearly beyond the capabilities of the already overtaxed JDC, and that it would, moreover, "turn especially to the regular contributors to the yeshivoth," rather than to the wider Jewish community to avoid interfering with the UJA.[27] As it turned out, however, the Va'ad ultimately did not abide by a single one of these declared intentions.

25 Rabbi Yitzhak Grozalsky interview by Efraim Zuroff, November 14, 1973; Jacob Hellerstein interview by Efraim Zuroff, November 29, 1973.

26 For details on Rabbi Silver's personality and communal activities, see Rakeffet-Rothkoff, *The Silver Era*, pp. 68–94; Menachem Glickman-Porush, *Ish Hahalaha Vehama'ase* (Hebrew) (Jerusalem: n.p., n.d.); Rabbi Alex Wiesfogel interview by Efraim Zuroff, July 22, 1973. On the differences between Rabbi Silver and Rabbi Henkin, see Shmaryahu Hacohen Margalit interview by Efraim Zuroff, October 22, 1973.

27 Letter from Rabbi Simcha Wasserman to Abraham Horowitz, December 19, 1939, ACJFWF, I-69, box 149.

Over the course of the years 1939–1943, there were four specific occasions in which the JDC and the Va'ad found themselves at odds over the relief efforts to specific groups of Jewish refugees. In each case, the JDC sought to assist all the Jewish refugees, while the Va'ad insisted on helping rabbis and yeshiva students exclusively. The differences of opinion were primarily over rescue priorities, but the two organizations also debated rescue tactics and the practical question of whether and to what extent to abide by American regulations that hampered relief and rescue activities. The cases in question are presented below in chronological order:

1. Relief for the Polish Jewish refugees who fled to Vilna.
2. Relief for the immigration of refugee scholars to the Far East, the United States, Canada, and Mandatory Palestine.
3. Relief for the Polish Jewish refugees in Soviet Central Asia.
4. Relief for the Polish Jewish refugees in Japanese-occupied Shanghai.

Relief for the Polish Refugees Who Fled to Vilna, Autumn 1939–Summer 1940

From mid-October 1939 until spring 1940, approximately 15,000 Polish Jewish refugees escaped to Lithuania, including 2,440 yeshiva students and 171 rabbis.[28] The Va'ad's efforts during this period focused exclusively on providing emergency aid to this latter group to enable them to continue their Torah studies, while at the same time, they were also the beneficiaries of assistance from the JDC. The rabbis realized within a relatively short time that they could not possibly raise the funds that they needed if they confined their fundraising efforts to the Orthodox community, so they began to approach the federations and welfare funds, which conducted the local fundraising campaigns for the UJA. In most cases, the local fundraisers were presented with an ultimatum by a local Orthodox rabbi, by a delegation of rabbis from outside the city, or through correspondence from the Va'ad's main office

---

28 Yehuda Bauer, *American Jewry and the Holocaust: The American Jewish Joint Distribution Committee, 1939–1945* (Jerusalem and Detroit: The Institute of Contemporary Jewry at the Hebrew University of Jerusalem and Wayne State University Press, 1981), p. 112.

in New York. Either the federation would allocate the sum demanded by the rabbis or the Va'ad would conduct a separate fundraising campaign of its own in the middle of the local campaign, something that most local community officials were anxious to prevent.

The rabbis' fundraising efforts caused considerable confusion and anger among the local community officials, as well as the ire of the JDC, which tried very hard to convince local communities that sought to help the refugee yeshivot in Vilna to transmit the funds in question via the JDC. In response after response to the local welfare funds, Moses Leavitt, the JDC secretary, Henrietta Buchman, the JDC secretary of its Committee on Cultural Affairs, and Blanche Renard, the secretary of the Committee on National Jewish Agencies of the Council of Jewish Federations and Welfare Funds (CJFWF), harshly criticized the Va'ad, questioned its ability to carry out the task it was established to undertake, and accused it of misrepresenting its goals.[29]

In an effort to defuse the looming crisis, JDC officials met in early June 1940 with Rabbi Abraham Kalmanowitz of the Mir yeshiva, who had recently arrived from Vilna and was one of the key leaders of the Va'ad, and tried to convince him that the best course of action for all involved would be for the rabbis to join forces with the JDC. According to Buchman,

> Of course, the greater the contributions to the JDC, the greater will be the measure of aid we shall be in a position to make available to yeshivoth and rabbis, as well as for the many other urgent requirements not only in Vilna, but in all parts of the world. It seems to us, therefore, that it would be more advantageous to all concerned if the Orthodox leaders sponsoring your appeal would lend their active assistance to the UJA to help raise the funds so sorely needed.[30]

We have no indication that the rabbis ever seriously considered Buchman's proposal. On the contrary, the Va'ad's success in raising funds

---

29 See, for example, the letter from Moses Leavitt to Rabbi Shaw, May 16, 1940, ACJFWF, I-69, box 149; letters from Henrietta Buchman to Elkan Voorsanger, April 24, 1940, and to Jacob Lightman, April 10, 1940, ACJFWF, I-69, box 149; letters from Blanche Renard to Louis Greenberg, February 8, 1940, and to Florence Hunter, April 1, 1940, ACJFWF, I-69, box 149.

30 Letter from Henrietta Buchman to Rabbi Karlinsky, June 11, 1940, JDC, Va'ad Hahatzala file.

helped strengthen its resolve to continue its efforts independently. By June 1940, it had raised approximately $100,000, which was distributed among the refugee yeshivot in Lithuania.[31]

Relief for the Immigration of Refugee Scholars to the Far East, the United States, Canada, and Mandatory Palestine

In the fall of 1940, in the wake of the Soviet occupation of Lithuania on June 15, 1940 and its annexation to the Soviet Union in August of that year, the focus of the Va'ad's efforts reverted to their original goal of relocation.[32] Less than a year after fleeing Communist rule in Eastern Poland, the refugee rabbis and yeshiva students had suddenly found themselves in the original predicament that had prompted their escape to Vilna. If until this point emigration had been an option but not an absolute imperative, now the Soviet occupation forced the *roshei yeshiva* and their supporters in New York to urgently seek havens abroad.

The problem was, however, that the rabbinic rescue organization lacked the resources and technical and logistic expertise to realize such an ambitious project and was, therefore, forced to try to enlist the assistance of other organizations, primarily the JDC, which was far from enthusiastic about the idea of bringing more than two dozen Orthodox yeshivot to the United States. The JDC and the Va'ad Hahatzala decided to convene a meeting of representatives of several of the major American Jewish organizations on August 15, 1940, to discuss the latter's proposal for the mass relocation of the refugee yeshivot. In addition to the leaders

31 Memorandum from Carol Kuhn to Blanche Renard regarding the Emergency Committee for War-Torn Yeshivoth, July 5, 1940, ACJFWF, I-69, box 149.

32 The Soviet takeover was preceded by a Russian ultimatum to the Lithuanian government on June 14, 1940, in which the latter was accused of signing a military pact with Latvia and Estonia in violation of the Soviet–Lithuanian defense treaty of October 10, 1939, and of arresting and torturing Russian soldiers in order to obtain information on Soviet military bases in Lithuania. The Russians demanded the establishment of a new government that would be "friendly" to the Soviet Union, the trial of Minister of the Interior Skučas and of Povilaitis, the chief of the security police, and the admission of an unlimited number of Soviet troops to Lithuania. Before the Lithuanian government could reply, Soviet forces invaded Lithuania and took over the country. See Owen J. C. Norem, *Timeless Lithuania* (Chicago: Amerlith Press, 1943), pp. 174–175; Arad "Concentration of Refugees in Vilna," p. 212.

of both the JDC and the Va'ad, among those in attendance were Rabbi Stephen Wise, who headed both the World Jewish Congress and its American affiliate; Nahum Goldmann of the World Jewish Congress; and Henry Monsky of B'nai B'rith.

The meeting began with the presentation of the rabbis' proposal to bring all the Polish refugee yeshivot currently in Soviet Lithuania to the United States, a total of about 3,500 persons, and to approach the State Department to grant special visas for the group. The rabbis' plan encountered considerable opposition, which was led by Rabbi Wise, probably the most influential American Jewish leader at that time, who considered the project both unfeasible and problematic, advising against any attempt to try to pressure the State Department to grant special visas for the entire group. In his opinion, if the American Jewish community would be able to absorb the refugees from three to five yeshivot, that would be an important contribution to the preservation of Jewish culture, but attempting to bring more could have negative consequences.[33]

Neither side was able to convince the other, and there are conflicting accounts regarding the number of visas requested and those actually obtained, but it is clear that by September 18, 1940, as many as 732 "alleged leaders of the intellectual thought of the Jewish religion and leading exponents of the Talmudic schools and colleges, together with their families," were approved for entry visas to the United States.[34] In the meantime, starting in early September 1940, a significant number of rabbis and yeshiva students were able to obtain permission to leave Soviet Lithuania on the basis of visas to the Dutch possession of Curacao and of Japanese transit visas. Most had no funds to pay for their travel expenses, which the Soviet authorities demanded in foreign currency, and they appealed to the Va'ad for urgent assistance. These pleas naturally increased the pressure on the Va'ad to raise additional funds as quickly as possible, which also exacerbated the tensions between

---

33 Letter from Moses Leavitt to Samuel Goldsmith, January 27, 1941, JDC, Va'ad Hahatzala file.

34 *Foreign Relations of the United States,* 1940, vol. 2 (Washington, DC: U.S. Government Printing Office, 1957), pp. 239–240. The number of visas obtained was 1,200, but there is no documentary proof to support this figure; see *Churbn un Rettung,* p. 205. According to Moses Leavitt, the State Department had agreed to recommend that visas be issued "to a few hundred of these people." See letter from Moses Leavitt to Samuel Goldsmith, January 27, 1941, JDC, Va'ad Hahatzala file.

the rabbis and the leaders of the JDC and the CJFWF, who were also facing increased demands for assistance, but in their case, from Jews in distress all over the world.[35]

The evolving situation in Lithuania added two new arguments to those hitherto presented by the JDC and the CJFWF to discourage allocations to the refugee rabbis and yeshiva students through the Va'ad. The first was the uncertainty regarding the actual existence of the refugee yeshivot in the wake of the Soviet occupation, and the second was the claim that the method used by the Va'ad to transfer funds to Lithuania was in violation of U.S. government regulations.[36] Once again, the officials of the Va'ad met with their counterparts from the JDC and CJFWF to clarify these issues, but were unable to reach any agreement. Moses Leavitt stressed that the Va'ad's arrangements for the transfer of funds from Lithuania—persons leaving for the United States gave funds to the yeshivot and were repaid in New York by the rabbis—were "dangerous and illegal as far as U.S. regulations were concerned," and emphasized "the danger to Jews from a public relations standpoint of acting counter to U.S. regulations." The rabbis' response was "where lives are at stake, chances must be taken...legal or illegal."[37]

This issue continued to be a serious bone of contention in the following months. The Va'ad kept trying to convince the CJFWF to encourage its member federations and welfare funds to forward all monies designated for the refugee yeshivot via its office, but the CJFWF refused to do so. Moreover, although the CJFWF and JDC refrained from expressing opposition to the Va'ad's method of transferring funds to Lithuania in their official bulletins,[38] in their correspondence with individual federations, the CJFWF and JDC officials were highly critical of the Va'ad, clearly indicating that they would not recommend working together with it.[39]

---

35 Bauer, *American Jewry and the Holocaust*, pp. 119–128.

36 Letter from Blanche Renard to Amos Deinard, August 5, 1940, ACJFWF, I-69, box 149.

37 Representatives of the Federated Council of Palestinian Institutions also participated in the meeting; see "Meeting Re Yeshivoth, September 10, 1940," September 18, 1940, ACJFWF, VH-600.

38 "Status of East European Yeshivoth, Methods of Transmitting Funds and Activities of Emergency Committee for War-Torn Yeshivoth (Replacing Bulletin #116)," Budgeting for Member Agencies, No. 123, October 1940, ACJFWF, I-69, box 149.

39 Letter from Blanche Renard to Norman Dockman, October 18, 1940, ACJFWF, I-69, box 110.

The major arguments presented by Moses Leavitt and Henrietta Buchman of the JDC and Blanche Renard of the CJFWF can be summarized as follows: The primary ideological claim against the Va'ad's campaign was that it was created to obtain preferential treatment for one specific group of Jews at the expense of all the other Jews in distress. The practical arguments were basically threefold. The first was that allocations by local community fundraising agencies to the Va'ad ultimately reduced the funds made available to the JDC, which was responsible for the major burden of American Jewish relief and rescue work overseas.[40] The second was that it was highly doubtful that 3,000 visas to the United States could actually be obtained for the entire group of rabbis and yeshiva students as the Va'ad publicly claimed.[41] The third was that the JDC was already helping the recipients of the aid sent by the Va'ad, since half of the $150,000 allocated by the JDC for the transportation expenses of Polish Jewish refugees to Japan had been earmarked specifically for refugee rabbis and yeshiva students, not to mention the large sums spent by the JDC for the sustenance of all the Jewish refugees who had arrived in Japan since the autumn of 1940.[42]

These criticisms were, however, only part of a bigger picture concerning the emigration of Polish Jewish refugees from Soviet Lithuania. For example, there was no mention in the CJFWF reports about the Va'ad Hahatzala, or in its correspondence with individual federations and welfare funds of the fact that, in November 1940, the JDC had advised Moses Beckelman, its representative in Vilna, against sending refugees with Curacao visas to Japan. When he, nonetheless, continued to assist refugees to leave for the Far East, Moses Leavitt actively attempted for several months to stop that emigration by refusing to authorize payment for the refugees' transportation expenses. The reason for this policy was that the JDC was unexpectedly forced to pay tens of thousands of dollars for the sustenance of these refugees in Japan, an expense that it had not originally anticipated. Fortunately for

---

40 See, for example, letter from Moses Leavitt to Samuel Goldsmith, January 27, 1941, JDC, Va'ad Hahatzala file.

41 Letters from Blanche Renard to Edward Kahn, January 23, 1941, and to Louis Greenberg, February 25, 1941, JDC, Va'ad Hahatzala file; letter from Moses Leavitt to Samuel Goldsmith, January 27, 1941, JDC, Va'ad Hahatzala file.

42 Letter from Moses Leavitt to Jacob Kammen, executive secretary of the United Jewish Welfare Fund of Rochester, April 14, 1941, JDC, Va'ad Hahatzala file.

the refugees, the JDC covered those expenses, thereby preventing their deportation back to the Soviet Union.[43]

In the meantime, in early 1941, the Va'ad's separatist stance received significant support from two different sections of the Orthodox community. The first was from the more modern Orthodox organizations, which had originally been skeptical about the necessity of establishing a separate rescue and relief agency, and preferred that the rabbis work within the framework of the JDC and the UJA.[44] By the time the Va'ad had launched its tickets campaign, however, modern Orthodox organizations, such as the Rabbinical Council of America, Young Israel,[45] and the Union of Orthodox Jewish Congregations[46] were fully supporting it, along with the Ze'iri Agudath Yisrael, which had provided very important assistance to the rabbis from the very beginning.[47]

The second event of importance in this regard was the arrival in the United States in the spring of 1941 of several, extremely prominent, Polish, refugee *roshei yeshiva* and communal rabbis, who had emigrated from Soviet Lithuania via Japan with the Va'ad's support. The most prominent of these new arrivals was Rabbi Aaron Kotler of Etz Chaim Yeshiva of Kletzk, who was known throughout the Orthodox world as a brilliant Talmudic scholar and was also active in communal affairs.[48] Other *roshei yeshiva* who reached the United States during this period were Rabbi Reuven Grazowsky of Kamenetz, Rabbi Mendel

---

43 Bauer, *American Jewry during the Holocaust*, p. 122.

44 "Distress of the Yeshivot," *Jewish Outlook*, 4: 6 (February 1940), p. 4; Elijah Stein was the financial secretary of the Young Israel Movement; see Elijah Stein interview by Efraim Zuroff, April 16, 1974. Herman Hollander was a leader of American Mizrachi; see Herman Hollander interview by Efraim Zuroff, December 18, 1973.

45 Rabbi Joseph Konvitz, "Greetings," *The Young Israel Viewpoint*, March 23, 1941, p. 34; Amos Bunim, *A Fire in His Soul: Irving M. Bunim 1901–1980: The Man and His Impact on American Orthodox Jewry* (Jerusalem and New York: Feldheim, 1989), pp. 75–92.

46 "Orthodox Union to Cooperate with the Va'ad Hahatzala," *The Orthodox Union*, March–April 1941, p. 11.

47 *Churbn un Rettung*, pp. 201–205. Gershon Kranzler, "Setting the Record Straight," *Jewish Observer*, 7:10 (November 1971), pp. 9–14.

48 Rabbi Aaron Kotler assumed the leadership of the Etz Chaim Yeshiva after his father-in-law, Rabbi Isser Zalman Meltzer, immigrated to Mandatory Palestine. During the two decades in which he headed the yeshiva in Europe, Rabbi Kotler attracted many students from all over the world because of his original teaching methods. In addition, he was one of the leaders of Agudath Yisrael and served on its Mo'etzet Gedolei HaTorah (Council of Sages), which made all the movement's policy decisions. See Aaron Shurin, *Keshet Giborim*, pp. 244–248.

Zaks of Radin, and Rabbi Avraham Yaphin of Bialystok. Among the communal rabbis who arrived were Rabbi David Lifshitz of Suwalki and Rabbi Moshe Shatzkes of Lomza.[49] The three *roshei yeshiva*, it should be noted, had left behind almost all their students, only a few of whom had already managed to reach Japan,[50] and so they were very determined to become active on behalf of the Va'ad. Rabbi Kotler, for example, practically from the moment of his arrival in the United States, became one of the most important leaders of the rabbinic rescue organization, and his unflagging efforts on the Va'ad's behalf lent it considerable prestige.[51]

In March 1941, the Japanese authorities issued instructions to stop granting visas to Jewish refugees, which further complicated the efforts to extricate the refugee rabbis and yeshiva students still in Soviet Lithuania.[52] Subsequently, the Va'ad and the refugee rabbis and yeshiva students became involved in two partially successful initiatives designed to help clear the Japanese bottleneck. The first was an attempt to secure entry permits to the International Settlement at Shanghai, which was governed by the representatives of the foreign powers that had extraterritorial rights in the Chinese port, then under Japanese occupation.[53] The second was an attempt to obtain visas to Canada

49 "Va'ad Hahatzala" (Hebrew), *Hapardes*, 15: 4 (Tammuz 5701/July 1941), pp. 3–4.

50 Unlike the students of the Mir yeshiva, almost all of whom obtained the necessary travel documents and were thus able to leave Lithuania, very few of the students of the other yeshivot secured the visas and exit permits. As a result, the overwhelming majority of these students were still in Lithuania at this point, and few ever reached the Far East; see Zuroff, "Rescue via the Far East," pp. 167–168.

51 See, for example, Rabbi Kotler's telegrams to Rabbi Ashkenazi in Shanghai regarding the efforts to rescue the yeshiva students still in Lithuania, April 27, May 5, and May 13, 1941, YUA, Va'ad Hahatzala Collection (AVH); Bunim, *A Fire in His Soul*, pp. 96–112.

52 All 1,119 refugees who arrived in Japan from July 1 to September 30, 1940, stayed for only a brief period and had left the country by the latter date. Of the 852 refugees who arrived during October, November, and December, 693 were able to leave by the end of 1940. This situation changed dramatically in January and February 1941, when 1,325 Jewish refugees were admitted to Japan, but only 383 left the country. The author would like to thank Rabbi Marvin Tokayer, formerly of Tokyo, for providing him with the "Report of the Activity of the Committee for Assistance to Refugees: The Jewish Community of Kobe (Ashkenazim), July 1940–November 1941," Kobe, 1942, p. 9.

53 Entries of February 25 and 29, 1941 in the diary of Frank Newman, the Va'ad Hahatzala emissary sent to Japan. The diary was made available to me by the late Dr. David Kranzler; see also Warhaftig, *Palit Vesarid Beyemei Hashoah*, p. 229.

for a group of rabbis and yeshiva students stranded in Japan.[54] In both cases, the Va'ad found itself at loggerheads with the JDC, or in the case of Canada, with its Canadian affiliate.

In the former case, 1,200 permits were obtained by late June 1941, while emigration from Soviet Lithuania was still possible, but unfortunately only about half were secured prior to the German invasion of the Soviet Union.[55] We know with certainty that these permits enabled the entry to Shanghai of two groups, totaling at least sixty-five refugees who had been stopped by the Soviets in Vladivostok and were threatened with deportation back to Lithuania, unless they could leave for a destination other than Japan by the end of March.[56] The successful transfer of the first group of fifty refugees, which included an unknown number (at the time) of rabbis and yeshiva students, is of particular interest in evaluating the relations between the JDC and the Va'ad Hahatzala. In this case, the leaders of the refugees in Japan decided that the permits would be allocated to this entire group, regardless of religiosity or ideological affiliation,[57] and the Va'ad provided the necessary funds for all the fifty refugees, even though at that point it was already known that only about half of them were rabbis and yeshiva students.[58] Thus, the entire group, which had been facing deportation back to Lithuania, was able to go to Shanghai, thereby saving them from almost certain death. The JDC, it should be noted,

---

54 Zuroff, *Response of Orthodox Jewry*, pp. 170–190.

55 Efraim Zuroff, "Attempts to Obtain Shanghai Permits in 1941: A Case of Rescue Priority during the Holocaust," *Yad Vashem Studies*, 13 (1979), pp. 349–350.

56 Telegram from Rabbi Shmulewitz to Frank Newman, March 28, 1941, YIVO Archives (YIVO), file 49; letter from Dov Amster to Zerach Warhaftig, March 28, 1941, YVA, P.20/8.

57 Letter from Zerach Warhaftig to Rabbi Ashkenazi, April 11, 1941, Papers of Rabbi Meir Ashkenazi (Ashkenazi Papers), YVA, P.20.

58 Unsigned telegram from Shanghai from Rabbi Ashkenazi or Tugendhaft to Frank Newman, April 17, 1941, YVA, P.20. The decision to provide assistance to the non-Orthodox refugees was apparently quite difficult for Rabbi Ashkenazi and Tugendhaft, who viewed the rescue of the Torah scholars as their primary objective and, therefore were reluctant to allocate resources for the rescue of others. Thus, following the arrival of the boat from Vladivostok, Tugendhaft wrote to Newman, "Although the other group [of non-Orthodox refugees] cost us money, we were forced in the interest of the *bnai Torah* who were to be saved to undertake to pay these costs ourselves." See letter from Tugendhaft to Frank Newman, May 4, 1941, Irving Newman Papers, USHMM, 1995.A.0753.1.

later paid for the voyage of all these passengers,[59] which made this an episode marked by successful cooperation between the two American Jewish rescue organizations.

This was also the case in regard to the second initiative launched by the Va'ad in 1941 to help extricate at least some of the refugee rabbis and yeshiva students who were stuck in Japan. In early May 1941, the Va'ad learned that the Canadian government had agreed to admit 1,000 Allied nationals who managed to get to neutral countries during the war, including some of the Polish Jewish refugees in Japan, specifying that they could remain in Canada only until the end of the war.[60] It immediately sought to ensure that at least some of the places allotted to those refugees would be set aside for rabbis and yeshiva students. This effort, which the Va'ad coordinated with the Federation of Polish Jews in Canada, put it on a collision course with the JDC's Canadian affiliate, the United Jewish Refugee and War Relief Agency (UJRWRA), in a manner exactly analogous to its problematic relations with the JDC in the United States.[61]

As could be expected, Rabbi Oscar Fasman, the local advocate for the Va'ad, emphasized the unique importance of the scholars who "embody a wealth of Jewish sacred learning, the likes of which can no longer be duplicated," and thus whose rescue would be the "saving not only of people, but [of] a holy culture which cannot be otherwise preserved."[62] The director of the UJRWRA, Saul Hayes, was more concerned with practical matters, preferring to give priority to refugees who had no other possible emigration destination and especially to those with relatives living in Canada, who obviously had a better chance of being admitted.[63]

---

59 Letter from Tugendhaft to Frank Newman, May 4, 1941, Irving Newman Papers, USHMM, 1995.A.0753.1; letter from M. Birman to Moses Beckelman, May 8, 1941, JDC, Shanghai file. Birman wrote that 52 persons arrived, but the passenger list had only 50 names. See "List of recent arrivals," May 2, 1941, JDC, file 461.

60 Federation of Polish Jews in Canada, "Memorandum Regarding Permission to Enter Canada of Polish Jewish Refugees from Japan and Elsewhere," May 6, 1941, Archive of the Canadian Jewish Congress (ACJC); Archive of the United Jewish Refugee and War Relief Agency (UJRWRA), file 174. At this point, Podoski thought that about 500 Polish refugees from Japan would be brought to Canada. See letter from Podoski to Peters, May 8, 1941, ACJC; UJRWRA, file 174.

61 Letter from Hayes to R. L. Zion, May 28, 1941, ACJC; UJRWRA, file 174.

62 Letter from Rabbi Fasman to Hayes, May 18, 1941, ACJC; UJRWRA, file 174.

63 Letter from Peters to Podoski, May 15, 1941, ACJC; UJRWRA, file 174; Saul Hayes diary, May 15, 1941, ACJC; UJRWRA file 174; see the letter from Rabbi Fasman to Petruska, May 16, 1941, ACJC.

In early August 1941, the Canadian government agreed to admit 200 Jewish refugees from the Far East, including 80 rabbis and yeshiva students,[64] but ultimately only 29 reached their destination. Four rabbis, 23 yeshiva students, and the widow and son of the "Chofetz Chaim" sailed on September 30, 1941, from Shanghai to San Francisco,[65] but 16 refugee rabbis and yeshiva students with Canadian visas refused to sail on the same boat for fear that they might have to fast for two whole days of Yom Kippur as the ship crossed the International Date Line. Ultimately, 51 rabbis and yeshiva students remained in Shanghai for the duration of the war.[66]

Thus, prior to the outbreak of war in the Pacific, which effectively halted all movement to and from Japan and Shanghai, a total of approximately 625–635 refugee scholars and the members of their families were able to escape from Soviet Lithuania to the Far East; about 180 of them subsequently were able to reach other destinations. Most went to the United States and the others to Canada and Mandatory Palestine. Their escape was the raison d'être of the Va'ad Hahatzala, but if we examine the sums spent by the Va'ad for transportation, it is obvious that the rabbinic rescue organization could not possibly have paid for the emigration of all the persons it claimed to have successfully resettled. During the period of January 1, 1940–December 10, 1941,

---

64 Blair, "Memorandum for File," August 9, 1941, Canadian National Archives (CNA), RG 76, vol. 441, file 673931.

65 The 80 visas were originally supposed to be distributed as follows: Mir (44), Lubavitch (9), Kletzk (6), Lublin (6), Radin (2) Bialystok (2), Telz (1), Kollel (2), and rabbis (2). When the initial arrangements were made for the first 41 scholars to sail to the United States, 16 visas were issued to students of the Mir yeshiva and the rest were distributed among the other yeshivot. Only 3 students from Mir utilized the visas, whereas all those from the other yeshivot sailed on the *President Pierce*, despite the Yom Kippur problem; see letter from Rabbi Levinson to Moses Leavitt, August 26, 1941, JDC, Va'ad Hahatzala file; Yoseph Epstein, "Yeshivat Mir," in Samuel K. Mirsky, ed., *Mosdot HaTorah Be'Eropa Bebinyanam Ubehurbanam* (Hebrew) (New York: Ogen Publishing, 1956), p. 127; letter from Birman to the JDC, New York, and the telegram of the HICEM—the acronym of the Hebrew Immigrant Aid Society and Jewish Colonization Association that merged—Shanghai, to the JDC, New York, September 30, 1941, and October 24, 1941, Archives of the Shanghai Office of the HICEM–JDC, Jerusalem (HICEM–JDC), CNA, RG 76, vol. 441, file 673931.

66 Letter from Birman to the JDC, New York, September 2, 1941, CNA, RG 76, vol. 441, file 673931. See also, for example, telegram from British Chief Rabbi Hertz to Canadian Prime Minister Mackenzie King, December 7, 1941, and letter from Blair to Podoski, December 13, 1941, CNA, RG 76, vol. 441, file 673931.

the Va'ad expended $97,052 for the transportation expenses of rabbis, yeshiva students, and the members of their families, but the costs for transporting 525 adults and 100 children from Lithuania to Japan was at least $103,500, not to mention the costs involved in the immigration of about 180 additional scholars to the United States, Canada, and Mandatory Palestine.

Therefore, it was the JDC that ultimately bore a significant portion of the transportation expenses for the rabbis and yeshiva students. In fact, about half of its expenditures of $150,000 on "the Lithuanian emigration project," were earmarked for that group, even though they constituted only about 30 percent of all the Jewish refugees who reached the Far East.[67] In fact, during the course of 1940–1941, the Va'ad was forced time and again to turn to the JDC for help in funding various expenses related to the emigration of refugee rabbis and yeshiva students,[68] despite the declared intention of the rabbis to pay all such expenses. Ironically, it was the JDC that funded the transportation of several of the most prominent rabbis who were able to emigrate from Soviet Lithuania to the United States, including Rabbi Aaron Kotler, Rabbi Mendel Zaks, and Rabbi Avraham Yaphin, and to Mandatory Palestine, such as Rabbi Eliezer Yehuda Finkel and Rabbi Shabtai Yogel.[69] The Va'ad's dependence on the JDC in connection with these individuals, whose rescue was undoubtedly considered to be among the rabbinic rescue organization's crowning achievements, clearly manifests the Va'ad's weaknesses and inability to fully achieve its primary goals.

The Va'ad's failure to fulfill its promises, which resulted in additional burdens being placed on Jewish communal fundraising agencies, was also apparent in the case of the refugee scholars who were rescued and sent to Canada. The Canadian authorities had approved the immigration of the refugee rabbis and yeshiva students only after the UJRWRA, the JDC's local affiliate, had provided the financial guarantees demanded by the government for their sustenance, a commitment it made based on promises by a number of American Orthodox organizations to provide the required funds. The Va'ad had assumed responsibility

---

67 Zuroff, *The Response of Orthodox Jewry*, pp. 195–196.
68 See, for example, memorandum from Henrietta Buchman to J. C. Hyman and Dr. Joseph Schwartz, July 7, 1941, JDC, file 360; letter from J. C. Hyman to Rabbi Albert Gordon, September 4, 1941, JDC, file 360.
69 Letter from Rabbi Simcha Wasserman to Dr. Bernard Kahn, January 19, 1942, and the response of Bernard Kahn to Rabbi Simcha Wasserman, January 22, 1942, JDC, file 360.

for the pledges made by the UOR, the Union of Orthodox Jewish Congregations, Agudath Yisrael, and Young Israel, but they only sent a total of $900 by the end of May 1942. Therefore, the UJRWRA had to expend about $10,000 for the sustenance of this group, part of which should have been paid by the rabbis.[70]

Relief for the Polish Jewish Refugees in Soviet Central Asia

The events of the autumn and early winter of 1941 posed two new challenges for the Va'ad Hahatzala. One was the plight of several hundred Polish rabbis and yeshiva students who were living under very difficult conditions, scattered in different cities in Soviet Central Asia. These were the Jews who had been arrested and deported from Soviet Lithuania during the week before the Nazi invasion, or who had been exiled by the Soviets during their occupation of Eastern Poland, or who were among the hundreds of thousands who had fled to the Russian interior during the days immediately after the Nazi invasion. The deportees who had been arrested were initially sent to labor camps, and those exiled were taken to rural settlements in Siberia and near the Arctic Circle; in both cases, the living conditions were particularly harsh.[71] Their situation changed dramatically, however, in the wake of the Sikorski–Stalin Agreement of July 30, 1941, which granted Polish citizens pardons and allowed their release from detention.[72] Thereafter, many of the Jewish refugees moved to cities in Central Asia, especially Bukhara, Samarkand, Dzhambul, Chimkent, and Kokand.[73] The rabbis and yeshiva students among them

70 Letter from Henrietta Buchman to Joseph Talamo, May 28, 1942, JDC, file 360.

71 Yoseph Litvak, *Plitim Yehudim MiPolin BeVrit HaMo'atzot, 1939–1946* (Hebrew) (Jerusalem: The Hebrew University of Jerusalem, 1988), pp. 18, 70, 128–148; Shimon Redlich, "The Jews under Soviet Rule during World War II" (PhD diss., New York University, 1968), p. 60; Dov Levin, "Arrests and Deportations of Lithuanian Jews to Remote Areas of the Soviet Union, 1940–1941," *Crossroads*, 11 (1984), pp. 85–86.

72 Litvak, *Plitim Yehudim*, pp. 171–174; Edward J. Rozek, *Allied Wartime Diplomacy: A Pattern in Poland* (New York: John Wiley, 1958), pp. 50–67. In Labor Camp No. 7, for example, three Polish refugee yeshiva students were released on August 30, 1941, whereas more than fifty others were not released until October of that year; see Alter Pekier, *From Kletzk to Siberia: A Yeshiva Bachur's Wandering during the Holocaust* (New York: Mesorah, 1985), pp. 71–78.

73 Litvak, *Plitim Yehudim*, pp. 184–185; Eliyahu Dobkin, "Report Concerning the Refugees

tried to form groups that would help them maintain some semblance of their original lifestyle. They appealed to the Va'ad Hahatzala for financial help to enable them to do so.[74]

The Va'ad's efforts to send aid to the refugee rabbis and yeshiva students in Soviet Central Asia were particularly fraught with difficulties, because the Soviet authorities had prohibited all relief efforts on behalf of the Polish refugees, except for those by the Polish Red Cross. Under those circumstances, the JDC signed an agreement in January 1942 that allowed it to send American clothing, medicines, and concentrated food to the Polish Embassy in the Soviet Union for distribution to Polish refugees through the local committees that it had established for that purpose. These committees included several Jewish leaders, who ostensibly would prevent any discrimination against the Jewish refugees.[75] The Va'ad, needless to say, refused to abide by such an arrangement, which could not guarantee that the funds it raised would go exclusively to refugee rabbis and yeshiva students, and opted for the shipment of clothing and the transfer of money directly to individual rabbis and Torah scholars.[76]

When the Va'ad launched a nationwide campaign for this cause, it aroused the anger of the JDC, which claimed that the rabbinic relief organization was duplicating its efforts on behalf of the Polish refugees in the Soviet Union and, thus, had no justification to appeal for funding to "the same sources...from which the JDC receives its contributions." However, it noted, that if the Va'ad would raise money from "their own Orthodox circles in ways that would not affect the fundraising campaigns of the communities from which the JDC receives its incomes," the JDC would not object.[77] The Va'ad countered by pointing out that since the JDC's aid was distributed on a nonsectarian basis to about 2 million Polish refugees, there was no way that the refugee Torah scholars, who had special needs, such as kosher food, could possibly receive the assistance that they required. Moreover, it reiterated that the

Arriving in Teheran," September 24, 1942, part 1, p. 1, YVA, M-2/343; Redlich, *Jews under Soviet Rule*, pp. 81–83.

74 See the invitation to the meeting, December 1, 1941, YUA, AVH.

75 Letter from Henrietta Buchman to Seligson, January 16, 1942, JDC, file 360.

76 Ibid., p. 2; "Va'ad Hahatzala," January 1942, p. 3, ACJFWF, I-69, box 150, Va'ad Hahatzala reports.

77 "Va'ad Hahatzala," Budgeting Bulletin B-13 of the Council of Jewish Federations and Welfare Funds, February 1942, pp. 3–4, JDC, Va'ad Hahatzala file.

Va'ad's goal was not only to ensure the physical survival of these groups, but also to enable them to continue their intensive Torah studies.[78]

Tensions between the relief and rescue agencies reached a boiling point in May 1942 after the JDC clearly communicated its displeasure with the Va'ad's campaign appeals to appeal to several local federations. In the words of Henrietta Buchman,

> The JDC cannot veto or approve the fund-raising campaigns of any of the separate groups, which out of an interest in special problems, desire to do a 100 percent job. We must take the position, however, that they should not appeal to the same sources for income that the JDC does and at the same time expect the JDC to carry the major part of the burden in the same area, in addition to all the other responsibilities we are called upon to shoulder.[79]

In response, Rabbi Silver asked to meet with the JDC leaders and on June 4, 1942, he and Rabbi Yisrael Halevi Rosenberg met with Joseph C. Hyman and Henrietta Buchman in New York. No transcript of that meeting has ever been found, but subsequent correspondence between the participants reveals what transpired. The rabbis accused the JDC of minimizing the Va'ad's activities and emphasized their unique assistance to the yeshivot, which was essential for their continued existence. They also accused the JDC of sabotaging the Va'ad's fundraising efforts by questioning the legality of its operations and claiming that it does not deserve the support of American Jewry.[80] In response to a letter from Rabbi Silver and Rabbi Rosenberg presenting the Va'ad's claims, the JDC threatened to respond in a manner "which would not be helpful" to the Va'ad,[81] and ultimately a compromise of sorts emerged. For the first time ever, Hyman, on behalf of the JDC, acknowledged that since his organization was incapable of meeting "in toto or 100 percent any of the

---

78 Ibid., p. 2; "Va'ad Hahatzala," January 1942, p. 3, ACJFWF, I-69, box 150, Va'ad Hahatzala reports.

79 Letter from Henrietta Buchman to Philip Bernstein (Cleveland), May 14, 1942, JDC, Va'ad Hahatzala file; see also letter from Henrietta Buchman to Joseph Talamo (Worcester), May 28, 1942, JDC, file 360.

80 Letter from Rabbi Rosenberg and Rabbi Silver to J. C. Hyman, June 9, 1942, JDC, Va'ad Hahatzala file.

81 Henrietta Buchman's handwritten notes in the margin of the letter from Rabbis Rosenberg and Silver, JDC, Va'ad Hahatzala file.

requirements that are so close to the needs and heart of Jewish life," it was understandable why organizations like the Va'ad Hahatzala deemed it necessary to launch special fundraising campaigns.[82]

Indeed, in subsequent responses to local federations regarding possible allocations to the Va'ad, JDC officials noted that the rabbinic rescue organization had

> [A] valid claim for community support, since whatever they are doing to extend aid to refugee yeshivoth and their students is done on the basis of keeping alive traditional cultural–religious institutions. The funds that they make available are over and above the sums which we are able to provide for the maintenance of needy refugees, including the yeshiva groups.[83]

At the same time, however, the JDC continued to harbor a degree of skepticism and suspicion regarding the Va'ad's operations,[84] which were most probably fueled by the inflated figures publicized by the rabbis for their fundraising appeals. For example, as late as the summer of 1942, the Va'ad was still citing the figure of 3,000 refugee rabbis and yeshiva students, whom they were trying to help,[85] which had absolutely no basis in fact. According to the Va'ad, 1,202 of the 4,000 Torah scholars whom they sought to relocate from Soviet Lithuania had managed to reach safer destinations—also a gross exaggeration[86]—which meant that "the remainder (2,798) had been evacuated to Siberia."[87] In fact, at this point in time, the Va'ad possessed the names of, **at most**, only a few

---

82 Letter from J. C. Hyman to Rabbi Rosenberg and Rabbi Silver, June 18, 1942, JDC, Va'ad Hahatzala file.

83 Letter from Moses Leavitt to George Sherman, June 25, 1942, JDC, file 463.

84 See, for example, the August 27, 1941, letter from Joseph Hyman to Rabbi Chavel and Rabbi Strull in Louisville in which he said that he had no way to check the veracity of the Va'ad's claims and advised them to make their decision based on their confidence in the leaders of the Va'ad, adding that normally the JDC would conduct an inquiry, but under the current circumstances, it was "impractical" to do so; see JDC, Va'ad Hahatzala file.

85 "Va'ad Hahatzala," Budgeting Bulletin B-13, February, 1942, p. 2, YUA, AVH; "Kriya Nilhava MiVa'ad Hahatzala" (Hebrew), *Hapardes*, 16:3 (Sivan 5702/June 1942), p. 4; "Bihiyot Veyilalot Belishkat Va'ad Hahatzala" *Hapardes*, 16:4 (Tammuz 5702/July 1942), pp. 3–4.

86 Zuroff, "*Response of Orthodox Jewry*," pp. 195–198.

87 "Va'ad Hahatzala," Budgeting Bulletin B-13, February 1942, p. 2, YUA, AVH.

hundred rabbis and yeshiva students who had relocated there.[88]

During 1943, Iran became the most important center for the shipment of aid by Jewish organizations to the Polish Jewish refugees in Soviet Central Asia. Therefore, the Va'ad sent Rabbi Yitzchak Mayer Levi of Jerusalem to Teheran as its special representative to facilitate its activities. From the very beginning of his mission, Levi encountered both logistic and ideological problems. The former was due to Iranian regulations limiting the shipment of aid parcels, and the latter prompted the objections of the Teheran representatives of the JDC and the Jewish Agency to Rabbi Levi's modus operandi. Levi was more than happy to send as many parcels as he could to refugee rabbis and yeshiva students, even if some of those individuals received multiple parcels, whereas the representative of the Jewish Agency, Dr. Moshe Yishai, objected on the grounds that, as a result of this duplication, many refugees were deprived of any assistance at all. He also claimed that many of the persons on Levi's list were not Torah scholars but were somehow connected to a rabbi or a yeshiva student and that, in certain cases, the same individual was listed at several different addresses.[89]

During 1943, the Va'ad sent a total of 3,101 packages to the approximately 900 Polish refugee rabbis and yeshiva students in Soviet Central Asia, with the largest number (1,748) sent from Teheran,[90] and the others from Mandatory Palestine (821)[91] and the United States (532).[92] In addition, the Va'ad sent $48,778 in cash to the refugee scholars to pay customs duties on the parcels and for the purchase of additional items, as well as the transportation expenses of the refugees seeking to relocate. These sums constituted approximately 50 percent of the Va'ad's relief budget.[93] By comparison, the JDC and the Jewish Agency

88 Letter from Rabbi Silver to Rabbi Chavel, June 12, 1942, JDC, file 360; telegram from the UOR (Rabbi Silver and Rabbi Rosenberg) and the deans of Polish rabbinical colleges (Rabbi Kotler and Rabbi Kalmanowitz) to Ignacy Schwarzbart, July 8 and 11, 1942 (same telegram), YVA, M-2/560.

89 Moshe Yishai, *Tzir Belo To'ar* (Hebrew) (Tel-Aviv: Tversky, 1950), pp. 150–151.

90 "Current Needs and Activities of the Va'ad Hahatzala," YUA, AVH; letter from Rabbi Levy to Rabbi Rosenberg and Rabbi Kotler, January 6, 1944, YUA, AVH.

91 Yishai, *Tzir Belo To'ar*, pp. 150–151.

92 "Va'ad Hahatzala," Budgeting Bulletin B-49 of the CJFWF, August 24, 1943, p. 2, YUA, AVH.

93 "Va'ad Hahatzala Statement of Income and Payments For Year Ending December 31, 1943," YUA, AVH; Va'ad Hahatzala, Budgeting Bulletin B-16 of the CJFWF; June 1944, JDC, file 362.

sent 6,827 parcels, at least 2,000 of which were apparently paid for by the Va'ad Hahatzala. The JDC and the Jewish Agency had originally allocated $190,000 for this project, but only about half of that sum was actually spent, because of technical and logistic problems.[94]

Relief for the Polish Jewish Refugees in Japanese-Occupied Shanghai

In the case of aid to Shanghai, the Va'ad used a legally questionable transfer arrangement to continue to make it possible for the rabbis and yeshiva students to get funds from local Jews in Shanghai, which remained a bone of contention between the rabbis and the JDC. The issue related to the American Trading with the Enemy Act, which barred the transfer of any funds to Japanese-occupied territory, including Shanghai, after the outbreak of the war in the Pacific. This development created serious difficulties for the Jewish refugees in the city, who were to a large extent dependent on assistance from the JDC. The veteran relief agency solved the problem by allowing its local representative, Laura Margolis, to take loans of $180,000 every six months from the wealthy Jewish residents of Shanghai in return for a promise of repayment in dollars by the JDC after the war.[95] The Va'ad, on the other hand, solved the problem by promising to immediately deposit equivalent sums in dollars for every cent that the Shanghai residents would give to the refugee Torah scholars. Contact between the United States and Shanghai was forbidden, so the Va'ad established a channel of communication, initially via Rabbi Aaron Milewsky in Uruguay[96] and Rabbi Wilhelm Wolbe in Sweden;[97] both countries were neutral at the time. By the summer of 1942, the Va'ad had sent $22,000 to the rabbis and yeshivot in the Chinese port city through this arrangement.[98]

---

94 "Statement of Relief Activities of the JDC for Refugees in the USSR," May 31, 1944, JDC, file 1056.

95 Moses Leavitt, "Memorandum on the Refugee Situation in Shanghai," June 17, 1942, JDC, file 463.

96 See, for example, the telegram from Rabbi Kalmanowitz to Rabbi Milewsky, January 21, 1942, YUA, AVH. Rabbi Milewsky had studied in the yeshivot of Grodno and Slobodka, and was the unofficial leader of the Orthodox community in Uruguay.

97 Telegram from Rabbi Kalmanowitz to Rabbi Wolbe, January 22, 1942, YUA, AVH.

98 Letter from Rabbi Aaron Milewsky to the Va'ad Hahatzala, October 23, 1942, Rabbi Aaron Milewsky's private archive.

During 1943, the rabbis reimbursed a total of $90,709.70, which had been given to the refugee rabbis and yeshivot, a sum that enabled the scholars to continue their regimen of intensive Torah study, despite the worsening economic conditions and the forced transfer of all the stateless Jewish refugees to a ghetto in the Hongkew quarter of the city in May 1943. It should be noted that the assistance provided by the Va'ad was over and above the relief that they received as Polish Jewish refugees from the JDC, and thus the average refugee rabbi and yeshiva student received approximately $20 a month—three-quarters of which was arranged by the Va'ad—whereas the other Polish Jewish refugees in Shanghai received only $5 a month, all from the JDC.[99]

This discrepancy, as well as the fact that the rabbis and yeshiva students in Central Asia who were receiving parcels and/or cash from the Va'ad Hahatzala were also the recipients of the assistance that was financed by the JDC and the Jewish Agency, made the Va'ad's demands for funds from local federations and welfare funds a continuing source of anger and frustration for the JDC leaders in New York. This situation became even worse in the latter half of 1943,[100] in the wake of the Va'ad's harsh criticism of the JDC's ostensible inability to help the Jews who were being assisted by the rabbis, which the Va'ad claimed was only possible because of its own innovative relief methods.[101] The JDC tried very hard to discourage federations and welfare funds from allocating funds to the Va'ad by reiterating three basic accusations: the Va'ad was duplicating what the JDC was already doing far more successfully than the Va'ad; the Va'ad's methods were either illegal; and/or the rabbis' claims of success were figments of their imaginations. In letter after

---

99   Laura Margolis, "Report of Activities in Shanghai, China, from December 8, 1941, to September 1943," JDC, file 463. The calculation is based on the following statistics: The approximately $90,000 raised by the Va'ad was distributed to 500 persons over a period of twelve months. Assuming that the level of aid provided by the JDC to the Polish refugees in Shanghai from their arrival remained approximately the same, those assisted by the rabbis received four times as much money as their nonobservant counterparts.

100 David Kranzler, *Japanese, Nazis & Jews: The Jewish Refugee Community of Shanghai* (New York: KTAV, 1975), pp. 456–485, 489–504.

101 See, for example, the letters from Sidney Cohen (Boston), David Watchmaker (Boston), and Max Bretton (Kansas City) to the JDC, July 2, 6, and 26, 1943, respectively, JDC, file 361; letter from J. C. Hyman to Rabbi Wohlgelernter, September 16, 1943, ACJFWF, I-69, box 150; letter from J. C. Hyman to Butzel (Detroit), June 11, 1943, JDC, Va'ad Hahatzala file.

letter to local community leaders, JDC officials stressed that all the relief programs in the Soviet Union were nonsectarian, that cash transfers to the refugees in Central Asia were not effective, and that American relief agencies were forbidden to communicate with people in enemy territory like Shanghai. In other words, the Va'ad's claims of assisting thousands of refugees in Central Asia and hundreds in Shanghai were bogus or, if accurate, had been achieved in violation of Soviet regulations and/or U.S. laws, steps that the JDC staunchly opposed.[102]

Although the frustration of the JDC officials regarding the Va'ad's inflated claims of successes was justified, the arguments they used to discourage allocations to the Va'ad were not entirely honest. For example, the JDC began sending parcels directly to Jewish refugees, which the Va'ad had proven to be a successful means of helping the Polish Jewish refugees in distress.[103] Another misleading claim was that of the sum of $400,000 cited by JDC officials as having been allocated for aid to Central Asia, less than half of which was actually spent due to technical and logistic problems.[104] In the case of the financial assistance arranged for the refugees in Shanghai, the JDC implied that if the rabbis' claims were accurate, they must have been in violation of American laws, but legally that might not have been the case, at least with respect to the transfer of funds, since no money was ever actually sent from the United States to Japanese-occupied territory. In fact, the JDC was doing exactly the same thing, but with one major difference. Whereas Laura Margolis took loans from wealthy Jews in Shanghai in return for a promise of repayment after the war and did not maintain any contact with JDC headquarters in New York,[105] the rabbis did maintain communication with Shanghai and deposited funds immediately to facilitate the loans taken by the rabbis and yeshiva students there. Furthermore, whereas the JDC claimed that the funds sent to Shanghai by the Va'ad were merely

102 See, for example, letter from Henrietta Buchman to Pearlstein, March 8, 1943, JDC, file 423; letter from J. C. Hyman to David Watchmaker, July 9, 1943, JDC, file 361.

103 See, for example, the letter from Moses Leavitt to Mrs. Stameshkin (St. Paul), May 7, 1943, JDC, file 361; letter from Henrietta Buchman to Saloman (Tulsa), May 25, 1943, JDC, file 423.

104 See, for example, letter from Moses Leavitt to *Hapardes* magazine, May 26, 1943, JDC, file 361; "Mr. James N. Rosenberg's Statement to the Emergency Administrative Committee Meeting Held on Tuesday, June 8, 1943," JDC, file 423; "Statement of Relief Activities of the JDC for Refugees in the USSR," May 31, 1944, JDC, file 1056.

105 Laura Margolis, "Report of Activities in Shanghai, China from December 8, 1941, to September 1943," JDC, file 463.

supplementary to those provided by Laura Margolis,[106] the truth was, as far as the rabbis and yeshiva students were concerned, just the opposite.

In summation, the relations between the Va'ad Hahatzala and the JDC during the slightly more than four years reviewed in this essay illuminate four major issues that faced the American Jewish relief and rescue organizations during the Holocaust—communal unity, rescue priorities, rescue tactics, fundraising strategies, and organizational credibility—all of which proved to be sources of deep conflict between the rabbis and their JDC counterparts. Due to the ideological roots of the positions taken by both groups and the fact that Jewish lives were at stake, it was extremely difficult to reach compromise solutions, but there were instances of practical cooperation on some rescue projects. To the JDC's credit, it never threatened to refrain from assisting rabbis and yeshiva students in order to try and force the Va'ad to stop its fundraising efforts to attain monies from federations and welfare funds. To the Va'ad's credit, it was willing to use Shanghai permits obtained for Torah scholars to save nonobservant Jews stranded in Vladivostok, who were facing the threat of expulsion back to Soviet Lithuania, and to pay for their passage to Shanghai.

It is clear, however, that the existence of the Va'ad did focus far more public attention on the plight of the refugee rabbis and yeshiva students than would have been the case otherwise and, as a result, more individuals from this group were ultimately rescued than would have been had the Va'ad not been established. The success in obtaining the eighty Canadian visas for rabbis and yeshiva students is, for example, one clear accomplishment that can be attributed to the Va'ad's activities. However, we will never be able to ascertain the following: What would have been the impact of a decision by the leaders of the Va'ad Hahatzala to disband their organization and join forces with the JDC? What impact would such a step have had on the issues of rescue priorities and the policies adopted vis-à-vis American regulations that hindered Jewish relief and rescue operations. Under these circumstances, it is difficult to judge the protagonists in this chapter of Holocaust history.

At the same time, it is important to note that during the period reviewed in this article, the differences of opinion between the rabbis of the Va'ad and the leaders of the JDC were also reflected in the realm of

---

106 JDC comments regarding CJFWF bulletin on Va'ad Hahatzala, August 11, 1943, CJFWF reports, ACJFWF, I-69, box 149.

politics. Whereas both agencies ostensibly dealt exclusively with relief and rescue activities, their "parent" organizations were active in the American Jewish political arena and, as could be expected, very rarely saw eye to eye on critical issues. Even in the wake of the revelations in late 1942 of the scope of the murder of Jews by the Nazis and the plan for the annihilation of European Jewry, attempts to unite the community for political action invariably were short-lived.[107]

In January 1944, two dramatic developments were to further complicate the relations between the Va'ad Hahatzala and the JDC. On January 5–6, 1944, the Va'ad announced at its annual conference that it was officially expanding its mandate to attempt to save all Jews, regardless of religiosity or affiliation and, on January 22, 1944, President Roosevelt announced the establishment by the U.S. government of the War Refugee Board, a special agency to attempt to rescue potential victims of the Nazi regime.[108] These two events significantly influenced the relations between the two American Jewish relief and rescue organizations, but they did not change the basic pattern of fundraising competition and begrudged rescue cooperation between them, which had evolved from the beginning of World War II. [109]

107   Zuroff, *Response of Orthodox Jewry*, pp. 219–238.
108   Ibid, p. 273.
109   Yehuda Bauer, *Jews for Sale? Nazi-Jewish Negotiations 1933–1945* (New Haven and London: Yale University Press, 1994), pp. 196–251; Zuroff, *Response of Orthodox Jewry*, pp. 273–287.

Religious Perspectives Interpretations and Acts

Jewish Unity, Disunity, and Assigning Blame for the Holocaust

GERSHON GREENBERG

T he explanations for the Holocaust by Jewish thinkers, which also address responsibility and blame for the catastrophe, disclose different views about the solidarity of the nation.[1] Some held that the People of Israel were inherently united, and they responded to the catastrophe in unitive terms. They spoke of collective suffering, innocence, culpability, and the failure of mutual responsibility or of collective participation in a cosmic, kabbalistic drama. Others did not assume that unity was inherent. To the contrary, Jewry had split apart. Some Jews had separated themselves in such a radical manner from authentic Judaism as to have strengthened the enemy. Those who separated themselves included assimilationists, *maskilim* (proponents of the Haskalah movement[2]), secular Zionists, and Jews who resisted *aliya* (immigration to *Eretz Israel*). In some instances, thinkers, such as Shlomo Zalman Ehrenreich, Yissachar Shlomo Teichtal, and Hayim Yisrael Tsimerman, were inclined in both directions, depending upon the issue at hand.[3] The language used by them blended history with metaphor and metahistory, and metahistory with ontological categories.

---

1   My study does not include responsa literature, which constitutes a separate desideratum. Michal Shaul writes that the *mevo'ot* (authors' introductions) to rabbinic responsa literature of the Holocaust almost never focused on any particular sin that brought the disaster about, nor do they blame specific groups, e.g., Zionists or secularists. See Michal Shaul, *Pe'er Tahat Efer: Hahevra Haharedit BeYisrael Betzel Hashoah, 1945–1951* (Hebrew) (Jerusalem: Yad Yitzhak ben Tzvi and Yad Vashem, 2014), p. 75.

2   The Haskalah movement—the Jewish Enlightenment—is an intellectual movement that emerged at the end of the eighteenth century and early nineteenth century in Europe that sought to further the integration of Jews in western society, while at the same time renewing the spiritual and cultural aspects of Jewish society and preserving a distinct Jewish identity.

3   The Scriptural passage that serves as a foundation of the theme of unity and mutual responsibility is Leviticus 26:3–7.

Suffering

Polish Hasidic thinkers and individual representatives of the *Musar* (ethics)[4] school addressed Israel's suffering in collective terms. They did not distinguish between Jews who suffered and those who did not. They also set matters of blame and sinfulness aside and focused instead on offering consolation. Hasidic *Admorim* [5] blended the suffering with dark reality—but one with implications for illumination and ultimately for *geula* (redemption) itself. The *nekuda penimit* (inner sacred spark) both drew light from and contributed to the *Shechinah* (Divine presence, associated with light). The turmoil of empirical history with its agonies constituted a separation between the *nekuda penimit* and the *Shechinah*, so that time–space existence was surrounded by a dialectical relationship between the individual Hasid and the cosmos. In turn, that dialectic moved linearly, from dark suffering toward messianic salvation. As the interchange between the *nekuda penimit* and the *Shechinah* intensified and historical events became more and more absorbed into the dialectic, the *Admorim* held that the darkness would recede and there would be progress toward *geula*. The relationship between the spiritual (light) and material (darkness) and suffering was nondual: the spiritual emerged from within the material and through it, over time, the material would become increasingly sublimated into the spiritual.

The *Admor* of Bobov, Bentsion Halberstam, tied the plight of the Jews who had been expelled from Germany before the *"Kristallnacht"* pogrom to God. The perpetrators' malice was beyond comprehension in terms of natural behavior and so could only be ascribed to God. Insofar as the plight was under Divine aegis and God's intentions were ultimately for the good, the descent into darkness necessarily meant that illumination and Israel's ascent toward *geula* would follow. The *Admor* called upon fellow Jews to plead to God and to act benevolently, so that their *nekuda penimit* would interact with the *Shechinah* and assist in advancing salvation. The *Admor* of Gur, Avraham Mordechai Alter, responded to the suffering of the People of Israel by urging Jews

---

4   The Musar Movement was a moralistic movement of Orthodox Judaism founded by Israel Salanter in Lithuania in the early nineteenth century.

5   *Admor*, an acronym in Hebrew for *"Adonenu, Morenu Verabenu"* (our master, our teacher, our rabbi), is the leader of a Hassidic community and a scion of a dynasty of *Tzadikim* (righteous men) who led communities of Hasidim for generations.

to draw from the *nekuda penimit* by observing Torah and trusting in the *Shechinah*. This would lessen the distress and enable participation in the advent of the Kingdom of Heaven.[6]

In the Warsaw ghetto, the Piaseczner, Rebbe Kalonymous Kalman Shapira, instilled his sermons with the theme that God's sacred light filled the entire universe, illuminating the smallest detail. The good was present in the bad, and holy sparks were present within the agonies of the profane ghetto. He also sought to explain how individual suffering could be lessened. Finite human suffering was incomparable to God's infinite suffering over His people's plight. Shapira beseeched his listeners to dwell on the suffering of God, trusting that this would ease their pain. As the ego would become diminished and the *Shechinah* would grow, the tribulations of the self would subside.[7] The metahistorical drama of illumination articulated by the Hasidim did not include any distinction between Jews who suffered and Jews who did not. When some Jews suffered, the whole of Israel suffered.

There were also *Musar* thinkers who addressed the collective pain of their people. Culpability and sinfulness were marginal concerns. The head of the Telz (Telšiai) Yeshiva, Avraham Yitzhak Bloch, focused on the tragic situation in Telšiai brought on by the invading Germans and their Lithuanian collaborators. He sought to instill *bitahon* (trust and confidence) in God. *Bitahon* reflected consciousness of the Divine, Who was present in historical events. The certainty that God was present and, thus, that the suffering would be for the good, instilled endurance on a spiritual level. *Teshuva* (repentance), prayers, and charity fostered *bitahon*.[8] In Jerusalem, the head of the Hevron yeshiva, Yehezkel Sarna, identified a higher, ontological triad composed of *din* (judgment), *teshuva*, and *geula* guided by *hesed* (benevolent love) and *rahamim* (compassion). The three interacted with one another dialectically. They were also evident across the path of Israel's history: God had sowed the

---

6   Gershon Greenberg, "Hasidic Thought and the Holocaust, 1933–1947: Optimism and Activism," *Jewish History*, 27:1 (2013), pp. 26–52.

7   Kalonymous Kalman Shapira, *Sefer Esh Kodesh: Imrot Tehorot Mishenot Hashoah 5700, 5701, Ve 5702, Shene'emru Beshabatot VeY[om]T[ov] Begeto Varsha Hadeviya* (Hebrew) (Jerusalem: Va'ad Hasidei Piaseczno, 1960).

8   Gershon Greenberg, "Holocaust and Musar for the Telšiai Yeshivah: Avraham Yitshak and Eliyahu Meir Bloch," in Alvydas Nikžentaitis, Darius Staliūnas, and Stefan Schreiner, eds., *The Vanished World of Lithuanian Jews* (Amsterdam and New York: Rodopi, 2004), pp. 223–261.

seed of *geula* during the *hurban* (destruction) of the ancient Temple in Jerusalem. The Holocaust—also referred to as the *hurban*—was the manifestation of *din*, which would be followed by the *ikveta dimeshiah* (onset of the messiah)—the manifestation of *rahamim*. God allowed for the Holocaust, Sarna believed, as a way to induce *teshuva*—although he did not identify specific sins. Because the despair over suffering was so deep, God would enter the heart of each Jew in an act of *siyata dishmaya* (with the help of Heaven) and open it for *teshuva*. *Teshuva* aligned the suffering people below with the transition process above, from *hurban* to *geula* through *teshuva*.[9] Here, too, the people were presumed to be in unity, so that the suffering of some Jews meant that the people as a whole suffered.

Innocence

Another unitary mindset posited an Israel–Gentile nations dualism with Jewry being collectively innocent. The enemy (the non-Jew) was the culprit, not the Jew. In May–June 1943 in Jerusalem, Mizrahi leader Shlomo Zalman Shragai wrote that Israel bore no blame whatsoever for the bloody strife. Jews neither caused nor contributed to it. Any focus on *teshuva* as a response to the persecution was wrong. For that matter, *teshuva* was an activity that belonged solely and directly to God and the People of Israel. It was not mediated by any outside force, such as inducing *teshuva* by persecuting Israel. Indeed, *teshuva* was not the issue. Shragai rejected the notion that it was up to the Jews to take self-corrective action to bring an end to the crisis and stop the bloodthirst and cannibalism. The nations, not Israel, committed the crimes—and it was for them to rectify themselves.[10] Shlomo Zalman Ehrenreich in Şimleul Silvaniei, Transylvania, held that the nations of the world, as descendants of Esau, were inherently evil and intent upon hurting the Jews. He cited Levi Yitzhak of Berdichev.

9   Yehezkel Sarna, *Liteshuva Velitekuma: Devarim Shene'emru Bekinus Lemasped Uteshuva Shehitkayem Ba'ir Biyeshivat Hevron Keneset Yisrael Beyom 18 Kislev 5705* [December 4, 1944] (Hebrew) (Jerusalem: Tevunah, 1945).
10   Shlomo Zalman Shragai, "Hamashber Haruhani Shebiyamenu," in Shragai, *Tahalihei Hatemura Vehageula* (Hebrew) (Jerusalem: Mossad Harav Kook, 1959), pp. 184–185. See also Shragai, "Bemabul Damim," in *Bametzar: Lishe'elot Hazeman* (Hebrew) (Tel Aviv: Haberit Ha'olamit Litenu'at Torah Ve'avodah—Mazkirut Hano'ar, 1942), pp. 10–26.

Were the intentions of the evil ones to tyrannize the People of Israel and destroy the Temple, in order for the *mitzvot* [commandments] of the Creator to be carried out, it would be conceivable that they should not be punished. But their intentions were purely malicious and solely evil. Had God not decreed anything, they would still be evil and they still would have brought suffering. They were inherently both stupid and evil. [For example] had their intention been to follow the will of God, they certainly would have allowed the people to do *teshuva*—and not force Israel to violate His *mitzvot*.[11]

Sinful Culpability

There were also Orthodox thinkers who focused on the sins, not on the innocence, of the People of Israel in collective terms. Given the oneness of Jewry, whatever transgressions existed infected the nation as a whole. Writing in Piestany and Budapest during 1942–1943, Yissachar Shlomo Teichtal pointed to the ongoing internal enmity and fragmentation that had overtaken Jewry. God had endowed the nation with a sacred unity. The People of Israel constituted a soul, Hayim Halberstam wrote, and every part of the body was crucial to it. The people were enjoined by God to reject all sectarian and societal disparateness as alien to their true nature. In ancient times, dissension brought about the destruction of the Temple, a source and symbol of unity. Over the generations, assimilation coupled with obliviousness to *Eretz Israel*—where unity was uniquely possible—evoked Divine punishment. In modern times, assimilation shattered unity. The Holocaust was, in part, the eventual consequence of the dismemberment of the nation—presumably because it made Israel vulnerable. There could be no remedy for Israel's suffering until all Jews would join together and return to Jerusalem— the center of unity under God.[12]

11 Levi Yitzhak of Berdichev, "Kelalut Hanisim," in *Kedushat Levi Al HaTorah* (Hebrew) (Lublin: n.p., 1926), pp. 77–84; Shlomo Zalman Ehrenreich, "Ma She'amarti Beshabat Hol Hamo'ed Pesah 5699 [April 8, 1939]," in *Sefer Derashot Lehem Shlomo* (Hebrew) (Brooklyn: Y. Katz, 1975), pp. 128–129; Ehrenreich, "Bo" in *Even Shlomo Al HaTorah* (Hebrew) (Jerusalem: Keset Shlomo, 1962), pp. 7–8.

12 Hayim Halberstam of Sanz, "Hashma'ut Leparashat Re'eh," in *Divrei Hayim* (Hebrew) (Kraków: Y. Fisher, 1892), p. 230; Yissachar Shlomo Teichtal, *Em Habanim Semehah* (Hebrew) (Jerusalem: Mahon Peri Ha'aretz, 1983), pp. 242–265. For an English

As with other Polish Hasidic thinkers, Abraham Heschel viewed historical events in terms of sacred illumination and profane darkness. In 1943 in Cincinnati, Ohio, where Heschel had found refuge from war-torn Europe, he described a world in which "snakes" were sending their "venom" into the bloodstream of humanity—bringing paralysis, numbing nerves, and dulling the mind. The difference between good and evil was blurred, force was worshipped, and compassion held in contempt. Raw appetite ruled; greed, envy, and unrestrained will for power reigned. God was defied and abandoned, and sanctity was at the brink of death. The People of Israel, as a collective, shared in the eclipse of the sacred, and Heschel called upon Jews to assume their rightful office as "ministers of the sacred," and to welcome God back into their lives. Upon doing so, their sacred inner sparks would effectuate changes in the tragic condition of history.[13]

Eliyahu Eliezer Dessler, in Gateshead, England, and in Bnei Brak as of 1947, wrote that Jews, as a unit, were called upon to instill the objective, ontic morality that pervades the God-imbued universe into their subjective realm. Instead, they assimilated into Western European culture, dissipating morality to the point of creating a void in the world— the Holocaust. Dessler called for *teshuva* and for utilizing the suffering as a means of purification so as to fill the void with ethical life. *Teshuva* on the subjective level, he believed, would restore the objective–subjective nexus in terms of morality and even lead to *geula*.[14]

Irresponsibility

A further reflection of unity held that Jews were responsible for one another—not only in the present but cross-generationally. In the wake of the *"Kristallnacht"* pogrom, Eliezer Gershon Fridenzon in Łódź, editor of the journal *Beit Ya'akov*, wrote that persecution was punishment for failure to abide by the principle that "All Israel are guarantors for

translation of this essay, see Teichtal, *Em Habanim, Semeha* (Jerusalem: Kol Mevaser, 2000), http://israel613.com/books/ERETZ_EM_HA_BANIM-ENG.pdf (accessed May 11, 2022).

13 Abraham Heschel, "The Meaning of this War: 'Either You Accept the Torah or Be Crushed,'" *Jewish Weekly*, 8 (July 14, 1943), p. 1.

14 Eliezer Schweid, "An Ethical Theological Response to the Holocaust as It Was Evolving: The Teachings of Rabbi Eliahu Eliezer Dessler," *Henoch*, 17:1–2 (1995), pp. 171–196.

each other."[15] This included the Jews' responsibility for the sins of other Jews—predominantly for the current sin of assimilation. The Nazis served as the instrument of Divine punishment for the failure of this responsibility.[16]

In Petah Tikvah, Chief Rabbi Reuven Katz evoked the biblical narrative of a corpse by an unknown slayer that was discovered near a certain city.[17] The city's elders assumed responsibility and sacrificed a heifer lest the innocent blood be borne by all the People of Israel. In this vein, Katz wrote that the Holocaust atoned for earlier and ongoing (unspecified) sins. The 6 million killed were a collective *Akedat Yitzhak*[18] sacrifice in which righteous Jews atoned for the trespasses of their predecessors.[19]

In Tel Aviv in 1947, Hayim Yisrael Tsimerman explained that should a sin be so serious that the appropriate punishment was more than any individual could absorb, the punishment would overflow to the nation as a whole. He also cited Rambam, noting that a pious person was guilty of trespass if that person stood by and let an evil individual do as he wished.[20] For example, Tsimerman offered, if one witnessed a household member sinning, one was obliged to intervene, and if one did not, one was liable.[21] Before the Holocaust, pious Jews failed to take responsibility for the transgressions of other Jews.[22]

The Cosmic Aspect

For some, the unified experience of the People of Israel also had a cosmic context—that of the Lurianic Kabbalah about collective suffering, sinfulness, and responsibility in collective terms. Sins took the

---

15 Numbers Rabbah 10:5.
16 Eliezer Gershon Fridenzon, "Nokh Alets Farblendinishn" (Yiddish), *Beit Ya'akov*, 16:153 (1938–1939), p. 1.
17 Deut. 21.
18 Isa. 57:1.
19 Reuven Katz, "Parashat Behukotai: Sevel Yisrael Ugeulato," in Katz, *Sefer Duda'e Re'uven: Derushim Uve'urim Al Hamisha Humshe Torah* (Hebrew), vol. 2 (Israel: Hotza'at Hasfarim Ha'eretz Yisraelit, 1954), pp. 72–78.
20 Hilchot Deah 51, Halacha 7.
21 Shabbat 54a, 55b.
22 Hayim Yisrael Tsimerman, *Tamim Po'alo: She'elot Uteshuvot Bidevar Hahashmada Ha'ayuma Shel Shishah Milyon Hayehudim, Hashem Yinkom Damam* (Hebrew) (Jerusalem: Beit Hayitomim Diskin, 1947).

form of *klippot*—shards that were dispersed upon the shattering of the vessels containing Divine light at the beginning of creation. *Mekubbalim* (kabbalists) who responded to the Holocaust differed as to whether the sinful content of the *klippot* belonged to the People of Israel or to the enemy. For Rabbi Aaron "Areleh" Roth and Yehiel Meir Morgenshtern, the sins were committed by Jews. For Ya'akov Moshe Harlap, the *sitra ahra* (negative being), the enemy, was able to infect the People of Israel with the *klippot*. According to these thinkers, whatever defects existed within Israel were a collective matter, even if only some individuals had trespassed.

Rabbi Aaron "Areleh" Roth, who fled Beregszasz, Hungary, for *Eretz Israel* in 1939, held that over time the sparks within the Jewish soul had become trapped in *klippot* of materialism, egoism, and immodesty. The suffering of the Holocaust was a painful process of purifying souls, of sifting the sparks within the *klippot*. It was also inevitable: God's plan for Creation included the trials of the People of Israel. Jews would have to pass through *Gehinnom* (netherworld), he wrote, before they could enter *Gan Eden* (Garden of Eden). The souls currently on trial included those of earlier generations that had yet to atone and had transmigrated, which are referred to as *gilgulim* (transmigrations of souls). The sifting included a return to the *emunah peshuta* (pristine faith) of Abraham, where the ego was annulled and replaced by the *Shechinah*. With the sifting process coming to an end, *geula* was now imminent. Accordingly, the *tikkun* (mending) was underway on a massive scale. As the suffering of Jewish people is part of a transgenerational *tikkun*, it is to be viewed as ultimately for the good.[23] The motif of *gilgulim* was also employed by Tsimerman. *Geula* required the purification of souls of all generations. Reportedly, there was a Jewish population explosion in the interwar years, which Tsimerman interpreted to mean that all the unrectified souls had transmigrated and were being purified with the bodily suffering of the Holocaust.[24]

For Ya'akov Moshe Harlap, head of the Merkaz Harav Yeshiva in Jerusalem, the *klippot* that were dispersed upon the creation of the world

---

23 Gershon Greenberg, "R. Areleh Roth: Pristine Faith Through Holocaust to Redemption," *Journal of Modern Jewish Studies*, 14:1 (2015), pp. 72–88. Aaron "Areleh" Roth, *No'am Halevavot* (Hebrew) (Satmar: Meir Leb Hirsch, 1934), p. 21b; Roth, *Shomer Emunim* (Hebrew) (Jerusalem: Eshkol, 1942), pp. 4a, 102a/b, 117a/b, 225a; Roth, *Kunteres Hatzava'ah* (Hebrew) (Jerusalem: Horeb, 1947), p. 23b.

24 Tsimerman, *Tamim Po'alo*.

became included in the *sitra ahra*, the "other," negative being. Jewish souls were never sinful[25]—if sinful *klippot* did envelop them, they were imposed from the outside—for example, when persecution led to a loss of faith. However, the messianic process was now underway and the sparks of Israel were being sifted. In the first stage, that of the messiah son of Joseph, Divine light would enter the world, separating history into light and darkness. (Had light entered all at once, the encounter would have shattered historical reality). Divine illumination struggled against the *sitra ahra*. The *sitra ahra*, sensing the imminent advent of Torah-filled *geula* and thus its own annulment, assaulted the People of Israel as the advent's vessel. However, as the People of Israel were the only source that fueled the *sitra ahra*, the assault was self-destructive. Harlap also identified the *klippot* among the People of Israel with the physical (but not sinful) body. At the moment a Jew was slaughtered during the Holocaust, the soul burst forth and its spark ascended and adhered to the *Shechinah* of the messiah son of Joseph. It would then ascend further into the fully illuminated redeemed universe of the messiah son of David.[26]

In London in 1947, Yehiel Meir Morgenshtern, a great-grandson of Menahem Mendel of Kotsk, who had escaped Poland in 1939, wrote that over the generations the *klippot* that had been dispersed upon the cataclysmic creation of the world became the sins of Israel. Sacred sparks from the macrocosmic head of *Adam Kadmon* (primordial man) had been enveloped by the *klippot* and they descended together until they landed in the heavy darkness and thick materiality of the feet. As sacred sparks were indestructible, the descent went no further. Instead, the sparks became sifted and reversed course for a radical ascent. The violence of the reversal was the Holocaust.[27]

---

25 Zohar Vetosafot 3:42b.

26 Gershon Greenberg, "The Holocaust Apocalypse of Ya'akov Mosheh Harlap," *Jewish Studies*, 41 (2002), pp. 5–14.

27 Yehiel Meir Morgenshtern, "Hakdamah," in Ya'akov Arieh Guterman, *Bikurei Aviv: Al Seder Parshiyot HaTorah* (Hebrew) (London: Narod Press, 1947), pp. 5–12; Gershon Greenberg "Jewish Mysticism (Kabbalah) Through the Holocaust," in Sara Horowitz, ed., *Lessons and Legacies, Vol. 10: Reexamining Perpetrators, Victims and Bystanders* (Evanston: Northwestern University Press, 2012), pp. 37–67.

Divisions among the People of Israel

A different set of responses to the Holocaust reflected internal national division, whether retroactively, actualizing a potential, or de novo. Some Jews held that others had separated themselves from the true religion and thus shared responsibility for the suffering. Those responses focused on cultural assimilation, the Haskalah movement, and failure to make *aliya*.

Cultural Division

Leading up to and following the "*Kristallnacht*" pogrom, Lithuanian and Polish Jewish thinkers tied the disaster to assimilationist Jews. Some correlated and associated assimilation with persecution, whereas as others drew a causal relationship. They all invoked the motifs of Divine aegis and measure for measure punishment. In Telšiai, Lithuania, in October 1938, Avraham Yitzhak Bloch, head of the yeshiva, wrote that to suggest that Germany, a country feared by the world for its military prowess, was so apprehensive of Jews that it was compelled to attack made little sense. The reason had to lie elsewhere. Jews should have kept their "*geza*" (cultural–racial identity) and religion separate from others. Instead, they denied their religion and tried to ingratiate themselves and become absorbed into German culture. God intervened to rein in the attempt and did so by allowing radically nationalist Germany, ever poised to annihilate the Jewish enemy, free to attack. The assault was measure-for-measure.[28]

In Vilna (Vilnius), on May 31, 1939, Hayim Ozer Grodzinsky, who shared the leadership of Eastern European Haredi Judaism with his brother-in-law Elhanan Wasserman, upon learning of the life-threatening plight of the Jews, who were stranded on the German–Polish border, and the burning of houses of learning and Torah scrolls, pointed to the coincidence between assimilation and Reform Judaism in Western Europe, and the persecution and expulsion that was then spreading eastward.[29] In Łódź, Eliezer Gershon Fridenzon attributed the tragedies surrounding the "*Kristallnacht*" pogrom to a punitive reaction coming

---

28 Avraham Yitzhak Bloch, "Otot Me'et Hahashgaha," *Dos Judisze Togblat* (Yiddish) (1938), pp. 8–10.

29 Hayim Ozer Grodzinsky, "Hasdei Hashem Azkir," in Grodzinsky, *Sefer Ahi'ezer* (Hebrew), vol. 3 (Vilna: Sh. P. Garber, 1939), preface.

from God to the sins of Reform Jews. They had immersed themselves in German society, thinking that by assimilating they would become as secure as the Germans themselves. They tore themselves from their Jewish roots so they could serve the "Moloch" of German culture, with all its scientific study and art, "blindly dancing a devil's dance of Jewish denial."[30]

In Warsaw, Alexander Zisha Frydman distinguished between Jews dwelling in the realm of Torah (of "fire") and the realm of Esau–Amalek dwelling in the non-Torah realm (of "water"). Assimilators removed the wall of separation, whereupon God allowed water to drown out the fire, and it did so in terms of measure for measure suffering.[31] For these thinkers, the self-separation of a portion of the people through assimilation split the nation apart, whether by actualizing a potential disunity or creating one. Albeit indirectly—for it was God who allowed the assault—it was the assimilators who were responsible for Israel's troubles.

The division that manifested itself between the assimilators, with their indirect responsibility for the persecution, and those who regarded themselves as authentic Jews continued into the war. In Bratislava, Shlomo Zalman Unsdorfer, the de facto leader of the Orthodox community after Akiva Sofer left in 1940, identified a range of measure for measure punishments set off by assimilation: When Jews decided to do away with their traditional garb, the enemy forced them to wear patches of yellow stars. Following their participation in Christmas celebrations, Jews were compelled to remain indoors during the holiday.[32]

In Brooklyn, New York, the Lubavitcher Rebbe Yosef Yitzhak Schneersohn went further and positioned Jewish assimilators alongside the Nazi perpetrators. Whereas Jewish assimilators denied election of Divine chosenness, German Nazis prided themselves on being the chosen people who were too holy to share the same planet with the "pathetic" Jews, who had to be destroyed. The ensuing destruction was measure for measure and under Divine aegis. The *Admor* declared that "Jewish Nazism" had torn Israel's special status asunder. It was as insane and barbaric as "superior" German Nazism. Only God knew, he wrote

---

30 Fridenzon, "Nokh alets farblendinishn," p. 1. Fridenzon died in the Warsaw ghetto.

31 Aleksander Zisha Frydman, "Hasina Layehudim," in Frydman, ed., *Ketavim Nivharim* (Hebrew) (Jerusalem: Moreshet Sofrim, 1960), pp. 51–55; Frydman, "Sirtutim venitsotsot," in Frydman, *Ketavim Nivharim*, pp. 156–157.

32 Gershon Greenberg, "Shlomo Zalman Unsdorfer: With God Through the Holocaust," *Yad Vashem Studies*, 31 (2003), pp. 47–74.

on January 6, 1943, how much blood would be poured before German-pride Nazism would destroy Jewish self-degrading Nazism.[33]

The Haskalah Movement

The Haskalah movement was its own source of categorical division. Elhanan Wasserman, a leading exponent of the *Da'at Torah* principle—whereby Torah is the fundamental program of the universe and the inner essence of each Jew—identified the Haskalah movement as a reprehensible Jewish activity related to the decline and descent that was to precede the advent of the messiah. It was a "stupid" attempt—Wasserman spelled *Haskalah* with the letter *samech* instead of the correct *sin*, to mean "stupidity"—to emulate the nations with the byword of "We will be as the nations,"[34] and to "Be a Jew at home and a man abroad."[35] As the Torah foundation crumbled within, violating God's separation of Israel—"And have set you apart from other people that you should be Mine"[36]—nations reacted from without by expelling and murdering Jews. This was under Divine aegis: "In that you say, we will be as the nations....Not [so] at all. Surely with a mighty hand and with an outstretched arm and with fury poured out."[37] In the summer of 1939, Wasserman accused the advocates of the scientific study of Judaism—historian Heinrich Graetz, theologian Abraham Geiger, and historian of the Oral Law Isaac Hirsch Weiss—along with unnamed authors of modern Hebrew literature, of cultivating the "Torah of Satan."[38]

---

33 "Unzere Fier Rosheshones: Nissan, Ellul, Tishrei, Shevat," *Hakriya Vehakedusha* (Yiddish), 3:29 (February 1943), pp. 8–10, https://hebrewbooks.org/pdfpager.aspx?req=12162&st=&pgnum=8 (accessed April 25, 2022). On exclusion, see Adam S. Ferziger, *Exclusion and Hierarchy: Orthodoxy, Non-Observance and the Emergence of Modern Jewish Identity* (Philadelphia: University of Pennsylvania Press, 2019).

34 Ezek. 20:32.

35 This is a famous dictum by Moses Mendelssohn; see Lionel Kochan, "Mendelssohn: True or False Prophet," *European Judaism: A Journal for the New Europe*, 19:20 (1985), pp. 41–45.

36 Lev. 20:26.

37 Ezek. 20:32–33.

38 Elhanan Wasserman, *Ma'amar Ikveta Dimeshiha Uma'amar al Ha'emuna: Ah Belaykhtung fun der Yetstiger Tekufa* (Yiddish) (New York: n. p., 1938); Wasserman, "Torah Megina Umitzale" (Hebrew), *Kol Yisrael*, 19:33 (1939), p. 2; Gershon Greenberg, "'Da'at Torah Neged Amalek: R. Elhanan Vaserman," in Binyamim Brown and Nissim Leon, eds., *Hagedolim: Ishim She'itsvu Et Penei Hayahadut Hahareidit BeYisrael* (Hebrew)

In Tel Aviv, Chief Rabbi Moshe Avigdor Amiel identified a divinely set metahistorical dualism between the nations of the world and Israel. He accused Moses Mendelssohn and the *maskilim* who followed him of violating the separation. By seeking absorption into European culture, by replacing Jewish identity with a quest for equal rights, and by setting any land that they happened to be in as a land of Scripture above *Eretz Israel*, they breached their protective perimeter, which created an opening for the nations to burst into the realm of Judaism with their hatred.[39]

Yosef Yitzhak Schneersohn also targeted the *maskilim*. The *teshuva* expected by God and required to alleviate the suffering of exile, which had resulted from sins in *Eretz Israel*, did not take place. The *maskilim*, who abandoned the Torah altogether, brought the failure to a head. When they sought to integrate themselves into modern civilization, they were greeted by the Angel of Death. The satanic nation of Germany set out to annihilate Jewry, armed with a whip provided by the Jews themselves. Schneersohn correlated the Haskalah drivel—declaring war against the Torah and faith—with the nonsense of Hitler's *Mein Kampf*. The assault, under Divine aegis, was measure for measure: "The Haskalah [movement] prompted the Torah's destruction and inscribed a *Mein Kampf* for Jews, while Hitler's *Mein Kampf* advertised how he would destroy the Jews."[40]

Secular Zionism

A division also manifested itself between secular Zionist and Orthodox Judaism. Orthodox thinkers correlated and drew a causative relation between secular Zionists and European persecution. In 1937–1938, Elhanan Wasserman, head of the Yeshiva Ohel Torah-Baranovich, alleged that the transgression of Torah by secular Zionists in *Eretz Israel*, including the settlement of the land by force, presumably by defying

(Jerusalem: Magnes Press, 2017), pp. 209–233.

39 Gershon Greenberg, "Rabbi Moshe Avigdor Amiel's Religious Response to the Holocaust," in *World Congress of Jewish Studies Proceedings* (Jerusalem: World Union of Jewish Studies, 1984), pp. 93–100.

40 "Bakent Zich mit der 'Himlisher Tochter,'" *Hakriya Vehakedusha* (Yiddish), 3:26 (1942), pp. 14–15; "Bakent Zich mit der Tzivilizatzie," *Hakriya Vehakedusha*, 3:34 (1943), pp. 11–13; "Farvos G–t B"H Shvaygt!" *Hakriya Vehakedusha*, 3:29 (1943), pp 11–12; "Zeman Herutenu," *Hakriya Vehakedusha*, 2:19 (1942), pp. 8–11.

the British, in violation of the three oaths,[41] amounted to a declaration of war against Torah. God would respond against them in kind. The Mizrahi and Poalei Agudath Yisrael movements, which were affiliated with the Zionists, were also at fault. All were enemies of Torah. Indeed, they belonged to the realm of Amalek, whom they internalized. The absence of Torah within Israel objectified itself in the form of the Nazi assault from the outside.[42] In Bnei Brak, Moshe Sheinfeld, a disciple of Elhanan Wasserman, wrote that secular nationalists created a chaos within Judaism, which attracted Nazi aggression. Zionists also failed to help Torah-true Jews escape from Europe.[43]

Wasserman's view was echoed by Shlomo Zalman Ehrenreich, a devotee of anti-Zionist Hayim Elazar Shapira of Mukačevo (Munkács). Although he distinguished collectively innocent Israel from the evil nations of the world, he condemned the Zionist, anti-Torah developments in *Eretz Israel*, and the Mizrahi and Agudath Yisrael movements that associated with Zionist organizations. He specified the transgressions: violating the *shmita*—the commandment to leave the land fallow every seven years;[44] mingling of woman and men in public; wearing clothing that left parts of the body uncovered; raising children as heretics; and violating the rabbinic proscription against settling *Eretz Israel* by force,[45] that is, in opposition to the British. All this angered God and brought the punishment of the European catastrophe. Ehrenreich feared that

41 Ketuvot 111a. The three oaths are that Israel should not forcibly break the wall to enter the land of Israel; Israel should not rebel against the nations; and the nations should not excessively oppress the people of Israel in the Diaspora.

42 Wasserman, *Ma'amar Ikveta Dimeshiha*, p. 25. On *Ketuvot* 111a, see Shlomo Aviner, "Be'irurim Be'inyan Shelo Ya'alu Kehoma" (Hebrew), *No'am*, 20 (1980), pp. 2–28; Greenberg, "'Da'at Torah' Neged Amalek," pp. 209–233.

43 Sheinfeld translated Wasserman's book *Ma'amar* into Hebrew and wrote an introduction to it, which was published in parts in several issues of *He'atid*; see Wasserman, "Ikveta Dimeshiha" (Hebrew) *He'atid*, 4 (1939), p. 3; *He'atid*, 5 (1939), p. 3; *He'atid*, 6 (1939), p. 3; *He'atid*, 7 (1939), p. 2; *He'atid*, 9 (1939), p. 2; *He'atid*, 12 (1939), p. 3; *He'atid*, 13 (1939), p. 2; *He'atid*, 14 (1939), p. 3; Moshe Sheinfeld, "Ha'am Beyaguno, Hamanhigim Bepisham…Vehamaskanah," *Haderech*, 13 (1942), p. 4; Sheinfeld, "Hamosifim Het Al Pesha" (Hebrew), *Haderech*, 15 (1943), p. 3; Sheinfeld, "Di Gedolei HaTorah Hobn Dos Vort" (Yiddish), *Di Vokh*, 7 (1947) p. 2; Sheinfeld, "Uvaharta Behayim" (Hebrew), *Diglenu*, 2 (1946), pp. 2, 11. On the issue of *Shmita*, see Arye Edrei, "From Orthodoxy to Religious Zionism: Rabbi Kook and the Sabbatical Year Polemic," *Dinei Israel: Studies in Halakhah and Jewish Law*, 26–27 (2009–2010), pp. 45–145.

44 Exod. 23:11.

45 Ketuvot 111a.

1937–1938 would be filled with murderous activity—the Hebrew letters for 5968 (1938), *tav-resh-tzadi-het,* are also the letters for "murder." According to his son-in-law, Hillel Likhtenshtayn (Lichtenstein), during his internment in a ghetto near Şimleul Silvaniei prior to deportation to Auschwitz, Ehrenreich paced back and forth, sobbing "The Zionists alone brought this on."[46]

Yosef Yitshak Schneersohn, who considered secular nationalism a response to the Jews' rejection by European nationalists, condemned the Jewish Agency in Mandatory Palestine for tearing Jewish children away from Poland and away from their religion to make their way to *Eretz Israel* via Teheran. What would happen next in *Eretz Israel?* Would Torah scrolls be torn apart? Jewish scholars burned to death? Cemeteries desecrated? Schneersohn coupled the Nazis' burning Jewish bodies in lime kilns in Europe with the burning of Jewish souls by the Yishuv (Jewish settlement in *Eretz Israel* prior to 1948) nationalists.[47]

Finally, while the Mizrahi Movement was being criticized by Wasserman and Ehrenreich, the Mizrahi leader, Chief Rabbi Moshe Avigdor Amiel of Tel Aviv, drew comparisons between secular Zionists and non-Jews. Both wanted to live in a land devoid of spiritual meaning and to speak a language and observe a weekly day of rest devoid of sanctity. Ultimately, Amiel contended, the secular Zionists were out to abandon God and anything sacred—as Hitler was doing. The nationalist "*mitzvah*" of assimilation opened a path for latent hatred against Jews to take effect. To stop it all, Amiel proposed a set of Nuremberg-like laws to restore Jewish identity in the *Yishuv* by setting boundaries.[48] Another

---

46 Shlomo Zalman Ehrenreich, *Kol Yisrael Saba* (Hebrew) (Shamloh: Dafus Zahav, 1939); Hillel ben Baruch Lichtenshtein, "Hakdamah," in *Shu"t Kavanat Halev* (Hebrew) (New York: A. Y. Friedman, 1966), p. viii.

47 Yosef Yitshak Schneersohn, "Divrei Ha'admor MiLubavitsh" (Hebrew), *Kol Yisrael,* 19:34 (1941) p. 1; Schneersohn, "Mimechtivei Admor Shlita [to Ya'akov Klatzkin]" (Yiddish), *Hakriya Vehakedusha,* 33 (1943), pp. 9–14; Schneersohn, "Ofener Brief fun Admor Shlita," *Hakriya Vehakedusha,* 35 (1943), pp. 6–7; Schneersohn, "Ah Brief fun Admor Shlita," *Hakriya Vehakedusha,* 36 (1943), p. 3; Schneersohn, *Di Reyd fun Kavod Kodsho Admor Harav Yosef Yitshak Shlita Shnayrson, 11 Merts 1944* (Yiddish) (New York: Merkaz Hayeshivot Tomhei Temimim, 1945); Schneersohn, *Sihot…Yeshivot Tomhei Temimim Lubavitsh, 7 Mai 1941* (Hebrew) (New York: Merkaz Hayeshivot Tomhei Temimim, 1944). On the Teheran children, see *Yaldei Teheran Ma'ashimim: Odot Gezel Haneshamot Hana'aseh Al Yaldei Hasochnut Be'Eretz Yisrael* (Hebrew) (New York: Yidishe Shtime, 1944).

48 Moshe Avigdor Amiel, "Veha'aretz Ezkor" (Hebrew), *Hayesod,* 9:296 (1940), pp. 1–2;

Mizrahi leader, Shlomo Zalman Shragai, also coupled nonreligiosity in *Eretz Israel* with the tragedy in Europe and compared the mass desecration of the Sabbath by members of Kibbutz Dalia and the immolation of millions of European Jews who died in the sanctification of God's name.[49]

Accordingly, secular Zionists were accused of separating themselves from Judaism to the point of turning against it. They pulled their adherents away from authentic—that is, Torah—Judaism; generated Nazism; provoked God into punishing Jews by means of European persecution; and, in their own way, mirrored Nazi profanity and its burning of Jewish bodies.

Generators of Pathological Hatred

Avraham Yitzhak Bloch and Alexander Zisha Frydman held that non-Jewish animus and Jewish assimilation combined to foment disaster. A number of Orthodox thinkers probed the details of this dynamic. In America, Joseph Eliyahu Henkin of the Ezras Torah relief society in New York and Mordechai (Martin) Schwartz of Cleveland elaborated on the disastrous consequences of Jewish intrusion into non-Jewish society. At the end of 1939, Henkin wrote that non-Jews were like "animals of prey"—with a raw antagonism toward Jewry that sooner or later would burst out into attack. Assimilation provided pretext and provocation. The non-Jewish world did not look kindly on Jewish attempts at emulation. On the contrary, he said, non-Jews were convinced that Jewish assimilation was an underhanded maneuver to sabotage Christianity from the inside, while Jews were enriching themselves materially and advancing politically. Henkin accused Reform Jewish leader Stephen S. Wise in particular of provoking a hatred so deep that it would devour all of Israel. Jews who were ready to trade their chosen

---

Amiel, "Sakanat Hahitbolelut Be'Eretz Yisrael," *Hayesod*, 15:353 (1942), p. 2; Amiel, "Al Hanisim," *Hayesod*, 10:340 (1941), p. 3.

49 Shlomo Zalman Shragai, "In Pustn Roym: Nokh di Tenz in Daliya" (Yiddish), *Di Yidishe Shtime*, 2:2 (1947), pp. 2, 8; Shragai, "Ayropeisher Kinus fun Mizrahi Torah Veavoda in Antverpm," *Di Yidishe Shtime*, 2:19 (1948), p. 2; Shragai, "Orah shel Mashiah: Im Tekumata shel Medinat Yisrael," *Di Yidishe Shtime*, 2:33 (1948), p. 8. Avraham Yitzhak Bloch also associated nationalism in *Eretz Israel* with the troubles in Europe; see Bloch, "Otot Me'et Hahashgaha," pp. 8–10.

status for the "pot of lentils"[50] of foreign culture were bringing nothing but persecution.[51] Schwartz was convinced that the People of Israel, both the observant and the nonobservant, would continue to be hated. However, had they not assimilated, there would not have been such an outburst of hatred. Every attempt to assimilate by Reform Jews and others—whether by neglecting the Sabbath, kashrut (Jewish dietary laws), family purity, or Torah study; by rushing into the professions; or by pursuing university degrees—backfired. The current hatred, deeper than any before, was resulting in the theft of Jewish property, beatings, and, ultimately, concentration camps.[52]

In Tel Aviv, Chief Rabbi Moshe Avigdor Amiel described how the animosity toward Israel was traceable to the conflict between Jacob and Esau. It ran through Amalek and continues into the present. Nevertheless, it would have stayed within non-Jewish bounds and not reached Judaism had secular Zionism and the Haskalah movement not created an opening through which the contempt would pass.[53] Shlomo Zalman Ehrenreich cited Levi Yitzhak of Berdichev, declaring that the nations were evil, and were out to injure the Jews and to attack them, regardless of whether or not God used them as instruments to restore the People of Israel to their authentic selves. In February 1939, a transport of Jews from Grosswardein (Oradea) passed through Şimleul Silvaniei. The passengers had swastikas burned on their faces, their fingernails ripped out, and their fingers bitten off. How could such inhuman cruelty, especially in cultured Germany, be explained? Ehrenreich cited Rabbi Moses Hayyim Efraim of Sudlikov's *Degel Mahaneh Efraim*,[54] noting that Esau could not take over the world and rule harshly as long as Jacob's voice was that of the Torah. He claimed that German and Austrian Jews had turned to other cultures and abandoned the Torah. He pointed specifically to intermarriage, declaring that once Esau took

50 Gen. 25:31–34.

51 Joseph Eliyahu Henkin, "Sinat Ha'umot" (Hebrew), *Hamesila*, 4:11/12 (1939), pp. 4–6; Henkin, "Itzumo Vekiyumo shel Yisrael Ve'amim," *Hamesila*, 6:2 (1940), pp. 2–4; Henkin, "Ten Li Yavne Vehahameha" (Yiddish), *Di Yidishe Shtime*, 1:1 (1940), p. 15.

52 Mordekhai Tzvi (Martin) Schwartz, "Yafeh Liyemei Hateshuvah Ulehol Et," in *Derushei Hohmah Veda'at* (Hebrew) (St. Louis: Quality Printing, 1940), pp. 163–169.

53 Greenberg, "Rabbi Moshe Avigdor Amiel's Religious Response to the Holocaust," pp. 93–100.

54 For the English translation, see Moses Hayyim Ephraim of Sudlikov, *Rabbi Moses Hayyim Ephraim of Sudlikov's Degel Mahane Ephraim* (Ann Arbor: University of Michigan, 1986).

over, there was no distinction between pious and impious Jews, citing Metzudat David on Isaiah 10:5.[55]

Jews Who Refused to Make *Aliya*

Another group alien to Orthodox thinkers, which they held responsible for the catastrophe, was made up of Jews who refused to make *aliya*. As explained above, Yissachar Shlomo Teichtal maintained that Jewish unity was essential for *geula*. This was possible only in *Eretz Israel*, where Jews could unite around adherence to the *mitzvah* to settle the land, a *mitzvah*, he added, equal in importance to all the other *mitzvot* taken together. Over the generations, God punished the people for their indifference toward settlement, but this failed to incentivize their return. God now brought the Holocaust, and Jews had no choice but to make *aliya*—lest they die. Mandatory Palestine was the only refuge; every other country closed its gates. Teichtal focused on those Orthodox who waited passively for God to act and bring them to *Eretz Land*. It was owing to them, he concluded, that pure Jewish blood was being poured in Europe.[56]

Others asserted that God brought the Holocaust as a way to create a new and fresh generation—one ready and able to make *aliya* en masse. Aharon Petshenik, a nephew of the *Admor* of Belz Yissachar Dov Rokeach, citing Abraham ibn Ezra on Exodus 14:13, wrote that the Israelites who were liberated from Egypt had so internalized their slavery that they had to turn to God before counterattacking the Amalekites. In order for there to be a generation with the self-confidence needed to take *Eretz Israel*, God let the older males die out in the desert.[57] In Tel Aviv, Hayim Yisrael Tsimerman wrote that the *geula* had already begun when *Eretz Israel* began to flourish before the war, citing Ezekial

---

55 Efraim Misudylkov, *Degel Mahaneh Efraim* (Hebrew) (Warsaw: N. Shriftgiser, 1883), p. 14a; Ehrenreich, "Ma Shedarashi Beyom Alef Parashat Tetsaveh" in *Sefer Derashot Lehem Shlomo*, pp. 283–285; Gershon Greenberg, "Shlomo Zalman Ehrenreich's (1863–1944) Religious Response to the Holocaust: February 1939–October 1943, Şimleul Silvaniei, Transylvania," *Studia Judaica*, 9 (2000), pp. 65–93.

56 Teichtal, *Em Habanim, Semeha*, pp. 21–32, 41–56.

57 Aharon Petshenik, "Oyfn Eretz Yisrael Front" (Yiddish), *Der Mizrahi Veg*, 5:1 (1941), p. 3; Petshenik, "Golus im Geula," *Der Mizrahi Veg*, 8:6 (1944), pp. 5, 13; Petshenik, "Al Hanisim ve'al Haniflaot," *Der Mizrahi Veg*, 6:1 (1941), pp. 6, 16; Petshenik, "Der Mizrahi oyf Shaydeveg," *Der Mizrahi Veg*, 8:3 (1946), pp. 7–13.

36:8. When Jews failed to ascend en masse, God let the generation die off so that a new and more capable one would replace it. Tsimerman attributed the Holocaust to the single trespass of not making *aliya* in time.[58]

In Mexico City, the Aleppo-born Jerusalem kabbalist Mordekhai Atiyah wrote that over the course of 1,900 years of exile, the sparks that had dispersed with the shattering of the vessels at creation had descended into deep darkness. The tension between the *klippot* of the shattered vessels and the sparks within them reached an explosive point in the present world. The explosion was the Holocaust. Once it began, he added, citing Yalkut Shimoni, Remez 432, there was no distinction drawn between the pious and the impious. As Jews made their way to *Eretz Israel*, many sparks were sifted out of the *klippot* and, together with the *Shechinah*, which had accompanied the people into exile, returned to *Eretz Israel*. Many pious Jews, whose sparks were required for the advent of the messianic era to follow the Holocaust catastrophe, nevertheless resisted *aliya* and in so doing delayed the *geula*, leading Atiyah to conclude that another Holocaust would follow. Then, any Jew who did not make *aliya* would descend into oblivion.[59]

Conclusion

Most of the thinkers cited herein, including Halberstam, Teichtal, Fridenzon, Amiel, Bloch, Frydman, Schneersohn, Wasserman, Ehrenreich, Petshenik, and Tsimerman, maintained that enemy nations acted as instruments of Divine intervention. Given the Orthodox commitment to God's oversight and instrumentalization of history and metahistory, could the disunity have been part of a plan for higher unity? Could the identification of assimilators, *maskilim*, secular Zionists, and those who resisted making *aliya* as alien "others" belong to a higher Divine plan for collective Israel, namely, to bring the alienation to the surface so that it could be overcome? Was self-separation a divinely set, dialectical prelude to greater unity? Perhaps.

However, the direct reading of the sources indicates that Orthodox

---

58 Tsimerman, *Tamim po'alo*.

59 Gershon Greenberg, "Mordekhai Yehoshua Atiyah's Kabbalistic Response to the Holocaust," *Iggud*, 2 (2008), pp. 72–99.

Jewish thinkers, who successfully steered religious thought throughout the Holocaust, wavered between unitive and divisive dispositions. Those who deliberated in unitive terms viewed the suffering as a collective experience; held Jewry as either generally innocent or generally guilty; as failing to attend to one another's religious derelictions; or as pertaining to an all-inclusive cosmic drama. Others were prone to identify division. Whether they believed that divisiveness was inherently potential in Judaism or that it surfaced de novo with the Holocaust, the division not only existed but existed to the point that those to whom the Orthodox were opposed were deemed to have been serving the enemy.

Requests for Atonement in Responsa Literature
Complex Dilemmas regarding Jewish Solidarity during the Shoah[1]

MOSHE TARSHANSKY

"Because of the wrongs of your brother Jacob, shame will cover you."[2]

"Esau has to be ashamed of causing the sons of Jacob to do wrong."[3]

esponsa literature has accompanied the Jewish people for generations.[4] The limitations of using this literature for historical research, as already discussed,[5] are due mainly to the purpose of writing responsa literature, which was not meant to serve as a historical source but rather as a guideline for the study of Halacha (Jewish law) and to establish legal precedent for future rulings. For this reason, basic historic details are missing from the responsa, such as the names of the people involved, dates, names of places, etc. Without these details it is not possible to draw a clear and full picture of the historical events that were a basis for the halachic discussion. However, despite the fact that responsa writings

---

1   This study is dedicated to the blessed memory of my father, my teacher, Isaac W. Tarshansky, deceased in March 2021, who taught me right from wrong and greatly assisted me in my research, translating and advising. His knowledgeable comments are embedded in this article as well.
2   Obad. 1:10.
3   As opposed to the simple interpretation that Esau should be ashamed for the crimes that he inflicted on Jacob, Rabbi Shimon Efrati quoted one of the commentators; see Rabbi Shimon Efrati, *Migey Hahariga* (Hebrew) (Jerusalem: Yad Vashem, 1961), p. 30.
4   For a general discussion of responsa literature, see Menachem Elon, *Jewish Law: History, Sources, Principles*, vol. 3 (Philadelphia and Jerusalem: The Jewish Publication Society and Hamilton Printing, 1994), pp. 1453–1528.
5   Haym Soloveitchik, *Shut Kemakor Histori* (Hebrew) (Jerusalem: Shazar Center and Hebrew University, 1990).

lack a historical approach, there are many historical details within the lines and between them that may be utilized in research.

Even during the Shoah, people continued to ask questions, and rabbis continued to respond, in spite of the difficult conditions that made proper study and discussion impossible. The subjects on the agenda were issues of life and death, subjects that traditionally required the rulings only by the leading rabbis, which were presented to the rabbis who were available then, regardless of their position in the rabbinical hierarchy. These rabbis had to address the questions without the possibility of consulting other rabbis, in many cases without books and sources for study, without the peace of mind that is necessary for dealing with momentous subjects, and sometimes under time constraints that did not allow for sufficient thought. As Rabbi Zvi Hirsch Meisels wrote,

> How can I give a clear halachic ruling…during the time that the Temple was intact a question of life and death such as this would be presented to the Sanhedrin [supreme court of sages], and I am here in Auschwitz without any reference book for Halacha and without other rabbis and without peace of mind due to the many hardships and troubles.[6]

Presumably, the material available to us covers an infinitesimal fraction of the issues discussed at the time, since many of the rabbis and the questioners did not survive, and their discussions were generally oral and were not recorded in writing.

Among the works available to us in the genre of the Shoah responsa, the work with the widest scope and the best known is the work of Rabbi Ephraim Oshry *Questions and Responsa from the Depths*, which includes 112 questions and replies, originally published in Hebrew in five volumes during the years 1959–1978.[7] Rabbi Oshry was imprisoned in the Kovno ghetto, and was one of the few who managed to hide and survive during the German retreat in the summer of 1944. After the liberation, he

---

6   Rabbi Zvi Hirsch Meisels, *She'elot Utshuvot Mekadeshei Hashem* (Hebrew), part 1 (Chicago: International Printing, 1955), preface, "Sha'ar Mahamadim," letter C, p. 8.

7   Rabbi Ephraim Oshry, *She'elot Ut'eshuvot Mima'amakim* (Hebrew), parts 1, 2 (New York: Modern Linotype Co., 1959, 1963); parts 3, 4, 5 (New York: Modern Linotype Co. and Gross Bros. Printing Co., 1968, 1975, 1978); Ephraim Oshry, *Responsa from the Holocaust* (New York: Judaica Press, 1983).

served as the rabbi of the community of survivors until summer 1945.[8] Other rabbis who wrote responsa books regarding the Shoah were Rabbi Meisels and Rabbi Shimon Efrati.[9] There are also isolated responsa of other rabbis, which were not published in separate collections devoted to this specific subject. The material in this field has been compiled in the CD *Responsa of the Shoah.*[10]

8   Rabbi Ephraim Oshry thereafter headed a yeshiva for young Holocaust survivors in Rome and later in Montreal. He then became the rabbi of a congregation in New York. For more regarding his biography, communal activity, and literary works, see Moshe (Moss) Tarshansky, "The Communal Activity of Rabbi Ephraim Oshry and the Importance of His *Responsa Mima'amakim* for the Development of a Religious Historiographical Narrative of the Holocaust" (PhD diss., Bar-Ilan University, Ramat Gan, 2016). Regarding the authenticity and level of historic accuracy of his writings, see Tarshansky, "The Writings of Rabbi Ephraim Oshry of the Kovno Ghetto: Orthodox Historiography?" *Yad Vashem Studies*, 47:1 (2019), pp. 59–103.

9   Meisels, *She'elot Utshuvot Mekadeshei Hashem*, part 1; Meisels, *She'elot Utshuvot Mekadeshei Hashem* (Hebrew), part 2 (New York: Deutsch Printing and Publishing Co., 1967); Efrati, *Migey Hahariga*; Efrati, *Me'emek Habaha* (Hebrew) (Jerusalem: Mossad Harav Kook, 1948). Regarding these writings, it should be noted that Rabbi Meisels, who was born in Hungary in 1902 and served there as a rabbi, collected responsa of European rabbis who were murdered in the Shoah. Actually, these are not responsa written during the Nazi occupation. A great majority of them were written before the Holocaust or during the war, before the Nazis conquered the towns in which the responding rabbis lived. Only in Meisels, *She'elot Utshuvot Mekadeshei Hashem*, part 1, preface, "Sha'ar Mahamadim," does the author quote several questions that he was asked mainly while he was in Auschwitz, and their major importance is that these are practically the only questions and responsa from the extermination camps. After the liberation, he served as rabbi of the survivors in the British zone in Germany and later as a rabbi of a community in Chicago. It should also be noted that Rabbi Efrati, who was born in Galicia in 1908 and served as a rabbi in Poland and Serbia, was exiled to Russia during the war, and therefore the questions that he deals with are not from the period of the Nazi conquest but deal with the consequences of the Holocaust, which he dealt with as a rabbi in Warsaw after the liberation. Later he came to Israel and served as a rabbi in Jerusalem.

10   Rabbi Yitzhak Gutman, ed., *Shut Hashoah* (Hebrew), CDs 1 and 2 (Alon Shevut: Mahon Netivei Hahalacha—Torah Databases, 2006 and 2012); see online, https://www. responsa-holocaust.com (accessed April 26, 2021). The quotations from the Holocaust responsa literature quoted in this article, as well as the biographies of the rabbis, are based on this online version, unless otherwise noted. For a literary review of this database, see Isaac Hershkowitz, "Holocaust Responsa Project," *Holocaust Studies: A Journal of Culture and History*, 15:3 (2009), pp. 97–99. Mention should also be made of the collection of Holocaust responsa collected by the journalist Itamar Levin; see Itamar Levin, *Otiyot Shel Esh: Eduyot Mitkufat Hashoah Basifrut Hahilhatit* (Hebrew), expanded 2nd edition (Tel Aviv: Miscal, 2002).

Historical research regarding the Shoah neglected the subject of religious life for many years.[11] Only in the 1970s was the subject dealt with by researchers. Among the first to publish books on the subject were Hirsch Jakob Zimmels[12] and Irving J. Rosenbaum.[13] Additional books were published later, including the books by Esther Farbstein[14] and Yehezkel Lichtenstein,[15] as were various articles.[16] These researchers emphasized the halachic aspect, the observance of the Jewish commandments, both in the domain of commandments between man and his Creator, such as the observance of the Sabbath and abstaining from eating non-kosher food, and in the domain of man and his fellow. They focused on the halachic questions relevant to the Shoah, as well as on questions raised after the liberation, which dealt with its consequences. A central issue posed during the Shoah, which many researchers have addressed, involved the German orders that the Judenräte submit lists of Jews for deportation,[17] a

11 For a discussion of this subject, see Dan Michman, "Research on the Problems and Conditions of Religious Jewry Under the Nazi Regime," in Israel Gutman and Gideon Greif, ed., *The Historiography of The Holocaust Period: Proceedings of the Fifth Yad Vashem International Historical Conference* (Jerusalem: Yad Vashem, 1988), pp. 737–748.

12 Hirsch Jakob Zimmels, *The Echo of the Nazi Holocaust in Rabbinic Literature* (New York: Ktav, 1977).

13 Irving J. Rosenbaum, *The Holocaust and Halakhah* (New York: Ktav, 1976).

14 Esther Farbstein, *Hidden in Thunder: Perspectives on Faith, Halachah, and Leadership during the Holocaust*, 2 vols. (Jerusalem: Mossad Harav Kook, 2007); Farbstein, *Hidden in The Heights: Orthodox Jewry in Hungary during the Holocaust*, 2 vols. (Jerusalem: Mossad Harav Kook, 2014).

15 Yehezkel Shraga Lichtenstein, *Vehasne Einenu Ucal: Sugyot Miyemei Hashoah Biri Hahalaha* (Hebrew) (Jerusalem: Yad Vashem, 2015); Lichtenstein, *Ve'emunatha Baleylot: Sugyot Miyemei Hashoah Biri Hahalacha* (Hebrew) (Jerusalem: Carmel, 2017). It should be noted that Lichtenstein does not approach the subject as a historian but from the viewpoint of a researcher of the Talmud who concentrates on the rabbinical considerations regarding the rulings.

16 An early article on the subject was published by Rabbi Yosef Šafran; see Yosef Šafran, "She'elot Halacha Biyemei Shoah Vehurban Be'Eropa" (Hebrew), *Sinai*, 64: 1–6 (1969), pp. 190–198. For additional articles see, for example, Meir Eyali, "Sifrut Hashut Mitekufat Hashoah" (Hebrew), *Bitzaron*, 11: 49–51 (New Series) (1992), pp. 131–141. Bitzaron has a new series and appears with that designation.

17 See, for example, Yosef Nedava, "Ba'ayot Hahalacha Bageta'ot" (Hebrew), *Dapim Leheker Hashoah*, (Series A) (1979), pp. 44–56; Farbstein, *Hidden in Thunder*, vol. 1, pp. 185–223; Pnina Feig, "Pesikat Rabanim Be'inyan Selektzia Bitkufat Hashoah" (Hebrew), *Shana Beshana*, (1991), pp. 321–340; Moshe Tarshansky, "'Metim Behufsha' Tehushat Klu'ei Geto Kovna Kenidonim Lamavet Vehishtakefuta Bifsikat Hahalacha," in Michal

question that Trunk defined as a "particularly grave dilemma,"[18] which in some cases was referred to rabbis. Another primary issue that the postliberation responsa contended with was that of *agunot*—women whose husbands were missing but no proof of death was available.[19]

However, it appears that there is an area of questions involving both periods, which did not receive the adequate attention of researchers.[20] These are questions posed to rabbis generally after the liberation by people who sought the proper way of repentance and atonement for sins committed during the Shoah. Study of these questions reveals a variety of halachic and moral dilemmas with which the questioners were confronted due to the Shoah and its consequences. Many of their questions and the rabbis' responses also illustrate issues regarding Jewish solidarity during the Shoah.

The questioners wished to know if they were in need of atonement for actions that they had taken, and if so, they wanted clear guidance regarding specific acts of repentance that would lead to the desired atonement. It should be noted that traditional Jewish thought focuses on the inner–spiritual aspect of repentance and demands recognition of the sin, including regret, and commitment to refrain from committing the transgression again in the future.[21] However, during the height of the Ashkenazi Hasidim period,[22] a new approach was developed,[23] calling

Ben-Ya'akov, Gershon Greenberg, and Sigalit Rozmarin, eds., *Hakayitz Hanora Hahu…: 70 Shana Lehashmadat Hakehilot Hahayehudiot Be'arei Hasade Belita* (Hebrew) (Jerusalem: Michlelet Efrata, 2013), pp. 53–65; and Zimmels, *The Echo*, pp. 49–51.

18 Isaiah Trunk deals at length with the various approaches of the Judenräte and of rabbis who confronted this issue; see Isaiah Trunk, *Judenrat: The Jewish Councils in Eastern Europe Under Nazi Occupation* (New York and London: Macmillan and Collier-Macmillan, 1972), pp. 420–433. Zimmels too claimed that this was the most difficult dilemma that they faced; see Zimmels, *The Echo*, p. 49.

19 See, for example, Farbstein, *Hidden in Thunder*, vol. 1, pp. 365–392; Tehila Darmon-Malka, "'Our Unfortunate Sisters, the Daughters of Israel': Holocaust-Survivor Rabbis Confront the Problem of Post-Holocaust 'Agunot,'" *Yad Vashem Studies*, 47:1 (2019), pp. 143–173.

20 Eyali partially dealt with it; see Eyali, "Sifrut Hashut Mitekufat Hashoah," pp. 134–135.

21 See for example Maimonides, *Mishne Torah: Sefer Hamada*, Hilchot Teshuva 2: 2.

22 The thirteenth century, during which Rabbi Judah the *Hasid* and his student Rabbi Elazar of Worms and other rabbis were active.

23 Yitzhak Ber and others suggested that these means of repentance are an innovation that reached Judaism through Christian influence; see Yitzhak Ber, "Hamegama Hadatit Hahevratit Shel 'Sefer Hasidim'" (Hebrew), *Zion*, 3 (1938), p. 18; Efraim Elimelech Urbach, *Ba'alei Hatosafot: Toldoteyhem, Hibureyhem Veshitatam* (Hebrew) (Jerusalem:

also for acts of atonement named *Teshuvat Hamishkal*, which required a person to inflict pain upon himself as a means of compensating for any pleasure gained by way of sin. Some demanded explicit forms of asceticism, such as immersion in ice water or sitting on ant nests. However, the focus was usually on days of fasting and, in cases of grave sins, tens of days of fasting were demanded.[24] Actually, the rabbis in the modern period took different approaches to this issue. In addition to stressing that inner feelings of repentance are the core of atonement, some demanded acts of asceticism and fasting as a means of waking and purifying one's heart and soul, and also as a means of being saved from punishment,[25] while others refrained from these measures for various reasons and emphasized only inner repentance and strengthening devotion to Torah.[26]

Mossad Bialik, 1956), p. 326; and Yosef Dan, *Sifrut Hamusar Vehadrush* (Hebrew) (Jerusalem: Keter, 1975), p. 131.

24 Dan, *Sifrut Hamusar Vehadrush*, pp. 129–133; Ya'akov Elboim, *Teshuvat Halev Vekabalat Yisurim: Iyonim Beshitot Hateshuvah Shel Hahmey Ashkenaz UPolin, 1348–1648* (Hebrew) (Jerusalem: Magnes, 1993), pp. 11–17.

25 In a case of a man who had sexual relations with a married woman, Rabbi Yehezkel Landau, who was born in Poland in 1713 and served as rabbi in Prague, ruled that fasting is secondary to repentance but "exoneration without any is not possible," therefore, the man should fast for two days per week for six years; see Rabbi Yehezkel Landau, *She'elot Utshovot Noda BiYehuda: Mahadura Kama, Mahadura Tinyana, Teshuvot Nosafot: Ora Hayim* (Hebrew) (Ashkelon and Netanya: Mif'al Noda Bi'Yehuda, Mahon Yerushalayim, 1993), § 35. Rabbi Moshe Sofer, who was born in Frankfurt in 1762 and served as a rabbi in Pressburg (Bratislava), wrote that whoever had a forbidden sexual relation should observe forty to sixty fasts to be saved from punishment; see Rabbi Moshe Sofer, *Hatam Sofer, Ora Hayim: She'elot Utshovot*, part 1 (Hebrew) (New York: E. Grossman's Publishing House, 1958), § 173. Rabbi Moshe Feinstein, who was born in Russia in 1895 and immigrated to the United States before the Holocaust, where he was considered a central religious authority in his time, wrote that it is proper that a woman who had done ugly deeds of hugging and kissing before her wedding and then repented should do acts of repentance, "which are absorbed in the inner body and soul." In fact, he did not specify acts of asceticism for her, because of her obligation to her husband and to raising her children for which she needed good health and strength of body and soul. He ruled that it is sufficient for her to read Psalms and to recite the *Vidui* (confessional prayer); see Rabbi Moshe Feinstein, *Sefer Igerot Moshe: Ora Hayim*, part 4 (Hebrew) (Brooklyn: Noble Book Press, 1982), § 117. It should be noted that the sources quoted in this article from the responsa literature, which is not from the Holocaust period, and the biographical sketches of those authors, were taken from the *Proyekt Hashut* database (Hebrew), issued by Bar-Ilan University.

26 Rabbi Avraham, the brother of the Vilna Gaon who lived in Vilna in the eighteenth century, emphasized only repentance and increase of Torah study. "In these generations when people are of weak demeanor and it is impossible to fulfill *Teshuvat Hamishkal*…

Atonement for Actions between Man and his Creator Taken during the Shoah

Part of the requests for atonement involved actions between man and his Creator, such as using Christian identification documents and posing as a non-Jew. Rabbi Moshe Feinstein was asked in 1961 regarding a woman who had been hidden by a non-Jew together with her young children. The non-Jew had demanded that they be baptized in exchange for being hidden. Immediately after the liberation, they returned to Judaism. The rabbi ruled that since the baptism was done under duress it is not considered apostasy. The woman was allowed to repent and try to sanctify the Divine name by her conduct and, if her health permitted, to fast each year on the day that she was baptized.[27]

A wide range of practical questions during and after the Shoah involved the prohibition of eating non-Kosher foods.[28] In his writings Rabbi Yehoshua Moshe Ahronson posed a question of whether the survivors of the camps "require repentance and atonement for forbidden food…and desecration of the Sabbath and other Torah prohibitions under duress which we committed in the camps?" The rabbi did not answer this question in his notes. However, it is interesting that of all the prohibitions that may require repentance, Rabbi Ahronson viewed forbidden foods to be a major prohibition with special consequences. In the notes for his sermon on the occasion of his appointment as rabbi of the displaced persons camps in Austria, he wrote, "how many times did I decide that I will no longer serve as a rabbi, [because] my body is impure due to forbidden foods." He accepted the appointment, since "I alone survived from a meeting organized by the Joint in Warsaw, which was attended by 200 rabbis." According to one testimony, he also said in his speech, "if enough rabbis of the rabbis of Poland who were not made repulsive by forbidden food will be found, I will resign from

---

asceticism…and if man lived 1,000 years…he could not fast for all the details of his sins…we haven't other than to strengthen ourselves in Torah"; see Rabbi Avraham brother of the Gaon, *Ma'alot HaTorah* (Hebrew) (Jerusalem: Luria, 1942), preface, https://www.hebrewbooks.org/pdfpager.aspx?req=33866&st=&pgnum=14 (accessed April 28, 2021). For additional opinions, see Azriel Shohat, *Im Hilufei Tekufot: Reshit Hahaskalah Beyahadut Germanya* (Hebrew) (Jerusalem: Bialik, 1961), pp. 42–44.

27 Rabbi Moshe Feinstein, *She'elot Utshuvot Igerot: Yoreh De'ah* (Hebrew), part 2, § 129, https://www.responsa-holocaust.com (accessed April 26, 2021).

28 See for example Oshry, *Responsa from the Holocaust*, p. 22.

my position."[29] Apparently he assigned a metaphysical value to this prohibition of eating non-kosher food that defiled the human soul.[30]

A request for atonement regarding this matter was presented at a very early stage even before the start of World War II. In June 1939, a Jew from Vienna who had been imprisoned by the Nazis in Dachau[31] and had eaten non-kosher foods during his imprisonment asked for instructions for appropriate repentance. Rabbi Hayim Yitzhak Yeruham dealt with the matter and established the principle that he who acted under coercion does not require atonement. However, from the words of the questioner, it appeared that he had eaten in a situation that was not life threatening on a few occasions. In his reply, the rabbi referred to the tortures that he had suffered during this period in Dachau and wrote that they themselves were an act of atonement. Nevertheless, the heart of the questioner continued to burden him and he wanted to know a way to repent. The rabbi instructed him to fast on Mondays and Thursdays for a number of weeks—approximately forty days of fasting.[32]

29 Rabbi Yehoshua Moshe Ahronson, *Alei Merorot: Yomanim, She'elot Utshuvot, Hagut Bashoah* (Hebrew) (Jerusalem: Mossad Harav Kook, 2014), pp. 242–243, 250. Rabbi Ahronson was born in Warsaw in 1910 and was the rabbi of the town of Sanok in Poland. During the Holocaust, he passed through the gates of hell of the ghettos and the camps, including Auschwitz, and after the liberation, he served as a rabbi in the displaced persons camps. Later he immigrated to Israel and served as rabbi in Petah Tikva.

30 Lev. 11:43; B. Yoma 39a. This verse deals with the prohibition of eating vermin: "neither shall you make yourselves unclean with them, that you should be defiled thereby." As the sages interpreted it, "read not that you should be defiled, but that you should become dull hearted." It is interesting to note what Zorach Warhaftig wrote in a short report regarding the situation of the Jews in the displaced persons camps in the French occupation zone in Germany after his visit there in September 1945. He quoted many religious survivors who defined their liberation day not as the day they were liberated by the Allied forces, but rather as the day they were able to abstain from non-kosher food. See Zorach Warhaftig, *Situation of the Jewish Deportees in Camps and Localities in the French Occupation Zone as of September 28, 1945: A Study on the Basis of a Tour of these Places between September 18–28*, (n.p.: n.p., 1945), p. 4.

31 Dachau Camp was established by the Nazi regime as a prison camp for enemies of the regime as early as March 1933; Barbara Distel, "Dachau," in Israel Gutman, ed., *Encyclopedia of the Holocaust*, vol. 1 (Jerusalem, Tel Aviv, New York, and London: Yad Vashem, Sifriat Poalim Macmillan, and Collier Macmillan, 1990), p. 339.

32 Rabbi Hayim Yitzhak Yeruham, *She'elot Utshuvot: Birkat Hayim* (Hebrew), § 42, https://www.responsa-holocaust.com (accessed April 26, 2021). Rabbi Yeruham, born in Galicia in 1864, served as a rabbi and fled with his family to Vienna during World War I. When the Nazis entered Austria, he fled to Poland. He was arrested by the Nazis in the summer of 1942 and died in the Altstadt ghetto on Succoth in 1942.

An unusual dilemma was presented much later, more than forty years after the war had ended. In September 1989, a woman posed a question to Rabbi Hayim David Halevi.

> She experienced the Shoah in the Auschwitz camp and abstained from eating the pieces of meat in the soup that they got once a week... she was fourteen years old then. After the liberation, she was brought to a non-Jewish convalescent home, where she was taken care of with much concern and attention...After being there for several days, she once ate a piece of the meat. Also, it happened once that she was asked to sign some document on the Sabbath, and she signed it as did the other children. She was about sixteen years old then. Now she is asking how to atone for the fact that in the most difficult conditions she withstood the temptation but, after the liberation, she surrendered to social pressure and committed the sins of eating non-kosher food and desecration of the Sabbath...She is truly repentant for this and is looking for a means of reparation; she cannot rest and the matter disturbs her to the point of distraction.[33]

Although the question focuses on pangs of conscience that accompanied the questioner for not paying sufficient attention to observing Jewish law in the convalescent home after the liberation, where she was surrounded by help and sympathy, from the story we learn about her devotion to abstain from forbidden food while she was in Auschwitz. Her failure to observe matters that she believed in after the liberation is in the realm of psychology but, in any case, she is an example of the unique difficulties that religious survivors suffered even after the liberation. In this case, the rabbi did not propose acts of repentance but tried to calm her spirit with words of encouragement. She should not be sorry for a short hour when she did not resist temptation, and she should be happy for the entire period during which she behaved with self-sacrifice and abstained from non-kosher meat.[34]

Rabbi Ephraim Oshry describes another sphere where Jews asked for an appropriate way to atone. In the beginning of the Nazi conquest of

---

33 Rabbi Hayim David Halevi, *Sheelot Utshuvot: Mayim Hayim* (Hebrew), part 1, § 68, https://www.responsa-holocaust.com (accessed April 26, 2021). Rabbi Halevi, born in Jerusalem in 1924, served as the rabbi of Rishon LeTzion and later as the rabbi of Tel Aviv.
34 Ibid.

Lithuania in the summer of 1941, the Nazis ordered gathering all dogs and cats in one of the synagogues of Kovno, and shooting and killing them there. Thereafter, they commanded Jews to tear the Torah scrolls with their own hands and to cover the carcasses with the parchments of the Torah scrolls. Those who had participated in and saw this terrible sight turned to the rabbi of Kovno, Rabbi Shapiro, and asked him to instruct them in the way to repentance. Rabbi Oshry noted that those who had torn the Torah scrolls were told to fast, even though they had been coerced. Those on the sidelines who had seen the act were also required to fast, provided that they were physically able. Other ghetto inhabitants who had heard the details were not required to fast but to give charity and to meditate on repentance.[35] This case, or a similar case, was the basis of a question posed to Rabbi Oshry after the Shoah.

> Immediately after the liberation…a respected Lithuanian Jew poured out his heart to me. He related how he had seen the Germans beat an old rabbi and, under pain of death, forced him to burn a Torah-scroll with his own hands. Since the witness owned a Torah-scroll himself, he began to worry lest they compel him to burn his Torah-scroll too. He woke up in the middle of the night, took his Torah-scroll to the river and let it sink to the bottom to keep the accursed Germans from desecrating the sanctity of the Torah.

---

35 Oshry, *Responsa from the Holocaust*, pp. 9–10. Rabbi Oshry wrote that this event took place on August 27, 1941. Avraham Tory, the secretary of the Kovno ghetto Ältestenrat, described in his diary a similar event on January 14, 1942, in which an order was issued to gather dogs and cats in one of the synagogues where they were shot to death. The carcasses were left for months and Jews were forbidden to remove them. See Avraham Tory, *Surviving the Holocaust: The Kovno Ghetto Diary* (Cambridge and London: Harvard University Press, 1990), p. 67. It should also be noted that Rabbi Ahronson described an incident when a rabbi was ordered to tear a *mezuza* (door post) scroll. He refused at first, but after being beaten viciously, his will weakened and he tore the *mezuza*. A few days later, after he had recovered, he cried bitterly, sat *shiva* (seven days of mourning), and abstained from giving halachic rulings; Ahronson, *Alei Merorot*, p. 234. Esther Farbstein, the editor of this book, addresses the question of whether there is a halachic obligation to sacrifice one's life in order to avoid desecrating sacred writings; see Ibid., p. 235.

Nevertheless, he was troubled by doubts[36]...After liberation the first thing he did was hurry down to the river in the hope of dredging up the Torah-scroll from the bottom so that he could bury it in the traditional manner. But his efforts were in vain...Then he came to ask whether he needed to atone for his action.[37]

Rabbi Oshry ruled that since the deed was done with good intentions to save the scroll from desecration, he did not require atonement. But, if his economic condition allowed, it would be proper for him to have a new Torah scroll written at his expense and thus to sanctify the Divine name, which was desecrated.[38] This is an example of the complex dilemmas in many situations faced by Jews, who questioned whether it is better to commit a minor sin or a small moral transgression in order to prevent results that are far worse? The choice was not between good and bad, but between bad and worse. There were many questions of this nature in the realm of relations of man with his fellow.

Atonement for Actions Between Man and His Fellow Man Taken during the Shoah

The questions in this realm expose moral and halachic dilemmas that tested the boundaries of proper solidarity during those tragic times. They caused pangs of conscience and pain, which accompanied those involved for many years. A prime example of this deals with an incident of quieting a crying baby so as not to give away the group in hiding. The question was posed to Rabbi Shimon Efrati as follows:

He who hears this question, his hair will stand on end...in a hiding place there was a group of Jews hiding from the enemy...and while the wicked ones were searching for these desperate people, a

---

36 According to this description, his doubts were whether it was preferable to wait and not throw the Torah scroll into the river, since he might have succeeded in hiding it from the Germans, and even if he failed to hide the holy scroll and was ordered to desecrate it, it may have been preferable to do so under coercion rather than to hastily decide to throw it into the river. It should be noted that the letters in the Torah-scroll are written in ink, and being thrown to the river definitely caused the letters to be erased.

37 Oshry, *Responsa from the Holocaust*, p. 173.

38 Ibid., p. 174.

baby, who was among the hidden, started crying and there was no possibility of quieting him. If he would have been heard outside, all would have been captured and executed. The question was: is it permissible to put a pillow on the mouth of the baby to quiet him... There was a danger that the child would be asphyxiated...One of the people put a pillow over the baby's mouth. After the wicked left... they removed the pillow and to their horror they saw that the child was dead. The question is: was it permissible to put the pillow [over the baby's mouth] in order to save the rest of the people...and does the person who did it, although unwillingly, have to undertake an act of repentance for forgiveness for the sin?[39]

Rabbi Efrati's answer indicates the complexity of this matter. On one hand, he writes that the person who put the pillow on the baby "does not need to have pangs of conscience, since he acted within the law in order to save lives of Jews" and, therefore, he does not need a procedure of repentance. On the other hand, he writes "[Those] (and there were such cases in my family may the Almighty revenge their blood) who did not choose to save their lives by asphyxiating a Jewish child sanctified the Divine name."[40] Although according to Jewish law, he finds it permissible to do what was done, he hints that this case is a situation in which it would be fitting to act beyond the letter of the law, as did members of his family.

It is interesting to compare this reply to several responsa that were given years earlier in the matter of a mother who was breastfeeding her child and fell asleep. When she woke, she found a dead baby in her arms. The fear is that she lay on top of him and caused his asphyxiation. Rabbi Moshe Sofer freed her of the obligation to fast, since her intentions were for the good of the child, when she breastfed him and she fell asleep unwillingly.[41] In a similar case, Rabbi Bezalel Ze'ev Shafran proposed

---

39 Efrati, *Migey Hahariga*, p. 23. It should be noted that the details of this event, the place and time, are not cited, as well as the date that the question was posed. However, there are known cases of such incidents, as the one related by Moshe Sonnenson of Eishishok, for example; see Moshe Sonnenson testimony in Yigal Lossin, *Pillar of Fire* (Jerusalem: Shikmona, 1997), p. 315.

40 Efrati, *Migey Hahariga*, p. 30. This ruling was dealt with at length by Lichtenstein, who delved into the halachic aspects of endangering one trying to save him and others; see Lichtenstein, *Ve'emunatcha Baleylot*, pp. 157–182; Zimmels, *The Echo*, pp. 72–74.

41 Sofer, *Hatam Sofer, Hoshen Mishpat: She'elot Utshuvot* (Hebrew), part 5 (New York: E. Grossman's Publishing House, 1958), § 184.

that the mother fast every last day of the Jewish month for a period of a year.[42] Rabbi Binyamin Aharon Solnik was severe and ruled that the mother fast more than 100 days over a period of a year.[43] Comparing the deeds committed, while disregarding the Shoah conditions, it appears that the intentional act of silencing the child while endangering him is certainly more severe than the case of the mother who fell asleep while breastfeeding. Nevertheless, Rabbi Efrati was lenient in this case. The exemption from fasting perhaps is due to his general approach toward *Teshuvat Hamishkal*, but his statement that "he does not need to have pangs of conscience" teaches us how far rabbis went to express understanding of the unique circumstances of the Shoah even though, in this case, the rabbi thought that it would have been proper to act otherwise.

Additional questions involving seeking atonement are found in the Shoah responsa literature, and they may be classified as cases of substituting another person for one condemned to death; participation in mercy killing; the attitude toward those who breached the limits of Jewish solidarity; and indirectly causing a person's death.

Substituting Another Person for One Condemned to Death

The issue of saving one condemned to death at the price of another person arose in a number of cases. An incident that reflects the highest degree of Jewish solidarity and readiness to help another is found in a question posed to Rabbi Meisels. A group of over 1,000 boys was selected because of their short stature and were confined in a closed barrack in Auschwitz.[44] Those of short stature were assumed to be unsuitable for physical labor, therefore, the fate awaiting them was clear to all. Rabbi

---

42 Rabbi Bezalel Ze'ev Shafran, *Sefer She'elot Utshuvot HaRabaz* (Hebrew), part 1 (Warsaw: Levin–Epstein Bros., 1930), § 16. Rabbi Shafran was born in Galicia in 1867 and served as a rabbi in Bacau, Romania until his death in 1929.

43 Rabbi Binyamin Aharon Solnik, *Sefer Ma'aset Binyamin: She'elot Utshuvot* (Hebrew) (Vilna: Avraham Tzvi Publishing, 1894), § 26. Rabbi Solnik wrote that he had to be strict with this woman, since "this was the second time that this happened to her." Rabbi Solnik, who lived in Poland from about 1550–1620, was a student of Rabbi Moshe Iserlis and others, and was known as one of the leading rabbis in Poland in his generation.

44 Farbstein researched this case and wrote that it occurred on the eve of Yom Kippur in the autumn of 1944; Farbstein, *Hidden in the Heights*, vol. 2, pp. 617–619.

Meisels was approached by a young man of about fifteen who wanted to substitute himself for his scholarly friend, who was imprisoned in the barrack of those condemned to death and said, "I accept with great joy to be sacrificed instead of him." The rabbi forbade sacrificing himself for his friend.[45]

However, another case of substitution for a condemned person is found in a request for atonement, which was presented years after the Shoah and indicates a low boundary of solidarity. As in other cases, it raises difficult emotions, even though there were good intentions behind it. The matter was disclosed in a question that was posed in 1959, about fifteen years after the Shoah, to the Tzieshinov Rebbe, Rabbi Shalom Yehezkel Shraga Rubin-Halberstam in Brooklyn, who transmitted it to Rabbi Matzliah Mazouz in Tunis.

> One of the confined in the ghetto inferno during those days of rage... was a member of the ghetto leadership. Whenever the Germans wanted someone, they would order the head of the Jews to capture him and hand him over. Once, they asked for a healthy man named Kahane. The Jews knew that they were searching for him in order to kill [him] and that, if they failed to capture him, the Germans would seize ten other Jews in his stead and kill them as a penalty for not having captured him. But there was another man, by all accounts, with the intellect of a two-year-old,[46] whose name was also Kahane. Therefore, they sent the mentally challenged man instead of the man of sound mind and [the Germans] killed him and the other was saved. Now [the questioner] has regrets, [thinking that] perhaps he should not have done it.[47]

---

45 Meisels, *She'elot Utshuvot Mekadeshei Hashem*, part 1, "Sha'ar Mahamadim," Letter D, p. 9. In the question preceding this one, he quotes a father, who wanted to save his son but refrained from doing so, because he knew that another boy would be seized to take his place; see also Zimmels, *The Echo*, pp. 112–116; Lichtenstein, *Vehasne Einenu Ucal*, pp. 167–216; Meir Eyali, "Adam Temurat Adam Behatzalat Nefashot Besifrut Hashut Shel Ha'aharonim Umiyemei Hashoah" (Hebrew), *Dapim Leheker Tekufat Hashoah*, 3 (1984), pp. 43–59.

46 It appears to be an exaggeration since, if his mental age was two, how could they fool the Germans and substitute him for the other man?

47 Rabbi Matzliah Mazouz, *Sefer Ish Matzliah: Vol. 1, Yoreh De'ah* (Hebrew), § 18, https://www.responsa-holocaust.com (accessed April 26, 2021). Rabbi Mazouz was born on Djerba Island in 1911, and was known as one of the leading Tunisian Jewish authorities. He was murdered at the entrance to his house in 1971.

According to the text of the question, the decision to save the mentally sound individual at the expense of the mentally challenged person rested on a halachic consideration, as discussed below, that gives preference to saving the life of a Jew who is obligated to fulfill the commandments.[48] That the man of sound mind was more likely to survive and perhaps be more useful to the community than would the mentally challenged man may also have been a consideration. It should be noted that this was not the only case in which a mentally challenged person rather than a mentally competent person was handed over to the Germans.[49]

In his response, Rabbi Mazouz asked whether there had been any doubt about whom the Germans had in mind. Rabbi Halberstam, speaking for the questioner, answered in the negative. The order was to surrender a man named Kahane, who lived at a specific street address. Although both men had the same last name, lived in the same building, and were in fact related, the community leaders knew that the Germans were looking for the healthy Kahane.[50] The rabbi did not mince words: "It is unquestionably a criminal transgression...and I find no aspect of merit in it." The preference of saving a Jew who is obligated to fulfill the commandments applies only in a situation in which two people are in similar danger and only one can be saved. It is totally forbidden to hand over one Jew as a substitute for another Jew who is condemned to death. According to the rabbinical ruling, this case crossed the boundary! The rabbi concluded

---

48 A mentally challenged person is absolved from the observance of commandments; see Maimonides, *Mishne Torah: Sefer Korbanot*, Hilchot Hagiga 2:4. Regarding preference in saving lives, see B. Horayot 13a.

49 When Moshe Marin, the head of the Central Judenrat in Upper Eastern Selesia, was ordered to hand over Jews for deportation, he asked to choose "Informers, thieves, immoral or sick and mentally ill persons, and retarded children"; see Trunk, *Judenrat*, p. 428. Another case occurred in the Kovno ghetto in November 1942, when during a failed escape attempt a Jew shot at a German soldier. As a result, the Jewish Police were ordered to imprison twenty hostages, and they were collected from "prostitutes, thieves, imbeciles, and a few sick people." They were released later. See Leib Garfunkel, *Kovna Hayehudit Behurbana* (Hebrew) (Jerusalem: Yad Vashem, 1959), pp. 135–138. It should be noted that in these two cases, a quota of Jews was demanded and not any specific person, and they were collected from among the marginal members of the community, as opposed to the case described by Rabbi Mazouz in which a specific Jew was demanded and a mentally challenged person was sent instead.

50 Mazouz, *Sefer Ish Matzliah: Vol. 1, Yoreh De'ah*, §18. A general question of great importance is: Was it permissible to hand over to the Germans a specific man whom they demanded in order to spare other victims? Regarding this issue, see Lichtenstein, *Vehasne Einenu Ucal*, pp. 276–337.

his answer by quoting other rulings regarding unintentional murderers who were commanded to fast approximately forty days, and he added that in this case, in which the act was committed willfully, the questioner himself certainly should fast.[51] As for the reason that the question was forwarded from Brooklyn to faraway Tunis, perhaps the answer to this has to do with the gravity of the case. It may have been intended to limit the possibility of the questioner's identity being revealed.[52]

Participation in Mercy Killing

Much ink has been spilled over the question of mercy killing. Halacha categorically forbids euthanasia, instead requiring action to preserve life, even if the life in question will obviously be brief.[53] Two complex questions arose in the context of the Shoah. One question was also posed to Rabbi Halberstam in Brooklyn in 1972, almost thirty years after the Shoah, and was referred by him to a number of rabbis.

> [This concerns] a man who wishes to be shown a path to repentance. It happened during the time of Nazi rule…He was…in Poland together with his parents. [The Germans] were collecting furs,[54] and

51 *Sefer Ish Matzliah: Vol. 1, Yoreh De'ah,* §18. He added that the ruling depends on the individual's physical ability to withstand such fasting and, therefore, only a rabbi who is personally acquainted with the questioner should give a ruling.

52 However, it should be noted that Rabbi Halberstam was in contact with Rabbi Mazouz regarding other matters, and in the same volume of his book *Sefer Ish Matzliah* in which he listed his answers to approximately 160 various questions, five of them were presented by Rabbi Halberstam; see Mazouz, *Sefer Ish Matzliah,* part 1.

53 Halacha forbids active termination of a dying person's life; see Rabbi Joseph Karo, *Shulchan Aruch,* Yoreh De'ah 339:1. The Sabbath is to be desecrated to save even a wounded person who is plainly about to die; Karo, *Shulchan Aruch,* Ora Hayim 329:4. Halacha distinguishes between the categorical injunction against shortening life and the absence of a requirement to prolong it artificially in certain cases. See, for example, Rabbi Ben Zion Firer, "Hibur Goses Lemehonat Hanshama—Mitzvah O Issur" (Hebrew), *Tehumin* 7 (1986), pp. 219–225.

54 Due to the absence of identifying details, it is not possible to determine in which ghetto this incident occurred. Confiscations of fur were declared in various ghettos, such as Warsaw, Lublin, and Kovno at the end of December 1941; see the entries for Warsaw, Lublin, and Kovno (Kaunas) in Guy Miron and Shlomit Shulhani, *The Yad Vashem Encyclopedia of the Ghettos during the Holocaust* (Jerusalem: Yad Vashem, 2009); see also, Garfunkel, *Kovna HaYehudit Behurbana,* pp. 123–124.

the Nazis announced that they had to surrender everything to the authorities by a certain day, and that thereafter anyone caught with a piece of fur in their possession would be liable to death. Furthermore, three Jews who were elders of the community were placed in charge of the operation and they too would be killed, if a fur were to be found in anyone's possession after the deadline. Of course, everyone handed over any garments and hats they owned that contained fur. When [the Nazis] conducted a search several days later, however, they found one man with a fur hat in his possession. They killed him at once and began to severely torture the three elders whom they had placed in charge of the operation as the public looked on. After one of [the elders] died of his agonies and another was in his death throes, they began to beat the third, who happened to be the questioner's father. Then one of the overseers of the lethal beating made his son an offer: If you give me a gold watch, I'll shoot him to death with my handgun. That way, he'll go easily and won't suffer as did those who came before him. So it was; they shot him to death. Now[55] [the son's] conscience is troubling him: Perhaps he had not done well by helping to cause his father's death indirectly and has come to ask for instructions on how to repent, thinking that had [the German] not shot [his father] to death, a miracle might have happened.[56]

The first to answer was Rabbi Menashe Klein (Hakatan) in June 1972. His decision was that since the Nazi was determined to kill his father, it was not possible to bribe him to save his life. Thus, the son who saved the father from torture performed a commandment and should not regret his deed. He should just increase his study of Torah and performance of the commandments.[57] A month later, in July, an answer was received

55　The wording of the response suggests that the son may have thought for decades that he had behaved commendably and only now began to doubt it. However, it appears to be more probable that doubt and pangs of conscience were troubling him during all those years, and perhaps even became stronger, and only then did he dare to pose the question to a rabbi.

56　Rabbi Yitzhak Ya'akov Weiss, *Sefer She'elot Utshuvot: Minhat Yitzhak* (Hebrew), part 6, § 56, https://www.responsa-holocaust.com (accessed April 21, 2021). Rabbi Weiss was born in Poland in 1902, and was a dean of a yeshiva in Hungary and a *dayan* (Jewish judge) in Rumania. He survived the war and, after the liberation, was appointed as a *dayan* in England. He immigrated to Israel in 1970 and was appointed to the chief justice of the court of the Eda Haredit (ultra-orthodox community) in Jerusalem.

57　Rabbi Menashe Klein, *She'elot Utshuvot Sefer Mishne Halachot: Mador Teshuvot* (Hebrew), from Rabbi Yitzhak Ya'akov Weiss, stating that within the bounds of the law, the son does not need deeds of repentance, because of the tragic circumstances of the incident, and also because he made the decision at a time in which he did not have a clear mind. He ruled that charity donations and acts of kindness performed by the son in memory of his father's soul would suffice.[58] However it is not clear from his words if it was right to bribe the Nazi at the outset to kill his father quickly.

It is interesting that this did not relieve the questioner or Rabbi Halberstam. The question was presented in August to another rabbi, Rabbi Avraham David Horwitz, who answered in September. Rabbi Horwitz disagreed with the preceding rabbis and wrote that the son had not acted properly and, therefore, he should perform acts of repentance. However, Rabbi Horwitz found it difficult to propose proper deeds of repentance, because this depends on the personal situation of each individual.[59] Apparently, the last rabbi to answer this question was Rabbi Gestetner, who answered over a year later in December 1973. He too thought that the son had not acted properly and needed to atone. However, considering the difficult circumstances and mental stress that the son was subject to, the procedure of repentance should not be too strict. Therefore, he did not specify the requirements for atonement.[60]

It seems that the strict replies that required the son to perform deeds of repentance were the ones that brought peace to his restless soul and,

part 6, § 314, https://www.responsa-holocaust.com (accessed April 21, 2021). He added in his conclusion that his words should not be interpreted as allowing quickening the death of a sick person who is suffering pains, even on the brink of death. Rabbi Klein was born in Slovakia in 1925. During the Holocaust, he survived several concentration camps. After the liberation, he reached the United States and led the Ungvar community in New York and Jerusalem.

58 Weiss, *Sefer She'elot Utshuvot: Minhat Yitzhak*, part 6, § 56.

59 Rabbi Avraham David Horwitz, *She'elot Utshuvot: Kinyan Torah Bahalacha* (Hebrew), part 1, § 121, https://www.responsa-holocaust.com (accessed April 26, 2021). Rabbi Horwitz was born in 1912 and was a rabbi in Transylvania. During the Holocaust, his wife and five children were murdered. After the liberation, he served as a rabbi in the displaced persons camps and later in France, until he immigrated to Israel in 1978.

60 Rabbi Natan Gestetner, *Sefer She'elot Utshuvot: Lehorot Natan, Helek Yoreh De'ah* (Hebrew), part 2, §§ 65–67, https://www.responsa-holocaust.com (accessed April 26, 2021). Rabbi Gestetner, born in 1932 in Hungary, was in hiding in Budapest during the Holocaust. His parents and sisters were murdered. After the liberation, he immigrated to Israel in 1949 and was recognized as a young prodigy. He was later appointed to teach in yeshivot and to lead a community in Bnei Brak.

as far as is known, the question was not sent to any other rabbis. In any case, since all the rabbis who replied were Shoah survivors themselves, it is not possible to attribute the different approaches to a greater or lesser understanding of those who were there, as opposed to those who had not experienced the Shoah personally.[61]

Another question is described by Rabbi Oshry in his writings. It was posed to him shortly after the liberation of Kovno by the Red Army in early August 1944. The High Holidays, Rosh Hashana, and Yom Kippur were to take place in September. The small community of survivors in Kovno was searching for a cantor who would lead them in the prayers. A qualified Jew was found, but there were rumors that he had killed a Jew during the Shoah and, therefore, he was not qualified to serve as a cantor. Rabbi Oshry investigated the matter. The details of the incident that had occurred during the march[62] to the site of forced labor were as follows:

[O]ne of these marchers, unable to walk any longer because of his own unbearable suffering, said to his friend struggling right behind him, "Please do me a favor. Give me a push so that I will fall. If I rise, push me down again. And again. Eventually my strength will give out and I will not be able to rise again. I cannot bear the pain and the suffering. I prefer to be dead."

Unable to convince his stronger friend to carry out this act, he had to beg him again and again. Finally the man took pity on the broken Jew, saying to himself…"He is better off dead than living in so much pain. Since he begs me with the last ounce of strength, how can I not do what he asks?"

So the friend pushed him down and, when he rose up again, he pushed him down again. Although the man was able to get up each

---

61 For comparison, Farbstein writes that regarding the question of the *agunot*, the Holocaust survivor rabbis showed responsibility and acted more quickly to allow *agunot* to remarry compared to rabbis who were not Holocaust survivors, due to their greater awareness of the tragedy and to having been witnesses to what happened. See Farbstein, *Hidden in Thunder*, vol. 1, pp. 370–375; Darmon-Malka, "Our Unfortunate Sisters," pp. 172–173.

62 Even though a detailed description is not provided, it may be assumed that the question deals with the group marching to labor at the airfield, which was considered to be the most difficult forced labor performed by those imprisoned in the Kovno ghetto. In addition to a long shift of twelve hours of hard labor, they also had to march about 5 kilometers to the work site and back. See Garfunkel, *Kovna Hayehudit Behurbana*, p. 86.

time, when he got to his place of work, he was so weak that he simply collapsed and died.[63]

In this case, the rabbi ruled that, despite the unique circumstances, the assaulter acted improperly and must repent and immerse himself in a ritual bath. He did not add additional requirements for atonement. The latter accepted the verdict, had remorse for what he had done, and repented for his deed. Thereafter, he was allowed to lead the High Holiday prayers, which he recited with sighs and weeping, greatly inspiring the congregation.[64] In this case, the initiative to repent and to atone for this deed did not come from a long, internal struggle of the person involved but rather from external pressure exerted immediately after the liberation. From the description it appears that the repentance was sincere.

The Attitude toward Those Who Breached the Limits of Jewish Solidarity

Another question was raised regarding the prayer leader's lectern in the synagogue of the Kovno survivors, which deals with the attitude toward those who breached the limits of Jewish solidarity during the Shoah and who wanted to repent. Rabbi Oshry describes the following:

> Jewish Kapos. Serving the Germans, they yelled and beat and informed against their fellow-Jews...
> When the enemy was finally crushed and...our suffering brothers within the confines of the ghetto walls burst out into the open spaces...That was when I was asked about one of the Jewish policemen. Claiming that he regretted his actions and had repented fully for his evil deeds, he sought to be appointed as cantor and to lead the prayers.[65]

---

63 Oshry, *Responsa from the Holocaust*, p. 212; Zimmels, *The Echo*, pp. 324– 325.

64 Oshry, *Responsa from the Holocaust*, pp. 213–214. According to this source, many of the worshippers were Jewish soldiers in the Red Army, who visited the synagogue to worship with their fellow Jews, "and they too were greatly inspired" by the performance of this prayer leader.

65 Oshry, *Responsa from the Holocaust*, p. 206.

Rabbi Oshry's response in this case was that a prayer leader must have a completely clean record. One who treated fellow Jews cruelly and inflicted curses and blows should not be appointed to the post. From the answer, it seems that in addition to doubts regarding the sincerity of the repentance of this man, Rabbi Oshry established limits that not every public position is open to a person who repented, even following sincere repentance.[66] A comparison of the two responsa reveals the distinction that Rabbi Oshry made between one who hit a person at the latter's request and with the intention of trying to aid him, and one who delivered blows on his own initiative in the service of the Germans. In Rabbi Oshry's eyes, members of the Jewish police in the ghetto were not free of responsibility.

In this context it is worthwhile to mention another response of Rabbi Oshry concerning a Jew who collaborated with the Nazis. "One man who had served the Germans...was about to be put to death [by the Nazis]. In the presence of his fellow-Jews he bemoaned his sins, cried bitter tears, and begged [for] forgiveness." The question dealt with mentioning the name of the collaborator when his son is called to the Torah. Should the customary version be used in which the name of the father is also proclaimed, or should they abstain from mentioning the name of this person? Rabbi Oshry answered that, since the father repented, the son should be called up according to the customary version.[67] Although collaborators with the Nazis who sought repentance were disqualified from certain public positions, they were not among those whose names were to be erased.

Indirectly Causing a Person's Death

During the Shoah, questions were raised as to what extent a person is required to endanger himself to save others. He who volunteers to sacrifice himself in order to save many others is considered a *Harug Malkhut* (martyr) to whom no being can come close in paradise.[68]

---

66 Ibid. Rabbi Oshry based himself on the halachic rule that a prayer leader must be a decent person who does not have a bad reputation, even as a child. See Rabbi Joseph Karo, *Shulchan Aruch*, Ora Hayim 53:4; Rosenbaum, *The Holocaust*, pp. 154–155.

67 Oshry, *Responsa from the Holocaust*, p. 207.

68 This term is found in the sages' description of Lulianos and Paphos, who confessed to a murder that they had not committed and sacrificed themselves to save the Jews of Lod; B. Ta'anit 18b with Rashi's commentary; B. Bava Batra 10b.

However, to what extent is an individual obligated to endanger himself to save others? Rabbi Oshry considered this question at the beginning of the Nazi conquest of Kovno, when he asked Rabbi David Itzkovitz to go to the Lithuanian authorities, in spite of the pogroms raging in the streets, to try to free a number of yeshiva students who were imprisoned there.[69]

Another question dealt with an opposite situation of saving a few but endangering many. It was posed in real time to Rabbi Yehoshua Greenwald, rabbi of the community of Khust, who was asked whether it is permissible to help a few Jews to escape from an imprisonment camp, despite the expectation that the remaining prisoners would be subject to collective punishment. Normally, the welfare of many would be preferred but the rabbi ruled that, in this unique situation, it is permissible to help the escapees. His reasoning was based on the difficult conditions to which they were subjected and the cruel fate that awaited them, since "in any case, they were condemned to death,[70] and everything that could be done to inflict pain on them was done…therefore, it is a commandment…to aid the escape…and may the remnant of Israel not be lost."[71]

Those who felt that they had not done enough to save others and perhaps indirectly had caused their deaths suffered inner doubts and pangs of conscience after the Shoah. One question was asked by a man who felt very responsible for the death of his brother, who died when they were marching together in a death march. It was presented

---

69 Oshry, *Responsa from the Holocaust*, pp. 1–2. The conclusion drawn from this is that there is no obligation to endanger one's self for others, but a person with a soul will not be overly careful and will try to save Jews. Therefore, Rabbi Itzkovitz accepted the task and was successful.

70 Regarding the unique feelings of those facing death and their influence on rabbinical rulings, see Tarshansky, "Metim Behufsha," pp. 53–65.

71 Rabbi Yehoshua Greenwald, *Hesed Yehoshua* (Hebrew), part 1, § 20, https://www.responsa-holocaust.com (accessed April 26, 2021). Rabbi Greenwald was born in Khust in Hungary in 1909, where he served as rabbi. During the Holocaust, he was sent to Auschwitz and from there marched in death marches to camps in Austria. After the liberation, he was a rabbinical judge in Hungary and dealt with allowing *agunot* to marry. Thereafter, he served as rabbi in New York. It should be noted that the rabbi does not mention the date that he was asked this question, and it is not clear whether it happened during the Hungarian conquest, which started in March 1939, or during the Nazi conquest in the spring of 1944. From the description of being condemned to death, it seems that it was during the Nazi conquest. Regarding Khust during the Holocaust, see S. Y. Gross and Yitzhak Yosef Kohen, eds., *Sefer Marmarosh: Me'a Veshishim Kehilot Kedoshot Beyishuvan Uvehurbanan* (Hebrew) (Tel Aviv: Beit Marmarosh, 1983), pp. 219–223.

to Rabbi Izrael in New York who transmitted it to Rabbi Mordechai Ya'akov Breisch.

The evildoers gave us some minutes of rest and allowed us to sit on the side of the path. Often it occurred that when one of the suffering dosed off, he fell into a deep sleep due to exhaustion and weakness, so when the command came to continue marching, he did not wake up, and soon the murderer came over to him and killed him without saying a word. Therefore, the miserable ones walked in groups, and when they sat to rest, one was to wake the others.

And one man...accused [himself] in front of him [the rabbi], that he marched together with his younger brother...and when they sat down, he told the brother that he could sleep a little and he would awaken him. The resting time extended for a long period, and he himself dosed off a little. Suddenly the shout "LOS, LOS" was heard, meaning to continue on. Panic stricken, he ran over to where his fellows stood in the line of march. He was not yet fully alert and they immediately started marching. Then he remembered his brother but could not return to his [brother's] place without endangering his own life. Since then, his brother has been missing...and it is clear to him that he was killed, and it is close to thirteen years that he has pangs of conscience and guilt, and he approached [the rabbi]...is he obligated to repent for this or not?[72]

Although Rabbi Breisch did not note the date that the question was presented, it is stated that the questioner had guilt feelings for thirteen years and, therefore, it may be concluded that the question was asked at the end of the 1950s. The rabbi answered that the brother does not need to atone, and that his heart should not suffer feelings of guilt, because "this is a source of sadness, which is a greater sin that prevents him and disturbs him from serving God, which should be done with joy." However, "the right thing is to perform *Teshuvat Hamishkal* for a small fraction

---

72 Rabbi Mordechai Ya'akov Breisch, *Helkat Ya'akov: She'elot Utshuvot: Helek Hoshen Mishpat* (Hebrew), § 33, htttps://www.responsa-holocaust.com (accessed April 26, 2021). Rabbi Breisch, born in Poland in 1896, was a rabbi in Poland and later in Germany. Following the Nazi rise to power, he emigrated in 1934 to Zurich and served there as a rabbi until his death in 1977. See also Malka Weingarten, "'Nafshi Bish'elati': She'elot Utshuvot Benoseh Mesira Vehatzala Bitkufat Hashoah" (Hebrew), *Yalkut Moreshet*, 83 (2007), pp. 164–165.

of the sin" of not keeping his promise to wake his brother. Therefore, he should be particularly careful not to insult anyone, because insulting someone is like shedding blood, and he should also try to perform the commandment to be fruitful, and should raise an orphan in his house, and support Torah students. Thus, he will contribute to preserving a life and atone for the loss of a life.[73]

An additional case is described in a question that also was presented to Rabbi Izrael in New York, which he transmitted to Rabbi Israel Weltz in 1956.

> While in the accursed Buchenwald camp, [the questioner] had a Jewish overseer, a Kapo…who discharged his duties with great cruelty and beat and murdered people. On one occasion, this Kapo assaulted him with his bloodstained hands and beat him so severely that he could not arise and go to work the next day. When the SS officer came around…and asked him why he had not gone to work, he told him what had happened and showed him his body, injured from head to toe with bruises and fresh wounds everywhere. At once [the SS officer] led the Kapo away and placed him in detention, and they beat him to death, as was their wont, and he died of his injuries…[74] Now, long after the fact, he fears for his soul: Is he not guilty…of the crime of *moser* [handing over][75] for having surrendered the Kapo and causing…his death by doing so? Does he need to atone for it?[76]

73 Rabbi Breisch, *She'elot Utshuvot: Helkat Ya'akov, Helek Hoshen Mishpat*, § 33.
74 The SS officer killed the Kapo, evidently for diminishing the German labor force. It is interesting to compare this event with what happened to Rabbi Ahronson in Auschwitz, where he was beaten by a Kapo and his hand was severely wounded. A group of Germans who witnessed the incident harshly scolded the Kapo for his brutal behavior toward the prisoners in his charge. Rabbi Ahronson was hospitalized for a month; from there, he sent a message to the Kapo that he had declared to the Gestapo that the Kapo is not guilty in this incident. Therefore, when he returned to work, the Kapo went easy on him for a period of time; Ahronson, *Alei Merorot*, pp. 214–215.
75 It is a serious transgression for a Jew to hand over the person or the property of another Jew to a non-Jew. The penalty for this is losing his share in the world to come. See Maimonides, *Mishne Torah: Sefer Hamada*, Hilchot Teshuva 3:12.
76 Rabbi Israel Weltz, *She'elot Utshuvot: Divrei Yisrael* (Hebrew), part 3, § 150, https://www.responsa-holocaust.com (accessed April 26, 2021). Rabbi Weltz, born in 1887, lived in Budapest where he served as a dean of a yeshiva and as rabbi of a community before the Holocaust. He was sent to a forced labor camp during the Holocaust. After the liberation, he returned to Budapest and revived the community. Later he immigrated to Israel, where he died in 1973.

It is extraordinary to see how a Jew, who was severely beaten by the Kapo, resulting in his inability to go to work and thus endangering his life, suffers pangs of conscience for over ten years for indirectly causing the death of the cruel Kapo, and asks if he needs to make atonement. It appears that the one who was beaten identifies himself with the beater only for reasons of Jewish solidarity. The rabbi replied at the end of July 1956 and ruled, "he is not at all guilty and does not require any atonement."[77] It is interesting to point out that more than a month earlier, Rabbi Weiss replied to a similar question from Rabbi Izrael, declaring that the Kapo was a *rodef* (pursuer) who endangered another person, and it was permissible to kill him. However, he raised the possibility that the Germans forced him to serve in that capacity and, therefore, he concluded that whoever caused his death should repent "in accordance with the ruling of a great and righteous man," but did not propose specific acts of repentance.[78]

It is not clear whether the question was originally sent to both rabbis or perhaps, because of the delay in Rabbi Weiss' reply, the question was sent also to Rabbi Weltz. Rabbi Weiss apologized for not replying on time due to ill health. In any case, the two rulings are not necessarily a difference of opinion, since it appears from Rabbi Weiss' text that he understood that the beaten Jew went on his own initiative to the SS men and informed on the Kapo. Perhaps that is why he ruled that repentance was required.[79] This is opposed to the presentation of the event by Rabbi Weltz, who wrote that, only after being questioned by the SS, did the man show them his wounds and identified who had beaten him. Therefore, it was possible to be lenient.

Conclusion

A study of the questions that were posed to rabbis as the events occurred indicates what people considered they might do. A study of those questions that were posed after the events informs us of what people actually did, on the basis of the faith and values instilled in them, and also of spontaneous instinctive decisions. From the replies of the rabbis,

---

77 Ibid.
78 Weiss, *She'elot Utshuvot: Minhat Yitzhak*, part 6, § 55. The letter is dated June 21, 1956.
79 Ibid.

it is possible to learn what Jewish law considers proper and permissible, or improper and forbidden, and what was the reaction after the fact to the deeds that were done.

Very difficult circumstances and dilemmas are described in most of the requests for atonement found in the Shoah responsa literature. There was no possibility to consult rabbis or other authority figures, and decisions had to be made instantaneously when facing these dilemmas during the Shoah. Doubts and pangs of conscience about the actions that they had taken accompanied them for many years. The time frame—when the questions were posed from the time of the event or the liberation—varies up to thirty and even forty years later. The first questions that were asked had practical consequences and did not involve atonement only, such as the right to act as a cantor in the synagogue of survivors in Kovno. Many questions were asked during the second half of the 1950s. Apparently the questioners needed some time to sort out their thoughts and also to establish themselves before they gathered the strength to examine the past and to seek atonement. It appears that the shame connected to their actions was also a reason for the delay in consulting the rabbis. It is possible that for this reason the last question was asked in 1989 by one who had behaved with self-sacrifice during the Shoah but had transgressed after the liberation.

The requests for atonement reveal a wide range of behavior, from passive to fully active; from a brother, whose sin was that, while confused and under pressure, he neglected to wake his brother and thus indirectly caused his death, to an improper decision to substitute a mentally competent man with a mentally challenged man with the same name, and also to asphyxiating a baby, fearing that his cries would be heard, endangering others. They all sought atonement. The questioners were mainly ordinary persons. Among those who requested atonement in the responsa literature, Jews who held leadership positions in the Judenräte, as well as those who served as Jewish policemen and Kapos, are relatively absent. It could have been expected that they would hold a larger part in this literature. Their absence may be explained by a wide range of psychological explanations: from acceptance of the acts that they had committed under impossible conditions, to severe embarrassment and difficulty to face their past.

The questions in which the questioners sought atonement reveal the complex dilemmas that the Jews faced during the Shoah. These include relations between man and God, but mainly relations between man and his fellow. As opposed to normal situations, when solidarity and help are clear, and include all that is done to aid a person in distress, during the Shoah the boundaries were blurred. There were cases where help and solidarity involved harming another person. Mordechai Chaim Rumkowski, the head of the Judenrat in Łódź, solved this dilemma by a rational mathematical computation that gave preference to the welfare of the many over the few and, as he said in his famous speech, "I must cut off limbs in order to save the body!"[80]

In the responsa literature, there are various questions that examine the boundaries of proper solidarity and present the complexity of the definition. In these circumstances, what is considered a good deed? And where is the line distinguishing between a good deed and a bad deed? Was giving a gold watch, which saved one's father from torture but accelerated his death a good deed? Was helping a few to escape and be saved, knowing that collective punishment would be inflicted on the remaining prisoners, a deed of Jewish solidarity? Was silencing a baby and asphyxiating him to prevent the baby and all the others from being found and probably killed a proper act?

From the descriptions in the pages of responsa literature, it appears that in the vast majority of the cases, there were positive intentions to aid others and to help the community, and thus to fulfill the ideal "All Israel are responsible for each other," even in those incidents in which the rabbis ruled that they had acted improperly. The pangs of conscience that are revealed in the question presented by a Jew who was beaten severely by a Kapo and in an unexpected turnabout led to the execution of the Kapo are an extreme reflection of unconditional Jewish solidarity, even toward a sinful brother.[81]

---

80 See Rumkowski's speech in the Łódź ghetto, where he asked to surrender the ill and the children in order to try and save the others; Yitzhak Arad, Israel Gutman, and Abraham Margaliot, ed., *Documents on The Holocaust: Selected Sources on the Destruction of the Jews of Germany and Austria, Poland, and the Soviet Union* (Jerusalem: Yad Vashem, the Anti-Defamation League, and Ktav Publishing, 1981), p. 283.

81 Unconditional solidarity toward a sinful brother appears in another response, not discussed in this research. Rabbi Yitzhak Isaac Liebes was asked in September 1944, shortly after the liberation, regarding a Jew who had murdered a fellow Jew in the forest and also had abused the rabbi himself. The Jewish survivors asked the rabbi if they should hand the murderer over to the Russian authorities, as they were ordered to hand over all those who had committed crimes under the Nazi rule. The rabbi ruled that although the man had sinned and, according to the Torah laws, deserved punishment, they should not hand him over to the non- Jewish court, which would judge him

The rabbinical rulings make it clear that the rabbis took into consideration the tragic reality of the Shoah and were not strict with the questioners. Even the man who covered the baby's mouth in order to quiet his crying, which led to the baby's death, was not required to atone, although the rabbi praised those who had acted differently in a similar situation and had chosen to sacrifice themselves and die. The lenient rulings that did not require acts of atonement did not always satisfy the questioners, and they sometimes continued to seek atonement. In such cases, the rabbis tried to convince them that atonement was not necessary, or else suggested simple acts of atonement in order not to make it hard on the questioners. In the majority of the cases, the deeds of atonement did not include the common penance of fasting, but rather specific acts were suggested to compensate for the specific transgression. For example, the atonement for participating indirectly in the killing of a Jew was to bring children into the world, or to adopt orphans. For acts of destroying Torah scrolls, the penance was to have a Torah written and to encourage Torah study.

Nevertheless, along with the lenient approach, the rabbis drew red lines. Even in the tragic reality of the Shoah, there was no automatic forgiveness on the basis that all acts were done unwillingly. Deliberate injury to Jews by a Jewish policeman required repentance and atonement. Substituting a mentally challenged Jew for a mentally sound Jew who was condemned to death was forbidden—no justification was given for it, and the way to atone for this was to fast for many days.

From the responsa of the rabbis it appears that there is also a difference between personal atonement, which is less stringent, and qualification for public positions, for which a high level of clean hands is required. The policeman who beat Jews was not permitted to serve as cantor in the synagogue, even though he had repented. On the other hand, repentance by the Jew who had pushed his fellow at his request and participated in a type of mercy killing was sufficient to qualify him for the same position. It should also be noted that there were those who considered the specific sin of eating forbidden foods a unique sin with

according to their laws. See Rabbi Yitzhak Isaac Liebes, *Sefer She'elot Utshuvot Beit Avi: Helek Hoshen Mishpat* (Hebrew), part 1, §158, https://www.responsa-holocaust.com (accessed April 26, 2021). Rabbi Liebes was born in Greiding (Horodok) in Galicia in 1906. His family was murdered in the Shoah, and he survived after hiding in the forests for many months. After the liberation he was active among the survivors. In 1948, he immigrated to New York where he served as a rabbi.

metaphysical consequences, which impaired one's qualifications for a leadership position in the rabbinate.

This study, which is based on varied sources from the Shoah responsa literature, indicates the wide range of this literature, including a variety of books and various subjects. The responsa presented in this research demonstrate the importance of this literature and its uniqueness. Questionable acts that people were ashamed of and that they perhaps had kept strictly secret were revealed to the rabbi as the religious authority in an attempt to atone. It may very well be that the rabbinical answers are the only documentation of these events.

Renée Reichmann and Her Rescue Enterprise in Tangier

ESTHER FARBSTEIN

D
ozens of documents and letters sent to a single addressee reveal a hitherto unknown rescue effort. Sent in the fateful years of 1942–1945 from Auschwitz, Theresienstadt, Bratislava, Vienna, Paris, Spain, Portugal, Switzerland, and the United States, they were all addressed to Renée Reichmann in Tangier. Renée Reichmann is rarely mentioned in historical research on the Holocaust, but documents found in her personal archive and in other collections[1] disclose a special story of rescue at the initiative of a mother and her daughter: Renée and Eva (Maidi) Reichmann.

The Reichmanns left Vienna in good time—March 1938, during the first days of the *Anschluss*. After brief stays in France and Spain, they reached Tetuán, Spanish Morocco, where the local Jews welcomed them. They eventually moved on to Tangier, the international free-trade city that had been occupied by Spain since the middle of 1940, which was the destination of hundreds of Jewish refugees from Central and Western Europe. As long as Tangier remained an international zone, refugees were admitted without difficulty, but after the Spanish occupation, they were deprived of the right to work. The local community and the American Jewish Joint Distribution Committee (JDC) helped them.[2] Despite the fact that the Jews were victims of Nazi propaganda, which was promoted by German merchants, and were harassed by the Spanish

---

1 They include the Reichmann family archive, in the possession of Esther Reichmann of Jerusalem; the archive of the Rabbinical Rescue Committee at Yeshiva University in New York (RRCA); the archive of the American Jewish Joint Distribution Committee in New York (JDC); the archive of Agudath Yisrael in New York (AIA); the archive of the U.S. War Refugee Board (WRB) in Washington, DC; and the Ganzach Kiddush Hashem Archive in Bnei Brak, Israel.

2 After April 1944, the JDC spent $12,000 monthly on behalf of these refugees; see Michael M. Laskier, *The Alliance Israélite Universelle and the Jewish Communities of Morocco, 1862–1962* (Albany: SUNY Press, 1983), p. 68.

police at times, their situation remained relatively secure.[3] It was against this background—and while her husband was developing the family business, and she was raising six children in a world at war and worrying about the family that she had left behind—that Renée Reichmann decided to devote her years in Tangier to relief and rescue efforts on behalf of the Jews in occupied Europe.

What insight inspired her to do this? What tools and connections did she amass at such a distance from occupied Europe? How did her activity become possible under the political conditions in which she lived? How did the Jewish community of Tangier relate to it? What makes Renée Reichmann unique as an initiator of rescue in general and as a woman in particular? How can her accomplishments be assessed from a historical perspective? These questions are addressed in the pages that follow.

First Steps: Parcels to Jews in the Occupied Countries

Renée Reichmann's efforts began with small steps. Concerned about family members whom she had left behind in Europe, she was eager to find a way to alleviate the existential distress of European Jewry—without imagining what awaited them later. As she corresponded with relatives in Hungary and Slovakia and with friends whom she had made in Western Europe, she became a conduit for the forwarding of letters from one country to another. Discovering the uniqueness of living in neutral Tangier, she allowed her address to serve as a way station for correspondence among Jews in different areas. Her postal activities grew and branched out, and what began as a family project became an effort on behalf the community. Her son Eli (Edward) wrote, "She had a small Hermes portable typewriter and began to write letters by the hundreds to every part of Europe."[4] Her right-hand woman throughout this

---

3   See Isabelle Rohr, *The Spanish Right and the Jews, 1898–1945: Antisemitism and Opportunism* (Sussex: Canada Blanch Centre for Contemporary Spanish Studies and Sussex Academic Press, 2007), pp. 110–120; Michel Abitbol, *The Jews of North Africa during the Second World War* (Detroit: Wayne State University Press, 1983), pp. 73–74. Laskier writes, "Politically speaking, the Jews of Tangier enjoyed the highest level of freedom attainable under an authoritarian regime"; see Laskier, *The Alliance Israélite Universelle and the Jewish Communities of Morocco*, p. 71.

4   Edward Reichmann, *Memories and Recollection: The Personal History of My Family* (Jerusalem: Mazo, 2009), p. 65.

activity was her seventeen-year-old daughter, Eva (Maidi), an intelligent, charismatic, and multilingual girl, who recruited additional participants among her friends.

In late 1941, Renée Reichmann also began sending parcels to Jewish friends in Western Europe who had become the targets for persecution of the Nazi occupation. After paying a family visit to Hungary in early 1942—itself a hazardous journey that reflected her courage—she became aware of the first transports from Slovakia in which many members of her family, among others, had been deported. Most shocking to her was the deportation of young people from Slovakia, who, as she soon learned, had been sent to Auschwitz. The first group of deportees from Slovakia—999 young women—were sent to Auschwitz in March 1942. The camp authorities ordered them to send postcards to Slovakia in a ploy to show that they were being treated well. Although these postcards were censored, based on them and other information that she received through channels directly from Slovakia, Renée Reichmann learned of the existence of a labor camp in Auschwitz but did not know that it was an extermination site. The rescue activity to help the deported girls began in the second half of June 1942.[5] During her travels, she encountered refugees and activists, including Rabbi Boruch Rabinowicz of Munkács[6] and Jacob Griffel, the Haredi rescue activist, who was a member of the Rescue Committee of the Jewish Agency in Istanbul.[7] Upon her return to Tangier, she began sending an ever-growing number of parcels to Slovakia, Auschwitz, and Theresienstadt,[8] using deportee address lists that she received via Budapest and from her brother Yechezkel Gestetner in Bratislava.

---

5   This refers to the first deportation from Slovakia in which 999 girls were shipped to Auschwitz to build the camp office infrastructure. According to Danuta Czech's records, a total of 999 Jewish women from Slovakia reached Auschwitz on March 26, 1942; see Danuta Czech, *Auschwitz Chronicle 1939–1945* (New York: Henry Holt and Company, 1990), p. 148.

6   On Jacob Griffel's activities for the refugees, see Esther Farbstein, *Hidden in the Heights: Orthodox Jewry in Hungary during the Holocaust* (Jerusalem: Mossad Harav Kook, 2014), pp. 172–175, 283–285; and Farbstein, "Harav, Hano'ar, Vehaplitim BeBudapest 1944" (Hebrew), *Dapim Leheker Hashoah*, 20 (2006), pp. 85–111.

7   On Griffel's activities in Istanbul, see Chaim Shalem, *Et La'asot Lehatzalat Yisrael* (Hebrew) (Tel Aviv: Agudath Ysrael, 2007), pp. 170–184.

8   Letter from Renée Reichmann to the Rabbinical Rescue Committee (RCC), New York, October 2, 1946, RRCA, Reichmann archive.

It should be noted that the rescue activist, Rabbi Michael Ber Weissmandel of Nitra, was also aware of the deportations as soon as they started but only began to understand their full implications later. In his memoirs, he wrote,

> It was between the festivals of Purim and Pesach 1942, and no one knew then that deportation meant immediate murder in the crematoria of Bełżec and Auschwitz. They feared starvation and disease; they feared multiple natural deaths as a result of the terrible exile, and this was sufficient to instill the fear of death in everyone… Our rabbi [Rabbi Samuel David Ungar, head of the Nitra yeshiva] did not speak of the deportation in terms of mass murder.[9]

It was at this time that the Working Group was established in Slovakia, and one of its first acts was to send couriers to document the fate of the deportees in Poland. As early as July 1942, they reported a high mortality rate among them and noted that starvation had been the cause of many of those deaths. The Working Group conveyed this information to their contacts in the West. In October 1942, they reported the disappearance of deported Jews, and couriers were sent to confirm the authenticity of the reports. In November, they returned and reported the annihilation taking place in Bełżec and Treblinka. From then on, the Working Group sent news of the murders as part of the appeals to contacts abroad concerning the rescue of Jews.[10]

Renée Reichmann already had the support of the Spanish Red Cross when she set out for Hungary and, after returning to Tangier, she received authorization from this organization to use its stamp to ship parcels to deportees at no cost, which was very significant assistance indeed. Thanks to her daughter Eva's friendship with Bebe Arias, a niece of Ángel Sanz-Briz, who would become the Spanish embassy chargé d'affaires in Budapest three years later, these connections, as well as others with the high Spanish officialdom in Morocco, were established. The friendship endured and would prove fruitful in subsequent years. Renée Reichmann mobilized her five sons and her daughter, Eva, to

9   Rabbi Chaim Michael Ber Weissmandel, *Min Hameitzar* (Hebrew) (New York: Emunah 1960), p. 24.
10 For more on the activity of the Working Group, see "Bratislava During the Holocaust: The Working Group," https://www.yadvashem.org/yv/en/exhibitions/communities/bratislava/working_group.asp (accessed May 1, 2022).

collect essential items and to send parcels. They also recruited friends in Tangier—offspring of refugees from Hungary—and even local comrades among the Jews of Morocco.

In late 1943, the parcel project expanded, owing to changes on the front. The Moroccan Jews had stopped fearing for their fate and the Spanish government, no longer considering Germany invincible, became more amenable to offering aid than it had been before.[11] The enterprise broadened again after the Nazis occupied Hungary in the winter of 1944. The destinations of the parcels now spread to Budapest and the labor camps to which Hungarian and Slovakian Jews were being taken. Reichmann received letters and postcards in response to her parcels in which the correspondents expressed gratitude, pleaded for food, and also asked for *matzot* for Passover.[12] Those in Bratislava also asked her to help Jews who were in hiding.[13] The packages were filled for the most part with food, medicines, and items that could be bartered. In a special operation, clothing was collected for Hungarian Jews ahead of the winter of 1944–1945.[14] For this purpose, Renée Reichmann and her associates also visited Madrid, Barcelona, Melilla, Gibraltar, and other localities.[15]

Due to wartime postal regulations, Renée Reichmann, like other activists who were trying to send parcels, encountered many difficulties, among them lack of addresses, German censorship, and problems in arranging shipping services for her parcels. Even after most of the addressees had been murdered, not knowing about their deaths, she

11 Reichmann, *Memories and Recollection*, pp. 61–66, 70–73; David Kranzler, *Thy Brothers' Blood: The Orthodox Jewish Response during the Holocaust* (New York: Mesorah, 1987), pp. 247–251.

12 Letter from Shimon Lebensfeld of Bratislava in which he asks Renée Reichmann to send parcels to his family in Auschwitz, January 10, 1944, and a letter from Heinrich Gestetner of Bratislava, who requests food packages and *matzot* to be sent to specific addresses in Birkenau and Theresienstadt, March 12, 1944, Reichmann family archive.

13 Confirmation, August 11, 1944, that Mr. Grossgut and his daughter, Mrs. Brandman, hiding in Slovakia, received a parcel, AIA, Sternbuch Collection, and HIJEFS (Hilfsverein für Jüdische Flüchtlinge in Shanghai [im Ausland]) Collection. The correspondent sent additional names and described how difficult it was to find a hideout there.

14 Telegram from Renée Reichmann to the HIJEFS, October 3, 1944, and letter from Renée Reichmann to the RCC, January 15, 1945 (summary of activities), RRCA, Reichmann archive.

15 Letters Renée Reichmann to RCC, March 14, 1945, January 15, 1945, and October 2, 1946, RRCA, Reichmann archive.

continued to inquire into their fates and whereabouts.[16] In one letter, Renée Reichmann made an audacious proposal: "If we get some more money, we'll be able to rent a little boat to cruise on the Danube"[17] to take Jews to safety.

Ties with affluent families in Spanish Morocco and Hungarian Jewish families in Tangier led to the establishment of the Committee for Aid to Refugees in Tangier. The new panel drew its membership from the refugee population, as well as from affluent and respected families in the Tetuán community, including those of the brothers Aaron and Jacob Cohen, the Salamas,[18] and the Ben-Haroushes. Thus, sending parcels was more than just a humanitarian enterprise; it figured importantly in raising awareness among the local Jewish population and set an interesting precedent as a partnership of fate with European Jewry.

The JDC also joined the providers of relief through the offices of the community head, Isaac Laredo, one of JDC's representatives in the city. The parcel operation continued to expand with support from the Spanish Red Cross that, from 1942 onward, allowed Renée Reichmann to make enormous numbers of shipments with hardly any objections and almost no limit, even allowing her to affix its official labels to her boxes. Views about Franco's policy in this matter are divided. Did he support these activities or did he ignore them? His motives are also subject to debate.

The packages were distributed by the German Red Cross, resulting in the strange paradox of relief for people who were facing that country's policy of annihilation.[19] This was probably the result of opposing German interests, for example, schemes involving the exchange of "war prisoners," the need to maintain friendship with Spain, or yet another deception for the rest of the world. Clearly, too, the Germans appropriated many of the parcels.

Only in July 1944 did the International Committee of the Red Cross (ICRC) also involve itself in these rescue efforts, including, but

---

16 See, for example, the letters from the HIJEFS to Reichmann, August 23, 1944, from Reichmann to the HIJEFS, August 25, 1944, and from Reichmann to the HIJEFS, September 16, 1944, AIA, Sternbuch Collection.

17 WRB, file 1127.

18 The paterfamilias was Isaac—a wealthy businessman, a socialist, and a friend of Franco.

19 Meir Dworzecki, "The International Red Cross and Its Policy vis-à-vis the Jews in the Ghettos, and the Concentration Camps in Nazi-Occupied Europe," in Israel Gutman and Efraim Zuroff, eds., Rescue Attempts during the Holocaust (Jerusalem: Yad Vashem, 1977), pp. 71–110.

not limited to, support for various rescue organizations around the world and for Renée Reichmann as well. In the spring of 1944, the Rabbinical Rescue Committee (RRC) recognized Renée Reichmann as its representative and authorized her to act for the rescue of any Jew anywhere, irrespective of the cost.[20] Renée Reichmann corresponded directly with the heads of the RRC in the United States, Rabbi Aaron Kotler and Rabbi Abraham Kalmanowitz, and with the RRC agent in Switzerland, Recha Sternbuch. The partnership that developed between Reichmann and Sternbuch in the intensive rescue work is mirrored in their correspondence, which stretched from spring 1944 to several years after the war.[21] Writing to Dr. Jacob Rosenheim, Renée Reichmann stressed, "We have asked neither you [RRC] nor the JDC for one cent for [our] work, because the wrapping of such large numbers [of parcels] has been taken care of by my children and our friends, who have done it through superhuman effort."[22]

Did the Parcels Reach Their Destinations?

Given the paucity of letters from the camps in reply to the relatively large number of parcels sent, everyone involved in the project wondered whether the packages were actually reaching their addressees. Each letter that arrived from the camps in response to their efforts was greeted with joy and inspired those involved to keep going. One of these letters was written by Regina Lebensfeld (Steinberg). In her testimony to Yad Vashem, she said that while in Auschwitz she had received parcels from Renée Reichmann in Tangier for three years.[23] Her letter is one of 635 thank you

---

20 Telegram from Renée to the HIJEFS, August 25, 1944, AIA, Sternbuch Collection.
21 See AIA, Reichmann Collection. Recha and Yitzchak Sternbuch plunged into rescue work when the war began and subsequently functioned as an extension of the RRC under the aforementioned initials HIJEFS. Since they headed this organization at the time of concern in this article, letters sent in their name and those sent to the HIJEFS overlap. On Recha Sternbuch and the HIJEFS, see Joseph Friedenson and David Kranzler, *Heroine of Rescue: The Incredible Story of Recha Sternbuch* (New York: Artscroll History Series, 1984).
22 Letter from Renée Reichmann to the RRC, October 2, 1946, Reichmann family archive; letter from Renée Reichmann to Stefan Klein, August 12, 1944 and letter from Renée Reichmann to Sternbuch, September 16, 1944, RRCA, Reichmann archive.
23 Regina Lebensfeld (Steinberg) interview, August 15, 1996; copy in RRCA, Reichmann archive.

notes addressed to Renée Reichmann from Jews all over Europe, which are in the family archive.[24] Although aware that the Germans confiscated much of what she sent, Renée Reichmann believed that the project should continue, even if only some of the packages reached their destinations.

An interesting and lengthy correspondence took place between Renée Reichmann and two girls from Slovakia, Ida Unger and Rivka (Regina) Heinovitz, who maintained contact with Renée Reichmann, and through her, with their families in 1942–1943. Raya Cohen, a survivor of Auschwitz, offers an interesting description of the girls from Slovakia and their moral values.

Pesah was approaching....The devout were resolved to live on potatoes....I eavesdropped on Ida and Rivka'le, sitting behind me, as they talked. They were worried about having to spend the eight days [of Pesah] without bread....

Rivka'le was very devout; some even considered her benighted. But everyone knew that she was willing to help everyone, believers and atheists alike. Fearful and totally daunted where her own self was concerned, she did not hesitate to break the law and disobey orders when it came to others' welfare. Late that winter, a former acquaintance, someone from her hometown, happened to appear before her in the woodshed where we would sometimes work. Ill and starving...he cried out to her in an anguished tone of voice: Rivka'le! From then on, she made it her business to look out for him as best she could and spared no effort to help him. He recovered thanks to the food that she had denied herself with love.[25]

---

24 For examples of postcards, dated March–April–May 1944, and one postcard dated July 1944, confirming the receipt of parcels in Theresienstadt, see Kranzler, *Thy Brother's Blood*, pp. 248–254. Eva also testified about this: "We knew that the Auschwitz inmates were receiving the packages, because of the postcards we received. The Nazis made them write postcards so the world would think they were treated well, but they were afraid to write to their relatives in Slovakia, for fear of giving away identities"; Ibid., p. 248. Also preserved in her archive is a list of girls to whom parcels had been sent, and their "addresses" in the camps. (There is something innocent about recording Auschwitz as a permanent address.) Additional examples are postcards to the Ehrenfelds, Rosenfelds, and Reichmanns in March–May 1944, confirming the receipt of parcels in Theresienstadt. These documents were collected by Eva Reichmann in Jerusalem.

25 Raya Cohen, *Nashim Belishchat Hagehinom* (Hebrew) (Tel Aviv: Hakibbutz Hame'uhad: Sifriyat Po'alim, 1947), pp. 148–149, 222.

One may surmise that some of the commodities that Rivka'le shared with her friends had come from Renée Reichmann. A letter that Ida Unger sent from Auschwitz to Renée Reichmann in October 1943 reflects the spirit of the rest of the letters, as well as her own emotions.

> I think of you all the time....We have received 11 letters, 9 parcels, 2 parcels from Portugal....I cannot describe what I feel about you....I wanted to keep it all, they were so delicious and precious....The cookies...the chocolate...It all tasted so wonderful....Why aren't they writing to Rosie Klein? I'm in good health and I'm thinking only about you. Kisses from me, love, Ida.[26]

On the margins of the letter, her friend Rivka (Regina) added: "I also send kisses to my parents and greetings to all of you, Regina Heinovitz."

Rivka (Regina) Heinovitz was grateful to Renée Reichmann for the rest of her life. She kept all of the letters that she had received during that period, most of which had arrived via Renée Reichmann, until her last day, keeping them in a cloth pouch that her friends had devotedly made for her on the occasion of her nineteenth birthday in 1942.[27]

Relief or Rescue by Jews and Jewish Organizations

Along with Renée Reichmann, Zionist organizations sent parcels to Jews in the occupied countries. Key among those involved were Richard Lichtheim of the Jewish Agency and the Zionist Organization, Nathan Schwalb of the Hehalutz Youth Movement,[28] Abraham (Alfred)

---

26 Author's translation of the original letter in German from Ida Unger in Auschwitz to Renée Reichmann, October 1943, Reichmann family archive. Also, the letter from Rivka Heinovitz to Leo Unger via Renée Reichmann, October 15, 1943, and the letter from Leo Unger to Renée Reichmann, May 18, 1944, Reichmann family archive.

27 Reported by Asher Heinovitz, Rivka (Regina) Heinovitz's cousin, August 2015; see Rivka (Regina) Heinovitz testimony, USC Shoah Foundation Visual History Archive (VHA).

28 Avraham Milgram, "*Bivediduti Ani Toleh Et Kol Tikvotai*" (Hebrew), *Yalkut Moreshet*, 83 (April 2007), pp. 85–104, particularly pp. 93–95; Raya Cohen, *Bein "Sham Lekan": Sipuram Shel Edim Lahurban, Shvaitz 1939-1942*" (Hebrew) (Tel Aviv: Am Oved, 1999), pp. 78–112. Schwalb sent parcels to Jews in the Generalgouvernemen, France, and Theresienstadt; they were intended for perspective immigrants to *Eretz Israel* and youth

Silberstein of the World Jewish Congress, and the power behind the aid organization, the Relief Committee for the War-Stricken Jewish Population (RELICO).[29] Others who engaged in this activity were Saly Mayer, the JDC representative in Geneva,[30] and Haredi activists, who appear to have operated on a vast scale—Chaim Yisroel Eiss, the Agudath Yisrael representative;[31] Recha and Yitzchak Sternbuch of Montreux,[32] representing the RRC in various locations; Rabbi Chaim Michael Ber Weissmandel of Nitra; and others.[33]

Like Renée Reichmann, they initially sent parcels to personal addresses but, from 1942 onward, they did so via public organizations. In Poland, the principal intermediary was the Jüdische Unterstützungsstelle (Jewish Relief Office, JUS), centered in Kraków and headed by Dr. Michael Weichert.[34] Most of the activists lost contact with Poland during the course of 1943 and rerouted their parcels to Theresienstadt. Their motives were also similar: Most had relatives, or relations with members of their movements, in the occupied countries; and they acted out of compassion for their fellow Jews and took initiatives of their own, even when they received funding from others.

How should this activity be viewed—as relief for the Jews or as rescue? "Historiography realizes that this was but an illusion that burst. For this reason, it tends to disregard the relief activity on the grounds that

movement members in the ghettos and training facilities. These parcels were also sent from Lisbon, additionally via Silberstein's organization, RELICO, and subsequently in additional ways. His activity was funded by the JDC.

29 Cohen, *Bein "Sham Lekan,"* pp. 156–177. For documents about the matter, see Abraham Silberschein Archive, YVA, M.20.

30 Cohen, *Bein "Sham Lekan,"* pp. 178–198.

31 In regard to Chaim Yisroel Eiss, see Shalem, *Time to Rescue,* pp.155–170; Ganzach Kiddush Hashem, Chaim Yisroel Eiss file.

32 For information about Recha and Yitzchak Sternbuch, see Friedenson and Kranzler, *Heroine of Rescue*; Shahar Shapira, *Eihaha Uhal Vera'iti* (Hebrew) (Jerusalem: Tzuf, 2012); Ganzach Kiddush Hashem, Sternbuch file; AIA, Sternbuch file.

33 By the time Rabbi Weissmandel began to ship parcels, most of Slovakian Jewry had been deported to Poland; he received letters of gratitude that encouraged him to keep going. See Abraham Fuchs, *The Unheeded Cry* (New York: Mesorah), pp. 31–32. Concerning those who sent parcels, see Nathan Eck, *"Nisyonot Hatzala Be'emtza'ut Darkonim,"* in Eck, *Hato'im Bedarkei Hamavet: Havai Vehagut Biyemei* (Hebrew) (Jerusalem: Yad Vashem, 1960), pp. 99–106; Dina Porat, *The Blue and the Yellow Stars of David* (Cambridge: Harvard University Press, 1990).

34 During the Holocaust, Weichert headed the JSS, the Jewish self-help organization in Poland, that operated under official Nazi auspices in that country.

the annihilation campaign rendered it unimportant, as it were," as Raya Cohen noted in one of the principal studies on this topic.[35] Some are in doubt about defining food parcels as "rescue operations," because the rescue was temporary. Another question is whether the focus on sending parcels numbed the senses to the mass murder that was underway and whether this pattern of activity was poorly suited to the time.[36]

These doubts are countered by the argument that the parcels provided an anchor for survival amid the war and represented an attempt to stanch the toll of death from hunger, cold, and epidemics.[37] Often, the food thus delivered gave Jews a chance to endure a little longer than they would have otherwise—who knows what the morrow would bring?[38] Each parcel also had moral significance: It gave the recipients a measure of mental fortitude that helped in the struggle against despair and loneliness by proving that someone remembered and was looking out for them.[39] A parcel from the free world sent a signal of still-extant love. It gave encouragement by showing that someone out there remembered them. It conferred hope and mirrored the profound traditional value of Jews' responsibility for one another.

Decisive Measures: Rescue Visas to Tangier

The Idea behind the Visas

The mass deportation of Hungarian Jews to Poland following Germany's occupation of Hungary on March 19, 1944, presented Renée Reichmann and her rescue efforts with a new and very difficult challenge. As the fate of Hungarian Jews, her intimates by country of birth and by kinship, was at stake, she worked to arrange visas for them for Tangier.

Procuring such visas entailed intensive political activity and depended on Hungarian and Spanish policies to issue them, and on

---

35 Cohen, *Bein "Sham Lekan,"* p. 177.

36 Raya Cohen, *"Solidariyut Bemivhan Hashoah: Pe'ilut Ha'irgunim Hayehudim Ha'olamim BeGeneva"* (Hebrew) (PhD diss., Tel Aviv University, 1992), pp. 280–281.

37 Cohen, *Bein "Sham Lekan,"* p. 167.

38 Dalia Ofer, "The Yishuv Mission in Constantinople," *Yalkut Moreshet*, 28 (November 1979), pp. 55–76; Dan Michman, *Holocaust Historiography: A Jewish Perspective* (London and Portland: Vallentine Mitchell, 2003), pp. 179–204, esp. 179–180.

39 Milgram, *"Bivediduti."*

German policy to allow them to be used for the emigration of their holders from Hungary. The possession of such a visa also had immediate protective value, because both citizens and noncitizens were subject to the same laws in Hungary. Although most foreign legations in Budapest had been closed by then, their countries' interests were represented by neutral legations; for example, Britain was represented by Carl Lutz, the Swiss envoy. Obtaining visas for Spanish-occupied Tangier should be credited to the efforts of Renée Reichmann, who powered the idea and its implementation.

The idea of requesting visas for Tangier was raised by Pinchas Freudiger—a member of the Budapest Judenrat and a leader of the Haredi rescue committee in that city[40]—and by two rescue activists, Shmuel Frei and Haim Róth.[41] The request was submitted in late April or early May 1944,[42] when the impending deportation of Hungarian Jewry to Auschwitz first became known, or roughly at the time it began.[43] It stands to reason that Freudiger, Otto Komoly, and Miklos "Moshe" Krausz sought ways to save children at this time by using their connections abroad. Freudiger forwarded similar appeals to the Haredi rescue activists in New York, Istanbul, Britain, and elsewhere.

The Visas: Switching from Emigration to Protection and Rescue

To obtain a visa for Tangier from the Spanish government involved concerted efforts in both Spain and Tangier, as well as the approval of General Luis Orgaz, high commissioner and commander in chief of Spanish and native forces in Spanish Morocco. Renée Reichmann set this stage of the process in motion by using her connections with high-

40 On the Haredi rescue committee, its heads, and its activities, see Farbstein, *Hidden in the Heights*, pp. 172–243.

41 In regard to Róth, see Shlomo Róth, *Der Vanderlikher Klal Toer fun Budapest* (Yiddish) (Jerusalem: 2007); on Shmuel Frei, see Moshe Holczler, *Budapest '44: A Story of Rescue and Resistance, 1944–1945* (New York: Mesorah, 2004).

42 Summarizing letter from Renée Reichmann to the RRC, October 2, 1946, RRCA, Reichmann archive.

43 On the information that reached Budapest, see Rudolf Vrba, *I Escaped from Auschwitz* (London: Robson, 2006), chaps. 15–17; Yehuda Bauer, *Jews for Sale? Nazi-Jewish Negotiations 1933–1945* (New Haven: Yale University Press, 1996), p.157; Ayala Nedivi, *Bein Krausz LeKasztner: Hama'vak al Hatzalat Yehudei Hungariya* (Hebrew) (Jerusalem: Magnes, 2014), pp. 116–118, 165–186.

ranking Spanish officials. Her emissaries operated under Spanish law regarding visa applications. The visas were to be for children and to be used for a temporary stay in Tangier, without allowing the number of refugees to grow and with a commitment to assume the expenses for their upkeep. In a process that need not be detailed here, Orgaz approved the issuance of the visas under these conditions.[44]

The success of this phase of the project owes much to the support of James Rives Childs, the American chargé d'affaires in Tangier and a friend of General Orgaz.[45] Attached to the application was a commitment by the Jewish communities of Tangier and Tetuán, signed by the heads of the Tangier community, to support the children. This was the first application for the rescue of children that these two communities officially presented to the government of Spain.

The second stage was the willingness of the Spanish envoy in Budapest, Ángel Sanz-Briz, to issue the visas and implement the rescue scheme. Sanz-Briz, who was appointed to his post at the time of the deportations as Miguel Ángel de Muguiro's successor, was one of several diplomats who used their power to save Jews. His beneficiaries were Jews of Spanish extraction, who under de Muguiro could obtain Spanish citizenship, as well as a large number of Ashkenazi Jews. Sanz-Briz has been recognized as Righteous Among the Nations.

Sanz-Briz issued provisional passports to children, which made Spain officially responsible for their holders. In the meantime, conditions came about in Budapest that made child rescue easier. Primarily in mid-May, the Swedish Red Cross began to engage in humanitarian activity with the Hungarian government's consent and was willing to help to move Jews to neutral territory, or to shelter them in conjunction with the International Red Cross. This led to the establishment of orphanages in Budapest under the patronage of the Swedish Red Cross, where nearly 1,000 children, Jewish and non-Jewish, were placed. The buildings were granted extraterritorial status. About five months later, the idea of sheltered homes for children became the main venue for large-scale rescue.

On June 26, 1944, the Hungarian regent, Miklós Horthy, issued the

---

44 Letter from Renée Reichmann to the RRC, October 2, 1946, RRCA, Reichmann archive; Haim Avni, *Spain, the Jews, and Franco* (Philadelphia: Jewish Publication Society of America, 1982) p. 195.
45 See Rohr, *The Spanish Right and the Jews*, pp. 125–126.

statement known as the "Horthy Plan" or "Horthy Offer." It included a decision to halt the deportations and to allow 7,000 holders of immigration visas to Mandatory Palestine to relocate there,[46] and a three-month de facto moratorium on deportations began around two weeks later, on July 9, 1944. It was on that very day that Raoul Wallenberg reached Budapest to immerse himself in rescue operations as an attaché to the Swedish mission in Budapest.

The visas for Tangier reached Budapest on August 25, 1944, and were followed by an immediate effort to expedite the emigration of children to Tangier and to other neutral destinations. Each legation mobilized to protect "its" Jews by issuing immigration visas to them. These efforts were augmented by the Committee for Aid to Refugees in Tangier, which granted permission to move the children to Tangier, and added a list with the names of 200 youngsters, proposed by Renée Reichmann, and 300 others chosen by the Budapest Judenrat. Renée Reichmann also corresponded about the matter with the RRC, which funded the operation.[47]

In Budapest, Sanz-Briz, heads of the ICRC, and heads of Jewish organizations began to screen the children who were candidates for rescue. Concurrently, Sanz-Briz extended protection to forty-five Spanish Jews—fifteen families—whom he could declare as citizens of Spain.[48] In the meantime, the ICRC placed the youngsters in protected camps.[49] Amid these measures, Renée Reichmann prepared an infrastructure to receive the children in Tangier. Childs, having heard about this from Orgaz, reported it to the War Refugee Board.[50] Renée Reichmann also

---

46 David Kranzler, *The Man Who Stopped the Trains to Auschwitz* (New York: Syracuse University Press, 2000), pp. 122–143; Randolph Braham and Nathaniel Katzburg, eds., *Toldot Hashoah: Hungariya* (Hebrew) (Jerusalem: Yad Vashem, 1992), p. 351; Nadivi, *Bein Krausz VeKasztner*, pp. 187–216. The book was greatly expanded by Moshe Krausz.

47 Letter from Shemaya-Shmuel Reichmann to Stefan Klein, Brooklyn, July 14, 1944, RRCA, Reichmann archive; letter from the RRC to Shmuel Reichmann, July 19, 1944, WRB, file 1104; Chaim U. Lipschitz, *Franco, Spain, the Jews, and the Holocaust* (New York: Ktav, 1984), p. 59.

48 Avni, *Spain, the Jews, and Franco*, p. 199.

49 Letter from the HIJEFS to Renée Reichmann, August 15, 1944, AIA, Reichmann family archive; Renée Reichmann to the HIJEFS, August 25, 1944, ibid. See also David Kranzler, "Renée Reichmann and the Tangier Rescue Connection," *The Jewish Observer*, February 1991, p. 29; Randolph L. Braham, *The Politics of Genocide: The Holocaust in Hungary* (Detroit: Wayne State University Press 1994), pp. 1242–1244.

50 Childs, Tangier, to Department of State for War Refugee Board, August 12, 1944, WRB, file 1104.

managed to obtain visas for some of the children's parents.[51]

The Germans, however, obstructed the children's emigration and, in October, four days after the Arrow Cross coup, announced officially that they would not issue visas.[52] From then on, during the moratorium on deportations and after the Arrow Cross insurrection, the visas served to protect the children and, in turn, allowed the Spanish legation in Budapest and the ICRC to protect the special orphanages within the framework of the municipal orphanage system.[53] To her great distress, however, Renée Reichmann was unable to rescue her family members and their children. "I cannot save my brothers' and sisters' children.... My heart bleeds but I must comfort myself that other souls were saved in lieu of them. We should pray to God that in His compassion he will save all our hapless brethren."[54]

Protecting 700 Additional Jews

Observing the efficacy of the principle, the method, and the connections, Renée Reichmann sensed that a door had opened to seek the rescue of 700 additional Jews. Again, she availed herself of the Tangier community, its head, individual Jews of means, and General Orgaz.[55] On September 14, 1944, she turned to a higher political channel, the Spanish Consul

---

51 Kranzler, "Renée Reichmann," pp. 32–33.

52 Letter from the HIJEFS to Renée Reichmann, October 19, 1944, AIA.

53 Shortly before Budapest was liberated from Nazi occupation, more than fifty protected homes for Jewish children operated in the city, which saved 5,000 children and 1,500–2,000 adults. See Asher Cohen, *The Halutz Resistance in Hungary 1942–1944* (*Social Science Monographs*) (Boulder: University of Colorado, 1986); Hava Eichler, "*Hatzalat Hayeladim BeHungariya*" (Hebrew), *Yalkut Moreshet*, 22 (April 1994), p. 17; Robert Rozett, "Jewish and Hungarian Armed Resistance in Hungary," *Yad Vashem Studies*, 19 (1989), pp. 271–272. Today we speak of more than fifty houses. See Peretz Révész, *Standing up to Evil* (Jerusalem: Yad Vashem, 2019) pp. 274–285.

54 Letter from Renée Reichmann to the RRC, October 18, 1944, RRCA, Reichmann archive.

55 On September 20, 1944, Orgaz advised the Spanish Foreign Minister that the public council in Tangier had sent him an application for entry and provisional-stay visas in Spanish sovereign territories in Morocco for 700 members of Budapest Jewish families, whose names were specified. See Matilde Rosillo Morcillo, "Las relaciones entre el régimen franquista y Hungría durante la Segunda Guerra Mundial: Petición de entrada de judíos procedentes de Hungría en el Protectorado del Marruecos Español," *Anales de Historia Contemporánea* (Universidad de Murcia, 2002), pp. 469–488.

431

in Tangier, through whom the Foreign Minister in Madrid was asked to instruct his consul in Budapest, Sanz-Briz, to grant 700 additional Jews Spanish protective papers.[56] Two days later, on September 16, 1944, she received approval in principle,[57] and Childs forwarded the information to the American ambassador in Madrid on October 4.[58]

The Arrow Cross coup on October 15, 1944, and the acceleration of the Final Solution in Budapest stopped the exodus from Hungary. However, the neutral legations' protection of those who had applied to emigrate remained in effect, and after Sanz-Briz left Budapest in December, his successor, Giorgio Perlasca, maintained it as well. On November 2, 1944, the ICRC gave the Spanish legation in Budapest authorization in principle to distribute the 700 visas as it had for the 500 children; even with no emigration possible, this still would serve to help protect the visa holders. Renée Reichmann thanked Childs for his assistance in obtaining these 700 documents, and he responded to her words of gratitude by expressing appreciation of her efforts and the hope that she would surmount the obstacles.[59] The relevant archives reveal that Renée Reichmann both initiated these rescue efforts and was involved in them by recruiting Childs and Orgaz, and by mobilizing community pressure to have the visas approved and sent on to Budapest. Historical research has overlooked this activity, attributing it to anonymous activists as well.

The estimate is that the Spanish mission issued 2,795–5,200 protective documents; the lower figure is Avni's and the higher one is Morcillo's.[60] Nearly 1,500 of these visas were distributed at the initiative of Renée Reichmann and her associates. Researchers such as Avni and Braham attribute the initiative to rescue children via Tangier to the

---

56 Especially after the German invasion of Hungary in March 1944, various neutral governments and organizations issued letters of protection in their name to thousands of Hungarian Jews, mostly in Budapest.

57 See Lipschitz, *Franco, Spain, the Jews, and the Holocaust*, p. 59.

58 Sent by the treasurer of the High Commissioner of Spanish Morocco, General Orgaz, to the Foreign Minister, Tetuán, October 6, 1944. The number evidently includes escorts and Jews who acquired Spanish visas in other ways. See Morcillo, "Las relaciones entre el régimen franquista y Hungría"; p. 481; Lipschitz, *Franco, Spain, the Jews, and the Holocaust*, p. 59.

59 December 8, 1944, Reichmann family archive.

60 Avni, *Spain, the Jews, and Franco*, pp. 191–200. Kranzler estimates the number of Jews saved by Spanish patronage at 3,000. See also Kranzler, "Renée Reichmann," pp. 32–33; Morcillo, "Las relaciones entre el régimen franquista y Hungría," p. 481.

Tangier Jewish community and, primarily, to wealthy Jews from Hungary and the Committee for Aid to Refugees in Tangier, without mentioning Renée Reichmann's central role.[61] Documents that have gathered dust in various archives, however, show that she was the catalyst behind the political démarches, and the one who pulled the local community and the Committee for Aid to Refugees in Tangier into the mission in the same way as she had earlier when sending parcels to the occupied countries.

In his memoirs, written twenty years after the events, Childs described the connection with Renée Reichmann and her role in obtaining the visas.

> From 1941 to 1945, I served as charge d'affairs of the American Legation in Tangier with jurisdiction over American interests in the whole of Morocco. About 1943, I had a call from Mme. Renée Reichman, a Jewish refugee concerned with philanthropic activities affecting her co-religionists. Her plea to me was a very earnest and moving one [so], in light of my now close personal relationship with General Orgaz, Spanish High Commissioner at Tetuán, Spanish Morocco, I appealed to him to support the issuance by the Spanish Legation in Budapest of Spanish Moroccan visas to 500 Jewish children in Hungary threatened with extermination. Mme. Reichman represented that the granted [visas] would not necessitate the physical transfer of the children to Morocco but would be a means of placing them under Spanish protection. I informed Mme. Reichman that it would be entirely irregular for me to intervene with Orgaz officially, but that in view of the humanitarian aspect, it was impossible for me to decline to transmit the request....I drove to Tetuán....As I anticipated, he immediately agreed to transmit the request to Madrid and support it with this approval.
>
> After a few weeks, Mme. Reichman called on me again to inform me that the visas had been issued and the children saved "and now, sir, would you be willing to approach General Orgaz again and ask him for visas for 700 adults?"...Later Mme. Reichman called to inform me that the additional 700 adults had joined the original 500 children."[62]

---

61 Avni, *Spain, the Jews, and Franco*, pp. 194–195.
62 James Rives Childs' memoirs, Reichmann family archive; Kranzler, *Thy Brothers' Blood*, p. 251; Reichmann, *Memories and Recollection*, pp. 97–99; see also Childs' letter to Rabbi

After the war, at Renée Reichmann's request, the Reichmann family postponed its departure to Canada.[63] She remained active in relief, mainly in aiding Jews in displaced persons camps and arranging visas for them to Tangier and to the United States, receiving refugees in Tangier, and, further, trying to ensure the survival of the Moroccan Jewish tradition. The last was an extraordinary enterprise, which led to the founding of the Otzar HaTorah school system[64] and, thus, brought about a meaningful change in the sense of Jewish identity and upbringing of the young generation of Moroccan Jewry.

Renée Reichmann's Unique Role in the Rescue of Jews

Renée Reichmann was one of those Jews in the free world who were galvanized by an impulse not to stand aside but to rise up and pledge themselves to rescue activity. Most of these individuals launched these devoted efforts in a personal initiative that gradually expanded into an international public activity. Sooner or later, global relief and rescue organizations became involved. They first became active at a relatively early stage of the events and thought it important to ward off the Jews' demise for even the briefest duration. As the Nazis' annihilation plans became increasingly evident, they began to attempt rescue, mostly with the help of passports or clandestine border crossing.

Unlike rescue activists who did their work in neutral countries, mainly Switzerland and Turkey, or in Allied countries, primarily Britain and the United States, where consuls served and rescue organizations operated, Renée Reichmann acted in a far distant place where she too was a refugee, and in association with a community that until then had not been involved with the fate of European Jewry at any practical level. Her mobilization of Moroccan Jewry for rescue activity was a singular and exceptional act that led to the rescue of hundreds of Jews, in addition

Lipschitz, concerning his cooperation with Renée Reichmann during the war, July 23, 1970, document no. 3, Reichmann family archive.

63 "We too are thinking about coming to America, but before we emigrate we want to help those who have come here"; letter from Renée Reichmann to Stefan Klein, January 1946. This is one of many documents that I received from Dr. David Kranzler, whose archive was transferred to Yad Vashem.

64 On Otzar HaTorah, see Ora Zagouri-Ohana, "Em Habanim, Otzar HaTorah, Vehahinuch Hayehudi BiMoroko Bein Hashanim 1860–1960" (Hebrew) (master's thesis, University of Haifa, 1988).

to those who may have owed their survival in the camps to the lifesaving parcels that her enterprise had placed in their hands.

Several impressive women engaged in rescue work during the Holocaust, the most prominent of them being Gisi Fleischmann of Slovakia, but with regard to Renée Reichmann, the right comparison is with women who operated out of neutral countries. Another woman in this group, whose activity has only come to light in recent years, is Hélène Cazès-Benatar (1898–1979), who was born in Tangier and was a lawyer and an activist with the Alliance Israélite Universelle and WIZO in Casablanca and with the JDC and the Red Cross in Morocco. In Casablanca, she aided refugees from Europe who suffered under the Vichy laws, were deported to labor camps in Morocco, and encountered difficulties in their daily lives. At her initiative, a relief committee was established—the Comité d'Assistance aux Réfugies Étrangers—and subsequently the JDC appointed her as its Morocco representative. After the war, among her other activities, she obtained visas to Casablanca for a group of children from France. She eventually moved to Paris, where she engaged chiefly in welfare work, facilitated emigration to Israel from Northern Africa, and participated in Zionist activities. Her tombstone carries the following epitaph: "To our mother, a legendary woman who saved so many from distress."[65]

Thus, Renée Reichmann and Hélène Cazès-Benatar were active in roughly the same geographical area: in Spanish Morocco and French Morocco, respectively. Both tackled the problem of Jewish refugees, each from her own angle, and both had the merit of saving children by arranging visas to Tangier. Both drew Moroccan Jews into the sphere of relief, both were living spirits behind refugee relief committees, and both were supported by Jewish organizations. Despite different cultural backgrounds, both had similar motives. The main difference lies in the breadth of their activity: Whereas Hélène Cazès-Benatar focused on the situation in Morocco, Renée Reichmann acted in response to what

---

65   See Michal Ben-Yaakov, "Hélène Cazès-Benatar et ses activités en faveur des réfugiés juifs au Maroc, 1940–1943," in Dan Michman and Haim Saadoun, eds., *Les juifs d'Afrique du Nord face a l'Allemagne nazie* (Paris: Perrin, Yad Vashem, and Yad Ben Zvi, 2018), pp. 177–198; Shalom Bar-Asher, "*Pelitim Yehudim Me'Eropa Hanatzit BiTzefon Afrika: Te'uda Mi'Archion Cazès-Benatar*" (Hebrew), *Pe'amim*, 114–115 (May 2008), pp. 257–262. The Cazès-Benatar Archive is now kept with the Central Archives for the History of the Jewish People Jerusalem (CAHJP), Hélène Cazès-Benatar Collection, 1979.

was going on in Europe and went as far as the concentration camps in a display of audacity and original initiatives. An additional distinction was that Hélène Cazès-Benatar operated in a political and geographical habitus of which she was a part, whereas Renée Reichmann lived in continual fear and acted in an environment where she herself was a refugee. Unlike Hélène Cazès-Benatar, however, who remained active into the 1970s—until her son died—Renée Reichmann terminated her public activity when her family relocated to Canada in the 1950s.

There are also commonalities between Renée Reichmann and Recha Sternbuch of Switzerland: Both were Haredi women whose religious appearance was striking, both were mothers, and both managed households that were always open to the indigent and to guests. Although devoted to their household labors, when trouble struck, they plunged into rescue activity that entailed working at home and away from home, traveling, and contacting representatives of governments and international organizations.

Recha Sternbuch's activity, which also began as her own initiative and continued in her capacity as an agent of the RRC, was more comprehensive than Renée Reichmann's in breadth and duration. Like Renée Reichmann, Recha Sternbuch dealt with parcels and visas and, after the occupation of Hungary, she too was involved in negotiations between the Jews and the Nazis for the rescue of the vestiges of Hungarian Jewry and the ghettos. After the liberation, Recha Sternbuch traveled to seven countries that had accepted Holocaust refugees in order to retrieve Jewish children from non-Jewish hands and relocate them. Recha Sternbuch's base of operations was Switzerland, where it was relatively easy to communicate with rescue organizations in both occupied and free countries. Renée Reichmann and her daughter, Eva, in contrast, overcame geographical distance and relative isolation to establish a supportive environment and a new communication system.

Once Renée Reichmann and Recha Sternbuch developed a relationship, they collaborated on a basis of mutual respect and trust. Several features stand out in these women's activities: sensitivity to the other, compassion and empathy for fellow Jews, the values of mutual responsibility that are embedded in Judaism, bravery and resolve, and a quest for original and diverse ways to be helpful. In the case of Renée Reichmann, this was also evident in her initiative to overhaul the schooling of the young generation of Moroccan Jews.

After the war, Renée Reichmann built her life around her home and did not seek personal publicity, honor, or glory. It is likely that her life, like that of Recha Sternbuch, was clouded by her success in having managed to rescue many Jews but not her parents and relatives, despite her strenuous efforts toward that end.

List of Contributors

Verena Buser is an affiliated researcher and codirector with Dr. Boaz Cohen of the project Children after the Holocaust, War, and Genocide at Western Galilee College, Akko. She received a PhD from Potsdam University of Applied Sciences and did her postdoctoral studies at the Alice Salomon University of Applied Sciences. Her research, which focuses on the areas of *hachshara* (training) and non-Zionist emigration preparations, childhood and youth during and after the Shoah, and Jewish functionaries under Nazi rule, has been supported by the Memorial Foundation for Jewish Culture and the Leo Baeck Institute in New York, the Hadassah Brandeis Institute in Waltham, and the Edith Saurer Fonds in Vienna. She is the author of *Überleben von Kindern und Jugendlichen in den Konzentrationslagern Sachsenhausen, Auschwitz und Bergen-Belsen* (Metropol, 2011) and of a number of articles, and the editor of the memoirs of Heinrich Demerer, *Als Kind in NS-Konzentrationslagern: Aufzeichnungen* (Metropol, 2009).

David Engel is the Greenberg professor of Holocaust Studies, professor and chair of Hebrew and Judaic studies, and professor of history at New York University; a senior fellow of the Goldstein–Goren Diaspora Research Center at Tel Aviv University; and a member of the Carnegie Commission on Ethics and International Affairs and the Commission on Polish–Jewish Relations since 2002. He holds a PhD in history from the University of California in Los Angeles, and did postdoctoral study at the Division of Holocaust Studies, Institute for Contemporary Jewry, the Hebrew University of Jerusalem. Engel received the honor of Outstanding Lecturer at Tel Aviv University, 1986–1987, and the 1996 Golden Dozen Award for Excellence in Undergraduate Teaching at New York University. His publications include *Bein Shihrur Lebriha: Nitzulei Hashoah BePolin Vehama'avak Al Hanhagatam* (Between Liberation and Flight: Holocaust Survivors in Poland and the Struggle for Leadership, 1944–1946) (Am Oved, 1996); and *Facing a Holocaust: The Polish Government-in-Exile and the Jews, 1943–1945* (University of North Carolina Press, 1993).

Esther Farbstein is the director of the Holocaust Research Center of the Jerusalem College; academic advisor at the Ganzach Kiddush Hashem Archives, Bnei Brak; and the head of the project "Zikaron Besefer" (Memory in a Book), an online database of rabbinic memoirs originally written as prefaces to their religious volumes. She has conducted groundbreaking research on the response of religious Jewry to the Holocaust, has published many articles in prestigious academic journals, and has edited several Holocaust diaries, among them the diary of Rabbi Chaim Stein. Her books include *Hidden in Thunder: Perspectives on Faith, Halacha and Leadership during the Holocaust* (Feldheim, 2007); *The Forgotten Memoirs: Moving Personal Accounts from Rabbis who Survived the Holocaust* (Sha'ar Press, 2011); *Hidden in the Heights: Orthodox Jewry in Hungary during the Holocaust* (Mossad Harav Kook, 2014); and *Tal Shel Tehiya: Michtavim Rishonim Shel Anshay Emuna Aharay Hashoah* (Dew of Revival: First Letters from Jews of Faith after the Holocaust) (Mossad Harav Kook, 2020).

Jeannine Levana Frenk, a scholar who participates in projects for Yad Vashem and Moreshet, earned her PhD in history at Tel Aviv University with a dissertation that deals with the Holocaust and representations of the "Other" in French and Israeli cinema. After publishing various articles on this topic, she then focused on researching rescue attempts in France and in Belgium during World War II. Yad Vashem published the results of her comparative study on the attitudes of Righteous Among the Nations in these two countries, as well as her research on children houses in France and on the Jewish Defense Committee in Belgium during the war period. Her monograph on the youth movement Hashomer Hatza'ir in France was published by Moreshet, Yad Ya'ari, and the Havazelet group in 2021.

Idit Gil is the academic director of the interdisciplinary program M.A. in Democracy Studies at the Open University of Israel. The subjects of her research are Jewish forced labor in Poland and in concentration camps in the Reich, particularly on the economic and ideological aspects of the Nazi labor policy, and Jewish reactions to them; Israel and the Holocaust, collective memory, teaching the Holocaust, Israeli society, and the Holocaust; and Yosef Giser's diary, which was written in three concentration camps and during a death march. Her book *Masa'a: Bein Ha'ishi Vehahistoria* (The Holocaust: Between the Personal and History) (Carmel, 2017) interweaves a personal memoir with original research on the development of the Holocaust in Poland. Her research currently focuses on the correlation between beauty and sexual abuse during the Holocaust.

Gershon Greenberg is a visiting professor of Jewish philosophy at Bar Ilan University, and professor of philosophy and religion at American University in Washington, DC. He previously taught in the Department of Jewish Thought of the Hebrew University of Jerusalem, in the Judaistik Faculty of the Free University of Berlin, and in the Oxford University Center for Hebrew and Jewish Studies. The primary fields of his published research are the real-time Orthodox Jewish responses to the Holocaust and the history of modern Jewish thought. The secondary focus of his research is the history of Jewish religious thought in America and America–Holy Land studies. He recently translated to English and wrote an introduction to Eliezer Schweid's *Siddur Hatefillah*, entitled, *Siddur Hatefillah: The Jewish Prayer Book. Philosophy, Poetry, and Mystery* (Academic Studies Press, 2022), and coedited with Asaf Yedidyah, *Mishpateha Tehom Rabah: Teguvot Hagutiot Ortodoksiot Lashoah* (The Vast Abyss of Your Trials: Orthodox Reactions to and Reflections on the Shoah (Mossad Harav Kook, 2016).

Steven T. Katz holds the Slater Chair in Jewish and Holocaust Studies at Boston University, is a member of the Academic Committee of the United States Holocaust Memorial Museum, and is chair of the Kagan Fellowship Committee of the Claims Conference. From 2011–2017, he acted as academic advisor to the thirty-one countries belonging to the International Holocaust Remembrance Alliance (IHRA), where he is the founding director of the Elie Wiesel Center for Jewish Studies. He writes on the Holocaust, Jewish philosophy, and comparative mysticism, and edits the journal *Modern Judaism*. He is the author of numerous works, including a two-volume study *The Holocaust and Black Slavery: A Comparison* (Cambridge University Press, 2019), which was awarded the 2019 PROSE Award for Professional and Scholarly Excellence, and a book of essays entitled *Holocaust Studies: Critical Reflections* (Routledge, 2019), and the editor of *The Cambridge Companion to Antisemitism* (Cambridge University Press, 2022).

Rami Neudorfer is a PhD student at Tel Aviv University, who is writing a dissertation about life in the Kovno ghetto. His master's thesis, entitled

"The Jewish Police in the Kovno Ghetto: A Story of Contradictions," won the 2016 Goldhirsch Prize for Best Thesis on the Holocaust and Rebirth from the Ben-Gurion Institute for Research of Israel and Zionism. Neudorfer organized a concert at Yad Vashem in 2018, reenacting a Zionist concert that took place in the Kovno ghetto in 1943. He also holds a BS degree from the Tecnhion—Israel institute of Technology, and an MBA from Tel Aviv University.

Dalia Ofer, Max and Rita Haber professor of Holocaust and East European Studies at the Hebrew University of Jerusalem (emerita), was the director of Avraham Harman Institute of Contemporary Jewry, 2003–2007, and of the Vidal Sassoon International Research Center for the Study of Anti-Semitism, 1995–2002; a visiting professor at Harvard, Yale, Brandeis, and the universities of Maryland and of Sydney, Australia; and a Charles H. Revson Foundation Fellow at the USHMM. Her publications include *Escaping the Holocaust: Illegal Immigration to the Land of Israel* (Oxford U. Press, 1990), which won the Ben Zvi Award and Jewish Book Award for the Hebrew and English versions respectively; *Women in the Holocaust* (Yale U. Press, 1998), coauthored with Lenore Weizman; and *Her Story, My Story: Writing about Women and the Holocaust* (Peter Lang, 2020), coauthored with Judy Baume. She also coedited with Sarah Rosen both the Hebrew and English versions of Lipman Kunstadt, *Diary from Hell in Transnistria 1942–1944* (Yad Vashem, 2020 and 2022). She is the recipient of the Distinguished Achievement Award in Holocaust Studies from the Holocaust Educational Foundation of Northwestern University in 2018.

Miriam Offer, an expert researcher of Jewish medicine during the Holocaust, is a senior lecturer at Western Galilee College; cochair of the international conference Medicine in the Holocaust and Beyond, Western Galilee, 2017; member of the Lancet Commission on Medicine and the Holocaust: Historical Evidence, Implications for Today, Teaching for Tomorrow; a researcher at Hadassah–Brandeis Institute; head of research team on Medicine, Morbidity, and Childhood during and after the Holocaust, which is funded by the Israel Ministry of Science and Technology; and cofounder and former director of the Hedva Eibeshitz Institute for Holocaust Research, Haifa. She is the author of *White Coats in the Ghetto: Jewish Medicine in Poland during the Holocaust* (Yad Vashem, 2020); coeditor with Sabine Hildebrandt and Michael A.

Grodin of *Recognizing the Past in the Present: New Studies on Medicine Before, During and After the Holocaust* (Berghahn, 2021); and editor of *Nashim: A Journal of Jewish Women's Studies & Gender Issues: Jewish Women Medical Practitioners Before, During and After the Holocaust*, 36 (Spring 2020).

Liliana Picciotto is an Italian historian and essayist at the Jewish Contemporary Documentation Center Foundation (CDEC) in Milan. Her main field of studies is the history of the Italian Jews during the Fascist regime. She has published numerous articles and essays on this subject. Her most important work is her research on the deportation of the Jews from Italy, which she published in *Il libro della Memoria* (Mursia, 1991). A second publication, *Salvarsi: Gli ebrei d'Italia sfuggiti alla Shoah* (Einaudi, 2017) explains and describes how the Jews in Italy survived the Shoah. Picciotto is currently involved in a three-year research project on the contribution of the Jews to the resistance struggle against Fascism and Nazism in Italy during the two-year period 1943–1945.

Michaela Raggam-Blesch is a senior research fellow at the Institute for Contemporary History at the University of Vienna, where she is currently completing her habilitation on intermarried families during the Nazi period in Vienna, funded by the Elise Richter Programme of the Austrian Science Fund and the Fondation pour la Mémoire de la Shoah. She worked at the Leo Baeck Institute in New York from 1999–2003 and was among the first fellows of the Center for Jewish History Fellowship in 2003; and she has curated several exhibitions on the Holocaust. Her research interests include Austrian Jewish history of the nineteenth and twentieth centuries, antisemitism studies, gender studies, oral history, microhistory, and Holocaust and genocide studies.

Avihu Ronen is a retired professor of Tel Hai Academic College and the University of Haifa. He has published several books and papers on Jewish youth movements and Jewish resistance during the Holocaust, including *Hakrav Al Hahayim* (The Battle for Life) (Yad Ya'ari, 1994); "Women as Leaders," in *Jewish Women: A Comprehensive Historical Encyclopedia* (Shalvi, 2006). His book *Nidona Lehayim: Yomana Uhaye'a Shel Chajka Klinger* (Condemned to Life: The Diaries and Life of Chajka Klinger) (University of Haifa Press and Yedi'ot Sefarim, 2011) was awarded the Yad Vashem International Book Prize for Holocaust Research and will be published in English by Yad Vashem. Ronen also published several books and papers on the subject of leadership. He coedited with Michael Popper, including *Al Hamanhigut* (On Leadership) (Israeli Ministry of Defense, 1989–2006), and edited *Tzava Ve'etica* (Army and Ethics) (Israeli Ministry of Defense, 1996).

David Silberklang, senior historian at the International Institute for Holocaust Research, Yad Vashem, also teaches at the University of Haifa's International MA Program in Holocaust Studies and at the Hebrew University of Jerusalem. Among his past functions at Yad Vashem, he was the editor of *Yad Vashem Studies*, the series editor of "The Holocaust Survivors' Memoirs" project, and the chief historian of the "Museum Development" project, for which he wrote the conceptual historical outline for the Holocaust History Museum. He represented Israel at the International Holocaust Remembrance Alliance for many years on the Academic Working Group, the Committee on Antisemitism and Holocaust Denial, and on numerous steering committees and planning teams. His book *Gates of Tears: The Holocaust in the Lublin District* (Yad Vashem, 2013) was a finalist for the National Jewish Book Award and for the Yad Vashem International Book Prize in Holocaust Research.

Moshe (Moss) Tarshansky is an educator, independent researcher, and lecturer, who immigrated to Israel from New York in 1971. He studied at Har Etzion Hesder Yeshivah, combining military service and religious studies from 1984–1992, received rabbinical ordination from the Israeli Chief Rabbinate in 1993, and received a PhD in history in 2017 from Bar-Ilan University with a dissertation entitled "The Communal Activity of Rabbi Ephraim Oshry and the Importance of His *Responsa Mima'amakim* for the Development of a Religious Historiographical Narrative of the Holocaust," advised by Prof. Gershon Bacon. He continues to research religious life during the Holocaust, particularly the rabbinical responsa literature, and to publish articles on religious and historical topics.

Kim Wünschmann is the director of the Institute for the History of the German Jews in Hamburg. She obtained her PhD from Birkbeck, University of London as a member of a major Arts and Humanities Research Council (AHRC)-funded research project on the prewar concentration camps. She held postdoctoral fellowships at the Hebrew University of Jerusalem and the Center for Research on Antisemitism at Technische Universität Berlin, and was Deutscher Akademischer Austauschdienst (DAAD) lecturer at the Centre for German Jewish Studies at the University of Sussex and research fellow at the Department for Modern and Contemporary History at Ludwig-Maximilians-Universität (LMU) Munich. Her research centers on Holocaust studies, modern European Jewish history, legal history, and comics studies. She authored *Before Auschwitz: Jewish Prisoners in the Prewar Concentration Camps* (Harvard University Press, 2015), which was awarded the Yad Vashem International Book Prize for Holocaust Research, and she coedited with Jörg Osterloh, *"...der schrankenlosesten Willkür ausgeliefert": Häftlinge der frühen Konzentrationslager 1933 bis 1936/37* (Campus, 2017).

Efraim Zuroff is the chief Nazi-hunter of the Simon Wiesenthal Center and the director of its Israel Office and Eastern European Affairs, who has discovered the escape destinations all over the world of more than 3,000 suspected Nazi war criminals, and has facilitated the exposure and prosecution of dozens of them. A leading spokesperson in the world on Holocaust-related issues, he has played a key role in identifying the phenomenon of Holocaust distortion in post-Communist Eastern Europe in recent years, and is one of the leading opponents of this dangerous campaign. He has authored four books, which have been translated into fifteen languages, and more than 500 articles on Nazi-hunting, Holocaust history, and contemporary Jewish life and identity. His most recent book, coauthored with Ruta Vanagaite, *Our People: Discovering Lithuania's Hidden Holocaust* (Rowman & Littlefield, 2020), deals with Lithuanian complicity in Holocaust crimes and the false narrative promoted by successive governments.

Index of Names and Places

Abraham (biblical figure), 44, 48, 374
Abraham ibn Daud, 51
Abramovich (deputy of Kopelman), 147
Abadan, 24
Abyssinia, 154
Adamowicz, Irena, 133
Adler, Amek (Abraham), 202
Adler, Benjamin, 202
Adler, H. G., 181n6
Adriatic coast, 326
Adriatic islands, 323
Ahan (biblical figure), 45
Ahan (son of Karmi), 46
Ahimeir, Aba, 135
Ahronson, Yehoshua Moshe (Rabbi), 393,
    394n29, 396n35, 410n74
Aichinger, Ilse, 158
Akiva ben Joseph (Rabbi), 49
Albania, 323
Aleppo, 385
Alexander, Leo, 22, 23
Alexander S., 217–219
Almansi, Dante, 318, 321, 323
Alten, Marek, 279, 280, 284n39
Alter, Avraham Mordechai, 367n2
Altman, Tosia, 251
Altstadt (ghetto), 394n32
Amalek, 377, 380, 383
America
    See United States of America
Améry, Jean, 260, 264
Amiel, Moshe Avigdor (Rabbi), 379, 381, 383,
    385
Anderson, Benedict, 310
Andrén, Greta, 159
Annaberg (labor camp), 233
Antwerp, 294, 302, 307

Aprica, 325
Arad, Yitzhak, 413n80
Arctic Circle, 355
Arias, Bebe, 420
Aristotle, 51
Arlosoroff, Chaim, 136
Arnielewicz, Mordechai, 251
Ashkenazi, Meir (Rabbi), 351n58
Asolo, 326
Atiyah, Mordekhai Yehoshua, 385
Atlantic Ocean, 322
Auschwitz-Birkenau (concentration camp
    complex), 11, 15, 16n14, 197, 221, 230,
    234, 236n52, 240—242, 244, 259 –265,
    305, 308, 327, 328, 333, 381, 388, 389n9,
    394n29, 395, 399, 408n71, 410n74, 417,
    419, 420, 421n12, 423–425, 428
Australia, 283
Austria, 12, 33, 153, 155–157n14, 159,
    166n46, 174, 200, 258, 279, 293, 323, 329,
    393, 394n32, 408n71
Avni, Haim, 432

Baader, Cecilia, 167
Baader, Gerhard, 158n19, 167
Baader, Oskar, 166, 167
Bacau, 399n42
Bachya ben Asher (Rabbi), 42
Bach-Zelewski, Erich von dem, 22–24, 27,
    28, 40
Back, Ted, 213, 215
Bacon, Gershon, 444
Baden, 38n42
Badoglio, Pietro, 325
Bakauer, L., 88
Baquis, Federico, 320
Barale, Giovanni, 328

Baranek, Andzia, 92–93
Barani (repair man), 330n49
Baranowicze, 23, 337
Barcelona, 324, 421
Basel, 271
Bassi, Ettore, 318
Bavaria, 230, 234, 269, 272
Beccari, Arrigo, 330
Beckelman, Moses, 348
Będzin, 247, 252, 254, 255, 257
Będzin (ghetto), 59
Belarus, 22
Belgium, 12, 230, 258, 291–299, 301, 303,
    308, 309
Belgrade, 323
Belz, 384
Bełżec (death camp), 271, 275, 277–280,
    283–286, 420
Bełżyce, 281n27
Bemporad, Giulio, 320
Bendix, Ludwig, 191–194, 196
Ben-Haroush family, 422
Berdichev, 370, 383
Beregszasz, 374
Berek (concentration camp inmate), 204
Bergen-Belsen (concentration camp), 239n62
Berger, Franz, 163, 164, 168
Berglas, Haim Arieh (Rabbi), 289
Berlin, 32, 37, 99n8, 111n43, 113n44, 153n3,
    167n48, 179, 192, 194, 241, 329
Bessarabia, 291n1
Bettelheim, Bruno, 182
Biała, 233
Bialik, Hayim Nahman, 255, 283
Bialobrzegi, 208
Białystok, 23, 90, 250, 252, 254, 350, 353n65
Białystok (ghetto), 133
Bichlmair, Georg, 156
Bielicka-Blum, Luba, 106, 112
Bielitz, 233
Bielorussia, 59
Bielsko-Biała
    See Biała
Biłgoraj, 277
Bines, Eliahu, 209
Birkenau (concentration camp), 234, 236, 240,
    421n12
Birman, M., 352n59

Birnbaumel (concentration camp), 241
Bisingen (labor camp), 221
Blechhammer (concentration camp), 15, 223,
    228, 229–230, 232–235, 237–239
Bleichröder, Gerson, 32
Blevis, Meir, 204
Bloch, Avraham Yitzhak, 369, 376, 382, 385
Bnei Brak, 372, 380, 404n60
Bocchini, Arturo, 317
Bohemia, 323
Böhm, Berta (Weisz), 283
Bohn, Frank, 295
Boimal, Max (Melech), 208
Bolaffio, Eugenio, 323, 329
Bologna, 320
Bondy, Curt, 182
Bondy, Hugo, 172
Borgo San Dalmazzo, 326–328
Bories, Georg (Boris Jochvedson), 330
Born, Ludger, 157, 174, 175
Borochov, Dov Ber, 292, 294, 309
Borsari family, 330n49
Bosnia, 323
Bosnia-Herzegovina, 324
Boves, 326
Braham, Randolph L., 432
Brajtman, Abram, 87
Brajtman, Chil, 79–81
Brand, Jokel, 287
Brandeis, Louis, 36–37n39
Bratislava, 38, 392n25, 377, 417, 419, 421,
    421n12
Braude, Ruth, 250
Braude-Heller, Anna, 105, 111
Brazil, 23, 324
Breisch, Mordechai Ya'akov, 409
Breitenau (concentration camp), 180
Brinberg, Bajla, 75–77
Brisk, Haim (Rabbi), 50, 337
Britain
    See Great Britain
Broder, Israel, 304
Broder, Pinkas (Pierre), 307
Brondello, Francesco, 328
Brooklyn, 377, 400, 402
Brunner, Gertrude, 161
Brussels, 293, 294, 297, 299, 307
Bruzzi family, 330n49

Brzezinska, Fela, 89, 91
Buben, Verena, 157
Buber, Martin, 46
Buchenwald (concentration camp), 167, 194, 226, 231n35, 232, 410
Buchman, Henrietta, 344, 348, 357
Bucovina, 291n1
Budapest, 13, 38, 259, 371, 404n60, 410n76, 419, 421, 428–433
Budzyn (concentration camp), 208, 213, 215, 216, 219–221
Bukhara, 355
Bulgaria, 32, 291, 323
Bunim, Irving, 341n22

Cadbury, Emma, 156
Cain (biblical figure), 49
California, 126
Campagna (concentration camp), 322
Canada, 11, 136n16, 335n1, 343, 345, 350–354, 434, 436
Cantoni, Raffaele, 316, 318
Capogreco, Spartaco, 322
Casablanca, 435
Casari, Romolo, 330n49
Caspi-Serebrovitz, Josef, 129, 134, 135, 137–141, 143, 144, 147, 148
Cazès-Benatar, Hélène, 435, 436
Central Asia, 343, 355, 356, 359, 361, 362
Chaim, Chofetz (Rabbi Yisrael Meir Kagan), 353
Charleroi, 307
Chavel, Charles (Rabbi), 358n84
Chełm, 284n37
Chełmno (death camp), 274, 276, 277, 285
Childs, James Rives, 429, 430, 432, 433
Chimkent, 355
Cholawsky, Shalom, 59
Cincinnati, 339, 372
Cleveland, 382
Cohen, Aaron, 422
Cohen, Boaz, 439
Cohen, Jacob, 422
Cohen, Raya, 424, 427
Colle della Finestra, 326
Colle di Ciriegia, 326
Conegliani, Aldo, 320
Cooper, Nathan, 205

Cosel, 230
Côte d'Azur, 317, 326
Criba, Franziska, 163
Croatia, 326, 329
Cuneo, 326, 328
Curacao, 346, 348
Cymlich, Yisrael, 286
Czechoslovakia, 258
Czerniaków, Adam, 104, 111, 116, 117
Częstochowa, 254

Dachau (concentration camp), 179–197, 183, 394
Dalla Volta, Alberto, 264
Dalmatia (Italian), 323, 324, 329
Danube, 422
Dautmergen (concentration camp), 221
David (King of Israel), 49, 375
Davidson, Shamai, 205
Dawidowicz, Lucy, 124
De Angeli, Guido, 328
Demerer, Halina (daughter of Karl Demerer), 233, 238
Demerer, Heinrich (cousin of Karl Demerer), 234
Demerer, Heinrich (Heniek; son of Karl Demerer), 233, 238, 239
Demerer, Henia (wife of Karl Demerer), 233, 238
Demerer, Karl, 15, 223, 228, 233–241, 243
Dessler, Eliyahu Eliezer, 372
Dizengoff, Meir, 97
Dolezal, Arnold, 158n19
Domb, Abraham, 297, 298
Donat, Alexander, 207, 215, 218, 219
Donati, Salvatore, 320
Dornstrauch, Hala (Halinka), 170
Draenger, Gusta Davidson, 254
Drancy (transit camp), 327
Durkheim, Emile, 124
Dymlecht, Bela, 87
Dzhambul, 355

Eckstein, Walter, 167
Efraim, Moses Hayyim (Rabbi), 383
Efrati, Shimon (Rabbi), 387n3, 389, 397–399
Egypt, 42, 282, 384
Ehrenfeld family, 424n24

Ehrenreich, Shlomo Zalman, 367, 370, 380, 381, 383, 385
Eibeshitz, Yehoshua (Rabbi), 15
Eichmann, Adolf, 153
Einstein, Albert, 113n44
Eisenberg (prisoner at Blechhammer), 236
Eiss, Chaim Yisroel (Rabbi), 270, 426
Ejbuszyc, Necha, 284n39
Eleazar ben Judah, of Worms, 391n22
Elkes, Elchanan, 130, 131, 136, 145
Emilia, 324
Entracque, 326, 327
Eretz Israel, 57, 97, 247–251, 255–257, 262, 263, 294, 295, 302, 311, 312, 329, 367, 371, 374, 379–382, 384, 385 425n28
See also Israel; Palestine (Mandatory)

Esau (biblical figure), 370, 377, 383, 384, 387n3
Eschen, Heinz, 190–193
Estonia, 232, 345n32
Ethiopia, 154
Europe, 8n4, 10, 11, 60, 89, 98, 99, 113n46, 225, 269, 272, 274, 283, 294, 349n48, 367n2, 380–384, 418, 424, 435, 436
Eastern, 13, 32, 33, 65, 67n4, 68, 181, 275, 309, 339
Southern, 275
Western, 39n45, 293, 376, 417–419
Ezekiel (biblical figure), 46

Fabiszkiewicz (refugee activist), 318
Falco, Mario, 320
Fano, Giuseppe, 320
Far East, 250, 343, 345, 348, 350n50, 353, 354
Fasal, Erich, 155
Fasman, Oscar (Rabbi), 352
Fay, Stefan (Stefka), 270
Feinstein, Marek, 220
Feinstein, Moshe (Rabbi), 392n25, 393
Fels, Ferdinand, 283
Fenigstein, Henry, 212, 218
Ferdman, David, 308
Ferramonti di Tarsia (concentration camp), 322
Ferstman, Hela, 281n27
Finkel, Eliezer Yehuda (Rabbi), 337, 354
Finzi, Mario, 320
Fishman, Avraham, 206, 207

Fiszelzon, Baruch, 287n50
Fiszelzon, Berek, 287n50
Fiume, 324
Flam, Leopold, 300, 302, 307
Fleischmann, Gisi, 435
Florence, 327, 328
Flossenbürg (concentration camp), 239
Forell, Friedrich, 158
Fossati, Maurilio (Cardinal), 328
Fossoli (concentration camp), 333
France, 12, 13, 34–35n31, 113n44, 210, 230, 258, 291, 293, 295, 298, 309n23, 318, 319, 325–327, 404n59, 425n28, 435
France, Anatole, 66
Franco, Francisco, 422
Frankl, Viktor, 182, 263, 264
Fransman, Harry, 235
Fredler, Beniek, 89–90
Frei, Shmuel, 428
Freiberg, Dov, 275n11
Freiberger, Lotte, 167, 168
Freiberger, Mimi, 167
Freiberger, Moritz, 167n49
Freiburg, 126
Freier, Recha, 329
Freisinger (Lieutenant), 290
Freud, Sigmund, 125
Freudiger, Pinchas, 428
Fridenzon, Eliezer Gershon, 372, 376, 385
Frieda, Ryfka, 284
Friedheim, Władysław, 212n47, 216
Friedländer, Saul, 9, 228
Friedmann, Gino, 318, 320, 330
Friedmann, Yehoshua, 184
Fruchtgarten, Tadek, 90, 91
Fry, Varian, 295n9
Frydman, Alexander Zisha, 377, 382, 385
Frylegsztejn, Beniek, 86, 87
Fuchs, Lotte, 161
Fürnberg, Hermann, 152, 154
Fürstengrube (concentration camp), 244

Galicia, 163n36, 284, 389n9, 394n32, 399n42, 413, 414n81
Galilee, 256
Gar, Yosef, 135, 137, 148n63
Gardinas, 143
Garfinkel, Mieczysław, 280

Garfunkel, Leib, 130, 131, 135–137, 140, 144
Gateshead, 372
Gdańsk, 107n31
Geiger, Abraham, 378
Geneva, 98, 113n44, 282, 303, 426
Genoa, 320, 323, 324, 327, 328, 331
Gens, Jacob, 59, 60, 140n32, 142
Germany, 8, 10, 12, 22n3, 23, 25, 27, 33–37,
    39, 90, 97, 111n42, 136, 137n19, 157n14,
    184, 200, 230, 235, 242, 243, 258, 269,
    279, 293, 304, 315, 316, 318, 321–323,
    329, 367n2, 376, 379, 383, 389n9, 394n30,
    409n72, 421
Gestel, Hela, 87
Gestetner, Heinrich, 421n12
Gestetner, Natan (Rabbi), 404
Gestetner, Yechezkel, 419
Gheel-Gildemeester, Frank van, 151–154
Gibraltar, 421
Giser, Yosef, 206, 207, 209, 216
Glazman, Yosef, 140, 141
Glicensztejn, Luba, 81, 82, 83
Göcke, Wilhelm, 148
Goffman, Erving, 183
Goldberg, Oskar, 214n51
Goldmann, Nahum, 10, 11, 346
Goldminc, Hava, 280
Goldnadel, Jacques, 283n33
Goldnadel, Rafael, 283
Goldwasser, Shlomo, 287
Goldzand, Hela, 89
Golub, Avraham
    See Tory, Avraham (Golub)
Góra Kalwaria, 80, 81
Goriely, Georges, 300, 302
Grabiner, Charles, 299, 301
Grabów, 276
Graetz, Heinrich, 378
Granat-Horn, Malla, 161
Grazowsky, Reuven (Rabbi), 349
Great Britain, 33, 39, 137, 160, 273, 372,
    403n56, 428, 434
Greenwald, Yehoshua (Rabbi), 408
Greiding, 413–414n81
Greif, Gideon, 226
Griffel, Jacob, 419
Grinberg, Ika, 59, 136
Grochów, 247, 256

Grodin, Michael A., 442
Grodno, 88, 90, 143, 250, 360
Grodzinski, Chaim Ozer (Rabbi), 338, 339,
    341, 376
Grojnowski, Jakub
    See Winer, Szlamek
Groß Rosen (concentration camp), 239
Grosser, Berl, 320
Grosser, Bernardo, 318
Grossman, Chaika, 254
Grosswardein (ghetto), 383
Guerzoni, Marcellina Nascimbeni, 330n49
Gutfreund, Jacob, 298
Gutkowski, Eliahu, 282n28
Gutman, Elek, 203
Gutman, Hyman, 203
Gutman, Israel, 86, 253, 413n80
Gutman, Jacob, 203
Gutterman, Bella, 226, 259

Hacker, Johannes, 214
Haifa, 283
Halberstam, Bentsion, 367n2
Halberstam, Hayim, 371, 385
Halberstam, Shalom Yehezkel Shraga Rubin
    (Rabbi), 400, 401, 402, 404
Halevi, Hayim David (Rabbi), 395
Hanasi, Yehuda (Rabbi), 41
Harlap, Ya'akov Moshe, 374, 375
Hayes, Saul, 352
Hedenquist, Göte, 158, 159
Heidelberg, 111n43
Heinovitz, Rivka (Regina), 424, 425
Hellerstein, Jacob, 341n23
Hellman, Martha, 158
Henkin, Yosef Eliyahu (Rabbi), 342, 382
Hering, Gottlieb, 271, 272
Herschthal, Klara, 284n39
Herzl, Theodore, 255
Heschel, Abraham, 372
Hesse-Nassau (Prussian province), 179
Hessental (concentration camp), 14, 199–222
Hilberg, Raul, 23, 40
Hildebrandt, Sabine, 442
Himmler, Heinrich, 230
Hindenburg, Paul von, 179
Hirsch, Markus, 284
Hirszfeld, Ludwik, 111

Hitler, Adolf, 25, 35, 36, 97, 135, 180, 210, 379, 381
Hochberg, Shlomo, 295
Hoffmann, Erich, 236
Hofmekeker, Michel, 146
Holland
    See Netherlands
Hollander, Herman, 349n44
Horodok, 413–414n81
Horthy, Miklós, 257, 429
Horwitz, Avraham David (Rabbi), 404
Höss, Rudolf, 236n52
Hrubieszów, 287
Hrubieszów (ghetto), 282
Huberband, Shimon, 281
Hungary, 11, 12, 113n46, 200, 257–260, 262, 323, 374, 389n9, 403n56, 404n60, 408n71, 418–421, 427, 428, 432, 433, 436
Hurwitz, Ariel, 335n1
Husserl, Edmund Gustav Albrecht, 126
Hyman, Joseph C., 357
Ibn Daud, Abraham ben David, Halevi, 51
Ibn Ezra, Abraham ben Meïr, 384
Imber, Naftali Hertz, 262n52
Indig, Josef (Ithai), 258, 329, 330, 332, 333
Innitzer, Theodor, 157n14
Ippas, Leibas (Ipp, Leib Arie), 140, 141
Iran, 359
Iraq, 240
Isaac (biblical figure), 53
Isaiah (biblical figure), 53, 57
Iserlis, Moshe (Rabbi), 399n43
Israel, 30, 41–46, 48, 49, 53, 56, 57, 97, 228, 246, 262n52, 378–380, 385, 389n9, 394n29, 404n59, 410n76, 435
    See also Eretz Israel; Palestine (Mandatory)
Israel F., 240
Isserles, Moses ben Israel (Rema) (Rabbi), 56
Istanbul, 428
Italian Riviera, 318
Italy, 12, 258
Itzkovitz, David (Rabbi), 408
Ivarsson, Johannes, 159, 161
Izbica (ghetto), 286
Izrael, Avraham Meir (Rabbi), 409, 410, 411

Jacob (biblical figure), 383, 387n3
Jakob (bunkmate of Moshe Kuperwajs), 205

Japan, 348–354
Jarach, Federico, 316, 317
Jarosław, 86
Jarzebski, Hejnoch, 81
Jedlińsk, 205, 216
Jeremiah (biblical figure), 49
Jerusalem, 359, 369–371, 374, 385, 389n9, 403, 404n57, 424n24
Job (biblical figure), 53
Joselson, Janina, 272
Joseph, Hermann, 244
Joseph ibn Tzaddik, 51
Joseph Soloveitchik (Rabbi), 43
Joshua (biblical figure), 45
Jospa, Hertz, 305
Jospa, Yvonne, 305, 306

Kadlecik, Rene, 283
Kahana-Shapira, Avrohom Dov Ber (Rabbi), 59
Kahane (ghetto inhabitant), 400, 401
Kalisz, 81
Kalk, Israel, 321
Kalmanovich, Zelig, 58, 141
Kalmanowitz, Abraham (Rabbi), 344, 423
Kamenetz, 337, 349
Kammen, Jacob, 348n42
Kantorowicz, Jozef, 88
Kaplan, Chaim, 125, 281, 286
Kaplan, Mordecai, 48
Karay, Felicja, 221, 259
Karmi (biblical figure), 45
Karo, Joseph, 49
Karski, Jan, 286
Kassel, 180
Kassow, Samuel D., 277n14, 297
Kasztner, Rezső (Israel, Rudolf), 113n46
Kattowitz (Katowice), 233
Katz, Reuven (Rabbi), 373
Kazahstan, 250
Keitel (Gestapo man), 148
Kermish, Joseph, 115
Kesselbrener, Yehezkel, 286
Khust, 408
Kielmansegg, Emanuela von, 156n12
Kinneret (Lake), 256
Kirshen (Kirshenworcl), Joseph, 209
Kishinev, 283
Klein, Harry, 320

Klein, Menashe (Hakatan) (Rabbi), 403
Klein, Rosie, 425
Klesów, 247, 248
Kless, Shlomo, 250
Kletzk, 337, 349, 353n65
Klukowski, Zygmunt, 286
Kogon, Eugen, 190n30
Kohensius, Frederika, 235
Kohn, Erich, 140
Kokand, 355
Kollel, 353n65
Komoly, Otto, 428
Kopelman, Michael (Moisei), 130, 142, 147
Korczak, Janusz, 60, 121
Korczak, Rozka, 254
Kostenwein (née Ringler), Rosa, 172, 173n68
Kotler, Aaron (Rabbi), 337, 341n22, 349, 350, 354, 423
Kotsk, 375
Kovner, Abba, 140n32
Kovno (Kaunas), 129–131, 135, 136, 138, 140–142, 147, 396, 405, 408, 412
Kovno (ghetto), 15, 55, 56, 59, 129–131, 133, 137, 141, 148, 149, 181, 226, 388, 396n35, 401n49, 402n54, 405n62, 406, 412
Kraków, 25, 56, 252, 254, 279
Kramer, Dwora, 168n55
Kramer, Rubin Wolf, 168
Kranzler, David, 350n53, 432n60, 434n63
Krausz, Miklos (Moshe), 428, 430n46
Krępiec, 279
Krigsman, Zanwel, 78, 79, 81, 82
Kropotkin, Peter, 125
Kruk, Herman, 141, 142, 144n47
Krzeszów, 275n11
Kubowitzki, Aryeh Leon, 295, 302
Kuffler, Arthur, 152
Kuperwajs, Moshe (Kfir), 205

Landau, Yehezkel, 392n25
Langnas, Mignon, 170, 171
Laredo, Isaac, 422
Łaskarzew, 283
Latvia, 345n32
Laurence, Alfred E., 192
Lazewnik, Fajga, 88
Leavitt, Moses, 344, 347, 348
Lebensfeld, Regina (Steinberg), 423

Lebensfeld, Shimon, 421n12
Łęczna, 283
Lederman, Izrael, 80–83
Leibowitz, Boruch Ber (Rabbi), 337
Leitner, Isabella, 241
Lemberg, 284n39, 286
Lenczner, Chawka, 254
Lenin, Vladimir Il'ich, 292
Lensky, Mordechai, 120, 124
Leonardi, Ernesto, 330n49
Lerman, Yisrael, 209
Lesno Brdo, 329
Levi, Primo, 189, 197, 223, 227, 229, 241–243, 260, 264, 265
Levi, Yitzchak Mayer (Rabbi), 359
Levin, Dov, 139n28, 141
Levin, Hirsch (Zvi), 130, 139, 141, 143
Levin, Moshe, 59
Lévinas, Emmanuel, 126
Lewin, Avraham, 281
Lewkowicz, Daniel, 281
Libon, 425, 426n28
Lichtenberg, Uziel, 254
Lichtenburg (concentration camp), 179–197
Lichtenstein, Yehezkel Shraga, 390, 398n40
Lichtheim, Richard, 321, 425
Liebes, Yitzhak Isaac (Rabbi), 413n81
Liège, 292, 307
Lifshitz, David (Rabbi), 350
Likhtenshtayn (Lichtenstein), Hillel, 381
Lipovsky, Franz, 156
Lipowa (POW camp), 275n9
Lipson, Alfred, 221
Lipzer, Benjamin (Benno), 129, 132n8, 134, 139, 143–148
Lisbon, 113n45, 154, 324
Lithuania, 11, 58, 133, 135, 136, 140, 246, 250, 336–338n14, 341, 343, 345–351, 353–355, 358, 363, 368n4, 376, 396
Litzmannstadt, 168n55
Litzmannstadt (ghetto), 224, 242
Ljubljana, 323, 329
Ljubljana, Province of, 323
Łódź, 205, 252, 254, 255, 256, 276, 372, 376
Łódź (ghetto), 59, 129n1, 168n55, 181, 196, 226, 256, 412
Lomza, 350

London, 35, 160, 272, 273, 375
Louisville, 258n84
Löw, Franziska (Franzi), 174, 175
Löwenherz, Josef, 162, 164, 170, 171
Löwenherz, Sophie, 170, 171
Lubavitch, 353n65
Lubetkin, Zivia, 251
Lublin, 277, 279, 283, 353n65
Lublin (ghetto), 11, 271, 274, 275, 278, 279, 280, 281, 282, 283, 284, 285, 287, 288, 402n54
Lucca, 328
Ludwig, Alfred, 234, 235
Ludwigsburg, 235
Luisada, Renzo, 316
Łuków (ghetto), 288, 289
Lutz, Carl, 428
Luxemberg, Bernard (Dov), 269n1, 270
Luzzatto Pardo, Enrico, 323
Lwów, 59, 286n44

Macedonia, 291n1
Mack, Julian, 35n33
Madrid, 421, 432, 433
Mahler, Raphael, 293
Maimonides, Moses (Rambam), 43, 51, 52, 56, 373
Majdan Tatarski (ghetto), 278, 279, 284n39, 287, 289
Majdanek (concentration camp), 218, 221, 271, 272
Malc, Kalman, 211
Maly Trostinec, 174n74
Manasse, Ignatz, 194
Mandelbaum, Robert, 306
Mapen, Murray (Moses), 207
Margaliot, Abraham, 413n80
Margolis (Dr.), 61
Margolis, Laura, 360, 362, 363
Marin, Moshe, 401n49
Maritime Alps, 317, 325, 326
Markuszów, 287
Martin, Victor, 309
Marysin, 256
Mayer, Saly, 113, 307, 321, 425, 426n28
Mayzel, Baruch, 299, 301
Mazouz, Matzliah (Rabbi), 400–402
Mead, George Herbert, 125

Mechelen-Malines (transit camp), 305, 308, 310
Meed (Miedzyrzecki-Meed/Miedzyrzecki-Peltel), Wladka, 213, 215
Meisels, Zvi Hirsch (Rabbi), 388, 389, 399, 400
Melilla, 421
Meltzer, Isser Zalman (Rabbi), 349n48
Mendel, Menahem, 375
Mendelssohn, Moses, 378n35, 379
Merin, Moshe, 59, 255, 257
Merinfeld, Loszek, 305
Metschl, Johann, 168
Metschl, Stefanie, 168
Metschl, Susanne, 168, 172n65
Mexico City, 385
Mielec (labor camp), 279
Migdalek, Charles (Cudyk), 202
Migdalek, Samuel (Szmul), 202
Milan, 316, 317, 318, 320, 321, 331, 332
Milejkowski, Israel, 111, 117, 121–123
Milewsky, Aaron (Rabbi), 360
Mir, 337, 353n65
Modena, 320, 324, 325, 329, 332
Moghilev, 23
Monaco, 317
Mongolia, Outer, 34, 35n31
Monroe, Kristen Renwick, 127
Monsky, Henry, 346
Montalcini, Emanuele, 320
Montenegro, 32
Montreux, 426
Moore, Bob, 39n45
Morcillo, Matilde Rosillo, 432
Moreali, Giuseppe, 330
Moreno, Armand, 329, 330
Morgenshtern, Yehiel Meir, 374, 375
Morocco, 417, 420–422, 428, 431n55, 433, 435
Morpurgo, Carlo, 320
Morpurgo, Vittorio, 323
Mortara, Eugenio, 331n50
Moses (biblical figure), 43, 44, 46, 53, 57
Moses ben Nachman (Rabbi), 50
Mualem, Zahava, 236n51
Mugiero, Miguel Ángel de, 429
Mukačevo, 380
Müller (Captain), 326, 327
Munich, 190

Munkács, 380, 419
Murmelstein, Benjamin, 224
Murnau (POW camp), 269, 272
Mussolini, Benito, 11, 315

Nahman, Haim, 283
Nahon, Umberto, 316
Napoleon III, 309n23
Natzweiler (concentration camp), 199, 244
Nemirov, 283
Netherlands, 12, 13, 200, 208, 230, 236, 258
Neumayer, Käthe, 156, 161
Neurath, Baroness von, 203
Neurath, Konstantin, Freiherr von, 203, 214
Neurath, Paul Martin, 182, 186, 187
New York, 11, 26, 99n8, 295, 312, 340, 344,
     345, 347, 357, 361, 362, 377, 382, 389n8,
     403, 404n57, 408n71, 409, 410, 413,
     414n81, 428
Newman, Frank, 350n53, 351n58
Nibeks (Karl Demerer's deputy), 236
Nice, 327
Niethammer, Lutz, 190n30
Nitra, 420, 426
Nizza, Alberto, 320
Noah (biblical figure), 44
Noah, Raffaele, 320
Nonantola, 324–326, 329–332
North America, 320, 338
Northern Africa, 435
Nuremberg, 12, 23n6
Nusfeld, Anna, 70
Nykerk, Benjamin (Beno), 307, 308

Ohio, 372
Opatów, 208
Opochinsky, Peretz, 119
Opoczno, 252
Opole-Lubelski, 283
Opole-Lubelski (ghetto), 283, 284
Oradea (ghetto), 383
Oranienburg (concentration camp), 183
Orgaz, Luis, 428–432
Oshry, Ephraim (Rabbi), 55, 388, 395–397,
     405–408
Osterloh, Jörg, 445
Ostmark (Austria under National Socialism),
     152, 154

Ottmuth (labor camp), 233
Otwock, 88

Pacific Ocean, 353, 360
Pacifici, Aldo, 331, 333
Pacifici, Goffredo (Cicibù), 330, 331, 332, 333
Palestine (Mandatory), 22n4, 28, 99, 137, 247,
     248, 252, 283, 297, 304, 308, 329, 336,
     343, 345, 349n48, 353, 354, 359, 381, 384,
     430
     See also Eretz Israel; Israel
Pammer, Thomas, 159n21
Pappenheim, Ludwig, 179, 180
Pardo, Enrico Luzzatto, 320
Paris, 33–35, 99n8, 113n44, 158, 283, 299,
     327, 417, 435
Pavelić, Ante, 324
Pearl Harbor, 274
Penson, Jakub, 107
Perec, Yitzhak Leibusz, 286
Perechodnik, Calel, 70, 71
Perelman, Chaïm (Charles), 300, 302, 305, 306
Perelman, Fela, 301, 302
Peretz, I. L., 309
Perk, Kalman, 131, 132
Perlasca, Giorgio, 432
Perlis, Rivka, 247n5, 257
Perrone, Lorenzo, 265
Petah Tikvah, 373
Peterson, Anna-Lena, 159
Petliuk, Sima, 69, 70
Petshenik, Aharon, 384, 385
Piaseczno, 78
Piasek, Abe (Abram), 209, 215
Piazza, Elio, 320
Piccinini, Emilia Sitti, 330n49
Piedmont, 328
Piestany, 371
Pignatti, Mauro, 330n49
Piotrków, 205
Piwowszczyzna, 163n36
Plock, 107n31
Plotnick, Frumka, 251
Poch, Alexander, 158n19
Poland, 10, 37, 68, 73n21, 88, 90, 98n4, 100,
     104, 107n31, 109, 111, 113, 123, 125, 130,
     133, 163n36, 200, 219, 246, 247, 248,
     249n12, 250, 251, 252, 253, 257, 258,

270n2, 272, 273, 274, 280, 282, 283n33, 285, 293, 307, 309, 323, 337, 338n14, 375, 381, 389n9, 392n25, 393, 394n29, 394n32, 399n43, 402, 403n56, 409n72, 420, 426, 427
   Eastern, 336, 345, 355
Poltava, 309
Pompan, Alexander, 168
Poniatowa (concentration camp), 269–272
Ponte Chiasso, 331
Ponte Tresa, 332, 333
Popper, Michael, 444
Portugal, 417, 425
Poschiavo, 333
Povilaitis, Augustinas, 345n32
Pozner, Chaim, 303, 304
Praga, 83, 85, 86, 94
Prague, 392n25
Prešov, 284n37
Pressburg
   See Bratislava
Prussia, 192
Przygoda, Zdzisław, 203, 218

Rabinowicz, Boruch (Rabbi), 419
Radin, 350, 353n65
Radom, 199, 200, 208, 210–215, 217, 221, 293
Radom (concentration camp)
   See Szkolna (concentration camp)
Raimondi family, 330n49
Rakishok, 135
Rapoport, David, 299
Rashi, 9, 41, 42
Rauca, Helmut, 136–138, 143
Rawa Ruska, 277, 286n44
Regensburg (concentration camp), 239n62
Reichman, Renée, 11, 417–428, 430–437
Reichmann family, 424n24
Reichmann, Eli (Edward), 418
Reichmann, Esther, 417n1
Reichmann, Eva (Maidi), 417, 419, 420, 424n24, 436
Renard, Blanche, 344, 348
Ringelblum, Emmanuel, 121, 125, 293, 297, 299
Ringler, Rosa
   See Kostenwein (née Ringler), Rosa
Ritter (Dr.), 240
Rixinger, Johann, 164

Roizman, Isser, 283
Rokeach, Yissachar Dov (Rabbi), 384
Rokiškis, 135
Romania, 32, 68, 291, 399n42, 403n56
Rome, 154, 320, 324, 327–329, 389n8
Roosevelt, Franklin Delano, 364
Rosenbaum, Irving J., 390
Rosenberg, Marshall B., 126
Rosenberg, Yisrael Halevi (Rabbi), 357
Rosenfeld family, 424n24
Rosenheim, Jacob, 423
Ross, Steve (Rosental, Szmul), 204, 205
Rosulna, 284
Rotgold, Edzia, 283
Rotgold, Fajga, 283
Rotgold, Mordechai, 283
Roth, Aaron (Areleh) (Rabbi), 374
Róth, Haim, 428
Rozenblum, Chana, 91, 92
Rozenblum, Cyla, 87, 88
Rozenblum, Jakob, 110
Rozman, Mordechai, 250
Rozniatow, 240
Rubenstein, Richard, 48
Rubin, Moses, 284n37
Rubinstein (Rubin, Felix), 195
Rubinsztein, M., 89
Rudniki (forests), 131
Rudorff, Andrea, 226
Rufeisen, Hela Schüpper, 253
Rumkowska, Regina, 196
Rumkowski, Chaim, 224, 242, 255, 256, 412
Russia, 22n3, 32, 35, 389n9, 392n25
Ryba, Abraham, 299, 307
Ryki (ghetto), 286
Rzeczyński, Ada (Adela), 270
Rzeczyński, Adam, 270
Rzeczyński, Feliks (Efraim), 269–272, 289
Rzeczyński, Inia (Irena), 269–270n1
Rzeczyński, Nusia (Anna), 269–270n1

Saar (region), 36
Sachsenhausen (concentration camp), 190, 226, 231n35
Saerens, Lieven, 302n15
Saint Petersburg, 113n44
Saint-Martin-Vésubie, 325, 326, 328
Sakowska, Ruta, 277n14, 282n28

Salamas, Isaac, 422
Salanter, Israel, 368n4
Salerno, 322
Salonika, 111, 112n43
Samarkand, 355
San Francisco, 353
Sanok, 394n29
Sanz-Briz, Ángel, 420, 429, 430, 432
Sarna, Yehezkel, 369, 370
Sarnoff, David, 36
Scheck, Manfred, 214n51
Schelvis, Jules, 208, 209, 211
Schier, Max, 192
Schiff, Jacob, 32
Schlaph, Enrik, 318
Schlesiersee I (concentration camp), 232
Schlesinger, Israel, 304
Schmalkalden, 179
Schmelt labor camps, 230, 232, 234
Schneersohn, Yosef Yitzhak (Rabbi), 377, 379, 381, 385
Schnitzer, Sam, 237
Schoky, Marco (Marek Silberschatz), 330, 331n50
Scholem, Gershom, 194
Scholem, Werner, 194
Schultz, Fritz Emil, 271, 272
Schwabisch Hall, 202
Schwalb, Nathan, 282, 283, 307, 332, 425
Schwartz, Mordechai (Martin), 382
Schwartz, Mordechai Tzvi (Martin), 383
Segalson, Arie, 134n12
Segalson, Moshe, 134n12
Sémelin, Jacques, 292
Senise, Carmine, 323
Serafini family, 330n49
Serbia, 32, 111n43, 389n9
Shafran, Bezalel Ze'ev, 398, 399n42
Shamir, Josef, 249
Shanghai, 11, 343, 350, 351, 353, 360–363, 421n13
Shapira, Carlo, 321
Shapira, Chaim Nachman, 130, 135
Shapira, Gedalia, 205, 215
Shapira, Hayim Elazar, 380
Shapira, Kalonymous Kalman (Rabbi), 216, 369
Shapiro (Rabbi), 56

Shatzkes, Moshe (Rabbi), 350
Shaul, Michal, 367n1
Shavli (ghetto), 58
Sheinfeld, Moshe, 380
Shimon Bar Yochai (Rabbi), 102
Shragai, Shlomo Zalman, 370, 382
Siberia, 355, 358
Siegfried, Josef, 279, 280
Sierakowiak, Dawid, 13
Silberstein, Abraham (Alfred), 425, 426
Silberstein, Adolf, 174
Silesia
  East Upper, 229–230, 233
  Lower, 232
  Upper, 233, 309, 327
Silver, Eliezer (Rabbi), 339, 340, 342, 357
Şimleul Silvaniei, 370, 381, 383
Simon, Joachim (Shushu), 258
Simons (Dr.), 240
Sinai (Mount), 41, 46
Skarzysko-Kamienna (labor camp), 221
Skučas, Kazys, 345n32
Slobodka, 129, 360
Slobodka (ghetto), 135
Slovakia, 10, 11, 252, 257, 279, 283, 403, 404n57, 418–421n13, 424, 435
Slovenia, 258, 323, 324, 329
Sobibór (death camp), 282, 284
Sodom, 44, 46
Sofer, Akiva, 377
Sofer, Moshe (Rabbi), 392n25, 398
Sofsky, Wolfgang, 185, 186, 226
Solnik, Binyamin Aharon (Rabbi), 399
Solomon (King of Israel), 58
Soloveitchik, Yitzchak Ze'ev (Rabbi), 337
Sonnenson, Moshe, 398n39
Sorani, Settimio, 320
Sorek, Israel, 101
Sorin, Nicholas (Nicolas), 34, 35, 37n41
Sosnowiec, 233, 234, 236, 255
Sosnowiec (ghetto), 59
South America, 320
Soviet Union (USSR), 22, 90, 200, 272, 274, 276, 337, 345, 349, 351, 356, 362
Spain, 12, 13, 417, 422, 429, 430
Spalato (Split), 323, 329
Spielhofer, Sheila, 155
Środula (Szrodula) (ghetto), 234

St. Gallen, 114
Stanisławow, 284
Starachowice (labor camp), 221, 225, 235
Staszów, 208, 209
Stein, Elijah, 349n44
Stein, Josef, 104
Steinberg, Maxime, 291
Steinitz-Metzler, Gertrud, 157
Sternbuch, Elias, 114
Sternbuch, Recha, 423, 426, 436, 437
Sternbuch, Yitzhak, 423n21, 426
Sterno, Ida, 305
Stockholm, 272
Strull (Rabbi), 258n84
Stuttgart, 202
Sumpf, Grete, 156
Supovitz, Yehuda, 59
Sušak, 323
Suwalki, 350
Sweden, 360
Switzerland, 111n42, 113n46, 114, 258, 270,
    293, 296, 302, 303, 307, 308, 318, 321,
    325, 331–333, 417, 423, 434, 436
Sylman, Yaakov (Rabbi), 276
Szac-Wajnkranc, Noemi, 71
Szálasi, Ferenc, 259
Szalavec, Josef, 283
Szatan, Icek, 303
Szeps, Fela, 71
Szifman, Lejb, 269n1
Szkolna (concentration camp), 199, 200, 201,
    215, 217–221
Szulcman, Gitla, 87
Szuzman, Chana, 90
Szwajger-Blady, Adina, 60
Szymánski (Polish lawyer), 271

Tabakman, Israel, 296, 298, 299, 304
Tabakman, Meyer, 296, 297, 298
Taft, William Howard, 32
Talmud, Zvi Elimelech (Rabbi), 289
Tangier, 11, 417–423, 427–435
Tardini, Ennio, 330n49
Tarshansky, Isaac W., 387n1
Tatarski, 278
Tausig, Otto, 160
Taussig-Löw, Edith, 172
Tchorsh, Katriel Fishel (Rabbi), 56

Teheran, 359, 381
Teichtal, Yissachar Shlomo, 367, 371, 384, 385
Tel Aviv, 56, 97, 373, 379, 381, 383, 384
Telšiai, 369, 376
Telz, 353n65
Tenenbaum, Hanoch, 221
Tétuan, 417, 422, 429, 432n58, 433
Theresienstadt (ghetto), 11, 158, 181n6, 224,
    258, 279, 417, 419, 421n12, 424n24,
    425n28, 426
Thon, Ozjasz, 25, 28, 37
Thrace, 291n1
Tiberg, Judah, 293, 295
Ticino, 331
Többens, Walther Caspar, 271, 272
Tokayer, Marvin (Rabbi), 350n52
Tokyo, 350n52
Tomaszow-Lubelski (ghetto), 280
Tory, Avraham (Golub), 131, 139, 140, 144n44,
    145, 146, 396n35
Tosatti, Erio, 330n49
Toselli, Mario, 318
Transnistria, 291n1
Transylvania, 370, 404n59
Trawniki (concentration camp), 272, 277, 278
Treblinka (Treblinka II) (death camp), 60,
    110n39, 121, 269–270n1, 285, 286, 288,
    289, 420
Treblinka I (labor camp), 286
Tresa (river), 331
Treviso, 326
Trieste, 320
Trocki, David, 293, 295–297, 299
Trunk, Isaiah, 391
Tschlenoff, Boris, 113
Tsimerman, Hayim Yisrael, 367, 373, 374,
    384, 385
Tunis, 400, 402
Turin, 320, 328
Turkeltaub, Symcha, 280
Turkey, 434
Turobin, 275n11
Tydor-Baumel, Judith, 259

Ukraine, 163n36
Ungar, Samuel David (Rabbi), 420
Ungar-Perner, Luise, 157
Unger, Ida, 424, 425

Ungern-Sternberg (Baron), 35n31
Ungern-Sternberg, Roman von, 35n31
United Kingdom (UK)
    See Great Britain
United States of America (U.S.), 10, 11, 28,
    32, 33, 39, 81, 95, 110n40, 114, 115, 137,
    154–156, 158, 171n61, 271, 274, 295,
    296, 322, 335, 338, 341, 343, 345–350,
    352–354, 359, 360, 362, 564, 382, 392n25,
    403, 404n57, 417, 423, 434
Unsdorfer, Shlomo Zalman, 377
Unterriexingen (concentration camp), 221
Uruguay, 360
Uzbekistan, 250

Vaihingen (concentration camp), 14, 199,
    201–203, 205–215, 217, 221, 222
Vaivara (concentration camp), 232
Val d'Aosta, 324
Val di Gesso, 326
Valdieri, 326, 327, 328
Valobra, Lelio Vittorio, 320, 321, 323
Vanagaite, Ruta, 445
Vanves, 34n30
Varese, 331
Velvel, Shlomo, 282
Veneto, 324
Ventimiglia, 317
Veziano, Paolo, 317, 318
Viale, Raimondo, 328
Vienna, 151–153, 155–157, 161, 163, 167, 168,
    170, 171, 174, 233, 235, 293, 329, 394, 417
Vilijampolė, 129, 134
Vilna (Vilnius), 25, 38, 58–60, 133, 140–142,
    144, 181, 246, 248n10, 249, 251, 254, 276,
    293, 336, 337, 338, 339, 340, 341, 343,
    344, 345, 348, 376, 392n26
Vilna (ghetto), 60, 133, 140–142, 181
Vladivostok, 351, 363
Voigt, Klaus, 329
Vojvodina, 324
Volterra, Gustavo, 320

Wachsmann, Nikolaus, 226, 242
Wahrhaftig, Zorach, 394n30
Wajnblum, Emanuel, 237
Wallenberg, Raoul, 430
Walloon (region), 291

Warsaw, 66, 72, 73, 75, 77–81, 83, 85,
    85–90, 100n10, 104n20, 107n31, 109n38,
    110n39–40, 111n43, 112, 115n50, 116, 121,
    133, 181, 208, 210, 212, 213, 215–221,
    252, 254, 259, 269–272, 275–277, 281,
    282, 287–290, 293, 297, 299, 377, 389n9,
    393, 394n29
Warsaw (ghetto), 13, 27, 59, 60, 65, 66, 71–73,
    75, 78, 100, 101, 103, 104n20, 108, 110–
    112, 114–118, 121, 122, 124, 128, 129n1,
    133, 181, 210, 218n65, 220, 221, 226, 256,
    269–272, 275–277, 281, 282, 284, 287,
    289, 290, 309, 369, 394n32, 402n54
Wasser, Bluma, 277
Wasser, Hersh, 277
Wasserman, Elhanan Bunim (Rabbi), 337, 376,
    378–381, 385
Wasserstein, Isak, 204
Wdowinski, David, 218, 219
Węgrow, 75
Weichert, Michael, 114, 426
Weiner, Zehava, 329
Weinryb, Leon, 204
Weisbord, Tobias, 203
Weiss, Isaac Hirsch, 378
Weiss, Yitzhak Ya'akov (Rabbi), 403n56, 404,
    411
Weissmandel, Michael Ber Dov (Rabbi), 10,
    11, 420, 426
Weizmann, Chaim, 97, 136
Weltz, Israel (Rabbi), 410, 411
Werber, Abusz (Zerubavel), 293–297, 299,
    302–307
Werber, Sziffra (Sophie), 293, 299, 300, 305,
    306
Westerweel, Joop, 258
Widawska, Sara, 81, 82
Wilczek, 235
Winer, Szlamek (Jakub Grojnowski), 276, 277,
    285, 286
Wise, Stephen S. (Rabbi), 26, 28, 34–37n41,
    346, 382
Wittenberg, Itzhak, 59
Włodawa, 282
Włodawa (ghetto), 282
Wlodawer, H., 85, 86
Wohlfuss, Yehoshua, 286
Wolanów, 205

Wolbe, Wilhelm (Rabbi), 360
Wolf, Albert, 307
Wolf, Grigory, 130, 135, 137n19
Wolmann, Icek (Richard), 306
Wrocław, 112n43
Wygodzki, Jakub, 25, 28, 37

Ya'ari, Meir, 251
Yaphin, Avraham (Rabbi), 350, 354
Yeruham, Hayim Yitzhak (Rabbi), 394
Yishai, Moshe, 359
Yitzhak, Levi, 370, 383
Yogel, Shabtai (Rabbi), 354
Yugoslavia, 258, 322–325, 329

Zagdanski, Jehezkel (Henry), 204
Zagłębie, 255
Zagreb, 324, 329
Zajdner, Aron, 92
Zakai, Yochanan Ben (Rabbi), 339

Zaklików, 208
Zaks, Mendel (Rabbi), 349, 350, 354
Zalewas, Szlama, 88, 89, 92
Zamość (concentration camp), 277, 280, 283, 286, 287
Zeitlin, Aaron, 216
Zeitlin, David, 206, 207, 216, 217
Zeitlin, Elhanan, 216
Zeitlin, Hillel (Rabbi), 216
Zerah (biblical figure), 45
Zilberberg, Israel, 205
Zimbardo, Philip, 240, 241
Zimmels, Hirsch Jakob, 390, 391n18
Zimri (biblical figure), 45
Zitomirski, Shmuel, 282
Zoboli family, 330n49
Zuckerman, Yitzhak, 254
Zupovich, Judel, 143, 147
Zurich, 111n43, 170, 270, 290, 409n72
Zweibaum, Juliusz, 112